I0124347

LIKE FIRE

THE PALIAU MOVEMENT AND MILLENARIANISM IN MELANESIA

LIKE FIRE

THE PALIAU MOVEMENT AND MILLENARIANISM IN MELANESIA

THEODORE SCHWARTZ AND MICHAEL FRENCH SMITH

MONOGRAPHS IN
ANTHROPOLOGY SERIES

Australian
National
University

PRESS

ANU
PRESS

Published by ANU Press
The Australian National University
Acton ACT 2601, Australia
Email: anupress@anu.edu.au

Available to download for free at press.anu.edu.au

ISBN (print): 9781760464240
ISBN (online): 9781760464257

WorldCat (print): 1247150926
WorldCat (online): 1247151119

DOI: 10.22459/LF.2021

This title is published under a Creative Commons Attribution-NonCommercial-NoDerivatives 4.0 International (CC BY-NC-ND 4.0).

The full licence terms are available at
creativecommons.org/licenses/by-nc-nd/4.0/legalcode

Cover design and layout by ANU Press. Cover photograph: A Paliau Movement Supporter, Manus Province, Papua New Guinea, 2000, taken by Matt Tomlinson.

This edition © 2021 ANU Press

Contents

List of illustrations

Acknowledgements

We owe our greatest debt to several generations of the people of Manus Province, Papua New Guinea, which was the Manus District of the United Nations Trust Territory of Papua and New Guinea when the research for this book began. Too many people have contributed to name individuals. Those named in the book (we do not use pseudonyms) account for only some of the major contributors. We also would be staggeringly remiss not to thank Margaret Mead. In this book we take issue with some of her writings on Manus and Paliau, but we also draw on her findings. Above all, there would have been no book at all if she had not introduced Theodore Schwartz to Manus in 1953.

We are deeply grateful to our spouses, Shirley Otis (Theodore Schwartz) and Jana Goldman (Michael French Smith). Aside from the encouragement and material support they have provided, they have put up with a lot of aggravation. We would not want to have been our own roommates during the many days and nights we each obsessed about the book. In Del Mar, California, Cecelia Gomez and Arlene Olivarria made it possible for us to swan about being scholars without thinking whence our next meals or other creature comforts were coming.

We received an important early grant from Mary Catherine Bateson and the Institute for Intercultural Studies. As we continued, Steve and Paula Mae Schwartz made it possible for Smith to travel coast to coast to work with Schwartz as often as necessary without worrying about the expense. Adan Schwartz covered most of the costs of preparing the completed manuscript for publication, with help from Steve and Paula Mae.

Aletta Biersack proved herself a colleague of unparalleled endurance. She read several drafts of each chapter and gave us detailed and thoughtful comments. Anything, however, that readers may find amiss with the final product is our fault alone, and probably something Aletta warned us about. Ton Otto, a leading scholar of things Manusian, gave us valuable comments on the penultimate draft of the book.

Matt Tomlinson was our vital connection to ANU Press and cheered us on through all the stages of manuscript submission and approval. At that point, Emily Tinker took over and saw us to the end with great efficiency. It is hard to overestimate how important and how taxing copyediting and creating a book's index are, and Tracy Harwood accomplished these tasks with elan. Diane Buric skilfully made our maps and other images, and prepared for print our photographs, some of which we feared were too old and worn to salvage.

Preface: Why, how, and for whom

In early 2012, when I visited Theodore (Ted) Schwartz at his home in Del Mar, California, he had recently finished digitising audio recordings of interviews he had conducted with Manus people in Papua New Guinea (PNG) from 1953 through 1995; the annotated catalogue went on for many pages.[1] Ted gave me an audio tour and we listened to Paliau, his supporters, and his detractors talk about the Paliau Movement, Paliau as saviour, Paliau as betrayer, and topics ranging from the politics of local-level Movement leadership to when the dead ancestors would return to life. There was more than enough material here for a book that would not simply update Ted's early-career monograph (Schwartz 1962), but replace it as the primary scholarly source on the Paliau Movement. A lot had happened in the Movement since the monograph was published, and much of the data Ted had collected since the 1950s called for thinking again about Paliau and the events described in the 1962 volume. By early 2013, Ted and I had decided to collaborate on a new book on the Paliau Movement. I don't remember exactly how we reached that decision, but it was obvious that we would regret not writing the book and writing it was clearly a two-person job.

We knew that such an intimately detailed record of so many decades in the life of a social movement in the Pacific Islands—or almost anywhere—was rare, and we felt that making it widely available was virtually an obligation. Also, although his failing vision made it difficult, Ted had been reading some of the recent anthropological literature on cargo cults, of which the

---

1   These recordings and Schwartz's other original research records are now housed at the Archive for Melanesian Anthropology at the University of California, San Diego, library (library.ucsd.edu/research-and-collections/collections/special-collections-and-archives/collections/melanesian.html). The archive provides a searchable online catalogue.

Paliau Movement provides dramatic examples. I had been doing the same and I agreed with Ted that many anthropologists were entertaining ideas about cargo cults and millenarianism that needed firm rebutting.

We also agreed that neither of us could write the book alone. It would require analysing decades of Ted's still-raw data and reviewing literature in several fields. But Ted's vision was going from bad to worse and he was feeling his 80-plus years in painful and limiting ways. Similarly, I couldn't interpret Ted's data on my own. Even though I spoke the language of Ted's cache of interviews fluently, I couldn't hear in them all that he could.[2] Every time we listened to an interview, Ted broke in frequently to add remembered details or draw my attention to something that I hadn't noticed but that leapt out at him because of his long familiarity with the people speaking and the larger context.

In 2013, I had just finished a third book about my work in Kragur (Smith 2013) and I was free to start another major project—preferably, one that would stretch my abilities as this one surely would. I was also flattered that Ted regarded me as a worthy collaborator. I first met Ted in 1970, when I entered the PhD program in cultural anthropology at the University of California, San Diego (UCSD), where he was a faculty member. I quickly gravitated towards studying with him and I served as his teaching assistant whenever I could. That led to him offering me a position as one of his three research assistants in Manus Province, PNG, from mid-June through early September 1973.

This was my first time in PNG and a major event in my life. That year I had been seriously wondering if I really wanted to pursue a university career—the amount of sitting indoors it entailed was one mark against it—but by the time I returned from Manus I was eager to get back to PNG to do my own research, whatever I might do next. With Ted as my adviser, I went back to PNG (in 1975–76), did research in a village called Kragur in East Sepik Province, wrote my doctoral dissertation, and got my degree.

I knew from Ted's example that doing research in PNG could be habit forming, and this proved true for me as well. Although my PhD did not lead me to a university career, I found ways to go back to PNG several

---

2   Most of the interviews were conducted and transcribed in Tok Pisin, the major lingua franca of PNG, about which we provide more information in 'Spelling and pronunciation of Tok Pisin words and Manus proper names'.

times while making a living outside the academy. I moved in university circles only fitfully after leaving UCSD, but I kept in touch with Ted, who was always more interested in my last trip to PNG than in how I was earning my keep. He encouraged me to keep visiting Kragur whenever I could, despite excellent reasons for putting this interest aside and concentrating on paid employment. For this I will always be grateful. And because of this, in 2013 I could share Ted's passion for getting a more complete Paliau Movement story on record and for having a say in related anthropological debates.

That is why we decided to collaborate on this book. Here's how we wrote it. One of the first things we did was listen to dozens of the recorded interviews at Ted's home in Del Mar. This entailed a lot of sitting down indoors while the sun shone brightly outside. From this we both needed the relief of conducting some of our discussions while pacing the long driveway between the pens where the goats, sheep, chickens, rabbits, and a Vietnamese pig live, and the paddock that belongs to Arturo the wild burro and Tiny the miniature horse, with a final turn on the paths through Ted's large collection of bonsai.

The interviews were our richest source of data, and many of the most important had been transcribed years ago. But we listened to these again, as Ted commented and I took notes. We initially ignored the transcripts so we could base our thinking as much as possible on people's words in their own voices, with their original emphases and inflections. This engages the recesses of memory and stimulates questions of interpretation better than reading the most precise written records. In early working sessions we also had long conversations about what topics the book should address and what we should say about them. We recorded these and had them transcribed.

Between visits to Del Mar—where I travelled from my home in Silver Spring, Maryland (just outside Washington, DC)—I continued delving into the relevant literature. Drawing on this work, Ted's theoretical writings, transcripts of our discussions, sections of the 1962 monograph, and notes on the interviews, I began drafting and expanding book outlines and chapter summaries. As these took shape, I returned to Del Mar where I read them to Ted, we discussed them, and I made notes for revising them. We proceeded in this way more or less chapter by chapter with a lot of circling back to revise all that had been written before. Ted's health problems prevented him from typing or even writing by hand as well as from reading, so composing and revising fell to me. But the reading aloud and critique of my efforts that we conducted together was intense.

Unfortunately, by the time we reached the concluding chapter, Ted's health had deteriorated so much that he could no longer take part in this process. We had discussed many times the issues this last chapter addresses and I believe that what I wrote continues the trajectory of the book's analyses and arguments and that Ted would not raise any significant objections. Still, I bear more responsibility for the final chapter than does Ted. (Similarly, I wrote the note on spelling and pronunciation of Manus proper names that follows this preface without Ted's knowledge of linguistics or the languages of Manus.)

The 'whom' in this preface's title is primarily anthropologists who focus on social change in PNG and other Melanesian locales.[3] But we also commend it to scholars in any field who are interested in millenarianism—the hope for and pursuit of a miraculous, supernaturally mediated transformation of the world—wherever it occurs. As we argue, millenarianism is almost always a timely topic, but it may be unusually relevant now, because— as Ted has argued with great force—millenarianism inclines people to embrace highly implausible explanations for events and reject explanations for which there is sound evidence. It is no coincidence that this is also the kind of thinking characteristic of conspiracy theorists and to which they incite their audiences.

I am writing this at my new home in western upper-lower Michigan, where in normal times social distancing means staying clear of bears emerging from hibernation, hungry and grumpy. But the COVID-19 pandemic has changed that. The effects of this novel coronavirus on physical health are horrifying. But the way in which people in many parts of the world are reacting psychologically to the pandemic is also chilling. Just as though they were caught up in millenarian fervour, they are cutting loose from reasonably sober everyday logic. They are denying things for which there is overwhelming empirical evidence—for example, that there really is a virus that is killing people at a great rate. Simultaneously, they seize on the idea that reports of such deaths are part of a massive conspiracy to, for example, undermine national economies or impose totalitarian regimes. Here in the United States, conspiracy thinking—

---

3   We explain the Melanesian label in Chapter 1.

the shadow side of the millenarian mind—is undermining civic life. Perhaps the most malignant conspiracy fiction (spread by outgoing President Trump, among others) is that the Democratic Party candidates, Joseph Biden (President) and Kamala Harris (Vice-President), won the 2020 presidential election only by conspiring to carry out nation-wide election fraud. Despite abundant evidence to the contrary, thousands of Trump supporters reacted by attacking the United States Capitol on 6 January 2021, flaunting racist and anti-Semitic messages and symbols and causing several deaths. Although Biden and Harris have assumed their offices, the irrational belief that dark forces conspired to steal the election continues to infect American life. I am sure Ted would join me in hoping that this book will encourage readers to ponder the roots of such outrageous credulity; to recognise how common it is, even in better times among ordinary people; and to be alert to the ways in which it works against improving life in virtually all human societies.

Michael French Smith
Honor, Michigan
April 2021

Spelling and pronunciation of Tok Pisin words and Manus proper names

Tok Pisin spelling and pronunciation

Tok Pisin is the modern name for what used to be called Pidgin or Melanesian Pidgin. It was the principal lingua franca of Papua New Guinea in the colonial era and it remains so today. Indigenous PNG languages provide Tok Pisin's grammar. PNG languages, other western Pacific languages, and several European languages, chief among them English, provide the vocabulary. It is technically a creole, not a pidgin. In brief, this means that it has a more complex grammar and a larger vocabulary than a pidgin and is a first language for many people. Pidgins develop as a means of communicating across language barriers. Creoles often do the same job, but they differ from pidgins as noted above. Creoles often develop from pidgins.

To the extent that it is standardised (as used in newspapers and government documents, for instance), Tok Pisin spelling is strictly phonetic. Consonants are pronounced as they are in English, except that 'r' is sometimes trilled and 's' is pronounced as both the English 's' and the English 'z'. Single consonants are pronounced as follows:

a   as in father

e   as in set or name

i   as in hit or machine

o   as in squawk, fork, or home

u   as in soup

Diphthongs are pronounced as follows:

ai   as in t**i**me or tr**y**ing

au   as in c**o**w

After introducing them, we use a number of Tok Pisin words for which there are not good English equivalents. The only confusion this might cause is when distinguishing singular and plural forms: in Tok Pisin, plural and singular forms are the same. So, if there is one *kiap* (Tok Pisin for colonial government officer) in a village and another arrives there are now two *kiap* in the village.

We use quotations from interviews and personal conversations throughout the book. Except where otherwise indicated, all quotations from Manus people are translated from Tok Pisin. We supply the original Tok Pisin where we think it helps clarify a point.

Spelling and pronunciation of Manus proper names

We have retained from Schwartz's 1962 monograph most of the spellings of proper names. Our spellings are not all consistent with local Manus pronunciation. For instance, many placenames in Manus are prenasalised. This means that the placename that sounds to the untrained ear like Dropwa actually includes an almost inaudible initial 'n' sound. Thus, it is often spelled Ndropwa, as we do. Similarly, the placename that sounds to the untrained ear like Bukei actually includes an almost inaudible initial 'm' sound. Thus, it is often spelled Mbukei, as we do. But we also use Bunai and Baluan as placenames. Pronounced properly these are also prenasalised. But in the anthropological literature on Manus they are spelled so often without a nod to the initial touch of 'm' that we do also.

There is only one complication in our spelling of personal names. Manus people pronounce the male personal names that sound to the untrained ear like Chamilo and Cholai more like they contain a subtle 'y' sound that might be indicated by spelling them Chyamilo and Chyolai. To convey this nuance more subtly, Schwartz renders them as Tjamilo and Tjolai, respectively, a practice we follow.

Finally, Paliau is pronounced pay-lee-ow, with the accent on the first syllable.

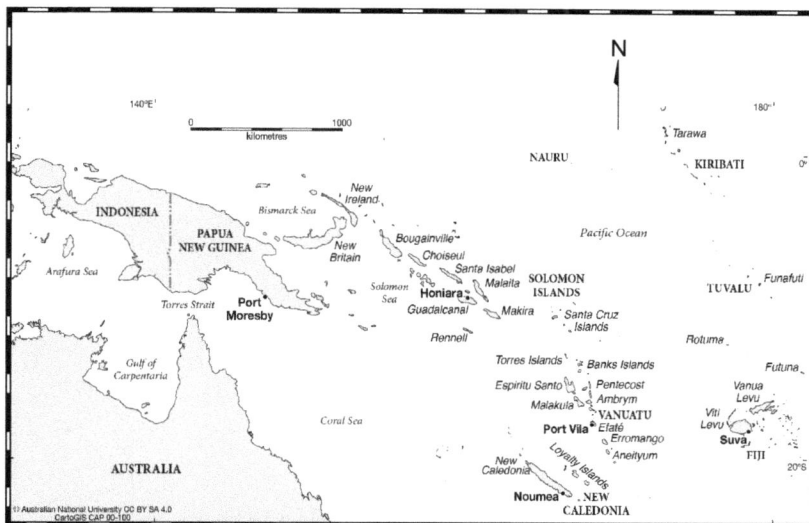

Map 1: The location of contemporary Papua New Guinea in relation to its closest neighbours.

Source: Map reproduced with the permission of CartoGIS Services, ANU College of Asia and the Pacific, The Australian National University. Prepared for publication by Diane Buric.

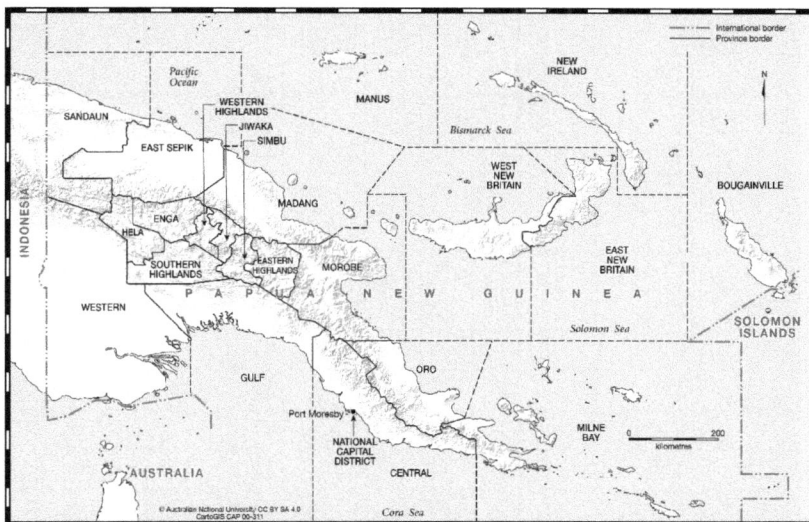

Map 2: The boundaries of the provinces of modern Papua New Guinea.

Source: Map reproduced with the permission of CartoGIS Services, ANU College of Asia and the Pacific, The Australian National University. Prepared for publication by Diane Buric.

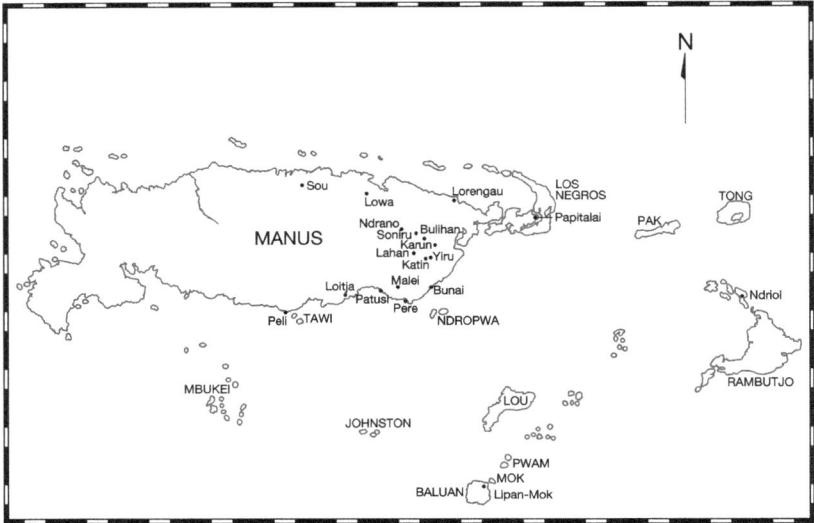

Map 3: The principal places in the Admiralty Islands involved in the events in 1953–54 as discussed in the text.

Islands are labelled in capital letters. With the exception of Lorengau, the only town in Manus then and now, the other locations are all villages, linked only by sea or rough trails through the interior.

Source: Created by Diane Buric and Michael French Smith, based on a map in Schwartz (1962).

1

'The last few weeks have been strange and exciting'

In April 1954, Theodore Schwartz wrote to Margaret Mead in New York City from Bunai village, Manus District, Territory of Papua and New Guinea. He was reporting on the remarkable events Lenora Shargo (his wife at the time) and he were witnessing. He began his letter: 'The last few weeks have been strange and exciting', and he was not exaggerating. He and Shargo were Mead's research assistants on her second trip to the Admiralty Islands, which today comprise the Manus Province of the independent country of Papua New Guinea (PNG). Mead had conducted research there in 1928 with New Zealand–born anthropologist Reo Fortune, her husband at the time. When Schwartz became her assistant in 1953, she was already famous for writing *Coming of Age in Samoa* (1928) and *Growing Up in New Guinea* (1930), the latter based on her 1928 research in the Admiralties. Schwartz was a graduate student in anthropology at the University of Pennsylvania, Shargo was an art student, and neither she nor Schwartz had ever been outside the United States or even west of the Mississippi. The party of three arrived in New Guinea in June 1953. Mead returned to the United States in December, as planned. Schwartz and Shargo stayed on for another eight months, to collect more data for Mead and complete their independent work. By the time Mead left they were taking in stride much that at first had been arrestingly exotic. But they had yet to encounter the revelation that would force them to reconsider their earlier impressions and draw Schwartz into a lifetime research project.[1]

In 1953, Schwartz and Shargo lived in Bunai village and Mead lived in Pere village, about 1.5 miles west of Bunai. Both Bunai and Pere are on the south coast of the largest land mass in the Admiralties, Manus Island, a name derived from that of one of the principal ethnic groups in the Admiralties, the Manus. Under the Australian administration, Manus District comprised the Admiralty Islands; the district became Manus Province after PNG gained independence in 1975 (from Australia, which was then governing PNG as a United Nations Trust Territory, having accepted responsibility for preparing the Territory for independence after World War II).

From here on, when we mean the Manus as an ethnic group within the larger population of Manus Province, we will refer to them by the name of the language they share; we will call them the Titan (pronounced, approximately, tee-tun, emphasising the first syllable). Anthropologists generally distinguish two other groups within the indigenous population of Manus: the Usiai (who, in precolonial times, lived exclusively in the island's mountainous interior) and the Matankor (who inhabited offshore islands, but were not as thoroughly amphibious as the lagoon-dwelling Titan). Although, like the Titan, the Usiai and Matankor inhabited distinct ecological niches, unlike the Titan neither group shared a single language. When we need to refer to all the indigenous peoples of the Admiralties, we will lump them together as Manus people.[2]

---

1   Schwartz was not Mead's student. He was a student of A.I. Hallowell at the University of Pennsylvania, preparing to do his doctoral thesis research in Africa. Seeking an assistant for her 1953 trip to Manus, Mead contacted several anthropology departments with strong graduate programs. Hallowell urged Schwartz, who hadn't yet secured funding for his proposed research in Africa, to apply for the position. Mead wanted not only a well-trained young anthropologist but also someone with expertise in still and motion picture photography and able to repair photographic equipment. Schwartz was a competent amateur photographer and after Mead offered him the position he took a crash course in photographic equipment repair. Mead agreed to hire Shargo as well, assuming she could learn to do ethnographic research, which she did quickly. Mead also thought that travelling and working with a married couple rather than an apparently unattached young man would raise fewer eyebrows in the conservative white colonial society of the Territory. Among their other tasks, Schwartz and Shargo did all the photography for the team.

2   Carrier and Carrier (1989: 35–36) note a number of complexities in this three-part division of the population. Mead (2002 [1934]: 5) called it a reflection of the Titan point of view, that is: 'a reflection of the typical sea-dwellers' point of view towards people landbound and wholly without canoes, the Usiai, and those who live on land but who also use canoes with more or less frequency, the Matankor. As a matter of fact, those Matankor who live near the Manus [i.e. the Titan] use canoes very infrequently, while the Matankor of the north coast seem to be as habitual and fearless sailors as are the Manus [Titan] themselves'. At least since the 1980s, and perhaps earlier, some Usiai have rejected the Usiai moniker. We know that members of one 'Usiai' language group, Nali speakers, prefer to be known as Nali rather than Usiai.

Figure 1.1: Schwartz films while Mead takes notes, 1953.

Theodore Schwartz and Lenora Shargo did all the still and motion picture photography for Margaret Mead when Mead returned to Manus in 1953 for the first time since her sojourn there with Reo Fortune in 1928. Here, Schwartz, photographed by Shargo, films a public event in the centre of Pere village while Mead takes notes.

Source: Lenora Shargo, from the collection of Theodore Schwartz.

Schwartz and Shargo often walked to Pere to confer with Mead, taking a well-used path along the shoreline and across a wide river mouth they could wade at low tide, but to stay in more regular contact they engaged villagers to carry written notes back and forth.[3] Such a life was the height of novelty for them, but on first arriving in Pere, Schwartz could not suppress a pang of disappointment. He had read Mead's *Growing Up in New Guinea* (2001 [1930]), her more technical treatises on Titan culture and society, and Reo Fortune's *Manus Religion* (1965 [1935]), with its detailed descriptions of seances in which Titan people communicated with the ghosts of their dead through spirit mediums.[4] He had also seen Fortune's photographs of Pere in 1928, the thatched houses set above the water on timber posts, people making their way from house to house by canoe, women in skirts made of plant fibre (so-called grass skirts), men in breechcloths (which would have been made of beaten bark in earlier times), widows with shaved heads, and both men and women sporting ornaments of dogs' teeth. But Pere and its inhabitants looked nothing like this in 1953.

Even when Mead and Fortune first arrived in Manus in 1928, the region was not isolated from the Western world. Alvaro de Saavedra, a Spanish trader, was the first European to record a sighting of the Admiralties, in 1528. Dutch explorers Willem Schouten and Jacob LeMaire noted them again in 1616, as did the English buccaneer and explorer William Dampier in 1686. In 1767, Philip Carteret—exploring with the support of the British Admiralty (which administered the Royal Navy)—named the group the Admiralty Islands, in honour of his sponsor.[5] European powers began to take proprietary interests in the region, including the Admiralties, in the nineteenth century. The Netherlands, Germany, and Great Britain each claimed a portion of what is still known geographically as the island of New Guinea. The Netherlands appropriated the entire western half as part of the Dutch East Indies, and Germany claimed the northern half of what was left, which became known as German New Guinea. Great Britain claimed the southern remainder as British New Guinea. This it placed

---

3   Evelyn Waugh (1938: 58–60) speaks of using cleft sticks to convey such correspondence, but Mead, Shargo, and Schwartz did not find this necessary.

4   Mead's principal academic works based on the 1928 research are her well-known paper 'An investigation of the thought of primitive children, with special reference to animism' (1932) and her treatise 'Kinship in the Admiralty Islands' (2002 [1934]).

5   For this information and other details in this paragraph we draw on Bogen (n.d.: 61) and the following Princeton University webpage: lib-dbserver.princeton.edu/visual_materials/maps/websites/pacific/wallis-carteret/wallis-carteret.html.

under Australian administration in 1906, and Australia rechristened it the Territory of Papua. At the beginning of World War I, Australia took control of German New Guinea, merging it with Papua following the war to govern under a League of Nations mandate as the Territory of Papua and New Guinea (the Territory). Throughout the colonial era, Christian missionaries of several stripes proselytised in the region.[6]

Such incursions, though, were minor compared to the upheaval of World War II. In 1944, an American military invasion, including a smaller Australian force, ousted the Japanese forces that had occupied the Admiralties with the larger aim of sweeping south to invade Australia. The Americans established a massive air and naval base on Los Negros Island, the detached eastern tail of Manus Island, separated from it by a narrow strait. After the war, the military hoards disappeared as quickly as they had arrived, but they left behind an indelible impression of apparently limitless material wealth and coordinated human effort on a scale utterly unknown in indigenous New Guinea.

Meeting the Paliau Movement in its Sunday clothes

Mead returned to Manus in 1953, primarily to document what she had heard was a spontaneous effort by the people of the south coast and smaller southern islands to discard their old ways and adopt what they understood from their experience of colonial government and wartime occupation as the way of life of 'white' people. They saw American military forces as especially impressive representatives of the white way of life. Although black American soldiers were segregated in construction units, many indigenous people saw their very presence, and their mastery of powerful machines, as evidence that black New Guineans, too, could attain all the benefits of white life.

By 1953, most of the people of Manus spoke not only one or more of the several indigenous languages of the Admiralties, but also the lingua franca of the Territory. In the form spoken today, this is called Tok Pisin. Mead and many other anthropologists of her era called this language

---

6   Moore (2003) provides an excellent and compact history of New Guinea, from prehistory to the present era. Gavin Souter's *New Guinea: The Last Unknown* (1963) remains very worthwhile.

Neo-Melanesian, invoking a still-common division of the Pacific Islands into three geographic and cultural regions: Polynesia, Micronesia, and Melanesia.[7] In the Tok Pisin of the 1950s, people of the Admiralties called the new pattern of life of which Mead had heard the *Nufela Fasin*, which translates as the New Way. The New Way was the program of what soon came to be called the Paliau Movement, after its founder and leader, Paliau Maloat.[8]

Under the influence of the New Way, many Manus people—mostly Titan, but also some Usiai and Matankor (Paliau himself was Matankor)—had publicly repudiated many of their longstanding customs and were trying to appropriate as much as they could of the way of life, as they understood it, of the Americans and other Western foreigners who had descended on them—often literally, at the Los Negros air base—during the war. So, in 1953, rather than the lagoon villages of 1928, Mead's party found villages built on land in orderly rows, like military bases or colonial towns. People wore whatever Western-style clothing they had and there were few signs of traditional music, dance, ceremonies, wood carving, personal decoration, or the seances Fortune had witnessed. New Way leaders summoned people twice daily to gatherings in the New Way's own Christian church, in which they practised a version of Catholicism revised to support the New Way. The New Way's effort to organise all aspects of village life entailed what sometimes seemed incessant mandatory gatherings of all men, women, and children to discuss, and settle by a show of hands, matters as diverse as scheduling fishing expeditions, responsibility for cutting the village grass, and standards of child care.

When Mead, Schwartz, and Shargo first arrived in Pere by outrigger canoe from Lorengau—the district's only town in 1953, as it remains today— the first man stepping forward to greet them as they came ashore wore

---

7   The lines on a map showing this tri-part division suggest neat boundaries. It is more accurate to say that there are contrasting social and cultural tendencies in the Pacific Islands that correspond roughly with geographic areas. The contemporary political entities included in Melanesia with the least quibbling are PNG, the Indonesian province of Papua (adjacent to PNG and formerly part of the Dutch East Indies), Vanuatu, Solomon Islands, and the French colony of New Caledonia. The governments of several contiguous countries of the south-west Pacific have adopted the collective label Melanesia to pursue shared geopolitical interests, as in the Melanesian Spearhead Group, established in 1986. Today, if you can speak Tok Pisin, you can quickly master the analogous creoles of Solomon Islands and Vanuatu. Moore (2003: 1–14) provides a useful discussion of the origins and current significance of the Melanesian label.
8   Stephen Pokawin (1983b) distinguishes the Paliau Church from the Paliau Movement, and places both under the rubric Paliau Phenomenon. The Paliau Movement is a multifaceted phenomenon, but to emphasise the integral relationship among its different dimensions we do not follow Pokawin's practice.

white pants, a white dress shirt, a necktie, and leather shoes, all store-bought. Schwartz and Shargo, however, eventually found that things had not changed quite as drastically as this costume portended. Beneath the surface of the New Way an apparently very different kind of effort to transform life was gaining momentum. Schwartz's interest in seeing something more exotic than people trying to live like Americans would not be disappointed.

Proponents of the New Way advocated collective efforts to amass money for new economic ventures; greater equality between young and old, men and women, and those of different indigenous hereditary ranks; abandoning the indigenous marriage system, which required exchanges of large quantities of material wealth between the families of the bride and groom; and abandoning the indigenous obsession with the spirits of the dead. Catholic missionaries had been discouraging the latter since establishing themselves in Manus in the 1930s, having first arrived in New Guinea late in the German era. But several months after Mead's departure, Schwartz and Shargo found that the ancestral ghosts were back in a dramatic new role.

Stumbling on a cargo cult

In the 1920s, as Reo Fortune (1965 [1935]) documented, the Titan believed that spirits of the dead punished wrongdoing with illness. (Spirits of the dead played a similar role among the Usiai and Matankor, although we have no detailed accounts of these practices like those Fortune provides for the Titan.)[9] To diagnose serious illness and explain other kinds of misfortune, the Titan consulted the ghosts to find out who had committed what offending impropriety. The ghosts were especially strict regarding economic and sexual behaviour. In early 1954, Schwartz and Shargo discovered that many Bunai villagers, whom they thought they knew well, were consulting the ghosts almost every night, but keeping this secret from them. The villagers were not, however, trying to cure illness. They were trying to open a way for the dead to return, bringing with them virtually unlimited quantities of Western manufactured goods, from

---

9   We are sceptical of recently published descriptions of indigenous Usiai belief in a 'supreme deity and creator' similar to 'the Christian Triune God' (Minol et al. 2014: 10–12). Minol et al. (2014: 12–16) also note the importance of spirits of the dead, which they describe as less 'aloof' (p. 15) in everyday Usiai life than other categories of non-human beings.

food and clothing to construction materials and machinery. Schwartz and Shargo knew that something similar—called the Noise (in Tok Pisin, *Nois*)—had happened in 1947, but they had been led to believe that it was defunct. Anthropologists used to routinely call this kind of thing a cargo cult. Some now object to this term (a topic to which we return below and in Chapter 2), but it was the label that first sprang to mind for what Schwartz and Shargo found in Bunai. This was a chance discovery, but far from distracting them from their study of the Paliau Movement, it led them deeper into it.

Distinctive features of our approach

Our approach in this book is distinctive in several ways. Perhaps most distinctive is the breadth and depth of our data. They are especially rich in comparison with the data available to most studies of millenarian movements—that is, studies of efforts to achieve not merely a better world, but a perfect world, either gradually or through sudden miraculous transformation. The cargo cults within the Paliau Movement were of the apocalyptic variety of millenarianism. By apocalyptic we mean simply that the transformation sought or expected is dramatically abrupt; we do not mean that it necessarily entails, as in the Christian Bible's Book of Revelations, the world's destruction.[10] Most scholarly accounts of millenarian movements of all kinds rely primarily on data collected after the movements have already failed or lost all but a rump following.[11] To the best of our knowledge, our account is unusual because it apprehends a millenarian movement in action close to its inception and follows it to the present.

That we recognise the strong millenarian tendencies within the Paliau Movement does not mean that we must call it a religious phenomenon, for millenarianism also comes in secular varieties. In any event, we find the term 'religion' vague in the extreme and we will use it sparingly. Further, our data incline us to part company with those who have tried to tease apart what they see as distinct religious and political dimensions of the Paliau Movement and Paliau Maloat the man. We also part

10   Landes (2011: 31–6) identifies several types of apocalyptic millenarianism. Recognising a single general type, however, suffices for our purposes.
11   Landes emphasises this point throughout his 2011 work *Heaven on Earth: The Varieties of the Millennial Experience*; see especially pages 60–1 and 144–5.

company with views of cargo cults—a characteristically Melanesian form of millenarianism—many anthropologists currently take for granted. We expand on these features of our approach and note their principal advantages in what follows.

Drawing on decades of observation and intimate access

Schwartz observed the Paliau Movement for several decades—an unusual feat of what anthropologists call longitudinal ethnography. His long intimacy with Movement people and events helped him obtain exceptionally detailed data on many dimensions of the Movement. Within a few years of the Movement's birth, Schwartz and Shargo collected from many participants and bystanders firsthand accounts of how it began and spread. Schwartz continued to observe the Movement periodically over more than 40 years.

Figure 1.2: Schwartz and Paliau in Lorengau, late 1980s.

Schwartz first met Paliau in 1953 and subsequently discussed developments in the Movement with him on visits to Manus spanning more than 40 years. Here, Schwartz and Paliau chat at a pub in Manus's only town, Lorengau, in the late 1980s.

Source: An unidentified colleague of Paliau's took this picture with Schwartz's camera.

We emphasise the years from 1953 through 1995, for which we can rely primarily on Schwartz's firsthand observations from about seven years of field research spread among some dozen visits. Schwartz last saw Paliau the year before the latter's death in 1991, and he last visited Manus in 1995. Several other anthropologists began research pertaining to Paliau and the Movement in the 1980s. Their work helps us extend the Paliau story into the current millennium. Ton Otto began his research in Manus in 1986. His work—including his doctoral thesis (1991) and a series of later articles—is especially valuable. Other anthropologists who have observed aspects of the Paliau Movement include Alexander Wanek (1996), who conducted research in Manus in the middle to late 1980s, Berit Gustafsson (1992), who conducted research in the early 1990s, and Steffen Dalsgaard, whose 2009 volume is based on research conducted post-2000. Smith worked with Schwartz in Manus for three months in 1973 as one of three assistants. He conducted research in PNG's East Sepik Province in succeeding decades and returned to Manus briefly in 2015 to talk with leaders and rank-and-file members of the current incarnation of the Paliau Movement, Wind Nation (in Tok Pisin, *Win Neisen*) in Pere village and on Baluan Island, where Paliau is buried.

Explaining the details of movement and cult distribution

The depth in time of Schwartz's research and his intimate access to events allow us to describe in detail how, in 1946, Paliau's call to action spread from place to place. We know who carried the news and how people in different villages received it. As in other social movements, the power of the message was not necessarily enough in itself to draw followers, and we can identify reasons why Paliau's message took root in some places and not in others. Schwartz and Shargo were able to obtain similarly detailed accounts of the cargo cult—the Noise—that emerged within the Movement in 1947. And they were on the scene in 1953–54 for a second cargo cult episode, observing events kept hidden even from Manus people who stayed outside the cult, and seeing firsthand what enabled or impeded its spread.

Including a full (and shifting) cast of characters

Our chronicle of the Movement over the years draws heavily on Paliau's own commentary and conversations with both long-time adherents and new generations of Movement members and leaders. But Schwartz also took pains to obtain the perspectives of opponents of the Movement, apostates, and rivals. Studies of social change movements in general and millenarian movements in particular tend to fixate on their adherents. But such movements seldom sweep all before them and their participants are often a shifting cast. Those who stand aloof or drop out along the way are part of the full picture, and we include some of this variety in our account.[12]

Illuminating the irreducible complexity of a charismatic leader

Paliau was a protean figure, melding politician and prophet, moving smoothly between creating revolving loan funds and reinterpreting the Bible in a Melanesian idiom. Seeing him at only one point in his career or in relation to only one of the many groups with which his career brought him into contact could not reveal his complexity. Our data transcend these limitations. Further, we can glean insights from Paliau's many private conversations with Schwartz over the years.

Efforts to understand Paliau the man by distinguishing secular from non-secular aspects of his identity are especially problematic. From the beginning of his career, many of Paliau's followers believed he was inspired by God. Paliau gave his followers a mythic explanation, featuring the Christian God, for their relative poverty and powerlessness, but he also gave them programs with this-worldly rationales for change through this-worldly action. At times, the Movement has shown a primarily secular face, while at other times a focus on supernatural forces has been more visible. At no time, however, have all Movement adherents clustered densely at one pole or the other. Paliau's natural aptitude for inspirational ambiguity helped him appeal to people with many, often contrasting proclivities. Whether he did so with conscious intent must remain an open question. He was a keen judge of an audience and skilled in the kind of multilayered speech common in indigenous Melanesian oratory, a skill that allowed

---

12 This is the minimum required by what Schwartz calls a distributive model of culture, a topic he addresses in other publications (Schwartz 1978a, 1978b; Schwartz and Mead 1961). Ulf Hannerz (1992: 14) describes the major implications of a distributional model. It is not, he writes, 'just some nit-picking reminder that individuals are not all alike, but [rather] that people must deal with other people's meanings … At times, perhaps, one can just ignore them. Often enough, however, one may comment on them, object to them, feel stimulated by them, take them over for oneself, defer to them, or take them into account … They may be understood or misunderstood. And as these responses occur, or even in anticipation of them, [others] may respond to them'. Thus, the lack of uniformity of culture in a population also contributes to constant cultural change. Hannerz (1992: 12–14, 271–2) discusses the history of models of culture that emphasise diversity rather than sharing, including Schwartz's work. Edwin Hutchins, a member of Schwartz's research team in Manus in 1973, discusses this tradition and its place in his work in cognitive science (1995: 176–7).

people—including outside observers—to find in his words what they wanted to find. Also, at different points in his career, he turned different facets of a complex personality more to the light than others. The most stable, although not necessarily the 'deepest', aspect of his character was probably his steadfast determination to be recognised as a leader. We find it impossible, however, to reduce Paliau to politician, prophet, or even a consciously canny manipulator of complementary roles.

Emphasising the human penchant for millenarianism

The term 'millenarian' comes from passages in the Christian Bible (principally, the Book of Revelation) predicting Christ's Second Coming and his subsequent 1,000-year reign of peace and justice (the Millennium).[13] But some millenarian movements have been Christian, some non-Christian (such as the late nineteenth-century Ghost Dance among Native Americans, and some varieties of Islam) and some anti-Christian (e.g. the Boxer Rebellion of c. 1899–1900 in China). Christian millenarianism itself may have roots not only in Judaism but also in Zoroastrianism (Hall 2009; Hunt 2001: 2, citing Cohn 1970). There were also movements seeking to realise a vision of a perfect world substantially before the time of Christ. Richard Landes (2011: 149–84) provides an example in his discussion of what he calls the 'imperialist millennialism' of Pharaoh Akhenaten (1360–1347 BCE). Common in human history throughout the world, millenarianism, as Kenelm Burridge (1995 [1960]: xvii) puts it, 'seems to be a universal human proclivity'.

We use the term millenarian in the same sense as Landes (2011), who observes that millenarianism as used by scholars 'designates the belief that at some point in the future *the world that we live in will be radically transformed into one of perfection*—of peace, justice, fellowship, and plenty' (p. 20). Some utopian doctrines verge on millenarianism without invoking the supernatural, but they usually argue that abstract forces

---

13 The most familiar of these passages is Revelation 20:4 (King James Version): 'And I saw thrones, and they sat upon them, and judgment was given unto them: and *I saw* the souls of them that were beheaded for the witness of Jesus, and for the word of God, and which had not worshipped the beast, neither his image, neither had received *his* mark upon their foreheads, or in their hands; and they lived and reigned with Christ a thousand years'. The 1,000-year reign is followed by the Last Judgment, an element of biblical doctrine that is less popular.

of some kind—such as the progress of reason or justice—shape history. A telos—a purpose or preordained end—takes the place of supernatural powers, but it is no less metaphysical.[14]

Christianity has made critical contributions to the Paliau Movement, in particular its apocalyptic millenarian tendencies. Catholic missionaries were the major conduit of Christian ideas to Manus people in the Movement's formative period. As has happened frequently in the history of the Catholic Church, its teachings helped inspire people to expect an imminent world transformation despite the church's efforts, at least since St Augustine (354–430 CE), to expunge from doctrine the idea of an impending Second Coming for fear of exactly the kind of events that transpired in Manus.[15] Paliau's version of Christianity was clearly heretical, but he had something essential in common with defenders of church orthodoxy. To maintain a stable institution he too had to walk the fine line between instilling hope and committing to impossible promises, as our chronicle of his career will show.[16]

The Movement spread rapidly at first—'like fire', as a Movement slogan of later years proclaims—but it ultimately remained confined to Manus. Yet it persists, as do its deep millenarian tendencies. Whether trying to unite mutually hostile villages for economic self-help; waiting for the dead to rise, bringing unlimited material wealth; backing candidates for the national parliament; or cultivating ties with international conservation organisations, many Movement adherents have held fast to the hope that perfecting their world is possible and that perfection is almost within their reach.

Garry Trompf wisely advises against assuming that everything that someone calls a cargo cult is necessarily a millenarian effort. He writes: 'one should … be cautious about the varying degrees to which the cults reflect so-called millenarist features' (1991: 193–6). His extensive review of documented cases illustrates that not all cargo-centric ritual efforts or movements have necessarily sought a total, final transformation of the

---

14   See Landes (2011: xviii, 20–21, 292ff.) on secular millenarianism.

15   This is a commonplace in the literature on Christian millenarianism. For instance, many of the chapters in Hunt (2001) note this point. See in particular Watt (2001: 91) and Hamilton (2001: 21). See also Landes (2011: 48–9).

16   Regarding millenarianism and heresy, Hunt (2001: 2) writes: 'The millennium dream is therefore at the center of the faith and consistent with its principal dogmas. It is the *preoccupation* with the millennium to come … which separates the fanatics and the heretics from the rest of Christendom'.

world—an aim that many definitions of millenarianism require. It is also likely that *within* any ritual quest for cargo, participants may well differ in the degree to which they seek cargo as part of a total, final world transformation as opposed to seeking primarily the material goods. This seems to have been true of the Noise and the second cult episode, which we call the Cemetery Cult. The strongest proponents of these efforts, however, were fervent millenarians.

That proviso aside, it appears that anthropological interest in cargo cults as instances of a more widespread phenomenon has declined over the years. Peter Worsley's *The Trumpet Shall Sound: A Study of 'Cargo' Cults in Melanesia* was first published in 1957. Kenelm Burridge's major study of a particular cargo cult, *Mambu: A Melanesian Millennium*, first appeared in 1960, and his study of millenarianism in general, *New Heaven, New Earth: A Study of Millenarian Activities*, first appeared in 1969. We should add to the list of anthropological works giving millenarianism its due in the matter of cargo cults Weston La Barre's 1970 volume *The Ghost Dance: The Origins of Religion*. But the closer one gets to the present, the harder it is to find anthropological works on cargo cults that attend to millenarianism in general for more than a sentence or two. Landes (2011: 145) draws a similar conclusion in a review of anthropological writings on cargo cults: 'Aside from Garry Trompf … most recent anthropologists working on cargo cults seem to know far less about non-Melanesian millenarianism than did Peter Worsley'.[17] Landes also gives Kenelm Burridge credit for such a wider view.

Aletta Biersack (2013: 110–12) advocates eloquently for 'de-exoticizing' cargo cults by recognising their kinship with Western millenarianism, citing the work of Andrew Lattas (1992) and Joel Robbins (2004b) in support of her argument.[18] We are not, then, breaking a new trail, but the road we will take is still a road less travelled. Anthropological works that at least recognise the millenarian nature of cargo cults often fail to use that fact to elucidate their subject. Lamont Lindstrom (1993a, 1993b) notes literature that identifies the kinship of cargo cults with millenarianism in general, but he discards this avenue of analysis as unimportant.[19]

---

17   See Worsley (1968 [1957]) and Trompf (1994, 1991: 155–281).

18   Anthropologists have also produced a number of valuable studies of instances of Melanesian millenarianism that are not cargo-centric, among them Biersack (2013, 2011a, 2011b, 1991), Robbins (2004a), and Schmid (1999).

19   In the process, Lindstrom (1993a: 51) seriously misconstrues Schwartz's thoughts on cargo cults and millenarianism.

Nancy McDowell (2000: 378) almost grasps the point, but she lets it slip through her fingers: 'Melanesians may … long for the cargo, but their behaviour and desires are no more cult-like than the fervent Christian's belief in and preparation for the Rapture'. Unfortunately, McDowell takes this insight as a point of departure for questioning the existence of cargo cults rather than as a clue to understanding both cargo cults and the Rapture better. But McDowell is only one among many contemporary anthropologists who cannot look at cargo cults in such a larger context because they are preoccupied with dipping the concept in what Lindstrom (1993a: 42) calls the 'acid baths of deconstructionism'—principally, finding in the concept residues of colonialism that distort or pervert understanding of Melanesian reality.

Our reasons for bringing millenarianism in general into our discussion are simple.[20] First, it is beyond debate that many cargo cults are indeed instances of millenarianism. In fact, some of the over-extension of the cargo cult concept that concerns Lindstrom and others may flow from the fact that, in Landes's words (2011: 130), 'cargo cults illustrated so many of the dynamics characteristic of millennial movements that they soon became for some scholars the epitome' of millenarian phenomena. Second, we acknowledge that some people regard cargo cult as a stigmatising label, but we think that recognising the pan-human features of cargo cults helps remove this stigma. It demonstrates clearly that they are not a fringe form of human naivety. Rather, cargo cults are instances of a deep and wide human tendency, a tendency that does not lose its attraction in societies possessing greater scientific knowledge and more sophisticated technology than those of indigenous Melanesia. Third, keeping millenarianism in the discussion may help us understand cargo cults better by allowing us to distinguish common features of millenarian thought and action from those that are characteristically Melanesian. Finally, millenarianism—not necessarily of the explicitly cargo variety—is a potent force today in PNG, as it is in the world in general. It is not necessarily either benign or dangerous. But it may be easier to assess its influence on events if we can see it in a larger historical and cultural context.

---

20   We do not intend, however, a point-by-point comparison from which to derive theoretical conclusions.

Eschewing 'religion': Almost terminally amorphous

Both indigenous cosmology and Christianity influenced the Paliau Movement. Even so, many treatments of the Paliau Movement either regard as incidental or deliberately diminish aspects that do not look like secular politics; that is, politics focused on changing people's circumstances 'within the world of time and history' (Landes 2011: 21) with little or no supernatural assistance. Some observers of the Movement try to distinguish its political from its religious aspects, but this oversimplifies it. It also raises a more fundamental problem.

Anthropologists generally agree that politics has to do with obtaining and using power and that politics exists in virtually all spheres of life, even where it is not overt. But there is no consensus on even a broad definition of religion. Anthropological literature generally either fails to define the term or stretches it to baggy uselessness. Even anthropologists who are admirably subtle in treating religion and politics as at least analytically distinct, as is Roger Keesing, have found it, in Keesing's words, 'a difficult anthropological balancing act' (1982: 246). We prefer to avoid this precarious situation as much as possible. Fortunately, we can describe most of the aspects of the Paliau Movement that have been called religious more precisely as manifestations of what Schwartz calls a cosmology of animate and personal causation, a topic we return to in Chapters 2 and 3.

Recognising cargo cults: Because they exist and they are about cargo

Millenarian movements throughout Melanesia have often made access to unlimited quantities of material goods a centrepiece of a vision of a perfect world. Many indigenous millenarian movements in Melanesia have focused on obtaining—through ritual appeals to the Christian deities, the spirits of ancestors, or other indigenous supernatural powers—the kinds of goods that white colonial populations could call up, without obvious physical effort, as deliveries of 'cargo' (in Tok Pisin, *kago*) by ship and/or aeroplane. Hence, white colonials dubbed these indigenous Melanesian efforts to transform the world 'cargo cults'.[21]

---

21 Lamont Lindstrom (1993a) provides what is probably the most thorough history of the term cargo cult.

The name cargo cult stuck, but many anthropologists have promoted interpretations of the phenomenon that de-emphasise the overt obsession with material goods. Preferring to hypothesise about long-term political significance, Peter Worsley (1968 [1957]: 193) famously labelled the Paliau Movement, among others, as 'proto-nationalist'. Similarly, R.J. May (1982: 7) identified it as one among many 'micronationalist' movements in PNG. Burridge, in the introduction to a more recent edition of his classic *Mambu: A Melanesian Millennium* (1995 [1960]: xvi), notes numerous adjectives—most now fallen from use—scholars have attached to such Melanesian movements, among them acculturative, adaptive, nativistic, and revitalisation. Each involves a different focus of interpretation, although all tend to draw attention away from the participants' apparent focus on cargo.

More recently, some anthropologists object that the term cargo cult is inherently pejorative. A less ideological objection is that cargo is primarily a symbol of more complex, less concrete aims. We can speak with full confidence only of the cargo cult episodes within the Paliau Movement, but the facts of the Paliau Movement case suggest that discounting too vigorously participants' interest in material cargo—from canned goods to automobiles—seriously distorts participants' own understanding of their aims. The material wealth Paliau's followers sought *was* fraught with meaning for them. We think that easy access to the cargo meant restoring the self-worth of which their colonial situation deprived them and relieving deep anxieties characteristic of precolonial indigenous life. Cargo cult participants knew that white ascendency rested in large part on material superiority (in manufacturing, transport, communication, and armaments), and many of the core anxieties of indigenous life flowed from the highly competitive struggle to excel in trading, producing, and exchanging material goods. Yet, as we discuss further in Chapter 2, the broader hopes of most participants in the Noise and the Cemetery Cult were indistinct. There is a case for interpreting the more specific object of their yearnings—material goods—as a symbol. But our data indicate that material goods in themselves were critical. In a phrase anthropologist Paula Levin suggests (personal communication, July 2017), material cargo was sufficient for some cult participants and necessary for all.

In 1976, generalising about cargo cults from the case he knew best, Schwartz wrote that when people said 'It's not the cargo—it's the principle', he replied, 'it's the cargo' (1976a: 177; cf. Otto 2004: 222–3). We would not draw quite such a crisp line between cargo and more abstract things today. But we still insist that, whatever else they may have sought, cargo was fundamental to the visions of a perfect world that moved participants in the cults we will describe. Many who joined them hoped they would bring not only cargo but also reunification with their ancestors. But, as Schwartz has also observed, if the dead had returned as prophesied, cult adherents would have given a chilly reception to any who returned without cargo. And if the returning dead had somehow purged the islands of white colonial domination, cult adherents would have been aghast if white colonial cargo had also disappeared.

When the adherents of today's most visible version of the Paliau Movement, Wind Nation, talk about their organisation, many strongly deny that it is a cargo cult. Through Wind Nation, they say, they will someday find 'true freedom' (in Tok Pisin, *tru fridom*). This does sound 'more profound and less tangible than European goods themselves', to use Garry Trompf's phrase (1994: 160). But to Wind Nation adherents, this freedom comprises very tangible things: it is freedom from hard work, illness, old age, and death. This is clearly a millenarian aim. But could one call Wind Nation a cargo cult? We will return to this question in Chapter 15.

Preview of the chapters to come

In Chapter 2, we give more detailed attention to the issues broached above—the futility of trying to separate politics from religion in the Paliau Movement, or of separating the identities of politician and prophet in Paliau the man; the need for a less shapeless concept to describe what is often glossed as religion in Melanesia and elsewhere; and the case for keeping cargo cult in our professional vocabulary and recognising the importance of material goods in understanding cargo cults. Keeping faith with our data on the Paliau Movement helps drive our concern with these matters. In critiquing some trends in anthropological analysis of cargo cults, we also urge our colleagues not to ignore the ubiquitous human propensity for irrationality.

In Chapter 3, we show why forging even fragile unity among dozens of villages in the Paliau Movement was a remarkable accomplishment and illuminate the cultural and historical circumstances that gave Paliau's call for radical change its appeal. We also dwell on the nature of a pervasive cosmology of animate and personal causation, because it is of the Movement's essence, not simply its context or background. The latter discussion would be incomplete without pointing out that although understanding this aspect of the indigenous Manus world is critical to understanding the Paliau case, cosmologies of animate and personal causation—and their dark side, which informs what Schwartz has christened a paranoid ethos—also flourish in the modern West. Everywhere they occur, they contribute to the strength of millenarianism, including its deep implication in current events of international political importance. We return to this fact and the questions it raises in our final chapter. Chapter 4 summarises European contact and colonialism in Manus, the dramatic events of World War II in the Admiralties, and early efforts by indigenous innovators to make fundamental changes in Manus society inspired by the resonance of visions stirred by the European presence with chronic problems of indigenous life.

In Chapters 5 through 11, with the help of data Schwartz collected from the 1960s to the 1990s, we cast new light on the events of the 1940s and 1950s that Schwartz first described in his 1962 monograph, 'The Paliau Movement in the Admiralty Islands, 1946–1954'. Chapter 5 takes us from Paliau's early life through the Movement's beginning. Chapter 6 tells of the irruption of the Noise in 1947 and its failure. Chapter 7 describes the period of drift in the Movement after the Noise subsided, during which (in 1953–54) Mead, Schwartz, and Shargo arrived to document the Movement. It was not apparent at first that the Movement was foundering. But as this became more visible, and after Mead's departure, Schwartz and Shargo became witnesses to a second cult episode, which interrupted the Movement's apparent turn away from the Noise. Chapter 8 describes how Schwartz and Shargo finally became aware of the cult. Schwartz wrote to Mead of these 'strange and exciting' events, but this news did not please her. In an exchange of letters she questioned him closely about his report, suggesting that he and Shargo might be mistaken. She even speculated that exposure to the nervous imaginings of members of the tiny white colonial community on Manus might have led Schwartz and Shargo astray. Mead might also have found it galling that she had failed to notice such dramatic goings on, or that Pere villagers had kept them from her. There is no doubt, however, that she would have preferred there simply had been no cargo cult. Schwartz (1983: 928) later recalled: 'Before we left for the field Mead told me that if Manus turned out to be another cultural shambles—a slum culture, undermined and demoralised as a result of the drastic culture contact and change they had experienced—

she would not write about it. What the world needed was a success story'. In Mead's view, success did not include abandoning what she portrayed as a systematic modernisation program to turn to petitioning Jesus for immediate salvation. Mead herself was an ardent Christian, but many Manus people clearly did not interpret the Christian message as did Mead, an Episcopalian. Fortunately, Schwartz and Shargo persisted, and their observations of this second cult, presented in Chapter 9, are perhaps the most powerful argument that material wealth was a defining objective of the Manus cults.

Schwartz dubbed the second cult the Cemetery Cult because it required building new cemeteries constructed according to the instructions of the cult's tutelary ghosts. Comparing the Noise with the Cemetery Cult, as we do in Chapter 10, gives us the rare opportunity to see how a history of millenarian thought and action can influence a particular instance. In the Manus case, our knowledge of what was the relatively recent and spectacular failure of the Noise casts light on many features of the Cemetery Cult that distinguish it dramatically from its predecessor. Schwartz's detailed observations also allow us to understand why within a single population people took radically different attitudes towards the cults.

It was especially important to the course of the Movement that some Cemetery Cult adherents began to see it as an alternative to Paliau's program, not—as in the Noise—as its fulfilment. Keenly aware of this, Paliau took dramatic steps—described in Chapter 11—to end the Cemetery Cult before it inevitably failed on its own. Here we also see Paliau at the height of his powers. He was a charismatic leader, but his charisma was not some ineffable aura. His sway over people rested to a great extent on rhetorical skill, remarkable physical energy, and perhaps overweening self-confidence, as well as on people's belief in his occult knowledge and power.

Paliau stopped the Cemetery Cult at a time when the Australian administration was accelerating its efforts to introduce new political and economic institutions in Manus. He quickly grasped the import of these efforts, and—as described in Chapter 12—he pursued secular Movement goals through participating in the Territory's emerging electoral political system. But as Paliau's star rose in secular spheres, morale declined among those of his followers who still hoped for a sudden supernatural transformation of their lives. Nevertheless, Paliau was elected first president of the new regional Native Government Council he had pressed the administration to create, and in 1964 and 1968 he won four-year terms as Member for Manus District in the first Territory-wide House of Assembly, the precursor of independent PNG's parliament. But his political fortunes declined rapidly after he lost his 1972 bid for a third term in the House.

Chapter 13 begins with Schwartz (accompanied this time by Smith, Edwin Hutchins, and Geoffrey White) returning to Manus in 1973 after several years' absence. They found Paliau in retreat on Baluan Island, despondent and in poor health. Paliau told Schwartz that this visit, lasting several weeks, reinvigorated him. But he was already pondering reviving the Movement on a more explicitly mystical footing. Paliau soon attracted a small but enthusiastic band of new followers, including university-educated members of younger generations. Schwartz watched Paliau and this new core of adherents create a new version of the Movement that combined a new theology with cultural pseudo-revival and a theocratic political ideology chronically opposed to independent PNG's provincial and national governments. Under its current name—Wind Nation—this iteration of the Movement has enjoyed limited success in the electoral sphere, but it remains to this day vitally interested in metaphysical knowledge that will banish hard work, want, illness, ageing, and death.

By the time the Movement morphed into Wind Nation, Paliau had been made an Officer of the Most Excellent Order of the British Empire (PNG is a member of the British Commonwealth of Nations) in honour of his worldly accomplishments. He had also proclaimed himself the Last Prophet of the World. By the end of his life, his followers had begun to identify him with Jesus. We cannot claim to know how Paliau regarded himself at this point. When, in 1953, Paliau first spoke to Schwartz about the development of his ideas for the Movement, he refrained from telling of a dream in which he had received a revelation from Jesus. But Schwartz, having already heard of this from Paliau's followers, wanted to hear it directly from Paliau. Paliau demurred, saying 'Who am I that God should talk to me?' But he finally responded to Schwartz's prodding. He may have been reluctant to do so at first because he expected Schwartz, as a white, to be openly sceptical, even scornful. But he came to understand that Schwartz was merely deeply interested. Schwartz visited Paliau for the last time in 1990, the year before Paliau's death. He had heard that Paliau had told his followers that he (i.e. Paliau) was Jesus. Schwartz asked him bluntly if he had done so. Paliau's reply was equivocal, perhaps studiously so, perhaps not. Paliau told Schwartz: 'I said to them, who else in the world has such good things to say? It's Jesus! He is a man with good things to say. I said: I'm your Jesus. I'm your Jesus, I told them.'[22] Paliau added that he had told his followers that he was merely Paliau Maloat, but that he got his teachings from Jesus.[23] He then turned to Schwartz and said: 'So, what do you think?'[24] Rather than give an opinion, Schwartz prompted Paliau to expand on his prior remarks, but Paliau either would not or could not offer a glimpse into a neater self-understanding. In 2015, some Wind Nation adherents were firmly convinced that Paliau had not only said he was Jesus, he indeed was—in a sense—Jesus. But we will argue that while Paliau may have dissembled in his conversation with Schwartz, he was not a fraud.

As described in Chapter 14, Smith found in 2015 that some aspects of Paliau's life and teachings were in dispute, but Wind Nation endured. There is no accurate count of current participation in Wind Nation and, as far as we know, there is no formal membership status. Some activists claim that Wind Nation still has members in all 33 villages Schwartz identified as participating in the Movement in the 1950s. In Pere, a Movement stronghold since the 1950s, Wind Nation adherents still gather regularly at the spacious meeting house they maintain in the centre of the village, adjacent to 'Margaret Mead's Resource Center'.[25] But they face increasing competition for attention and allegiance in Pere and in Manus Province. There is even danger of schism within Wind Nation. Even so, on Baluan Island, the Nation's official leadership was overseeing construction, to an architect's specifications, of Freedom House, a small but impressive octagonal structure intended as the focal point of Wind Nation International.

In Chapter 15, the final chapter, we observe that to many of the people of Manus Paliau still represents communitarian values and a spirit of self-help. But some also see him as the prophet of something grander.

---

22   In Tok Pisin (the lingua franca in which the conversation took place, which we describe in Chapter 2): *Mi tokim tok olsem, na husat moa i ken mekim gutpela toktok long olgeta man long worl? Em Yesus tasol! Em i man bilong gutpela toktok. Mi tok, mi, mi Yesus bilong yupela. Mi Yesus bilong yupela mi tokim ol.*

23   In Tok Pisin: *Mi tok long maus bilong mi olsem, 'Mi Paliau Maloat, tasol mi kisim olgeta toktok olsem long Yesus'.*

24   In Tok Pisin: *Na yu ting wanem?*

25   This is a spacious, multi-room structure of manufactured materials, built in part with funds provided by American friends of Mead.

Earlier generations of Movement participants could not have imagined obtaining today's material comforts without supernatural aid: mobile phones and wristwatches (that function) are common and many Manus villagers enjoy reliable electric lights in their homes, powered by movable solar panels that charge lightweight batteries (even though many village houses are still made from forest timbers and palm-leaf thatch). But the attachment to the millenarian face of Paliau's doctrines many maintain indicates they would like something more. In the last stage of his career, Paliau held out the possibility of attaining a perfect world through the favour of a supreme being (but not the Christian God). But he gave no detailed formula for achieving it. Nor did he promise when it would arrive; he only spoke cryptically of signs for which people should watch. His last teachings and prophecies may have drawn new participants and reinvigorated some of the old guard, but we know that they also alienated some second- and third-generation Paliau admirers. Some Wind Nation adherents appear to be settling in for a long wait, but the possibility of a millenarian transformation is still Wind Nation doctrine.

It is hard to see allegiance to Wind Nation today as a reaction to the inequality and powerlessness of direct colonial rule. Many adherents of Wind Nation were either very young when PNG achieved independence—in 2015, 40 years had passed since that event—or born thereafter. They know nothing of the open racism and both the legal and de facto segregation of the colonial era. Anthropologists familiar with PNG before and in the years just following independence know that the racial climate changed only gradually as Papua New Guineans took over running the country and assumed more prominent roles in business and civic institutions. Changes in relations between indigenes and whites are sometimes most dramatically apparent in mundane situations. Smith recalls that in the early decades of independence, when he travelled from his research site on Kairiru Island to Wewak, the principal town in East Sepik Province, he often stayed at one of Wewak's few small hotels, most of which resembled rather spartan versions of what Americans call motels. The staff of these hostelries—even if they were Papua New Guineans— often looked askance at the barefoot, shabbily dressed villagers from Kairiru who accompanied Smith and helped him with his baggage. And members of Smith's escort—the older ones in particular—often felt uneasy, and hovered near the doors of the small lobbies.

Things have changed a lot since then. When Smith arrived in Wewak after several weeks on Kairiru in 2015, the desk clerk at the Airport Lodge was unperturbed when he asked for a double room for him and his barefoot companion, Stephen Umari. A junior hotel manager, Charlie Numbos, born and raised on Kairiru and now studying the hospitality business, came out to greet them warmly. A few weeks later, Smith was returning to Lorengau after a stay in Pere village. Three mature Pere men accompanied him, managed his baggage from the open boat up a steep, muddy bank, and helped hoist it into the back of a truck, already crammed with passengers, for the trip to town. Arriving at the Harbourside Hotel, the security guards at the gate in the chain link fence surrounding the hotel grounds waved the entire party through. Inside, the desk clerk gave the Pere elders no more than a glance as they waited for Smith to check in and then saw him to his room. When they got there, one stretched out on the bed and pronounced it worthy of a nap. Another checked the contents of the small refrigerator and helped himself to iced water. And the third disappeared into the bathroom for a long sojourn from which he emerged looking refreshed. (In Pere, people still have to fetch fresh water from inland sources by canoe, and toilets are thatched structures reached by log bridges over the lagoon.) These may seem like small things. But if you remember the past, they feel like big changes.[26]

As we also discuss in Chapter 15, such changes in PNG and considerable scholarly literature incline us to recommend reducing the widespread emphasis on oppression and deprivation in explaining both particular instances of millenarianism and the larger phenomenon. We propose that to understand people's *susceptibility* to millenarianism as a response to suffering—which is universal, whereas millenarianism is not—anthropologists should probe more critically two near-universal human tendencies: people's difficulty accepting the role of chance or impersonal forces in shaping events (that is, the tendency to personify causation), and people's tendency to imagine that they are the focus of malign or benign attention, from the local level to the cosmic.

This view is at odds with tendencies to romanticise millenarianism, wherever it occurs. As we point out, millenarianism in the United States also provides excellent current examples of its highly problematic potential. Conspiracy theories, many of them noxious, are more than just

---

26 We should add that such changes also make life more pleasant for anthropologists. It is maddening to watch one's companions treated as inferiors or, worse, see them appear to accept that role.

millenarianism's frequent companions. Millenarianism and conspiracy thinking are, as political scientist Michael Barkun (2006 [2003]: 10) points out, symbiotic: 'Conspiracy theories locate and describe evil, while millennialism explains the mechanism for its ultimate defeat.' And both rest on a cosmology of animate and personal causation and what Schwartz calls a paranoid ethos and Barkun calls a 'conspiracist worldview'. Like a paranoid ethos, a conspiracist worldview assumes 'a universe governed by design rather than by randomness' and 'a world based on intentionality, from which accident and coincidence have been removed' (Barkun 2006 [2003]: 3–4). Hence, millenarianism can have unfortunate tendencies. For instance, the passion for 'spiritual warfare' of Pentecostal and other millenarian Christian sects in PNG today makes them aggressively less humane than the Paliau Movement in any of its phases.

Why we wrote this book

We have the privilege of adding something to the world's historical record from somewhere—PNG—that gets little attention, unless it is the site of a disaster or gets pulled into the affairs of more prominent nations. We also have the unusual opportunity to chronicle a substantial portion of the life of a charismatic leader and the evolution of his social and metaphysical doctrines from the standpoint of people who are not disciples or apostles. An anthropologist or journalist watching at close range the life of Jesus of Nazareth, chatting with him behind the scenes, and interviewing both his close associates and his detractors, probably would have produced an account rather different from that found in the New Testament.[27]

Parts of the Paliau story are forever beyond recovery, but we can fill many gaps. Current followers and critics of Paliau, many too young to have witnessed the events of which they speak, are already busy filling in gaps with their own versions of the past, often shaped by their present interests. This includes describing well-known events in new ways. No one today denies that in 1947 people threw their valuables into the sea in an effort to

---

27   Wind Nation adherents have already found fault with Schwartz's 1962 account of the Movement. Kakak Kais (1998: Chapter 1) writes that Schwartz 'denies Paliau's reasoning capacity and his ability to plan', apparently because Schwartz reported Paliau's own accounts of knowledge received in dreams. But Paliau himself deemed his dreams important in the development of his thought. A more careful reading of Schwartz's 1962 account clearly shows his admiration for Paliau's skill in planning and organisation.

bring the cargo. In 2015, however, some Movement members described this as an act of 'repentance'—using the English word—a description never conveyed to Schwartz in the 1950s or in subsequent decades.[28]

In addition, the value of considering the Paliau Movement as a case study in millenarianism extends beyond PNG. Barkun describes the current era in the United States as marked by 'a dramatic proliferation of millenarian schemata, both in terms of the number of competing visions and … their diversity' (2006 [2003]: 21). Millenarianism embraces both fear— usually of evil conspiracies—and hope, often inspired by utopian visions. But the hopes as well as the fears fatten on the human willingness— even eagerness—to believe what is founded only in imagination and to deny reality. Although millenarian hopes date from ancient times, they thrive in what we have recently learned to call a 'post-truth' era and they nurture it.[29] This should give us pause.

---

28   A similar but more trivial case: In 2015, some Pere villagers told Smith that Margaret Mead chose Schwartz's first wife, Lenora Shargo, for him. She did not. Nor did Mead have a hand in selecting his subsequent wives.

29   Oxford Dictionaries chose 'post-truth' as Word of the Year for 2016 (languages.oup.com/word-of-the-year/). It is defined as an adjective 'relating to or denoting circumstances in which objective facts are less influential in shaping public opinion than appeals to emotion and personal belief'.

2

Taking exception

We are eager to get to the islands, beaches, and lagoons of Manus and the flesh-and-blood people and remarkable events of the Paliau Movement. But before we do, we need to say more about some of the distinctive aspects of our approach and the issues they entail that we summarised in Chapter 1.

Problems with portrayals of the Paliau Movement and Paliau the man

Histories of Papua New Guinea (PNG) that mention the Paliau Movement ignore or minimise almost all its dimensions that aren't easy to depict in conventional political terms (Griffin et al. 1979: 99; Souter 1963: 241n; Waiko 2007: 11–13; White 1965: 151–6).[1] The Movement did have significant lasting effects on political institutions in Manus. But focusing narrowly on conventional politics does not do justice to the complexity of the Movement, its founder and leader, and the motives and experiences of Movement participants.

---

1   Other histories of New Guinea or PNG we know of (Dorney 1990; Moore 2003; Turner 1990) make no mention of Paliau.

The fallacy of opposing the political and the religious

Trying to distinguish what is political from what is religious is no more helpful for understanding Manus in the 1950s than it is for understanding contemporary Europe or America.[2] For instance, Christian reconstructionism (Ingersoll 2015; McVicar 2015) is a millenarian doctrine holding that Christ will return only after the faithful have established biblical law on Earth. It is influential on the right wing of American politics and virtually obliterates any but the most tortured distinction between politics and theology. Closely examining Paliau's career, as we will show, has much the same effect. We can also see both the man and the Movement more clearly if we largely dispense with the concept 'religion'.

Keeping politics but eschewing religion

Politics is a much more helpful concept than religion. The definition of politics generally accepted in anthropology is simple and useful: politics is behaviour concerned with obtaining and using power, something one can find in virtually all spheres of life—including those pertaining to metaphysical concerns—although frequently it is not overt. But not even a similarly broad definition of religion unites anthropologists. Roy Rappaport, a leading anthropological scholar of religion, does not dispute this, but he doesn't let it slow him down either: 'The concept of religion is irreducibly vague, but vagueness is not vacuity, and we know well enough what people mean by the term to get on with things' (1999: 23). Some prominent scholars of Melanesian religion also avoid proposing a definition of religion. Garry Trompf (1994: xv) chooses to think of religion in Melanesia 'much more as a people's "way of life" than merely worship or approaches to the "non-empirical realm" in particular'.[3] In the same spirit, Swain and Trompf (1995: 15) prefer to

---

2   Jebens (2004b: 167) and Otto (1992b: 4–5) are among those who have stressed the inadequacy of such categories for interpreting millenarianism in both Melanesia and Europe. Landes (2011) is particularly useful on this topic. See especially Chapters 8–12.

3   Trompf's references to the Paliau Movement in his 1994 work on Melanesian religion show a sound grasp of Paliau's and the Movement's complexity, which he does not try to parse using simplistic categories.

write about *The Religions of Oceania* without committing to a definition, opting instead for 'an open-ended and flexible understanding of the religious dimension'.[4]

Many anthropologists appear to regard whatever the term religion refers to as something not only inseparable from human life but also essential to it, like digestion. Rappaport (1999: 1–2) opines that, given the vast amount of time and energy human beings have devoted to 'religious considerations' over the ages, 'it is hard to imagine that religion … is not in some way indispensable to the species'.[5] This compounds the confusion.

In this book, we use the terms religion or religious sparingly. When we do use them, we do so to refer to phenomena pertaining to human relationships with supernatural beings and powers, albeit recognising that many Manus people past and present may not subscribe to an opposition between natural and supernatural.[6] But the natural/supernatural distinction is useful for understanding aspects of the Manus case, which

---

4   Speaking of 'religiosity' or 'spirituality' rather than religion (as, for example, in Douglas [2001]) does not clarify anything. Bruce Kapferer and colleagues (2010: 9) only muddy the water more by trying to define religiosity, calling it 'an urgency to total commitment that is a force of the religious and that tends to find legitimation of its truth in the evidence of experience, in the qualities of its lived relations, and its capacity to rid the world of the perceived humiliations and injustices of encompassing realities'. As a definition, it is not only borderline inscrutable, it is also much too broad to allow one to distinguish 'religiosity' from myriad other human passions. In his classic discussion of millenarianism, Burridge (1969: 6–7) offers a definition of 'religion and religious activity' that appears to overlap with what Kapferer et al. are struggling to say. Equally prolix, it also fails to distinguish an easily recognisable object, to wit: 'the redemptive process indicated by the activities, moral rules, and assumptions about power which, pertinent to the moral order and taken on faith, not only enable people to perceive the truth of things, but guarantee that they are indeed perceiving the truth of things'.
5   Here, Rappaport seems to be recommending religion as much as trying to understand it. This calls to mind Daniel C. Dennett's observation that many more people nourish 'belief in belief' in God than could be said to actually believe in God (2006: 200–46). It is easier to find religion indispensable to the species if you contrive, as some anthropologists do, to find it even in people's efforts to avoid it. Kapferer et al. (2010: 3), for instance, argue that 'the apparent rejection of the religious in much secularism masks the secular subsumption of religious orientations'. They are correct to a certain extent. Forms of millenarianism that attempt to expunge all traces of the occult, such as some forms of Marxism, may nevertheless invite it in by assuming a necessary direction or purpose in human history. Such prominent intellectuals as Bertrand Russell (1997 [1935]) and Raymond Aron (2001 [1957]) have argued that various political isms are forms of religion. But it would be a mistake to argue that people are incapable of seeing things in fully secular ways, no matter how rare this may be. Hans Kelsen's combatively titled *Secular Religion: A Polemic against the Misinterpretation of Modern Social Philosophy, Science, and Politics as 'New Religions'* is of special note regarding this issue. Kelsen completed *Secular Religion* in the early 1960s, but he deferred its publication during his lifetime and the book was not published in English until 2012. We rely on Stewart (2012) for this information and for insight into Kelsen's arguments.
6   We join many other social scientists in choosing such a definition. Barrett (2000: 29), for example, adopts the following definition: 'a shared system of beliefs and actions concerning supernatural agency'.

we describe in Chapter 3. It fits many other cases just as well, if one doesn't confuse religion with theology. Theology is speculative, and it is often concerned with challenging rather than elaborating accepted definitions of religion. Everyday religion—working religion or religion in practice—is generally a matter of applying comparatively simple ideas without pausing for speculation.

The concept we need: A cosmology of animate and personal causation

Even given the above qualification, we will avoid speaking of religion when we can. To the extent possible, we will focus on a feature of the Paliau Movement's cultural context that has often been described as religious, but that we can define much more precisely. This is the strength in Melanesia—past and present—of what Schwartz calls a cosmology of animate and personal causation. Schwartz has also used the terms 'personalism' and 'personalistic explanation' to describe a cosmology that assumes the world is governed by conscious forces with many of the attributes of persons. That is, forces that have intentions and emotions and are sensitive to human will and emotion. Thus, there is little or no room for randomness or chance or the impersonal natural forces to which science, and people with a scientific bent, turn for explanations of many phenomena (Schwartz 1972: 33; 1973: 165). Other anthropologists have come independently to use personalism, personalistic, and similar terms to describe world views in which animate and personal causation hold sway, among them Stanley Diamond (1974: 144–6), George M. Foster (1976), George M. Foster and Barbara G. Anderson in their pioneering work on medical anthropology (1978), and Roy Wagner (1981: 87), who speaks of the prevalence of 'anthropomorphic or sociomorphic explanation' in Melanesia.

We have to eschew the term personalism because it has long been associated with more than one school of philosophy, none of which address questions usefully related to our purposes here.[7] Anthropomorphism does not serve either. Anthropomorphism as usually understood—ascribing human attributes to non-human entities—suggests something narrower than what we have in mind. So, we will settle for speaking of a world view or cosmology of personified causation or simply personification of the world, with special emphasis on personifying causation.

---

7   See, for instance, the definitions offered in Blackburn (1994: 283–4).

Personification underlies much of what anthropologists call religion (e.g. Trompf 1994: xvi), with the exception of what are sometimes called non-theistic religions, such as forms of Buddhism, Taoism, or Confucianism, although personification figures in the folk versions of these traditions.[8] Personification, however, is not simply another name for religion or for what E.B. Tylor, in defining 'animism', called 'the doctrine of spiritual beings' (1871: xii, 287, 420). Personification as we use it embraces a range of assumptions regarding the vital role of human or human-like forms of consciousness in shaping events, either as specific interested parties responding to human actions or intentions, or as vaguer moral forces, like karma or fate. While some people may conceive of the latter as impersonal characteristics of the universe, cognitive psychologists Konika Banerjee and Paul Bloom (2014: 285–6, cf. 300) suggest that at least some Euro-Americans tend to personify fate 'as a type of goal-directed intentional force'.

A. Irving Hallowell (1955: 181) provides a classic example of a common kind of personified cultural construction of the world—what Hallowell might have called a personified behavioural environment—among the Ojibwa people of what is now north-eastern Canada: 'All the effective agents of events throughout the entire behavioural environment of the Ojibwa are selves—my own self and other selves. *Impersonal* forces are never the causes of events. *Somebody* is always responsible'. Elsewhere (1960), Hallowell refers to conscious non-human agents in the Ojibwa cultural world as 'non-human persons'.[9] But the concepts of personification and animate and personal causation embrace an even

---

8   The Christian theologian Paul Tillich is well known for his efforts to free religion from personification by elaborating a concept of God as something other than a being. Rather, he argues for conceiving of God as the 'ground of Being-Itself', an idea that has not passed into folk Christianity. His best-known exposition of this idea appears in his 1952 work *The Courage to Be*.

9   Graham Harvey leans heavily on these items from Hallowell's work and gleanings from the work of other anthropologists in *Animism: Respecting the Living World* (2005). This volume has received considerable attention as a statement of what is sometimes called the 'new animism'. Curiously, some proponents of the so-called ontological turn in anthropology (Holbraad and Pedersen 2017: 161) cite it as such uncritically. Harvey's work, however, should not be mistaken for anthropology. Among other things, he appears to be unfamiliar with the concept of the behavioural environment, which is essential to understanding Hallowell's work. In brief, Hallowell uses the term behavioural environment to refer to the culturally constructed environment within which people perceive and act in the world, specifically allowing not only for constructions shared by members of a group but also for universal features of human behavioural environments and features derived from individual experience (Hallowell 1955: 40, 75–110). While the ethnographic vignettes of 'animism' Harvey presents also illustrate varieties of personification, we hope it is clear that when we speak of forms of personification we are speaking of *culturally constructed* realities. Harvey is ambiguous on this vital issue.

wider variety of phenomena. Some degree of personification is probably a human universal. One can find vivid examples of this bias even in supposedly modern, highly rationalised settings. The work of W. Edwards Deming (1982), for instance, provides many examples of how, in Western business organisations, when things go wrong, managers often look first for inadequate employees rather than for weaknesses in the systems within which people work (cf. Smith 1994: 44).

To the extent that assuming a guiding purpose behind events implies a shaping consciousness of some sort, teleological thinking, which is rampant virtually everywhere, clearly qualifies as a form of personification. Teleological views of history are arguably attenuated forms of personifying causation, but couched in the language of materialist naturalism. And Banerjee and Bloom (2014: 277) report that teleological thinking—'the perception that human life is guided by unseen intentional forces'—is common in the West, and that 'it is not solely the consequence of culturally transmitted religious views, but rather reflects a general cognitive bias to perceive purpose in social and natural worlds' (p. 287).[10]

Although personification is not the same as supernaturalism, naturalism is its antonym.[11] From a naturalistic standpoint the non-human world (with the exception of our more cognitively complex fellow animals) comprises entities and forces—such as viruses and the shifting of tectonic plates—that not only do not care about human thoughts or actions, they are not capable of taking an attitude of any kind, either towards human beings or towards each other. Anthropology as a science doesn't necessarily require insisting on the ontological truth of naturalism; it must, however, insist on naturalism as a heuristic stance.[12] In Chapter 3 we discuss factors that give personification its strength in Melanesia, and we look at personification's pronounced dark side. It is enough at this point to say that a personified understanding of the world is integral to all phases and faces of the Paliau Movement.

---

10   Bias towards both personifying causation and teleological thinking might be seen as a form of illusory pattern perception, a widespread cognitive bias that social psychologists have linked to belief in the supernatural and the paranormal (van Prooijen et al. 2017). Exploring the relationship between these phenomena, however, is beyond the scope of our book.

11   Foster and Anderson (1978: 54) help clarify why 'supernaturalism' is not an accurate antonym for naturalism when the latter term is used as we use it here.

12   We are aware that not all anthropologists regard the field as a science. Those who find our position troubling may want to consult Jarvie (1984), especially pages 51–4, Kuznar (1997), and Spiro (1986). We are also aware that there is a case for a historical relationship between millenarianism and modern science (e.g. Noble 1997); but the esteem in which Schwartz and Smith hold science does not extend to finding in it a route to social perfection.

Paliau's irreducible complexity

Undoubtedly, some who discuss the Movement and the man largely in terms of politics as a pragmatic, secular endeavour are simply uninterested in their other dimensions. Other oversimplified depictions, however, flow from their authors' biases. Margaret Mead's bias helps explain why Douglas Dalton (2004: 203–4) finds 'disagreement' between observers who describe Paliau's early mission as 'primarily a practical one' and those who 'describe in detail the dream-inspired biblical millennial message with which Paliau began his movement'. Dalton cites Schwartz's work and Otto's as examples of the latter emphasis. He relies on Worsley's *The Trumpet Shall Sound* (1968) for an example of the former—that is, an emphasis on Paliau's 'practical' mission. In an essay written many years later, Worsley does refer to the 'First and Second Paliau Cults' (1999: 151); but, in *The Trumpet Shall Sound* he relies on Mead's *New Lives for Old* (2001 [1956]). Mead's commitment to drawing optimistic lessons for the world in *New Lives*, the first published account of the Paliau Movement, led her to discount evidence that Paliau was engaged in anything other than a self-conscious effort to, in Mead's words, 'incorporate the values and institutions of the Western world' and 'build a real modern culture' (ibid.: 16). She stressed Paliau's commitment to 'a limited earthly paradise to be realistically attained only by hard work and controlled behaviour' as opposed to sudden, supernaturally mediated transformation as promised by cargo cults (ibid.: 205).[13] Journalist Osmar White's one-dimensional portrait of Paliau (White 1965: 151–6) also owes much to Mead's influence. White's only encounters with Paliau were in Mead's company (Mead 2001 [1956]: 196–204), and he depended for additional information on *New Lives for Old* (White 1965: 151n).

Some of Paliau's admirers carry on the tradition of asserting emphatically his fundamentally 'practical', 'secular', 'reformist', and 'rational and sceptical' orientation, as Biama Kanasa did in his 1991 obituary of Paliau in *The Times of Papua New Guinea*. Kanasa is clearly intent on distancing Paliau from any association with cargo cults. But he finds it impossible to ignore Paliau's deep entanglement with metaphysical concerns and recognises the importance for the Movement of what he calls Paliau's 'religious' ideas. Similarly, Mead noted the importance of the 'religious

---

13   For some of the lessons Mead found, and may have intended to find, see in particular her preface to the 1975 edition of *New Lives for Old* (2001 [1956]: xix–xxvi).

sanction' Paliau claimed for his leadership (Mead 2001 [1956]: 225). It is more to the point, we think, to acknowledge that Paliau lived fully within a personified world, as much when he ran for elective office as when—late in his career—he failed to demure, at the least, when followers identified him with Jesus.

Paliau was born on Baluan, one of the Admiralty Islands, about 25 miles south of Manus Island and substantially smaller. New Guineans of his generation did not usually keep track of their birthdates, but Paliau probably was born in the early years of the twentieth century.[14] Unlike most of his contemporaries, he never joined a Christian mission and thus never received one of the many Christian names—such as Francis, John, Mathew, or Thomas—the missions bestowed on their converts. He remained Paliau Maloat throughout his life.[15] Paliau is a common name in Manus, but from here on when we refer to Paliau without qualification we mean Paliau Maloat.

In *New Lives for Old* (2001 [1956]), Mead repeatedly emphasised Paliau's exceptional ability: he was 'a political genius' (p. 204), she wrote, with 'a mind as gifted as that of men who have led millions and changed the face of the earth' (p. 199). She also praised his charisma ('vice-regal … carries an air of aristocracy about him' [p. 193]), and pronounced him manifestly superior to his contemporaries: he 'towered over his followers in statesmanship and planning' (p. 192) and was 'intrinsically superior to his fellows' (p. 204). Paliau did stand out from the crowd. His success in recruiting and retaining followers, however, depended to a great extent on what he had in common with the other indigenous people of Manus. He shared their hopes for a changed way of life, but he was also able to inspire his contemporaries to accept his leadership because he and they were immersed in the same cultural world. Like his contemporaries, Paliau did not question the prevailing personification of the world. He was also completely at home in a culture in which indirect and figurative speech

---

14   Paliau's obituary in *The Times of Papua New Guinea* (Kanasa 1991: 20) states that he was born in 1907. Paliau himself has given that date (Maloat 1970: 144), but in 1984 and 1986 respectively he claimed in conversation with anthropologist Alexander Wanek to have been born as early as 1892 or 1884 (Wanek 1996: 198).

15   Maloat was Paliau's father's name. Using one's father's name as a surname is probably a practice adopted from Christian missionaries. Such a change in naming practices was common in PNG (see e.g. Smith 2013: 205n2). It apparently had not yet taken hold when Fortune and Mead conducted research in Manus in 1928. Fortune (1965 [1935]) identifies Manus people by single names, using the names of their places of residence or a kinship relationship to another person to provide further identification.

was the norm and people were on constant alert for hidden meaning. Both Schwartz and Smith have seen the latter tendency so ascendant in various Melanesian locales that people assumed that speakers' intended meanings completely contradicted the literal sense of their words. The historic upheaval that gave rise to the Paliau Movement exacerbated this tendency and it metastasised during certain phases of the Movement.

Among the traits that Mead admired most in Paliau was that he 'adeptly and responsibly, tried to be "all things to all men"' (2001 [1956]: 192). She wrote of his ability to interact confidently with government officials and anthropologists as well as with both the 'level-headed' and the 'mystical fanatics' among the people of Manus. There is no denying Paliau's ability to seize and hold people's attention and loyalty. He was a skilful orator and had the organisational ability to build on his rhetorical triumphs. But underpinning his talents was the fact that he shared with his listeners cultural orientations that enabled him to convey a compelling vision in an idiom they understood.[16] He also probably knew that he could depend on many of them to hear from him what they wanted to hear. When Paliau did not explicitly play on themes of personified causation, many of his followers undoubtedly filled them in.

In his obituary of Paliau, promoting his image as pre-eminently a secular reformer, Kanasa (1991) suggested that those among his followers who took him as anything other than a 'practical' man were victims of their own 'misunderstanding' of what he was trying to achieve; they 'had their own expectations … contrary to Paliau's aims'. Indeed, some degree of misunderstanding is almost certain in a cultural world in which people expect layered discourse and figurative speech. Paliau was undoubtedly aware of this. To the extent that people's 'misunderstanding' kept them within the Movement, it was very much to his advantage, even when their expectations were a poor fit with his immediate plans. Schwartz's reconstruction of the events of 1946–47 strongly suggests that what many people expected from Paliau in the early days of the Movement was a path to a sudden, supernaturally mediated and radical transformation of their world. Hence, to some it mattered little exactly what words Paliau used. Some participants in the events of both the 1940s and the 1950s probably made little or no distinction between ritual appeals to the ancestors to

16 Otto (1992c: 436–40) shows how Paliau's rhetorical success in Baluan rested on the consistency of his message with indigenous notions of a 'hierarchy of the reliability of knowledge' that did not necessarily pertain throughout Manus.

bring the cargo and what Mead would have called 'practical' efforts, like imposing more coordination on village life or wearing trousers, shirts, dresses, and other kinds of European clothing.

To the best of our knowledge, Paliau never doubted the animate, conscious foundation of things and the primacy of animate and personal causation. But within that world, Paliau was a free thinker. He promulgated ideas and practices at odds with both indigenous and Christian orthodoxies. Some of what he advocated was potentially dangerous by indigenous standards. For instance, ceasing to scrupulously avoid one's future spouse in the course of daily life—a practice he sought to abolish—could bring punishment from an ancestral ghost. But Paliau spoke and acted as though he were immune from indigenous supernatural sanctions. And, unlike many Christian converts in PNG, he did not claim that he was protected by more powerful supernatural entities. We cannot see him, however, as someone driven by the conviction of having discovered new metaphysical truths. He never tired of metaphysical speculation, yet in his conversations with Schwartz—as illustrated in Chapter 1—he often sounded more like a man testing ideas than a prophet sharing revelations.[17]

Schwartz has described Paliau as a 'social fantasy producer and as such … demand oriented' (1976a: 183). Nonetheless, Paliau gave no hint that he regarded the cosmological visions and theological constructions he purveyed as implausible. It is likely that he was as concerned with their value in attracting followers as with their ontological truth, but we cannot be sure that this distinction was important to him. On one occasion in 1965, Schwartz asked Paliau which religions he thought were 'true'. Paliau responded that maybe one or two religions were 'true', but that most just relied on what the Bible reports of Jesus's teaching. (At that time, Paliau was probably unfamiliar with non-Christian religions from outside PNG.) Asked if his own religion—his own interpretation of the Bible—was 'true', he said he thought that ordinary men had written some of the Bible, and that a lot of what Jesus really said had probably

17   Otto (1998: 74) comments on how the 'Long Story of God', which Paliau presented to audiences as a foundation of the New Way, differed from an autobiographical narrative Schwartz recorded. 'The contrast between the two stories', observes Otto, 'is striking indeed. Whereas the Long Story is a religious narrative about creation, revelation and redemption, Paliau's autobiography is characterized by rational analysis and psychological insight'. Otto goes on to suggest that while the 'Long Story of God' was directed at followers and potential followers, the autobiography Schwartz recorded 'may perhaps be seen as a reflective exercise in which he used the anthropologist as a sparring partner' (ibid.: 84).

been lost.[18] Apparently taking 'true' to mean complete, Paliau said thus his own religion wasn't 'true' either. Later in his career, Paliau would make grander claims for his cosmology and theology; but, in 1965, at least in private, he was more tentative. He undoubtedly, however, found his own creations more useful than those of others as rationales for action and visions that could move people. Whatever questions might have vexed him when, in a philosophical mood, he pondered the nature of things, he was pre-eminently a creator of things to inspire others and in which they could invest their hopes. We know that his flexibility regarding his own creations—his ability to revise as he saw fit—has troubled some of his followers. But it was also one of his great strengths.

While Paliau did not fit the conventional mould of a prophet, neither was he an ordinary politician. He advanced some highly specific programs for social change, and he never wavered in some of his positions, such as his opposition to the grand-scale exchanges of durable wealth for food characteristic of precolonial Manus. He was quite capable of assembling and leading a parade, and he knew how to work his way to the head of a parade that was leaving without him. Yet Paliau was also conspicuously indifferent to the potential material rewards of leadership. Some opponents accused him of amassing a fortune illegitimately, but if he did so—and no proof was ever produced—he did not spend it on himself. He maintained a spartan standard of living throughout his life. During part of the last phase of his career, in the 1980s, he lived in makeshift, virtually open-air quarters on the concrete slab beneath the elevated house of one of his followers in Lorengau.[19]

The most consistent thread in Paliau's life was the importance he attached to maintaining a following, whether to listen to him tell the 'Long Story of God' (see Chapter 5), help him build a new kind of society, support his candidacy for the House of Assembly, or—towards the end of his life—listen to him orate about the real nature of a supreme being and the path to 'true freedom'. Otto (1998: 85–6) ponders what he considers Paliau's contrasting identities as 'rational cultural innovator' and 'divinely inspired prophet' and the possibility that Paliau 'was able to consciously use his different identities as a resource and that he manipulated them,

18 Paliau was, of course, correct about this, and in tune with modern mainstream biblical scholarship.
19 Granted, he was also accused of sexually exploiting his 'midwives', female followers whom he trained in herbal medicine. He did enjoy the attention of these women, but no one ever produced evidence that he also enjoyed them carnally.

at least partly, according to circumstance'. But Otto rejects this simple hypothesis in the light of what he sees as Paliau's ability to maintain a more complicated 'self-understanding' throughout most of his career.

Paliau was surely what people call a natural leader. He demonstrated this dramatically in his exploits during World War II (described in part in Chapter 5). Under intensely trying circumstances, while others hesitated, he could make decisions and act on them, rallying support as he went. He was also a thinker and a consistent critic of the status quo. These inclinations fed each other. He could not be satisfied with thinking and criticising; he needed to act, and action required followers. In the end, however, he may have needed followers as much to support his sense of self as to support his efforts to change the world.

Assessing critiques of the cargo cult concept

A substantial number of anthropologists have dismissed or attacked the very idea of cargo cults. They argue that the term cargo cult is not only inaccurate, it is also demeaning; that it reinforces white supremacy; that reports of cargo cults are often reflections of the irrational preoccupations of outside—mainly 'Western'—observers, including anthropologists; and that cargo cults aren't really about cargo. Some have concluded that cargo cult as an anthropological concept has had its day. Lamont Lindstrom, for instance, allows only that 'for a time, it became part of standard anthropological jargon' (2013: 182; cf. Stewart and Harding 1999: 287). Lindstrom is too hasty.

What are cargo cults?

Instances of what some might call cargo cults have been identified outside Melanesia (see e.g. La Barre 1972 [1970]; Peires 1989). What Ton Otto (2010) calls 'material religions' can be found throughout the world. A type of Christian Pentecostalism spreading rapidly on several continents rivals Melanesian cargo cults in its emphasis on gaining material wealth (Kapferer et al. 2010: 4). America continues to produce new varieties of what are sometimes called 'prosperity gospels' (e.g. Bowler 2013). But what we call cargo cults in this volume are distinctively Melanesian, engendered by a historically distinctive meeting of peoples.[20] Not only did the Melanesian and the intruding white or European societies have radically different capacities for material production, material goods had very different cultural significance in the respective societies. (Many Papua New Guineans still use European as a synonym for white people of all geographic origins—including, for instance, Americans and Australians. We will sometimes do the same.)[21] And while the intruders exhorted Melanesians to better themselves through hard work and frugality, the Christian missionaries among them also implied—both in their doctrines and by their prominence in colonial society—that white wealth rested more on acumen in relations with the supernatural than on technological savvy, sweat (not necessarily ones' own), and a capacity for deferred gratification.

Lindstrom (1993a) and Tabani (2013: 15; cf. Sullivan 2005) are correct that the term cargo cult has been greatly overextended. When used carelessly, it can be just as unedifying a term as religion. From its beginning until today, the Paliau Movement has harboured millenarians. We reserve the label cargo cult, however, for the aspect of the Movement that made obtaining European goods—that is, cargo (in Tok Pisin, *kago*)—with supernatural assistance the central element of a sudden and momentous transformation of the world. We can speak with complete assurance only of the cargo cults within the Paliau Movement, but our study of the literature and our experiences elsewhere in Melanesia suggest that they are substantially similar to many—but not necessarily all—phenomena called Melanesian cargo cults.

Melanesian cargo cults feature variations on a few core doctrines. The central doctrine usually holds that performing the proper ritual with the right attitude can bring the return of the ancestors, and/or in some cases Jesus Christ—sometimes at a prescribed time and sometimes not, as we will see—bringing a bounty of the white world's wealth. One or more alleged prophets—claiming revelation from God, Jesus Christ, or the spirits of the dead—usually conveys to other participants instructions for performing the necessary ritual. Frequently, it is also revealed that whites

---

20   Otto (2010: 89) observes, citing Trompf (1990): 'only millenarian movements in Melanesia and the West appear to have a cargoist character, while … case studies from Timor, Jamaica, and Africa completely lack this dimension. This confirms that there is a discernible quality that collectively sets a group of movements apart from others'. We are not entirely in accord with Otto, however, on the similarity of the Melanesian and the Western movements in question.

21   In Tok Pisin, Melanesians may use *Yuropian*—that is, European—interchangeably with *ol waitpela man* or simply *ol waitman*; that is, the whites.

have deliberately withheld knowledge of such ritual from Melanesians. The cargo usually comprises the kinds of material goods Melanesians have seen delivered to the whites by ships or aeroplanes. In Manus in 1960, for example, followers of the prophet Sua prepared a list of items they wished to acquire in the form of the kind of order for goods some had seen whites prepare, listing items and quantities. They presented it to Manus District Commissioner W. O'Malley, along with a sum of money intended either as payment for the goods or as a gratuity to the commissioner for passing the order along to the appropriate powers.[22] The list illustrates the range of imported manufactured goods with which Sua's followers were familiar. Here are a just a few items from the list: 1,000,000 sheets of corrugated steel (of the kind used for temporary construction during World War II), 10,000 pigs, 16,000 writing pens, 4,900 sewing machines, 9,000 razor blades, 14,000 refrigerators, 16,000 radios, 40,000 drums of fuel, 4,000 warships, 500 pistols with cartridges, 28,000 chairs, 10 tractors, 10 motorbikes, and 5 bicycles.[23]

Most cargo cults are much less specific in their material requirements. More central to cargo cult doctrines than the particular material goods sought is the idea that the ultimate source of the wealth of the whites is supernatural, but that whites have conspired to keep the means of producing such wealth a secret. Some cults have contended that the ancestors themselves create the cargo but devious whites intercept it and purvey it to the indigenous people, its rightful recipients, only in miniscule quantities in exchange for hard labour or money, of which they have almost none. Typically, cult doctrines are vague on what life will be like after the cargo arrives. Some doctrines hold that Melanesians will shed their black skins for white ones. Others envision God or the ancestors driving out the whites. Still others anticipate that once indigenes have fair access to the cargo they will live with whites as equals. Some cult prophets have also promised transformations of the landscape: mountains will be levelled and islands will be joined together, making travel and food production easier. Others promise that crops will grow without human effort and fish will jump into people's nets.

---

22 District Commissioner O'Malley showed Schwartz the document and told him how he had acquired it. Schwartz copied it by hand.

23 Lindstrom (1993a: 139–42) argues at some length that 'European' descriptions of the goods participants in the John Frum movement (on Tanna, in Vanuatu) sought that include refrigerators cannot be 'accurate, in the ethnographic sense'. He argues that including refrigerators in what he calls 'cargo catalogs' reflects 'European fancies rather than Tannese'. We cannot speak for John Frum adherents, but Sua's followers apparently included refrigerators in their list on their own.

Cargo cult as insult and instrument of oppression: A weak case

One objection to calling something a cargo cult is that it echoes the efforts of white colonials in Melanesia to deny the status of 'serious religion' to ritual or organisational activities that colonial authorities saw as subversive (Lindstrom 1993a: 34). Nancy McDowell (2000: 378) argues that the cargo cult label implies that 'others' indulge in cults 'while we have religion'. This, she contends, allows 'we rational, intellectual academics' to see ourselves and our 'Western tradition' as superior.[24] We grant that in everyday English speech, calling something a cult is usually not a compliment. It can, for instance, imply that an institution is founded on deceit by a cunning and charismatic manipulator. Some Melanesians take it that way, too; for example, in 2015, opponents of an emerging Wind Nation splinter group condemned it as a 'cult' (using the English word) and portrayed its leader as a fraud.

But scholars have long used the term cult with neutral intent. Anthropologist Martha Macintyre (2010) notes that 'medieval historians write about the rise of the "Cult of Mary" and people recognise that it refers to a specific movement within broader (Catholic) Christian ritual traditions' (cited in Tabani 2013: 14).[25] Barkun (2006 [2003]: 25) describes 'the predominant usage' of the term cult in the sociology of religion as not inherently pejorative. Daniel Dennett (2006: 194), following Stark and Finke (2000), endorses a non-pejorative definition of cult, or sect, that applies to some, but not necessarily all cargo cults, employing a distinction between higher-tension and lower-tension religious groups: 'Tension refers to the degree of distinctiveness, separation, and antagonism between a religious group and the "outside" world' (2000: 143). In Dennett's words, 'in a spectrum from low to high, large established churches are low-tension, and sects or cults are high tension' (2006: 194).

The term cult is also used to denote a kind of germinal religion. For instance, Scott Atran (2002: 271) contrasts 'starter cults' with 'established religions' (cf. La Barre 1972 [1970]: 60, 343). Further, many anthropologists

---

24 Two of McDowell's apparent assumptions here are much too broad. First, that 'we have religion'. Many Westerners do not, including many 'rational, intellectual academics'. Second, she appears to associate religion with rationality, a notion we address later in this chapter.

25 Schwartz refers to the 'Christ cult' (1973: 170) and 'the early Christian cult (and its Judaic and earlier antecedents' (1976a: 186), and Smith refers to the 'Jesus cult' (2002: 25), but it is probably unfair to cite our own works as precedents.

routinely use cult to refer to indigenous ritual institutions in Melanesia, such as men's cults or *tambaran* cults, although they may qualify this by identifying these institutions as Melanesian forms of 'religion' (e.g. Tuzin 1980). Even Lindstrom (2011: 256) is comfortable speaking of the 'Melanesian fondness for culting' as a means of coping with threats to social unity.

Joining cargo to cult, however, is more controversial. Lindstrom (1993a) argues that the term has deep roots in noxious colonial attitudes towards indigenous Melanesians. He identifies Lucy Mair as the first anthropologist to include the term in the index of a publication, in which she bluntly criticised disdainful attitudes towards cargo cults. Long before Worsley urged the progressive political significance of cargo cults, Mair wrote: 'the idea that [cargo cults] are mere nonsense, and can be stamped out by being treated as such, is a fallacy, as the younger officers of the [Australian New Guinea] District Services are well aware. In their view the motive force of the cargo cult is a feeling of helpless envy of the European with his immensely higher material standards' (1948: 67, quoted in Lindstrom 1993a: 36). But Lindstrom contends that the efforts of anthropologists to forestall or roll back the sensational and demeaning implications journalists, missionaries, and colonial administrators have given the term have failed.

We grant that some anthropologists have deliberately used the term cult in a derogatory way. In *New Lives for Old* (2001 [1956]), Mead was very clear that she approved of religion (see e.g. pp. 81–84, 94), in particular 'higher religions' (p. 309). But she almost invariably hung such modifiers as 'mystical' and 'semi-religious' (p. 208) on the words cult or cargo cult, and she contrasted participants in cults with 'responsible' people (p. 40). The bulk of more recent objections to the term, however, focus on supposed unintentional damage. Elfriede Hermann (2004: 52) contends that by adopting a term with such allegedly potent pejorative implications, 'anthropological discourses … produced knowledge conducive to ruling over and colonising others so characterized'. In this she echoes Lindstrom, who argues that the notion of cargo cults as characteristically Melanesian— even given anthropology's 'context-sensitive, sometimes empathic cultural readings'—has encouraged outsiders to discount Melanesian aspirations of all stripes (Lindstrom 1993a: 71, 146–68). Early in his career, Michael Somare, who would become independent PNG's first prime minister, made a similar complaint: 'If Niuginians are organised, Europeans mark them as "cultist", e.g. [Pita] Lus, [Paliau] Maloat … They are good examples of people with organisational abilities, but Europeans brand them as "cargo cultists'" (Somare 1970: 492).[26]

It would be impossible to determine empirically the extent to which anthropological use of the term cargo cult has helped blight Melanesian aspirations. Paige West (2016: 78, 84) describes cargo cult as a term that "'got loose" from anthropology to become a rhetorical means of branding people as incapable and depriving them of control of their natural resources and their lives in general'.[27] Yet, while this may be a plausible hypothesis, the supporting evidence West provides is weak at best. Similarly, Lindstrom, Hermann, and other anthropologists who charge that anthropologists contribute to colonial and post-colonial oppression by using the term cargo cult provide no specific examples we know of that link anthropologists' written words, on which they focus their criticism, with concrete damage done.[28] Lindstrom's exploration of the history of the term also suggests that the denigration train was well down the tracks by the time anthropologists—like Lucy Mair—provided more neutral, sympathetic ways of understanding cargo cults.

No one, however, has proposed an alternative label that captures the distinctiveness of cargo cults. Weston La Barre (1972 [1970]) includes them among what he calls 'crisis cults', Gesch (1990: 223) likens them to what he calls 'enthusiastic movements in the West, both religious and political', and Burridge (1995 [1960]: xvi), as noted earlier, reminds us of other descriptors attached to Melanesian movements, among them acculturative, adaptive, nativistic, or revitalisation (cf. Whitehouse 1995: 203). One could legitimately describe cargo cults that invoke missionary teachings as Christian sects. A definition of the 'ideal-type [Christian] … sect' Burridge offers (1969: 125, following Wilson 1961) fits many cargo cults

---

26 Cited in Schmid and Klappa (1999: 108). Pita Lus, later to become Sir Pita Lus, was a member of the first PNG national legislative body to include indigenous Papua New Guineans chosen by popular vote (the pre-independence House of Assembly, first seated in 1964).

27 West's (2016) analysis of the larger issue of rhetoric and sovereignty in PNG does not rest on her views on cargo cults. But she is on shaky ground calling cargo cult a term 'generated and popularized by anthropologists' (2016: 78). Lindstrom (1993a) contends that the term first appeared in print in the *Pacific Islands Monthly*, a publication largely devoted to business issues, in 1945, in an article by a member of the Australian administration in PNG. Anthropologists did indeed begin using it soon thereafter, but—unless their works were more widely read than are those of today's anthropologists—it may be exaggerating to say that they 'popularized' it.

28 In this, their efforts are disturbingly familiar to what Herbert Lewis (2014: 129) calls 'textual fetishism' in his trenchant defence of Franz Boas against charges that his work furthered colonialism and scientific racism.

neatly (cf. Hamilton 2001: 23–4). Or, one could label them heresies, as the Catholic Church judged millenarian movements sprung from official Christianity in medieval Europe (Watt 2001: 91), and as some missionaries surely did in Melanesia.[29] Marc Tabani (2013: 16) seconds Lindstrom's (1993b) suggestion that cargo cults be understood as a form of *kastom*, a Tok Pisin term (roughly analogous to the English word 'custom') some anthropologists have adopted to refer to self-conscious indigenous formulations of local ways, created in response to their perceived erosion by colonialism and institutions of foreign origin.[30] Otto (2010) includes cargo cults among what he calls 'material religions'. Some scholars include cargo cults among what they call New Religious Movements or NRMs (Lewis 2004). But we agree with Burridge (1995 [1960]: xvi) that of all the general categories into which scholars have proposed placing cargo cults, '*millenarian* smells the sweetest', and it stimulates useful avenues of analysis.[31] But substituting a more inclusive label for cargo cult dodges the question of what to call the specific, characteristically Melanesian phenomenon.[32]

The importance of showing Melanesians proper respect looms large in cargo cult criticism. McDowell (2000: 378) does not inveigh against calling things cargo cults, but she recommends that anthropologists treat cargo cults 'with the same respect we treat other new or transforming religions'. But mere levelling doesn't necessarily grant cargo cults greater dignity. Fokke Sierksma's tone was as even-handed as McDowell's but unambiguously less respectful to all concerned when he wrote, in 1965: 'Jesus standing before Pilate is just another messianic prophet standing before a District Officer'.[33]

---

29 Fortunately, Christian missionaries in colonial Melanesia could do no more to discourage heresies than deny their adherents communion, sparing Melanesia campaigns of extermination (e.g. Oldenbourg 1961 [1959]) or the equivalent of a Spanish Inquisition.

30 Most of the anthropological literature on this phenomenon uses, like Tabani and Lindstrom, the spelling *kastom*. In Manus, *kastam* is the usual spelling and the one we will use when we return to this topic in Chapter 13.

31 It is interesting that Burridge (1995 [1960]: xvi) notes that at one time both millenarian and messianic were rejected as categories for 'cargo activities' because they were considered 'too loaded'.

32 Biersack (2013: 107) argues that the Mata Kamo movement in PNG should not be called 'cargoist' because it was millenarian; that is, its aim was not primarily to acquire wealth—although wealth was not irrelevant—but it 'sought a total transformation' of human life and the advent of a 'cosmically privileged "blissful" condition'. Biersack's argument that the concerns of Mata Kamo adherents were not 'materialist' depends on a particular reading of the meaning of this term. In any case, we regard cargo cults as a form of millenarianism, not a distinct phenomenon. Currently, Biersack (personal communication) tends to agree.

33 This remark appears in Sierksma's 1965 review of Vittorio Lanternari's *The Religions of the Oppressed: A Study of Modern Messianic Cults* (1963) and is cited in La Barre (1972 [1970]: 254).

Lindstrom contends that cargo cult 'always carries along a circus aura of sport and faint mockery. Its roots in the politics of ridicule cannot fully be erased. The term is never entirely decorous or tasteful' (1993a: 34; cf. Hermann 2004: 52).[34] Other scholars, however, provide contrary examples from within Melanesia. Tabani (2013: 21), citing Lattas (1998) and Macintyre (2013), notes instances of Melanesians using the Tok Pisin label *kago kult* 'as one that is inherently powerful, not shameful'. Lindstrom himself (1993a: 162) observes that while 'cargoism serves negatively within island political debate to label and denigrate anything that may threaten established orders', it also 'serves, positively, as a metonym of Melanesian culture. Cargo stories record a proud history of resistance to colonial domination. As a philosophy and protoscience, the cargo cult distinguishes Melanesians as Melanesians'. Lindstrom's interest, however, is largely in the negative use, and we cannot deny that even scholars sometimes condescend more to cargo cults than to other forms of millenarianism. Despite a sound grasp of cargo cults as millenarian movements, Landes (2011: 140) is also prey to the notion that cargo cults 'have an indelible element of the silly'.

Despite the controversies surrounding the term, we are not the only anthropologists who still find it useful (e.g. see Lattas 1998; Leavitt 2004; cf. Robbins 2004b). We grant the vagueness of the term cult, but *cargo* cult refers to something quite specific, as described above. Otto (2010: 92) distinguishes cargo cults from similar phenomena 'elsewhere in the world', referring to 'the specificity of the cargo millennium', and argues for keeping cargo cult because anthropologists need a distinct term for such a distinct phenomenon (ibid.: 88). If we thought an alternative term were necessary we would suggest cargo millenarianism. But we cannot recommend a wholesale purge of cargo cult, for the reasons given above. Further, if one wants to make the term's referent look less humorously exotic to the uninitiated, changing its name isn't likely to produce a long-lasting effect. The long game requires us to recognise the phenomenon's profoundly pan-human dimensions. If anthropologists have demeaned Melanesians by writing about cargo cults, they have done

---

34 Schwartz has fought this tendency hand to hand. In 1971, *Psychology Today*, a magazine for general audiences, invited Schwartz to submit an article about the Noise. After a brief editorial process, he didn't see the article again until it appeared in print, when he was shocked to see that the magazine had titled it 'The Noise: Cargo Cult Frenzy in the South Seas'. A capsule description of the article referred to a 'cargo cult freak-out'. In his article, Schwartz had taken pains to point out parallels between cargo cults in Melanesia and similar phenomena in the West. The article could not be recalled, but Schwartz returned his payment for it with a letter of protest.

so by not stressing enough that what Melanesians do in cargo cults is what people elsewhere and throughout recorded history have done over and over again, drawing their inspiration from Zoroastrianism, Judaism, Christianity, Islam, Buddhism, and a host of other cultural traditions that many people regard with respect.

Neither a name change nor the long game we propose, however, would satisfy all critics, many of whom hold that phenomena like those Schwartz witnessed in Manus do not exist, or—if they do exist—that they are not about material cargo. We turn to these arguments next.

Cargo cults as illusion: An even weaker case

The problem of how to talk about cargo cults with appropriate delicacy goes away if we deny that they exist. Jebens (2004a: 8) concedes cautiously that 'there might in fact be a correspondence between the term [cargo cult] and the Melanesian ethnographic reality'. There are anthropologists, however, who disagree.

Lindstrom (1993a, 2004) has been the leading voice for the argument that Western *interest* in cargo cults, including anthropological interest, has more to do with an irrational Western obsession than with empirical phenomena (1993a: 207–10). The object of the Western obsession, writes Lindstrom, is 'unrequited love' (p. 184): 'The story of the cargo cult is just another avatar of the prosaic Western romance' (p. 198). Lindstrom marshals many colourful examples of Western popular culture stretching the cargo cult concept far beyond the limits of its use in ethnography. He declines, however, to provide any evidence that the obsession he ascribes to Westerners has led anthropologists to see cargo cults where they are not, on the grounds that his concern is with 'discourse rather than with ethnographic reality' (p. 13).[35]

Others are less circumspect. Karl-Heinz Kohl (2004: 90–1), for instance, contends that cargo cults are projections of Westerners' own 'hopes, desires, and fears' regarding 'the pursuit of wealth and money' in a time of rapid economic change in the West.[36] And Papua New Guinean scholar

---

35   Careful readers, however, will find that Lindstrom sometimes fails to maintain this distinction (cf. Otto 2010: 88).

36   Hermann (2004: 52) writes that Epeli Hau'ofa (1975: 285) makes a similar suggestion, that is, 'the Westerner's tendency to construct the Melanesian as a caricature of the Western capitalist has been instrumental in moving scholars to concede priority to the "cargo" notion'. One can find such a suggestion in Hau'ofa's article, however, only by reading between the lines with one's imagination in high gear.

Regis Tove Stella (2007: 117) declares—without offering evidence—that 'the myth of the cargo cult' was created by white colonials in aid of subjugating the indigenous people.

If our account of the Paliau Movement does nothing else, it presents empirical evidence of cargo cults that is hard to ignore. Empirical evidence, however, is easy to discount if ideology clouds one's vision. Many anthropologists' objections to both the idea and the empirical reality of cargo cults appear to reflect their conviction that anthropology has its roots in colonialism and is perforce neo-colonial in its outlook, its aspirations to objectivity cloaking a hidden (or perhaps merely inadvertent) agenda of oppression (e.g. Keesing 1994).[37] We reject this point of view, but we leave more focused criticism to the penetrating scholarship of Lawrence Kuznar (1997) and Herbert S. Lewis (2014).

Cargo cults are about cargo: Sufficient for some, necessary for all

But what if, beneath the surface, what we call cargo cults aren't really about cargo? Roger Keesing protests that, although Melanesians may talk about cargo and seek supernatural aid in obtaining cargo, this is not an expression of 'simple materialism' (Keesing n.d., paraphrased in Tabani 2013: 8). But we know of no anthropologist who has ever argued that Melanesians seek cargo solely for some primal joy of possession, uninformed by cultural significance and historical context. The closest one can come to examples of 'simple materialism' in human life occur in fables (King Midas) or literature (Ebenezer Scrooge or Silas Marner before their respective redemptions), and in instances of real people whose attachment to material things was truly pathological, like New York City's Collyer brothers. But even the Collyers doubtless found some meaning in their hoarding.[38] One can also find examples of 'simple materialism' in crudely stereotypical descriptions of the industrial capitalist world like the one Dalton offers: it is 'a dead materialist one', he writes (2013: 48).[39]

---

37 Roger Keesing's 1994 essay 'Theories of culture revisited' propounds such a view succinctly. The anthropology he criticises, however, is a caricature of the field.

38 On the Collyer brothers, see E.L. Doctorow's novel *Homer and Langley* (2009), based on the real-life brothers.

39 Dalton defines a 'dead materialist' world in part by contrast with the world of the Rawa people of PNG, which is grounded in 'an epistemology which assumes a consciously aware universe' (2013: 42) and in which 'things in nature possess an unseen interior living subjectivity which is continuous with human intelligence' (p. 37). We would call this a personified universe, and it may be that from the Rawa perspective a universe seen through secular and scientific eyes would be less interesting. But if one does not insist on pervasive conscious awareness as a criterion for a lively universe, what we can see of it through secular and scientific eyes is far from moribund.

Annelin Eriksen (2010: 69), following (rather recklessly) Lindstrom (1993a) and Jebens (2005), contends that the ostensible aim of cargo movements, 'the reception of Western goods', might not be their 'most important aspect. The very act of organising the movement might have been of equal importance'. Thus, 'cargo cults were efforts to create new forms of local solidarity in periods characterized by great upheavals'. As we will show in our chronicle of the Paliau Movement, this generalisation does not describe *motives* for participating in the Manus cults, and the *effects* on social solidarity in the Manus case were considerably more complicated.

A more subtle argument is that cargo is indeed important in cargo cults, but largely as a symbol. Jan Pouwer (2000: 339) speaks of cargo as 'a totalizing symbol which stands for physical well-being, freedom from want, economic wealth, social dignity and equivalence, political freedom and eternal bliss'. Garry Trompf (1994: 160) argues that the cargo symbolises 'something more profound and less tangible than European goods themselves'—something he characterises as 'new, enigmatic, even "eschatological" forces impinging on the time-honoured primal fabric of life' (ibid.: 161). Referring to a cargo cult in PNG's East Sepik Province, Donald Tuzin also minimises the importance of physical cargo. The cargo people seek, he argues, should be understood 'in a mythic rather than a literal sense' (1990: 368).[40]

It is not entirely clear, however, if the scholars cited above intend to say that cargo is *only* a symbol (for Melanesians, that is; it certainly has become so for some anthropologists). Otto's (1992b: 5) assertion that cargo 'is not matter', however, is quite plain.[41] But this assertion is manifestly untenable in the Manus case. Consider the list of manufactured goods followers of the prophet Sua prepared in 1960, discussed earlier. And here is how one cult adherent described cargo to Schwartz in the 1950s: 'Cargo is things, like what we see in stores. We think like this. We work hard, work hard, work hard until we die to get one shilling to buy a little something. In a short time it is used up. Now we think that it is true; all these things that we desire are near now if we hold fast to what they [the dead] say. They say it is not hard. Money, too. They say if they want to give us money, they can'. Some participants in the same cult also

---

40   Explaining what Tuzin (1990) means by this would require a considerable detour. Tuzin himself, however, makes it adequately clear to patient readers.
41   This is not Otto's last word on the subject. He takes a more nuanced position elsewhere (2004: 210–11).

reported seeing its tutelary ghost holding a bag of money. And, as we describe in Chapter 6, during the Noise, the people of some participating villages chased away visitors arriving by canoe, determined to keep for themselves the wealth they were expecting.

These data do not, of course, show that cargo has *no* symbolic value. Such a conclusion also would be untenable. Anthropologists agree that material objects in Melanesia and in human society in general have rich symbolic functions. This is true even in Western capitalist societies, wherein—in the words of Mary Douglas and Baron Isherwood (1979: 10)—material goods are 'part of a live information system' necessary for constructing 'an intelligible universe' (p. 65) (cf. Smith 1994: 8–9).[42]

Our descriptions of the Manus cults will show that some participants were after something more than material goods. The Manus case, however, also suggests that to understand such cult participants anthropologists should interpret material cargo not as a symbol—which can have an arbitrary relationship to that which it represents—but as a synecdoche, a part of something that stands for the whole.[43] Further, as we argue below, the Manus case strongly suggests that material cargo was the part of the whole that could do the work of a synecdoche most effectively.[44]

Much about the kind of larger transformation—beyond access to material wealth—that some Manus people hoped for in the 1950s was at least as vague as the notions of Heaven of most Christians. (Will one have to learn to play the harp, or can one work on one's golf game?) But it is easy to see how Manus people could have attributed larger significance to the whites' material possessions and devices. They made indigenous forms of wealth, implements, and manufactures look virtually worthless and thus no longer able to underwrite Manus social and psychological desiderata—such as self-esteem, reputation, or power—as they had in the past (see Chapter 3). Judging from some of the rhetoric of the Paliau

---

42   Much of the work on this topic takes as its theoretical beginning Marcel Mauss's thesis on the 'well-nigh indissoluble' links between people created by exchanging objects that 'are never completely separated from the men who exchange them' (Mauss 1967 [1925]: 31).
43   When we say that a symbol has an arbitrary relationship to that which it represents, we do not exclude the possibility that one can find a historical reason for the association of a symbol and its referent.
44   Otto (1992b: 5) comes close to saying this when he calls cargo 'a cultural idiom … in which millenarian visions are cast'. Lattas (1998: xi) may have something like this in mind when he writes that the 'desire for commodities' found in cargo cults is 'a way of objectifying the realization of a new Melanesian self and a new Melanesian social order'.

Movement and the cults within it, for some participants, obtaining the cargo did imply achieving social and political as well as material parity with Europeans. But we doubt that anything other than material cargo could have represented such a whole as effectively, if at all. Material cargo was by far the most tangible aspect of white life with which Manus people were familiar; and, given the indigenous significance of material wealth, some Manus people probably did understand it, if not explicitly then inchoately, as the portal to a less tangible and more complex whole. But for others (as illustrated above) cargo was primarily 'things, like what we see in stores … money, too', as a cult adherent once described cargo to Schwartz. To repeat Paula Levin's formulation, cargo was sufficient for some, but necessary for all.

Numbers of anthropologists continue to promote readings of what cargo cults are 'really about' that push interest in material goods far into the background. In doing so, some take considerable liberty. Frederick Errington and Deborah Gewertz (2004: 7) argue for the primarily symbolic nature of cargo when they take on Jared Diamond's depiction of the cargo cult leader Yali in Diamond's popular volume *Guns, Germs and Steel* (1997). Diamond introduces his grand scheme for understanding human history with an account of a 1972 conversation with Yali in which Yali asked Diamond: 'Why is it that you white people developed so much cargo and brought it to New Guinea, but we black people had little cargo of our own?' (Diamond 1997: 14). Errington and Gewertz are correct that Diamond fails to appreciate the culturally specific importance of material wealth to Melanesians; they observe that Diamond seems to think Papua New Guineans want foreign material goods because they are 'inherently desirable'. But they go a little too far when they assert that 'Yali was really asking less about cargo per se than about colonial relationships between black and white people' (Errington and Gewertz 2004: 25). This is plausible speculation, but it is speculation and does not merit the adverb 'really'.

Dalton (2004: 207) far surpasses Errington and Gewertz in putting words in people's mouths.[45] He tells of how a Papua New Guinean asked him in the early 1980s: 'How is it the Whitemen ever thought to make machines?' Dalton writes that he took the question to mean: 'Are you Whitemen really the gods you pretend to be or not?' Regarding cargo cults among

---

45   See also Landes's (2011: 415) criticism of Lindstrom for the same tendency.

the Ilahita Arapesh of PNG, Donald Tuzin (1990: 368) argues that 'cargo is not really what the cults are about'. The cargo people seek is 'an image of Self-Person unity', not unlike what they seek in their indigenous ritual institutions. Tuzin's argument for the reality of Ilahita concern about self-person unity is coherent and based on impressive ethnography. But his conclusion that this is what cargo cults are 'really about' is a jump that should leave readers restive. What does he mean by 'really about'? And how can Errington and Gewertz or Dalton be so confident when they tell us what someone was 'really' asking?

Doubtless Yali was *concerned* about colonial relationships, but he *asked* about cargo. There is unseemly haste here to discard people's own words, even acknowledging Melanesian fondness for indirect and layered speech. We, Schwartz and Smith, have found many Papua New Guineans ready and able to ask questions about white wealth and Melanesian poverty in ways that leave little room for reinterpretation. A sample from among the questions Papua New Guineans have asked us: Is it true that Catholic priests know how to get money from the dead? Will you go to the cemetery with me some night and show me how to get money from the dead? When did whites get factories and machines; when Jesus died? Patrick Gesch (1990: 222–3) writes of similarly blunt questions asked of him 'in moments of quiet friendliness', including 'Will you speak out the Secret to us now?'—that is, the secret of how to obtain material wealth without physical effort.

Anthropologists are trained to look beneath the surface of what people say and do, but it is easy to go too far. One can speculatively relate virtually any aspiration, intention, or concern human beings express to more abstract interests. This sometimes illuminates an issue, and sometimes it helps make what seems exotically inexplicable less so. But sometimes it simply glosses over something an anthropologist finds discomfiting—like an apparent obsession with material things.

Anthropologists who insist that material cargo is *not* central to cargo cults are concerned in part with countering popular ethnocentric tendencies to depict Melanesians in demeaning ways. Some may also be trying to counter their own ethnocentric discomfort. We agree with Andrew Lattas (2001: 161) that anthropologists' 'ethical apologies for the natives' materialism imply their own ethnocentric ontologies. They imply a materialist-spiritualist opposition—where the desire for material goods and wealth is seen to corrode the legitimacy and integrity of politicalethico concerns', thus suggesting a 'Christian-inspired, God-versus-Caesar dichotomy'.[46] A tendency to denigrate the material world is present in many philosophical or theological traditions. But it is probably most familiar to Euro-Americans in its Christian form, as often expressed in the Christian Bible: 'Lay not up for yourselves treasures upon earth, where moth and rust doth corrupt, and where thieves break through and steal: But lay up for yourselves treasures in heaven, where neither moth nor rust doth corrupt, and where thieves do not break through nor steal' (Matthew 6:19–20, King James Version).

Melanesians do not generally feel that material wealth stands in opposition to virtue or that material wellbeing is separable from social and metaphysical wellbeing. Bruce Knauft (1999: 35), for instance, sums up the relationship of food and the human body in Melanesia as follows: 'material substance cannot be divorced from social and spiritual life; food is irrevocably tied to personal relationships and to unseen effects that may enhance or alter its potency. Social and spiritual relations form the precondition for nourishment and growth, and the body is conceptualised in terms of these'. Biersack (2001: 74) describes such a relationship more vividly in her analysis of a ritual pertaining to boys' maturation among the Paiela people of PNG's Enga Province. Pieces of bark used in the ritual symbolise boys' skin 'and the wealth that the boys will accumulate'. This reflects a Paiela conception that 'wealth "comes to the skin", meaning that it becomes integral to a person's reputation and image'. Integral, we should add, in a socially desirable way.[47] This conception is common in PNG. For example, as Marilyn Strathern (1975) reports, struggling unskilled migrants to Port Moresby from rural areas describe their plight as having 'no money on our skins'. In a related vein, Smith (1994) explores the integral connection between collective material wellbeing and right relations among the living and with the dead that the people of Kragur village, East Sepik Province, felt in their bones in the 1970s. Similar

---

46   Lattas notes, however, that such a dichotomy may appear 'nowadays' among 'informants influenced by charismatic forms of Christianity' (2001: 161).

47   Biersack (2011b) tackles a similar issue regarding the Cult of Ain in what, in 2011, were PNG's Enga and Southern Highlands provinces. (Parts of Southern Highlands Province have since been incorporated into Hela Province, formed in 2012.) Anthropologists studying its manifestations in different times and places have reached different conclusions on the relative importance to its adherents of 'an ascent to the sky', to dwell eternally in what some might call a spiritual realm, and acquiring material wealth. Biersack's review of the research leads her to conclude that 'these two goals not only did not compete but were substantially the same' (2011b: 238).

conceptions are not, of course, absent in the West. But in Melanesia they do not strain in tension with a common interpretation of a major cultural tradition, that is, Christianity.

Allowing people to be irrational

Errington and Gewertz also object that Diamond, by vastly oversimplifying the significance of cargo, casts Papua New Guineans as 'the agents of their own domination' (2004: 25). Diamond can be faulted for aspects of his methods, but we disagree that it is wrong on principle to depict people as unwittingly complicit in their own oppression. To understand human behaviour, one has to leave open the possibility that people sometimes help create and maintain self-destructive illusions.

Doing so looks irrational, but it is indisputable that people *are* often irrational. As Schwartz has written: 'Belief systems cannot be explained entirely on the basis of a rational calculus of experience. The social scientist who attempts such an explanation is rationalising on behalf of the people he is studying because he takes the irrational as pejorative. But such an explanation does not have an invidious implication when the irrational is considered a potential component of all human behaviour' (1976b: 219).[48] Regarding cargo cults, Worsley (1999: 154–5) accepts that they can be irrational, but argues strenuously that they are no more irrational than various 'fundamentalist' versions of the major world religions and such ideologies as racism, nationalism, fascism, communism, and World Bank-sponsored structural adjustment. He concludes: 'To single out Melanesian Cargo [Worsley's capitalisation] cults as if they were the most striking contemporary instances of irrational ideology, religious or otherwise, is … supremely ethnocentric arrogance'. We cannot imagine any anthropologist disagreeing.[49]

Worsley could have included non-fundamentalist versions of world religions among ideologies that might be called irrational, for they often proudly divorce themselves from quotidian reason. Kierkegaard's

48   Robert Coles (1999: 56) quotes Anna Freud making much the same point. Discussing with Anna Freud her father's comparison of religious faith to infantile neurosis in *The Future of an Illusion*, Coles notes that he found the tone 'uncharacteristically harsh, even scornful, not the way Freud usually addressed readers'. Anna Freud replied: 'As you know, to speak of "infantile neurosis" in connection with anyone is to describe them as a fellow human being!'
49   And, contrary to McDowell (2000: 378), we find it hard to imagine any anthropologist offering much resistance to 'acknowledging our own irrationality'.

commentary (2012 [1843]: 7) on the Old Testament story of Abraham and Isaac (Genesis 22:2–8) is a vivid example: 'Abraham was … great by reason of his wisdom whose secret is foolishness, great by reason of his hope whose form is madness'. The New Testament continues this theme, as in St Paul's praise for the precedence of imagination over empirical evidence: 'Now faith is the substance of things hoped for, the evidence of things not seen' (Hebrews 11:1, King James Version).[50] Yet, the implication of irrationality is among the most heartfelt complaints some critics make of the term cargo cult (e.g. Biersack 2013; Hermann 2004: 52; Lindstrom 1993a: 66–72). Again, many fear that this unfairly diminishes Melanesians. McDowell (2000: 377) opines that to call cargo cults irrational perpetuates the assumption that '"we" are rational and "they" are not'. This allows 'us' to 'distance ourselves and continue the hierarchy implicit in colonialism'. Hence, to be on the side of the angels 'we' (an unspecified 'we') must find the rationality in cargo cults.[51]

The most typical anthropological argument for the rationality of cargo cults is that they have a coherent inner logic given the cultural and social context: that is, they are logical given indigenous Melanesian notions of causality and the circumstances of the Melanesian encounter with the West. As Burridge puts it in *Mambu* (1995 [1960]: xvii), cargo cults make sense in terms of 'a particular cultural idiom within a historical bracket'. But, at the very least, as the historical bracket shifts, such an analysis may become less applicable. In Manus and elsewhere in Melanesia, people adhere to cults after decades of intensive involvement with, and practical mastery of, material technologies from the industrialised world—including, in Manus, participating in wartime construction projects and working as mechanics and clerks with the occupying military forces. Some of today's leading members of Wind Nation are highly educated and have held important positions managing PNG's economy and infrastructure. It is difficult under these circumstances to see cargo cult beliefs as simply rational constructions of all the available

---

50   The English Standard translation is even more explicit: 'Now faith is the assurance of things hoped for, the conviction of things not seen'.

51   Like many others who make such an argument, McDowell is very free with the pronoun 'we'. (Enclosing it in single quotation marks in in the passage cited is a rare gesture on her part toward greater care.) It is generally difficult to determine to whom precisely she and others are referring, although the possible referents appear to be anthropologists, sympathisers with colonialism, heirs of the Enlightenment, or some combination of these categories. Most often, however, the referent seems to be people of the West. Thus, in defending Melanesians against unfair representation in this way, McDowell and others provide excellent examples of what James Carrier (1992) aptly calls 'occidentalism'; that is, a tendency to represent 'the West' stereotypically that mirrors the 'orientalism' Edward Said (1979 [1978]) criticises.

information. We find it impossible to ignore the degree to which cargo cult beliefs and hopes—like the key doctrines of the major world religions—require those harbouring them to abandon the pragmatism they exhibit in everyday life.

Does this constitute irrationality? We propose a conception of rationality that is not culturally limited: we hold that all human beings share an objective reality that is distinct from any particular cultural construction, a reality to which we all must adapt. To be rational is to formulate and pursue aims that appear achievable in terms of *what one knows* of that shared reality, one's cultural construction of an ultimately shared reality. Conversely, setting and pursuing goals that depend on a version of reality that flies in the face of *what one knows* of that reality—what Schwartz calls a person's or group's accessible reality (a term we will use again)—is irrational. We do not mean, of course, that there are no *reasons* for irrational behaviour; they are simply not reasons that make sense within a particular accessible reality. Hence, we give no rationality credits for the internal coherence of an actor's reasons or salutary unintended consequences of their behaviour.[52]

This conception of irrationality does not provide a finely calibrated instrument for measuring the rationality or irrationality of particular ideas or behaviours. A major obstacle is the impossibility of apprehending the boundaries of anyone's accessible reality. We insist, however, that respect for the people they observe does not require anthropologists to strain until they can expunge from their analysis all hints of irrationality as we have defined it, an effort that can easily lead them to positions beyond what their data justify. Certainly, in cases of millenarianism, we can and must leave open the possibility that people may want something so much that, in the hope of attaining it, they put aside understandings of reality—accessible realities—that previously have served them well. Landes (2011: 99) writes that 'the prophet must overcome the innate common sense of most people'. We prefer to think of 'common sense' not as something 'innate' but as the taken-for-granted culturally constructed understandings of the world that enable a society to survive and reproduce. But we take Landes's point. In our Manus case, it appears that many people were eager for someone to help them overcome their reluctance to abandon old, reliable

---

52 Nicholas Bainton (2010: 94) suggests that a tendency among anthropologists to focus on functional analyses emphasising the 'socially positive' aspects of cargo cults is an effort to 'side-step' sensitive issues pertaining to rationality.

ways of understanding the world for something untested but infinitely more exciting. In the early years of the Movement, some of its adherents yearned for a prophet and found one in Paliau. And those who wanted a more unambiguous cargo prophecy found it elsewhere, as we describe in Chapter 6. In both cases, Movement adherents who seized on cargo prophecies could do so only by putting aside their working knowledge of their accessible reality.

We are aware that some anthropologists are not comfortable with the idea of a reality that is not a social construction. To pursue anthropology as a science, however, one must assume a reality independent of culture, at least during business hours (cf. Jarvie 1984: 53). We are, however, more than comfortable, at all hours, with philosopher John Searle's dictum that 'there is a way things are that is independent of how we represent how things are' (1995: 156).[53]

Fortunately, there is a lot of latitude for creating versions of reality that have at best tenuous relationships to what Searle calls the 'brute facts' of existence; that is, reality distinct from cultural constructions.[54] People can do so without harm, and perhaps much to their benefit, in dream life, play, or art. They can even build substantial institutions around notions that depart radically from the brute facts without impairing their ability to survive and reproduce. But, ignoring some brute facts may not only diminish the quality of group life but also—for example, in the cases of racism or nationalism—threaten the survival of other groups.[55]

---

53 There has been considerable critical discussion of Searle's ideas among cultural anthropologists. See especially *Anthropological Theory*, volume 6(1), 2006. No critiques we have seen, however, incline us to disagree with Searle's (2006: 81) fundamental proposition that there is an observer-independent world and that 'the real observer-independent world does not give a damn about us. Things such as hydrogen atoms and tectonic plates do not become something different "once observed and interpreted by human agents". They remain the same ... In this respect they differ from money, property, government, marriage and other social institutions'.

54 It's hard to speak about this without seeming to equate 'brute fact' reality with nature as opposed to culture, especially because the most ready examples of brute fact reality come from what we are accustomed to calling nature, such as hydrogen atoms and tectonic plates. But—if we read Searle correctly— it seems apparent that 'a way things are that is independent of how we represent how things are' is not merely another way of saying 'natural' as opposed to 'cultural' phenomena.

55 George Orwell made a similar point in his 1946 essay 'In Front of Your Nose': 'We are all capable of believing things which we *know* to be untrue, and then, when we are proved wrong, impudently twisting the facts so as to show that we were right. Intellectually, it is possible to carry on this process for an indefinite time: the only check is that sooner or later a false belief bumps up against solid reality, usually on a battlefield'.

We stress that acting irrationally is not the same as acting immorally. It can, however, be extremely dangerous. People do not have to penetrate to the quiddity of being to survive, but neither can they live completely divorced from it. In the end, to survive, let alone flourish, people must allow for a certain amount of what Schwartz calls reality seepage. The Breatharian belief that people can survive on light and air alone poses little threat to non-Breatharians, except innocents under their influence. But it puts individual Breatharians in immediate peril, like a woman in Scotland who died while fasting according to Breatharian principles.[56] Some groups with millenarian ideologies have posed far greater dangers to both their members and others than the Breatharians. Well-known cases included Heaven's Gate (best known for a 1997 mass suicide in California), the People's Temple of the Disciples of Christ (founded in California, but best known for a 1978 mass suicide/murder in Guyana), the Order of the Solar Temple (associated with a string of murders and suicides in Europe in the 1990s), and Aum Shinrikyô (infamous for poison gas attacks in Japan).[57]

But we do not have to go to darkest California, Europe, or Japan to find examples of the danger of ignoring brute-fact reality. Landes (2011: 91) calls the Xhosa cattle slaying of 1856–1857, in what today is South Africa, a case of 'suicidal millennialism'. Home-grown prophets convinced the Xhosa that if they 'would slay all their cattle, destroy their grain stores, cease planting crops, and purify themselves of all witchcraft, a great day would dawn when the British would vanish from the land and the ancestors would live again, bringing with them new and more plentiful cattle and grain'. Enough people heeded this prophecy to cause 30,000–50,000 Xhosa to starve and to enable greater consolidation of the British regime and extended white settlement on Xhosa lands—a 'self-inflicted catastrophe', in Landes's words (2011: 91).[58] Biersack (2013) writes of a catastrophe on a smaller scale among the Ipili-speaking followers of the Cult of Ain in PNG. Under the influence of a cult leader, many came to believe that they would find wealth at the bottom of a pool to which the leader took them. 'Despite the fact that Ipili speakers fear water and

---

56   BBC Online Network (21 September 1999) reported that a woman died in Scotland while fasting in accord with Breatharian principles (news.bbc.co.uk/2/hi/uk_news/scotland/453661.stm).
57   There is substantial literature on each of these cases. Also, *The Oxford Handbook of New Religious Movements* (Lewis 2004) places these and similar cases in context.
58   Although this horrifying episode is often mentioned in the literature on millenarianism, Landes notes that the 'only extant scholarly monograph' on it is by J.B. Peires (1989), and that a critique of that study is available in Andreas et al. (2008).

do not swim', Biersack writes, 'they entered the water and ... drowned' (ibid.: 96). This may sound apocryphal, but Biersack's (2011a, 2011b) careful research on the Cult of Ain suggests that it is not.

We will not argue that all the people involved in the highly disturbing incidents noted above were indisputably irrational; that is a tough call and would require extensive information on their accessible realities. Could one then argue that they must have been behaving rationally in their own terms? That would be a stretch, because they clearly ignored whatever reality seepage had hitherto allowed them to survive or forestalled their attacks on others. The 'rational in their own terms' interpretation is arguably more pejorative than suggesting that they were exhibiting a capacity to ignore accessible reality of the kind Kierkegaard admired in Abraham.

It is hard to imagine the Titan people of Manus—famously at home on and in the water—suffering the fate of Biersack's Ipili speakers. During the 1946 cargo cult, however, some of them destroyed their canoes, seriously jeopardising their livelihoods. Titan have impressed observers with their empirical bent and pragmatism, even in their dealings with the spirit world. This makes the fact that they were core participants in the cargo cults within the Paliau Movement all the more worthy of explanation. In the next chapter, we describe the principal features of indigenous Manus life, including the Titan's predominately hard-headed relationship with brute-fact reality. This sets the stage for our chronicle of the Manus encounter with the European world and the Paliau Movement's response.

3

Indigenous life in the Admiralty Islands

Direct knowledge of life in the Admiralty Islands before European contact is beyond our grasp. But the works of Fortune and Mead, based on their 1928 research among Titan speakers, describe in great detail major features of life at a relatively early point in the Australian colonial era, and Nevermann (1934) provides a useful compilation of observations from the German colonial era. We also rely in this chapter on what Schwartz learned of the precolonial and early colonial eras from his research in the 1950s. In addition, in the 1960s, to get a wider view of life in the Admiralties, Schwartz circumnavigated Manus Island and travelled the surrounding waters by motorised outrigger canoe to visit scattered Titan and Matankor villages, and he trekked to Usiai villages in the interior. His research confirmed the wider relevance of Mead's, Fortune's, and his own earlier findings on the south coast and in the southerly islands. It also allowed him to understand better how, despite the many things that divided them, the peoples of the Admiralties comprised what he calls an integrated areal culture (Schwartz 1963). We refer to this substantial body of research to illuminate why forging even fragile unity among dozens of villages in the Paliau Movement was a remarkable accomplishment; the circumstances that gave Paliau's call for radical change its appeal; and the aspects of the Admiralties areal culture that contributed to people's susceptibility to the Movement's millenarian aspects.

We first describe the relevant dimensions of precolonial or early colonial life in the Admiralties and the links among them in a couple of paragraphs, before addressing them in more detail. The precolonial Admiralties were highly fragmented politically; trust and solidarity were fragile at all levels, from the major ethnic groups down to the nuclear family. Nonetheless, in the quest for leadership and prestige, ambitious individuals built networks through which they amassed goods for the exchanges associated with marriage. As Mead and Schwartz put it (n.d.: 19–20): 'Among any sample of individuals from the same village, there would be no exact correspondence in the range of their allegiances, the areas where they could travel safely, the villages into which they might move, or the quarrels and combats in which they might become involved'. To the extent that lineages, clans, or villages collaborated in a venture, it was because 'the individuals initiating the proposed … exchange, trading voyage, or raiding party invoked lineage or clan or village membership as a reason for temporary cooperation'.

What Fortune called Manus 'religion'—more concretely, people's relationship to the ghosts of the dead—reinforced the marriage exchange system by punishing failure to meet trade and exchange obligations and breaches of sexual morality, for the latter endangered the stability of marriages, thus affecting the exchange system and all that it entailed. The role of the ghosts of the dead was the most prominent feature of a prevailing disposition to see the world as governed by conscious forces, vitally interested in human affairs. Here was fertile ground for both the comparatively gradualist millenarian hopes interwoven with the secular efforts of the Paliau Movement and the apocalyptic cargo cult visions that took hold within the Movement. Despite the great cultural similarity of all the peoples of the Admiralties, some villages remained outside the Movement and its cults while apparently similar villages joined enthusiastically. There is no simple explanation for this. It is to a great extent, however, the result of the play of micropolitics described in later chapters. And these micropolitics often reflected the way in which particular locales specialised—beyond the limits imposed by local environments—in producing goods for trade, and the constant struggle of established and would-be leaders to avoid the ignominy of subordination to others.

We begin below a more detailed description of the features sketched above by describing the social fragmentation of the indigenous Admiralties, ranging from the fault line at the heart of the nuclear family to the omnidirectional armed hostility among villages. Yet, as we consider next, the people of the Admiralties were integrated in a dense pattern of interlocking networks centred on individuals seeking leadership and prestige, a quest in which the exchanges of material goods surrounding marriage were crucial. The central role of such exchange is important in the story of the Paliau Movement because it became the most obvious focus of young men's discontent as precolonial ways began to lose their hegemony. This despite the punishment household ghosts visited on those who failed to honour the system's requirements. Paliau and others eventually rejected these ghostly enforcers, but—ironically—the ghosts were merely one face of an all-embracing cosmology of animate and personal causation without which there would probably have been no Paliau Movement.

A fragmented social world

In 1953, Schwartz estimated that the total indigenous population in the Admiralty Islands was about 15,000. The postwar Australian administration, the Australian New Guinea Administrative Unit (ANGAU), also estimated the indigenous population *during* World War II at about 15,000 (ANGAU 1944). Bogen (n.d.) estimated a total *postwar* population of 12,500, divided among about 1,200 Titan in some 10 villages, about 6,500 Usiai in some 70 villages, and about 4,500 Matankor in about 45 villages. The people of each of these three ethnic groups considered themselves distinct in numerous ways from the people of the others and tended to marry within their respective groups. Many Manus people told Schwartz that in the past some people of the Admiralties had practised cannibalism, but—they said—while they married endogamously, their ancestors had eaten only members of other ethnic groups; that is, they had practised exophagy. But none of these three groups acted in concert in other ways, and warfare was as common among people of the same ethnic group as among members of different groups.

Villages varied considerably in size. They were the largest units with any degree of internal cohesion, but this cohesion was loose. Most villages comprised one or more patrilineal clans—that is, families related by descent through men from common male ancestors several generations in the past. A village was usually known by the name of the dominant clan or the name of the village's location. The most prestigious adult male of a clan functioned as its leader. In a multi-clan village, people recognised the most prestigious clan leader as the village leader; as long, that is, as he maintained his prestige. The leaders of some villages were more skilled in trade, exchange, or warfare than the leaders of others, but this did not confer on them any authority over other villages.

Figure 3.1: In Pere village in 1928, houses and other structures were built on pilings over natural or artificial lagoons. People moved around the village by canoe.

Source: Reo Fortune, from the collection of Theodore Schwartz, now housed in the Archive for Melanesian Anthropology, University of California, San Diego.

Villages with populations diminished by warfare or disease sometimes ceded their autonomy to join more populous villages. Villages and clans, however, were also prone to splitting. Given sufficient strength in numbers, lineages—that is, segments of clans[1]—sometimes claimed recognition as entities distinct from their clans of origin, with their own leaders. Pursuing such a split was the only option for an ambitious man wishing to escape subordination to another: 'To have a "name" required that one have a "place" and public of one's own, however small, if one's feats of warfare and exchange were not to redound to the credit of another' (Schwartz 1975: 110). Individuals could increase their own prestige and authority by creating autonomous places, but the overall effect was to dilute the value of leadership by keeping villages from getting very large.

---

1   More precisely, segments comprising descendants through men of common male ancestors closer to the present than the common clan ancestor, but still some three to six generations above their senior members.

As we will see below, neither warfare nor ritual institutions fostered unity beyond the clan or the village, which were themselves fragile, schismatic entities. Individuals dispersed among several clans or villages sometimes collaborated in waging war. Warfare 'usually established or involved participation in extended chains of retaliation', but it did not produce 'resolution, cohesion, [or] linkage' (Schwartz 1963: 83). Neither did tending the critical relationships between the living and the dead create even temporary episodes of any wider unity. It was, to the contrary, very much a household affair in which even the interests of husbands and wives could diverge.

Warfare, village vulnerability, and divided households

Lack of political units larger than the village and the absence of any overarching authority that might mediate disputes between people of different clans or villages provided an ideal environment for chronic armed hostility. Cases that have been recorded suggest that, both within and between the ethnic groups, some fights were about control over locations favourable for trade: for instance, Titan groups competing for control over sea or river routes giving easy access to trade with Usiai; Usiai competing with other Usiai for easy access to the coast, where they could trade with Titan and Matankor; or Titan and Matankor struggling over routes favourable for sea trade. Nevermann (1934) drew from German colonial records evidence of near-constant raiding between the Titan of Mok and Mbukei islands between 1906 and 1910, under the leadership of particularly aggressive war leaders, although he did not comment on the raiders' motives.[2]

Schwartz (1963) describes features of social networks that would have helped avert conflict, but they were at best only moderately effective. A temporary truce prevailed when people from several villages and different ethnic groups met on comparatively neutral ground, such as a beach or a riverbank, to trade products of the sea for products of the land and to barter the various manufactured items in which particular groups specialised. Even so, Admiralties oral history includes accounts

---

2   We have not been able to locate a page number for this reference. It appears in Schwartz's notes without one.

of instances in which groups took advantage of such markets to ambush their enemies, willing to disrupt the vital flow of trade to exact revenge for a death suffered or captives taken in a previous encounter.[3] To a great extent, each village stood on its own.

Some inter-village raiding probably had little to do with trading prerogatives. While in the long run this perpetuated cycles of violence, in the short term it might have made villages more secure by demonstrating their capacity for violence. The preferred weapon for most fighting was a spear, preferably with an obsidian point, used without a shield. Practising spear skills was a common pastime among boys and young men, and their elders occasionally organised raids so that youths could validate their manhood by killing or wounding an enemy. While individual participants gained prestige from a successful action, the greatest prestige accrued to a raid's leader. Men kept count of the number of enemies they had killed by adding to a bundle of sticks; a war leader was also entitled to add a stick for every enemy killed by a member of one of his war parties.

Warfare was not a clear-cut affair of village against village. Like trade and exchange, it was something individuals organised, recruiting participants from among those having obligations—perhaps related to trade or exchange—to the leader and those eager to increase their own prestige. People belonging to a war leader's village or clan who had close kin or trading partners in a group to be attacked could choose not to take part in a particular action. But this was not necessarily without cost. If it appeared that someone had alerted the targets of a raiding party, their kin and associates in trade and exchange would have been obvious targets of suspicion. Many men, of course, were related to people in other villages through their wives, placing them in a delicate position with respect both to war leaders to whom they might have obligations and to their wives. If a man calculated that joining a raid in which he might encounter members of his wife's family was more to his advantage than sitting it out, he still had to try to keep his wife from alerting her kin, or face suspicion, if the raid went awry, that she had done so.

---

3   Children taken as captives generally would have been adopted; women might have become wives, or they might have been held to serve as prostitutes. Titan people of recent generations have disputed this last assertion, but the accounts that Mead, Fortune, and Schwartz collected from older generations support it.

Prestige, exchange, and obligation

Hereditary rank was a feature of all groups in Manus. Some version of a two-rank system appears to have been present in each of the three ethnic groups, as confirmed by Otto (1991: 69), citing Romanucci (1966: 36), and Carrier and Carrier (1989: 69). Titan speakers recognised two hereditary ranks. Persons or lineages of the higher rank were called *lapan*; those of the lower rank were *lau*. All members of a lineage shared the same rank. But to maintain a lineage's status as *lapan*, at least some members in each generation had to act as *lapan* were expected to act; although one could gain prestige without being *lapan*. To be *lapan* meant little if one did not validate the rank through prestige-building endeavours.

As noted above, a man could gain prestige by taking part in or leading successful war parties. But by far the most important route to prestige was success in organising the exchanges of goods central to the marriage system.[4] Mead (2002 [1934]) and Schwartz (1963) have described the complexities of the relationships formed by marriage in the Admiralties in some detail. For our purposes, it is enough to understand the bare bones. People married outside their lineages.[5] Such a marriage either created or continued an enduring relationship between the lineage of the groom and the lineage of the bride. A man or woman on the side of the bride (in Titan, *lom pein*) established by a previous marriage had the right to demand from the side of the groom (in Titan, *lom kamal*) a daughter in marriage to his or her son. Once a match was agreed—which did not require the consent of the prospective bride and groom—it was formalised by an exchange of goods between the bride's side (*lom pein*) and groom's side (*lom kamal*). The groom's side presented to the bride's side durable wealth, which in precolonial and early colonial times would have included dog's teeth, decoratively incised and worked into elaborate body ornaments, and so-called shell money—that is, small shell discs drilled with centre holes and strung on hand-made cord or fashioned into body ornaments. The bride's side presented food to the groom's side. In precolonial or early

---

4   Otto (1991: 74) confirms that war leadership was also an important source of prestige on Baluan Island. There, too, 'the general picture of the leader as an economic entrepreneur is certainly valid', although 'investment in other people's marriages may not have been prominent' (cf. Carrier and Carrier 1985, 1989).

5   Readers who are not anthropologists need to remember that in a patrilineal system like that of the Titan, a lineage is *not* a group of men descended through men from a common male ancestor. It is a group of men *and women* descended through men from a common male ancestor. Both men and women belong to their father's lineage, but only men pass that membership on to their children. A woman's children belong to their father's lineage.

colonial times, this would have been both cooked food (pigs, taro, yams, sago, and fish, accompanied by coconut oil), on which all those attending the ceremony feasted, and uncooked quantities of the same items that members of the groom's party carried home.

This initial exchange, however, was not enough. To maintain the prestige of the parties and continually validate the marriage and the relationship between lineages it created or maintained, further exchanges of the same kind were necessary at various stages in the marriage and the life cycle of the children resulting from the marriage, including their deaths. One generation, then, might have to carry on a series of exchanges begun by the previous generation. It is better to call these affinal exchanges—that is, exchanges between people related through marriage—than marriage exchanges, because, although begun with marriage, they eventually involved a much wider variety of events. Since members of a single lineage could contract marriages with members of several other lineages—in some providing a husband, in others providing a wife—they could be involved simultaneously, but in different roles, in several affinal exchange series.

Figure 3.2: Pere village men, photographed in 1928.

They were probably not resting, but planning a prodigious exchange of wealth to seal a marriage and build their social status.

Source: Reo Fortune, from the collection of Theodore Schwartz, now housed in the Archive for Melanesian Anthropology, University of California, San Diego.

Although both sides in an exchange had firm obligations, greater prestige attached to giving durable wealth, and Titan spoke of the durable wealth given by the groom's side as a payment and of the food given by the bride's side as simply the return. But, although a lineage therefore gained more prestige by carrying out the exchanges entailed by the marriage of one of its young men, his sisters and their descendants were believed to have the power to bless or curse the brothers' children and their descendants by invoking the spirits of the dead—the power of *tandritanitani*.

It was impossible, however, for a prospective bride or groom or their immediate families to accumulate the wealth needed for even an initial exchange without help. Even all the members of a man's or woman's lineage working together could not muster either the labour power or all the skills and resources to produce the goods needed. Affinal exchange also depended at least as much on trade as on production. Trade took many forms, including barter at markets, where people could chose with whom to exchange their products on each occasion, and established trade partnerships between individuals. The latter were ongoing relationships, sometimes passed from generation to generation, between suppliers of specialised products. Thus, trade partnerships crossed ecological zones and ethnic lines. In contrast to the barter at markets, such trade could be delayed. That is, one partner could supply goods to the other, sometimes in response to a direct request, and not receive the agreed-upon return in goods of another type until much later.

Some specialisation in production depended on having specialised skills or access to particular raw materials. For instance, villages with access to the few locales where one could find obsidian specialised in producing spear points and knives. But specialisation in manufacturing many other items—such as clay pots, carved wooden sleeping platforms, or particular types of baskets—was largely based on a locale's claim to priority and people's recognition of that claim. This kind of arbitrary specialisation would have helped foster networks crossing lineage, clan, village, and ethnic boundaries. But it is unlikely that anyone honoured claims to manufacturing precedence with this result in mind. It is more likely that people simply recognised that the costs of violating such claims outweighed the benefits. Locales probably defended their rights in such matters fiercely. In Papua New Guinea (PNG) today, fierce disputes still erupt between villages or clans over rights to use particular designs for dance regalia or to practise certain kinds of magic. But it is perhaps more fundamental that people recognised that imitation was a losing tactic in the constant competition for prestige and distinctive local identity, a point we will return to when we look at the distribution of participation in the Movement and the cargo cults within it.

A man vigorously seeking prestige through playing a central role in numerous affinal exchanges would need many trading partners, involving him in a complicated web of what an accountant would call payables and receivables. A lot of wealth would have passed through his hands, but he would have held none of it for long. He would have poured some into new or ongoing series of affinal exchanges, used some to pay debts to trading partners, and used other goods to put trading partners in debt to him so he could count on the goods owed him for a future affinal exchange.

If a man was active and skilled in the wheeling and dealing required to 'finance', as Mead put it, affinal exchanges, he could do so to obtain spouses for his children. If not, a male kinsman could take on the responsibility—and the potential additional prestige—of arranging their marriages and organising and accumulating the goods, or the promises to provide the goods, for the series of exchanges the marriages would entail over many coming years. Marriage immediately placed both women and men under heavy obligation to those who had organised their unions, committing them to work off their debts by producing and trading for goods that their sponsors could put into other prestige-building exchanges.

The affinal exchange system put great pressure on people to remain married; if a union dissolved, all the networks of payables and receivables focused on the exchanges validating the union were thrown into disarray. But the system did nothing to mitigate men's and women's resentment at being forced into marriages not of their choosing or the resulting tension in the relationship. On the contrary, Mead (2002 [1934]: 61) noted, after marriage, husbands and wives remained bound to those who made the required payments and returns, thus beholden to the opposite sides of tense relationships between larger groups. Even at this intimate level, then, there was a significant barrier to trust and solidarity.

Mead also observed that, once betrothed, the young often resented the elders to whom they now owed years of labour and subservience, and she called the constant production, trade, and close accounting of debts of the affinal exchange system an 'economic treadmill' from which it was virtually impossible to step down (2001 [1956]). Mead described the limited choices a man had within this system: he could remain permanently indebted to whomever had financed his marriage, not attempting to free himself from obligation and remaining merely a helper in his sponsor's endeavours; he could work off his initial obligation and then take control of the further exchanges entailed by his marriage, but not attempt to engage in financing the marriages of others; or he could work off his obligation, take control of the further exchanges entailed by his own marriage and work towards becoming a financier of others' marriages.

Gaining prestige on one's own—becoming a man of renown—was the reward for taking the latter course. But once established as a successful financier of affinal exchange a man could not relax. One's prestige lasted only as long as one kept up with ongoing series of exchanges and continued initiating new ones. Even a man who chose to remain subordinate to the sponsor of his marriage had continuing obligations to provide goods for the sponsor's endeavours and even men with very limited ambitions risked loss of their limited status if they did not meet their correspondingly limited obligations. Women were expected to produce and trade for those who had arranged the bride's side of their betrothal, wedding, and subsequent exchanges, as well as for their husband's endeavours. They managed their individual networks of payables and receivables, and their good names depended in significant part on their skill and vigour in producing and trading for goods for exchange.

Ghosts, morality, and exchange

In addition to the repercussions for one's status, there were powerful supernatural sanctions, applicable to both men and women, for shirking exchange obligations. The constellation of beliefs and practices revolving around men's guardian spirits that Fortune observed among Titan speakers (that Fortune called their religion) had parallels among Usiai and Matankor. The preferred guardian spirit was the ghost of a man's father, whose skull would have been decorated and kept in a wooden bowl stowed securely in the house rafters. Fortune translated the Titan term for this deceased household member, *moen palit*, loosely but memorably as Sir Ghost. Sir Ghost punished moral lapses of those under his scrutiny. He also was expected to protect household members from misfortunes, such as an accident at sea, and attacks by the Sir Ghosts of other households, which could be motivated by pure malice. Titan attitudes towards Sir Ghosts regarding their responsibilities as protectors were severely practical. If a man's Sir Ghost failed to protect members of his household from misfortune and, as was inevitable, death, he replaced him with the ghost—and the skull—of another recently deceased male kinsman. Titan never took death as 'natural', and if they did not regard it as punishment for sin they usually attributed it to the malice of another household's Sir Ghost or to malicious magic, hence the need for a Sir Ghost's protection. Fortune (1965 [1935]: 8) described the fate of a discredited Sir Ghost as follows:

> His skull may be battered to powder, and the powder thrown into flames, or it may merely be hurled into the sea. Sir Ghost becomes a vague lurking danger of the middle seas, not very seriously regarded—then a sea slug. But the system goes on. A new skull is bleached from the corpse of the recently dead. It is installed in the house front with the women wailing at the reminder of the death.

The Sir Ghost's role as moral watchdog is more germane to the system of affinal exchange and its relationship to the Paliau Movement than its role as protector. Sir Ghosts could mete out misfortune or illness to household members who violated moral rules or to members of the violator's family not resident in the household. Sir Ghosts were especially concerned with sexual morality and meeting obligations in trade and exchange, but they also found indolence morally offensive. Sexual offences could range from incest or adultery to more subtle but, in the ghost's view, equally dangerous acts, such as bodily immodesty or neglecting to avoid any of the categories of opposite-sex kin with whom an individual was forbidden to have contact. Young men and women, for instance, were forbidden even the most casual contact with their betrothed and men and their mothers-in-law were to avoid each other sedulously.[6]

Confirming that an illness or misfortune was ghostly punishment for immoral behaviour required the services of a diviner or a medium, the former generally a man and the latter generally a woman. Men and women got their powers of detection ultimately from the Sir Ghosts, but they paid established diviners or mediums to be 'consecrated' in their roles, in Fortune's language (1965 [1935]: 29ff.). A major difference between male divination and female communication with the spirit world (relevant to events in the Paliau Movement that we will describe later) was

---

6   Mead (2002 [1934]: 52ff.) discusses a variety of types of avoidance behaviour, as well as relationships in which joking and familiarity are permitted, that she and Fortune observed among the Titan in 1928.

the medium's use of a spirit intermediary—often the ghost of her dead child—which announced its presence by whistling (that is, whistling via the medium).[7]

Mead (2001 [1956]: 55) emphasised how these beliefs and practices spurred unremitting attention to trade and exchange:

> This system ensured that the rich and enterprising were punished if they paused for a moment in pursuing their far-flung enterprises, and that the man who had elected to remain a dependent of some entrepreneur was chastised for not fulfilling his simple dependent role. The man who had elected to stand aside from the complexities of high finance and simply fish was chastised for not returning some very small debt or for letting his house floor get dilapidated.

Since the people of the Admiralties did not entertain naturalistic explanations for illness and death, they must have found it disturbingly easy to find evidence that they or others were moral laggards.

Mead's portrayal of the burdens imposed on Titan adults by the system of affinal exchange, including the harsh moral regime the ghosts enforced, is so relentlessly dark that one could easily wonder if she was exaggerating or maybe overlooking some dimension of Titan life that softened the rough edges. We have already noted that trade, including arbitrary local specialisations that inhibited local self-sufficiency, would have helped integrate a fragmented social world. Marshall Sahlins (2013) finds more metaphysical significance in the complexities of Admiralties affinal exchange. Drawing on a theme in anthropology with deep roots, he argues that, to the people of many societies, distant strangers who are potentially dangerous are also a source of life-giving power. Hence, affinal exchange was much more than an exhausting and stressful way to organise sexual reproduction or promote industry; it was a way of sustaining 'existence' (p. 285)—not just the social status quo, but being/existence

---

7 Fortune (1965 [1935]) describes in detail the methods diviners and mediums used to contact, question, and obtain answers from the spirit world; social influences on their findings; and the expiatory payments made, on both the mortal and spirit planes, to produce cures. Women did not enjoy the same degree of protection from a Sir Ghost as men did (ibid.: 25ff.), but their moral lapses could trigger more widespread consequences. As Fortune explains: 'In case of a woman sinning sexually, she and her husband's kin, and also her brother's kin may be punished by the Sir Ghosts of the respective kin ... where[as] sexual sin or other sin by a man is dangerous only to himself and to his own kin, his wife alone among affinal kin being added' (ibid.: 27).

itself—through transactions with a 'spiritually charged outside' (p. 287). That is, trade for and exchange of 'foreign wealth' (p. 285) revitalised the parties involved on a metaphysical level.

This sounds less grubby and more deeply rewarding than scrambling to keep one's footing on Mead's 'economic treadmill'. But if the people of the Admiralties recognised, even inchoately, this metaphysical significance, it does not appear to have made the system less onerous. According to Fortune (1965 [1935]: 7), many Titan found the strict moral oversight of the household ghosts—an integral part of the system—hard to take, not only because the ghosts punished moral lapses, but also because they subjected people to the shame of public confession. He observed in 1928 that there was talk among the Titan of 'throwing all the ancestral skulls into the sea, thus throwing out all their Sir Ghosts, and adopting instead the Christian God [as represented by the Catholic Mission]. The advantage stated … is the substitution of private confession and private expiation of sin for public confession, public indictment, and public expiation of sin'. Many Titan did affiliate with the Catholic Mission within a few years of Mead's and Fortune's sojourn with them. The presence of an alternative—Catholicism—undoubtedly helped move people to recognise and articulate their discontent. We will see in Chapter 4 how experience with wage labour and life among white colonials influenced later critics of affinal exchange, including Paliau.

A world of animate and personal causation

One cannot understand the indigenous world of the Admiralties without recognising the critical role of the household ghosts. But to comprehend some aspects of the Paliau Movement, it is even more important to recognise that the beliefs and practices pertaining to the ghosts are part of something more fundamental: a cultural world in which impersonal natural forces and processes play minor roles at most, and people typically invoke conscious entities—human, alive or dead, and non-human—to explain events, especially unwelcome events. Fortune emphasises that, in 1928, Titan assumed that ghosts were not only capable of causing illness and death, they were virtually the only cause: 'there is no secular attitude towards the life and death of the body or towards the body's ills. Death is regarded as punishment of sin. It is not accepted as impersonal' (Fortune 1965 [1935]: 8). Neither was serious misfortune of other kinds accepted as impersonal. In a world governed by entities with human-like motives and emotions, events of human significance could not be accidents.[8]

There are people everywhere prone to personifying the forces and processes that shape life, but such a view is not dominant everywhere. Its significance in a particular society may be most obvious in how people understand disease. In their classic volume *Medical Anthropology*, George M. Foster and Barbara Gallatin Anderson (1978: 54) distinguish naturalistic from what they call personalistic explanations of illness. They emphasise that personalistic is not a synonym for supernatural. Personal causes, for instance, may include human witches and sorcerers who might 'draw on the supernatural', but they are human. Foster and Anderson (1978: 56) also emphasise that a naturalistic approach to medicine is not necessarily a mainstream, contemporary Western approach, citing as examples humoral pathology, Ayurvedic medicine, and traditional Chinese medicine.

Foster and Anderson also observe that people in a given society may resort to both personalistic and naturalistic explanations of disease, the type of affliction often determining the type of diagnosis and treatment deemed appropriate.[9] A personalistic or personifying understanding of disease, however, is still strikingly dominant in rural PNG and would have been considerably more so before the introduction of Western naturalistic medicine.

Many anthropological studies of Melanesian peoples build on the thought of Marcel Mauss, as expounded in his 1925 volume *The Gift: Forms and Functions of Exchange in Archaic Societies*. Mauss argues that where gift exchange predominates, people construe the things exchanged, particularly on ceremonial or ritual occasions (e.g. in affinal exchange

8   We have already introduced Schwartz's other name for this cultural construction of the world: a cosmology of animate and personal causation. Since it pertains to fundamental ideas about the nature of being, one might want to call it an ontology. But, without losing anything, we could also speak of this conception of things as a type of world view; a phenomenological ecology, to use a term Schwartz also favours (1991: 185–6); a type of behavioural environment, following Hallowell (1955); or an aspect of what Pierre Bourdieu calls habitus (1977). There are many acceptable options. We will, however, stick with cosmology to remain consistent with Schwartz's earlier work.

9   When people distinguish general categories of diagnosis and treatment that mirror the naturalistic–personalistic divide, they do not necessarily understand the distinction in these terms. In rural PNG, for instance, people often distinguish afflictions that can be treated with European medicine from those requiring indigenous methods, that is, methods based on personalistic understanding of disease. But we have never heard rural Papua New Guineans speak of such specific distinctions in terms of broad abstractions.

in the Admiralties), as parts of persons or as partaking of the substance of the giver. More recently, Marilyn Strathern (1988: 178) writes of exchange in Melanesia that 'things are conceptualised as parts of persons … They are not, of course, apprehended as standing for persons: that is our [i.e. an outside observer's] construction'.[10] Writing of the Gimi people of highlands PNG, Paige West (2016: 93) affirms that in societies based on gift exchange, 'identity and personhood are made through social relationships with others'. Further, these are relationships of 'exchange and transaction', and the Gimi see themselves as having social relations with 'animals, plants, people, and spirits' (ibid.: 98). The result, as West conveys vividly (without, however, using our terminology), is a deeply personified world. She explains that the Gimi call 'the force that animates a living person' *auna*, and continues:

> When a person dies, her auna leaves her body and migrates to the forest. Once there, the auna slowly turns into kore ('ghost', 'spirit', 'ancestor', and 'wild') and lodges in plants, animals, streams, mountains, birds, and other bits of what we call forests. The life force of a person becomes the forest, with the 'wild' parts of the forest becoming filled with and 'animated by' the kore of the deceased Gimi. Once the auna goes to the forests and begins to infuse itself into wildlife, it becomes part of not only the forest but also the never-ending cycle of Gimi existence. (West 2016: 93)

When a hunter kills and eats a marsupial, 'The [marsupial] as food makes the hunter's body while the [marsupial] as embodied ancestor or kore makes the auna of the hunter' (West 2016: 95).[11]

The dark side of a personified world

It is easy to find the dark side of personification in Fortune's description of the role of household ghosts in Titan life. Fortune's and Mead's view of Titan life in general in 1928 teeters on the edge of negative romanticism. West's depiction of the Gimi world teeters on the edge of positive

---

10   Marilyn Strathern's *The Gender of the Gift* (1988) explores the implications for anthropology of this theme in Mauss in Melanesia and beyond, with special emphasis on its implications for understanding gender. Her work has become a taken-for-granted starting point for much current research. In discussing Schwartz's work on trade and exchange in the Admiralties, Sahlins (2013: 284), for example, speaks of the 'inalienable person-attributes of the things exchanged'.

11   The type of marsupial West uses in this example is known as a *kile* in the Gimi language and in Latin as Macropodidae *Dedolagus goodfellow* (West 2016: 95).

romanticism. But even in such positive romanticisation there are hints of the dark side of personification, an important topic for understanding aspects of the Paliau phenomenon.[12]

West describes the social relations that make up the Gimi world as 'familial and poetic' (2016: 93). And the Gimi world as she describes it sounds like one in which people would be untroubled by the anxiety regarding salvation Christianity generates, the deep unease of life in a modern world the inhabitants of which suspect has no inherent meaning, or the existentialist vertigo of confronting one's freedom from the past and responsibility for the future. To the Gimi, 'everything that "is" and that ever will be is the physical incarnation of their ancestors' life force' (West 2016: 93), a perception we can imagine would make one feel profoundly at home.[13]

But it might not necessarily make one feel profoundly at ease. Life in a deeply personified world is not necessarily more humane than life in a world shaped by naturalistic assumptions. As Stephen Leavitt's work (2004: 183–4) illustrates, a world in which one is defined by one's exchange relations with others has characteristic rough edges. Leavitt's research among the Bumbita people of East Sepik Province of PNG convinced him that, despite the intricate web of relationships comprising Bumbita society, people sometimes longed for personal autonomy in a way that rootless, self-reliant (or aspiring to be so) Westerners would find familiar. But for the Bumbita this creates tension with 'an overwhelming sense that one is in fact defined by one's relations with others', and 'that for each action one must consider a myriad of factors relating to one's relatives and associates'. He concluded that many Bumbita find this dilemma 'a severe burden'. Leavitt worked among the Bumbita in 1984–86, when they had been exposed to deracinated Europeans for some time, so it is hard to say if precolonial Bumbita felt a similar conflict, but—as we shall see—young men of Paliau's generation in the Admiralties would have recognised it.[14]

---

12 West's work on the whole is not as unremittingly romantic as our selections might suggest. Her focus is on the grittier issues surrounding Gimi self-determination in the face of powerful external forces eroding their sovereignty.

13 It is not clear why West encloses the word 'is' in quotation marks.

14 Leavitt (2004: 183–4) also observes: 'Social conditions like these [i.e. those he found among the Bumbita] prevail in face-to-face societies [i.e. small-scale societies, where everyone knows everyone else] everywhere. In Melanesia though, researchers have sought to establish the "sociocentric" bases of self-understandings without asking much about what this means for individuals trying to live their lives on a day-to-day basis'. Day-to-day living in such social conditions, he contends, 'can seem oppressive to individual actors'.

In addition to the burden Leavitt observed, personification is also associated with chronic suspicion and mistrust. Stanley Diamond (1974: 94) wrote that the intense personal interaction characteristic of small-scale societies often produces not only 'sophistication and subtlety' about people, it also fosters 'dangerous sensitivity'. He was speaking in part of how personification can breed mistrust, begat by the assumption that when bad things happen, other people are generally to blame. Fortune's *Manus Religion* (1965 [1935]) provides a surfeit of illustrations of this in his detailed cases of diviners and mediums seeking the causes of illness, death, and misfortune (cf. Foster and Anderson 1978: 55). Similarly, Hallowell (1955: 145) writes of the attitude of the Ojibwa of north-eastern North America in early colonial times, 'if something goes wrong, it is somebody's fault'.

Throughout the world, where personification dominates, what Schwartz and Smith and their ilk would construe as accidents engender recriminations. West (2016: 97) shows this principle at work among the Gimi, when she explains how a Gimi man understood why his daughter was killed by a falling tree. Since the daughter had been in a part of the forest associated with the *kore* of her ancestors, she should have been safe; therefore, her father concluded, sorcery—the intentional use of malicious magic—must have killed her. This diagnosis is incidental to West's main point, so she doesn't elaborate on its implications. In PNG, however, a diagnosis of sorcery can be like a match set to dry brush. Such a personified explanation can cast a pall of fear over a community's everyday life, starting—or reviving—generations of hostility within or between communities, and inciting retaliatory violence to the point of torture and murder.

Explaining rampant personification

We will not linger on some proposed ways of explaining the human tendency to personify the world, other than to strengthen the point that although it is a nearly universal human tendency, the fact that it is stronger in some societies and social contexts than others is subject to explanation. It is not, as Rappaport (1999: 1–2) contends (rather carelessly) of religion, 'indispensable to the species'. And although many members of our species find it impossible to see the world otherwise, we have the potential to make other choices. Only large-scale social and cultural change is likely to deprive this tendency of its strength. Banerjee and Bloom (2014: 299), however, provide a hopeful note. Regarding the human propensity for teleological reasoning, they argue that 'although teleological beliefs about life events and nature may be highly intuitive and automatically generated, they can be explicitly overridden by engaging in reflective thought and by inhibiting default causal explanations'.

A number of scholars discuss a human tendency to personify causation as a product of cognitive evolution and a vital element in the general human receptivity to religious concepts. For instance, the work of scholars like Scott Atran (2002) and Pascal Boyer (2001) builds on the work of Stewart Guthrie (1993) to elaborate the hypothesis that evolution equipped human beings with a hyperactive tendency to detect agency in their environments. Hence, as ably summarised by Justin L. Barrett (2000: 31): 'people have a bias towards detecting human-like agency in their environment that might not actually exist. Thus, people are particularly sensitive to the presence of intentional action as the cause of a given state of affairs when data is [sic] ambiguous or sketchy ... such a biased perceptual device would have been quite adaptive in our evolutionary past, for the consequences of failing to detect an agent are potentially much graver than mistakenly detecting an agent that is not there'. Boyer (2001: 33) emphasises that this line of reasoning is not an effort to identify a '*historical* origin of religion in the sense of a point in time ... when people created religion where there was none'. Rather, the point is to get at the possible evolutionary roots of a cognitive bias that has been culturally elaborated in many ways, such that 'it is part of our constant, everyday humdrum cognitive functioning that we interpret all sorts of cues in the environment, not just events but the way things are, as the result of some agents' actions' (p. 145). Daniel C. Dennett (2006: 109) draws on an evolutionary perspective when elaborating what he calls a tendency to adopt 'the intentional stance' and commenting on the human 'disposition to attribute agency' (p. 114).[15] Bruce M. Hood focuses on ontogeny rather than phylogeny. He hypothesises that what he regards (probably prematurely) as the inevitability of 'supernatural belief' (Hood 2009: xvii) and the difficulty human beings have handling 'the possibility that things happen randomly by chance' (p. 11) are natural products of *individual* human cognitive development.

---

15   For a more recent examination of research on human cognitive bias and religion see Van Leeuwen and van Elk (2019).

None of the above, of course, explains why a universal tendency to personify is more highly developed in some contexts than in others. Schwartz (1976a, 1978b; cf. Smith 1994: 44–69) has proposed the relevance of social scale to the strength of personification in different cultural worlds. An important point in his argument (greatly simplified here) is that small-scale societies provide social environments more consistent with a personifying view than do large-scale societies. In small-scale societies, what Schwartz calls face-to-face ratios are low, perhaps as low as one-to-one if everyone is known relatively equally to everyone else. Hence, the interpersonal ramifications of people's actions are relatively direct and obvious. This is consistent with (Schwartz does not argue for causation) assuming that conscious agents who are intimate with the details of people's lives are among the world's prime movers. To use Peter Berger's (1967) language, life in a society in which all or nearly all are known to each other provides a strong 'plausibility structure' for personification, especially where there is no strong tradition of naturalistic explanation. In contrast, the comparative anonymity of life in large-scale societies can foster the perception that one is unknown (and probably wildly unimportant) to powerful distant institutions. Such a perception is consistent with assigning impersonal causality a central role in events and accepting the importance of specific natural forces, such as gravity, natural selection, weather systems and tectonic shifts, and a social world in which the chance confluence of unrelated events can have effects that neither human actors nor other-than-human entities intended .

Nonetheless, even in large-scale societies that depend on technology that is the fruit of naturalistic understanding of the world, and in which anonymity is not only possible but common, people continue to indulge in teleological thinking and invoke supernatural entities and metaphysical forces to explain things. A prime example: even as more and more of the world's people become entangled in global social networks and depend on complex digital technologies, theism thrives. As Schwartz (1978b: 225) writes, 'The notion of an omnipresent, omniscient god, aware of and concerned with the detailed behaviour of each person, is obviously a small-scale concept extended to the most extreme asymmetrical face-to-face ratio', that of all of humanity to a single deity. But this is something to be explained, not evidence of the inevitable nature of things.

It is apparent that—as noted in Chapter 1—the conspicuously dark form of personification that Barkun (2006 [2003]) calls conspiracism is gaining strength in the world at large, including the technologically highly developed West. We return to this topic in Chapter 15, our final chapter.

Personification is a critical concept in our discussion of the Paliau Movement. Paliau grounded all his efforts to revolutionise indigenous society at least in part in a cosmology of animate and personal causation entirely in keeping with indigenous orientations. That Paliau's cosmology drew extensively on a personifying European mythology—mission Christianity—gave his vision greater weight as the basis for a plan to attain parity with the Europeans. To be complete, any explanation or interpretation of Melanesian cargo cults must acknowledge that the prevailing personifying orientation is something to be explained as well as part of the explanation.[16] The dark side of personification is especially relevant to the mixture of credulity and suspicion characteristic of cargo cults at their peaks.

Personification and pragmatism in indigenous Manus

Emphasising the ubiquity of a personifying tendency in our species should make cargo cults look less like an especially exotic kind of otherness and more like people doing something familiar—millenarianism—in a historically and culturally distinctive way. It is also important to keep personification in the forefront because the sphere in which naturalistic views are not only accepted but valued in PNG (for instance, consider the growing number of indigenous medical professionals) is expanding even as millenarianism remains common. It is hard to appreciate the full significance of this if we relegate personification to the background.

Yet despite the densely personified world of indigenous Admiralty Islanders—the strength of a cosmology of animate and personal causation—a number of observers have commented on the high value people of the Admiralties have placed on empirical evidence. Both Mead and Fortune observed that Titan adults had enormous respect for accuracy

---

16   Nor are explanations of most instances of apocalyptic millenarianism in the West complete without considering the strength of personification in Western societies.

in describing the physical world, Fortune (1965 [1935]: xi) noting that 'the Manus [i.e. the Titan] delight in facts and argument … They debate questions about entirely useless matters for the love of truth'. One of Mead's favourite anecdotes was of a Titan man who carried the jawbone of a fish with him for several days so that he could show it to someone with whom he'd argued about the number of teeth the type of fish in question had.[17]

In 1928, the Titan often sought the reasons for troubling events by communicating with the dead, but Mead and Fortune saw Titan adults reject the findings of seances, even though this risked arousing the anger of the ghosts (Mead 2001 [1930]: 90; Mead 2001 [1956]: 95–6). Fortune (1965 [1935]: 2) argued that people rejected the findings of a medium or 'oracle' not simply because they did not like them, but because they thought the medium had not given 'a judgment derived from the will of the [ghost], but rather one derived from the oracle's too clearly human capacity'.

We must recognise, however, that to strengthen the case for Titan practicality, Mead played down some contrasting aspects of Titan life. In *Growing Up in New Guinea* she described Titan culture in 1928 as not only sober and pragmatic, but also poor in fantasy. That was probably a step too far. Schwartz points out that Titan people showed considerable capacity for fantasy in the same seances that provided Fortune and Mead with evidence of Titan pragmatism. Indeed, one could regard the mediums through whom people communicated with ghosts as specialists in elaborating culturally provided fantasy, in unwitting collaboration with the audience. (This does not, of course, conflict with the idea that on occasion some members of the audience withdrew their collaboration for pragmatic reasons.)

Mead also wrote that the Titan language was 'rigorously matter-of-fact where ours [i.e. American English] is filled with imagery and metaphor' (Mead 2001 [1930]: 95). Schwartz, who has much greater command of the Titan language than Mead had, also observes that everyday speech is relatively nonfigurative. But Schwartz has observed that Titan commemorative ballads, a form of language use different from all others in Manus life, make considerable use of imaginative language. They

---

17 Fortune (1965 [1935]: xi) employs the same anecdote. We do not know with whom—Mead or Fortune—it originated.

employ a vocabulary not used in ordinary speech, many words are archaic or foreign, and even common words are pronounced in distinctive ways. Granted, when in need of a ballad to express sorrow or feelings for the dead, those who cannot do it themselves go to a specialist—a man or woman who can invest language with the required emotional richness.[18]

Fortune and Mead, however, made a good case for Titan pragmatism even without such questionable claims. Regarding other Admiralty Islands people, Otto observed similar respect for visible evidence on Baluan Island and presents what he calls a Baluan 'hierarchy of the reliability of knowledge' as follows: 'the highest status belongs to those things you have seen with your own eyes; in second place comes knowledge you have seen the effects of, whether that knowledge comes from dreams, divination or from other human beings; a much lower status is attributed to those things you have only heard about' (Otto 1992c: 437). Similarly, Anders Emil Rasmussen (2013: 104) observes that Mbukei Islanders place high value on 'visible proof' in assessing the reliability of knowledge. The point here is not that Admiralty Islanders value visible evidence more than other Melanesians.[19] It is to help show how far those who participated in the cults had to depart from their quotidian orientations.

A paranoid ethos

It is difficult to understand the apparent ease with which Manus people involved in cargo cults dropped their usual empirical orientation without recognising an aspect of indigenous Manus life that pulled against

---

18   The ballad form seems to have derived its style from the pattern of speech in formal kinship avoidance behaviour. Among relatives such as cross-cousins, between whom obscene joking was expected, the joking was direct, raw, literal, and vulgar. This was potentially dangerous, but it was considered safe as long as it was clearly labelled as joking. For relatives in an avoidance relationship, one had to use oblique reference, never mentioning anything that could be seen as identifying that person directly. This taboo on direct reference was extended to all of the deceased.

19   The literature undoubtedly provides many examples of indigenous empiricism elsewhere in Melanesia. We offer only one. Smith (1994: 78) notes that despite the great importance of spirits of the dead in the lives of Kragur villagers in the 1970s, at least one man found it hard to accept prevailing views or to sympathise with common fears. He was blind and often walked around the village and its environs at night, as confident of the paths then as during the day. He told Smith: 'I never hear a ghost. Nothing makes a noise in the bush or touches me. During the rains when the nights are completely dark everyone says, "Oh, now is the time the ghosts walk around". But I … don't meet anything'.

empiricism and pragmatism even in normal times. Schwartz calls this a paranoid ethos. As we will emphasise below, this is not something unique to Manus or Melanesia, but it is vital to understanding the Manus case.

Gregory Bateson introduced the useful concept of ethos in *Naven*, a study of a ritual he observed among the Iatmul, a Sepik River people, in the late 1920s and early 1930s.[20] He defined ethos as 'a culturally standardised system of organisation of the instincts and emotions' (1958 [1936]: 118–19). George De Vos (1976: 9) also offers a helpful phrasing of the concept: 'The *ethos* of a culture is the characteristic spirit or prevalent tone or sentiment of a people, institution, or system'. Although an ethos develops in relationship to the history and particular circumstances of a population or institution, it can linger as circumstances change: 'In situations of change, patternings in the emotional tone or implicit feelings underlying behaviour may persist in spite of revision in ... behavioural forms' (ibid.). Schwartz (1973) argues that an important element in the typical indigenous Melanesian ethos was a tendency to see and feel the world as a place of ubiquitous danger, requiring constant vigilance, and fostering suspicion of *personally relevant* meaning beneath the surface of events. Such an ethos militated against entertaining the possibility of chance or coincidence.

Schwartz summarises as follows the conditions conducive to a paranoid ethos in indigenous Melanesia:

> The paranoid ethos in Melanesia derived from the uncertainty of life, from the high mortality rate and short life span, from the many births and few surviving children. It depended on the uncertainty of the yield of productive activities even though the technologies were ingeniously diversified ... Perhaps more fundamentally for Melanesia, the paranoid ethos related to the extreme atomism of social and political life, to the constancy and omnidirectionality of war and raiding, to the uncertainty of all alliances, and even to the uncertainty of village and clan cohesion. Uncertainty was experienced as a pervasive threat in terms of the premises of a cosmology of animate and personal causation. (Schwartz 1973: 155)

---

20 Bateson later became Mead's third husband, after Reo Fortune. But he did much of the research on which *Naven* is based before he encountered Mead and Fortune, who at the time were also engaged in research among Sepik River peoples.

It is easy to see how a chronic feeling that 'malice is … almost omnipresent beyond the narrow circles of relative trust', as Schwartz (1973: 157) describes the dark side of a paranoid ethos, could thrive in such an environment. Our description above of the nature of indigenous social life in Manus illustrates just how narrow those circles of relative trust could be, frequently not even embracing partners in marriage. And the indigenous Manus personification of the world exacerbated perceptions of the dangers of the natural and social worlds, in which objective risks to life and limb were already numerous. If every misfortune is caused by some conscious, but usually hidden agent—if nothing is accidental—then each misfortune is evidence of lurking malice.

Schwartz is not the only anthropologist to observe a similar orientation among particular Melanesian peoples. Most of Fortune's *Sorcerers of Dobu* (1932), reporting on his research among the people of Dobu Island, located in what is now PNG's Milne Bay Province—which he conducted prior to his 1928 research in Manus—is devoted to describing a social context that fosters an attitude that could have been crafted especially to illustrate a paranoid ethos.[21] We must be somewhat wary, however, of relying on this famous work for validation. It was Ruth Benedict, not Fortune, who used the term 'paranoid' to describe aspects of Dobuan life in her 1934 work *Patterns of Culture*, and Fortune is said to have objected to this characterisation (Antrosio 2013). Decades later, anthropologist Susanne Kuehling (2005) also saw Dobuan life differently from Fortune.[22]

But we do not have to rest on Fortune, or Benedict's interpretation of Fortune. A.L. Epstein (2000–2001) examines his data on the Tolai people of what is now PNG's East New Britain Province to assess the applicability to the Tolai case of Schwartz's conception of a paranoid ethos in Melanesia. Epstein (2000–2001: 17) concludes that his data give 'full support' to Schwartz's thesis. Specifically, he notes a 'pervasive sense of threat and vulnerability … characteristic of the response of the Tolai to so many aspects of their world' (p. 6), and reports that 'in so many ways … the

---

21 Schwartz (1976a: 198) summarises a key element of the Dobu social context as follows: 'The structure of trust and distrust, so important to the paranoid ethos, may have had one basis in the experience of the divided family. The dichotomy of owner and stranger found throughout Melanesia was exacerbated in a matrilineal context, such as that described by Fortune in Dobu … distrust was intensified by a pattern of alternating residence and alternating roles of owner and stranger between the husband's and the wife's villages'.

22 Antrosio (2013), however, has suggested that in her criticism of Fortune, Kuehling may not have given sufficient weight to changes in Dobuan life in the intervening decades. One should not, however, opt for Fortune's interpretation before reading Kuehling as well.

[Tolai] world appears [that is, it appears to the Tolai] … threatening and full of menace', replete with 'enemies in human or spirit form who seek to destroy one' (p. 9). Further, 'the Tolai language does have a word for accident, but I don't recall ever hearing it used to explain some misfortune one had suffered' (p. 11). Among the underlying factors he lists are belief in a panoply of 'generally malevolent spirit beings' (pp. 7–8), chronic 'jealousy over land' (p. 8) and 'elements of the Tolai scheme of domestic relations' (p. 16).

Maria Lepowsky (2011) is uncomfortable with Schwartz's use of the term 'paranoid' and the sweep of his claims, but she finds that the people of Vanatinai Island (also known as Sudest Island) in Milne Bay Province also experience the world as though under the sway of a paranoid ethos. She writes: 'While I would not agree that a paranoid cognitive orientation distinguishes all the cultures of the Southwest Pacific, and although the term bears distinctly unfortunate connotations of individual and societal pathology, I do recognise elements of a similar worldview and affective tone in Vanatinai people's powerful fears of the destructive agency of other persons, particularly other-than-human persons' (2011: 52). And, like Epstein, she emphasises the force of a personifying, chance-rejecting understanding of the causes of misfortune: 'The islanders believe firmly in the personal causation of misfortune. Virtually all deaths, serious illnesses, or misfortunes are attributed to the sorcery or witchcraft of another, or to the retributive acts of ancestors' spirits or place spirits, the result of the victim or a kinsperson having violated a taboo … a sacred proscription' (Lepowsky 2011: 46).[23]

Rejecting chance is probably a more important dimension of a paranoid ethos for understanding the cargo cults within the Paliau Movement than is the feeling that 'malice is … almost omnipresent beyond the narrow

---

23 Lepowsky is not alone in her concern that mention of paranoia 'bears distinctly unfortunate connotations of individual and societal pathology'. Epstein (2000–2001) addresses this issue at the outset in considering the relevance of a 'paranoid ethos' to the Tolai case, concluding that the term as Schwartz and others (e.g. Richard Hofstadter 2008 [1965]) have used it in social analysis is analytically fruitful. Lindstrom (1993a: 70), in service of his own argument, over-interprets Schwartz's own remark (1973: 156) that applying the term paranoid to Melanesian culture may entail 'something more than analogy'. To pursue this issue further, readers should consult Schwartz (1973), Epstein (2000–2001), the literature to which they refer, and Barkun (2006 [2003]: 8), who explores the relationship between Hofstadter's concept of a 'paranoid style', conspiracy thinking, and millenarianism, a topic we will also discuss in Chapter 15. (Hofstadter first aired his thoughts on 'the paranoid style in American politics' in a lecture at Oxford University in 1963 and *Harper's Magazine* published a shorter version in 1964. His longer essay has subsequently been published in a number of editions, most recently in 2008 [1965]).

circles of relative trust' (Schwartz 1973: 157). Regarding the Melanesian paranoid ethos, Schwartz (1973: 164) observed: 'There is an attitude towards events and language that rejects coincidence, radically rejects homonymy, and cannot accept rhyme as semantically irrelevant, so that words that sound the same or just similar must have some common meaning'. The strength of a paranoid ethos, then, helps explain Manus people's susceptibility—in their postwar situation—to abandoning their quotidian empirical and pragmatic bent and believing almost anything from almost any source. Those most drawn to the cults, Schwartz observed, simultaneously viewed the world with suspicion—nothing was as it seemed—and were prone to accept reports of events—such as ancestral ghosts piloting American cargo vessels—that they should have found suspect. 'Suspicion and cognitive rejection', observed Schwartz, were 'joined with extreme credulity' (1973: 157).

It takes more than a paranoid ethos, of course, to move people to millenarian fervour. But once it has taken hold, a paranoid ethos knows few bounds. Millenarian fervour virtually everywhere, Landes (2011) repeatedly reminds his readers, is marked by 'semiotic arousal'—that is, rejecting mundane meaning in favour of perceiving signs and wonders.

It is important here to emphasise that when he argued that a paranoid ethos was characteristic of Melanesia, Schwartz was careful to state that some degree of paranoid perspective was probably universally human. It is certainly easy to find examples in the ethnographic literature. Hallowell (1955: 147) linked what he saw as an Ojibwa tendency to assume that 'covert malevolence is always potentially present in one's dealings with others' to rejecting chance—'impersonal forces are never the causes of events' (p. 181)—and 'social atomism' (p. 147).

A paranoid ethos is not confined to small-scale, non-industrial societies. Regarding the enhanced perception of personal reference that is part of a paranoid ethos, Schwartz has argued that a perception 'of being the centre of malign or benign attention is natural to small-scale societies', but that it 'persists, just as village-size spheres of personal interaction persist, in large-scale societies' (Schwartz 1973: 169; cf. Schwartz 1972). Further, it is part of the common human heritage: 'It persists over the span of human history as a substratum of potential pathology in all societies' (1973: 168). A potential *pathology* because, taken to extremes, a paranoid ethos can impair a group's capacity to adapt and survive.

Although an ethos can have great endurance, even as the circumstances that formed it change, Schwartz opined in 1973 that the Melanesian paranoid ethos was changing: 'Many Melanesians have been able to attain a recalibration of expectations more realistic than that of the cults and are now capable of a more relaxed synthesis and selection of cultural features derived from both native and European sources … alternative modes of personal and group psycho-cultural adjustment are being opened up. For the Melanesian, the paranoid ethos is no longer without alternative' (1973: 172). Yet it remains a significant element in the millenarian dreams simmering today in Wind Nation, as discussed in Chapter 14, even though Manus people today live in a considerably changed social environment.

Now, however, we return to former times in the Admiralty Islands, how Manus people were drawn ever more deeply into a new world from earliest European contacts through involvement in two world wars, and how change coming from outside helped unleash internal demands for change.

4

World wars and village revolutions

World War II made a deep impression on the people of the Admiralty Islands, but they began getting to know Europeans, albeit in much smaller doses, hundreds of years earlier. Incorporation into the European world, even at its far edges, made them unwilling actors in two world wars. Their involvement with the European world inspired some Admiralty Islanders to reflect on their indigenous cultures, find them wanting, and propose truly revolutionary changes. Many were especially eager to alter the affinal exchange system, a radical aim since it was at the very centre of indigenous life, as discussed in the previous chapter. There was probably plenty of discontent with the demands and implications of this institution well before contact with outsiders, but it took new experiences and examples—even if only dimly understood—to stir systematic opposition. Most advocates of change had little success, but what we know of their efforts shows not only the extent to which Paliau lived in an era of widespread cultural ferment—his was not an isolated voice—but also how much his vision and talent distinguished him from fellow champions of change.

European contacts and colonial society through World War I

European explorers had noted the group of islands later named the Admiralty Islands as early as the sixteenth century, but for many decades the European presence in the Admiralties was limited and sporadic. In 1884, the German New Guinea Company (Deutsche Neuguinea-Kompagnie) obtained

a charter from the German government to do business and provide
civil administration in the areas of New Guinea claimed by Germany.
These were known at the time as the German Solomon Islands, Kaiser
Wilhelmsland (mainland New Guinea stretching south to the border with
Britain's claim), and the Bismarck Archipelago (encompassing the Admiralty
Islands, New Britain, New Ireland, and numerous smaller islands). In their
trade with New Guineans, Europeans sought shells for manufacturing
buttons and jewellery, usually from the nacre or mother-of-pearl; *beche-
de-mer*, an edible marine invertebrate, sometimes called sea cucumber; and
coconuts for producing coconut oil from the dried meat or copra.[1]

James and Achsah Carrier (1989: 75) note that in the early twentieth
century, Admiralties people were notorious for attacking trading vessels
and stations, looting them, and killing both white traders and their Pacific
Islander workers. The most active raiders were the Titan speakers, who
may have been defending their own prerogatives as the region's premier
maritime traders. Titan raiders sometimes captured firearms, which
probably exacerbated intra-indigenous warfare. The Germans attempted to
quell raiding by shelling villages from military vessels, but with little lasting
effect until Germany established a stronger, more consistent presence and
Admiralties people established stronger economic ties with the Europeans.[2]

For many years, German efforts at governing the Admiralties were negligible.
It was not until 1911 that Germany set up an administrative post at Lorengau.
At the same time, however, German companies were establishing coconut
plantations throughout Germany's New Guinea domain and recruiting
New Guinean labourers.[3] Plantations generally preferred labourers from
distant regions, to make it more difficult for them to decamp and return
home. Under both the German and Australian administrations in the
Admiralties there were also penal sanctions for New Guineans breaking their
labour contracts, including fines, flogging, and imprisonment. Although
New Guinean migrant workers had contracts (usually committing them to
two years of work), recruiting sometimes was little better than slaving, and
New Guineans often signed or, more often, simply made their marks on

---

1   Not all the trade was in European hands, however. Carrier and Carrier (1989: 75) observe that
the Japanese merchant Isokide Komine was a major figure in trade in the Bismarck Archipelago as
early as 1902.
2   The Carriers (1989) base their account of these aspects of history in the Admiralties on the work
of Biskup (1970), King (1978), and Sack and Clark (1979) in addition to their own field research in
the Admiralties.
3   Again, we rely on the Carriers (1989: 76), who draw on Firth (1973), King (1978), and Sack
and Clark (1979).

contracts under duress.[4] Even so, to obtain both European goods—such as steel tools, cloth, and tobacco—and cash, many New Guinean men went to work for the Europeans. Both German and Australian administrations also imposed a head tax on adult male villagers to create a need for cash obtained through wage work. Carrier and Carrier (1989: 76) point out that many Admiralties people avoided plantation work if possible, preferring work as domestic servants, on the crews of European vessels, or in the colonial police, an armed force composed of New Guineans, some of whom served as lower-level officers under white leadership.[5]

Christian missionaries were as active as traders and labour recruiters. German Catholic missionaries of the Sacred Heart were the first to create an outpost in Manus, initially at Papitalai on Los Negros, in 1913, and then in Bundralis, a village on the north coast, in 1916 (Carrier and Carrier 1989: 77). The Titan of the south coast of Manus Island adopted Christianity about 1930, shortly after Mead's and Fortune's sojourn in Pere village. Although most Christian converts never truly discarded their indigenous beliefs and practices, their affiliation with Roman Catholicism was voluntary. They assumed the missions played a central role in white society and that the new cosmologies and rituals were inseparably linked to white wealth, power, and longevity (as will be clear when we address borrowing from Christianity in the Paliau Movement). Also, unlike material wealth and political authority, Christianity was something the Europeans were willing, even eager, to share.

The Lutheran Evangelical Mission (also known as the Liebenzell Mission of the USA) established its first outpost in New Guinea on Manus in 1914.[6] Seventh-day Adventist missionaries entered the Pacific Islands in the 1920s and established themselves on Manus not long after.[7] By the beginning of World War II, most of the indigenous people of the Admiralty Islands had joined the congregations of one mission or another.[8]

---

4   Rowley (1965: 104–6) discusses major features of labour recruitment in colonial New Guinea.
5   Both the German and Australian administrations recruited New Guineans to serve in armed police forces.
6   lmi.tripod.com/pngmis.html.
7   encyclopedia.adventist.org/.
8   Christian missionaries first arrived in what is now Papua New Guinea in 1847 and they keep coming. In addition to Seventh-day Adventists, the Liebenzell Mission, and Catholics of diverse orders, PNG has drawn the London Missionary Society, Wesleyan Methodists, Lutherans, Anglicans, the South Seas Evangelical Mission, the Church of the Nazarene, the Apostolic Church, the New Tribes Mission, the Foursquare Gospel Church, the Christian Revival Crusade, the Philadelphia Church, and many others. The preamble to PNG's constitution pledges the country to Christian principles, but there is no state religion. Although most Papua New Guineans identify themselves as Christians, small numbers are followers of Buddhism, Hinduism, Islam, and Judaism (Gibbs 2014).

When World War I broke out in 1914, Australian military forces encountered little opposition from German personnel in the Bismarck Archipelago (Hiery 1995: 25). The Australian New Guinea Administrative Unit (ANGAU) governed the former German New Guinea for the duration of the war and, following the war, until the newly formed League of Nations gave the responsibility to Australia. Australian civil administration of what now became the Mandated Territory of New Guinea replaced ANGAU in 1921 (Souter 1963: 124–6).

In the Admiralties, Australia established government headquarters at Lorengau. The new administration adopted the German model for indirect rule, under which the colonial administration appointed New Guineans to act as its representatives in each village. The German administration took the titles for these officials from an indigenous language of New Britain, where Germany had established one of its first outposts. The highest ranking appointed official was the *luluai*, understood to mean a kind of chief. Someone of high rank in the indigenous community was usually chosen for this post, as the colonial imprimatur alone was not enough to give him authority among his peers. He was assisted by the *tultul*, a person often chosen in part for his ability to speak Melanesian Pidgin and thus to interpret between the *luluai* and Europeans. A paramount *luluai* was appointed for the north coast and another for the south coast to serve as intermediaries between the administration and the many village *luluai* in their regions.[9] But this only slightly lengthened the chain between the administration and individual villages and had little effect on inter-village relations. The political ties among villages remained insubstantial.

Although the Australian civil administration that replaced ANGAU in 1921 brought some improvements in New Guinean – Australian relations (Hiery 1995: 86, 92), Australia's liberation of New Guinea from German rule was not liberation from unapologetic white supremacy and colonial rule for profit (Hiery 1995: 65–97). But the combination of stronger colonial government and New Guineans' greater direct involvement with Europeans in the economic sphere and via the Christian missions gradually reduced both violent clashes between the colonial government and local people and diminution, if not complete cessation, of fighting among local groups. The indigenous people of several Pacific Islands locales had their own reasons for seeking an end to chronic warfare (Rodman 1979: 19–22), some of which may also have been at work here.

---

9   As indicated in our note on spelling and pronunciation at the beginning of this volume, Tok Pisin spelling does not distinguish plural from singular nouns.

Whatever the other effects of what historians and anthropologists often call the 'pacification' of the Admiralties, it did afford local people greater freedom of movement than had been possible before.

The other significant new freedom the colonial regimes offered was the opportunity young men now had to leave their villages and work for Europeans. Despite the often harsh conditions of such work, travelling beyond the narrow limits set by the political fragmentation of the indigenous world and seeing a sample of the European world up close became a rite of passage for younger men.

In the villages, life continued to centre around fishing, gardening, and ceremonial exchange. Migrant workers might have used the goods and money they brought home to mount the exchanges needed to acquire a wife and achieve full adult status, freeing them from the need to become indebted to their elders. But their elders usually appropriated the wealth young men brought home for their own exchanges, rendering the returned workers as dependent on their elders for position in society as before. The only escape was to leave the village permanently. This had been next to impossible in the past, and it was still too radical a measure for most. So the European currency and manufactured goods the young men brought home flowed to the elders and through them into the local system of arranged marriage and affinal exchange. (Although the Christian missions had some success in suppressing polygamy, the basic marriage system remained intact.) Alongside the strings of dogs' teeth and shell beads hung on the counting lines, the displays of wealth at exchange ceremonies began to feature European tools, cloth, and heavy strings of Territory shillings.[10]

But while elders and the *lapan* could turn these new sources of wealth to their advantage, they could not control the flow of new ideas. Working on plantations, crewing European trading ships, working as domestic servants, or—in some highly significant instances for the Admiralties— serving in the colonial police brought together New Guineans from all over the Territory. They learned from each other of conditions and events in other parts of the Territory and began to shape a pan–New Guinean

---

10   Territory shillings were distinct from Australian shillings. The former had their own design as well as holes in their centres through which the coins could be strung together.

culture. They abstracted from the similarities they found among their various home cultures an idea of a larger New Guinean way of life and its essential contrasts with the ways of the whites.

This was the situation in the Admiralties just prior to World War II. Colonial government had been imposed and accepted, although it would have been easy not to notice. Mead (1977: 63) reported in 1928 that the white population of Lorengau numbered only about two dozen. This had increased to only about 50 when World War II broke out (Jackson 1976: 388, cited in Carrier and Carrier 1989: 76). But warfare and raiding among indigenous groups had virtually ceased. The introduction of European-style currency was an important development, for it began the long and complex process of creating a cash economy, although people's desires for European goods far exceeded their capacity to purchase them with cash. Affiliation with Christian missions was spreading rapidly, without necessarily weakening the hold of old belief systems. Opportunities to leave the village to work had made it more difficult for village leaders and elders to bring younger men fully under their control. Despite the gross social inequalities and occasional violence to which both Germans and Australians subjected New Guineans, colonial authorities expropriated very little land—most villages lost little or none—and most people regarded as improvements to their condition the opportunities to work for Europeans, the presence of European towns, missions, and plantations, and access to European goods and money.

World War II: White wealth descends on Manus

What was then the Empire of Japan entered World War II by bombing the American naval base at Hawai'i's Pearl Harbor on 7 December 1941. Japanese forces soon sought to sweep down to Australia via Australian New Guinea. Having already overcome Australian resistance at Rabaul and bombed several Australian towns on mainland New Guinea, Japanese forces encountered little opposition to occupying the Admiralty Islands in April 1942. They built landing strips on Los Negros Island, set up artillery on the coast, and established garrisons. Assuming they would make New Guinea an enduring part of a greatly expanded empire, they started a school to teach the Japanese language to Admiralty Islanders. In 1953, the Mead party met Manus people who had lived through the occupation who told them that the Japanese had announced that, henceforth, they would be their rulers. Yet the Mead party found little evidence of enduring Japanese influence. People told stories about the distinctive customs of the Japanese and of how they forced villagers to work for them without compensation under the threat of cruel discipline. A number of those who had attended the school also could perform some Japanese songs. However, little else seemed to have survived to remind anyone of the occupation. It is possible that fear of being thought a Japanese collaborator encouraged expunging the record, or that events following the expulsion of the Japanese may have simply overshadowed the preceding years.

While the occupation had few obvious direct effects on local life, it had several important indirect effects. The Australians in New Guinea, easily routed by the Japanese, and the European missionaries, who had been evacuated as the Japanese approached, suffered some loss of prestige. But numbers of Admiralty Islanders trained by Christian missionaries as Bible teachers, or what Catholics called native catechists, carried on in the village churches, perhaps thereby acquiring a greater sense of independence. Several of the leaders of the Paliau Movement had been either Catholic catechists or Lutheran Evangelical teachers during the years of the war. Many Admiralty Islanders working on New Ireland or New Britain at the outbreak of war were stranded there for the duration in Japanese custody. This lengthened and intensified their contact with New Guineans from other parts of the Territory and seems to have nurtured wider ethnic identities. In the stories they told of their internment, Admiralty Islanders spoke of each other simply as Manus, dropping the invidious distinctions between Titan, Usiai, and Matankor. Younger men also told of how they discussed plans for changing the old way of life and subverting the authority of their elders on their return home.

The Japanese occupation of the Admiralties lasted less than two years. The first wave of a decisive American attack began on 29 February 1944. By the end of March, organised Japanese resistance had ended, at the cost of over 4,000 Japanese and just over 300 American deaths.[11] Casualties among the Manus people were mercifully few considering the scale of the fighting. The official ANGAU report on the campaign lists one indigenous

---

11   Several sources give approximately these same figures. They include the *Pacific War Online Encyclopedia* (pwencycl.kgbudge.com/A/d/Admiralty_Islands.htm) and *The Daily Chronicles of World War II: MacArthur Kicks Off Admiralty Islands Campaign* (ww2days.com/macarthur-kicks-off-admiralty-islands-campaign.html).

islander killed in combat and one wounded (many islanders served in combat, several of them receiving commendations), three men killed by the Japanese 'not in action', 20 men and women 'accidentally killed', and 34 'accidentally wounded' (ANGAU 1944: Appendix V).[12]

As soon as the fighting ended, American construction battalions began installing a military infrastructure that dwarfed that of the Japanese. Lachlan Strahan (2005: 10–11) writes that by October 1944 the Allied installation on Manus was 'one of the world's largest naval bases, with hundreds of warships anchored in Seeadler Harbor' (a name bequeathed by the German administration to the deepwater harbour embraced by the main island and Los Negros). The Americans expanded the Japanese airstrip at Momote and, near the present-day village of Mokerang, built a new 6 kilometre long airstrip (20,000 feet), capable of handling heavy bombers. The entire base covered some 64 square kilometres (about 25 square miles) and included housing for 150,000 troops. Over 1 million American military personnel at least paused there over the course of the war. The very success of the Allied war effort launched from this base, however, made it a fleeting presence. By late 1947, it had, in Strahan's (2005: 36) words, 'become something of a ghost town, quietly falling into disrepair in the tropical sun and rain, the jungle steadily reclaiming its own'. Australian military government remained, but with a decidedly unimpressive physical presence.

The people of the Admiralties saw first the Germans, then the Australians, the Japanese, and—once more—the Australians take control of their islands and, they supposed, their destinies. In the 1950s, however, Admiralties people tended to credit America with returning Australia to power and to regard the Americans as a superior people. The mass of men and materials the American invasion brought to Manus at remarkable speed was unlike anything the islanders had ever experienced. If any aspect of their relations with the Americans had been unpleasant, they appeared to have forgotten it.

Lamont Lindstrom and Geoffrey White document that in the Pacific Islands as a whole, indigenous people—'save for those who suffered the most' in the fighting—viewed Allied troops favourably in comparison with prewar colonials (1989: 12ff.). In Manus, the Americans paid the

---

12   By the end of the war, more than 3,500 Melanesians had served in Allied combat battalions (Nelson 1980: 19, cited in Lindstrom and White 1989: 31).

local people who worked for them well by Territory standards. Islanders often told members of the Mead party that the Americans had also been friendly—they let them ride in American vehicles and patrol torpedo boats and the Americans enjoyed fishing from the locals' canoes. And they had been generous, giving abundantly of their food, clothing, and other supplies. Even years later, Admiralties life was full of American army surplus. Many people wore parts of American military uniforms. To many of the people of Manus, their relationship with the Americans seemed to have dimmed the lines that separated colonial *masta,* the colonial term of address for male whites in Tok Pisin, from native *boi,* the colonial Tok Pisin term for male indigenes, regardless of their age.

Although while colonials often used the term 'native' in a highly pejorative sense, indigenous New Guineans in this era used its Tok Pisin cognate—*netiv*—to speak of themselves without negative connotations. It appears frequently in Manus people's Tok Pisin speech of the time. We will sometimes use it interchangeably with such terms as New Guineans, indigenous people, indigenes, and local people. At least by the current millennium, some younger indigenous Manus people had taken to calling themselves Manusians, although this is still a minority usage.

Manus accounts of their experiences of the war also emphasised the presence of black Americans in the construction battalions. To travel by sea from Pere to Lorengau, one still passes under a bridge connecting the main island (the Great Admiralty) and Los Negros. While passing under the bridge by canoe in 1954, a crewman proudly pointed it out to Schwartz, saying: 'Do you know that this bridge and that road were built entirely by black American soldiers?' In their pride that people with whom they identified had mastered this most impressive part of American culture, many people ignored or failed to notice that black American soldiers were doing most of the military's manual labour. What they saw instead was a clear sign that they, too, could accomplish such feats. This accords with what Lindstrom and White report of the Pacific theatre of war as a whole—that 'it was not the physical segregation of the U.S. forces that made an impression on island memories but their "similarity of condition" [of black and white troops] in terms of styles of dress, food, and work. The obvious abilities and achievements of American blacks personified the prewar aspirations of many Islanders' (1989: 18; cf. Robinson 1981: 161).

We must recognise that Neville K. Robinson (1981: 173) reports contrary perceptions of the relationships between Pacific Islanders and black Americans, and Lindstrom and White report numerous accounts of 'islanders' wariness and fear of black soldiers' (1989: 18). Even so, the evidence is strong that on Manus, in the flood of materials pouring from the cargo ships and the works of the black soldiers, islanders saw a new way of life in which—as they put it in Tok Pisin—life was set *stret*—that is, straight or as it should be. People lived in brotherhood and solidarity and, working in harmony, accomplished great things.

What people saw of white life during the war was, of course, smooth cooperation enforced by a steeply hierarchical military regime, not everyday life in white societies. Indeed, much of white life in colonial New Guinea took place within institutions—government, the colonial police, missions, plantations—that put a premium on hierarchical order and obedience. Smith (1994) has pointed out how, elsewhere in New Guinea, indigenous people assumed that whites were spontaneously more cooperative than New Guineans. He argues, however, that they did so because they knew little or nothing of the rigid discipline that enforced order in the white institutions with which they were familiar. But these perceptions in turn reinforced a conviction with deep indigenous roots that material wealth—that is, shared material wealth—was itself evidence of underlying social harmony (cf. Brison 1991; Errington 1974).

Such an analysis may well apply to Admiralties perceptions of American society and American wealth after the war. There is no doubt, however, that Manus people wanted fuller participation in the obviously superior knowledge, wealth, and power the Americans displayed. This new way of life had seemed within reach for a short time. But it disappeared as suddenly as it had arrived, leaving many wondering how they could come fully 'inside' (in Tok Pisin, *insait*) this new world—that is, how they could become privy to the knowledge underpinning it.

A home-grown impetus to change: The dark side of non-commercial exchange

Paliau would eventually give people a way to act on that grand frustration. But he was not the only grassroots activist to emerge in Manus in that era. Repeatedly seeing their elders appropriate the rewards of their wage labour to feed into the system of affinal exchange pushed a number of young men to challenge that system. We will tell some of their stories below. It is important to keep in mind that these iconoclasts were acting on discontent inherent in the indigenous system, their imaginations stimulated by exposure to hitherto unknown options. Their ambitions were more modest than those of the Paliau Movement, and this, in addition to their lack of Paliau's talent for organising, helps account for their limited success.

Mead's broad description—in both *Growing Up in New Guinea* and *New Lives for Old*—of the affinal exchange system ('an economic treadmill') depicted the indigenous system when it was already under pressure to change. But it rings true, especially in tandem with Reo Fortune's 1928 case studies, presented in *Manus Religion*, of divining causes of illness and misfortune in Pere village. A large part of the bad behaviour for which the ghosts were prone to punish the living concerned failing to meet affinal exchange obligations; for example, failing to provide food or dogs' tooth valuables for an exchange organised by someone who had provided for one of your endeavours; failing to support your kin in mounting exchanges or repaying their exchange debts; fecklessly consuming pigs, fish, or sago you could contribute to an affinal exchange; stealing goods destined for an exchange; or upsetting elaborate arrangements for affinal exchange by dallying with someone else's spouse or prospective spouse and upsetting an existing or planned marriage. Not participating in the system was almost inconceivable. It meant forgoing your prospects for status, respect, and marriage and family. In colonial Manus, then, even being able to imagine opting out by depending on wage labour or exploiting new opportunities in the emerging money economy probably increased longstanding tensions over the ways people could deploy their labour and wealth.

Following Marcel Mauss (1967 [1925]), anthropologists often call the general form of distributing goods that is dominant in indigenous Manus society 'gift exchange'. They distinguish gift economies from economies in which goods circulate via the exchange of commodities (that is, things that can be bought and sold without entailing further relations between the buyer and seller). They emphasise, however, that the commodity economy versus gift economy distinction is relative, not absolute (cf. Smith 1994: 10). That aside, in a hypothetical pure commodity economy, material goods circulate only through impersonal sale and purchase. People seek material gain rather than enduring personal relationships between the parties involved. In a hypothetical pure gift economy, in the words of C.A. Gregory (1982: 19), 'what a gift transactor desires is the personal relationship that the exchange of gifts creates, and not the things themselves'.

Formal occasions for giving and receiving in gift economies include births, marriages, deaths, initiation rituals, dispute settlements, and the grand-scale, long-duration cycles of gift giving for which Papua New Guinea (PNG) is famous: the Kula of the Trobriand Islands, described in Bronislaw Malinowski's *Argonauts of the Western Pacific* (1922), and *moka* in the Mt Hagen area, described by Andrew Strathern in *The Rope of Moka* (1971), are two examples. But a great many things—primarily food—circulate in less formal, daily, non-commercial giving and receiving among kin. Also, where gift exchange predominates, people usually do not work for others in exchange for immediate payment of any kind; rather, they work to fulfil social obligations.

The connotations of the word gift, however, make it easy to romanticise such a way of distributing material things and allocating labour. Paul Sillitoe (1998: 84–5) wisely suggests using the term sociopolitical exchange, which emphasises that the circulation of goods is governed not by market incentives but by social and political concerns and according to shared understandings about who should give what to whom and when. Sociopolitical exchange is central to societies throughout Melanesia. Some anthropologists argue that giving and receiving food in a sociopolitical exchange system not only reinforces bonds of mutual obligation, it creates deeper bonds. For instance, Melanesians may feel that food produced on ancestral land or using magic bequeathed by the ancestors is permeated by the spirits of these ancestors. Thus, as Bruce Knauft (1999: 47) puts it, a gift of food is 'a gift of oneself in a fundamental way'. Similarly, many anthropologists argue that giving and receiving food inclines Melanesians to experience themselves as embodying relationships among many people rather than as self-contained individuals.[13]

But as redolent of warm mutuality as such characterisations may be (although not necessarily intentionally), life in systems of sociopolitical exchange can be at least as fraught with troubles as life in a society where isolated individuals bear alone the stresses of impersonal buying and selling in unpredictable markets. As Mauss emphasised, the gifts in gift

---

13 Marilyn Strathern (1988) makes what is probably the best-known argument along these lines, an argument that remains highly influential.

economies are not voluntary, they are obligatory. Further, the personal relationships gift exchange creates or perpetuates are not necessarily pleasant. Mead and Fortune used the language of commerce—words like debt and credit—to describe Manus affinal exchange. But they recognised that the affinal exchanges on which indigenous Manus life pivoted were sociopolitical.[14] The parties relinquished the goods they received via other exchanges, gaining no permanent material advantage.[15] They did so to create or maintain personal relationships. But these were not relationships of trust and equality. Rather, they were relationships of obligation and invidious comparison. Participants in affinal exchange could gain prestige, but they could also lose it. They could earn greater respect, but they could also become objects of scorn.

As we said in Chapter 3, Leavitt (2004: 183–4) points out how today's Papua New Guineans can find life in a world in which one is defined by one's exchange relations burdensome. Ethnographic data suggest that discontent within sociopolitical exchange systems in Melanesia and other world regions probably predates contact with commercial societies. Biersack (2017) observes that, not only in Melanesia, but in other parts of the world where people often attribute death and misfortune to witchcraft or sorcery (that is, where they personify the causes of such events), they are also prone to assume that such malevolence is retaliation for failure to meet obligations to give of one's wealth to kin. Witchcraft, wherever people fear it, Biersack (2017: 296) observes, is the 'dark side' of exchange (cf. Smith 1994: 173–6).[16]

---

14 They did not, however, use this term.
15 Mead and Fortune tell us less about the trade through which people accumulated some of the goods for affinal exchange. We know that people did not use modern money in transactions, but it is also likely that transactions were not the same as bartering, either. Carrier and Carrier (1989: 155) describe what they could surmise about precolonial trade on the north coast of Manus Island from their research conducted in the 1970s: 'Trade partners should not have had a purely businesslike relationship, but instead were expected to give gifts openly and generously without haggling. It was expected that they would give small gifts to each other when they met, that they would make special visits to each other's villages occasionally to make large gifts or to participate in formal exchanges, and that they would be able to call on one another for help in collecting foodstuffs or other goods for formal exchanges or special projects such as house- or canoe-building'. Ian Hogbin (1935: 401) described participants' expectations in a trading system on the north coast of mainland New Guinea, as he observed it in the 1930s, in a similar way. He noted as well that 'if a man hands over a parcel of nuts and requests that he be given tobacco he definitely expects a bundle of a certain size … if he considers the return gift inadequate he has no direct redress, but in the future he will avoid this particular [trading partner]'.
16 The other chapters of *Pentecostalism and Witchcraft* (Rio et al. 2017) in which Biersack (2017) appears are worth consulting on this issue. Of the several additional works Biersack cites, Bercovitch (1994) is of particular interest.

The situation Schwartz observed in 1950s Manus was an instance of tension in a sociopolitical exchange system aggravated by contact with a commercial or commodity system. C.D. Rowley (1965: 110–11) argued that this state of affairs was causing friction between generations in many parts of the Territory. And Smith (2002: 48) observes that 'ever-increasing tension between the possibilities [people] see in the money economy and the pull of familiar forms of social and economic relations based on kinship and noncommercial exchange' persists in PNG today. It is a tension that is 'at the heart of cultural contestation' (Knauft 1996: 214) in contemporary Melanesia in general (cf. Smith 1994: 174–6; 2002: 48, 149).

Emerging local resistance to the traditional order: Some cases

Even the earliest exposure to the radically different European way of life may well have exacerbated Manus discontent with affinal exchange. After the war, many of the younger men—particularly those disposed to become leaders—found it hard to endure the fact that the old course of native life, separate and inferior to that of the whites, should return. For the people who were to comprise the Paliau Movement, life could never be the same again. They were not sure what would happen, but it was almost unimaginable that things would not change and change radically. Many of those who had been caught by the war in such distant Territory towns as Rabaul, Finschhafen, Talasea, or Lae, returned to their villages wondering what they might do to make their homes more fitting places for their altered selves.

Schwartz met the leaders of seven attempts other than Paliau's to formulate a new way of life, more satisfactory in itself and better integrated with the outside world than the ways of indigenous ancestors or the amalgam of old and new that was life before the war. Some of these attempts began before the Japanese invasion and had to be abandoned when the war broke out, but most reappeared with the peace. The innovators of whom we speak below confined their ambitions to their own villages or small groups of related villages. Although some spoke of a blanket repudiation of the past, most focused on specific practices or institutions, in particular the system of wealth production and exchange—that is, the affinal exchange system—dominated by the older men. This was not only burdensome in all the familiar ways; it stymied ambitions to take advantage of the new opportunities available in the postwar world.

Perhaps the most significant similarity among these attempts at innovation was their failure to recruit and sustain a broad base of adherents. It is important, however, to see the Paliau Movement in the context of the intensifying interest in social innovation of which these efforts are evidence. We will also meet the leaders of these efforts again in later chapters, for they all became important figures in the Paliau Movement.

Napo of Mbukei

Napo's attempt at transforming life in his own village is one of the earliest known in the southern Admiralties. Napo was from the village of Mbukei, the westernmost of the Titan-speaking villages. German planters had taken over the Mbukei chain of islands to create a coconut plantation. Mbukei people, however, continued to build their houses over the water and take their living from the sea, the reef, and the lagoon. Like most of the leaders of the Paliau Movement, Napo left the village in his early teens to work for whites, spending five years employed by a trading company, then joining the colonial police force. In about 1937, after three years serving with the police in mainland New Guinea, he returned to his village on leave. He was then, he estimated, about 23 years old. He did not want to return to the old routine, to years of indebtedness to the older men who would provide him with the wealth with which to obtain a wife and, that debt paid, to an endless round of work to amass wealth to achieve his own status.

Like other young men, Napo wanted eventually to return to his village, to marry, and to make a life there. But if he, a changed man, wanted a life into which he fitted, he would have to remake the world of his village. He wanted to terminate the unbroken lines of obligation and striving for status that came down from the past, but which offered his generation no satisfaction. He offered his age mates an iconoclastic attack on the keystone of the old system, calling for eliminating the great exchanges of wealth connected with marriage. Like the other people of Mbukei, he was a Christian and claimed that he had little fear of the ghosts who sanctioned failures to meet the heavy exchange obligations around which so much of the old culture orbited. But he still faced the opposition of older generations. They had already acceded to Catholic Mission demands to abandon such customs as polygamy, and they wished to retain as much as possible of what remained. According to Napo, although he saw his proposed reforms as modelled on white life, the local Catholic missionary, who was white, opposed him for what, in Napo's telling (below) sound like purely racist reasons.

When Napo's first efforts to recruit supporters for his plans proved unsuccessful, he left the village to serve another term in the police force in the Middle Sepik area of mainland New Guinea. Here, he said, he found scope for his abilities. He served his apprenticeship working with the Australian patrol officers who maintained superficial supervision of the area, and he learned the workings of colonial law from participating in government courts. Eventually, he was placed in charge of an outlying station for a year, responsible for keeping the peace and promoting and maintaining administration policies. It was clear in his telling that he was proud of his accomplishment, but he also continued to think of what he could do when he returned home, which had always been his plan. When Napo came back to Mbukei in 1940, he attempted again to lead his village into a new life. Again he addressed himself to the young men, this time denigrating the entire indigenous culture. He concentrated, however, on the economic activities that centred on marriage exchanges and he advocated abandoning native valuables—such as dogs' teeth and shell beads—in favour of Australian currency. As he recalled it in conversation with Schwartz, this was the essence of his message:

> Our traditional way of life is no good. All of the ways we act trouble our minds so that we don't think straight about God. Everything we do ruins us. We are always in anger. It would be better if we changed the way of our ancestors and made a new one of our own. Why is it that all of the white men have stores, but you and I are unable to take a dog's tooth or anything that we have to give to the store and get something?

Again the older men opposed him. The *luluai* complained to the missionary and to the paramount *luluai* of the south coast of Manus (Kisekup of Bunai village). It is impossible now to know the actual attitude of the Catholic Mission, but Napo described it thus:

> The Father heard about it and he was angry at me. He forbade me to go to church. He wasn't angry at me because I had any idea of changing the talk of the mission. 'No', he said, 'You are no *masta*, you are no white man. You are incapable of acquiring all that belongs to us white skins. You must confine yourselves only to the ways of the black man'. All the men in the village said that the Father told them this. But I said, 'Never mind. He is a white man and I am a native. I will do as I wish with my own village'.

Despite such opposition, Napo gained a following among the younger men. The mission, once satisfied that he was not attempting to interfere with its work, permitted him to receive communion again. The outbreak of the war, however, rendered all other concerns secondary. Nonetheless, Napo said that by the end of the war he had convinced the older men to promise that they would set a date for the termination of the affinal exchange system. But this was a highly qualified promise, because they held that villagers first had to meet as many of the obligations of the old system as possible; they still had to make the last big feast.

This was a limited victory, but by then there was excited talk of change all over the Admiralties. Napo was hearing of other men trying to introduce similar programs elsewhere. Although he was not sure exactly what it was, he told his followers that something of great importance was about to happen, and he saw that they were eager for it. Napo no longer saw his work as a purely local movement, depending solely on local ideas and initiative. But he was still looking for a plan of action that would move his village quickly and radically out of the past. For help and inspiration he sought out other innovators of whom he had heard. First he contacted Bonyalo of Pere. Later, he would hear news of Paliau.

Bonyalo of Pere[17]

In 1928, Mead and Fortune stopped in Rabaul, New Britain, on the way to Manus, to prepare for the next stage of their journey and to decide in which village they would conduct their research. Such decisions often turn on small things. In this case, they selected Pere partly because they found a student from Pere in the government school at Rabaul who knew enough English to act as an interpreter until they could get some grasp of the Titan language. Opportunities for formal schooling were rare in those days, but not particularly coveted among the Titan, many of whom preferred their young men to stay at home and work for their elders. Mead (2001 [1930]: 82) speculated that when government representatives visited Manus seeking young men to study in Rabaul, Bonyalo had been allowed to go because he was fatherless and thus more expendable than the son of an ambitious man. Whatever the case, immediately after the war it was Bonyalo who led Pere in its first movement towards a new culture.

---

17   Mead mentions Bonyalo in *Growing Up in New Guinea* (2001 [1930]) and *New Lives for Old* (2001 [1956]), in both of which she spells his name Banyolo.

In 1929, after working for Mead and Fortune, Bonyalo returned to school in Rabaul. He stayed away from Manus for most of the next 25 years. Among other jobs, just before World War II he worked as a clerk in a government store in New Britain, where one of his duties was issuing rations to the colonial police. While doing so he met Paliau, who was then a sergeant major in the force, the highest rank an indigenous man could reach. Bonyalo told Schwartz, however, that he and Paliau did not discuss plans for remaking the Manus world. Unlike most of the other early local advocates of change, Bonyalo claimed that for most of his years away from home he did not think about ways to change his village.

During the war Bonyalo worked—under duress—for the Japanese, along with hundreds of other Admiralty Islanders held in New Britain. After the war, he worked for ANGAU briefly and then returned to Pere in 1945. The intense fighting of the American invasion took place mostly towards the eastern end of the main island and did not extend to Pere's vicinity. Villagers had earned cash working on the American military bases, and they were using it in affinal exchanges, hanging American dollars alongside Australian shillings and the traditional dogs' teeth and shell beads in the displays of wealth. The village must also have been full of the material goods acquired from the Americans as gifts, payments for food or work, or from among their discards. These included tools, galvanised iron, electrical cable, metal airfield surfacing panels, lumber, army cots, lockers, blankets, mattresses, chairs, kitchen utensils, and clothing.[18] Villagers were wealthier than ever, but their aspirations had grown even more. In comparison with what they had seen of the American way of life, they were poverty stricken. For Bonyalo, who had spent more than half of his life in colonial towns, the village seemed too much like the village he had left so many years before.

Now in his mid-thirties, Bonyalo immediately began trying to move Pere towards a clean break with its past. But he began with an act reminiscent of the past. He killed a large sea turtle and called the young men of the village to a feast. At first he ignored the older men, whom he expected would resist. He hoped that he could gradually persuade them to discard the old culture, but Bonyalo was cautious. He avoided speaking of

---

18   Much of this probably wasn't visible at first glance. In 1953, Schwartz and Shargo noticed how much such goods had infiltrated village life only through mingling with Pere people at their work and in their homes. But photographs of Pere village exteriors taken by members of the American armed forces around the time of Bonyalo's return to Pere show almost no evidence of change in the material style of life in comparison with 1928, as seen in Fortune's photos.

matters pertaining to either the still-important household ghosts or to Catholicism. And to avoid trouble with the government, he kept a book in which he recorded the content of his meetings. The older men opposed him, as anticipated, but Bonyalo and his adherents persevered, going by canoe at night to a nearby uninhabited island where they met in secret.

When Napo visited, hoping to learn of a program more effective than his own, he was disappointed. Bonyalo's program was essentially the same as the one Napo had offered in Mbukei. Bonyalo called for standardising the obligation of the groom's side in affinal exchange at £10 Australian currency. This was to be a single cash payment, without reciprocal gifts of foodstuffs on the part of the bride's family. Bonyalo also advocated doing away with other feasts and exchanges related to marriage. There were to be no more *metcha* payments, for instance—what Mead (2001 [1930]: 61–4) called 'the silver wedding payment which a rich and successful man makes for a wife to whom he has been married fifteen or twenty years'. The payment a husband made to his wife's family in return for the care she received in her confinement, the *pwaro*, was also to be restricted. A wife's kin cared for her until 10 days after she had given birth, at which time the husband made the *pwaro* payment. Bonyalo declared that a woman should give birth in her husband's house under the care of two or three of her own female relatives. The husband's obligation would be met by a small cash payment to each of these women, who were to return to their homes 10 days after childbirth.

These would have been revolutionary changes, radically limiting the ability of the old to dominate the young. A young man, regardless of the status or wealth of his father, could earn through wage labour the cash he needed for the initial payment to the bride's family and for the *pwaro*. He would no longer be obligated to many years of service to the man who financed his marriage with large loans of dogs' teeth and shell money. The changes in postnatal care Bonyalo advocated would also have increased the privacy and autonomy of each household.

His elders may have considered the above elements of Bonyalo's program the most incendiary. His call for ending child betrothal must also have raised hackles, as would have his proposals that young men and women were to marry according to their own preferences and that premarital sexual relations should be permitted. He also proposed periodic village meetings to make decisions on community affairs and greater concentration on working for money. Since the village offered virtually no opportunities for earning money, the latter meant that more men would be going away to work.

Bonyalo told Schwartz that an ANGAU patrol officer who visited Pere encouraged him. The patrol officer read Bonyalo's record book with approval, but warned him to confine his activities to his own village. Other villages could copy his example if they wished, but Bonyalo was not to propagate his ideas beyond the village. According to Bonyalo, the ANGAU officer told him that if he and his followers continued their efforts to organise along the new lines and continued their meetings, the government would let them participate in a Native Government Council, an elected body that would give them a limited form of local participation in territorial government.

Bonyalo made a bold beginning, but his efforts in Pere soon collapsed. The prestigious older men continued to pull the younger men into the affairs of the old culture. John Kilepak, an articulate man of high status who might have been able to draw others of his station into a new system, made a large payment to obtain a wife for his young kinsman Karol Matawai in the neighbouring village of Patusi.[19] Pokanau, a former *luluai* of Pere, supported continuing the old marriage system, encouraged by Kisekup of Bunai, who—as paramount *luluai* for the south coast of Manus—had helped suppress Napo's activities in Mbukei before the war.

In the neighbouring village of Bunai, Samol was promoting changes similar to those Bonyalo was promoting in Pere. He joined Bonyalo in complaining to the Australian administration about the adamant support of the *luluai* for large exchanges of wealth between the families of bride and groom. Many colonial officers opposed the system of affinal exchange because they understood it incorrectly as bride purchase. So, Samol and Bonyalo were able to convince administration officers to tell Kisekup and Pokanau to withdraw their opposition if they wanted to keep their appointed positions.

---

19   Kilepak, like Bonyalo, had also worked for Mead and Fortune as an adolescent in 1928. He later became one of Schwartz's most valued collaborators. During Schwartz's travels throughout the Admiralty Islands in the 1960s, Kilepak often captained Schwartz's canoe crew. His work with Mead and Schwartz led to several visits to the United States in the 1970s.

This, however, didn't affect Kilepak's plans to provide the valuables Karol Matawai needed to marry. Since the intended bride was from Patusi village, which had no part in the struggling Pere reforms, Kilepak had little choice but to meet these demands. Bonyalo then insisted that Kilepak make the payment of durable valuables but refuse the return gift of foodstuffs from the bride's relatives. Such a move would have been almost as effective a blow against the old system as refusing to provide the groom-side payments. The system depended on reciprocal exchange between the families linked by marriage. The receiving parties rarely kept the payments. Rather, they passed on what they received to meet exchange obligations to others. It was impossible to step out of this continuing flow of wealth without sacrificing one's status among all those involved in the never-ending cycle.

Bonyalo's insistence that Kilepak could pay but not receive anything in return was also a part of his proposed approach to sexual morality, which held that licit sexual relations required some kind of payment to the woman. He argued that if Kilepak gave durable wealth and accepted a return gift, they cancelled each other out and it was tantamount to getting the bride for nothing (a position that administration officials might have seen as confirming their view of the system, had they known of it). That would entitle the bride's relatives to demand further payment in the future, and the old cycle of payment and repayment from which the young men sought to escape would continue.

When one of Bonyalo's own adherents made a *pwaro* feast to help his aged mother meet this traditional obligation, Bonyalo felt he had failed. There was no possibility of a real break with the past as long as the younger men lived with their elders, to whom they were obligated, and who jeered and taunted them when they failed to meet those obligations. At about this time, he heard that Samol's movement in Bunai (described below) was encountering similar obstacles. This had prompted Samol to recruit a group of young men from Bunai to move to land to which he had rights at a place called Lompwa, not far along the coast from Bunai. Samol and his followers built a new settlement there for those who wanted to follow his program.

Bonyalo had no land at his disposal. Among his young followers, however, was Makis, the son of a Solomon Island native who had come to the Admiralties as an indentured plantation labourer and who had settled there permanently. Makis told the Australian manager of a plantation on Ndropwa, one of two small islands about three miles offshore from Pere, about Bonyalo's dilemma. The manager invited Bonyalo to bring his men to Ndropwa where they could live and work as wage labourers, gathering coconuts and curing the meat to make copra. Bonyalo agreed, feeling fortunate to have the support of friendly Europeans.

By this time, Paliau had returned to Baluan from Rabaul, where he had remained for some time after the war (see Chapter 5), and hearing of Bonyalo's plan he came to see him in Pere. As Bonyalo recalls the visit:

> He [Paliau] spoke to me now. 'I have heard that you want to go to Ndropwa so I came'. I [Bonyalo] said, 'Yes, I am tired of the village'. Then he said: 'You can't tire. It is your village. You have to be strong about it. There is no one else who will make your village for you. Only you can do it'. He said: 'I didn't come to persuade you. I came to hear what you have to say. When I was still in Rabaul I heard of you. Everyone said that you were strong for this idea here'. Then he said: 'That is good. I have come to help you. You and I will work together. It is a good idea to hold meetings in the village and to let the government know about them. If you do something in secret there will be trouble. If you like, I can help by giving you some ideas. Now forget about Ndropwa. Let it go. Now you and I can talk here first, then in two or three days I will go back to Lipan [Lipan village, on Baluan]. We are making a meeting house on Baluan. We will open it on Friday. This is not a matter of persuading people. A man can come if he wants to'. Then I [Bonyalo] told him I was just going to work here and there for a while. I said: 'You do it in your own village. They will all see. Let them observe; then, if they want to do the same in my village. I will help them later'.

Bonyalo thought that removing enough young men from the village would help persuade the elders to accept his proposals for fundamental changes. Despite Paliau's advice, soon after his visit Bonyalo went to Ndropwa with young men from Pere and Patusi. According to Bonyalo, his followers included the most important and most intelligent of the young men of these two villages. Without them, he reasoned, the older men of Pere could not continue the ceremonial and economic activities of the past. Bonyalo's plan might have succeeded. Samol even told the plantation manager that he might bring his followers from Lompwa to join Bonyalo on Ndropwa. But before Bonyalo's men had collected their first month's wages, the Noise reached the south coast (as described in Chapter 6), disrupting this and all other local revolts against established village authority.

Samol of Bunai

Samol was of the same generation as Napo and Bonyalo. He also had left his village in adolescence to work for the whites. Unlike Napo and Bonyalo, he did not leave Manus but worked for about 10 years as a clerk in a store in Lorengau. From Lorengau he returned frequently to Bunai, which was only one day's travel by canoe. Samol learned to read and write Tok Pisin from other indigenous workers in Lorengau and he learned enough arithmetic to handle Australian currency. He never attended a government or mission school, yet in his late twenties he became a Catholic catechist. As a catechist he faithfully kept a record, in a neat Tok Pisin hand, of the church services he held. Like Napo, he impressed Schwartz as someone of quiet authority and quick intelligence. He belonged to a high-ranking family and Kisekup, the paramount *luluai* of the south coast, had announced that Samol was to be his successor (although the administration would have had to appoint him as such).

Samol spent the war years on Baluan Island, working as a catechist. Although the missionaries had been evacuated, Samol continued to hold services until the end of the war. After the war, he worked for a short time as a construction labourer at the American base. Like other local people, Samol was tremendously impressed by the American armed forces. One day, for example, as Schwartz and Samol walked along the road to Lorengau from where they had beached their canoe outside town on arriving from Bunai, Samol described in great detail how the Americans had built the first hard-top motor vehicle road in Manus with dynamite and huge earth moving machines. But 15 miles from all this activity, his village was still built on posts over the lagoon, much as it had been when he was born.

Samol's program for change in Bunai was almost identical to those Napo and Bonyalo campaigned for in their villages. A significant difference was that he advocated eliminating all avoidance behaviour between designated classes of kin, customs that profoundly affected relationships between men and women. Mead (2002 [1934]: 52–86) wrote that Manus interpersonal behaviour among kin as she observed it in 1928 fell into three categories: joking relationships, relationships like that between brother and sister marked by affectionate solicitude, and avoidance relationships. From the time of their early betrothal, engaged boys and girls avoided not only one another but also future in-laws of the opposite sex. They were taught to feel shame in the presence of these people. Women even carried a bark cloth cape with which to hide their faces in case one of their male relatives by marriage suddenly appeared. In addition to eliminating these avoidance relationships and the accompanying shame, Samol added to Napo's and Bonyalo's programs a call for husbands and wives to eat together, talk together, and walk together, just as he had seen white husbands and wives do.[20]

Samol wanted to remain in Bunai, but when his program for change brought him into conflict with his adopted father and brought his followers into similar conflicts, he moved them to Lompwa. He hoped that decamping with his adherents might bring Kisekup to agree to try his ideas for a new kind of society. Beyond that, his plans were vague. He hoped that he and his followers could find some means of making money and he began building houses at Lompwa. When the Noise came to Bunai, Samol and his group in Lompwa did not feel its early impact, but its effect in Bunai ruined his chances for pursuing his own plans for change there.

Lukas of Mok

Lukas must have been about 30 years old when he returned to the Admiralty Islands after the war. He had worked for a few years before the war as a mechanic at Vunapope, the Catholic Mission headquarters near Rabaul. Later he joined the crew of a small boat owned by an Australian and based at Rabaul. When the Japanese invaded, Lukas was with a group of other men from the Admiralties at Talasea in New Britain and he volunteered to help the remaining Australian troops in New Britain escape safely. His experiences won him a Loyal Service Medal and, Schwartz recalls, the respect of the Australians who knew him.

While Lukas was with the other Admiralties men at Talasea, the Lakalai and Kombe people of that area were in the throes of a cargo cult. Lukas said he thought these natives were 'crazy'. According to Lukas, the Lakalai, led by Batari of Kamalakese, took the Catholic missionary prisoner, smoked him briefly as if they were producing copra (to produce copra, coconut meat is smoked over a slow-burning fire; this is a detail that may be apocryphal), and later turned him over to the Japanese. According to

---

20   Although advocates of doing away with these restrictions had been exposed to Catholicism, it appears that they acted without mission prompting. Similarly, when native Hawaiian rulers abolished the *kapu* (taboo) system in 1819 there had been substantial European influence in Hawai'i for decades, but the European example was only one factor among many (Tanabe 2005).

Lukas, the Kombe, whose cult leader had proclaimed himself king, also expelled a Catholic priest from his island mission station. This missionary and another, fearing the anti-mission feelings of the cult followers, engaged Lukas and another Admiralties man to guard them. The arrival of the Japanese saved the missionaries from the cargo cult, but doubtless not as they would have wished.

The Japanese sent Lukas to Rabaul, where he worked as a labourer. Lukas told Schwartz that he thought a good deal about the indigenous way of life during his months in Rabaul, alternating working for the Japanese and hiding from the American bombing. He summed up his thinking as follows:

> The thoughts that I found went like this. God made all of the men on earth. But as far as the condition of the natives, I don't think that this was so. Why is it? All white men, they are men. They have two hands and two legs. We also have the same. What is it with us natives? They can fly in aeroplanes and sail on the sea in ships while we stay just as we are. Now these thoughts were always within me.

Lukas and nine others were able to surreptitiously build a canoe and escape from Rabaul, sailing down the coast to Nakanai and Karua where they found American and Australian troops. Lukas worked with them for a while, before they sent him first to Finschhafen, on the mainland, and, in 1944, from there back to Manus. When he returned to his village, Mok, a Titan-speaking village built over the water adjacent to the small island of Mok, just offshore from Baluan, he tried to put into effect the ideas that he had been formulating during his long absence. Like Bonyalo, Lukas met Paliau in Rabaul, where he too was trapped by the war and under Japanese authority. The Japanese had placed Paliau in charge of the local labourers they had commandeered, but Lukas did not recount to Schwartz any conversations the two of them might have had about revolutionising life when they returned home.

Back in Mok, Lukas called the village men to meetings, omitting the older men whom he believed would summarily reject calls to abandon the ways of the past. He told the younger men that the old ways were like a killing poison. As an alternative to leaving the village, he laid down a series of rules to follow in their relations with their elders. Following these rules, he argued, would bring about change. This is how he described to Schwartz what he told the young men of Mok:

If your father wants you to go look for food, you ask him what the food is for. If he says it is for a ceremonial exchange, you can't go with him. If he says it is for eating, all right, you can go help him find food. The meaning of my talk is as follows. You know, you of this village, we have no land. We work too hard to find food. We range from the Great Admiralty to Rambutjo. Our bodies are weary from all this work. When we carry food to the village, it isn't used properly as food, it goes for making ceremonial exchange. Our food supply is exhausted too quickly, then hard work finds us again. All this work is what makes you and me die. Now we have to rid ourselves of all this. Where is the mark of all this work? It leaves no mark, not the slightest. It is like this. If you can't comprehend it with your minds, you can see it with your two eyes. Look at Ndropwa. It is like all the plantations. The white man did not make them. The white man's work is only telling us to do the cutting. He says, 'You and I will cut the bush. You and I will clear it and plant coconuts'. Now our work is cutting the bush and planting the coconuts. He just sits down. He doesn't do it. Now why is it that you and I can't make something for ourselves? With everything it is the same. Things don't just appear for the white man. If we did not exist, if we didn't produce coconuts or work copra, where would his cargo come from? Or his store, what could he put in it? I think he could do nothing. It is our hard work that does it. Now today, why can't we do this on our own ground in the same way?

His speech, as he recalled it for Schwartz, went on in this vein, urging the young men of his village to work for their own benefit, to do the same work for themselves that they did for the white men, and to end the fruitless waste of their labour in the endless round of ceremonial exchange. The young men whom he harangued told their fathers of Lukas's program. Their fathers answered that Lukas was nobody. Who was he to talk of abolishing the past? He was not of a high-ranking family. When Lukas again called a meeting, few of the young men came.

Lukas stayed in the village, but shunned all the traditional exchange ceremonies. He had failed, but he was determined to find a way to move people towards a new way of life. In desperation, Lukas called those young men who were still interested to a secret meeting on a small islet near the village. He proposed running away to America on an American warship. They would go up to one in their canoe, ask to come aboard, and then plead to be taken to America. He set out with nine other young Moks. But older men took to their own canoes and pursued them, catching them and bringing them back before they reached the American naval base.

Later, Lukas heard of Bonyalo's activities in Pere. He went to Pere to see if Bonyalo had what he was looking for, a substitute for the past and for the past-in-the-present. Lukas's criticism of Bonyalo's plan casts light on why his and other local movements failed. He recalled the conversation as follows:

> I went to Bonyalo and asked, 'What are these meetings of yours? I want to hear'. When he [Bonyalo] spoke, it was not like something firmly rooted in the ground, it was like something that just floated. That was the essence of it. I didn't believe in his talk. First he said that he wanted to send all the young men to work copra on Mbukei Island. Then I asked, 'When you are through working copra, then what will you do?' 'Then I will send it to the plantation manager on Ndropwa'. 'Then what will you do?' Then he said, 'If we get a lot of money I want to make a store'. Then I answered: 'True, your idea is all right, but it is like a tree that has neither branches nor roots. You work only on the middle. You think about it'.

In this manner Lukas told Bonyalo that there was nothing really new in the plan he offered and that he had not defined its ultimate goals. Working for Europeans, he told him, left people with few tangible benefits after they'd spent their cash. He went on to tell Bonyalo that the idea of the store was naive and that the European stores had a government and, ultimately, Europe behind them.

Lukas returned to Mok to try again. He spoke against the old marriage system, arguing that marriages by the old system of infant betrothal followed by a series of exchanges between the contracting families were bad and created lifelong resentment between the coerced husband and wife. In Bunai, Samol also had argued that the system could be altered to produce better marriages, though he had focused on the avoidance behaviour that erected a barrier of shame between husband and wife. Mead's (2001 [1930]: 114, 146–8) observations on Manus marriage in 1928 support Lukas's and Samol's views of the strains in such traditional marriages. But, however Lukas formulated his attack on the past, he could add nothing significant to the fragmentary plans for the future that he, too, rejected as inadequate.

Lungat of Ndriol

Ndriol is the easternmost of the Titan-speaking villages. Just after the war it was still built over the water inside the reef adjacent to Rambutjo, one of the larger islands that fringe the Great Admiralty. Under favourable conditions a canoe from Ndriol under sail could reach Bunai, on the south coast of the Great Admiralty, in one day, Baluan in one day, or Mbukei in two. The nearest neighbours were the Matankor villages of Rambutjo.

Lungat demonstrated later that he could be an able leader on the village level (as did Napo, Bonyalo, Samol, and Lukas). But he was unique among the leaders of this period because he claimed that he received his calling and the content of his message in a dream. Lungat was younger than the others, in his early twenties, when he returned to Ndriol after the war. Shortly after the war his two brothers died. Both had been catechists and teachers in the village. Lungat says that he mourned them for a long time and thought of them constantly. The following is his report of his dream. (The Tok Pisin term translated here as 'religion' is *lotu*. It is a word of Polynesian origin, referring in its original context to metaphysical matters. It entered Tok Pisin via Christian missionaries who brought it to New Guinea from Polynesia and adapted it to the task of proselytising for their respective churches.)

> I was asleep and I dreamed. I dreamed about Tomas Sion [my brother]. He was in Heaven. He was holding a flag. He held a flag and he came down in a cloud from the east. He didn't come from Heaven directly, he came from the east. He came straight to me and he spoke to me as follows. 'Lungat, I am talking to you. You see, we, your two brothers, we are dead. Many men of Ndriol have died. They didn't just die [without cause], they died because of religion. This religion of the mission which was brought to Ndriol and shown to us and to all Manus villages as far as Mbukei … This religion, we haven't gotten it right. We aren't doing it right and it is killing many men in all villages. Ndriol is almost finished now. Now I am talking to you. Tomorrow, you tell our fathers … they are to get all the men of Ndriol together and tell them to get rid of all the customs of the past, throw them out—all the ways of the past, all the quarrels, all the feasts, all the ceremonial exchanges. You must lose completely the way of our ancestors. When you are clear of it, then you will be all right'. [In the Tok Pisin discourses of the Movement, to be 'all right' (*orait*) meant to be raised to the wealth, status, and condition of the European world. Thus, people said, 'Jesus made the white man all right',

or 'The Americans taught the American blacks and made them all right'.] When he came he held a ring and the feather of a bird like the kind they write with, a pen. He took the ring and he said, 'Lungat, this ring belongs to you. Put it on your hand'. Then he took the pen and put it in my hand. Then he made the sign of a cross on my shoulder. Then he said, 'This is the mark of us. It is the mark of all of us who are in Heaven. I have brought these three things that I give to you. This mark belongs to you'. He gave me this feather, this ring, and this cross. Then I awoke.

The other local movements, as reported to Schwartz, did not rest on supernatural revelations. Napo and Bonyalo tried to avoid coming into conflict with the mission and they attacked the old culture with specific criticisms. Samol continued to teach the standard catechism. Lukas said that the old system was killing them because of the ceaseless work that it involved. But Lungat claimed he had received the sanction of Heaven (that is, the Christian Heaven) through the ghost of his brother, a Catholic catechist. To Lungat, the ring, the feather, and the cross were indisputable signs of the validity of his revelation. At the same time, the idea that men were dying because they were not following 'religious' rules was reminiscent of the role of the guardian ghosts of house and village in punishing wrongdoing; it was a sanction quite in tune with longstanding beliefs.

Yet Lungat did not succeed either. He spoke to his elders as directed in the dream but, he told Schwartz, 'Nothing happened. No one responded'. He did not even have the partial successes of the others. As he put it, 'I was not a man of high rank. I was not an important man. I was young, just married, but with no children. I was ashamed to stand up to speak'. But the dream affected him deeply. Like the other early leaders, he travelled from place to place looking for other men with ideas that might succeed. He found nothing until he went to hear Paliau.

An Usiai case: Kampo of Lahan and Pita Tapo

The five men discussed above were Titan-speaking people from lagoon villages. Schwartz was able to learn of only one significant local effort to foment radical change in the villages in the interior of the Great Admiralty.[21] Its leader was Kampo, a catechist who also had a long history

---

21 It is likely that there were other movements among the Usiai and there may well have been some among the Matankor of the north coast. However, Schwartz was able to obtain reliable information only on the Lahan movement and the movements led by south coast Titan described above.

of work for Europeans. Working as a cook, Kampo had been to New Britain and mainland New Guinea. He spent the war in the Admiralties, working for the Japanese—again, under duress—until the American invasion. After the war he took casual jobs for a while if they allowed him to be near the remaining Americans. Gambling was nothing new in the Admiralties and games of chance using European playing cards were among the first customs borrowed from the whites. In the excitement and comparative prosperity of the immediate postwar period there were some epic gambling sessions that people still spoke of in the 1950s. The Usiai village of Lahan was the scene of some of the largest and Kampo took part for a while. But Kampo's interest in gambling did not last long. He felt an unusual sense of responsibility for his village and for the Usiai in general. He became the *luluai* of his village, but this office gave no scope for extending his influence to other Usiai villages.

Kampo possessed all the legitimate authority that a preferred position in the old social structure could give him. He was a *lapan* and early in life he had given some of the larger feasts needed to validate his rank. He was also literate in Tok Pisin and had the combined sophistication of a Catholic catechist and a man with considerable experience working for Europeans, with whom he had got on well. After the war, his greatest desire was that the Usiai form larger units from their small, scattered villages and make copra plantations of their own. Such a program was more plausible for the Usiai than for any Titan, although not without problems. The Usiai had ample land, only a small part of which they used for gardening, but it would have been hard to clear the dense tropical forest and keep it cleared for the approximately eight years needed for coconut palms to mature. Kampo, however, thought that the effort could provide the means to bring his village to a European living standard.

As *luluai* and an influential man by traditional standards, he tried to make as many changes as possible in his own village. He pushed people to build their houses off the ground, on posts, imitating in this both the Europeans living in Manus and the Titan. He encouraged them to build tables and chairs and buy the few essentials of European clothing that they could afford. Some older villagers opposed him, but his leadership rested on a firm foundation and his ideas could not be dismissed lightly. In spite of a promising beginning, however, he was dissatisfied.

He decided to send for Pita Tapo,[22] an Usiai who at the time was working for ANGAU, which still administered the Territory. Tapo was reputed to be intelligent and to know a great deal about the ways of the whites, whom he had come to know while working as a domestic servant. Then the war had trapped him in New Ireland, where he had worked—without choice—for the Japanese. The Japanese recognised his ability and sent him to school. The war ended before he could learn to speak more than token Japanese, but the other students taught him to read and write Tok Pisin. Tapo answered Kampo's summons and returned to Manus. Collaborating with Kampo, he went from one village to another on what had come to be called the 'Number Two Road' (in Tok Pisin, *Nambatu Rot*) in the interior. This was one of a few bush trails created or improved by the German colonial administration in the late nineteenth century. In the 1950s, the *Nambatu Rot* connected interior villages relatively close to the south coast, among which were those most involved in the Paliau Movement.[23]

Tapo sought to bring together in a single place a group of widely scattered villages sharing a common dialect. He found that most of the young men were absent, scattered among the various European centres, working. Few villagers he met felt there was any real possibility of living like Europeans. They wanted to have some of the things Europeans had, and to live as—in their vague conceptions—Europeans lived. But most were apathetic, for they could imagine no way of achieving this.

The people of a number of other Usiai villages regarded those of Lahan as too eager to be like Europeans and, Schwartz was told, sometimes ridiculed them as 'white men'. Kampo and his young followers, however, seemed to take pride in distinguishing themselves from what many of them regarded as the backward villages deeper in the interior. But Lahan—a settlement of no more than 90 men, women, and children—could not stand on its own. It was linked to other Usiai villages through intermarriage, which entailed, as it did for the Titan, obligations to conduct years-long series of feasts and ceremonial exchanges. Bulihan village had long tended to

---

22   By this time, many Manus people had acquired Christian names, which they placed in front of their single indigenous names. However, they did not necessarily regard the latter as Europeans regard a surname. Nor did they necessarily pronounce and spell their Christian names in the orthodox way. In Pita Tapo's case, Pita was not an indigenous 'first' name but represents Tapo's spelling and pronunciation of the English 'Peter'.

23   Minol et al. (2014: 1–2) write that the 'Namba 1 Rot', as they render it in Tok Pisin, led from Lorengau into the interior of the island and back to the 'central north coast'. They provide little detail on the route of the 'Namba 2 Rot'.

form a unit with Lahan, but its people were generally hostile to Kampo's efforts. Kampo was able to convince some of the people of Lahan to build their houses in a new style, favour European clothing, and make other superficial changes, but the obstacles to altering the fundamental pattern of life were substantial.

Kampo and Tapo understood that the Usiai of Lahan were too few for any economic undertaking large enough to make a real difference in their lives. They also understood that, even though they were not as deep in the interior as the majority of Usiai villages, carrying any copra they produced to the coast would be gruelling, even for people accustomed to the often barely perceptible trails of the Manus interior, trails slippery with red clay and that constantly climbed and descended steeply, almost never crossing level ground. And they would have to carry through the same terrain the galvanised metal sheets from which they hoped to build European-style houses. In the end, Kampo and Tapo could not get beyond convincing people to adopt a few symbols of the European life, such as eating on tables decorated with flowers arranged in beer-bottle vases.

The Admiralty Islands war veterans

A group of Admiralty Islands men who had volunteered to fight the Japanese in mainland New Guinea under Australian leadership also tried to organise for change in the immediate postwar period. Sayau of Yiru, an Usiai village near the south coast, estimated that his unit killed about 50 Japanese to each five of their own men lost. Whether or not he exaggerated, he was proud of the prowess of the Manus soldiers. Yet even among these volunteers there was little feeling that this war concerned them directly. When the war ended and they had received their medals and citations, they were returned to their villages. Many soon became bitter, claiming that the Australians had failed to keep the promises made to them. William Matbe, whom many considered the most outstanding Manus volunteer, came from a north coast Usiai community. After the war, he led a group of about 20 veterans who actively pursued their grievances until 1949. They claimed they had been told that when the fighting was over they would receive some kind of substantial payment for their service and that the government had promised other special help and consideration.

Schwartz was unable to confirm the validity of these claims, but Sayau also complained bitterly about a reward he did receive, and his complaint gives insight into the expectations of at least some of these former soldiers and the roots of their disappointment. Here is how Sayau described his grievance:

> They [i.e. the Australians] said, 'We want to give you a citation and a medal'. 'What is this?', I thought. I don't know what this thing is that they called me up for and gave me. You white men, you know about these things, but we natives, we don't understand. I think it is worthless. But I should rejoice in it and I should wear it. Why? You didn't explain its meaning to me adequately. I don't understand. If I put it on without knowing what it is all about and you see me, you will laugh very hard at me.

Sayau told Schwartz that he threw away the medal and citation. This is plausible, for other similar incidents have been confirmed. Sayau was sure that either there was some hidden meaning in the medal that was deliberately withheld or that he and others had been tricked into accepting these worthless and unredeemable tokens in place of the promised payment. In either case, he believed he had been put into a position in which he afforded the white man secret amusement. He felt shamed and angry.

Sayau said the veterans group presented itself to the government on two occasions to ask that wartime promises be kept, but without success. Neither Matbe nor Sayau wanted to return to their villages to try to change them. Instead, they stayed in Lorengau. Matbe persuaded the men in the group to pool their money to start a store. They put together about £300 Australian, and the store failed after five months. The group then broke up. Sayau and Matbe stayed in Lorengau, but as employees, not entrepreneurs.

In the local movements described here one can see maturing the conditions, attitudes, and ideas in the midst of which the Paliau Movement emerged. Paliau's prewar efforts were small and tentative. After the war, Paliau's efforts embraced a dramatically larger geographic area, became more organisationally sophisticated, and presented a much enlarged program for change, as described in the next chapter. Paliau's intellect and pragmatic political skills help explain his success, but it is difficult—as we will see— to separate these qualities from his penchant and talent for imbuing his program with metaphysical meaning.

5

The Paliau Movement begins

By the time Schwartz and Shargo met Paliau in 1953, he had cast off any trace of subservience to whites he may ever have felt. He assumed equality and expected mutual respect. Some government officers liked him, some gave him grudging respect, many disliked or distrusted him, and some hated him. But none could bully him, and all had to deal with him as an equal. Some missionaries considered him the Antichrist, and some Catholic missionaries thought him a Protestant, at best. Many Manus people, too, kept their distance, preferring to remain with one of the missions. But many others found Paliau a compelling figure. The best way to begin conveying a sense of who he was is to present his life story as he told it to Schwartz in 1954.

Paliau tells the story of his life

First, some background. Paliau was born in Lipan, one of the half dozen Matankor villages on Baluan Island. Baluan is a rocky but lushly forested volcanic cone not more than three miles long and a mile wide. On a clear day, Manus Island is easily visible about 25 miles to the north. In culture and language, the people of Baluan are most closely related to those of the islands of Pwam and Lou, and slightly more distantly to the Matankor people of Rambutjo. In the 1950s, other Manus people claimed to be able to distinguish the people of Baluan by their lighter skin colour, although this was never apparent to Schwartz or Smith. The indigenous people of Baluan were primarily gardeners, growing sweet potatoes, taro, and various fruits. They were not seafarers like the Titan, but they built canoes and they fished. They also traded for fish with the Titan living in houses built over the water at the edge of the small island of Mok, less than a mile from Baluan at the nearest point.

According to Paliau, in the indigenous system he would have been recognised as an important leader, by virtue of his descent from Lolokai, one of the best-known Baluan leaders of some five generations before. Otto (1998: 86n), on the basis of genealogical accounts he compiled in the 1980s, concluded that Paliau would have belonged to 'a junior and less-prestigious line descending from a younger son'. This, however, is not how Paliau construed his heritage.

The account below is a condensed version of a close translation of an autobiographical sketch that Paliau dictated to Schwartz. It begins with his childhood and continues through his return to Manus after the war. It is remarkable in that Paliau delivered it as an almost unbroken narrative. Schwartz had simply said that he wanted a detailed story of his life, and that Paliau could relate it at any length he wished. In what follows, ellipses indicate places where we have deleted repetitive or less informative sections. We have clarified some items in brackets. The translation from the Tok Pisin original is quite literal in order to maintain the simplicity of Paliau's style, a simplicity typical of storytelling in Tok Pisin. A few Tok Pisin terms that do not translate easily into English have been kept in the text, with notes on translation in brackets.

Paliau's youth

When I was born to my mother and father, they were still *kranki*. [This Tok Pisin term can mean 'confused' or 'foolish', but in this context it means 'backward'.] They couldn't tell me the time or the month in which I was born. I was the same as John here [Paliau gestured towards his son, then aged seven] when my mother died first, and my father died next. It was only a short time. I was still John's age. I cannot see [that is, remember] their faces at all. Then I just drifted around. They did not bear me a brother. They had one daughter, who died; then they had me. Soon after, they died. It is the same today, I am just one. When they died I didn't stay just with one person. I was not looked after properly then. I was midway between them all [that is, I belonged fully to no one's household]. I was in the middle between Joseph Pati and Ninow Namei. The latter and my mother had the same mother and father. Joseph Pati [a member of Paliau's father's clan, whom—within the Baluan kinship system—Paliau treated as a brother][1] is a man and Ninow Namei is a woman. I was in the middle between the two. But I wasn't properly cared for. Why? My parents were dead. Later when I was a little older Joseph lived in his own house and Ninow lived in hers. After my father died Ninow took me. She took care of me. But even as a child I didn't stay put. The two of them quarrelled over me. Joseph Pati angrily told Ninow she would have to let me stay with him sometimes. Both of them were right, but it was my way as a child not to stay put with either of them. I stayed here and there among all of the men now. Then I left the two of them altogether and stayed with Kalowin, an old man of Lipan. He was kin to my father and I stayed on my father's land. He looked after me. Later there was a quarrel between him and Joseph Pati … Later I used to play with other children. When we finished playing, I would follow them. I went to their mothers and fathers for meals. When their parents gave them food I took some too. I ate the food of everyone around the village.

While I was still young my eyes saw clearly all the big feasts they used to make. They made big feasts with pigs, gathered all the yams and sweet potatoes and heaped them together.[2] They could get as many as 100 or 200 pigs. Then they made a feast. Their money was dogs' teeth and shell beads. When they made the big feasts, they didn't just do it for nothing. One man would talk, saying he was the most important man on Baluan. Then he would hold a meeting of his men to make the feast. When it was time for the feast they beat the *garamut* [large logs hollowed out through a narrow longitudinal opening, used as drums, usually decorated with elaborate carving, sometimes called slit gongs in English] and danced to them. Each man would get a shell from the ocean, a white [cowrie] shell.

---

1   For non-anthropologists, we note that terms for kin in all the languages of the Admiralty Islands combine kin differently from standard Anglo-American terminology. Hence, in the Titan language, a man would describe (but not address) a male biological sibling, male children of his father's brothers, and, on occasion, almost any male kin of approximately his own age using the same term, *ndriasin* (Mead 2002 [1934]: 34). Describing people with the same term implies similar social expectations. Such systems are sometimes called classificatory, as opposed to descriptive, kinship systems. One can translate *ndriasin* loosely as brother, with the understanding that it covers a wider variety of male kin than the English term. When speaking Tok Pisin, Manus people are likely to use the Tok Pisin terms that translate roughly as brother and sister in a similarly classificatory sense. In translating people's accounts of events, we use loose English translations of the indigenous and Tok Pisin kin terms and do not try to distinguish people to whom they refer using standard Anglo-American kin terminology.
2   Like the Titan, the Baluan Matankor expended a great deal of time and energy on ceremonial exchange and displays of wealth in connection with marriage, although similar practices were also attached to death and mourning observances for important men. Otto (1991: 51–8) discusses the Baluan mortuary feasts as described to him in the 1980s by middle-aged men and women who had observed them conducted by members of their parents' generation.

They would put it on their penises and they would dance with them. Not the women though, they put on new grass skirts to dance. When they dressed up they adorned themselves with shell beads. The meaning of this dance was that they rejoiced in this feast that they made that everyone came to look at. Another meaning it had when all the men put on shells and went to dance was 'I am a man of know-how; I have a great deal of wealth; I have dogs' teeth and shell beads; the rest of you are just rubbish [that is, worthless] in the village; you are not accustomed to doing this dance'. It is like this. If I am 'rubbish' in having no dogs' teeth, no food and no pigs, then I can't make this dance. This is the mark of men who have much wealth, who raise many pigs, and who make large gardens. All of us children were schooled in this custom. Some learned and some didn't. I didn't learn. Why? Because I knew it was no good. I tried it once. This attempt was not my idea, it was Joseph's. He made what we call a *sinal* [a narrow wooden beam, carved and painted, on which this dance is done]. They put it on two posts. He sent me onto it. He told me to go up on it for the first time. Then I was to come down on the beam with one of my legs on one side and with my other leg on the other side. Then I return to the middle and make a speech, the speech Joseph had taught me. I came back to the middle and wanted to make my speech on top of this wooden beam. I wanted to speak but my mouth mixed it up. I don't know what I said. I was confused. I babbled. I jumped down and turned my back on all the men who were watching the dance. When I jumped down, I didn't go straight to a house. I collapsed onto the grass, along with all the decoration on my body, dogs' teeth, shell beads. They had put red paint in my hair and marked my eyes with red paint. I collapsed on the grass. I was extremely sick … It wasn't an hour till I became sick; I think it was only two minutes until I became sick. No one knew about me, no one saw me. Why? Because I fell down in the tall grass. When the feast was over late in the afternoon my body was a little strong then, I got up. I went home; then I was all right.

An old man, the aged father of Paliau [an older brother of Paliau's grandfather who was also named Paliau] whom Joseph Pati had called to this feast that Joseph was making for a woman [as an affinal payment to the old man] was there. The feast lasted two weeks. When it was over the old man for whom the feast was made died. When I was sick, if I had died, I think this old man would not have died. [Paliau did not explain this reasoning.] When my sickness was finished, I was all right, and then this man died. I knew this feast had been for him … He received it along with these pigs and distributed it among his clan. Then he died. Now my mind was decided like this. This custom was no good. I was through with it now. When they made big feasts I didn't go. I could hear them, I could see them when they were made but I wouldn't try it any more myself. When they made the feasts and when the feast was over a strong sickness used to break out in the village. When a feast was finished and the sickness occurred it used to kill 20 or 30 men. Later they used to say that spirits, *tambaran*, kill us. The meaning of *tambaran* was this: if one man dies first, his ghost takes all of us. The ghost of one goes and kills another … [Here, Paliau uses the Tok Pisin word *tambaran* for spirits of the dead. It was and still is used in many parts of New Guinea for both the supernatural patron of a men's ritual society and ancestral spirits.]

When a big feast is finished, there is a famine on Baluan. Why? If they make big gardens and then the gardens are ready, the man who is to make a feast sends word all over Baluan. Everyone digs up all the food to make a big feast. I considered it and I thought it wasn't right …

By the time I was a little older I found that all my age mates had died from this way of life. If an older man pulled them into it later they died from it. When one died many more in the village followed them. They all had to die. But I didn't believe this talk about the spirits of the dead. Why didn't I believe it? It was the way of children; they are ignorant. When I was a child my parents died. I never used to conform properly to any belief. Times when there was much sickness, the time of rain, darkness, thunder, and lightning, all the kin of my father and mother would be cross with me. They would scold me like this, 'When it is a bad time, when a man has died, when spirits of the dead roam about, you must sit down properly, you can't run about'. I wouldn't listen, I wouldn't stay put. If there was a big rain and they spoke to me, I would go out in the rain. Why? It is the way of children. They are ignorant. They can't be afraid. That's how it is that when I was older I didn't believe in *tambaran*. I said this talk of *tambaran* is a lie.

Going away to work

Time passed; then I was more grown up. I think I was about 15 years old when they put me down for government tax. I wasn't finished with all of these ideas. What ideas? The idea that I wouldn't accept the talk of the important men who said there were ghosts in the village and my thoughts about all the big feasts. Now that I was older I realised that these feasts caused the loss of many men of Baluan. This continued to stay in my mind. Now, at this time I didn't travel by canoe. I didn't go to the big place [Manus Island]; I just stayed with the men of the island [i.e. Baluan]. Just once, when I was younger, I heard the name Lorengau, and I thought it was one of the big places of the white men. Then once I was taken in a canoe. We went to Lorengau. When I arrived, I saw it was just another place like our own. I was not familiar with Mbukei, I hadn't gone there. I had gone to Lou; I had gone to Pwam. As for Mok [the Titan village adjacent to Mok Island], all the old men of before had said that I had an ancestor there. When I was still small my father used to take me to Mok. It is the way of children. If their father goes they cry to go with him. They used to go to a small islet here, Takumai [about one-tenth of a mile, or 150 metres, offshore from Baluan]. My Titan grandfather of whom they had spoken was named Sangol. He belonged to the same clan as Pwankiau, who is still alive. He is the old man here in the house over the lagoon. Following this line of relationship through this ancestor, my father used to take me to the house of Pwankiau. I also follow this story and I have taken this old man Pwankiau to live with me here. I associated only with the young men of Baluan. In Mok I just went straight to Pwankiau. When my father was still alive he used to send all sorts of food to Pwankiau. I only went around with the children of Pwankiau. And almost until I was 15 I just stayed in the village. Then I was marked to pay taxes to the government.

I heard this from the patrol officer who collected the tax. I stood up before his eyes and he said, 'Next year you will pay tax, now you cannot'. Then I thought, 'I am not a fully grown man yet, and they have marked me to be taxed'. Then I thought about finding money. I started working for a Chinese named Leu. I worked for two years. I didn't have whiskers yet. I was a young boy, not a young man. This Chinese looked at me and said I wasn't capable of hard work; I was just capable of cooking. He said I was too small. He wanted to send me back, but I was persistent. Why? Because the patrol officer had said I was to be taxed. I wouldn't have any money. This Chinese for whom I cooked, Leu, had a business collecting and marketing trochus shell.[3] Later he brought another Chinese to help him in this work. This Chinese who assisted was Akan … This Chinese Akan didn't have a servant. Soon Leu dismissed me as his cook and sent me to Akan. I worked as cook for him for two years. During this time that I cooked for him I received two

---

3   The nacre or mother-of-pearl of trochus shells is used for making buttons.

shillings a month, one length of cloth per month, and two sticks of tobacco, a few matches, and a little soap each week. When I finished, I was given £5 for these two years. When I finished my work I was angry; while I was at work I was also angry. My anger was for this reason; these two Chinese didn't pay well. I was angry, but I didn't quarrel with them. I wasn't lazy about work. I just kept it to myself. When I had finished the two years I divided the £5. For £2 10s [20 shillings = £1] I bought myself some things in the store. The other £2 10s I brought to the village. I gave it to Joseph Pati and all the kin of my father and mother. When they saw that I had come back, and they came to see me, they all cried. The meaning of their crying was this. I was lost for two years when their eyes couldn't see me. When I came back they all looked with recognition at my face that was like the face of my father who had died. They all saw that I looked like my mother who had died. Because of this all the kin of my father and mother came to cry over me. When Joseph Pati saw all these people he opened my box that I had bought at the store. He took all the small things that I had brought along with this £2 10s and he divided them among all these relatives of my father and mother who had come.

What I have just told is the same for all the men of Manus. The first time that I went to work I saw that this was not right. Why did I see it wasn't right? I went to find money for the government tax, so that I wouldn't go to jail over it. I had also bought a few little things such as *laplap* [Tok Pisin for lengths of cloth worn by both men and women like wrap-around skirts from waist to knees—a form of dress for indigenes introduced by colonial Europeans] and some other things from the store also. Then Joseph Pati divided it up among all these people, and I am again rubbish. This sort of thing didn't just happen to me; it happened to all the men of Baluan and Manus Island together. Others who had gone among the white men previously had come and received the same treatment also. They couldn't hold on to a single thing. They all thought it was all right. But I understood now, and I thought it was wrong. It made nothing of me. Why was this? They all valued all this money from before that belonged to our ancestors, the dogs' teeth and shell beads. They all valued all the ornaments of the past, the grass skirts and the leaves used for adornment. The women used leaves. The men pounded the bark of a tree and wore it [as a breechclout]. They all thought about all these things; then when they went to work for the white man and came back they threw away all their money on their kin. Now I was poor. Now what?

I was angry in my mind, but I didn't express anger with my mouth. Soon the *kiap* [*kiap* is a Tok Pisin term for an Australian government officer] would come for money and I had none.

I thought again of going to ask this Chinese if I could work for him. I went with him again for another two years. I went and stayed with this Chinese, Akan, who was still in the same business. I got my pay just as before. The monthly rate was the same. When the two years were up I received again £5 ... I sent the money on to the village, but I didn't go. Another Chinese wanted me again. He was named Akim. He wanted me to go shoot pigeons for him with a shotgun. I cooked, too. I stayed with him for six months. Then he beat me. He wanted me to herd the goats of the doctor into the house. I refused to obey. I said, 'These goats are not mine, they are the doctor's'. Then he beat me. I pushed his arm away. He went to get his gun to shoot me with it, but I ran away into the bush. Later I went to the government officer and told him. He said, 'Never mind; go back to the village. That's the way Chinese are. You two will always be cross and they don't think. Eventually he will really shoot you'.

I went back to my village. My money was gone. They had already divided it up among all the brothers, sisters, and other relatives of my mother.

The colonial police

I had no money. Now I wanted to go to work as a policeman. I joined for two years the first time. When I went away to the police I still did not have whiskers. I wasn't able to have the full outfit of a policeman. I just went with the *kiap*. After one year I was given the full equipment of a policeman. I worked in the bush [anywhere in the interior of the New Guinea mainland that was distant from the few European settlements on the mainland coast]. I worked at finding a *masta* that they [i.e. people in the interior] had killed, Master Bom. He was looking for gold and was killed by the natives of the bush. We went to right this wrong. We caught the natives, many of whom went to jail. They were not jailed to be killed but to teach them the ways of the white man and of the coast. [In this era, coastal New Guineans generally considered themselves more sophisticated than people of the interior.] When they had learned, we brought them back to tell those who were in the bush. The men of the interior had no knowledge of the coastal area. The white men called them the Kukakuka.[4] When they saw us they wanted to kill us, too. I worked in this part of the interior teaching them and stopping their fighting for two years. During these two years the Kukakuka killed two *kiap* and another white man who were on patrol [that is, seeking out indigenous communities to bring them under control of the Territory law]. They also killed a line [that is, a patrolling group] of native police and their sergeant, Hanis of Madang. I had finished two years now, and I returned to my village. While I worked as a policeman I was paid the same as when I had worked for the Chinese. When I was finished, I spent all this money on buying things. My box was full. I brought it all to Baluan. There was no difference. It was just the same. All the relatives came, and the old man Joseph opened my box and gave out everything. Joseph had taken the place of my dead father. All the Baluans are alike in this custom, should Joseph be different? He was the same as the rest. The Titan of the sea were the same. The Moks, too, are the same.

When they divide up everything, then they make a big feast just as in the past. If they get two cases of tobacco they will break open all the cases and string the tobacco along a line with all the other things of the white men that had come. Then they dance. The man who makes this will boast to all the other men of Manus that they are not up to doing this, bringing together so many things of the white men that they have all come to see. Some who looked at all this thought it was all right. Why is it that I knew it was wrong? I knew it was wrong, but I couldn't express my anger over it, I just thought it to myself.

I stayed in Manus for two years at this time. I just hung around. I went along with anyone who was going anywhere, just coming and going. If they made a big feast on Lou, I went along to observe. When they made a feast, I ate with them all. That in my mind I knew it all to be wrong, this I kept to myself …

I went to see every part of Manus. For what reason did I go around observing like this? I thought that this practice of letting everything of value be dispersed among everyone, does it exist only in Baluan or is it everywhere in Manus? I didn't speak out about it, I just thought about it like this. This way of doing things cannot help us. The way of our

---

4   Sometimes called the Kukukuku, they speak an Angan language. Their traditional territory is in a mountainous area where today Gulf, Eastern Highlands, and Morobe provinces converge. We thank Don Niles of the Institute for Papua New Guinea Studies for this information.

distant ancestors is still with us. It was becoming clearer in my mind. The white man has long been in our midst. Always he puts us to some task. When the patrol officer comes among us and one man isn't clean, the officer will be angry. If the government sends word to clean the road, and if they do not clean it, they will go to jail. With houses, too, if they don't build their houses well, they can go to jail. If they don't have money for taxes they go to jail. If there is no house *kiap* [a rest house for government officers] or no latrine, there will be jail. Many of us have been in jail. But they don't learn. They persist in all these ways of the past that I have already mentioned. I saw that everywhere in Manus people were the same as in Baluan.

When two years had passed I joined the police again for another two years. This time I went to Rabaul. As policeman I was sent out to work among the natives of the bush. Everything about the natives around Rabaul was no different from Manus. It was the same. All the specific customs were somewhat different, but as far as making big feasts and losing money as if it were something of no value, this was the same as in Manus. When I went back to work as a policeman, I didn't do it for nothing. I did it from anger at the natives of Manus. This was in my mind. When I left I thought that I would never go back to Baluan. I found that I didn't like the way of life of Manus. I could never go back. But when I went to Rabaul it was the same as in Manus. I left Rabaul and went to Salamau [a town on the mainland coast]. It was the same there. I went as policeman to Madang [a town on the mainland coast]. I took in all the ways of the natives of Madang. It was just the same. I went to Finschhafen [a town on the mainland coast] and observed the customs of the natives there. It was again the same. Lae [a town on the mainland coast] also, and Kavieng [a town on the coast of the island of New Ireland] were the same. Then I thought, our ways are only of one kind. Now where does this leave me? Well, I just stayed at work as policeman. I stayed for 12 years altogether. If I saw a man from Baluan I asked him, 'The ways of the old men of Baluan, do they still exist or are they finished?' And he would say, 'They still exist and what is wrong with this? It is still our way'. [After Paliau had been away three years, he took leave to visit Baluan again.] After three years I wasn't just taking a break. I came to look again at the Baluan culture and I came to bring a little money.

Prewar beginnings of the Paliau Movement

Always I received two shillings for one month. I didn't waste it, I put it away securely. I bought a case of tobacco that I sent ahead of me back to the village. It was sent to Joseph Pati with this message: 'You have wasted plenty of things of mine in the past but this case of tobacco you cannot touch. If you forget what I say I will come and I will be extremely angry'. This time he followed my instructions. This case of tobacco that I sent brought £15 [when divided and sold to villagers]. When I came back on leave after these three years I had £15 more in addition. Five pounds more was from the two shillings that I received each month that I saved. There was £20 altogether. I didn't buy anything. I just took this £20 and went to look over the Baluan way of life. This £20 along with the £15 that Joseph Pati had gotten for the case of tobacco made £35. I came and asked Joseph where the money for the tobacco was. He got it and now there was £35. I told him: 'This £35 does not belong to you, it is mine. I tell you this clearly. I have something to say about it. I want to talk to the *kukerai* [another Tok Pisin term for the government-appointed headman or *luluai*]. He has the hat given to him by the government. [A *luluai* received a military-style hat as a symbol of his office.] I want the *kukerai* and the *tultul* [the government-appointed interpreter, a lesser official]. I want to talk about this £35'. I told them, 'I want you to call together all your men, all the men and women of Lipan' … When everyone had gathered I took this £35 and I showed it to them all … 'These seven strings of shillings [Territorial shillings, made with holes in their centres, were typically strung together in £5 groups] is to stay with the *kukerai*. *Kukerai*, you take care of it. It is to look after all the men and women of Lipan. But it is not your money, it is mine. I give it to you for you to look after your people. The purpose of this money is this. Each year when the *kiap* comes to collect the tax, whoever does not have his tax money or is short on it, you must pay the tax for him. If you give a man ten shillings to pay the tax, you must write the name of this man; then, when the *kiap* has left, this man is to pay back the money. Why must he return the money? If it is returned to you, you can take care of everyone for all the years to come behind. I am showing you a good road, by which all your men can avoid going to jail. Why should they pay back the money? It would be no good if the money were used up. Now your men can stay in the village with you. This is the reason I left Baluan. I didn't have tax money when the *kiap* called me. If you get into trouble over these seven strings, if the *kiap* dismisses you and another boss is put in your place, you must turn this money over to him. The new boss can look after his men with it. Why? Because this is not your money, it is mine. I give it to you to look after the men over whom you are boss. And you can't just ignore a man of another *luluai* and another clan of Baluan if his man does not have money, you must send the money to him; later he will pay it back to you. You must help Lou and Pwam … When the *kiap* goes to collect the tax, you must go along with him to take care of whomever does not have tax money'. I said this. Then I put the seven strings into the hands of the boss, the *luluai*.

The *luluai* followed my instructions and paid tax for the men of Baluan, Mok, Pwam, and Lou. Then the *kiap* found out about this man who went around paying the tax on Baluan, Mok, Pwam, and Lou. I had previously instructed the *luluai* that if he is found out by the *kiap* he is not to mention my name, he must say that it is his money. When the *kiap* found out, he wrote the names of the men taxed on small slips of paper. These he gave to the *luluai* saying, 'If this man doesn't return your money, send me word and he will be jailed'. The *kiap* asked him whose money it was. He said that it was his own.

All this work was done quietly, just the way that I have told you. Everyone heard about it and supported the *luluai's* work. When the six months of my leave had finished, I went back to Rabaul. I was still a policeman. I finished another year. I took my £15, which I had saved out of my monthly two-shilling pay. I signed on again as a policeman and then took my leave to go home. I came, and with these three new strings of shillings there was now £50. The £35 from before was still there. The *luluai* paid the tax and then was paid back. I called for everyone to come together … [Paliau called a meeting and asked the people of Baluan if the money had been used properly and if they approved of his plan. They said yes.] 'You look. I am putting three more strings to go with the seven from before. Now if you think that this has been a good thing, you should put what you have with it to help'. They all thought about it, then they said: 'This road that you are making for us is clear to us. We will no longer go to jail'. Now I silenced them. I said: 'You keep quiet. This is the work of the *luluai*. It is not my work. You can't name me'. All right, they were all for it now. All of them put in their money. These were only the people of Lipan. The *luluai* was Ngi Asinkiau and the *tultul* was Lipamu. Everyone in Lipan put in £5 each until there was £500. The money was in the care of the *luluai*. I advised him. I told him: 'You cannot make court against a man of another boss. You can't be angry at them. Take care of all men from Lou, Pwam, and Mok. Look out for whatever trouble might arise among them. If they are angry, you must go quickly into their midst and stop it. If the men of another village come and fight with some of the men of your village, you can't seek revenge. You can't be too angry. You must do only what is good. All of these big feasts that are given on Baluan, sometimes you should think about them. If you get rid of a few of them, you won't regret it. They cause sickness, and many of our people of Lipan die'.

I told them this, then I went back. My leave was finished … As for this money, they saved more and more until they had £2,000.

Paliau in World War II

We break off the verbatim version of Paliau's autobiography at this point. His account of the war years is highly detailed. Much of this is extremely interesting, but it is tangential to the story of how Paliau came to found the Movement. The following is distilled from his longer account.

By the time the war started, Paliau had been promoted to sergeant major in the police and placed in charge of the 280 indigenous police stationed in Rabaul. The majority of Australians in Rabaul evacuated before the Japanese arrived in 1942, but many indigenous police remained. They fled to the bush with the Australian commander and a few remaining Europeans. Paliau and five other policemen stayed in Rabaul long enough to bury the police rifles and ammunition, making their escape at the last minute. The Australian military had told the police to hide in the bush and that they would return before long to drive out the Japanese.

Most of the local indigenous communities near Rabaul cooperated with the Japanese, for they had no choice. Some police gave themselves up to the Japanese and named Paliau as their leader, so the Japanese made a special effort to find him. Paliau said that the people of the local communities were afraid to harbour him and his men and reported him to a missionary. The missionary sent word to the Japanese, who came in two trucks to the house in which Paliau was staying. They fired at him as he fled into the bush, but he escaped. Finally, in August of 1943—feeling that he would soon be captured, weary of fugitive life in the bush, and short of food— Paliau gave himself up to the Japanese administration in Rabaul.

The Japanese asked him if he had hidden any Australians in the bush. He said that he had not and that he had had no contact with the Australians for over a year. Finally, the Japanese told him that he had to work for them as a police officer in charge of the indigenous population in Rabaul. Paliau feared that if he did not obey the Japanese they would cut his throat. He remembered also that the departing Australians had told the remaining police that if the Japanese captured them they were to obey to save their lives.

The Japanese made Paliau responsible for overseeing the New Guineans from all parts of the Territory, including many from Manus, who had been working in Rabaul and were now trapped there. He gathered them in groups according to their places of origin and assigned a policeman to supervise each group. He had them plant gardens to grow their own food while they worked for the Japanese. He judged disputes among members of this disparate community and brought their complaints about the actions of Japanese soldiers to the attention of the Japanese administration. He told Schwartz that when he reported an offence against local people by a Japanese soldier, the soldier was punished. He emphasised that he had nothing to do with the Japanese treatment of Australians or with Japanese executions of New Guineans.

When the Americans began bombing Rabaul in 1944, Paliau was wounded in the leg, but he was able to get out and find refuge in a Manus settlement outside the town. He stayed with this group of men from Admiralty Islands villages until the fighting was over in 1945. Among this group was Karol Matawai of Patusi (who was mentioned in Bonyalo's story in connection with the Pere local movement). When news came that an American warship was in Rabaul harbour and that the Australians had re-established their control, Paliau put on his old police uniform and presented himself to the government officer. He was sent back to bring in the other men from Manus. Many more Manus police returned to Rabaul with the Australians and they were overjoyed at finding Paliau alive. The Australian administration put the Manus to work clearing Rabaul of the war wreckage and building housing.

A group of police from the Sepik region of mainland New Guinea, however, wanted to kill Paliau, accusing him of helping the Japanese. They called him the *kiap* of the Japanese. Although the departing Australians had told the remaining police to obey the Japanese, on their return some of them suspected Paliau of collaboration because the Japanese had given

Paliau a position of considerable responsibility. Paliau was brought to court and tried for alleged war crimes. The rest of the Manus police were returned home, but Paliau was kept in Rabaul for a year while his trial continued intermittently. When he was not in court, he was put to work. At night he slept in the jail. But the Australian court could prove no willing collaboration.

In 1945, Paliau sent a letter from Rabaul to the *luluai* of the Baluan Island villages of Mok and Lipan, calling on the people of the two islands to build a large meeting house at the place in Lipan called Saponparunbuai to prepare for his return. When he arrived they were to assemble to hear his message. Adherents of the later Paliau Movement speak of this letter as the beginning of everything; it is the starting point of modern history for them.

The *luluai* of the several villages of the two islands decided to wait until Paliau's return before carrying out his instructions. According to Paliau they reasoned that he might yet be imprisoned or executed. Finally, in October 1946, the trials of New Guineans suspected of war crimes ended. Paliau was told he was free and would be assigned to a ship to return to Manus. But many ships came and went and he was kept waiting. He told Schwartz of going from one Australian official to another seeking a pass to board a ship, but with no success. It was clear to Schwartz that he was still bitter. 'If I had done anything wrong', he said, 'they had ample opportunity to convict me, but they didn't. They released me. Why did their anger persist?' The fact that he was not judged a collaborator did not sooth Paliau's resentment that the Australians—alongside whom he had served and fought—had treated him with suspicion.

The Manus people who had been in Rabaul with Paliau considered him a martyr and he had great prestige among them for his work on their behalf. He had organised the settlement of the heterogeneous mass of indigenous internees in Rabaul, taking it on himself to manage their internal affairs, calling meetings and holding courts. Many Admiralties people spent the war in a refugee settlement at Talasea, New Britain, some distance from Rabaul. Those with whom Schwartz spoke years later said that Paliau had acted on their behalf as well. Among other things, he had circulated a letter warning them to save their lives by obeying the Japanese and to bide their time, essentially what the departing Australians had told them.

Paliau felt that the Australian administration's treatment of him negated his many years with the police and the high rank he had reached. He decided to put this part of his life behind him. His sole interest now, he said, was leading a transformation of indigenous society. When he returned to Manus in 1946, he immediately began to gather a following from villages on the south coast.

By the time Schwartz came to know him, Paliau saw himself in the light of the Movement that bore his name, though not quite as his followers saw him. He gave Schwartz an introspective account of his thoughts and activities, asking aloud at several points, 'Why did I see that all this was wrong when the rest of them didn't?'

These are the points Paliau emphasised in answering his own question. First, he put great weight on losing his parents early in life. Among the Matankor people of Baluan there was probably a close relationship between father and son similar to that among the Titan. Having neither a brother nor sister, he felt that he belonged to no one after he was orphaned. He felt that he had been alone all his life and an outsider to his natal culture even before he knew any other. He associated his natal culture with his foster father, Joseph Pati, who had frequently caused him shame and anger. His disastrous attempt to dance on and speak from the *sinal* was probably a crucial point in his rejection of indigenous Matankor ways. And Paliau's emphasis on his relationship to the lagoon-dwelling Titan of Mok presages his later strong identification with Titan speakers.

Paliau also emphasised his expanding experience of the world beyond his home island. He travelled very little until his late teens. But he felt that his break with his natal culture preceded his travels. He dates his disbelief in the spirits of the dead, a nuclear belief in Manus, to his childhood. Paliau attributed his own scepticism to the fearless autonomy of a child too ignorant to be afraid of the ghosts that play such a large role in the adult world. This is consistent with Mead's assertion that Titan children were sceptical about adult beliefs (Mead 2001 [1930], see particularly Chapters 4 and 8). Although Paliau was ethnically Matankor, in his account of his early life there are more than echoes of Mead's discussion of the marked discontinuity in Titan socialisation. Titan adults, she observed, did little to prepare their children for adult responsibilities until they were suddenly required to accept them in their entirety. But unlike the Titan children of the 1920s whom Mead observed, Paliau was not suddenly and roughly initiated into a rigid adult role. Instead, to the extent possible, he struck out on his own.

Paliau rejected the adult explanation that a series of deaths following a feast was caused by spirits of the dead. Rather, he connected the deaths with a fault in the culture. People died because the feasts and dances required strenuous preparation, entailed too much eating and dancing, and used up all the food. But this was only part of his reasoning. He also thought that these events brought death because in some way, as yet undefined, they were wrong. They were wrong just as the dissipation of a returning worker's hard-won pay was wrong. No one achieved anything. Life was an endless round of work and dissipation of the rewards, which compelled people simply to return to work. His conviction that this was wrong showed the extent to which he had not internalised the value system of the old culture.

Paliau described his travels as opportunities to compare cultures. He had decided not to return to Baluan, but he found nothing better anywhere in other New Guinea societies. He abstracted from his experiences the basic similarity of the cultures he encountered. And he saw that New Guineans from many backgrounds who went to work for the whites found that when they returned their elders appropriated the wealth they had gained. Dissatisfied, some who returned remained aloof from their home cultures or, finding nothing desirable in their villages, returned to the European world to work.

Paliau's account of his attempt to change the culture of Baluan is also of great importance. Schwartz was able to check his story with enough people to confirm that he had indeed led local efforts as early as 1937. Paliau mentioned frequently, however, that as his ideas were developing he initially said nothing. He was too young, without prestige, and without a plan of action beyond abandoning the old culture in which his elders still participated. His earliest major project, however, made him known as a leader. As described above, he recruited others to help amass a sum of money larger than any single person could have, creating a fund that helped many people pay their taxes and remain out of jail. (The amount he named, £2,000, however, seems improbable for the prewar years. Others with whom Schwartz spoke who knew of the fund said they did not know its precise amount.)

LIKE FIRE

Even on his last return to Baluan before the war, four years or more after he initiated the revolving tax fund, he felt that he was not ready to call for a general break with the old culture. It was on his last leave from Rabaul before the war that he first mentioned his plan to build a meeting house on Baluan. Then, during his service and his detention in Rabaul, he cultivated men from many different Manus villages. Those Schwartz spoke with later said that Paliau had told them of his plans for transforming Manus when he went back.

In the 1950s, Schwartz usually felt that Paliau was speaking with him openly and freely, but he noted at least one significant exception: Paliau omitted almost any spontaneous mention of Christianity in his dictated autobiography. He spoke of his ideas about Christianity only when Schwartz questioned him. Paliau then said that Christianity had come slowly to Baluan. People who seemed about to die were baptised. If they recovered, they remained Christians. The Catholic Mission had been established while Paliau was away, working for Akim. Paliau was never baptised and was one of the few people Schwartz and Shargo encountered in Manus who had no baptismal name. When asked about his religion, he said he was a Catholic, and he had apparently acquired knowledge of mission Christianity from many different sources. In Rabaul and elsewhere during his years in the police force, he had occasionally attended mission worship services, usually Catholic. But he did not attend a mission school. He learned to read and write Tok Pisin from his peers. John Murphy, with whom Paliau served as a police constable in the Kukakuka area early in his career as a policeman, told Schwartz that Paliau kept to himself more than was usual among the police, and that he tried to learn anything he could, even trying to teach himself English from books.

When in the 1950s Paliau did speak to Schwartz of Christianity, he indicated that he accepted Christianity as true, validated by the obvious power and superiority of the whites who espoused it, and he accepted the reality of the God and Christ of the missions. We have seen, however, that in later years he expressed scepticism of the 'truth' of any religion or, in Tok Pisin, *lotu*. And even early in his career he revised much of the content of mission teaching, departing widely from orthodox Catholic doctrine and questioning the truth of the Bible as presented to New Guineans. He had rejected his natal culture before having intensive contact with Christianity, and he and others describe his local prewar movement in completely secular terms. During the war and just after it, however, his program became infused with his understanding of Christianity, an

138

aspect of his story he did not share with Schwartz at first. But it was well known to his followers. Many people told Schwartz of a revelatory dream—recounted below—they attributed to Paliau, long before Paliau told Schwartz his own version. And only just before Schwartz and Shargo left the field in 1954 did Paliau tell them of how he had recounted this dream in his early meetings on Baluan.

When Paliau finally filled in this dimension of his chronicle, he told Schwartz of how, as he renewed his efforts after the war, he presented his program as having come to him full blown in dream and vision, directly from the mind of Jesus. He presented himself not merely as a man with a program, but a man whose program was the latest chapter in the history of the relationship between man and God, a history revealed to him by a higher power.

In this mode, Paliau spoke of the war as a trial sent by God, a trial that would force open the minds of the New Guineans like a bomb striking a concrete building. He told of how, while he and his companions hid from the Japanese in the bush, he had dreamt several times that Japanese patrols had found them. Each time, he told the others of his dream and persuaded them to flee just in time to escape. He also told of how, during the American bombing, he had another dream that predicted the arrival of American bombers the next day and a bomb that would destroy the house in which he and his companions were staying. This dream also came true, but they had already fled the house. In another dream he predicted that 208 planes would appear the next afternoon. The next day, he said, 208 planes flew overhead. He held that dreams that prove accurate are sent from God and that he was being specifically favoured.

These dreams, however, came only after his crucial revelation: a dream in which a messenger, whom he usually identified as Jesus, appeared to him in the form of an ox, which then transformed into the figure of a white-skinned man. By the time Schwartz, Shargo, and Mead arrived in 1953, the story of this encounter was well known throughout large parts of Manus. Schwartz and Shargo collected versions of it from Europeans, from local people hostile to the Movement, and from many of Paliau's closest adherents. We will present below the version Paliau finally shared with Schwartz, but the varied versions that circulated spontaneously helped make Paliau's reputation. Most of those who told the story related it as if the events had had physical form. Some, however, described it as a dream that came in natural sleep; still others, as a vision that came to

Paliau as a kind of possession by Jesus. The accounts varied in their details, but despite this there can be little doubt that at least some narrators had heard the story directly from Paliau. Schwartz composed the following version of the story by combining the points of agreement among versions provided by several members of the Movement.

The revelatory dream

Jesus had sent the Americans to end the war and to act as his agents in bringing the truth to the natives. Jesus himself also came to select the native who would lead all the rest. He went to Manus but could find no one who was fit to lead. When Jesus saw how the Titan lived, landless, like fish in water, he felt great compassion for them. Jesus finally found Paliau in Rabaul. He was the only man capable of the task that Jesus had for him. Jesus came in a plane marked with a cross. When the plane appeared, Paliau was hiding, afraid that he would be hit by the Americans' bombs. Jesus appeared to him in the form of an ox. The thought came into Paliau's mind that he should not be afraid. The ox turned into a tall white-skinned man with a beard. The link between Paliau and this man was between their minds; they communicated without speaking. They went into a house together. The bearded white-skinned man sat down in one chair and bade Paliau sit down in another. The house was filled with a bright light that could be seen at a great distance. They also seemed to be surrounded by clouds of smoke. Jesus showed Paliau a book. It was the original *Buk Tambu*—the true Bible. [In Admiralties Tok Pisin of the 1950s, the Bible was *Buk Tambu*. This translates loosely as the powerful or sacred book. Forbidden Book is a possible translation, but things are forbidden—tabooed or, in Tok Pisin, *tambu*—because they are powerful or dangerous, not the other way around. Today, Tok Pisin speakers simply say *Baibel*. As we will see next, Paliau taught that the whites had concealed the true Bible from New Guineans.][5] It had been encased in concrete and the book itself was half metal, half stone. No one could open it and no hacksaw could have made an impression on the metal. Such was the knowledge that had been concealed from the natives. Now Paliau was given part of this knowledge, and he sometimes said that all the content

5   The Tok Pisin word *tambu* is closely related to terms from Polynesian languages, such as the Tongan *tapu* and the Hawaiian *kapu*, both meaning roughly set apart, potent, or—in more theological terms—sacred.

of the early meetings was revealed to him at this time. He was told that he and the rest of Manus people would be delivered safely to their homes. Paliau was to go straight to the people of Mok, who were singled out as an exemplar of the poverty of all natives. The Moks were the rubbish people who were to be the first to share this revelation. After this visitation, Paliau told his companions of his contact with Christ and implied that he continued to be inspired and empowered by his role as the chosen spokesman of Jesus.

***

When Schwartz first asked Paliau about this and other revelatory dreams of which Schwartz had heard from others, Paliau denied them, saying: 'Who am I that Jesus should come to me?' Later, when Schwartz pressed him again, he admitted to having had a dream that was the source of these stories. Here is the substance of the dream in which Jesus appeared to Paliau as an ox as Paliau himself finally recounted it to Schwartz:

> When he was being held in Rabaul by the Australians during the war crimes trials, Paliau was afraid that he would be imprisoned or executed. A friend who was still serving in the colonial police told Paliau that he would try to collect money to 'pay the court', which usually meant to pay a fine, though there was no question of a penalty as light as a fine. That night Paliau dreamt about the ox. He was frightened at first; later he was no longer afraid. The ox became a white-skinned man who told Paliau not to worry about the trial; Paliau would not have to 'pay'. He, the 'Master', would pay. Paliau was reassured. He understood the dream as a sign that he was favoured by God. He explained to Schwartz that all such dreams come from God; they are his way of communicating with men. He said that the men who conducted his trial wanted to punish him; that they did not do so confirmed his dream.

Some popular versions held that Paliau received his revelation while hiding in the bush, rather than while imprisoned. Most also added that, as a result of his encounter with Jesus, Paliau was able to prevail in interrogations by the Japanese and the Australians by mentioning the name of 'King Berra' at a crucial point in each trial. At the mention of this name, both the Japanese and the Australians were thrown into confusion. Not daring to kill Paliau, they released him. Schwartz first heard of King Berra in connection with these stories, but he later learned that the name appeared in cargo cult lore in various parts of what is now Papua New Guinea. It is apparently a distortion of the name Canberra, the capital of Australia. In Paliau's own account of his trial for war crimes, he told of how, after almost a year of intermittent court sessions, word came from Canberra, which he knew to be the capital of Australia, that all unconcluded war crimes trials against natives were to be discontinued.

Paliau knew of the various versions of his dreams circulating, and sometimes when speaking with Schwartz he called them distortions and exaggerations of what he had actually said. But publicly he accepted the legendary status that they underwrote. The more heroic versions of the history of his life became a part of the 'Long Story of God', which he related at the early meetings and which we will present later in this chapter.

Paliau's return to Manus

Paliau arrived at Australian New Guinea Administrative Unit (ANGAU) headquarters, near Lorengau, on 10 October 1946. As we have seen, at this time numbers of indigenous people were advocating change in their villages, but the local movements had all encountered intractable older generations. Some indigenous critics of the prevailing order were also saying that New Guineans should demand from employers a pound a day as a minimum wage. About the time of, or just before, Paliau's return to Manus, a paramount *luluai* from the north coast organised a movement to ask the Americans to take over Manus and a delegation presented a petition written in Tok Pisin to officers in charge of the American base. Nothing, of course, came of it. ANGAU was very unpopular among Manus people, who saw it as a barrier between themselves and the Americans. Paliau, however, had little interest in calling on the Americans to advance Manus society. His plan called for unifying Manus people and moving independently towards an approximation of their understanding of white life.

Paliau rejected others' schemes for Manus advancement brusquely, as he rejected William Matbe's plans to start a store. He had returned to Manus from Rabaul on the same ship that brought Matbe and other Manus men home. He had spoken to Matbe but could not enlist him in his own efforts. He described Matbe to Schwartz as an individualist and a gambler with little interest in becoming part of a larger endeavour. Paliau went to the store when it opened and predicted its failure within five months. The store was 'wrong' he said. The men who organised it were interested only in their own advancement, he told people, while they allowed their own villages to follow the old ways. In any event, such a small group had too little strength to make any appreciable change in indigenous society. Paliau's prediction that the store would fail proved correct.[6]

From Lorengau, Paliau sent word to Baluan, announcing his impending return and calling on people to build a large meeting house. Three days later he arrived in Baluan. It was impossible to trace all his activities during this initial period of organisation of the Movement. But before presenting the content of Paliau's talks to his rapidly growing group of followers, we will describe Paliau's recruiting method.

Paliau knew how to dramatise himself and his ideas. We noted his attempt to recruit Bonyalo in Chapter 4. Paliau's speech to Bonyalo—as Bonyalo recounted it—illustrates his initial approach. He came to see Bonyalo by canoe. He went straight to Bonyalo without attempting to speak to anyone else in Pere. When Bonyalo asked him why he had come, Paliau showed him his canoe. 'Do you see any cargo on it?' Paliau said. There was none. 'You see', said Paliau, 'I have not come to trade, I have come to talk'. This conversation made such an impression on Bonyalo that he recalled it—or some version of it—when Schwartz spoke with him seven years later. The empty canoe distinguished this visit from the visits of all other Matankor canoes to Manus villages. Having failed to persuade Bonyalo not to leave the village, Paliau invited the people of Pere to come to the meetings on Baluan. But despite Paliau's eloquence, Bonyalo did not promote the event and no one from Pere attended the early Movement meetings.

Napo of Mbukei, who had reached a stalemate in his own village, was ready to join anyone who had a plan that might succeed where his had failed. The men of Mbukei knew that Paliau had returned. They knew he had important plans; but, when they questioned the men of Mok who had already joined Paliau, the Moks would tell them nothing. Paliau had instructed them not to reveal the content of the Baluan meetings. But Napo saw that the Moks no longer wore *laplap* or grass skirts. Subsequently, 30 men of Mbukei went to Baluan in three canoes to try to learn more.

---

6   Indeed, as of 1954 no attempts at small group or private local business enterprise in Manus had succeeded.

Paliau attracted Lungat of Ndriol in the same way. As Lungat told the story, he had visited friends on the islands of Pak and Tong, hoping to find a person with ideas he could use. He had returned to Rambutjo disappointed. Later, a man from Pak who was on his way to Baluan told him, in strictest confidence, that he was going to help build a meeting house in which all men from all villages would gather to discuss the condition of the people of New Guinea. Lungat kept this information to himself until a canoe from Mok arrived one day, seeking sago palm leaves for thatching the new meeting house. Meetings had been going on since Paliau's return, but Lungat could learn nothing specific of the content. He asked one of the crew, who replied, 'I am unable to tell you'. Then Lungat said, 'I think this talk which you are all making at the meetings is the talk of God'. The other, seeing that he knew the truth, replied: 'That is it. It is nothing else. But I cannot tell you more. Whether you come or do not come, it is up to you'. Lungat thought of his two deceased brothers and of how they had appeared to him in a dream and one had made the mark of the cross on his shoulder. He approached another clan brother, Alois Ndreje, who agreed to accompany him to Baluan. They borrowed a canoe and, with their wives and another Ndriol man, Lukas Pomileu, started for Baluan. They took with them an aged woman who wanted to see her relatives. A headwind came up, driving them back to Rambutjo, which they reached just as the canoe was about to sink. Lungat reasoned that the old woman had been thinking about exchanges in which she and her kin were involved and that these thoughts of the old ways had brought the canoe to grief.

That night Lungat's clan brothers returned from Manus Island with their father's big canoe. With this added crew and the larger canoe, and without the old woman and her dangerous thoughts, they set out the next morning. This time there were the five clan brothers: Lungat, Ndreje, Muli, Pomileu, and Wapei, with three of their wives. A strong crosswind brought them to Baluan the following morning. They poled their canoe through shallow waters to Mok, where they tied it to the posts of Lungat's father-in-law's house. Paliau was in Mok, where he was holding meetings on the *arakeu* (a Titan word for the artificial island that served as a platform for work, displaying wealth during ceremonial exchanges, feasting, and dancing). The next morning Lungat went to find Paliau, but he met Paliau coming to him. That morning Paliau had met with Mok's leaders to ask about these men from Rambutjo, who were unknown to him. He asked the Moks who among the men of Ndriol could speak for them and, according to Lungat, they named him. Lungat was pleased. In his account, Lungat enumerated all the other men from Rambutjo who could have been named, most of whom were older. Paliau asked Lungat, 'Why did you come here to Baluan?' Lungat said: 'Yes, Paliau, I didn't come here to find food. I didn't come about the work of our ancestors. I came because I heard of this house you are building. We have come to hear the talk that you will make in this house'. Paliau replied:

> Your thought is a good one. This house belongs to all of us. I intended that it be built only by those who were here in Mok and Baluan, but he who comes from another place by his own volition can come inside. Now that you have come, I will tell you. You know that in the past all the white men have lied to us. All the missionaries have lied to us. They brought the name of Jesus and of his church. They told of his coming to earth, of his work, and of his death for our redemption. But the true talk of Jesus, this they didn't tell us. The inner meaning of the work of Jesus they didn't tell us. But now I have found this. I, myself, have found it.

According to Lungat, Paliau went on to say that the talk Jesus brought when he came among the white men had created great dissension among them. The white men had decided to conceal his message to keep it from reaching black people. It was as if they had wrapped it up, tied it, and encased it in cement. Then the war came and broke open this cement. He was glad that the men of Ndriol had come to hear the truth that he would soon reveal in the meeting house.

Kisakiu of Tawi village, on an islet just off the south coast, gave Schwartz an account of this period that illustrates other aspects of Paliau's recruiting. Kisakiu of Tawi and Manoi of Loitja, a south coast village, were young men. They were not leaders in their villages. They came to Mok in connection with preparations for a feast in Tawi. Mok was already in the Movement. The mood there was conspicuously excited, but the Moks were not talking. One of Kisakiu's mother's brothers told him that Paliau had taught them something, but they were not allowed to reveal it. Kisakiu responded, as Napo and Lungat had, by seeking to join in.

He and Manoi went across to Baluan where they saw the meeting house being built. They decided to see Paliau. Paliau shook hands with them, brought them to his private house, and told his wife to bring them food. Then they sat around a table and talked. Paliau told them that he knew who they were. Then he told them that what he had to say was absolute truth, but that they must want to hear it. They had to join voluntarily, knowing that a great deal of trouble would result from what Paliau would say. Without further explanation, he told them that they might not succeed; but, if they did, they would be all right. That is, they would achieve the envied condition of the whites. Paliau spoke at length to these two young men. Then he asked them if they would help in the 'work'. They agreed and were told: 'You, Manoi, will go look after the people of Loitja. The *luluai* is for the work of the government, whereas your work is to spread this talk [of the Movement] to all the men and women. You, Kisakiu, will be in charge of Tawi'.

Kisakiu and Manoi then returned to Tawi, appointed by Paliau as what were called in the Movement the local *pesman*, a Tok Pisin term translating literally as 'face men' and meaning spokespersons or representatives. (We note again that nouns have no distinct plural form in Tok Pisin. Plurals are formed by adding a modifier. Hence, we will use *pesman* as both singular and plural.) They were to relay Paliau's ideas and lead the Movement within their villages. In Paliau's name they urged discarding the ways of the past. The elders of their villages were unimpressed. Among the younger men, too, some answered that they did not want any change. Kisakiu and Manoi became angry, but others told them that until the government spoke, they would not listen. Kisakiu said he was angry for two months, but his arguments had no further success. Then he and Napo of Mbukei each received a letter from Paliau. Hearing of this, the people of Loitja asked Kisakiu to read his letter to them, but he said that it was addressed to Tawi and could not be read in any other place. In Tawi he waited until after church service on Sunday. The *luluai*, who had opposed Kisakiu, permitted him to read the letter to the village. It said that the meetings had begun and invited Tawi to send people to hear them.

The Tawi people did not want to remain outside now that the meetings were actually happening. The villagers agreed to hasten to complete a big feast that was already scheduled. They reasoned that they could not abandon an event that had been the centre of village activities for almost a year, but they could say that it was to be the last. This would satisfy the old men whose entrepreneurial exchange activities were to culminate in this event. Under similar circumstances twenty years previously Pere had planned the last big feast to include the phallic dancing (in which men swung and twirled the white cowrie shells they wore on their penises) of which the mission strongly disapproved. This done, they had called in the missionaries. Similarly, Napo in Mbukei had brought his local movement to a point at which the village promised to set a date before which all obligations derived from the old system would be met. But Tawi became preoccupied with making its final feast and did not send anyone to the meetings on Baluan. (And the feast was never properly completed, because the Noise broke out before preparations were finished, as described in Chapter 6.)

Only two men from Bunai went to Baluan to attend the meetings: Akustin Tjamilo and his brother Alois Posanau. Paliau invited Samol and anyone else interested from Bunai to come to the meetings, but Samol and most of the other villagers were sceptical. Tjamilo said that Paliau shook slightly when he spoke and that he spoke with great intensity, which impressed him. So when Paliau returned to Baluan, Tjamilo and Posanau followed. Tjamilo described his experience there as the most important in his life. As he saw it, he became a man during the weeks that followed.

The content of the early meetings

Schwartz and Shargo found much agreement on the content of these early meetings among the many people with whom they spoke, down to quite specific details. Most of what follows, however, is derived from conversations with three men who witnessed the meetings and whose accounts were the most complete and detailed: Paliau himself, Lukas of Mok, and Tjamilo of Bunai. Others' accounts confirm that the accounts of these three were either depictions of actual occurrences or widely shared standardised versions.

The meetings started in mid-October 1946. The meeting house planned for Lipan had not yet been built so people gathered on the *arakeu* (the meeting ground) of Mok village. Even after the meeting house in Lipan was nearly completed, many people from Baluan, Mok, and Pwam still gathered at night on Mok. During this early period Paliau travelled from village to village in search of support. Early in November, the talk in the meetings on Mok turned to building the Lipan meeting house. Paliau told of how he had dreamt of such a meeting house when he was in Baluan on his last visit before the war:

> I dreamt of something that rose up almost to the sky. It was very long. There were two things that projected down from the top. They looked like megaphones that are used for shouting. They

> started at the top and came down. It [i.e. this building] was very red. It looked red at the top. It came down, down, down straight upon this piece of ground here near the store [in the centre of Lipan village]. When it came down and reached the ground it looked like a cloth surrounding us. It had taken the form of a building. We were inside and its door was shut. It was a house with a door. I wanted to open the door to go outside, but the door was stuck. I pushed the door three times, but it was as if a man, though it was no man, pushed back. That was all. I found an image here according to which I could make a house.

In a meeting on 6 November 1946, Paliau began by describing his dream and talking about the importance of building the meeting house. God, he said, had sent this dream as he sends all good dreams. We give below a close translation of his speech as Paliau remembered it and as confirmed by Lukas and Tjamilo. It is full of what is called in Tok Pisin *tok piksa*—literally, picture talk—a term that covers parables, extended analogies, and metaphors. Paliau was considered a master of this form of speech. It was occasionally intended to refer indirectly to material well known to insiders in order to conceal the speaker's meaning from outsiders. It could occasionally be used to criticise or accuse a person or group present at a meeting, dramatising the content of the criticism but reducing overt incitement to conflict. Most often, parables were used to make a speech more striking, more memorable, and more convincing. The following account of his speech illustrates Paliau's style of speaking in parables. It also introduces part of the initial ideology of the *Nufela Fasin* (in English, the New Way).

> I pictured a house. I said this house is a good thing. As for the function of this house I said, 'Look at the framework of this house, all these timbers are the bones of this house; they are like the bones of human beings. This beam that rests at the top of the house is like our backbone. These, which form the sides, are like our ribs. The bones of the side are attached to the backbone. The floor inside the house is like the abdomen of men. The part of the house that has the front ladder is like the head of a man. There is a door in the other part that is like the anus of a man. The windows of this house are like the ears and nose by which a man gets his breath. The posts that support the house are like the legs and arms of a man. Everything that is inside the house is like all the organs and the heart of a man. Why is it that everything in the house is just like everything in a man? The part of the house that is like the anus of a man has another door that leads to the cook house.

The door near the house ladder is like the mouth of a man; as it leads back to the door of the cook house, it is like the bowels of a man. All the fastenings that bind the house together are like the muscles, ligaments, tendons, and blood vessels of our bodies'.

Everything for building a good house is needed also for making a good man. Who does this building? It is God himself who builds men. He knows that you and I, who are men, cannot sleep unprotected on the ground or the sea; we must sleep in houses. His building is to build the souls of we men that sleep within our bodies, which are their houses. If our bodies are broken, our souls have no houses and must go back to God, our father. Why? The breath of the souls of men is the breath of his mouth. While our souls are inside our bodies, these are their houses. But where are our bodies to sleep? The house is like the skin of the body. If our bodies had no house, we couldn't sleep. Would our bodies sleep under stones? No! Would they sleep on the water or on the ground? No! They must stay in houses, to protect them from the rain, to hide them from the sun. That is why we live in houses. When we talk, do we talk under a stone or do we sit down to talk on the water, or do we just sit on the ground? No, we must make a house in which men can talk. We must go inside to discuss what good way of life there is for us to follow that will make us and our villages all right. If we want to talk about anything on earth, if there is a place where we can talk, to straighten out the ways of our villages, this is good. But if one village does not have a meeting house, but talks round and about in every part of the lagoon or in the bush, this is not right. This place cannot be made all right. Why? Because all men and everything on the earth are, as I have said in this story about a house, all are only the buildings of God, the father of all.

The pattern for our work already exists on earth in the bodies of men. If we think intensely about God, our father, if all of our ways that are no good are thrown out, he is one who will have compassion on us, his children. He can make our heads become clear with good thoughts. With these good thoughts that will come to us, we can find good work and a good way of life. Only the meeting house will make us all right. It was like this with Jesus, whose name we have heard over and over, when he was on earth and went from place to place talking; sometimes he spoke here and there in the open, and sometimes he went inside a house to make some important talk to all men. He taught that that which is no good must be cast aside and not practised by us. He said we must think about and follow that which is good. He showed us that he was God, father of all of us. It is the same now. We must make a meeting house. We must think in it, we must meet in it. All of our ways that are no good, we must cast aside.

Paliau continued proclaiming the necessity of breaking with the ways of the ancestors. He argued that they had learned much from the whites. The government taught about the ways of the body and of the law and the word of God dealt with the spirit. But, said Paliau, if we combine the ways of the whites with those of our ancestors only death and ruination can result: 'The talk of God is like a sorcery charm. If you speak the word of God and you think good thoughts and do good things with it, that is all right. But if you mix the words of God with the evil ways of your ancestors, this will ruin you'.

To clarify Paliau's comparison of God's word as a sorcery charm: successfully performing many kinds of magic in the Admiralties required (and still requires) refraining from particular kinds of behaviour. The magic does good as long as people avoid the proscribed behaviour; otherwise it can result in death. So, people were unable to unleash the power of Christianity to make them 'all right' because they mixed it with the remnants of the old culture. Paliau frequently emphasised this idea and a large number of his followers often acted as though mixing Christianity with the old culture was not only ineffective but lethally wrong.

All who told Schwartz and Shargo of the meetings agreed that a central idea was that the first task for the Movement was thoroughly revising Christianity as taught by the missions. In the early meetings, Paliau expounded for the first time a story aiming to do this. He called this the 'Long Story of God'. Otto (1992a: 63) aptly calls this a historical cosmology—a description we will use again—that 'integrates cosmology and history'. Each new recruit to the Movement was told to learn it. Some learned it virtually verbatim simply by hearing it over and over again. Those who were literate wrote it out in the school exercise books that were the staple village stationery of the period.

The 'Long Story of God'

Tjamilo arrived in Lipan when the meeting house was almost completed and he attended the first meeting there. There was a platform in the middle of the floor on which Paliau stood when he spoke. Six of his more important followers sat behind him on a bench on the platform. As Tjamilo recalled, Paliau began his first rendition of the 'Long Story of God' as follows:

> A very long time ago God existed in the mists. [In Tok Pisin, this is '*God i stap insait long sno*'. *Sno*, pronounced like the English 'snow', denotes clouds that are indistinct or the mist that obscures a distant island.] We know of no mother or father for him. Heaven and earth did not yet exist. God was one and alone. The mists in which he stayed were cold. Then God thought. When he thought, the heavens opened up. When the heavens were made, he thought and brought the sun. Second, he thought and brought the moon. Third, he thought and the stars came. Now he created all the angels. All these angels were incorporeal. [We translate the Tok Pisin term *win nating*, that is, nothing but air or wind—as incorporeal.] They were the same as God. They stayed with him in Heaven. Then God thought and created the earth. First, he made stone. Then he made the ground. Then he made the grass. The grass was for firm ground. He made trees that were good. They grew unattended. The ground was brown. He put all the fish in the sea. Then he made the birds. He made cows and pigs. He also made the seas. When all this was ready, God thought and created Adam and Eve. Adam and Eve came down into Paradise. They were not human yet. One slept in one place and the other slept in another place. Their bodies were not fixed to their bones yet. Now God made the flesh to go on their bones. But they were still not human yet. They slept on the ground. God blew a little of his breath into their mouths and told them to rise.

At this point Lukas of Mok's version has God speak as follows:

> This is an order to you people of the earth. You two represent all people. I made you two first as the parents of all the people of earth. If you two are all right, all people will be all right. If you are wrong, all people must be wrong. Now I bring all the prophets upon the earth. The prophets cannot be born of the womb of a woman. They come from the strength of God. Now God spoke to Adam and Eve: 'You two live under my first order. You, Adam, you must stay at a distance. You, Eve, you must stay at a distance. Your house is ready. You two must go into the house. The rain can wash and the sun can burn everything in Paradise, but you two must live in a house. Still you must keep your distance from one another. You Adam, you stay to this side; you, Eve, you stay to this side. If you think, your thought will come to me, God, your

father. You have only to think and a child can appear to you. You, Adam, if you want a son, a son can appear. You, Eve, if you want a daughter, a daughter can appear. But you two must stay apart. If your belief is in me, God your father, you can have children. Food also can appear. Now you are living according to my first order. Now, for all the prophets that are created at the same time as you, you two are the face for all of them. Just as you two can think, so they can think, and whatever they desire can appear out of nothing for them. All right, you two stay here and I will go back to Heaven'.

Adam and Eve stayed in Paradise. Whatever they desired appeared for them. It was the same for the prophets. They lived in accordance with God's law. But after a short time some of the angels were envious of God. The First Angel thought: 'Why do we have to obey the talk of God? What is he and what are we? He is pure spirit; we are also pure spirit'.

One can say the close equivalent of 'he is pure spirit' in several ways in Tok Pisin. Paliau's followers used the following phrases most often: *em i no got mit* (*mit* is pronounced like the English meat; *em i no got mit* means 'he has no flesh'), or *em i win nating* (he is nothing but wind/breath/air), or *em i tingting tasol*. The Tok Pisin word *tingting* can be a verb meaning to think as well as a noun meaning roughly thought, mind, or spirit. Paliau and his adherents used *tingting* to convey all these, as well as such Movement concepts as the creative power of mind.

[The angels thought] 'when he [i.e. God] thinks, everything that he thinks of comes up through the power of his thought. It is the same with us also. Then why should we obey him?' God was not in their company. He was in another part of Heaven. But God is a true God. Why? Because he created all of them. He could perceive their thoughts. He asked them: 'Why do you speak ill of me among yourselves? It is true that you are incorporeal and I, too, am incorporeal. But you are angels and I am the one who created you. Now that you have envied me, I must divide you'. Then he divided them into two halves [one led by the rebellious angel, Lucifer, and the other led by the loyal Michael]. God said: 'All of you who are in Lucifer's group, get out. You who are in Michael's group, you must cast out all these angels who aren't good. They shall wander about in all places. Now all of you who belong to Michael's line will remain in Heaven. You will stay with me. You are my true followers'.

Shortly after this, one of the bad angels whom God had cast out came down to Adam and Eve.

Lukas's version differs from Tjamilo's here. Whereas Tjamilo, whose version we are following, gives a 'bad angel' the task of tempting Adam and Eve, Lukas gives this job to a snake or serpent, as does the Bible.

> He came to tempt them. He said: 'Now you two live under God's first order. Now today, if you listen to me you can be a spirit just like God. If you do not listen to me you will be in the wrong'. While he was still at a distance he projected these thoughts. Why? Because God had not taken away his power of mind [which was like that of God's thought] ... [The bad angel] looked into their minds and said: 'Adam has a better mind; Eve has a lesser mind. If I approach Eve, I will succeed, but if I try Adam I won't. He is a man and has the stronger mind'. Then he came to Eve, and he said: 'You two must lie together and copulate, then you will be like God. If you don't listen to me, I think you will not succeed in becoming like God'.

> Eve heard the talk of the evil angel. She aroused the desires of Adam who came to her. Adam could not resist because his desires were one with hers. He consented. The angel shouted in exultation from a distance. Adam went on top of Eve and the angel exulted because they had sinned. God already knew this. He came and called to them. They had run away and hidden. God called to them. They came. God spoke: 'Now you two have sinned. Now I retract my first order to you. You have followed the talk of Satan. You are his now. You have lost my favour. Now the First Order of things is revoked. All the prophets and the earth, too, are in the wrong. You two stood for all people of the world. Now that you are wrong, they are wrong with you. Now you will have hard work all the time. You, Eve, you belong to Adam. He will come to you. You two must work hard to have children. You, Eve, you must cry out and you must suffer pain as well. The child will be in your womb; you will cry and you will know pain'.[7]

---

7   According to the 'Long Story', maintaining the paradisiacal First Order of God required sexual abstinence. This is not, of course, the orthodox Christian interpretation of the original sin, the cause of humankind's fall from grace. Rather, the original sin was disobedience to God. The 'Long Story', however, states explicitly that intercourse was the sin and it elaborates on this theme. This is consistent with strict indigenous Manus sexual morality, but sexual intercourse as the original sin is also an idea common among Anglo-American Christians. Paliau could easily have absorbed it from contact with members of the white colonial population, including Catholic missionaries.

Note that 'first order' appears to have two closely related meanings: God's first instructions to Adam and Eve and the paradisiacal state of things before Adam and Eve disobeyed those instructions. The second meaning, however, rapidly became dominant in the Movement.

Again, Lukas's version contains a detail not in Tjamilo's. He includes an interaction between God and Eve, as follows, that is the beginning of shame. Following Adam's and Eve's sinning, God called to Eve, but she said she could not respond because she had no grass skirt. God asked her who told her about grass skirts. 'The snake', Eve said. Then God banished the snake from Paradise to live in the unsanctified bush. But shame had come among men and women. We now continue with Tjamilo's version.

> 'You, Adam [God said], now I will tell you what your work is to be. You must find food. If you work hard and long in your gardens you will have food. Now, you two get out. I no longer want to see you'. Before there was sin on earth, God would appear to the prophets. He would speak to them and they could speak to God. They knew all about the heavens above because they could talk to God. Now God was hidden from them. Everything was wrong on the earth now. All the prophets, who had been created with the earth, fought and quarrelled among themselves now. They could not know God their father now. He had hidden himself. The prophets scattered over the earth. Each went to stay in a place of his own. Each said that he was king of his territory. Everyone made war everywhere in the world. The world was completely wrong now.

Lukas, in his account, elaborated on the period after the Fall, equating it with the condition of the people of New Guinea before the coming of the whites. There was incessant warfare and great hardship. Men no longer knew God, as they had in the First Order. They worshipped many idols and devils. They thought that they had originated in stones, or trees, or animals. In Tjamilo's version, there follows a brief reference to the story of Cain and Abel; how Cain slew his brother Abel, after which God smeared Cain's forehead with the blood of Abel and condemned him to roam the world in misery. In Tjamilo's version, death in the world originated in this fratricide. In other versions, death is one of the results of the sin of Adam and Eve. Tjamilo's account continues the story:

> Now God saw that the earth was full of evil ... God sent a flood to all places. God told Noah: 'You must make a big ark. Then you must gather together your brothers, your fowls and pigeons.

My word is with you. If people do not listen to your message, you must go into this ark and you must go far away. All these other people will remain'. Now God sent the great flood upon them. Some people clung to the branches of trees. Some stayed on the ground and died. Those who climbed trees were struck by the tidal wave and fell. Now God watched. He thought of the world. He said: 'What will I do? I wanted to put an end to the world, but after all, who is it that created these men? No, I think I will send Jesus down'.

Now Jesus was given the power of his father. He came to earth together with 12 of his angels. These 12 angels were his councillors. They surrounded Jesus, who was their chairman. [In telling the story in the 1950s, Tjamilo used terms for positions of authority—councillors and chairman—that were not used in Manus in 1946.] He sent the angel Gabriel who went ahead to Maria. Maria was a German white woman. [The idea that Maria was a German is found only in Tjamilo's account. Others identify Maria simply as a white woman—a *misis*; that is, a Mrs, as New Guineans of the day had been taught to address white women in Tok Pisin.] The angels came down to Maria in Germany. Gabriel spoke to her, 'Maria, soon you will give birth to Jesus Redeemer, who will bring order to the earth'. Maria answered: 'I have no husband. How am I to give birth to Jesus?' Gabriel replied, 'It is through the power of God that you will give birth to Jesus Redeemer'. Maria consented: 'It is all right. I am just a woman. If it is the will of God to give him to me, that is good. But I am unworthy'. Now Jesus came down into the womb of Maria. Then everyone said to Joseph, 'Joseph, you brought this child into the womb of Maria'. Joseph denied it: 'We were not lovers. Why do you lie about me?' Then Joseph watched Maria. Maria took her ladle to fetch water from the well. Joseph followed her. He carried an axe to kill her. Then Gabriel appeared. He laid his hand on the handle of the axe saying, 'You cannot kill Maria and the child that is in her womb'. The angel threw down the axe from Joseph's hand: 'This child in the womb of Maria is not yours, Joseph. It belongs to God. Its name is Jesus Redeemer. He is to save the world which is full of evil. This child Jesus, you must watch over him. You must take care of Maria and the child that is in her. You two are not to marry. It is not your child. It is a sign to all the people of the earth. You must watch over him'. When the child was big in Maria and her time was finished an angel came to them telling them to take the child, Jesus, and go to a stable for sheep. Maria obeyed and brought Jesus to the house of the sheep. She laid Jesus on the half-shell from which the sheep usually ate, but first she covered it with a cloth. [Shells of giant clams (*Tridacna*) are sometimes used as containers in Manus.] While Jesus slept all the people who cared for the sheep came to worship him. An angel talked to all people saying: 'All of you go quickly. Maria has already given birth to Jesus the Redeemer. Everyone must go to see him and shake hands with him'. Some people worshipped him truly and knelt. Some people walked by on the road and scoffed. They said: 'He is small and insignificant. Why do you men come to obey him? You and I are already the kings of the earth, but he, what did he come for?' But the men who knelt said, 'He is the true child of God'. Their belief told them that he was the Son of God. He is the Redeemer to teach all men of the world.

In telling the story both Lukas and Paliau explain at this point why Jesus chose to come to earth via being born to Maria: it was to demonstrate to all people the dual nature of their being. All people are both *tingting* and *mit*; that is, all are both mind/thought and flesh, God and man.

Tjamilo's account continues:

When Jesus was a little older and stronger, Maria and Joseph brought him to the house of worship in Jerusalem. They showed Jesus to Simeon and Anna. [The Gospel of Luke tells of how Simeon and Anna each recognised Jesus as the Messiah when he was still a child. Here, Tjamilo gives his version of Paliau's version of this portion of the New Testament.] All the other prophets who had lived on the earth had died. The name of Christ had preceded him [to Jerusalem]. Johannes [that is, John the Baptist] had brought it. When people asked Johannes, he would tell them: 'I am just a man who cries out in the wilderness. Christ is yet to come. I am not Christ'. Now Simeon and Anna heard this from Johannes. They said that they wanted to see Christ before they died. They waited and waited. Finally, Maria and Joseph carried Jesus to Jerusalem. Now Anna and Simeon said to Jesus: 'We have seen you, Christ. We are very old; our eyes are nearly blind. We have looked upon you; we shake hands with you; now we can die'. Soon they died. When Jesus was in the house of worship in Jerusalem, he raised two of his fingers and said: 'I am God and I am man. All the men of the earth are God and man. My mind comes from God, my father. The minds of you people of the earth come also from God, our father. My body came from the womb of Maria. It is the same as your bodies which come from the wombs of your mothers'.[8] Jesus did not say this with his mouth. He was not old enough yet. He thought these words. Jesus stayed in Jerusalem for 30 years. When he was a man he did the work of a carpenter. He took a plank. Joseph gave him a saw. He sawed the plank saying, 'I have come first as a carpenter; I will be carpenter to all the people of the world'.

When his 30 years were finished and he had become a fully grown man, he travelled around to all the places of the Jews. [Tjamilo would have had only a murky notion of who the Jews were.] He took with him this big book the Bible. With his 12 apostles he went among the Jews. When Jesus spoke in a place, what did he say? Jesus said people should not be angry. They should not quarrel and fight. 'I am Jesus. I have come down because of all these ways of men. Everyone must listen and obey. All the ways of your ancestors from the past, now, at this time, you must be rid of them. I, Jesus, have come to take the lead in this. I, Jesus, I am like a dividing line; the sin of Adam and Eve lies behind me. I have come to the fore. All people must follow me, Jesus alone. The wrongs of Adam and of the angels lie behind me. I have come forward to teach all men. There must be no more dissension, no more fighting, no more struggle over land. It is because of things of this sort that I have come.' Whatever Jesus did or said in any place, his apostles wrote down. Jesus continued to work among the Jews. He taught continually and worked hard, very hard.

In describing some of the events in the life of Jesus, Lukas gives particular emphasis to curing the sick. Jesus accomplished this by sending his thoughts to God. Jesus said, 'You too, if you send your thoughts to God to cure the sickness of another man, you can succeed'. Lukas compares the work of Jesus to gardening: Jesus went from place to place clearing the ground and planting a garden. By the time he finished work at the next place, the previous place would be overgrown. The people of that place would have abandoned the good ways that he had shown them and returned to the ways of their ancestors. Tjamilo's account continues:

> When Jesus had finished his work, he looked over the world at the thinking of people everywhere. Some places were all right, some were not all right yet. Jesus knew that soon he would be killed. How did he know? Because he was both God and man. He knew

8   Aletta Biersack (personal communication) points out the clear identification here of men with mind (sacred), and of women with flesh (profane). Variations of the notion that women are dangerous to men's health and men's magical power are common in Melanesia.

that his day was near. He said, 'These parts that are not all right yet, when I die I can pay for them'. [Tjamilo used the Tok Pisin verb *paim*, which can mean both to pay and to buy. In this context, redeem would also be a plausible translation.] All the men of Juda caught Jesus now. [Tjamilo's recital betrays a murky conception of the meaning of Juda—the people of Judah, as we would write it in English today—that was common in Manus at the time. It was often used to refer to the people of a country called Judah, but there are contexts in which people extended its meaning to whites generally, and to white government functionaries specifically. It was not necessarily used as a synonym for Jews.] They pulled him along the road. They beat him. They said to him: 'What are you now? You are nothing but a boy. There are already mighty men in the world. Now you who come later, do you think that you will be king of the world?' They mocked him. They spit in his eye. But Jesus was not angry. He didn't return their talk. Jesus delivered himself into the hands of the policemen. They had made ready a cross of wood. Now they bound John Brown at the left hand of Jesus. [Paliau or his followers may have heard from American soldiers about John Brown, depicted as a martyr to the cause of abolishing slavery in America in the song 'John Brown's Body'. We know that many Manus people were familiar with the song.] Jesus was on the right. They put Jesus onto the cross on top of the mountain, Korokata [that is, Golgotha]. They put two nails in his arms and two nails in his legs. They bound thorny vines around his head. The leader of the police cried out loudly: 'Nail him to the wooden cross! Nail him to the wooden cross!' Then they put a spear into his breast. Maria and Joseph were nearby under the cross. Maria brought water to him, but the police threw it out. Jesus hung now from the cross. At three o'clock he died. He cried out to God, his father: 'My power is finished now. I have given my spirit and my body'. Then he died.

They put Jesus into his grave and stationed guards to watch over it. They were afraid that Maria and her women would steal his body and then spread the lie that Jesus had arisen from the grave. The guards stood watch. When Jesus was still alive, he had said, 'After three days I will arise again'. The men who had killed him scoffed. They said: 'What kind of talk is this? The prophets of old died and did not arise again. What man can die and then return?' When three days had passed, Jesus arose again from his grave. His light appeared and the earth shook. Now all the police near the grave were thrown down. When they got up, each said, 'Jesus is my

God, my master'. But Jesus answered them, saying: 'Why, when you saw me before, did you seize me? You said that I lied. Now I don't believe you'.

Then Jesus called for Thomas. 'Come touch the place of the nails and of the spear.' Thomas came close to him. He touched the wounds made by the nails and the spear. Then he spoke: 'It is true, it is true, my God, my master. Now I see you and I believe'. But Thomas had been one of Jesus's men. When pressure was brought against Jesus, the Jews had asked Thomas, 'Are you or are you not a follower of Jesus?' Thomas had answered that he was not one of Jesus's men. This was his lie. Now that he saw Jesus had risen from the grave, he believed. But Jesus was both God and man. He understood all this. He said, 'If I do not die, I think my word will last only until the sun goes down'. Jesus knew the intentions of the Jews. They wanted to confine his message to the house of worship in Jerusalem. They said, 'We must kill him together with his teachings, which must not be allowed to get out to all parts of the world'. But Jesus was God and he was man. He knew. At this time the advent of the law of Jesus was near. He told his apostles, all 12 of them: 'Bring my word everywhere from sunup to sundown. [Sunup and sundown are meant not only in the temporal sense but also in the spatial sense, in which the phrase means the entire world. In the 1950s, many Manus people thought of the sun coming up in the east among the whites and setting somewhere just west of Manus. Many also still thought of the world as a kind of inverted bowl, with islands scattered around an expanse of water enclosed by the dome of the sky.] Bring it to every place where God, my father, put people'. The apostles heard this from Jesus. Then Jesus left them to return to his father in Heaven. Now all the apostles wanted to bring the word of Jesus to us. But all the Juda they blocked this talk. The government said: 'You cannot bring this message to the native. If you do, we will cut your throats. Why? Because we have police and soldiers, you must obey us. You cannot spread these ideas. Wait, you must submit these laws of Jesus to an assembly. You must alter the book. The real talk of Jesus must be omitted. Instead, you must use talk picture. For the sake of deception, this must be made into a different book. You missionaries can take with you another book, but the true Bible must remain here. This book that changes the talk of Jesus will be passed off on the New Guineans'.

The 'Long Story of God' depicts events in the life of Jesus as happening in a distant land ruled by the Judah, the identity of whom, as noted above, is not clear. (Tjamilo, Lukas, and many other followers of Paliau equated the Judah with the authorities who killed Jesus.) Subsequently, the missionaries were either prevented from or unwilling to fulfil Jesus's intentions by proffering his teaching to New Guineans. Therefore, since the death of Jesus—an event many of Paliau's followers and other Manus people placed from three to six generations in the past—New Guineans had remained isolated, without access to the true teachings of Jesus, suffering the hard life that had been their lot since the sin of Adam and Eve. Some of Paliau's followers thought that with the coming of Jesus the whites had returned to the First Order of God, sometimes called the Number One Order, but this idea does not appear in the 'Long Story of God'.

The Long Story does not stop with the death of Jesus but continues into the present. Paliau told his listeners that God now felt compassion for the native again. He sent the sailing ships from Europe, Germany, and England. Captain Cook went from island to island leaving the markers of the government. (Paliau knew Cook to be English; Tjamilo called him German.) Then God sent the Germans, who brought law and government. They set up *luluai* in each village, with military-style hats and special sticks as their badges of office. The Germans banned warfare. They used the natives to clear plantations and work copra. With them came the Christian missionaries, but Tjamilo, in his telling of the 'Long Story of God', gave them little credit for improving New Guineans' lives. He continued:

> The Germans taught us nothing. They were here for many years. Now God said: 'They must get out. They must go back. They have used men as if they were trucks. Men are men'. All right, now he turned his thoughts towards Australia. Australia came and replaced Germany. They went on and on but didn't teach the native anything. The Australians treated the natives like oxen. Now God said that they must get out. Then God considered Japan. Now the Japanese came in the war and took Manus. The Japanese did not show us the road; instead they killed many people. God told them to clear out. 'All right', God thought, 'Each country that I tried was inadequate. They didn't show people the real road to me, God. Why? Because all the people of earth are only human. I made three loaves of bread. One was brown, one was white, and one was black. The pay for two of the loaves has come. I have seen

it. The pay for the black bread has not arrived … Did they throw it into a hole or what?' Now the man who made the bread [that is, God] thought about it. 'I will go take a look. Did the bread all burn up, or is some of it left?' All right, the man who was boss over this bread saw that a part of it still remained. Part had fallen upon America. Now Jesus said: 'You must go. I want to try you, America. I have already tried all other countries. Take my flag, take all this food and all these ships and go. Never mind Japan; you can defeat them. This flag of mine is the flag of the black men, you will fight under it'.

Japan came now to fight, but America came later. Jesus came ahead of them. He came as lightning and as an aeroplane marked with a cross. Now he came to Paliau in Rabaul. He had searched all over Manus without finding a single man whose mind was straight. He came down now to Paliau in Rabaul. America came after Jesus. America wanted to bring all these things straight to us, the natives of Manus. America wanted to show us the road that would make us all right. They kept in mind the words of Jesus. But the Australians blocked them. They put sentries along the road. They said to us, 'You cannot go to the Americans, stay at a distance'. Now the Americans did not speak to us. They returned to their own country. Everything they left, the Australians took. America did not forget the talk of Jesus, but the Australians kept them from us. Now God watched. These men who are with us now [the Australians], will they help us or not? We are watching. If they do not help us but continue to keep us down, then there will be another country that will come. Why? Because God has not forgotten the Territory of New Guinea. Soon he will get rid of them all.

The preceding account gives the 'Long Story of God' as Paliau presented it in the first meetings on Baluan in 1946, as recalled in 1953 by principal figures in the Movement (although parts of it seem to relate too closely to later phases of the Movement to have been part of the story in 1946). Tjamilo, on whose memory Schwartz relied heavily, was the main promulgator of the content of the Baluan meetings along the south coast. Whatever his particular distortions may be, they became the accepted version for a large part of the area affected by the Movement. His version also coincides very closely, and in many places exactly, with Lukas of Mok's version. What is given above is skeletal. Adherents of the Movement could add to it many other stories taken from mission teachings and additional twists and interpretations. Most of the adults who believed in the revision of Christian doctrine purveyed by the Movement (beginning with the 'Long Story of God') were also able to give the orthodox Catholic or Lutheran versions. They regarded these as the *tok piksa* of the mission, designed after the death of Christ to keep the truth of the Christian revelation from New Guineans. But Paliau had now upended the missionary effort to conceal the truth. Angered by the continued failure of the white men to share his teachings with New Guineans, Jesus had come directly to Paliau.

The Movement interpretation of Christianity

The 'Long Story of God' tells of a conspiracy between Christian missions and the colonial government to keep the natives ignorant of the truth of God and Christ.[9] Worse yet, the missionaries were teaching partial truths and false beliefs. The Bible the missionaries gave to New Guineans was not the true Bible but one in which the truth was disguised.[10] Hence, New Guineans often failed to discard old ways that were incompatible with true Christianity, which led to disease and death. Christianity in error is portrayed as more dangerous than unadulterated pre-Christian ways. To reveal the truth of the Bible, Paliau had to see past the teachings of the missionaries.

Paliau and his principal followers said the teachings of the mission were filled with lies and unexplained talk picture. Here, paraphrased, is one of the more important purported missionary lies and the Movement response: what did the missionaries mean when they said that the door of Heaven was closed, some Movement adherents asked. The missionaries never explained and we never questioned them, began the Movement reply. Now we have found its meaning. The closed door means that humans beings were barred from knowledge. But there is no actual door. But now Paliau is helping us to know the truth. When the angels and the

---

9   Otto (1992c: 442), following Gramsci (1971), describes the 'Long Story of God' as 'structured by a series of negations: It is anti-tradition, anti-mission and anti-government'. The latter two negations stand out most dramatically, but regarding the Long Story's anti-tradition character, Otto clarifies that 'the traditional indigenous culture is equated with the situation of all humankind after the fall'.

10   Such ideas were common among indigenous people in much of the Territory at the time. A full catalogue of relevant ethnography would fill many pages.

first humans were arrogant and thought they were equal to God, he made their *tingting* insufficient. People lived in ignorance of one another and of God. The white men had been given knowledge, but they continued to withhold this knowledge from the native. That was the meaning of 'the door of Heaven is closed'. This applies also to the key to Heaven that God put into the hand of Petrus (that is, St Peter). What kind of key is this that the missionary speaks of? It is not a key. It is the human mind. As long as men cling to the ways of the past and follow all of the bad ways of their fathers, their minds are closed and this key remains unturned in the lock. But now we have found the meaning of the key. Our minds must be cleared of the ways of Lucifer. We must think of God, then our minds will open. We will be all right. Now this key is in the hand of Paliau. It is just like the key that God gave to Petrus, but it is not a real key, it is knowledge. Paliau has gone ahead in finding knowledge. He holds the key that will open the door for us.

Paliau and his followers re-examined all mission teaching and practice in this manner. Followers of the Movement also rejected the need for confession to Catholic priests. They argued that confession could not purge people of their sins; therefore, purporting that it did led to natives dying for their unpurged sins. The only effective procedure when you have committed a wrong against another man, said Paliau, was to resolve it and to shake hands. Only this could prevent illness and death.[11]

Paliau did not overtly advocate breaking with the mission in the early days of the Movement, but his criticism of missionary teachings amounted to virtually the same thing. Nor did he advise his followers not to attend Catholic services. Yet when Paliau and others spoke of the lies of the missionaries, Schwartz and Shargo could hear the anger in their voices. This anger, however, cohabited with profound attachment to Christianity more broadly conceived. Paliau and his followers believed that the truth of Christianity had enabled the whites to rise to their present status. But if accepting Christianity and adhering to one or another of the local missions for decades had not brought them appreciably nearer to the condition of the whites, then it must be because they had not been given

---

11 Belief that unresolved anger or social conflict can cause illness is common in Melanesia, although even within a single community people may have different ideas of how this works. Whereas in Paliau's version, God or the spirit of a dead ancestor may punish anger with illness, Smith (1994) illustrates with case studies a belief common in Kragur village, East Sepik Province, in the 1970s, that the ghosts of a person's dead ancestors may act as agents of his or her anger, making the object of the anger ill.

the real thing. Death and sickness resulted from a defective relationship with God. Yet, Manus people said, the arrival of the missions had not led to fewer deaths; in fact, many claimed that more people were dying. It was thus clear that the missionaries were deliberately withholding true Christianity.

One of his followers attributed to Paliau the belief that the multiplicity of missions was also part of the conspiracy to maintain the backwardness of New Guineans. Why were there three different missions in Manus and still others elsewhere in Melanesia? Why did the Catholics denounce the Seventh-day Adventists as enemies of Christ, while the Seventh-day Adventists called the Catholics 'the beasts of Rome'? Obviously, there could be only one truth, but the missions divided the truth among them so that no indigenous member of any one mission could learn the whole truth. In their own land, this critic speculated, the whites must have only one church.

In practice, most of the doctrinal differences among the missions meant little to the people of Manus. They had generally affiliated with whichever mission arrived first in their vicinity, or they had chosen one that taught in Tok Pisin rather than in the local vernacular, or they had chosen one that taught in the local vernacular rather than in Tok Pisin. Most of Paliau's early adherents (of which the majority were Titan) had been nominally Catholic before joining the Movement, and many continued to regard themselves as such, despite the conviction that the missionaries were hiding the true faith from them. Hence, they regarded the motives of the missionary representatives of the Catholic and other Christian faiths with deep suspicion. Why would a missionary leave a comfortable home in Germany, Ireland, or America to spend six to eight years at an isolated mission station? Paliau declared in the early Movement meetings that 'the native is the copra of the missionary'. He suggested that missionaries got paid according to the number of converts they made or how many natives were under their supervision.

But there was another possibility, not necessarily contradictory. Some reasoned that Christ had established the missions to bring his word to the natives. The colonial government, however, prevented the missionaries from doing so. The government, they reasoned, was the lineal descendant of the men who had killed Christ and all the apostles, and it threatened the missionaries with a similar fate if they brought the real Bible to New Guineans. Even the Americans who had been sent to bring the truth had failed the New Guineans. There was no other channel now for the truth of Christianity; they would have to rely on direct revelation and experimentation. Paliau had brought the beginnings of knowledge. Once they got rid of the vestiges of the old culture, still more would be opened up to them.

An important aspect of the effort to find the truth of Christianity was developing the concept of the *tingting* in a way that joined the metaphysical and the material. The *tingting*, Movement thinkers determined, derives from God. It is God in each person; in this sense, all people are like Jesus, both God and man. The body is the house of the *tingting*. In death the body is like an uninhabited house and it is left to decay. In life the house must be a suitable residence for the *tingting*, so it must be kept in good condition. As in Paliau's parable, the house is like the body. Its front door is the mouth, its back door is the anus. Its windows are the eyes, ears, and nose. Paliau emphasised that anger—either overt or covert hostility—disturbed the equilibrium of the *tingting*. Lukas of Mok recalled Paliau's discourse on the subject:

> If you had no mouth or no anus, when your ears admitted something that provoked you, anger would remain within you. How could it get out? When you are angry inside, your mouth has to express it, it must get it out. Then the wind of this anger will escape. But if you keep your mouth fastened, the anger remains in your thoughts. This makes you sick. It is the same as with your body, if you eat a great deal your stomach will be filled up. If the road to your anus is blocked, this food cannot get out. You will become sick. If it goes out, you will be all right. God made everything to work this way. If you block the path of your thoughts, if your mind is clogged by bad thoughts, and if you don't talk it out, you will be sick and you will die … Mind cannot win over the body, body cannot win over the mind. The two are different, but inseparable. The *tingting* can go to another island, but the body is heavy, it cannot follow.

Health and life thus depend on the care of body and the *tingting*. People sometimes spoke of the relationship between sickness and the *tingting* as if disturbance in the latter automatically produced the sickness. At other times they made the more complex statement that when a person thinks or acts in bad ways, God is immediately aware and, in his anger, produces the body's illness. Those who either cleave to the good or who straighten out their *tingting* when they go wrong can live to be old. When their backs are bent, their eyes are blind, and their teeth are gone, then they can die, their age testifying to their virtue. If someone dies young, a wrong that has not been corrected is involved. A child, not yet responsible for its own *tingting*, can suffer sickness or death for its parents' sins.

Such concepts of the *tingting* were to ramify widely throughout Paliau's design of a new culture. The old life was permeated with bad ways. The laws of the new society were like a series of rules for a healthy life. The relationship between sickness and the state of the *tingting* was to be one of the main sanctions of the new society. But *tingting* was even broader in its meaning. It was also knowledge and understanding. Paliau did not say that his knowledge was complete and final. From the beginning of the Movement, he spoke of the need to find and to try new *tingting*. Even so, Paliau's ideas mixing metaphysics and mental hygiene were only one part of the guide to building a new way of life he offered.

The plan for reorganising society

Immediately on returning to Manus after the war, Paliau began to establish a new political structure, hoping to unite all the people of Manus. He had little precedent on which to draw. In the old world, Titan, Matankor, and Usiai were sharply divided, though their ecological differentiation made them economically interdependent (an interdependence which, we have seen, they elaborated through economic specialisation). Further, neither Usiai nor Matankor were united by a shared language, as the Titan-speaking lagoon dwellers were. Few villages of any ethnicity had populations of more than 300, and even the smallest villages rarely acted collectively. Within a village, the patrilineal clans had considerable scope for autonomous action. But there were virtually no enduring political institutions above the village level. The ability of important men to exert influence depended in part on hereditary rank, but it depended even more on constantly validating status through success in trade, feasting, and exchange. Economic relations between villages of different linguistic groups followed the lines of traditional trade partnerships, or occasionally the lines of marriages between people of different linguistic groups, although such marriages violated the generally preferred practice of linguistic group endogamy.

Sometimes more prominent *luluai* exerted influence on villages other than their own, but only informally. The Australian administration saw a need for native officials who had superior authority over village *luluai* and who could arbitrate inter-village disputes. In postwar Manus, there were two such paramount *luluai*, Sebaso on the north coast and Kisekup on the south coast. These *luluai* mediated between the many small and dispersed villages and the centralised administration, but without fundamentally altering the horizontal relationships among villages.

Paliau sought to build new, larger units. He tried to reverse the process of schism that maintained the settlement pattern described in Chapter 3. He attacked all the dividing lines of native society as inimical to a life similar to that of Europeans. 'Although the bodies of men have many parents', he said, 'the *tingting* of all men have only one source in God'. The meeting house symbolised the new unity. He himself was a Matankor of Lipan village, but he identified strongly with the Titan-speaking Manus and was particularly anxious to gain their support. Paliau said that since his youth he had deplored the division of the Manus people and the attendant mutual contempt and hostility. He preached that all indigenous New Guineans were alike in their condition and in the broad outlines of their ways of life. Their differences were to be of no importance to those who would follow him. These differences derived from the past and would be abandoned with it. The names Usiai and Matankor were no longer to be used. All people of the Admiralty Islands should call themselves Manus, after the fashion of the Europeans who applied the term Manus to the many islands of the Admiralties and all their peoples.

Usiai were largely uninvolved in the initial phase of the Paliau Movement. According to Paliau, Usiai leaders would have been welcomed, but his single attempt to enlist William Matbe and his followers had failed. Both Matankor and Titan participated in the early Movement meetings but from the first the Titan were the mainstay. In this early phase, Paliau leaned most heavily on the Titan of Mok, to whom, he said, Jesus had directed him to give priority. The Mok people were his emissaries. Their canoes gathered the building materials for the meeting house. The conspicuous secrecy about their doings that they maintained as they travelled on behalf of the Movement, their more European-like clothing, and the altered bearing they had adopted attracted many listeners to the early meetings. There was already a plan for the Mok people to move on to the land, where they would build a new village adjacent to Lipan. From the beginning of the Movement, Paliau urged the other Titan villages to abandon their lagoon homes, 'fit only for fish', in favour of new villages built on the nearby beaches.

Paliau appointed a *pesman* in each village represented at the early Movement meetings. His task—the *pesman* were always male—was to bring the program of the Movement to his own village. These were young men, upstarts by the standards of the old culture. All those who took these positions in this early phase had presented themselves to Paliau, seeking active roles in the Movement. For a while, some villages had both a *luluai* and a Movement *pesman*, the one representing the Australian administration, the other representing the New Way.

Within each village there was to be a new order of life. Paliau wanted to weld the people of each village into a community capable of working in unison. The old clans were to have no explicitly recognised role in the new village structures. Paliau called a clan a *banis*, a Tok Pisin word still used in other contexts to mean fence or a fenced area.[12] In condemning the past, he pictured the clans as 'each pulling in its own direction'. The *pesman* of the village was to be a leader for all its people, regardless of clan membership. He was to be impartial, not yielding to the pressures of kin and clan. Paliau also proscribed the two-rank system. He said that there was only one *lapan* (man of high rank) and that was God; all men were his 'boys'—echoing the colonial terminology that reflected the subordination of indigenous people to whites—and all were rubbish compared with God. This was consistent with the democratic tone that ran through Paliau's ideas about the ideal society.

Paliau also enjoined Movement members not to leave the village to work for white men, but to stay at home, at least for the time required to launch the new society. Such a plan would rule out the many possibilities for individuation and differentiation of personal experience migrant workers found in their explorations of the wider world. The men of the older generation also were to stop organising the exchanges that made them eminent among their age mates. The Movement strove to eliminate much that had socially differentiated child from adult, male from female, the older men from the younger men, entrepreneur from dependent, higher

---

12   Paliau used the term *banis* in place of the Tok Pisin term more commonly used for clan in Manus, *liklik ples*, meaning small place. The Tok Pisin term applied to clans or clan hamlets within villages. Paliau's choice of terms emphasised the clan as a mechanism of division, while the other term, 'small place', emphasised its social and territorial coherence.

from lower rank, migrant worker from villager, clan from clan, village from village, linguistic group from linguistic group, one sect of Christians from another, and native from European. Paliau's program, calling for brotherhood and de-emphasising the differences among individuals and groups, aimed at extending cooperation—in space and time—beyond that which individual strivers and local kin groups could muster.

Drawing on his observations of the Movement on Baluan years later as well as Schwartz's work, Ton Otto (1992c: 448) describes the major elements of Paliau's plan for reforming social relationships as embodying a 'logic of oppositional transformation'. He summarises the key transformations as 'communalism versus particularism; centralism versus particularism; equality versus inequality; unification versus differentiation'. Our descriptions of the Movement and the cargo cults that arose within it, however, will show that many of the differences between social groups in the old system still had a place in the new, although they were profoundly modified.

Paliau stressed the principle of 'hearing the talk' (in Tok Pisin, *harim tok*) to foster the larger, more solidary social and political groupings the Movement sought. Hearing the talk meant discipline and obedience. Adam and Eve did not hear the talk of God. The conditions after the Fall were the result. After the coming of Jesus, the white men were 'all right' because they knew and obeyed the laws of God. They had leaders who had real authority. White men could make a group decision and carry it out.[13] The natives also had to find and follow the laws of God. They would have to obey the leaders they chose. Eventually when they had their flag and government they would have jails and police to punish those who would not hear the talk.

But what was the talk? It was the word of God, transmitted through men whose ideas conformed or added to the New Way. It was the decisions reached through discussion at meetings or by a court trial. Such group decisions became the talk that Movement members must hear. In private life, hearing the talk meant not letting anger disrupt interpersonal relations. Hearing the talk of God and the community nourished and strengthened the *tingting*. Food and medicine were to the body what the talk was to

---

13   Similar perceptions of whites as cooperative and harmonious have long been widespread in Papua New Guinea. Smith (1994) discusses such perceptions, their genesis, and their implications in Kragur village, East Sepik Province, in the 1970s.

a *tingting* weakened by ignorance, sickened by sin, rendered immobile by obsession, or disrupted by anger. Not 'hearing the talk' by refusing to express a grievance so that it might be settled, or refusing to confess to a wrong, broke communication between members of a community and endangered the lives of individuals and the unity of the group.[14]

Paliau also stressed related dicta. Trouble within the group must be prevented, if possible, and contained when it occurred. He proposed 'laws' (in Tok Pisin, *lo*) against boasting to the disparagement of others, spreading malicious gossip, being suspicious or angry without definite proof of a wrong, taking sides in quarrels (even in cases in which close relatives quarrelled with non-relatives), and deliberately or carelessly provoking others to anger. The *pesman* and the community were responsible for seeking and hearing confession of unacceptable thoughts or acts, exposing grievances, and effecting reconciliations.

Paliau also spoke of physical causes of disease, such as dirt on the body or on food. He also believed that hard work and inferior food shortened people's lives. But sickness was primarily a disorder of the *tingting*, and death was the *tingting* returning to God. Paliau did not reject European medicine, but he argued that it could not in itself cure many sicknesses because the *tingting* had not been rectified. Only when the *tingting* had been rectified could medicine succeed.

These powerful moral sanctions were to be built into the new culture. Paliau offered his program as literally vital—a new way of life on which life itself depended. It clearly addressed a concern that lay close to the surface. The interval between funerals was short in Manus villages in the 1950s. People loved their children intensely, but the infant mortality rate was high.

Had Paliau succeeded in winning wide support during this early phase and had he been able to carry out those parts of his program that could have been realised in short order, the resulting way of life would have been a marked departure from the mixture of indigenous and introduced elements in the prevailing culture. But it would still have been far removed from the European way of life. Achieving some of the ultimate goals of the Movement obviously depended on mastering the wealth, technology, and

---

14   Again, this bears resemblance to conceptions of the importance of social harmony to human health and general material abundance found in many parts of Melanesia.

material culture of the European. Paliau understood this and considered improving people's economic condition crucial. This, however, was an even more intractable problem than instituting new ways of controlling anger and conflict.

Funding the Movement

The various accounts of the meetings during the initial phase of the Movement that Schwartz and Shargo collected agree on the details of Paliau's views of the economics of the new culture. He did not speak of achieving equivalence with the whites through supernatural means; rather, he spoke as a man trying to formulate a program for changing an entire way of life primarily through human effort and on human scale. His metaphysical ideas, however, were critical to his program. They placed the Movement in history, they explained the disparity between native and European, and they provided sanctions reinforcing the dicta of the New Way. They also gave the program God's blessing and cast Paliau as God's accomplice. God's support was a necessary but not a sufficient means to the Movement's ends.

Economic change had been a central point in a number of the local movements that preceded Paliau's return. They variously called for setting up stores or locally owned businesses and plantations, supplying all the labour for a white-owned plantation, and completing the transition to a cash economy by abandoning the remaining uses of indigenous wealth objects. But the few efforts that had gone beyond talk had not been part of comprehensive programs that recognised connections among all aspects of indigenous life.

Paliau presented an integrated economic plan. He offered a series of first steps based on his analysis of existing economic potential. In Tok Pisin, people often referred to the discussions in these early meetings that dealt with economic plans as *toktok bilong mani*, that is, talk of money. Paliau elaborated on his prewar idea of setting up as large a cash fund as possible for collective purposes. It was no longer necessary to keep such a fund to help people pay the colonial head tax, which the postwar government had not reinstituted. The new fund was to provide capital for Movement endeavours. But from where was the cash to come? This problem was acute, because Paliau also said that the young men should not go away to work for the whites. Their labour would be needed to rebuild the villages along new lines. Staying at home, however, would cut off the main source of people's cash income.

During this early stage of the Movement, Paliau announced that the Australian government was going to compensate indigenous people for losses of life and property resulting from the war. Manus people said in 1953 that they first heard of the coming payments of war damages from Paliau, who had heard of this in Rabaul. In 1945, the Australian government made surveys of the extent of war damage to New Guinean property and in 1946 it began to make payments. The announced purpose was to help rehabilitate communities and provide them with capital, but this was done in part in the hope that it would lessen New Guineans' postwar discontent. But the plan did little to increase indigenous traction in the commercial economy, because recipients spent much of the money on minor purchases from trade stores. Observing this, some Australian commentators criticised the Native Compensation Plan for making payments to individuals (Stanner 1953: 118ff.) rather than to groups, although the latter course would have been far from simple.

Even before war damages were paid, many Admiralties people had more money than before the war. Much of this was in American currency, earned from working on the American airbase or from selling souvenirs (such as wood carvings or traditional ornaments) and food to the Americans. Paliau wanted to prevent the dispersion of this wealth and he called for all the villages joining the Movement to collect as much of it as they could. On Baluan and Mok, Movement leaders immediately started funds, recording the names of all those who contributed and the amounts they gave. The money itself was kept in a locked box in Paliau's house. The *pesman* in each village was in charge of making the collections and trying to get a Movement cut of money coming into the village from other sources. The general idea was not new. In the past, returning wage workers had frequently pooled their wages, each one in his turn collecting the pool. Or a small group might pool wages to purchase a jointly owned guitar or phonograph. But few people had confidence in their ability to save their small wages or, if they did, to protect their savings from the requests of their kin. The government had established banking facilities for New Guineans but few of the south coast people used them. In the villages of Pere and Bunai, with a combined population of around 1,000, only one man had a bank book. But people accepted the idea of creating Movement funds enthusiastically.

Paliau's approach appealed to and elaborated on what seemed a generally accepted New Guinean economic theory at the time. New ways of obtaining money must be found and money must be amassed and concentrated. By acquiring and saving money, New Guineans could purchase ships, trucks, and galvanised metal sheets for building houses. They could set up and stock their own stores and companies. Paliau realised that any appreciable advance depended on finding new sources of money income. He spoke of Manus people starting their own plantations, having their own stores, and transporting their cargo with their own ships. All these Movement objectives were to be attained in the near future, but people had to wait until the first steps in organising the new society were completed.

The initial plan for economic change included abandoning old economic practices. The endless cycle of ceremonial exchange that persisted from the old culture would no longer drive production. People were to cease the feasts and exchanges and stop working to accumulate shell beads and dogs' teeth. Groom-side marriage payments were to be fixed at a single, small cash sum. The new economy would stress organising work at the village level. The collective work would focus on the immediate aims of the Movement, such as combining small, scattered, single-ethnicity villages into larger, multi-ethnic villages governed through communal decision making. Decisions concerning village work were to be made in meetings of its residents. Trade between villages or within villages was to be collectivised and conducted in a non-competitive spirit. Land rights were to be treated similarly. This communalisation was to be a general principle for all economic activity, a principle consistent with the emphasis on a new, solidary social and political life.

Paliau's plan for economic change demanded great effort of his followers. Yet, even if they could succeed in these first steps, they would still have travelled only a fraction of the distance to the condition to which they aspired. Paliau understood this, but he was primarily concerned at this point with getting the Movement started. He offered a program of planned change that would give its followers some parts of a new way of life immediately, a coherent new ordering of society that would be a vehicle for continued change in the direction of the ultimate goal—a way of life modelled after European society. Paliau called what he was offering a 'road' (in Tok Pisin, *rot*). This translates literally as road, but is probably best understood as way or direction. He could not map out the entire course of this road, but he could put the people of Manus on it, describe the end, and try to maintain people's belief that it was attainable.

From his base in Mok and his new meeting house Paliau's ideas spread with surprising speed over a wide area. Though he had recruited few entire villages, he had attracted and enlisted a significant number of men as energetic leaders. They carried Paliau's message—in part intact, in part transformed or reinterpreted—to their own villages and beyond, where it often thinned out into rumour. At the periphery, however, a different vision for transforming the Manus world arose in the form of the Noise. This would alter the course of the Movement drastically.

6

Big Noise from Rambutjo

Paliau depicted the indigenous way of life as one of endless hard labour leading only to sickness and death. He called for discarding it and adopting the white way of life. He had worked with whites for many years, but mostly in police and military settings, so what he knew firsthand of white or European life was limited. Most of Paliau's followers had to fill in even more details of white life from their imaginations than he did. Paliau proposed concrete steps for building a new society with a new relationship to God, but his message aroused anticipation of a rapid and complete transformation. While Paliau was still gathering followers and creating an organisation, rumours spread from Baluan Island that he was revealing a new truth—a truth that whites had hidden from natives. Word spread that Jesus had revealed this knowledge to Paliau and now the people of New Guinea could rise above the condition of humanity after the Fall and expulsion from the First Order. When the native was made all right, the last work of Jesus would be finished. This was the beginning of the Noise.

The rapid spread of the Noise strongly suggests that from early in Paliau's organising efforts many people expected him to bring them the magical secret of the cargo, not a program for gradual change. Rumours of his contacts with Jesus preceded his announcement that he would have much to say upon his return to Manus. He betrayed no details of what that would be, a sure way to elevate people's expectations. Although to the best of our knowledge he never overtly promised restoration of the First Order of God, when he finally returned to Baluan, he made much of the story of the First Order and the Fall from the First Order Paradise. And he did little or nothing to discourage radical expectations, even as he attended to promoting and organising the step-by-step Movement program.

In Manus in the 1940s, some members of the Paliau Movement clearly did see the call for change in mundane, secular time as a promise of sudden magical transformation. In Mok, the village where Paliau found his earliest support, people immediately started the community organising and communal work he called for. Almost as quickly, some Mok people saw signs that their activities were attracting supernatural attention.

The Noise then began and spread contagiously. Figure 6.1 shows the main routes by which people carried news of the Noise from place to place, events we describe below. Decades after the Noise had subsided, a comparatively staid Paliau Movement began using the slogan 'Like Fire!' on posters, leaflets, and T-shirts. But the spread of the Noise was more 'like fire' than the growth of the Movement as a whole, either before or after the Noise. The first manifestation of the Noise ran its course—at least in public—in less than three months. But they were months of intense activity and high emotion.

Lukas of Mok described the feeling of those days, when he was among those swept up by the Noise:

> At the time we started these ideas, we thought that all this trouble that we … have is not because of our own wrongs but because of the wrongs of the angels and of Adam and Eve. Why should we be burdened with all this pain and hard work because of them? We must leave this wrong of theirs behind us. We must start on the good way of life that was the First Order of God. If we lose these evil ways of theirs, eventually God will hear us. That is what we thought. We tried to follow this. We tried to live with only good *tingting*. At this time, when we worked according to good *tingting* exclusively, the Noise had not come yet, but everything came easy for us. When we went to clear ground for our new village we were completely occupied with that work; we did not need to fish. The fish just died and we gathered them up. In the past we used to build a shelter on our canoes, but now we needed no shelter. Why? Because the rain didn't wet us, there were only good winds for us to sail by. Birds used to come right up to us. Our thoughts were strong about all of this. Why was everything so easy now? If we thought something, God knew. Everything could come to us.

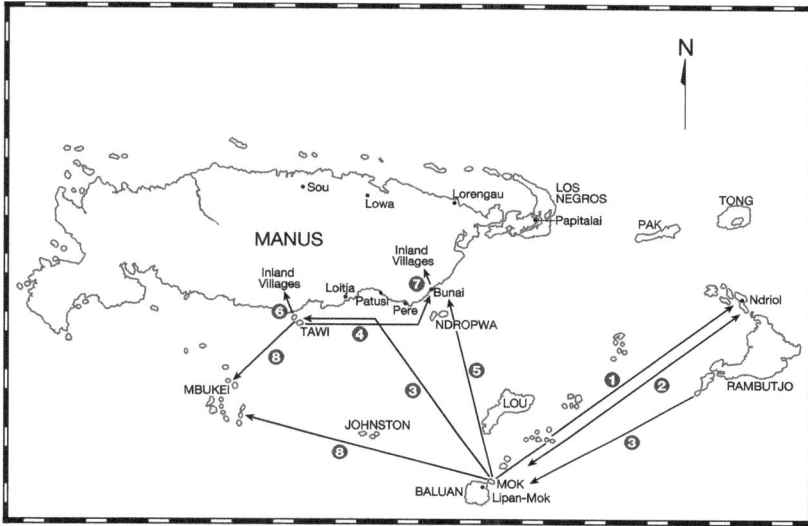

Figure 6.1: The routes of those who first conveyed from place to place news of Wapei's prophecies and the alleged deliveries of cargo already accomplished.

All the journeys shown here took place within less than a week. We know that the dramatic events of the Noise began with people carrying news of Wapei's prophecy from Ndriol to Mok. But we do not know the precise timing of the other journeys shown, so our numbering does not represent their sequence. The map key summarises what we do know. We expand on this in the main text. (*Guria* usually refers to violent shaking, as discussed in the main text.)

Source: Map created by Michael French Smith and Diane Buric, based on a diagram in Schwartz (1962).

Key to the map:
(distances are approximate)

- *Journey 1: Lungat, Wapei, and others return to Ndriol from Baluan (40 miles/65 kilometres).*

  Wapei began to prophecy the coming of the cargo after returning to Ndriol with Lungat from Baluan, where they had heard Paliau speak about the New Way. Lungat became an advocate of the New Way, but Wapei's contact with Paliau stirred a more apocalyptic vision.

- *Journey 2: Mok people (Tahan, Pwankiau, and others) travel to Ndriol and return home with news of Wapei's prophecy (a round trip of about 80 miles/130 kilometres).*

  The Mok people came to Ndriol to get sago palm leaves for thatching a New Way structure on Baluan. Wapei's followers on Ndriol told them of the cargo prophecy, but chased them away, telling them to go home and wait for their own cargo. The Mok people left and spent the night on nearby Rambutjo, where they began to *guria*. Impressed by this, when they reached Mok they endorsed Wapei's prophecy, sparking the *guria* in Mok.

- *Journey 3: Kosa travels home to Tawi from the direction of Rambutjo via Mok. On the way he stops in Patusi and Loitja, where he also conveys news of the Noise (70 miles/115 kilometres).*

177

Kosa of Tawi, returning to Tawi from the direction of Rambutjo, stopped at Mok, where people had begun to *guria*. The Mok people would not let Kosa land, but they told him of Wapei's prophecy. Kosa continued travelling, stopping on the way at Patusi and Loitja, where he told villagers of events in Mok, and finally arriving in Tawi, where on hearing the news people began to *guria*.

- *Journey 4: Piluan takes news of the Noise from Tawi to Bunai, conveying it to people of Patusi and Pere along the way (19 miles/30 kilometres).*

Several people from other villages were in Tawi when *guria* broke out, including Piluan of Bunai. She soon brought the news to Bunai, conveying it to people of Patusi and Pere along the way. The news sparked an outbreak of *guria* in Pere, and soon after Piluan arrived in Bunai its people began throwing their belongings into the sea.

- *Journey 5: Tjamilo and Posanau return to Bunai from Mok (25 miles/40 kilometres).*

Tjamilo and Posanau of Bunai were in Mok when the Noise broke out. They returned to Bunai soon after Piluan's return from Tawi and their report increased Bunai enthusiasm for the Noise.

- *Journey 6: Suan takes the news to Peli and other Usiai villages west of and inland from Tawi.*

- *Journey 7: Kampo of Lahan brings news of the Noise from Bunai to Lahan. From there, news spreads to other Usiai villages, including Yiru, Katin, Kapo, and Nuang, and villages further inland, including Bulihan, Karun, and Soniru.*

Kampo is among the Usiai people who heard of the Noise from other Usiai who had visited the coast to trade. Kampo went to Bunai to hear more about the Noise. He then brought what he heard back to Lahan, from where it spread further.

- *Journey 8: The news is conveyed to Mbukei.*

We are not sure who brought the news to Mbukei, but we know it reached there from either Mok (34 miles/55 kilometres) or Tawi (15 miles/24 kilometres).

The Noise in Ndriol

The Noise first appeared in February 1947, only about three months after Paliau began promoting the Movement from his base on Baluan. The canoes of the eager and the curious had begun to arrive there. His meeting house was crowded. He or his best-informed followers repeated the 'Long Story of God' and the details of his program for the benefit of each new arrival. Accounts of this period depict Paliau as constantly active, sleeping little, meeting and speaking at great length to new arrivals, and winning over with his skilled oratory small groups of curious visitors and the crowds at the twice-daily meetings.

When the group from Rambutjo Island was ready to leave, Paliau reminded them that he had entrusted Lungat of Ndriol, the only village on a small island adjacent to Rambutjo, with carrying out the Movement program in Ndriol and on Rambutjo. Lungat was to lead the young men of Rambutjo who had come to Baluan in winning over their elders and propagating the truth Paliau had taught them. Lungat was also to record people's dreams, for they contained the voice of God. But Paliau gave the voyagers to Ndriol this warning: The ideas he had given them were powerful and if they did not cleave to them closely they would bring ruin.

When Lungat's canoe returned to Ndriol, the men of the village were at their usual tasks, fishing on the reefs or cutting sago palms in the bush. It was the men to whom he wished to speak, and by nightfall he had gathered them for their first meeting. With the remarkable verbal recall typical of Titan people, Lungat repeated all that he had heard from Paliau. He proclaimed the break with the past, outlined the New Way, recounted much of the 'Long Story of God', and explained the way of the *tingting*. In the past, when he had presented his own dream-inspired attempt at local reform, villagers had rejected it. But now, he told Schwartz and Shargo, he was able to win over the older men, including the village *luluai*, to the new program. These men were deeply enmeshed in longstanding networks of affinal exchange obligations, and they spent the next few days settling their affairs by making at least token settlements of their debts from past birth, betrothal, marriage, and mourning feasts. Each night, they met with Lungat to discuss the new, 'true' version of Christianity and discuss, resentfully, the 'lies' of the missionaries.

Following Paliau's instructions, Lungat began collecting dreams. He interpreted some himself. Others he wrote down to take to Paliau, like the dream figuring in the following incident. A few days after his return from Baluan, Lungat and the most influential Ndriol converts to the Movement sent a large number of villagers to cut sago palms and extract the starchy pulp, a staple food in the Admiralty Islands and many other parts of Papua New Guinea. The process would require them to sleep several nights in the bush. The first night, one of Lungat's ancestors appeared in a dream to a member of the party. The ancestor commanded him to take the whole work group back to the village immediately because the men were hungry. But when the recipient of this command awoke in the morning, he decided to keep his dream to himself. That day the entire party paddled up a stream to cut some of the sago palms that grew in the damp soil on its banks. One of the palms they cut fell on one of their canoes and broke it. The dreamer immediately feared that ignoring the command he had received from his dead ancestor had brought this on, and he confessed this to the other members of the group. They decided to hurry back to the village to tell Lungat, who scolded the erring dreamer for disobeying the dictates of his *tingting*. But Lungat was not sure what the dead ancestor had been trying to communicate, so he prepared to leave for Baluan the next day to consult Paliau.

Titan were prodigious travellers by outrigger canoe, sailing when the winds permitted and paddling when they did not.[1] Even so, Lungat must have taken his responsibility for getting an authoritative interpretation of the dream very seriously, because Baluan was over 35 miles (more than 60 kilometres) away.

But Lungat did not leave the next day. The night before his intended departure, Wapei, an unmarried youth, had a dream that captured the attention of all the people of Ndriol. Lungat and his crew were at the beach preparing for their voyage when Wapei—with an excited but commanding air, strange for his youth and lack of status—accosted them and said they could not leave. Lungat argued at first, but then yielded to Wapei's urgent manner. Wapei said: 'Why are you going to Paliau to hear the word of God? Paliau has said that God is everywhere. He is here too'. Wapei insisted that the men of Ndriol should not listen to the talk of a man from any other village. He told them that Jesus had appeared to him in a dream. Jesus had told him that Ndriol was to receive its cargo on the coming Sunday. Jesus would come to Earth accompanied by the dead of Ndriol.

The cargo promised included every desirable material thing the whites possessed: planes, ships, bulldozers, sheet metal, money, and the food sold in stores. Ships and planes manned by the villagers' own ancestors would bring the cargo. And at the moment of the return of the dead, cargo would also appear in the graveyard.[2] As Wapei addressed the assembled village he trembled violently, his muscles straining against each other. All who saw him said that his eyes looked 'different' (in Tok Pisin, *arakain*, which translates literally as 'another kind'). Everyone, people told the anthropologists, believed Wapei instantly; they saw him as a prophet and acceded to his leadership.

---

1   Schwartz notes, however, that unless there was considerable reason to hurry, in the days of sail many Titan preferred to wait for a favourable wind rather than paddle any great distance.
2   Some Ndriol villagers also told Schwartz and Shargo that Jesus told Wapei that when the dead of Ndriol returned they would have white skins.

Paliau deliberately upset existing hierarchies by assigning young men with little status (but no women) to represent the Movement in their villages, but he tried to select effective advocates. When choosing spokesmen from among groups of visitors to Baluan to take his message back to their homes he asked who among them was the best and the boldest speaker. Still, some men so chosen, like Kisakiu and Lungat, recalled that trying to recruit prestigious older men to the Movement had taken all their courage. The Noise, however, generated leaders spontaneously and spread without skilled advocacy. The degree of authority Wapei was able to assume in Ndriol was exceptional. But in other villages, too, claims to supernatural revelations about the cargo almost immediately made young people and others with little status under ordinary circumstances into leaders. The mere rumour of the Noise generated great excitement and fevered expectations. People began destroying property on the strength of reports of a kind that ordinarily would have provoked scepticism and laughter, such as the reports of two old women, whom we will meet below.

Wapei told the people of Ndriol that a return to the First Order of God was at hand, but to ensure its arrival they had to purify themselves. This, he told them, required strict obedience to the commands of Jesus as conveyed through him, Wapei. Everyone was to think only good thoughts. No one was to gather food; they must fast, but they would not be hungry. Wapei also prohibited washing, sleeping indoors, and leaving the village. He told people to throw into the sea or burn everything in their houses; not only the dogs' teeth, shell money, fired clay pots, and coconut oil that represented the wealth and values of the past, but also all the white men's goods they had managed to secure from the trade stores and the scrap heaps of the American army. In his early meetings, Paliau had asked people to destroy a few items emblematic of the old culture, such as shell money, dogs' teeth, and grass skirts. He never suggested they destroy canoes, sails, fishing implements, war surplus tools, or American and Australian currency. But during the Noise, many people discarded things on which they depended for their livelihoods in nearly irrevocable acts of commitment. They abandoned day-to-day, life-sustaining activities, throwing out food and firewood and leaving their children unfed. They believed—or desperately hoped—that their next meal would be like the food of the Americans, a kind of manna in tin cans.

Wapei told the people of Ndriol to destroy their canoes and sails, an act akin to amputating a limb for these sea dwellers. Nothing could have been further from normal Titan inclinations. Yet people heeded his instructions, thus making a desperate investment in the validity of Wapei's prophecy. They accepted—or perhaps recklessly hoped—that discarding all their possessions was necessary to ensure and to display to higher powers a clean break with the past. Some also assumed they were making room for the abundant cargo soon to arrive. The cargo had to come. Committed to this outcome, many began to notice signs of its imminent arrival.

On Sunday, however, no cargo came. Wapei adapted quickly, saying this was the wrong Sunday. Jesus had really meant the next Sunday. Ndriol waited another week. Each day villagers spent long hours in church, praying intensely, their *tingting* concentrated on God, their bodies trembling violently with the feeling of God's nearness.

This was the *guria*, the trembling of the body which in some individuals became uncontrolled convulsions. In Tok Pisin, the word *guria* refers to various kinds of shaking, ranging from the trembling of the ground in an earthquake to the trembling of a person in fear or fever. *Guria* is a near cognate of the Tok Pisin word *nois*, which also refers to violent shaking. But during episodes like that in Ndriol, people were more likely to describe individual shaking as *guria* and to use *nois* to refer to the larger event. Soon, everyone in Ndriol shook with excitement, taking this as evidence of divine possession. Hence, being afflicted with *guria* validated people's visions or inspirations. Anything anyone said while in the grip of *guria* received rapt attention. (See Appendix A for further discussion of *guria* and other forms of what Schwartz calls pathomimetic behaviour associated with the Manus cults.)

Lungat, people said, became simply another of Wapei's followers. Wapei strode about the village making sure that everyone was following his instructions. Some villagers described his leadership in those days as a virtual reign of terror and told Schwartz and Shargo they had feared his increasingly erratic behaviour. Whether moved by belief or fear of Wapei, men and women walked about with their hands clasped in prayer. Many also communicated in dreams and visions with their ancestors, who always confirmed Wapei's original revelation. The dead spoke to one man by whistling. The sound of ghostly whistling had nearly disappeared from the Admiralties years before, when converts gave up the protection of their fathers' ghosts for that of Jesus and the Christian deity in the 1930s. Now, the whistles, familiar from seances many had overheard in childhood, assured them that cargo-laden ghosts would soon arrive.

One man claimed that money had appeared on a table he had built on the pattern of one he had seen in a dream. This, he reasoned, was a token gift from a dead brother.[3]

On Wednesday of this week of waiting, several Mok canoes arrived in Ndriol to pick up a load of sago palm leaf for thatching one of the structures Paliau had ordered built. The Mok people pulled their canoes ashore, but the men of Ndriol did not let them come beyond the beach. Wapei approached them and ordered them to return to Mok immediately so they would be on hand to receive their own cargo, which also would come on Sunday. He told them about Jesus's message and the promised return of the ancestors. But he grew angry when the Mok people seemed sceptical. He called the men of Ndriol to come to the beach. A group of men came and stood in attitudes of Christian-style prayer before the Mok visitors. Wapei said he and his followers were in contact with God, then they began to run around, shaking violently. The people from Mok were frightened, but seeing the Ndriol men *guria* helped convince them that Wapei spoke the truth. When they told Wapei they wanted to stay in Ndriol for a while, Wapei said, 'Look, your canoe is on fire'. The Mok visitors turned and, they reported later, they saw the flames. Wapei ordered the fire to stop, and (it was reported) it did, leaving no marks on the canoe. The Mok people then left, carrying news of the Noise with them, first to Pusu, another Rambutjo village, then to Mok and Baluan.[4]

Wapei continued to roam the village, threatening, scolding, and preaching. He whipped men with rattan switches. At one point he whipped a young man and woman after removing their *laplap* and exposing them before other villagers. But the people of Ndriol did not stop him, believing this was somehow necessary to prepare the way for the cargo.

As another Sunday approached, excitement mounted. On Friday, the *guria* became particularly violent. Some villagers fell down when they tried to walk. Wapei led prayers in the church; then he went outside, ripped the cross from above the door and threw it into the sea. He commanded the other men to tear down the church, offering no explanation. But people apparently assumed that the initial round of discarding and destroying property had not gone far enough, so they now had to finish the job. As some began to

---

3   Not necessarily a biological brother: see Chapter 5, footnote 1, explaining kin terminology in the languages of the Admiralties.

4   The accounts of this incident Schwartz obtained agree closely with those Marjorie Landman (1951) obtained from Mok people who were present in Ndriol at the time.

dismantle the church, others brought more possessions from their houses and began destroying them, and still others set fire to more of the remaining canoes. Ndriol people later told the anthropologists that although they did not eat they had felt no hunger, not even the children. Everyone stayed on the beach at night. Some saw the lights of aeroplanes. Others heard what they could not see: the sounds of ships, their winches lowering an invisible cargo, and the clank of metal objects being unloaded.

On Saturday, Wapei confirmed that the cargo would come at dawn the next day. Some villagers, however, suffering from the extremes of his rule, voiced doubts. Wapei became frantic and struck several older men and women, including the old *luluai*. He quarrelled with Alois Ndreje, whom he considered an older brother (within the Titan kinship system). Although he did not question Wapei's revelation, he protested the beatings. Wapei threatened Ndreje with a fishing spear, commanded him to kneel, then pressed the spear against Ndreje's chest, without breaking the skin. Ndreje said, 'If you want to kill me, you can'. Wapei relented and released him.

That night, Wapei lined up the people of Ndriol on the beach to await the cargo's dawn arrival. Although some saw lights again, no ships arrived. And no new way of life suddenly replaced the ways of the past that, with their dogs' teeth and other goods, they had tried to cast into the sea. Wapei held that he was not wrong about the cargo or the promise of a return to the First Order of God. But somehow, he told his deeply disappointed followers, he had spoiled this opportunity for the people of Ndriol. According to the account Lungat and Alois Ndreje gave Schwartz and Shargo, Wapei made the following speech to Alois Ndreje and another brother, Muli.

> You, my two brothers, I have completely spoiled the talk of God. This message from God was no lie. It is true. Lungat brought it and was teaching it to you and me, then I changed what he was saying. That I wanted to follow this through, that was all right, but I didn't do it right, and now I am fully in the wrong. Now what? I am not capable of setting everything straight now. Now I desire that you, my two brothers, should kill me. Lungat told us of it, and we all listened, but I drew this talk of his and this work to myself. I wanted to carry it out. Now I am wrong. Nothing will appear now. Now kill me.

Ndreje said that even on Saturday Wapei had told him that if the events of the coming Sunday proved him wrong, he wanted his brothers to kill me. Although Ndreje and Lungat denied it, others said that Wapei wanted to die so that he could go to the realm of the dead to see what had happened to the cargo. But it is certain from Ndreje's and Lungat's accounts that many still hoped for the cargo and some felt that Wapei's death might atone for his mistakes and bring a miracle. As an act of magical commitment, asking people to kill him was on a level far above even destroying canoes and fishing gear. No show of faith could surpass it. Yet if the Noise was genuine, no death would ever again be final. Wapei was making a speech on the beach when Muli, coming on him unaware, cleft his skull and then severed his neck with an American bush knife, retrieved from where it had landed on the reef when discarded with villagers' other possessions.

Schwartz studied the testimony from Wapei's murder trial, at which Ndreje and Muli were sentenced to prison terms, and he found it rather confused. It may be that by the time of the trial the people of Ndriol were anxious to attribute as much as possible of their behaviour to sheer madness and to blame as much as they could on Wapei. Those who testified asserted that they had come to their senses immediately after Wapei's death and that the Noise had then ended abruptly. But eight years later, Ndreje told Schwartz a different story shortly after his release from prison, explicitly denying that the Noise in Ndriol had ended with Wapei's death.

Lungat agreed with Ndreje. After the villagers buried Wapei, he said, they were filled with sorrow at his death and despaired of the cargo. Nevertheless, after the funeral the *guria* started again, as violently as before. Lungat ordered people to finish discarding their possessions. Despite declaring their complete commitment, during each episode of destruction some villagers had held a few things back. But now Lungat urged that they carry out Wapei's instructions to the fullest extent. For several more days some Ndriol villagers continued to fast. Some claimed they saw lights on the sea and in the sky. Some reported seeing planes and hearing the sounds of automobiles. People from as far distant as Tong and Pak islands later told Ndriol people that they had seen searchlights over Ndriol. But no one set another date. By the following Thursday—Sunday at the latest, depending on whose version of events one accepts—the Noise was finally over in Ndriol. 'Our heads cleared', one villager said. 'We knew our chance had been spoiled and was over. We were extremely hungry.' The people of Ndriol dispersed to find fish and sago. They were occupied with these tasks when Australian government officers arrived to investigate the strange and violent events of which they had finally heard.

But the people of Ndriol knew that although their village had given up on the Noise, it had spread. 'It ran like a wave from our village and broke over all the other Titan villages', one man told Schwartz. And Ndriol men said that after they went back to fishing and sago making they saw lights over Baluan like those reportedly seen over Ndriol when the Noise there was at its height.

The Noise on Mok

As they stood by their canoes, the Mok people who had come to Ndriol to gather sago palm leaves quickly dropped their scepticism and accepted the revelations Wapei shouted at them. Such prophecies probably were not entirely unfamiliar to them. Exponents of the Noise claimed direct revelations from God. They made no mention of cargo cults elsewhere or of previous cargo cults in the Admiralties, and Schwartz found no evidence of cargo cults in the Admiralties before 1947. But we know that Admiralty Islands people had heard of cargo cults occurring in Aitape (in what is now Sandaun Province, formerly West Sepik Province) and in Solomon Islands. Some of the Manus people caught in New Britain during the war also told Schwartz and Shargo of encounters with what has been called the Batari Movement there.[5]

Some also knew of the failure of cargo prophecies elsewhere, and a few agreed with the Europeans they knew that such events elsewhere had been a kind of temporary insanity. But when the Noise arrived, it swept up many sceptics. What else but the presence of God could shake people's bodies so violently? Why else would the senior leaders of the village obey an unimportant youth? Wapei had also caused the Mok canoe to catch fire and then made the fire disappear without a trace. But the people of Ndriol denied the Mok visitors any hospitality. Wapei told them to go home and wait for their own cargo. One might see this as selfless advice. But in the accounts Schwartz and Shargo collected, it is clear that Ndriol people did not want to share the cargo that had been consigned to them specifically and delivered by their own ancestors.

---

5   Jebens (2004b) examines manifestations of the Batari Movement in Papua New Guinea in the 1990s.

Wapei urged the Mok people to lose no time returning home, where on Sunday they could claim their own cargo from the ghosts of their own ancestors. The Mok travellers slept that night in a village on the larger, adjacent island of Rambutjo. In the morning, they prayed in a small church there. Several of the Mok men, among them Tahan and Pwankiau, an old man, began to shake, confirming the truth of Wapei's message. Joyful and excited by what they knew was coming, they set sail the next day for Mok, arriving after nightfall.

On Baluan, in Lipan-Mok village earlier that same day, Paliau had spoken at length about the importance of money and his plan for collecting it. This speech was for the benefit of newcomers to the Movement, including Tjamilo and Posanau of Bunai and 30 men from the Mbukei Islands, led by Napo. That night Paliau retold the 'Long Story of God', not in the meeting house on Baluan where the afternoon session had been held, but on the small islet in the midst of the houses built over the Mok lagoon. While he was speaking, the first of the canoes returning from Ndriol approached, the crew and passengers shouting their news. Coming close to shore, Tahan shouted:

> It is true! It is true! The talk of God is true. Our cargo is coming. The First Order of God has arrived. The way of the *tingting* is here. We must cry out to God. God said we must hurry to prepare ourselves. We must set our *tingting* straight. Hello! Hello! God our father says that our cargo is coming.

Throughout the night, Tahan told and retold of Wapei's message and the events at Ndriol. People said that, possessed as he was, he spoke in languages other than Titan or Tok Pisin; at times he even spoke the language of the Australians. As he spoke, his whole body trembled and his eyes rolled. People who heard him began to repeat his cries. They also shouted, 'Hello! Hello! God, our father!' They too began to tremble. Some fell to the ground, shuddering and convulsing. Many listened eagerly to every word of Tahan's revelations amidst these signs of its truth.

The accounts Schwartz and Shargo collected agreed that at some point that night, Tahan ran up to Paliau, knelt, and shook Paliau's hand, saying:

> It is true! It is all true! What you have said is true. Why, Paliau, did you bring this message to Baluan? God didn't designate Baluan. Jesus marked this place, Mok, specifically. Jesus said 'This village, Mok, it is rubbish. It has no land from which to get either food or fresh water. It has no rattan. It has no trees for making canoes.

It is truly impoverished. The Mok people must range over all the Admiralties. They find their food everywhere'. Now God is sorry and has great compassion for us. He came down upon you at Rabaul … He came as an ox, then as a spirit. There were two chairs. You sat in one. Jesus sat in the other. He brought this talk to you … 'This book', he said, 'I have put my breath into it'. When they wanted to throw it into the fire, they could not. When they wanted to cut it with a hacksaw they couldn't. Now you must bring my word straight to Mok. It is a poor place. There are coconut palms on it. You know it, near Baluan. You know it. You must bring it straight to them. Why did you go to Lipan? Why didn't you bring it exclusively to Mok?

Paliau, some said, replied that Tahan was telling the truth; Jesus had singled out Mok, but on returning from Rabaul he—that is, Paliau—had had to go first to Lipan to see his kin. Tahan then repeated that Paliau's teachings had all been true. They had been confirmed in Ndriol, and he, Tahan, had brought the message of God directly to the men of Mok. Tahan announced that Jesus had instructed him that everyone was to follow the way of the *tingting* wherever it might lead. Paliau allegedly replied: 'It is true. All this is just what I have already told all of you. The way is the way of the *tingting*; that is all. You must follow this carefully. Your thoughts must be strong and good'. But as Tahan made amply clear, God's message was not just that people should follow the way of the *tingting*; God's message was that the way of the *tingting* led to the cargo.

We would like to give Paliau's own version of the events following Tahan's dramatic arrival from Ndriol. Unfortunately, in Schwartz's conversations with him, Paliau always skipped lightly over this period to tell of how a few days later (as described below) he ended the Noise on Mok and Baluan, although it was still spreading elsewhere. Paliau never denied that at first he was inclined to give this new turn of events a chance to play out; but on the subject of his own actions from the time of Tahan's arrival until he assumed leadership again, he was tight-lipped.

Most firsthand accounts of his encounter with Tahan show Paliau thinking on his feet. He accepted Tahan's praise and made no effort to question or contradict his report that the cargo was coming. But, some witnesses told Schwartz and Shargo, Paliau also warned the Moks to beware, for the Noise might be a trial; that is, it might be a test sent by God or a deception sent by Satan. In these accounts, Paliau seems to be setting the stage to take charge again if the Noise comes to nothing.

Seeing people's ecstatic enthusiasm, Paliau may have judged that there was no point in opposing the Noise. It is possible, even likely, that Paliau also felt its grip. Numbers of people told Schwartz that this was indeed the case; that is, Paliau and his principal lieutenants—Lukas of Mok, Tjamilo of Bunai, and Napo of Mbukei—also assumed that they had nearly reached the marvellous end of the way of the *tingting*. Some said they even succumbed to the *guria* that ebbed and flowed through the gathering all night.

According to most accounts Schwartz and Shargo obtained in 1953–54, Paliau stepped back and let others lead for the first three days of the Noise on Mok, saying little in public. But it was easy for people to take Paliau's version of Christianity and the vague but portentous promises embedded in his program as prophecies of the Noise. Many years later, Lukas of Ndriol told Schwartz that Paliau had once said that those who followed the way of the *tingting* would be able to see their dead fathers and mothers. It is more telling that a number of people told Schwartz that Paliau had joined the prophets of the Noise in encouraging people to throw their belongings into the sea.[6]

Some of today's adherents of the Paliau Movement—under the name Wind Nation—describe the Noise as something other than a bid for cargo. Peter Kuwoh, a well-educated Wind Nation leader (whom we will meet again) has described the Noise (in English) as a 'spiritual revival' undertaken to revitalise the Paliau Movement.[7] When Smith visited Manus in 2015, although some Wind Nation members disagreed, others told him that Paliau had indeed told people to discard their possessions. Others said that people had discarded only war spears and the paraphernalia used to make war magic and enact sorcery. Whatever specific items were actually discarded, some called the entire episode—as they put it in English—an act of 'repentance'.

---

6   Typically, Mead diminishes Paliau's role in the Noise as much as possible without denying it outright, writing only that: 'Paliau himself was caught up in the mystical phase of the cult for several days before pronouncing against it' (2001 [1956]: 227). Gustafsson (1992: 121) writes that 'Paliau believed in the Noise, but preferred to remain outside it … He still encouraged people to join the Noise, while staying outside it himself … if and when the cult failed, he would be the only person to whom people could turn'. This is a plausible interpretation of Paliau's behaviour, but Gustafsson provides neither data to support it nor a source from which she may have borrowed it.
7   Kuwoh did so in a radio interview with Cyrus Pomat of the Papua New Guinea National Broadcasting Station in Manus Province. We have heard a recording of the interview but were unable to obtain the date for the broadcast, except that it was post-2000.

We return now to events in Mok in 1947 (where Paliau either did or did not throw himself fully into the Noise). A second canoe soon arrived, returning from Rambutjo. Pwankiau had made the passage from Rambutjo in the grip of the *guria*. But he had seen much, even though—people said—his eyeballs had rolled up, leaving only the whites visible. He had seen, he said, ships on their way to Mok, and they had been so near he could speak to the returning dead who crewed them. He had seen cars moving back and forth in the sky. He had seen bright lights over Mok and heard the sounds of many planes flying overhead. Mok's prize was ready, he announced.

But Mok people had to make additional preparations. Casting out everything in their houses was a prerequisite. Tahan had emphasised that the Ndriol people destroyed all they owned. Schwartz gathered, however, that in Ndriol (and other villages) people discarded and destroyed their property in bursts, hesitating after each bout, then discarding more goods each time someone received a further message from the dead.

The day after the Mok canoes arrived from Ndriol everyone gathered in the church, where they went into convulsions as they tried to reach out to God with all their strength. They also carried the way of the *tingting* to an extreme not contemplated in Paliau's original exposition of his philosophy. They turned the way of the *tingting* from a philosophy merging mind, body, and society into a rigidly ritualistic effort to restore to the *tingting* its alleged power to create any desired object through thought alone. Paliau taught that God was the *tingting* in each man, that God knew each man's thoughts, and that these thoughts had to be both morally good and 'straight'; that is, consistent and free of disturbance. Some adherents of the Noise elaborated on this, reasoning that once people thought of doing something, it was as if they had announced their intentions to God. Not carrying out those intentions but becoming distracted was tantamount to lying to God. If you thought of going to a certain person's house, you must go straight to it. You must control your eyes and ears so that nothing distracted you from your intention. If people called to you on the road, you must ignore them. When you arrived at your destination, you could think another thought, but then you had to act on it. As people described this version of the way of the *tingting* to Schwartz, he could visualise them moving in straight lines from point to point, setting aside their usual amiable receptivity to social interceptions, fearful lest they spoil their chances of realising that idyllic state which they thought of as the First Order of God. Schwartz later saw the same kind of behaviour in Bunai (described in Chapter 9).

Tahan and the others who led the response to the news of the Noise took other steps to remove the last barriers to the waiting cargo ships. Tahan ordered that two flags be set up. It was said that these were American flags. After the morning of prayer and *guria* in the church, the men of Mok marched between the flags throughout the afternoon. Marching has been part of cargo cult ritual in a number of Melanesian locales. In postwar Manus it is possible that people saw it as a quintessentially American behaviour that might tap American metaphysical power.

Tahan and others decided that no non-Moks (other than Paliau and a few visitors already there) were to be permitted to approach Mok. One night, two canoes under the command of a man called Kosa approached Mok. Kosa was from Tawi, a small island with only a single village, a short distance from Manus Island's south coast. As Kosa's canoe came near shore he shouted that he had seen European ships approaching Mok. But Tahan wanted no outsiders interfering with Mok's bid for the cargo and he told Lukas and several other men to repel the Tawi canoes. Tahan himself ran to the beach shouting, 'kill them, kill them'. Kosa and his party left in haste.

On the morning of the fourth day after news of the Noise reached Mok, Paliau spoke in church. He warned the people against doing anything that would spoil their chances in whatever was happening. Then he made the short crossing from Mok to Baluan.

While Paliau was on Baluan, a Mok man named Popau had a vision in which he learned that the cargo was to come that very night (this was either a Saturday or a Sunday night). The dead were to rise from their graves on the small islet the Mok people used as a cemetery. That night, everyone went to the cemetery. Throughout the night they waited, standing in a ring around the graves. As the morning uneventfully grew lighter and lighter they returned to the village, which they had stripped bare in the preceding days. They knew that something had gone wrong, and most of them realised that there would be no cargo.

Lukas of Mok had already gone to fetch Paliau back from Baluan. On Baluan, Lukas also collected the box containing the Movement's pooled cash and loaded it into his canoe. As the canoe neared Mok, one of the crew threw the money box into the sea. People told the anthropologists that Simon and Kusunan of Mok encouraged Lukas to do this, reasoning: 'That which is Caesar's, throw it away. Only that which is God's is of any consequence in his First Order of things'. Paliau may have agreed they had to discard the money to bring the cargo, or he may have reasoned that he could gain nothing by objecting. In either case, no one reports him objecting, and it is virtually impossible that Lukas and his crew could have obtained the box and thrown it overboard without his knowledge.

Despite this demonstration of complete commitment, on landing and surveying the situation in Mok, Paliau and Lukas found not cargo but the collapsing remnants of the Noise. The only signs of activity were a man wearing a metal bowl as a helmet, posted at the wharf to watch for the cargo, and a group of men watching a crab hole someone's revelation had identified as a place from which the cargo would appear.

Paliau spoke in the church the next morning and reasserted his leadership. He declared the Noise over and instructed everyone to recover as much of what they had discarded as they could. He interpreted the Noise and its failure in a way that gave it meaning compatible with the 'Long Story of God' but did not entirely repudiate it. He blamed the failure of the Noise primarily on Wapei, and claimed that he, Paliau, had predicted Wapei's murder. By revising his teachings, Paliau said, Wapei had brought ruin on Rambutjo and Mok. Some told Schwartz and Shargo that Paliau said that the Noise had been true, something sent by God, but Satan had embedded in it a trial. Wapei and the others had been the instruments of this trial. They had lied and misled the people into madness. Now the First Order was lost. During the Noise, God had come down to them, but now he had gone back to Heaven. Paliau cast Wapei as a figure in a drama like that of Adam and Eve; Wapei had led the people to re-enact the Fall. Now, Paliau told them, all that remained was a return to the Second Order and his original program of more gradual change. People told Schwartz and Shargo that everyone in the church cried in sorrow and self-pity. Some even began to shake again, but they inspired no contagion.

It is impossible to say what Paliau intended to accomplish by interpreting the Noise in relation to the 'Long Story of God' as he did. Did it reflect his true understanding, or did he simply want to proffer a plausible explanation to help dispel confusion and prevent panic? He apparently succeeded, however, in claiming understanding and authority superior to what Wapei, and a few other faces in the crowd, had claimed based on their revelations. And he did so without denying that God was indeed at work in Manus people's lives, not distant and indifferent. Whether he

Shortly afterward, Tuain and Matawai, two old men fishing near the reef, poled their canoes to the beach to report that they had seen a large ship anchored near Tawi. The ship had a flag and letters on its side which they, being illiterate, could not read. Kisakiu climbed to a high point to get a better look, but he could not see the ship. When he returned to the village, everyone saw a column of smoke on the horizon. They accepted the suggestion that this must be one of the ships bringing cargo to Mok.

Kisakiu then proposed to the assembled village that they had better get rid of everything connected with the feast: 'That's all that I said', Kisakiu recounted. 'Then everyone began throwing out everything they owned.' They threw into the lagoon their cooking utensils, the food for the feast, and the beads and dogs' teeth to be worn for the occasion. The women also discarded their leaf skirts and put on the cloth *laplap* they reserved for church. As the excitement built, Oto, one of Kisakiu's brothers, reported that God had visited him. He described God as a tall man with a long beard, whose face radiated light. God did not speak to Oto, but Oto's encounter convinced Kisakiu that Tawi's cargo was coming that very night.

Shortly thereafter, a youth named Kisokau reportedly received a visit from his dead father that caused him to break into convulsions. Villagers called Kisakiu, apparently assuming that his association with Paliau and the Movement gave him some insight in such matters. He found Kisokau shaking violently, shouting his father's name, pointing to the ghost that no one else could see. Kisokau claimed that he saw many more of Tawi's dead, and he called out their names as they appeared to him. A man named Kusunan, standing nearby, began to *guria* and to see all those Kisokau named. Everyone gathered around the two communicants, raptly observing them in the moonlight. Finally, Kisakiu sent everyone home to sleep except for Kisokau and Kusunan, who continued to shake and shout until the morning.

The next morning in the village church, Kisakiu again told of what he had learned from Paliau of the 'Long Story of God' and the way of the *tingting*. Thus encouraged, everyone joined in an effort to direct their prayerful thoughts to God. As they left the church they began to *guria*. Crying and shouting, they ran, fell, and rolled on the ground, their skins covered with sand. They called out the names of Jesus and Paliau. They saw and spoke to their dead brothers, fathers, sisters, and children. They saw the ships in broad daylight and heard the noise of galvanised iron sheets being unloaded. Then it rained. So hard, people said, that they could see only a few yards. They heard plainly the sound of an anchor chain. (Kisakiu interjected in his narrative at this point, 'Even I heard this'.) Some perceived that the spirit of Posangat, a man who had been *luluai* of Tawi a generation ago, captained the ship, and one of Posangat's living kin relayed this message from the spirit: 'The white men who teach us lie to us. Now everything that we want is here. You can see it'. Then, through his medium, Posangat told them that they must destroy everything before the cargo could be delivered. The Tawi men then began to set their canoes adrift and throw their sails into the sea.

At about this time, a canoe manned by men of Pere and Patusi arrived. The Australian manager of the Ndropwa Island plantation had sent them to investigate rumours of events in Tawi. A crowd of Tawi men chased them away, shouting threats and saying that this cargo was only for the followers of Posangat.

The Tawi people waited another day and night for the cargo and many people saw signs that it was tantalisingly near. Kisakiu smelled many white men. The odour, he said, was of powder and Vaseline, products some colonial whites used cosmetically in that era. He also smelled the food that was part of the cargo. (No one had eaten since the Noise started.) Each new bit of evidence revitalised excitement and belief during these days of waiting, but waiting became more difficult each day. Finally, a message from the dead broke the tension. Manoi, the Movement *pesman* of Loitja, who was in Tawi through most of the Noise, heard the whistles of his dead brother coming from inside the church. He saw no one when he entered, but he continued to hear his brother's whistles, which he said he could interpret. The message he relayed to the other villagers was that they should stop waiting for the cargo; it was not coming. Instead, the spirit said, they were to go straight to Paliau, who had a letter for them from God.

Kisakiu set sail for Baluan with several men deeply committed to the Noise. On arriving, he saluted Paliau, shook his hand, and then told him about events in Tawi. Paliau called a meeting of Mok and Baluan people and visitors from Mbukei. The men from Tawi related their experiences with the Noise, and then heard from the Mok people of its failure there. Paliau—thinking on his feet again—replied: 'You men of Mok, listen. I told you not to tell the people of Big Manus about the talk that I brought you. I told you that God would take care of these places. Now what you have heard from Kisakiu confirms what I told you. The spirit who appeared to Manoi said that I have a letter for you. It is true. I have your letter. It is the word of God. This is the letter I have for you'. Then Paliau repeated the 'Long Story of God'.

Paliau later took Kisakiu aside to brief him on what to say when the patrol officers would almost certainly arrive in Tawi to investigate. He told the party from Tawi to return immediately and take down the American flags which they, like the Mok people, had erected. They were to inaugurate the New Way as originally presented and to defy all attempts by the Australians to make them abandon it. According to Kisakiu, Paliau advised him how to reply to any threat that he would be killed. He must say: 'You may kill me, but my blood will spill on my own soil'. Kisakiu, still in his early twenties, said that he was afraid he would forget parts of what Paliau had told him when he returned to Tawi. Paliau reassured him that when he stood before his village the words would come because they were neither Paliau's nor Kisakiu's but belonged to Jesus. If Jesus willed it, Kisakiu would remember.

Back in Tawi, Kisakiu told the villagers that the Noise was over, the ships were gone, and the dead had retreated. Their belief had not been invalid, but for some reason they had lost their opportunity. The cargo, so nearly in their grasp, had been withdrawn. The Tawi people then retrieved from the sea what they could of their trade-store goods and their American war materials. But they willingly let the objects that represented the old culture sink beyond recovery.

Even as the Noise faded out in Tawi, it continued to spread to other villages. Suan of Peli village was the first Usiai person to encounter the Noise in Tawi. We know that he carried it to Peli and Bowai, villages in the interior. Schwartz and Shargo were unable to obtain accounts of events there, but we know something of the spread of the Noise in south coast villages.

The Noise in Patusi

Until the time of the Noise, no one from Patusi, a coastal Titan village not far west of Pere, had attended Paliau's meetings on Baluan. The young men had been absorbed in the endeavours Bonyalo of Pere had initiated. Led by Karol Manoi, they were on Ndropwa plantation making copra. But news of the Noise came to Patusi by several routes.

Kosa, returning to Tawi from Ndriol by way of Mok, spent a night in Patusi, on the south coast, and told the Patusi people that the cargo had already arrived in Ndriol and in Mok. When the Noise had begun in Tawi, Piluan and another elderly woman from Bunai village, who had been taking part in the feast there, left and returned to Bunai. As they left Tawi, Piluan saw ships unloading cargo there. She then carried her story all along the south coast. In Patusi, she told the villagers that they should wait no longer. Many ships manned by the dead were on their way to each village. Responding to these and other reports that had preceded her, the people of Patusi began throwing out or destroying their possessions that night. The next day the young men of Patusi working on Ndropwa saw carved wooden bowls drifting out to sea.

Patusi villagers heard the voices of the dead and their footsteps and, in the morning, they found their footprints. After church that day, the *guria* began, afflicting first a young man, Poselok, then an older man, Popeo, who brought from the dead assurance that everything thrown away would be replaced with money. While Popeo was conveying this message, his wife shouted to him to come quickly to his house where money had just appeared on the table. Popeo came back with a £1 note, the first tangible, indisputable evidence of the cargo. Then his wife shouted again. An additional ten shillings had materialised. Popeo and his wife passed the money around for everyone to hold and examine. A group of Pere men also saw this money and took news of it back to their village. Popeo said that he was in communication with his dead brother Popei, who had been *luluai* of Patusi.

Returning to Bunai, Piluan shared all she had seen and heard. From Bunai, travellers to Ndropwa brought the news of ships bringing cargo to Tawi. The young men of Pere and Patusi working there were sceptical at first. The Australian plantation manager sent a canoe to Tawi to investigate (as described above), captained by Gabriel of Patusi. Before the Tawi people drove them away, the men in the canoe heard about Posangat's ship and saw the Tawi villagers' ecstatic excitement. On the way back to Ndropwa, Gabriel spent a night in Patusi where he saw the money Popeo and his wife had allegedly received from Popeo's dead brother. He was also present during at least one seance in which Popeo communicated with the ghost of his brother Popei. In response to Popeo's questions, the ghost whistled if the answer was 'yes' and remained silent when the answer was 'no'. Gabriel's aged father also reported that when he approached the house where a seance was being held, he saw Popei, dressed in white shirt and white trousers, sitting in the doorway. Gabriel returned to Ndropwa the next day, disabused of his scepticism about the Noise. But he reported to the plantation manager that no one in Tawi had seen any ships bearing cargo. Then he and the rest of his work group deserted the plantation.

In Patusi, Karol Manoi still did not accept the validity of the Noise. He threatened to report the situation to the patrol officers. He, too, counted Popei as a brother, and—people told Schwartz and Shargo—he was angry that Popeo was invoking Popei's ghostly authority in support of the Noise. One night, Manoi attended one of the seances and served as Popei's interrogator. But when he questioned Popei, the ghost's answers indicated that the plan to work for money Manoi endorsed was mistaken and futile. Manoi left the seance angry with his dead brother, but he took with him the £1.10, to which he felt entitled.

In Patusi, the *guria* lasted four days, during which most villagers experienced it to some degree. Events in Patusi and nearby Pere were closely linked, so we now shift our focus to the latter village.

The Noise in Pere

When the Noise started in Pere, some of the most enterprising young men were absent, having gone with Bonyalo to work on Ndropwa plantation. For the time being, Bonyalo had refused Paliau's offer to collaborate as well as his invitation to Pere people to attend the meetings on Baluan. When Piluan stopped in Pere on her way home to Bunai, most of the men there were part of the conservative opposition to Bonyalo, and Pere people, like those of Patusi and Bunai, knew about Paliau's meetings—with their mystical aroma—only through rumour. It is the more remarkable, then, that they believed Piluan's report on the Noise. She told those present in Pere:

> There is a ship with many black men of Tawi on board. It is very big. It has already anchored at Tawi. Tawi village is completely filled with cargo. We saw all this, then we left. When we were near Loitja, we saw many, many more ships running beyond the reef. There is one ship for each village. Our ships are on the way; Tawi's has already arrived. These ships are bringing the cargo and everything that belongs to you. Listen, people of Pere, many big ships are coming. All our people who have died are now coming to us. The cargo has already been landed in Tawi. Why haven't

the ships come here? We are blocked by all the things of the past that we own. All these things of ours are like a reef keeping out the ships. The ships cannot come inside. If you throw everything away, then the ships will come with your cargo. When the ships unload the cargo, your village will be so full that you will have no room to walk. Your houses will be full.

The people of Pere spent that night discarding their possessions. Many even threw out their food, their firewood, and the clay platforms on which they made their indoor fires. (It is interesting, however, that in no village did people burn or destroy the houses themselves.)

The Catholic missionary for the south coast made his base in Pere. He woke up one morning to find his congregation's possessions littering the lagoon. When he figured out what was going on, he publicly denounced the Noise as the work of Satan. He saw the Noise as a dramatic aberration by people whom he regarded as the best Catholics in the Territory of Papua and New Guinea. In 1954, Pere villagers told Schwartz and Shargo that in 1946 they had defied the missionary, saying that what they did was their affair. Not only that, the mission had hidden the true word of Jesus from them, and they would no longer listen to the priest. They were taking their fate into their own hands, they told him, and whether it brought them ruin or success, it was their own concern.

The priest responded by ceasing to offer communion. Later, many people claimed they had not quit the church but had been cast out. Whatever the case, Pere people ignored the priest in their midst and pursued the Noise. This marked the beginning of what would soon become a complete break with the mission.

Each morning of the succeeding days, while they waited for the cargo-laden ships to arrive, the people of Pere filled the church. These were not the usual brief services; rather, villagers spent entire mornings in prayer, trying to open the way for the cargo by preparing their *tingting*. But nothing happened. Perhaps, people wondered, they were doing it all wrong; maybe they were ignorant of some vital prerequisite for receiving the cargo. They made short trips to the nearest of the villages also involved with the Noise for information. Pere men visiting Patusi learned about the contacts with Popei's ghost and the money. The money Popei had sent seemed a strong sign that the cargo was imminent, so when they returned home they encouraged Pere people to hold out longer.

Their empty houses like the skeletons of bridges burned behind them, Pere villagers waited, but less than patiently. They grew anxious lest Pere miss the reward that had already made other villages all right. They decided to send a canoe to Mok to learn what was happening there, but the young men picked for the mission refused to go for fear the cargo might come while they were gone. A few people in Pere had waking visions of incoming ships. But their dreams gave them their most vivid visions. Early in the Noise, Mikail Kilepak, a stable and respected man, dreamed that he saw a warship and an aeroplane at a passage through the reef near Pere. He saw the ghosts of ancestors on board. Tjolai, the deceased *luluai* of Pere, stood among them in a prominent position. A white man, whom Kilepak identified as Jesus, stood at the mast. But the ships went back. Something blocked their path. One woman dreamed that she saw the cargo being landed, making a great din. Planes, cars, and ships came to the village, which in her dream was no longer located over the sea but in a large clearing on land.

Some in Pere had heard that Akustin Tjamilo and Alois Posanau had returned to Bunai from Mok with full knowledge of Paliau's teachings and news of the Noise there. Tjamilo returned to Bunai from Mok in the third week after the beginning of the Noise on Ndriol. He brought new knowledge of Noise prophecy and doctrine, thus both revitalising interest and enhancing his authority. (Similarly, in Pere, would-be leaders in the Noise based their claims to authority on the fullness and freshness of their revelations.) In retelling the events from Mok, he presented what he regarded as evidence for the validity of the Noise prophecies. The ships had come, the dead had been with them, the cargo had been almost within their grasp; people had certainly seen and heard it. Unfortunately, he reported, Wapei's wrongdoing had thwarted the people of Mok and they had not yet succeeded in purifying their *tingting* and casting out the past. But Tjamilo reported this as merely a delay.

In fact, by this time the Noise had run its course in Ndriol, Mok, and Tawi. Tjamilo also brought news of Wapei's death. Nevertheless, Pere and Bunai had not abandoned their hope for cargo. Indeed, only after Tjamilo's return did Bunai and Pere begin holding regular gatherings devoted to the Noise and only now did they begin to *guria*. They also undertook to finish destroying property, although leaders urged discarding only the last of the dogs' teeth and shell money rather than all valuable or useful items.

Johannes Pominis had begun to *guria* while in Bunai. Returning to Pere, he brought Posanau, Tjamilo's brother, with him. He, too, had already begun to *guria* and others followed him into spasms of convulsive seizures. Pokanau, the *luluai* in Pere, had long been a bulwark against change. But, moved by the Noise, he assembled as many of the people of Pere as could crowd into his house to receive Posanau's instruction in the 'Long Story of God'. The late returnees from Mok, like Tjamilo, brought a version of the Noise mixed with elements of the Paliau Movement program. Some in this audience not only memorised but wrote down as much as they could of this revised, 'true' version of Christianity. The *guria* spread to several people, but Pere was never shaken by mass contagion.[8]

Meanwhile, Lukas Pokus left Pere quietly late one afternoon, heading for Mok, where he arrived close to midnight, having travelled about 25 miles (40 kilometres). He poled his canoe silently among the houses standing over the lagoon. He overheard groups of people sitting on verandas speaking of God, but he said that they acted suspicious, even hostile. Finally, someone recognised him and took him to see the Movement *pesman*, Lukas of Mok. Lukas of Mok asked Lukas Pokus of Pere whether the patrol officer or the mission had sent him or if he had come to trade. He replied that he had come to learn the talk of God. Lukas of Mok then received him hospitably, and all that night he and others tutored Lukas Pokus. They taught him the 'Long Story of God', the laws of the New Way, and the songs (among them 'John Brown's Body') they sang when marching. The next day, he watched the Moks practising the new, rigid, village routine, a routine that would be widely adopted in the post-Noise Movement.

By this time, an administration patrol investigating Wapei's death had come and gone from Baluan, taking Paliau with them to Lorengau. Unable to see Paliau after three days in Mok, Lukas Pokus returned to Pere. The wind was unfavourable and he paddled about half the distance. The sea became very rough after sunset. Afraid that his canoe would be swamped, Lukas prayed that God would calm the sea. His prayer, he said, was instantly answered. He heard the sound of an aeroplane in one ear and a whistle, as if a man were calling, in the other. God was heavy upon

8   Pere's participation in the Noise was subdued in comparison with Mok and Ndriol. Mead, however, was too eager to portray Pere people as superior and level-headed when she wrote in *New Lives for Old* (2001 [1956]: 228–9) that the Noise came to Pere 'not as a mystical religious seizure in which people felt themselves shaken by an unseen power, but as the practical preparation for the certain arrival of a wonderful cargo of European goods, which had already arrived elsewhere'.

him now, he told us. He could see him with his eyes but could not touch him. Then God spoke to him at length, repeating what the Mok people had taught him, prominently featuring the 'Long Story of God'. Driven by this experience, Lukas went ashore on Ndropwa before going to Pere. He was able to persuade most of the remaining plantation workers to return to the village. Only Bonyalo, John Kilepak, and Karol Manoi of Patusi remained from the first through the last month of Bonyalo's venture. Then they too returned to their respective villages, which they would help reorganise after the Noise passed.

On arriving in Pere, Lukas Pokus went immediately to the church, where, as he concentrated his thoughts on God, he began to *guria* violently. He silenced Johannes Pominis as a false prophet and attacked Tjamilo and Posanau as well. He told Pominis: 'You are not in true communication with God; this quaking of your body is merely something of the flesh'. Lukas Bonyalo (not the Bonyalo who began the Ndropwa venture, who had not yet left Ndropwa for Pere) had also experienced the *guria* during a vision in which the three persons of God (Father, Son, and Holy Ghost) appeared to him. On hearing that Paliau had ended the Noise on Mok and Baluan, Lukas Bonyalo aided Lukas Pokus in refuting Pominis. Pokus then dreamed that God instructed him to turn over his leadership of the village to Lukas Bonyalo. The dream was made known to the village in a meeting, as were all dreams that seemed to any degree significant. During the final days of the Noise, these two men were the teachers of the village. Lukas's house was filled to capacity, as Pokanau's had been when Posanau of Bunai had first brought the 'Long Story of God' to Pere.

But the urgent anticipation that had driven the Noise so quickly through its course among what today we might call early adopters could not be sustained. With relatively little drama, Lukas Bonyalo and Lukas Pokus began steering Pere towards a version of the New Way absent prophecies of cargo, but featuring ritualistic marching and singing and imposition of a strict schedule on everyday village tasks. Some still hoped that this would bring about a sudden miraculous change, but most realised they had returned to Paliau's original road, slightly modified, but still a road of uncertain length along which they could move only at a frustratingly slow pace.

Bunai and the Usiai Noise

When Piluan finally arrived at her home village of Bunai—having spread word of the Noise to several south coast Titan villages on her way from Mok—Tjamilo and Posanau had not yet returned. She was thus the first to report that, thanks to Paliau, Jesus was coming soon and so were Bunai villagers' ancestors, just as the ancestors had already returned to Ndriol, Mok, and Tawi. The people of Bunai and those of Pomatjau, a small village that was closely linked with Bunai, began discarding their possessions to prepare for the cargo. The *guria* seized some, and each night many saw the lights of ships beyond the reefs. One night, a young man in his late teens saw a glowing horse in the mangrove swamps, but it was gone by the time those who ran to see this wonderful thing arrived. The next day a group of adolescents and a young boy saw a white man, presumed to be Jesus, in the lagoon near the village.

These were rather feeble portents, however; just barely enough to keep hope alive. But Tjamilo's return from Mok resuscitated it. Tjamilo told the Bunai people that the Noise was real, but Wapei's wrongdoing and others' improvisations on the basic truths Paliau taught had made it go awry in Mok. Desperate not to repeat the Mok's errors, people listened raptly to Tjamilo's accounts of his firsthand experience of Paliau and the Noise. Men from Bunai, Patusi, Pere, and Pomatjau jammed Tjamilo's house, writing down or committing to memory the 'Long Story of God', the commandments of the New Way, and instructions for the synchronised mass activity other villages were undertaking to hasten the Noise.

The second day after his return, as Tjamilo was conveying his knowledge of the Noise to an outdoor assembly, his brother Posanau began to *guria*. He stood up in the midst of the crowd, calling the people to come close. He wept as he said: 'We must all love each other'. He then continued:

> We must all stay together. If there is only a little tobacco we must all smoke it. If there is only one small betel pepper leaf [the aromatic leaf chewed with betel nut], break it, we will all eat. However little food there is, we will all eat. We must love each other. We must have compassion for each other. One man must not be angry at another or think bad thoughts of another.

He went on like this, weeping with joy (or perhaps sorrow for his people's sins) and shaking. Thus, starting with Posanau, the *guria* spread to most of the people of Bunai. Accounts Schwartz and Shargo collected in the 1950s told of 50 or more men and women—most in their late teens or early twenties, but also a few of the oldest villagers—having convulsive seizures. Tjamilo was—as he put it—nothing before the Noise, but people now looked to him for leadership, and he remained the unquestioned leader of Bunai for the duration of the Noise.[9]

In every village in which the Noise took hold, older men who had resisted all proposed changes to the existing order joined enthusiastically in the Noise and, as part of their conversion, resigned their leadership. At Paliau's meetings, the most important men of the villages who attended were called on to publicly renounce the old culture and many did so. In Bunai, following the first pulse of the *guria* Posanau had triggered, Tjamilo led a meeting at which the older village leaders rose one by one to pronounce the dictum, '*nupela tingting, nupela man*' (that is, roughly, 'new minds/ideas, new men').

The Australian administrators assumed—based on their visits to Baluan and Mok—that the Noise had ended everywhere or was at least quiescent, even as it was just beginning in Bunai. Bunai people held their excitement in check when an official, who introduced himself to villagers only as 'Masta John', came to speak there. He had asked the *luluai* of Pere, Patusi, and Pomatjau, and of all the Usiai villages of the Number Two Road, to come to Bunai to hear him. He told this assemblage that the government was not angry with them and that it was good that they had broken with the past. He advised them to earn money by selling their labour and their produce. Villagers who worked hard to advance themselves would eventually earn limited local self-government in the form of Native Government Councils. He assured them that Paliau was not under arrest; rather, the administration was taking him to Port Moresby so he could learn more about the government.

This official visit did nothing to diminish enthusiasm for the Noise. The Usiai visiting Bunai were less impressed by Masta John than by the unanimity and determination with which the Titan people of Bunai adhered to the routines of the New Way. The delegation from the village of Lahan, led by Kampo and Pita Tapo, came to Bunai primarily to seek the 'inside meaning' of the Noise, which the Titan had made a show of concealing from them.

---

9   Samol—one of the local reformers described in Chapter 4—was still with the small group he had led out of the village before the Noise, when his adopted father, Kisekup, the paramount *luluai*, had blocked his reform efforts.

The Usiai had first heard of the Noise while trading their garden produce for the fish the Titan brought to the regular markets. At a recent market, some older Titan men had offered for sale to Usiai, many of whom still valued them above cash, large quantities of dogs' teeth and shell beads, which they had supposedly thrown into the sea. Kampo and Pita Tapo had heard rumours that God had sent special knowledge to the Titan through Paliau. Kampo implored a Titan friend, Gabriel Suluwan of Pomatjau, to teach him this New Way now taking hold in Bunai. We have seen that in villages committed to the Noise, many people believed that the cargo for each village was for that village alone, to be guarded against the people of other villages. In most accounts, people appear to simply be protecting what they regard as their exclusive property. Suluwan's reply to Kampo, however, suggests another reason some may have felt that the Noise required them to stay aloof from other villages: he feared that, used incorrectly, as Wapei had done, the new revelations would lead to disaster. 'It is true', Suluwan told Kampo, 'God is the father of all of us, but we are afraid. We are not adequate to tell you the ways of God. The ways of God and his words, it would be dangerous if we presented them incorrectly. It would be bad if later this talk turned to poison and killed us'.[10]

Suluwan also feared that Usiai people, whom many Titan people still mistrusted, might report them to the Australians. On the latter point, Kampo reassured him that if questioned by the administration he would insist that these ideas had occurred to him directly and had no other source than God. Suluwan finally allowed Kampo to copy from the book in which he had written much of the doctrine and ritual of the Noise. One passage read: 'God, Father, I desire the First Order. All of my strength comes from you. All my *tingting* belongs to you. But I am worthless; I am unworthy of you'.

Then—some three months after the beginning of the Noise—Suluwan brought Kampo and Tapo to Tjamilo, who, after a show of reluctance, agreed to confide in them, saying: 'All right, I will tell you. If you go report, or if you make trouble, it is all right. My body can be imprisoned, it can pay. But my *tingting*, no man can kill it. It is something which belongs to God'. (Such speeches of defiance—'let them kill me, let them beat me', and so on—appear in accounts of the Noise in every village from

---

10   The English word poison has a Tok Pisin homonym, *poison*, with a somewhat different meaning. Suluwan clearly had this meaning in mind. In Tok Pisin, *poison* can be translated as sorcery. Here, Kampo extended this basic meaning to embrace the more general idea of anything with supernatural power which, if not used properly, may harm the user.

which the anthropologists obtained them.) Tjamilo and Suluwan tutored Kampo's party for three days. When they left, Tjamilo walked with them to the beach. In parting he told them that soon after their return to their village in the interior they too would feel the full force of the *guria*.

Pita Tapo returned to his job with the Australian New Guinea Administrative Unit (ANGAU), but Kampo immediately began to reorganise his village, following the Bunai pattern. The first project was a new church. Leaders organised those building the church into coordinated work groups, imitating the way Manus people had come to believe whites worked. For example, in gardening, no longer were individuals or family groups permitted to go to their own plots at their own discretion. Instead, larger groups were to work communally in each garden, as directed by leaders, like the work groups coordinated by white managers on coconut plantations. When the church was completed, Kampo postponed using it until he could return to Bunai to finish transcribing the new liturgy, for the villagers were no longer to worship in the manner the mission had taught them.

Kampo then summoned Pita Tapo. He was still working for ANGAU in Lorengau, but he honoured Kampo's request, arriving in Lahan village close to Easter. Every day the people of Lahan concentrated only on God and their desire to return to the First Order. According to witness accounts, when the *guria* came, a mist or cloud enveloped the village, so dense that it was hard to see. (Recall that something similar was reported from Tawi.) Torrential rain fell while the sun shone. Several rainbows appeared. On the first day of *guria*, the *tultul*, named Lukas (yet another Lukas), and four young men fell to the ground, thrashing around. But they received no messages from God or the dead. On the second day, four women began to shake while they were working in the gardens. One of them, the wife of the *tultul*, saw her dead father and mother, but she was unable to touch them.

On the third day, Tapo began to *guria*. He saw the stars in the sky as if they were near him. He heard the voices of angels. He was filled with joyous compassion towards all the people he saw. He knew then that all he had heard from the Titan was true. He felt sorry for everyone for having to work so hard and he longed for the First Order of God in which people could satisfy their desires without effort. He described to those near him all that was being revealed to him. Late in the afternoon he fell into a coma-like state. Kampo publicly interpreted the coma as the result of some wrongdoing in the village that had never been resolved, and he confessed one of his own heretofore secret sins: He had seduced his brother's wife. Kampo and his brother then resolved to put this potentially explosive act behind them and shook hands. Kampo declared that the way of the past, in which each man must avoid the house and wife of his brother, was now at an end. He stopped short of speaking in favour of adultery, but he branded all the avoidances prescribed in the old system as evil ways of the past. Now there was to be no more shame.

After an hour Tapo revived. His mind was extremely clear. He had received instructions from God, which he proceeded to carry out, without opposition. First, he lined up everyone in the village, taking a long time to place them in strict order of birth, from the aged to the infants. Then he addressed them as follows:

> Soon we must get rid of all the hats of our *luluai* and *tultul*. God says they must all go. Then all the men who have died in the past will rise from their graves. God said this. Soon Jesus will come to hold court for us, for all whites and blacks. All the people who have died, they are many, we who are alive are few. Soon I will put all our houses into one long straight line. These houses must follow the law of God, they cannot be crooked; they must be perfectly straight, like God's word. All of us on Manus Island and in all places of the native will be one, one place and one people. One man will be our leader. When this leader is chosen, we will not choose him alone. Some white men, too, some men of Australia, of America, of China, and of other countries as well will be there. They will all meet in Lorengau to discuss this man who will be our leader. His name is Paliau. There will be another, from another part of Manus. He will be second. [Tapo later claimed he was marked to be second in command to Paliau.] America will take over Manus.

> While I slept, God came to me. As he came down, the sun hid, the moon hid, the stars hid. A mist came down with God inside. There were many angels with him, guarding him. When he does come down, he will come to hold court. All the men who have died will rise from their graves. Then God will hold a court to judge all who have died and we who are alive. Then I saw many houses appear. All these houses were in straight lines. There were a great many flowers lining the road. In this place, when men go inside a house, they go into something like a box, a pulley takes them up to the room above. They don't go up a ladder. There were plenty of cars. Later these cars will come to get us. And this place, we will see it also. Then I saw many white men sitting down to eat

at a table. I said, 'God says that he has forgiven us, yet we still must work'. Then God said: 'Soon all the whites and blacks will be good friends. They can live together, talk together, work together'.[11]

In America they have taught the black people. Now they are like the white Americans. When this war started the blacks of America arose to help America make war. They have their own ships. But as for us natives, God is extremely angry at the Australians. They didn't teach us correctly the word of God that Jesus brought. If they had taught it to us right, we would have been a country by now. But this didn't happen and God is angry. He sees us natives and is sorry for us, for so many of us died during the war. If they had given us knowledge before and many of us died, it would have been all right. But they didn't. We remain in ignorance and many of us die because of the many wrongs of our ways. If it weren't for America and its blacks we wouldn't be here now. All of us would be finished … Japan didn't believe in God and it lost. Australia, too, doesn't believe in God, and it lost. Why? Because they want only themselves to be all right. The Americans are truly men of Jesus. When they ask God, God gives them great knowledge. America likes us, it is sorry for us, but Australia is boss over us, and its way is blocked … In the future the Australians will no longer be able to do this work. We will have our own courts, our own offices, and our own government officers.

In keeping with this vision, God also told Tapo that not only the hats given to the village officials appointed by the government should be burned, but also the village census books.[12]

Adherents of the Noise regarded the Australian conspiracy to withhold the cargo intended for the natives as one of the most important of Kampo's revelations. This is Tjamilo's version:

When the *kiap* comes to collect taxes each year, he goes all around Manus. He collects ten shillings each year. When he has collected the tax, he writes down each person's name, and he asks 'Who is your dead father? Who is your dead grandfather? Which of your children are still alive, which have died?' All right, I give my father's

---

11   Americans and black Americans have a more prominent place in Tapo's revelations than in any other. Paliau had had less contact with the Americans than many of his followers, which probably explains why he places less emphasis than many others on this aspect of the First Order.

12   Although these ideas were part of God's revelation to Tapo, he had also heard them from Tjamilo. During the Ndriol Noise, Wapei attempted to induce the *luluai* to burn his hat and census book. Tjamilo, however, told Schwartz that Wapei got the idea from Paliau (although Schwartz never checked this point with Paliau).

name, Laloan. The *kiap* reads it, then he lies to me like this. 'I have taken out your father's name.' But he didn't take it out. He wrote it into another book. He does the same everywhere in Manus.

When he has collected the taxes and the names, he goes back to Lorengau. Then he types the names into a book along with the money collected. All right, he brings this to Port Moresby. The money stays in Port Moresby, but the book is sent to the true centre of the world. This place is near America, beyond America. The book goes straight to this place. Now this money, it is like the money that men brought to Jesus. Jesus looked at the money and said, 'This money has the head of Caesar on it. It doesn't belong to me. *Tingting* belongs to me and to God, my Father'. Now I [that is, Tjamilo] see it this way, this money belongs to Caesar [in Tok Pisin, *Kaisa*] and must go back to the government. But the names of men, these are really the most important road to God. The book of names is sent straight along this road. With the money, the government buys from all countries, from America, Japan, Germany, France. The money does not go to the true centre of the world. All the men who have died, the ancestors, do not receive this money, but this book, this is really the road of the native and of all the white men also. This book goes to this place which is the place of the *tingting* [that is, the place of the spirits of the dead and of God]. Jesus is there, together with the dead. There are angels there also. When these men who die think of Jesus, Jesus sends this *tingting* on to God, his father. Now God sends an abundance of goods back to him.

Now when this book arrives at this place, my father's name is in it and the name of my village. Now Laloan, my father, sends this cargo back. Laloan writes my name, Tjamilo, on the case along with his name. There is a book also in which all this is recorded. Now the ancestors just think, and a sling loads the cargo on the ship. This ship is extremely large. They have only to think and the ship is filled … All right, the ship now goes to Australia. They take all the cargo ashore. They look at the labelling and break open the cases. There is a customs official who inspects and breaks open the cases. They change the planks and put on new labels. [That is, they redirect the cargo, preventing it from reaching the New Guineans to whom the dead addressed it.] Now the British send it to all parts of the world. Carpenters [a major trading company in the Pacific Islands at the time] gets theirs, the company [Edgell and Whiteley Ltd, for which numbers of villagers had worked in Lorengau] gets theirs, the government gets theirs. Now we have thought out all this.

Thus, the *luluai* who were given hats, but no real power, were the guardians of the very books by means of which the Australians stocked their stores with the cargo that rightfully belonged to the natives. It was Tjamilo's own idea to elaborate on this and propose that the natives make their own books and get direct access to the world centre, which they would have if there were a restoration of the First Order of God. Tapo describes the world centre as a huge ship, bigger than Manus Island. A powerful but dimly perceived being, King Berra, is in charge of the ship. (Recall that Paliau allegedly secured his deliverance from the courts of the Japanese and the Australians by mentioning King Berra's name.) After his return from Mok, Tjamilo taught the village a song about Berra, 'Oh, Berra, You Come or I Wait' (in Tok Pisin, '*Yu Kam o Mi Wet*').

Schwartz tried to explain to Tjamilo that King Berra was not a person or a king but a misunderstanding of the name of the capital or centre place of Australia, Canberra. Tjamilo replied that a patrol officer had told them this, but they had naturally assumed the officer was lying. Tjamilo claimed that Paliau brought the King Berra story to the Admiralties. However, at least by 1953—and probably before that, given his long experience in the colonial police—Paliau understood perfectly well that Canberra was the Australian capital.

Tapo easily persuaded his own village of Lahan to burn its official hats and books. The Noise was transmitted from Lahan to other inland villages, including Yiru, Katin, Kapo, and Nuang, and received at least some support in Bulihan, Karun, and Soniru, in all of which villagers destroyed the hats of their *luluai* and the government census books. Kampo of Lahan and Bombowai of Yiru had also received instructions to destroy the hats and books in their own visions, which their episodes of *guria* had validated.

The Usiai had originally intended to put the New Way into effect while remaining in the interior, but Gabriel Suluwan and Tjamilo invited them to leave the interior and amalgamate with Bunai and Pomatjau in a village on the beach. Feeling emancipated and defiant after burning the symbols of their ties to the Australian administration, most Lahan families did move to Bunai.

Tapo tried to persuade other villages to join in the hat and book burning. His speeches were filled with hostility towards the government, and he spoke with the authority of one shaken by God's presence. He claimed that he was now second only to Paliau, who was at this time in Port Moresby. Kisekup, the paramount *luluai* on the south coast, refused to burn his hat. Tapo himself burned Gabriel Suluwan's book, the Pomatjau census book. In Bunai, the *tultul* Alphonse Kanawi burned his own hat, and a young man took another *tultul's* hat and burned it.

Pere did not join in this last manifestation of the Noise. Lukas Bonyalo heard Tapo speak in Bunai and he found Tapo's ideas attractive. He returned home, planning to bring the rest of Pere to hear Tapo. The canoes were filled for the trip to Bunai. In the new, regimented style, the fleet lined up, with Bonyalo's canoe in the lead, ready to signal the others to start moving simultaneously. On their way to Bunai they met a Pere canoe returning from Bunai where the Pere men had heard Tapo and had rejected his ideas. Many canoes in the convoy then turned back. The appeal of new revelations had worn off. Everyone—except a few who still believed the millennium was imminent—expected government action against those who had burned the hats and books. When the government patrol officers who arrested Tapo, Kampo, and others arrived in Pere, the village greeted the patrol with a conciliatory rendition of 'God Save the King'. Tapo spent 13 months in jail and Kampo served a year. Others served shorter terms.

An overview of the Noise

The Noise sought transformation through supernatural intervention. Living humans had a role to play, but it was largely confined to believing as intensely as possible in the imminent arrival of the cargo, a level of intensity that required active cultivation. It was essential to concentrate the *tingting* on the certain promise of cargo. This brought on the *guria*. And the *guria* not only brought God closer, it was also a sign of his nearness—a sign that in turn strengthened belief.

The advent of the Noise in any particular village curtailed the comparatively gradual progress of the Movement there and replaced normal, secular time with apocalyptic time, which is a prelude to the end of time as mortals know it. In Landes's (2011: 14) words: 'For people who have entered apocalyptic time, everything quickens, enlivens, coheres. They become semiotically aroused—everything has meaning, patterns. The smallest incident can have immense importance and open the way to an entirely new vision of the world … in which forces unseen by other mortals operate'. Within the world of the Noise, in the near future, there would be no future. On Christ's return, past and future, living and dead, would converge. Life would assume a perfection that admitted of no improvement, the highest condition possible for human beings.

All followers of the Noise agreed that soon everything would be good, but they were not clear about specifics. The transformation would, of course, begin with the cargo arriving and the dead returning. Those willing to speculate envisioned the returned dead as more substantive than ghosts, but they also entertained the apparently contradictory notion that all people—living and dead—would become like angels: pure spirit, pure *tingting*, like breath or wind—in Tok Pisin, *win nating*.

There were also other contradictions in ideas about the new world. Many parts of the expected cargo were tools or building materials, such as galvanised iron. But people also spoke of how, in the new world, they would be able to obtain material goods simply by thinking of them. People said that the cargo would include automobiles, but they also said they would be able to move from place to place by the power of thought. One man resolved the issue by imagining that there would be material cars, but people would be able to think them to their desired destinations. Some descriptions of the cargo included unlimited quantities of money; but it is not clear why anyone would need money. But people certain that the perfection of the world is at hand are unlikely to worry about inconsistencies in their visions of that perfection, for they would see perfection for themselves soon enough.

The Noise upended both Movement and pre-Movement forms of organisation, but it replaced them with only enough structure to prepare to receive Jesus and the ancestors. Pita Tapo, of the Usiai village of Lahan, had some of the most concrete political ideas about the post-millennial society. Destroying government-issued *luluai* hats and census books suggested that colonial authority would disappear and he spoke of black American soldiers helping drive out the Australians. Paliau would be the principal leader in the new world, appointed by Jesus, and Tapo would be second in command. He also had a vision in which people chose the American flag over the Australian flag. But most people were content to wait and see.

The Noise came and went within only a few months. Except for its extension among the Usiai and the later episodes of renewal in Pere and Bunai, the Noise reached the limits of its spread within two or three weeks. During the first week, villages accepted it almost instantaneously. It then reached the apex of intensity within a few days. In villages that entered the Noise earliest, the full cycle—from contact, to climax, to realisation of failure— ran its course within two weeks. In Pere and Bunai, it took much longer, probably because the full content of the Noise was transmitted in a series of episodes, each of which provoked a revival or a deepening commitment.

More people had convulsive seizures and behaviour in general was more extreme in the villages where the Noise manifested first. In fact, Mok was the only village in which the *guria* engulfed virtually all adults almost instantaneously. In the villages that followed Mok into the Noise soon thereafter, it took several confirming events to precipitate the same level of excitement. Even in Tawi, the first news of the Noise failed to entice most villagers. It took sightings of ships bearing cargo and God's visit to a young Tawi man to trigger a collective response.

Perhaps early participation in the Paliau Movement had put Tawi and Ndriol in a mood receptive to the Noise. Patusi and Pere were latecomers to the Movement, and the representatives of Bunai and Mbukei who had gone to the meetings on Mok had stayed to join Mok people in the Noise. The Noise began in Patusi only after repeated contacts with Tawi. The *guria* did strike some individuals in Patusi, a ghost appeared regularly, and a few Noise enthusiasts organised seances to converse with the ghosts, but there were no mass seizures. Pere and Bunai were even farther from the centres of the Noise. A series of rumours of the arrival of cargo moved some to try to initiate the Noise in these villages and, following the example of Patusi, throw their possessions into the sea, but—according to the accounts Schwartz and Shargo collected—they did so more hesitantly.

Paliau regained leadership after the demise of the Noise. In village after village, people abandoned expectations of an imminent, sudden realisation of a European Eden, and returned to Paliau's step-by-step program. The early New Way program called for moving towards a society that was not only more prosperous but also more focused on the common good. Thus, working collectively, abandoning gender and age hierarchies, doing away with taboos on interaction between certain classes of kin, and amassing money for collective ventures—none of which could be accomplished quickly—were among the program's key elements.

But some returned to this program reluctantly, and among these many hoped that Paliau still intended to lead them to the cargo, although by another route. It appears that they assumed that the mundane actions Paliau prescribed—building a meeting house, pooling money, strict coordination of daily activities, and so on—were in fact ritual acts; that is, symbolic communication meant to induce a higher power to fulfil their hopes. Such perceptions are common and durable in many parts of what is now Papua New Guinea. For instance, Eric Schwimmer (1979: 308–9) discusses the high rate of failure of small businesses among the Orokaiva people of Northern Province and concludes that they failed in the

European sense because many Orokaiva saw business as fundamentally a 'religious practice'. And Eugene Ogan (1972: 161–2, 175) observed that in the 1960s many of the Nasioi people of Bougainville Island 'never differentiated' between what looked to European eyes like efforts to conduct business more effectively and efforts to obtain riches by supernatural means (cf. Smith 1994: 156ff.; 1990; 1984).

Explaining the Noise

We have now provided enough information on the circumstances of the Paliau Movement to propose an explanation of the cargo cults within it—the Noise and (as described in Chapter 9) the re-emergence of millenarian action in the Cemetery Cult. We think it is likely that the key points of our explanation apply to most other Melanesian cargo cults as well.[13] But—as we will discuss in Chapter 15—our explanation of cargo cults falls short of applying to millenarianism in general.[14]

---

13 We will not review the major types of explanations for cargo cults offered in the literature. For such a review, we recommend Burridge (1969) and Schwartz (1976a). Although these works are not recent, few or no subsequent efforts identify circumstances that do not fall into one of the categories of explanation Burridge and Schwartz address, barring analyses that question the reality of cargo cults or focus on hypothesised inchoate functions that are not in themselves causal factors. Barkun's (1998 [1974]) treatise on the relationship of disaster to millenarianism also addresses most of the general categories of explanation on which Burridge and Schwartz focus. Similarly, Hamilton's (2001) discussion of hypotheses regarding Christian millenarianism addresses general categories of explanation that overlap substantially with those of Burridge and Schwartz.
14 Martin Holbraad and Morten Axel Pedersen (2017: 16), leading exponents of the ontological turn, recommend that the discipline pull away from the 'rather hackneyed choice' between interpreting social and cultural phenomena and explaining them, but they are more critical of explaining than of interpreting. They write: 'For anthropologists to imagine their task as that of explaining *why* people do what they do, they must first suppose that they understand *what* these people are doing. The ontological turn often involves showing that such "why" questions … are founded on a misconception of "what" …' [That is, what is being explained.] They acknowledge that how to conceptualise phenomena is the discipline's 'most abiding methodological concern' (ibid.: 5). But they want anthropologists to be warier about resting on well-worn conceptions, and they propose that anthropologists 'keep *open* the question of what phenomena might comprise a given ethnographic field and how anthropological concepts have to be modulated or transformed the better analytically to articulate them' (ibid.: 10). As we understand this school of thought, its proponents do not hold that explanation is undesirable or impossible, but they do not give it high priority. From the standpoint of the ontological turn, our efforts at explaining the Noise (and millenarianism in general) are premature (even though, as we see it, how one conceptualises things—or reconceptualises them—implies an approach to explaining them). But millenarian ideology and activity have immediate political importance (see Chapter 15); people have to react to millenarian ideas and movements now, not later at their leisure. And they can't do so without at least implicitly subscribing to some kind of explanation. Anthropologists will probably find better ways of understanding millenarianism than those available currently, including our own, but that is no reason to cede the field of explanation to others—most of whom are less qualified—today.

We have argued that cargo cults are about the cargo. By this we mean that the cargo is not merely a symbol for a less concrete desideratum; it is an *essential and integral* element of the desired new world. For some participants in the Noise it may have been enough that in that new world there would be less material want, pain, and suffering. For many, obtaining the cargo (and the secret of continuing easy abundance) may also have helped repair damaged personal and group self-worth, which in Manus (as in much of Melanesia) were tightly interwoven with material wealth. Indeed, we go further and contend that radically upsetting the fused moral/material foundation of indigenous society did more to inspire cargo cults in Melanesia than did subordination of Melanesians to colonial authority. In Schwartz's (1976a: 175) words, 'One can readily conceive of cults arising both in the known cases and all over the Melanesian area', he writes, 'even if colonial domination had not been attempted. The mere presence of Europeans and their possessions and the early contact disturbances to Melanesian … scales of values were sufficient'. Repairing this disturbance required cargo as cargo—that is, as material wealth.

What Burridge writes of the Tangu people in *Mambu* (1995 [1960]: 258) probably could have applied to many of the cargo cultists of Manus: 'Tangu would like to be men amongst men, not merely men among Tangu'. But to say that participants in the Noise perceived the cargo, either clearly or dimly, as primarily a means of achieving equality with whites goes too far.[15] A form of equality that did not include plenty of cargo for everyone would have been virtually inconceivable and, had it come to pass, unacceptable. Similarly, many participants wanted to be closer to God, but not in monastic austerity. And, just as returning ancestors with empty

---

15 Schwartz's (1976a: 175) discussion of 'value dominance' in cargo millenarianism is relevant here but it would divert us from our main argument. Schwartz's analysis foreshadows Marshall Sahlins's well-known essay 'The Economics of Developman in the Pacific', in which Sahlins suggests that 'humiliation' may be 'a necessary stage in the process of modernization' (Sahlins 1992: 23). Sahlins proposes that for people to reject their culture and attempt to create something radically different they 'must first learn to hate what they already have, what they have always considered their well-being. Beyond that, they have to despise what they are, to hold their own existence in contempt—and want, then, to be someone else' (p. 24). Robbins and Wardlow (2017 [2005]) provide perceptive analyses of the complexities of Sahlins's proposition in several Melanesian ethnographic contexts. Many of the chapters in their volume relate Sahlins's ideas to cargo cults and millenarianism in Melanesia (e.g. Biersack (p. 138) on Ipili 'millenarian expectations', Dalton (p. 106) on 'so-called "cargo-cult" activities' among the Rawa, Foster (p. 211) on Urapmin 'apocalypticism', Leavitt (p. 76) on Bumbita Arapesh 'cargo ideas', and Wardlow (p. 59) on the 'more millennial versions' of Melanesian Christianity). Sahlins's essay and these ethnographic cases largely support Schwartz's observations on the Manus cargo cults, although we would stop short of saying that Manus Noise participants had come 'to hold their own existence in contempt'.

hands would have received an ambivalent welcome (at best), participants in the Noise who hoped for immortality envisioned an everlasting life of material abundance. Thus, as we proposed in Chapter 2, the cargo in cargo cults—at least in those we know the best—is not a symbol but a synecdoche, a part of something that stands for the whole. And we hold that it is the only part of the whole (as variously imagined) that could do so.

Otto (2010: 90–1) proposes a motive for engaging in cargo cults that is more subtle than the desire for material parity with whites. He invokes the 'so-called New Melanesian Ethnography' and its 'key insight … that Melanesian personhood is constituted through the exchange of material and immaterial things, such as food, valuables, knowledge of ritual, magical spells, and proper names. Agency [that is, personal efficacy] is realised in the act of exchange, during which composite parts of the person [that is, material things or rights to such immaterial things as names, magical spells, or ritual knowledge] are given and received'. Hence, Otto writes: 'The theme of the white people keeping central parts of their personhood back from exchange with Melanesians runs through many cults'. Some participants in the Noise may have perceived and resented that whites refused to engage with them as full persons through exchange of esoteric knowledge and a wider range of material goods, just as some were angered by alleged white re-routing of the cargo the ancestors were trying to send. But of Manus participants in the Noise we are certain only of this: they were willing to take desperate measures to obtain command of the cargo—the unlimited wealth of which whites, they believed, had mastery—because they understood this as the one indispensable element of a sweeping transformation of their world, including their relationships with whites.

Why Manus people turned to the supernatural to obtain command of the cargo is a somewhat more straightforward issue. The prevailing and strongly institutionalised predisposition to personify the causes of events ensured the force of millenarian notions involving supernatural intervention in human affairs. Regarding specific indigenous Manus precedent for such a millenarian idea, Schwartz found in myths from throughout the Admiralties examples of 'mythological fantasies … about a work-free existence that preceded native versions of the Fall of Man, the time before the violation of a totemic taboo or some other act of spoiling a good thing' (1976a: 197; cf. Smith 1994: 139–40).[16] Even without such indigenous cultural material, by the 1940s Christian missionaries had long since introduced Manus people to a new vocabulary of human failing and redemption embedded in the Christian cosmology of animate and personal causation. It is impossible to say how Manus people would have reacted to colonial rule and the events of the war absent Christian missionary influence, but that is a moot point.[17]

In Manus, as elsewhere in indigenous Melanesia, there was also ample precedent for communication with occult entities (in Manus, principally ghosts of the dead) possessing knowledge exceeding that of mortal humans. Given a rich environment for millenarian thinking, it is not surprising that people would claim to be conduits for revelations from the occult sphere and that others would accept their claims. Many people took Paliau as a cargo prophet, whether or not he actually played or desired to play that role. The cargo prophets of Rambutjo Island (Muli and Wapei) made a critical contribution to the Noise and throughout both cult episodes numbers of people served as alleged messengers for occult beings. Finally, as we argued in Chapter 3, the nature of life in indigenous Manus (and much of indigenous Melanesia) pushed to an extreme a tendency to personify causation and find immediate personal relevance in events. This underlay

---

16   The ethnography of Melanesia also offers many examples of well-developed indigenous assumptions that the world is in chronic danger of ending and must be revitalised by ritual action (e.g. Biersack 2011a, 2011b; Dwyer and Minnegal 2000). One could call this a kind of defensive millenarianism.

17   Some anthropologists—Schwartz (1976a: 172, 177) and Smith (1994: 140–1) among them—have also suggested that a culturally constructed view of time as relatively shallow has been a factor in Melanesian cargo millenarianism, perhaps making an abrupt transformation of the world more plausible. Peter Lawrence (1989 [1964]: 241–3) has advanced one of the best-known arguments in this vein. Lawrence is also among those—including Frederick Errington (1974) and Nancy McDowell (1988, 2000)—who have suggested that an understanding of time and change as episodic, reported from some locales in Melanesia, may also help explain why Melanesians have found cargo cult doctrines plausible. A view of time as episodic is highly compatible with the quest for sudden, apocalyptic transformation, as is ignorance of the depth of human history. Some anthropologists, however, have questioned the importance of arguments in this vein on the basis of ethnographic evidence. For example, Joel Robbins (2004b: 342n7) speculates that in some parts of Melanesia where cargo cults have occurred, notions of episodic time and change 'are not indigenous but have been influenced by experiences of contact and colonialism and by encounters with Christian ideas'. More important, looking at cargo cults in a broader millenarian context inclines us to treat prevailing conceptions of time and history as of marginal value in explaining readiness to entertain millenarian hopes. The very nature of apocalyptic millenarianism, wherever it occurs, is that it seeks radically discontinuous transformation with no concern for any prevailing understanding of time and change. Hence, we find millenarianism even in times and places where an episodic view of history is not the norm and knowledge of how change in the human condition has come about gradually over many thousands of years is widely available.

an ethos—a paranoid ethos—that made many Manus people susceptible to putting aside the pragmatism that ensured their daily survival in favour of nearly full-time preoccupation with suspicions of hostile conspiracy and intimations of imminent miraculous deliverance. This was—and is— the world of cargo cults and other forms of apocalyptic millenarianism.

We know, however, that not all Manus people or even all the people of the south coast of Manus and the southerly islands participated in the cargo cults. Why not? Those who remained aloof from or opposed the cults lived in the same social and cultural world as those who participated. But this common world featured many structural tensions and incentives to compete for status, leadership, and material advantages. These did not make some people significantly more susceptible than others to millenarian hopes, but they channelled enthusiasm for becoming participants in particular millenarian efforts. In Chapters 8 and 9 we will show how the historical and sociopolitical context of the Manus cults helped shape distribution of participation over time and space within a population coping with the same larger circumstances. But we are not quite through with the Noise. Its aftermath is as important to the history of the Paliau Movement as are the events that comprised it. In Chapter 7, then, we look at the ways participants in the Noise reacted to its collapse and how the failure of the Noise set the stage for the idiosyncrasies of the Cemetery Cult, which Schwartz and Shargo were privileged to observe firsthand.

7

After the Noise

The Noise ended in village after village with the disappointed recognition that, at best, the arrival of the cargo and the First Order of God had been postponed. The retrospective accounts Schwartz and Shargo collected suggest that most people accepted this—at least outwardly—within a few weeks. People recalled clearly that Paliau had rallied them to return to his program where they had left off, even though this meant moving step-by-step through the Second Order.

Adjusting to the failure of the Noise

Many people, however, could not relinquish their hopes for something miraculous. They fed their hopes on what they took as the dual meaning of New Way practices and Paliau's version of Christianity. In addition, Paliau's pronouncements on the Noise were ambiguous. He said that it had been unsuccessful and that people must now take another path. But he did not say unequivocally that the idea of the Noise was wrong or that the many visions and manifestations reported had been mere delusions. Some Manus people told Schwartz and Shargo that the Noise had been temporary madness, often using the Tok Pisin word *longlong*. At its mildest, *longlong* translates as stupid or ignorant, but it can also denote what one would call madness in English. Yet the Noise had been a profoundly important experience in many people's lives and the anthropologists found only a few among those whom it had touched who did not feel that—despite their failure—they had indeed come close to God, the dead, and the cargo.

The desire for a direct relationship with God persisted. People pursued this most systematically in their separatist version of Christian worship, resisting overtures to return to the fold from the three missions active in Manus at the time—the Roman Catholic, Evangelical Lutheran, and Seventh-day Adventist. Distrust and rejection of the missions were almost universal within the Movement.

Some leaders of the Noise blamed Wapei—or Muli, his killer—for its failure, and many Noise participants suspected that Australians had somehow blocked the cargo. Still others said that Satan had deceived them. Even some who had been movers and shakers, however, held that the failure was their own fault. As one man put it, 'We were not ready; there was too much bad thought in our old culture and in ourselves for us to eliminate it so quickly'. Some speculated that the Noise had been a trial imposed by God and that the real Noise was yet to come. But no single explanation prevailed and many people seemed to find all explanations both equally plausible and equally unsatisfying. Only a few seemed truly sceptical, willing to entertain the idea that the strength of their own desires had generated people's prophetic visions.

Reluctantly turning back to life in the Second Order, people quickly recovered as much as they could of the valuables and other possessions thrown onto the Mok reef. Even as the aura of the Noise was fading, a few still reported signs and wonders, but their reports drew less and less attention. Many, however, regarded the ease with which they found the Movement funds as evidence that their Second Order efforts, although frustratingly slow, were on the right track.

The Noise and wider unity

Paliau was quite certain that the Australian administration would detain him in the course of its investigation of the Noise. He sent notes to a number of the Noise leaders on the south coast, conveying instructions on how to respond to government questioning about the Noise when it came. Local leaders, he counselled, should insist that the Noise had occurred independently within each village, that it was not fomented or directed by any central leaders. This was no deception. In fact, the Noise was not centrally coordinated and most participants did not see it as a collective effort on the part of several villages.

Some analyses of cargo cults hold that in the long term they help create greater political unity, paving the way for forms of political organisation—for instance, nationalist movements (May 1982; Worsley 1968 [1957]) and political parties (Kaima 1991)—that transcend local groups and precolonial networks. The Noise does seem to have created a new kind of solidarity *within* participating villages, the residents of which assumed that each village was to receive its own cargo. Noise adherents demonstrated this uncharacteristic assumption of village common interest most dramatically when, in several cases, they repelled visitors from other villages, fearing that they might try to take shares of the local cargo. This suggests that had the impossible happened and the cargo arrived, it would not have fostered greater trust and cooperation among villages. The *failure* of the Noise, however, did contribute to wider unity. This brings to mind Landes's (2011: 65) observation that 'in matters apocalyptic', wrong does not mean 'inconsequential'.

Schwartz and Shargo found wide agreement that the Noise ultimately involved approximately 33 villages. Its demise left their people with both the glowing embers of similar hopes and a common interest in putting the failure of the Noise aside and finding another path towards better lives. With Paliau's leadership, this proved the basis for inter-village unity of a scope and kind that had no precedent in indigenous Manus. Those who had gone through the Noise seemed to feel bound to one another by the experience. Many said that the Noise had changed them, that it had shaken them loose from their past. And many felt superior to the people of villages that had not been privileged to be near God during the Noise.

The ridicule and censure heaped on them by some who had remained outside the Noise, and by government officers and missionaries, also helped bind former Noise participants together. When they marched in the revived Movement, they marched with defiant pride. Paliau's detention and the jailing of leaders who burned hats and books also fuelled such feelings. When some Roman Catholic priests cut off participants in the Noise from the church, they succeeded only in creating additional unifying hostility towards the church among the ousted communicants. All else aside, people united around the person of Paliau, although many who had joined the Movement after the Noise had never seen or heard him in person. A series of ballads was composed about Paliau's triumph over the administration. It was said that the local administration officers and the missionaries had wanted to kill him. But they could not because Paliau had spoken so forcefully on his own behalf and because he was protected by both Jesus and the highest government officials.

Paliau realised that the wide reach of the Noise gave him a chance to broaden the influence of the Movement. The Noise spread rapidly, but its abrupt end left the people of many villages sunk in confusion and disorganisation. As they sought a steady compass, people's interest in Paliau's pre-Noise program grew. Granted, some did not perceive the Noise and the Movement as distinct, so cleaving to the Movement was for them a way to continue their quest. Yet as far as Schwartz and Shargo could ascertain, virtually all the villages involved in the Noise now turned to the Movement and looked to Paliau to tell them what to do next. Paliau was ready to do so.[1]

The post-Noise New Way

The administration held Paliau responsible for the Noise and assumed he had been its prophet. After detaining him and taking him to Lorengau, the administrators in Manus sent him to Port Moresby in mid-1947.[2] There, administration officials told him about the government's program for the people of the Territory of Papua and New Guinea, hoping they could enlist Paliau in its support. Paliau returned from Port Moresby later that year. In his absence, the Movement had continued along the lines laid down in the pre-Noise meetings and had done so with remarkable

1   Harvey Whitehouse (2000) uses the Paliau Movement as one of several cases illustrating what he proposes is a common process within religions in which episodes of 'imagistic religiosity' (in the Paliau Movement, the dramatic, emotionally compelling events of the cults) alternate with periods of 'doctrinal religiosity' (such as the focus on the 'Long Story of God', routine liturgical worship, and promulgation of New Way prescriptions and proscriptions during other phases of the Movement). The former, Whitehouse proposes, rejuvenates the latter. From this perspective, Whitehouse (2000: 145) suggests that 'it is probable that the Paliau Movement could not have survived as long as it has done without the intermittent outbursts of imagistic practices that rejuvenated religious commitment and overall cohesion'. This goes beyond what we care to claim for the contribution of either the Noise or the Cemetery Cult to greater solidarity within the Movement. Like Whitehouse, however, we do not believe the cults were conscious efforts to revive a flagging Movement or foster wider solidarity. Gustafsson (1992: 246) seems to suggest that in the cults there was conscious intent to 'accelerate the development of the Movement, or else to change its leadership structure', although she offers no evidence of this.
2   According to Kaima (1991: 175), Paliau was detained for 'misuse of his *luluai* title' without any explicit reference to the Noise.

vigour. Each village had its *pesman*, appointed by Paliau or elected after the Noise. Each village also had men called teachers, who taught the New Way, including the word of God as interpreted by Paliau.

In the immediate aftermath of the Noise, Paliau and his most loyal followers were able to institute a more fully developed and centralised New Way organisation. And as the Noise faded into the background, a more standardised version of Paliau's reinterpretation of mission teaching replaced the variegated beliefs characterising the Noise. Paliau wanted to encourage more consistent forms of worship and to excise from Movement teachings ideas that had crept in during the Noise. The immediate post-Noise Movement teachers preached or taught from written copies of the 'Long Story of God' rather than relying solely on memory. Taking a further step, Paliau also had each Movement village send one man to Baluan Island for training in a new liturgy to replace both recitations and readings of the 'Long Story of God'. Paliau borrowed much of the new liturgy from Catholic and Evangelical worship services and he reinterpreted some of these borrowings to make them explicitly compatible with the Movement. Nevertheless, local teachers were left on their own to elaborate Movement-specific meanings for some items in the liturgy or to leave them to their listeners' imaginations.

At some point after the Noise, the liturgical aspect of the Movement was more formally defined as the Baluan United Christian Church, sometimes called the Baluan Native Christian Church. The *Baluan United Christian Church Lotu Buk* (Baluan United Christian Church Worship Book)— bound in heavy, textured, red card stock—includes 18 pages of responsive readings in Tok Pisin, with places marked for singing and 25 pages of song lyrics.[3] Most of the songs are in Tok Pisin, but the English lyrics of several common Christmas carols (such as 'Silent Night' and 'Away in a Manger') are also included. The book gives the date of the church's founding as 1946, identifying it with the founding of the Movement. However, although the founding of the Movement and rejection of the Catholic Mission were virtually inseparable events, we know that Paliau's separatist Christianity assumed the identity of a named church only after Schwartz and Shargo left Manus in 1954.

---

3   Schwartz was unable to find out who paid for making *Lotu Buk*, the only document with a professional finish the Movement had issued at this point.

Figure 7.1: The Baluan United Christian Church in Lipan-Mok village, Baluan Island, 1953.

Paliau's followers built it according to his plan and under his supervision. At the time, it was probably the largest structure in the Admiralty Islands built with indigenous technology and local materials, and it boasted a balcony and a choir loft. The only non-local materials used were military surplus perforated metal sheets of the kind used to make temporary airfields.

Source: Theodore Schwartz.

Post-Noise, Movement adherents were less inclined than ever to regard its innovations merely as practical reforms for life lived in secular time. During the Noise, many people regarded secular activities as spiritually adulterating. Thus, Lukas Pokus of Pere village explained that, although the *guria* persisted in him longer than in others, he lost his ability to *guria* because he could not concentrate his thoughts sufficiently on God as he became increasingly preoccupied with building the new village and making his daily living. Some tried to avoid descending into the entirely mundane by giving the early forms of the Movement ritual and magical significance. As the New Way re-emerged from the ruins of the Noise, many treated its rules of behaviour as sacred.

We have mentioned some of these rules in previous chapters. We do not think there was ever a single definitive set of Movement rules. While writing this book, we came across a document Schwartz had forgotten he possessed: a small notebook that Paliau had given him containing numbered lists of New Way prohibitions and admonitions, written in Paliau's own hand. Apparently written with a fountain pen that occasionally blotted, some words—both Tok Pisin and Titan—are hard to decipher. Here, however, is the first of four lists, dated November 1946, translated into English.

> List of the things we ban from our villages because they are bad behaviour and cause us to die.
> 1. We won't argue about land any more.
> 2. Men can't have bad thoughts about their wives.
> 3. Women can't have bad thoughts about their husbands.
> 4. We can no longer [indecipherable word] women with their work.
> 5. We can no longer make feasts for people who die [indecipherable words].
> 6. We can no longer fight about trouble [i.e. sexual peccadilloes] between young men and young women.
> 7. We can no longer lie and talk behind people's backs.
> 8. We can no longer engage in [the word appears to be *palan*, a Titan term for a kind of gift or payment in the affinal exchange cycle].
> 9. We can no longer make feasts in the old way.
> 10. We can no longer arrange marriages; men and women must marry according to their own preferences.
> 11. We can no longer [indecipherable word].
> 12. We can no longer get angry.
> 13. We can no longer fight.
> 14. We can no longer steal.
> 15. We can no longer speak angrily in church.
> 16. We can no longer take things belonging to another.
> 17. We can no longer kill men, women, and children.
> That is all.
> Mi Paliau. [That is, 'I am Paliau'.]

There follows a list of things people *should* do, dated 1 November 1946. This is followed by two more lists of prohibitions, both dated 19 January 1948. Each of the three lists of prohibitions repeats some items that appear in the others and includes some distinct items. As fluid as it could be, however, the New Way was now considered the way of God, even if it was uncertain when God might reward those who followed it.

The post-Noise New Way emphasised coordinated, simultaneous behaviour. Movement leaders taught people to march in formation and instituted a shared routine for daily activities. There was no precedent for this in indigenous life; the models were the routines of plantation workers, the administration's quasi-military patrols, and the military camp.[4] In virtually every New Way village, people hung empty war surplus acetylene tanks from frames to serve as bells. (Many of these still hang in Papua New Guinea villages. Strike one with a piece of metal or a stone and the clang is impressive.) At the sound of the bell, people left their houses in the morning, bathed in the sea, went to church, and then lined up to receive assignments for the day's communal work. The bell then signalled the end of work, time to bathe again, to eat, and to attend church. Finally, after the bell announced curfew (at about nine o'clock), people remained in their houses.

Daily meetings, preceded by singing and marching, were filled with endless reiterations of the new rules of behaviour, the vices of the past, and the virtues of the New Way. A particularly troublesome New Way commandment was that people were to abandon shame. No one was quite sure what this entailed—how far they could go in acting on impulses that the norms of indigenous life called on them to suppress. Both in the late days of the Noise and for a short time during the initial post-Noise New Way, a few people experimented with nudism and mixed-sex bathing. Since Manus lagoon and beach dwellers bathed in the sea, there was still considerable scope for maintaining privacy. Still, these innovations did not catch on.

People were also enjoined to rid themselves of anger. Leaders constantly exhorted anyone who harboured bad feelings towards others to reveal them so that reconciliation could avert the sickness or death that such feelings might induce. When sickness did occur, the leaders elicited confessions of anger or other negative feelings that, it was believed, caused the illness.[5]

Paliau sought to eliminate longstanding horizontal and vertical social divisions and indigenous social fragmentation, and he regarded forming new composite villages as a step in this direction. He had planned that the Titan would move their villages from the lagoons to the beaches.

---

4   See Smith (1984) for discussion of a similar case.
5   Neither Fortune nor Mead speaks of such notions regarding anger and illness as indigenous among the Titan. Similar beliefs and practices, however, are definitely part of the indigenous heritage in other parts of Papua New Guinea. Smith (1994) gives a detailed account of such a case.

The Usiai were to leave their old villages and join the Titan on the beaches. Movement participants began relocating to beach villages in 1947. By the end of 1949 they had formed a number of Titan–Usiai composite villages. Paliau also urged contiguous or closely related sets of villages to amalgamate in larger settlements, and many did so.

Bunai as the anthropologists found it in 1953–54 was an amalgamated settlement, including both Titan and Usiai groups, formed late in the Noise. The original village of Bunai had itself been composed of the remnants of several formerly separate Titan settlements. These included a settlement of Titan people of the Ndropwa clan, who had left the island that became known as Ndropwa, seeking protection in numbers from constant raiding by other Titan; Titan of Tjalolo clan, a group that had split from Pere in the past; and Titan of Mpoat and Kupwen clans, which had constituted distinct places in the past. Another small, independent Titan settlement, Pomatjau, was the first separate village to join Bunai, by mutual consent, during the last days of the Noise. Several complete Usiai villages followed later, all from the area nearer the south coast known as the Number Two Road. These included Lahan and Yiru and later Malei and Lowaya. Before the move, the latter two had been linked by a distinct dialect and much intermarriage. Also, unlike the other segments of amalgamated Bunai, which had been Catholic prior to the Movement's break from the church, the people of these two villages had joined the Lutheran Evangelical Mission, but this did not seem to hinder their assimilation into the New Way version of Christianity. Small groups from the Usiai villages of Polisan and Kitan and individuals from a few other villages also gravitated to Bunai. Some of the latter had not committed completely to the Noise or the New Way, but they apparently saw advantages in becoming part of such a large unit in such a convenient location.

In 1953, amalgamated Bunai stretched in a single or double row of houses for almost a mile along the beach. It was a long, narrow settlement, with the sea in front, a bit of swampy land behind it, and behind that a steep rise into the forested interior. A wide, straight path of white coral sand ran from the western end of the village to the eastern end. Such a formal pathway was a distinctive feature of New Way villages. The Movement villages on Baluan built similar promenades. Even on Johnston Island, where there was only one village, people had built a formal pathway circling the island, leaving the village at one end and returning to it at the other.

All the Titan sections of Bunai were at the western end (nearest Pere) of the village, in approximately this order: Ndropwa, Tjalolo, old Bunai, Mpoat, Kupwen, and Pomatjau. Next came three houses from the Usiai village of Polisan. Then came Schwartz and Shargo's house. East of this were the remaining Usiai sections: Malei, separated from Lahan by a small stream flowing to the sea, then Yiru, Katin, and Lowaya.

Some villages became parts of larger beach settlements but retained much of their old autonomy by continuing to function as separate units. Yet both in size and in political complexity, these new villages were without precedent in the Admiralty Islands. Residents of the new villages adopted the slogan 'a new place for a new way of life'. Although remnants of their populations remained in their original locations, the majority of people from Usiai Movement villages moved to the beach en masse and burned the structures they left behind. People built each house in the new villages collectively, in the most linear pattern that space would allow. Many houses incorporated European features, having more windows and more separate rooms than common in indigenous dwellings. They were built largely of bush materials, but incorporated war surplus sheet metal, canvas, and plywood. Wherever possible, each village had a main gate and a wharf as well as a more formal demarcation of a clear central space—a kind of village plaza—where meetings were held. These suggested a kind of common village identity and a degree of centralised organisation absent from Manus village life as observed by Fortune and Mead.

As noted earlier, some men who played important roles in the Noise had not manifested such symptoms of supernatural favour as dreams, visions, and *guria*, but had exercised leadership by helping to organise, control, standardise, or interpret such behaviour. Many of them were able to retain some authority post-Noise. But those whose leadership had rested on their cult-specific behaviour lost most of their influence to people with special knowledge of the Movement's program and practices, like Paliau's *pesman* and teachers. Some leaders of the Noise ceded authority readily, at least in part because they did not wish to become entangled in what seemed to them the Movement's preoccupation with mundane matters and its apparent gradualism.

The New Way placed a high value on literacy, putting at a disadvantage the many illiterate villagers of all persuasions regarding the Noise. This included even Tjamilo, whose verbal memory was phenomenal. He knew by heart the 'Long Story of God' and every one of Paliau's speeches he had ever heard. A number of other men whose status had risen with the Noise were also illiterate or nearly so, among them Posanau of Bunai, Lukas Pokus and Lukas Bonyalo of Pere, and Pita Tapo of Lahan. Having lost what turned out to be their temporary status, some of these men went into rapid eclipse.

Accounts of the first years of the post-Noise New Way suggest that people adapted with surprising ease to the new economic practices. There was to be free exchange, with no strict accounting either within the village or between the Usiai and Titan participants in the Movement. The underlying principle was what is called in Tok Pisin *maremare* (má-ray-má-ray). This is a term still used extensively in Christian discourse in much of Papua New Guinea. It translates as compassion, mercy, or Christian charity. In New Way practice it meant giving without thought of return. Applied to exchange and the use of land and reefs, it amounted to a limited economic communalism. People retained the rights they held to land and other property by indigenous reckoning, but they were expected to share freely the yield of their fishing or gardening and to permit others to use gardening land, sago palms, fishing reefs, or other resources without paying compensation. New Way leaders tried to keep as much exchange as possible between villages as units. Each composite Movement village had a wharf with a shed on it, called the customs house, and an official, the customs officer. The customs officer recorded everything brought to the village from other villages so that a return could be made later. Inter-village travellers were expected to carry passes written by the heads of their own villages.

Every effort was made to make the network of Movement villages economically self-sufficient. Although leaders continued to collect cash in a common fund, they discouraged working for Europeans, even though this was one of the few sources of cash. Europeans in Manus accused Movement leaders of establishing a kind of totalitarian rule, coercing people to work for the Movement, and forcibly preventing villagers from working for the European dollar. The New Way economic system probably relied on strong peer pressure, but Schwartz and Shargo found no evidence corroborating the darker European accusations.

Each village held weekly meetings to decide to what communal tasks men, women, or children would be assigned at the daily morning assemblies. Sometimes a week was set for building up a supply of sago, or a day was set for communal fishing (several techniques of fishing among the reefs required a group to set and hold nets and drive fish into them), or for maintaining or improving the village paths. Specific days were set for individual work.

Paliau and a few of his followers continued to innovate. Paliau organised regular, Movement-wide meetings, rotating among participating villages. He added to his program much that he had learned in Port Moresby of the administration's program for rural improvement. Among other things, he had learned of administration plans to gradually introduce very limited local self-government in the form of what the Australian administration called Native Government Councils (NGCs). Under the NGC system, each village would elect someone to both represent the administration in the village and represent the village in dealing with the administration, in part through area organisations of these village leaders.[6] Paliau got a jump on the administration by putting in place in the Movement villages a system approximating this. He retired '*pesman*' as the title for leaders in Movement villages, replacing it with council (in Tok Pisin, *kaunsil*). The latter approximated the title proposed by the administration— councillor—for the elected village leaders once the administration's system was put in place. There was also a secondary village leader called the committee (in Tok Pisin, *komiti*). From here on, when we speak of the leaders of the new Movement villages, we will call them *kaunsil*. When we speak of village leaders under the NGC system, we will call them councillors. We will refer to the secondary leaders under both systems as *komiti*, as villagers did. Context should make it clear whether we are speaking of *komiti* under the Movement system or the NGC system.

The Movement wins a Native Government Council, but loses momentum

By 1949, the Movement was focusing on getting the administration to establish an NGC in the Movement area. Paliau, of course, would be at its head. The Movement also wanted the administration to hasten introducing non-mission schools and forming producers' and consumers' cooperatives. The cooperatives were to give producers of copra and other

---

6   Moore (2003: 196–7) provides an account of the growth of the council system from informal roots in the 1920s.

local products an alternative to dealing individually with European-owned traders and to provide a more economical source of the manufactured goods people wished to purchase with their cash earnings.

In 1950, the administration established an NGC area encompassing Baluan and Rambutjo and their adjacent islands. But what the administration called the Baluan Council included only part of the Movement area. Villages on the south coast of Manus Island were conspicuously left out. Still, this was a significant step. Australia created the NGCs as entities with statutory authority and financing only in 1949. The only NGCs other than the Baluan Council established within the next year or so were in locales with large indigenous populations and near the European centres of Rabaul and Port Moresby (Moore 2003: 196). Manus, let alone the Baluan area, had no such distinctions. Paliau and the Movement undoubtedly deserved some of the credit for drawing the administration's attention to Baluan. Paliau and the Movement villages had been pressing for an NGC consistently since the end of the Noise and it is reliably reported (Fenbury 1978: 279, cited by Otto 1991: 173) that among the administration's motivations for choosing the Baluan area at this point was the desire to calm what many officials regarded as Paliau's and his followers' anti-government agitation.

Things easily could have gone against Paliau. He was very unpopular with most administration personnel in Manus; one of them described him in a report as 'a pro-Jap, anti-White native with very evil intentions' (Otto 1991: 173–4). In January 1950, some months before the Baluan Council was established, an administration officer charged that Paliau had given an anti-government speech and produced alleged witnesses of this. The administration conducted an investigation, including a visit to Baluan, and charged Paliau with trying to inappropriately influence another *luluai* and making 'false reports which tended to cause trouble among the people'. Behind these spindly charges was the fear that Paliau was setting up his own government in opposition to the administration. The court in Lorengau found him guilty and sentenced him to six months incarceration with hard labour (Otto 1991: 172).

Paliau's followers protested, but their anger did not bear fruit until a United Nations Trusteeship mission visited Manus in May 1950. Paliau's supporters, including several village *luluai*, now addressed themselves to the United Nations representatives, protesting Paliau's harsh treatment and praising his accomplishments (Otto 1991: 172). Sensitive to the resulting pressure from the trusteeship mission, the district administration took a more subtle course. Paliau was released from prison before finishing his sentence, but only to be sent to Port Moresby. Once again, administration officials tried to enlist Paliau's support for government programs for improving village life, for instance, by taking him to visit examples of showcase programs near the city.

But administration officials took their time buttering up the potentially dangerous agitator. Paliau did not return to Baluan until March 1951, months after his release from incarceration. This suggests that the administration wanted to keep him out of Manus until the Baluan Council was in place. Paliau arrived home to find the council already established. People in Movement villages chose the men serving as Movement *kaunsil* as their councillors within the NGC system. More germane to Paliau's quest for leadership, the chair of the NGC's coordinating body was filled in his absence. But if the administration had hoped to keep Paliau on the sidelines, it failed. At the first opportunity, Paliau sought a seat on the coordinating body and soon after became its chair (Otto 1991: 173–4).[7] While many members of the administration would have preferred that he simply disappear, becoming chair of the Baluan Council did clip his wings. The Baluan Council area not only excluded the parts of Manus most loyal to Paliau (cf. Mead 2001 [1956]: 397), it also included villages on Baluan that had opposed the Movement. In addition, Paliau had to carry out his new responsibilities under the supervision of a resident assistant district officer (ADO) (Otto 1991: 174). Although the officer, James Landman, was dedicated to the Baluan NGC's success, as Schwartz knew from his personal conversations with Landman, his presence limited Paliau's freedom.

---

7   We assume he was eligible to contend for that post because he was still recognised as village councillor for Lipan-Mok. But we have been unable to find a detailed account of how he obtained the position as chair of the Baluan NGC.

Figure 7.2: Paliau greeting a young admirer.

In posed photographs Paliau often looks rather forbidding. Candid photographs like this one from 1953, however, show a more genial side of his personality.

Source: Theodore Schwartz.

Still, the situation had benefits for Paliau. Many Manus people saw granting the Baluan NGC as administration recognition of the Movement's own improvised system. Paliau exerted himself to provide an alternative to Christian mission schools in the Baluan Council area, for he had no sympathy with the missions. The first government school in Manus outside Lorengau with a European teacher—Marjorie Landman, the ADO's spouse—was established on Baluan in 1951 (Otto 1991: 184). In that era, many indigenous people saw a European teacher as an advantage, not a colonial imposition. Paliau also strove to acquire other government amenities for his NGC area, such as medical aid posts and cooperative societies. Again, many people gave Paliau rather than the administration primary credit. Decades later, anthropologist Steffen Dalsgaard (2009: 93) found that Paliau's followers on Baluan, who are still numerous, saw their schools and aid posts—even those acquired in later eras—as Paliau's accomplishments.

Paliau remained the Movement's leader. But the Movement began to lose momentum. The south coast villages had the rough form of but not the legal charter for an NGC. This situation lasted almost four years. But south coast villages, both Movement and non-Movement, were not content to be an audience for the successes of the Baluan Council, and Paliau and the other Baluan Council leaders were not blind to this. They regarded extending the Baluan NGC to the entire Movement area as a much-needed next step, but they could not make south coast people a firm promise.

Despite Paliau's success in bringing an NGC and the amenities it entailed to Manus, the accounts Schwartz and Shargo collected in 1953–54 show that by 1950 the Movement was struggling. Paliau's followers had become accustomed to a steady stream of new projects and pronouncements. Now, for the first time in the course of the Movement, the pace of change for all but those encompassed by the Baluan Council slackened. Perceptions played a role here. Although Paliau was adjusting the New Way program—for instance, by creating new leadership positions to prepare for the Movement area's full incorporation into the NGC system—he was doing so without the fanfare with which he had presented each innovation pre-Noise, perhaps because he now had to divide his efforts between the Movement and his Baluan Council duties. And extending the Baluan Council to include the south coast had to wait on the Australian administration, and many thought Paliau and the Movement had lost their leverage.

Formerly, each new development of the New Way had been the subject of many public meetings and presented as a significant innovation. Similarly, when Movement leaders called for abandoning aspects of the old culture, they had repudiated them openly and explicitly. If longstanding practices had been associated with material artefacts, these had been destroyed or buried. But by 1953–54, many elements of the New Way were being abandoned almost casually. The curfew; the customs house; the customs official, who had recorded everything that came in or went out in inter-village exchange; the marching and the singing at meetings—these were all falling gradually, almost surreptitiously out of use. When Schwartz and Shargo asked why some New Way practices had been allowed to atrophy, the responses were often vague and the responders uneasy. When Schwartz asked Lokes, the customs official in Pere, why he had ceased monitoring goods leaving and entering the village, Lokes said that people had gradually stopped bothering to follow the rules. There had been no public discussion or decision. People had simply stopped heeding his authority. Much the same, others said, had happened in other villages.

Paliau did not seem unduly concerned about such changes in themselves. Despite his rigidity on many matters of New Way practice, in conversations with Schwartz it was plain that Paliau took a longer view than most of his followers. He saw the New Way as a path, not a destination—what Schwartz (1962) has called a vehicular culture, intended to move people towards a still-undefined but better way of life. Paliau recognised the need to reassure his followers, but his efforts were falling short of the mark.

The best that could be said was that the Movement had reached a plateau. Some Manus people blamed this on administration opposition. But Schwartz's long-term observations suggest the opposite: When administration opposition to the Movement was strongest, Movement morale was highest. The period of sharpest decline in morale (particularly on the south coast) came after the administration established the Baluan Council and relaxed its opposition to the Movement. Declining morale led many to relax attention to the rigid social forms of the early Movement, causing consternation among those who attached magical significance to these forms, thus further damaging morale.

Materially, Manus people were better off than they had been before the war, but their aspirations had grown faster than their conditions had improved. Early in the history of their contact with Europeans they had chosen whites or Europeans as their reference group. Close contact with Americans and Australians during and after World War II strengthened what had been only a faint hope that Manus people could aspire to a European standard of living. Some saw no reason, other than selfishness and the desire to exploit the native, that Europeans could not help them realise their desires. But if Europeans would not help them transform their lives and take a place in world society, then they would have to find their own way.

Manus people rejected the colonial status quo, in which whites monopolised commerce and government, not because it had undermined the indigenous way of life, but because it fell far short of the European way of life they now desired. In the Movement area, most people considered the stabilised post-Noise New Way a step forward, but not far enough, and many felt becalmed.

The anthropologists' dawning awareness

Mead, Schwartz, and Shargo arrived in Manus in June 1953, as the Movement rested, in many adherents' eyes, on a plateau of uncertain duration. Preoccupied with a barrage of new experiences and distracted by villagers' excitement at seeing Mead again after some 25 years, Schwartz and Shargo initially noticed nothing suggesting a depressed mood. Also, they found themselves comparing the New Way villages with those outside the Movement and with the Manus of 1928 as Mead and Fortune had described it. Against this background, what they saw—first in Pere, then in Bunai—looked like a lively commitment to steady change in secular time.

As the excitement of the Mead party's arrival dissipated, Schwartz and Shargo began to see signs of drift, even in the central Movement villages. Although houses were now arranged neatly on the beach and incorporated new styles and materials, they were still constructed largely of local materials. In the composite village of Bunai the oldest houses approximated the New Way, quasi-European plan. Latecoming Usiai people had built houses of less ambitious design and many were still unfinished. Many houses looked ramshackle and it became apparent that people were neglecting to keep them in good repair. Exposed to brutal sun and heavy wind and rain, palm-thatch roofs need frequent repairs and must be replaced completely every few years. Out of sight, beneath ground level, the heavy posts supporting houses rot, often revealing their condition only when the house above begins to lean at a crazy angle. Although people were still using it, the Bunai church, where people practised the Paliau version of Christianity, was in ruins. Storms had torn off part of its roof about a year before but no one had repaired the damage. The wharves were collapsing and the Bunai customs house had finished its collapse but no one seemed concerned.

Aside from such physical deterioration, there were signs that support for the New Way was anything but unanimous. Unless the occasion was a special event, meeting attendance was poor. Those who did attend often straggled in more than an hour late. The leaders spent much of their time scolding the latecomers and shouting reproaches in the direction of the houses of those who, bored with the repetitious speeches, had stayed at home. Church attendance was also poor; only a handful of people attended most of the weekday morning and afternoon services. Some complained that the sermons were too long. People did, however, treat Sunday as a holiday, filling the church, dressed in their best European-style clothing.

At the church services in Bunai, where Samol did most of the preaching, he emphasised the prevalence of social sin. His orations often focused on condemning 'bighead' (arrogant stubbornness; in Tok Pisin, *bikhet*), adultery, and divorce. They were replete with invocations to obey the New Way social rules, to 'hear the talk' (in Tok Pisin, *harim tok*). On many Sundays, little or nothing was said of white deception and native redemption, the powerful themes with which Paliau had caught and held his audiences early in the Movement.

Not only had some New Way practices lapsed, its institutions were malfunctioning. The New Way had introduced new principles of organisation, many infused with forms borrowed from the Australian administration. But New Way leaders complained constantly that their supposed followers were *bikhet* who would not *harim tok* (that is, arrogant individualists who did not heed their leaders and the Movement rules of behaviour), and they were having trouble cultivating feelings of solidarity across village boundaries. It looked like people were reverting to the old pattern of individualistic village leadership and hostile inter-village relations. And although Movement leaders volubly disapproved, growing numbers of young men were leaving home to work for the whites.

The Usiai were having even greater difficulties than the Titan in these respects. A sizeable group of their younger men were losing interest in the Movement and treating their elders with disdain. In the past, Usiai had expected young men to be insubordinate, but this was incompatible with the aspirations of the new society. A conspicuous group of young men spent much of their time gambling, playing ukuleles and guitars, disrupting Bunai with their indiscreet adulteries, disdaining the New Way, and rarely doing any work. Schwartz and Shargo came to call them the minstrels. They got on well with them, for Schwartz and Shargo did not represent village authority and they often paused to talk with the idlers. These young men were the conspicuous extreme of a larger trend, but they didn't hesitate to point out to the anthropologists the widespread adultery and gambling with which many older men had begun to relieve their boredom now that the excitement of the Noise was behind them and the New Way was losing its novelty and sense of purpose.

While the south coast waited for an NGC, leaders holding the Movement title of *kaunsil* found themselves in an ambiguous and frustrating position. They were recognised within the Movement but they had no legitimacy in the eyes of the administration. From the point of view of the government, their roles were potentially subversive. Many government officers, however, conveniently overlooked the unofficial status of the Movement *kaunsil* because doing so helped to keep Movement members at least tenuously connected to the official system. But anyone disgruntled at a decision of a Movement court could complain to a government officer and possibly have Movement-appointed judges arrested for holding illegal courts.

Paliau had hoped to extend the Movement to all the Admiralties, but it never expanded more than slightly beyond the limits reached by the Noise. The efforts of the administration and the missions to stop the Noise helped set those limits. Perhaps more important, the accounts Schwartz and Shargo collected suggest that as news of the Noise travelled further from its origins it lost some of its power to inspire. Reports that ships were unloading cargo on a beach just a few miles away probably carried more weight than reports of more distant events, no matter how dramatic.

Another issue troubling the Movement was that it had created a superabundance of capable leadership, but it was crowded into an organisation without scope for it all. Paliau was applying himself to translating European concepts and programs into the New Way and teaching Movement members how to use the NGC system. But few saw these activities as significant steps towards the cultural transformation Paliau had pictured for them. Also, within the Baluan Council area the grit of everyday administration began to take some of the shine off Paliau's image. In the south coast villages, a visit from Paliau was still a novelty. His occasional appearances produced brief rallies of enthusiasm for the New Way, but nonetheless the New Way was beginning to feel old.

Amalgamated Bunai, a complex, composite village, was struggling to maintain the brotherhood between the Titan and the Usiai that the Movement prescribed. People unearthed quarrels over land rights, some dating back for generations, that they had put aside in the interests of unity. Titan contempt for the Usiai and Usiai reciprocal hostility came more nakedly into the open. Factions within the Titan and Usiai populations pressed grievances against other factions and the Movement leadership by threatening to withdraw from the composite village.

Problems with economic reform

Movement efforts to institute new economic practices lagged behind those pertaining to social and political organisation. Although new communal ways of working and distributing the products of people's labour seemed to work smoothly at first, they were not firmly established. From the beginning, problems also beset other aspects of the Movement's program for adopting a vaguely conceived European economic model. A first step in that direction succeeded. In accord with Paliau's plan, Movement members pooled the cash they had received for war damages and from working for the American military, amassing several thousand Australian pounds. The administration, however, feared that Paliau would appropriate the money for his own use and insisted that he turn it over for safekeeping. The Movement asked the administration to buy a boat with the money, but the administration refused to do so, on the grounds that Movement members had little use for a boat because they were producing negligible quantities of goods—such as copra or trochus shell—to transport to buyers for sale.

Movement participants had few ways to earn money without leaving home. Usiai people, who were not completely at ease with the sea, particularly with diving near the reef, left most trochus collecting to the Titan. But trochus were not abundant in the waters of Movement communities and yielded only sporadic income. The Titan hoped to find some way of converting their fishing skills into cash income, but there had been only a few, small-scale attempts to engage in commercial fishing, none of them Movement-wide. Neither were people producing much copra. The administration did not give such projects much direct help, other than acting as a marketing agent to help islanders avoid middlemen.

Paliau had told his followers that they would find their wealth in their waters and in their land. But he was little help in putting this vision into practice. On their own, some Titan people did make short inroads into commercial fishing, smoking their surplus fish (in the traditional way, to a board-like state of temporary preservation) to sell to indigenous labourers in the Lorengau market and at the Australian military base. Among the Usiai, Kampo had ambitions and plans for starting plantations rivalling in size those of the Europeans. But it would take as much as 10 years of hard labour before such plantations could yield a profit, so Kampo found it hard to drum up enthusiasm. He and his followers knew that they would probably need the administration's assistance and hoped that their project could be incorporated in administration plans for developing producer and consumer cooperatives. Manus people had built the foundations of the Movement in the face of opposition from the Australian administration, but by the early 1950s many felt that they couldn't make any more progress in the money economy without the administration's help.

Even so, hostility towards Australia and Australians persisted. Many of the leaders of the Movement—notably, Paliau himself—could judge whites as individuals and assess the actions of specific white institutions on their individual merits. But many Manus people were extremely suspicious of the motives of all whites (although Americans were often seen as exceptions to general white perfidy) and all white institutions. So, they looked askance at the possibilities for change the administration offered, even as they recognised—and probably bemoaned—the need for administration help.

The Movement tried to keep young men from going away to work for Europeans for more than very short periods so that they would put their energies into building enterprises within the Movement communities. But migrant work promised independence and adventure, in spite of migrants' justified discontent with poor wages and working conditions. Some within the Movement needed no encouragement to avoid wage work;

they took to refusing to work for Europeans as an expression of defiance, convinced that whites invariably exploited indigenous workers. But as the early solidarity of the Movement ebbed and activity and innovation slowed, more men began going to work for the whites. The men of some sections of Bunai and some male Mbukei Islanders earned appreciable cash by working on adjacent European-owned plantations rather than as migrants. They had negotiated agreements under which they were paid entirely in cash rather than in meagre wages supplemented by food and tobacco rations. But few Movement villages had such opportunities.

Even the most dedicated Movement participants felt the lack of opportunity to earn money in amounts remotely matching the level of their interest in European goods. They had to face the fact that in this very fundamental way they were still near where they had started. They had come to depend on, and to value over their indigenous products, American war surplus goods. But lanterns, tools, galvanised iron, gasoline drums, and clothing all eventually broke down, rusted, or wore out, and people did not have the money to replace them from stores in Lorengau. Moreover, as the extension of the NGC to include all the Movement area approached, they worried about how they would pay the taxes required or raise the capital to start a cooperative.

They began to realise that they might have to sacrifice an important symbol of the early Movement's communalism—that is, they would have to divert the money the administration held on behalf of the Movement from a possible collective project to paying individual NGC taxes and making individual investments in an NGC-sponsored cooperative. They had designated this money for the use of the Movement as a whole. They had told the government that they, as individuals, had no further claim to it. They had told Paliau that he alone was to decide how to use the money for the good of the Movement. But if they wanted whatever benefits the NGC system and associated administration plans for economic development offered they would have to go back on these pledges. In 1953, with much embarrassment, they did so by asking the administration to distribute the Movement funds it held among the individual contributors.

Paliau's initial plan for the New Way called for the Titan, Usiai, and Matankor to abandon their ecological specialisations. All groups were to have mixed economies. The Usiai and the Matankor were to give land to the Titan, and the Titan were to learn to maintain their own gardens.

The Usiai were to learn to build and use canoes to supplement their gardening with fishing. Only in this way could the Movement eliminate the differences between the three groups. All were to be simply Manus. Nothing more was to be heard of the names Titan, Usiai, and Matankor.

Along the south coast, after a few reluctant attempts to overcome their aversion to working the soil, the Titan abandoned their gardens, with the exception of Samol, Bunai's Titan leader, who maintained his conspicuously. The Usiai, on the other hand, changed more than they or the Titan had expected. While they did not acquire the skill and ease of the Titan, they did overcome their aversion to the sea sufficiently to learn to build, maintain, and manage canoes—albeit, in the eyes of Titan people, awkwardly. They began to supplement their diets with simple forms of fishing in the lagoon, carried on mainly by women, children, and older men. And they used their canoes to travel along the coast and up a river that took them close to their gardens in the interior.

This put the Titan at a disadvantage. The Usiai became less dependent on them, while the Titan were as dependent on the Usiai as before. The Usiai within the Movement used their improved position to press for greater prestige and respect, to the great annoyance of many Titan, long accustomed to looking down on the Usiai. It seemed unlikely that the Titan would overcome their aversion to gardening, even while the Usiai continued to improve their canoe skills. The system of communal exchange between the Titan and the Usiai in Movement villages collapsed. Titan and Usiai began trading as individuals or selling foodstuffs for cash. The Titan who had not joined composite villages continued to trade at regular markets with non-Movement Usiai.

Despite recognising that further progress might depend on administration help, Movement members suspected that the administration was deliberately isolating and suppressing them. The administration's introduction of an NGC to only half of the Movement area, its fear of the Movement as vaguely subversive, and widespread dislike for Paliau among administration officers in fact did check the Movement's spread. Attitudes and policies on both sides of the divide thwarted Movement ambitions for greater participation in the larger world.[8]

---

8   Against these odds, James Landman, the assistant district officer stationed on Baluan, where he oversaw the Baluan Council, doggedly maintained tenuous friendly contact between the Movement and the administration.

Stirrings of the next cargo cult

It is not surprising, then, that a second cargo cult episode broke the impasse. The Movement at this time did not require its adherents to put aside hopes for the closer relationship with God, Jesus, and the ancestors, but it did push such hopes into the background. During the Noise, however, it had seemed that the planes of existence of the living and of the dead had briefly come close together, as people imagined they had been in the pre-Christian past. Truly dramatic improvements in their lives achieved by secular means might have countered memories of such an intense experience, but life in a state of suspended progress could not. Although the Noise abated within a few months of its beginning, the hope of direct relationship to God persisted. Few of the erstwhile adherents of the Noise were fully disenchanted. The Noise had failed, but Schwartz and Shargo were to find that many still clung to the possibility of the kind of radical transformation it had promised.

8

The Cemetery Cult hides in plain sight

On 27 March 1954, Schwartz and Shargo had a profound shock. After eight months of work reconstructing the Noise, they suddenly discovered that they were in the midst of an event that in many respects appeared to be a re-enactment of the 1947 phenomenon they had regarded as over and done. They thought they had excellent rapport with Bunai people and that they were aware of the important events in villagers' lives. Now, they learned abruptly that they had been blind to the fact that Bunai village was in the throes of the most dramatic event since several Titan and Usiai villages had merged into one to pursue the New Way together some eight years before. In addition, they realised that they were witnessing, not the beginnings of a second cargo cult, but its climax, for it had begun in earnest more than a year before, in mid-1952.

Schwartz and Shargo had approached the subject of the Noise more cautiously than the subject of the Movement. The latter was out in the open and a matter of pride. Villagers did not try to hide the fact of the Noise and many were quite comfortable talking about it at length. But most gave the impression that the events of 1947 were an aberration in the development of the Movement that had left little or no trace. And yet, in some accounts of the Movement, Schwartz and Shargo heard the implication that the Noise in some way was the foundation of all major events since. They therefore tried to allow a picture of the Noise to emerge without much direct inquiry while they focused on topics that they assumed were less fraught. They would discover, however, that some Bunai people were also cautiously feeling their way towards speaking more candidly with the anthropologists.

Mead had picked up hints of lingering interest in cargo cults early in her stay in Pere. But she told Schwartz and Shargo she feared that if she pursued these some Pere people might take her interest as a validation of their desire to pursue the secret of the cargo. Mead wanted to encourage what she saw as the strengths of the Movement and she assumed correctly that people's perceptions of her opinions—and, to a lesser extent, those of Schwartz and Shargo—could influence them. But hints of lingering interest in cargo were stronger in Bunai. Schwartz and Shargo also learned that both the relatively few Pere people still strongly interested in a cargo cult and those who knew but disapproved of cult stirrings preferred to keep these things a secret from Mead. She had told Pere people that she was once more going to put their lives in front of the world and they did not want to be portrayed as cargo cultists. Of course, had a cargo cult dominated events in Pere during Mead's visit, she may well have decided not to write a book about it, given the intentions she shared with Schwartz before leaving for New Guinea: She wanted to write a success story.

Bunai villagers also kept Schwartz and Shargo from knowledge of the cult for eight months. Even the villagers to whom they were closest and those who spoke freely to them about the Noise kept mum about the current cult. People like Pita Tapo had given them uninhibited accounts of the Noise. But neither he nor others betrayed the fact that the ideas and hopes that had driven it were still thriving.

Missing the big story

On 29 November 1953, a young Bunai man, home from work on the Australian-owned copra plantation on nearby Ndropwa Island, mentioned to Schwartz that a group of young men were going to a big feast on Johnston Island. He told Schwartz there would be several days of gambling, dancing, and feasting on costly quantities of store-bought food. When Schwartz asked about the occasion for the feast the young man said only that it was for a dead man. Schwartz wanted to go, too, because he had never visited this tiny island many miles to the south, with its small Titan village. This also sounded like an event unlike any he had seen before. But the vigour of the attempt to dissuade him from tagging along, as was his wont, puzzled him. By this time, Schwartz had acquired his own outrigger canoe with outboard motor and a regular crew, so he could travel at will, weather permitting. But some of the young men insisted that his canoe was too small for the rough seas they were sure to encounter. Schwartz's older, more experienced crew members scoffed at this and they volunteered to take Schwartz to Johnston Island. Two other canoes from Bunai also went, one leaving before Schwartz and one after. A canoe from Pere, carrying the schoolteacher, Prenis Tjolai, and some of his male students, had gone a few days earlier.

After arriving on Johnston Island things became ever more curious. On the first night after their arrival, Schwartz found schoolboys from Pere and others of their age dancing to ukuleles. The dancing, which continued for the next few days, was different from any he had seen before in Manus. The boys danced as if it were a solemn duty. There was none of the usual joking or horseplay, none of the shouts from the musicians, no attempts to vary a monotonous repertoire of songs and dances. Schwartz set out to look for the village *kaunsil*, Kisakiu.[1] Although one could walk around the entire island in about twenty minutes, Schwartz could find no sign of him. Wherever he asked for Kisakiu, people told Schwartz that he was on the other side of the island. He did locate the *luluai*, who told Schwartz that the feast was merely to celebrate completing a new graveyard. They had worked very hard on it and decided to call all their relatives from other Titan villages to celebrate with them.

Schwartz had no obvious reason to doubt this. He saw and photographed the new graveyard—in Tok Pisin, the *matmat*. It was very impressive by Manus standards. During the day, the sun reflected glaringly from a fresh cover of clean white coral sand. And the graveyard was laid out in a regular pattern, unlike the usual graveyards that grew as the need arose, without much thought for their shape. Each grave in the several perfect lines of graves was marked by a cross carved with the name of the deceased and some crosses bore a date of death. A fence painted with white lime, which would have to be constantly renewed as the rain washed it off, surrounded the *matmat*. A large wooden cross stood at each end of the rectangular enclosure.

---

1   Not to be confused with Kisakiu of Tawi.

Two gates to the *matmat* stood side by side with a large wooden cross between them, each gate resembling the kind found in all New Way villages. His guides told Schwartz that if he wanted to go inside the enclosure he had to go in through the right gate and proceed around the graveyard counterclockwise before leaving by the left gate. A similar gate in good repair stood at the entrance to the village.

Schwartz attended church services and a meeting before leaving the island. Unlike the services and meetings he had attended in Bunai and Pere it looked like almost everyone on the island was there. Also, the meeting began with a half hour of singing and Schwartz noticed that the songs performed had been important in the ritualised New Way that followed the demise of the Noise in 1947.

Looking back, Schwartz can only marvel that he was so innocent that he did not at least suspect that he was visiting the very centre of a new cargo cult and witnessing a feast held to honour the cult's tutelary ghost. All the other visitors, including those from Pere and Bunai, had come to attend not only the feasting, dancing, and daylight meetings, but also the nightly seances, which they kept secret from Schwartz. He registered only that Johnston Island seemed to have preserved a distinctively ritualistic form of the early Movement. Two members of his canoe crew, John Kilepak and Johannes Lokes, knew exactly what was going on, and they had known for more than a year. Although they usually helped Schwartz energetically with his research, they didn't think he needed to know about this.

Schwartz saw for himself how much visitors from other villages admired the new Johnston Island graveyard and how they discussed building similar ones in their own villages. In Bunai, Tjamilo raised the subject in December 1953. He wanted to refurbish the old cemetery, which would involve cutting the coconut palms growing there. Samol, a Bunai leader, opposed the idea and Schwartz was surprised at the vehemence with which people debated this issue and how much some seemed to care about the coconut trees. Only later—again—did Schwartz realise that Samol was a staunch opponent of the cargo cult and, hence, of the cemetery plan. But Tjamilo and a few of his supporters cut the palms when Samol was out of the village and made plans to build a fence and gates.

Only weeks later, Schwartz and Shargo stood on the beach in Pere, watching Mead's canoe ease into the distance, taking her to Lorengau on the first leg of her trip back home. As they watched, Schwartz noticed an old man of Bunai digging a skeleton out of the gravel near the water's edge. The old man told Schwartz that it was his brother's skeleton and he pointed out how well the wood smoke enveloping the skull when it had resided in a bowl in his house rafters had preserved it. Schwartz soon learned that Tjamilo had told people to gather the remains of the dead buried in scattered beach graves near the old villages and bring them to Bunai to bury in the existing Bunai cemetery, for the cemetery built to cult design still was not ready.

In Bunai a few days later, Tjamilo was ready for a formal reburial of the remains that people had gathered. They had collected eight skeletons, including the skeleton of Tjamilo's father. They had cleaned each one, wrapped it in new cotton cloth, and carefully arranged it in its own wooden box. People did not hesitate to show Schwartz the skulls and they seemed to exhibit no particular reverence when handling the bones. They were as interested as he was in examining the skulls closely and they spoke freely of the deceased. When everything was ready, Tjamilo formed a procession to march the length of the village, beginning at the church, passing through the Usiai section (only Titan people marched in the procession), and ending at the graveyard. All the participants, some 30 adults and as many children, were dressed in their best clothing. The leading marchers carried wooden crosses to place on each grave. The children carried decorative bunches of green leaves. Tjamilo carried the Australian flag. Before they started, Tjamilo told Schwartz that they were going to sing a song that he would not know, 'a song belonging to all black men'. They then sang 'John Brown's Body' all the way to the graveyard. Schwartz knew that many Manus people had learned it from the Americans during the war, as well as 'Lay That Pistol Down' and many others. But Tjamilo's group had imbued it with ritual significance. After a brief ceremony at the graveyard, the marchers drifted off to join the general exodus to Baluan for the Movement Christmas celebration there.

Figure 8.1: The procession to the old Bunai cemetery that Tjamilo organised in December 1953 to re-inter the remains of Cemetery Cult adherents' deceased kin.

Source: Theodore Schwartz. Digital copy courtesy of the Archive for Melanesian Anthropology, University of California, San Diego.

Schwartz and Shargo also went to Baluan for the Christmas events and it proved a turning point in their research. During 10 days there they began a close relationship with Paliau, who was happy to discuss the old Baluan culture, of which he had considerable knowledge, especially considering the amount of time he had spent escaping it as a youth. Finally, he dictated to Schwartz a marathon autobiography, talking continuously for almost 10 hours one night. In effect, Paliau had now accepted Schwartz as 'inside' (in Tok Pisin, *insait*) the Movement. He was to be allowed to attend all the meetings Paliau held with his leaders. Paliau also told the Movement leaders that he had told Schwartz everything during their all-night session and that there were no longer any secrets from him. The latter, however, was by no means true. Schwartz would find that Paliau had been quite selective.

Another event on Baluan during the Christmas visit would also affect Paliau's followers' perceptions of Schwartz and Shargo. One morning while the two walked along a dirt road to James and Marjorie Landman's house, they noticed a white man bathing in the shallow water near the beach. They said 'Good morning' and he answered. They thought little of it, although it was an odd place and time to find a European bathing. A boat carrying a party of Australian naval personnel sightseers had come to Baluan the day before. But when Schwartz and Shargo mentioned meeting the white bather to Landman he said that there shouldn't be any whites on the island at the moment other than his family, unless the man Schwartz and Shargo had seen had stayed overnight somewhere, which didn't seem likely. Landman sent the indigenous police constable to find the mystery European. The constable returned saying that he could find no signs of such a person but he had warned everyone to watch for him. Another boatload of sightseers arrived later but no one saw the bather again. Schwartz and Shargo dismissed the incident, assuming there was some simple natural explanation, even if they did not know what it was.

Villagers, however, continued to search and to speculate. Paliau suggested to Shargo that perhaps she had seen an angel. That evening several leaders from several villages proposed and acted on a new explanation. They decided that the man was from the Australian Air Force and had been sent to kill Schwartz and Shargo because they were now 'inside' the natives and the Australians were thus jealous and afraid of them. A guard of 10 Native Government Council councillors, carrying glaring and hissing kerosene pressure lamps, was posted around the house where Schwartz and Shargo were staying. Other men continued to search the island. Schwartz and Shargo protested, but not too vigorously, for they had learned that if they expressed even mild disapproval of anything related to the New Way no one would discuss it with them again.

By the next morning the exhausted men who had kept vigil through the night reported that they had seen no suspicious Europeans. But the idea persisted that Schwartz and Shargo had to be guarded and it resurfaced every time an Australian came to the village while they were there. (Baluan people did not, however, suspect the Landmans of designs on Schwartz and Shargo, for they knew and trusted them, at least to this extent.) Even a plane flying low over Baluan brought a few people to the anthropologists' defence. It was not until March, when the secrets of the cult were revealed to them, that Schwartz and Shargo learned that while they were on Baluan with a crowd of celebrants many others were spending Christmas on Johnston Island, about 10 miles away. There, in a seance held just before Christmas, the tutelary ghost of the cult had prophesied that Christ would appear on Baluan on Christmas day. When this news reached Baluan after Christmas the whole episode became clear. It was generally agreed that Schwartz and Shargo had been the only ones who had seen Christ and some assured them that had they been closer they would have seen the stigmata on his hands. Schwartz and Shargo, however, did not learn of this until after other events led them to much deeper knowledge of the cult.

On their return from Baluan, a number of Bunai people volunteered to talk to Schwartz and Shargo about the Noise. They had wanted to ask some Americans about it for a long time, they said, but they had been afraid to do so until Paliau had told them it was alright. A group of four men came every night for a week to dictate their stories: Tjamilo, Talimelion, Alphonse Kanawi, and Kisekup. These were the four Movement *komiti* from the Titan section of Bunai. They said that Tjamilo knew and remembered more about the Noise than anyone else. A succession of others followed, eager to tell their own stories.

Throughout this period of intensive research on the Noise, public meetings to discuss building a new cemetery in Bunai continued. A few younger men began to throw their support to Tjamilo, among them Pwatjumel, Samol's brother-in-law and usually his close supporter. Pwatjumel had had a dream in which he saw a graveyard set up as it should be. His drawing of it closely resembled the Johnston Island cemetery that he had heard about but not visited.

Death and resurrection in Bunai

Early in the morning on 26 February 1954, the son of Ponram, an old man of Yiru, an Usiai village not far from the beach, came to fetch Schwartz, saying that Ponram was dead. It wasn't clear whether he meant his father had merely lost consciousness or that he was deceased. The two sound very much alike in Tok Pisin. To say that someone has lost consciousness in Tok Pisin you say *em i dai*. But to say someone is deceased you say *em i dai finis*. Ponram's son told Schwartz that his father had had violent convulsions, but now his body had died completely and he was limp and insensible. That is, in Tok Pisin, *em i dai olgeta*, which is still short of *em i dai finis*. Schwartz hurried to the house where Ponram lay, thinking it must be a case of cerebral malaria. He'd already seen several cases, and each had resulted in death. Ponram was unconscious, saliva running from his mouth, when Schwartz arrived. The village native medical assistant (in Tok Pisin, the *dokta boi*: a local man who had received very basic paramedical training from the Australian administration) had just arrived and was administering intravenous quinine. Almost instantly Ponram began to show signs of life, making chewing motions with his mouth. Schwartz dismissed the idea of malaria when he determined that Ponram's temperature and pulse were normal. Someone put a betel nut in Ponram's mouth and he began to chew.

The house was crowded with people, but instead of looking relieved at Ponram's revival they seemed to be waiting for something more. One of his six adult sons was supporting Ponram in a semi-upright position. Several old men and women were grouped around him, among them his wife and Sayau Bombowai, the *komiti* from Katin. Ponram's eyes were open, staring vacantly and his tongue lolled out. No one spoke or wailed. Everyone stared at him intently. Occasionally he made protracted, empty *aaaaaaa* sounds, apparently involuntarily. His body looked relaxed. He made sudden, random, but not spasmodic movements. His muscle tone seemed normal. Ponram made a motion with his hand that his sons interpreted as a request for another betel nut. So began several hours of communicating with gestures.

Ponram seemed dazed, but slowly his eyes began to focus on people and objects. For a while he stared at his hand. Someone made a commotion in the crowd, provoking immediate shouts of 'Hush, quiet'. It looked like word had spread that something significant was happening because people kept packing into the house, squeezing into places to sit on the already crowded floor. After opening and closing his hand several times, Ponram counted his fingers. The medical assistant explained that he was counting his sons. Someone else suggested that he was calling for those sons who were on Ndropwa. Sayau Bombowai did most of the translating, while others in the crowd occasionally made suggestions. Pantret, the *kaunsil* of Lowaya, moved close to Schwartz to translate for him from Titan, in which Schwartz was still a novice, and from scraps of Usiai languages to Tok Pisin. Sayau Bombowai began to question Ponram, using gestures like those Ponram was using, which were much like those used by a local deaf mute. Ponram was sitting up now, gesturing more vigorously and dramatically. Everyone seemed to know just what was happening, what to do, and how to translate, as if they had seen it all before. Sometimes Ponram would repeat a gesture until someone in the audience caught on and interpreted it aloud. Then Ponram would turn towards that person and smile. To an American, it resembled a game of charades.

Stretching his arms over his head, Ponram indicated—as Pantret translated for Schwartz—that he had been to Heaven. He had died as a punishment for his wrongdoing and had been brought to God. Now he had been sent back to report the many things revealed to him. He began to recite, using gestures, all the sins that he had ever committed. He had beaten his wife and children repeatedly and, when a child, he had stolen. He indicated that his son, Poteri, should stand up, then he acted out the message that one woman should not have two men. (Poteri was living with a woman in the same house with her aged husband, with the husband's consent.) Then Ponram spoke in gestures against divorce. He continued to pronounce against all the things so often condemned in the New Way. Although everyone had heard all this almost daily since the start of the Movement, it now came to them as direct divine revelation and they listened intently.

Ponram handed a shirt to two of his sons, instructing them to suspend it between them while he pretended to write on it, although it was well known that he was illiterate. As he pretended to write he shook his head approvingly. He next mentioned some of the people he had seen in Heaven. Sayau Bombowai and the people in the crowd interpreted his gestures through trial and error, guessing until Ponram indicated they had found the right name. But it also appeared that many were familiar with the larger story on which he was embarking. Ponram pantomimed putting on trousers, which the crowd took to mean 'I am an old man. I wear trousers and a shirt, while you young men wear *laplap*', although Ponram was actually wearing a *laplap*. He called for an enamel plate, showed that it was clean, and beamed his approval. He made motions as if eating with a spoon, indicating that this is good. He called for an old wooden bowl, threw it to the floor indicating that this was bad, for it was something of the past.

By this time, Ponram seemed fully awake, fully alert—although still unable to speak—and thoroughly enjoying being the centre of attention. He soon began to whistle an accompaniment to his gestures. The whistles were like the ones mediums used in seances to communicate with ghostly household guardians, which villagers had demonstrated for Schwartz previously. Continuing his account of revelations, Ponram kept looking about for props. He picked up a piece of cooked taro, took several bites, and spat each one out in disgust. This kind of food was no good, he thus indicated. Then he took up the enamel plate again in approval, indicating that only European foods were good. He took hold of the nipple of his breast, shaking his head approvingly, then again spat out taro, which the crowd took to mean that the common practice of women feeding children with pre-masticated taro was no good, they should feed them with the breast alone; taro and sago are fit only for pigs and dogs. For each point in a long list of contrasts, people in the crowd exclaimed '*tru!*'—Tok Pisin for true—or '*nru konan!*'—meaning true in Ponram's Usiai language.

The audience was more relaxed by this point and occasionally amused by Ponram's pantomimes. He continued to condemn all things indigenous and to praise all things European. He listed again everything he had done that was wrong (omitting several recent misdeeds for which he had been brought to court). He tore a scrap off a piece of newspaper for each sin and gave all the slips to the medical assistant. (In many parts of rural Papua New Guinea, people have long used newspaper for rolling cigarettes, hence its availability during these 1954 events.) He began to use Schwartz as a prop. He pointed to Schwartz's watch, making the '*plenti, plenti*' gesture a local deaf mute used when describing the wealth of the American army during the war.

Ponram eventually began to lose the audience's undivided attention, but he recaptured it when he began to construct a model of the gate to Heaven out of firewood. Here the Johnston Island cemetery came to mind again. Ponram said that he had been told to urge people to build a new cemetery for Bunai. The door that he modelled from sticks had a turnstile in it, like those each village gate had sported during the early part of the Movement. This finished, he seemed to run out of ideas and repeated much of what he had already done. As a variation, he called for his wife, whom he had just confessed to beating. He had her sit beside him. Taking the plate, he pretended to feed her with a spoon and he raised a cup to her lips, pretending to give her tea, while she very seriously pretended to eat and sip. This was the New Way model for the husband and wife, sitting together to eat as Europeans do. As the repetitious lecture continued, he again lost the crowd's attention. He then began to make noises with his mouth, as if speech were returning. The crowd again closed in around him, eager and expectant, as if they knew what was coming. He began to speak very rapidly in his Usiai language. His voice was a high-pitched falsetto. He repeated orally everything he had just acted out silently. His discourse took on the highly stylised form of New Way speeches. He recited long lists of formulas for all the virtues and vices approved or condemned in the New Way. At last, at about 2:30 in the afternoon, he lay back exhausted. The crowd dispersed.

Word of Ponram's death, vision, and resurrection spread through Bunai, to other villages along the south coast, and to Baluan. For months afterwards, orators at meetings used Ponram's death and resurrection as a warning to sceptics. For instance, Kampo of Lahan, in a speech berating the rank and file for their laxity and indifference to New Way leaders, proclaimed that the sceptics who said that they wanted to see Christ with their own eyes and hear him with their own ears should look at Ponram and be convinced. They might otherwise be taken to see Christ as Ponram had been taken to Heaven and perhaps not return.

Observing Ponram's resurrection helped Schwartz to understand a number of superficially unrelated events. For instance, Kampo of Lahan had allowed Schwartz to examine a journal he kept of outstanding events in which he had figured since the Lahan people's move to the beach. Here is Schwartz's summary of an entry for 17 September 1949:

> Kampo had quarrelled with his wife, Nambuleo. The next day, they went to present their grievances against each other to the government officer at Patusi Patrol Post. When they stopped to rest at a house on their way back to Bunai, Nambuleo suddenly collapsed, seemingly lifeless. Not until the following morning, back in her own village, did she regain consciousness, though she could neither hear nor speak. Her eyes were closed, but she ate, smoked, and walked about outside. She did not return to normal for two more days. Towards the end of her seizure she was able to explain that she had died and her *tingting* had gone to Heaven. When she came out of the house, she looked to the interior of the island, noting how rough and hilly the terrain was, and said that all this was no good. In Heaven the ground was perfectly flat, with a long, broad, clear road. All the houses were in perfect lines. There was no hard work carrying things. Anything you wanted, you had only to think and it was there. It was not even necessary to eat; if you were hungry, you just thought and your belly was filled. You had only to think and you were sitting in a car. You didn't have to climb into it. She saw people that she knew who had died. When she wanted to shake their hands, they said, 'Wait, you go straight to God first'. When she saw God, he wasn't sitting on something, he was just there. God asked her, 'What did you come here for?' She said, 'I don't know'. God told her: 'You must go back. You must change your ways—your stubbornness, your lying, your disobedience. If you don't I will bring you back here for good'. Then she saw her mother, father, and sister. She shook hands with them. Then she returned. Kampo added that Sayau

Bombowai's wife had died and returned shortly before his own wife's experience. He said: 'It was like what had happened to many people during the Noise. It happens occasionally, as a warning'.

Two months before Ponram's resurrection, Schwartz and Shargo had been involved in another event they initially took at face value. An elderly Usiai man of Yiru village, Jakob, had been fishing in the shallow lagoon at night. Schwartz and Shargo were called to see him when he was reported to be dying from the bite of a poisonous sea creature. His condition was roughly like Ponram's—limp paralysis, loss of speech and hearing, followed by gradual recovery within the next hour. People said that a sea snake had bitten him. Later he said it had been a crab, though it had not broken the skin. A house full of spectators carefully and sympathetically attended to his gestures and words as he came to consciousness. He was convinced that he was dying, that his throat was closed, and that he could neither eat nor drink. He communicated at first with his hands, later in weak and garbled speech. He went through a repertoire of revelations confirming New Way principles. His made a special point of cautioning people about the dangers of the sea. He said that the children should not be allowed to go into the water. His total recovery took about the same time as Ponram's, as his children spoon-fed him.

For some time afterward, people treated Jakob with unusual respect, but he elicited much less attention than Ponram. He was also less transformed by his experience than was Ponram, in whom the ready response of his audience produced a quick expansion of his personality as he moved into the role of righteous messenger, which for him was a novel guise. In fact, both he and Jakob were known as troublemakers. Most recently, Ponram had been brought into court for urging his sons to thrash the husband of his adopted daughter, and Jakob had instigated a quarrel that almost split his hamlet. Ponram in particular, however, took advantage of his experience to change his image. He had always worn a *laplap* in the past, but now he began to wear European clothing. He began to attend village meetings regularly, where people received with respect his pious but totally unoriginal speeches. He also lent his moral weight to the cemetery project.

Still naive, Schwartz found these deaths and resurrections worthy of close attention, but he regarded them as idiosyncratic expressions of the continued vitality of Noise ideology and the degree to which it had become an accepted part of local Christianity. He was mistaken. The dramatic events and the interest they aroused were part of an extant cargo cult of which he and Shargo were still unaware.

Schisms and secrets

Shortly thereafter, Schwartz left Bunai to visit Ndrano, an Usiai village in the interior. The route inland began in the coastal Titan village of Patusi. In Patusi, he noticed open hostility between the Patusi Titan and people of the two Usiai villages—Nuang and Kapo—that, under the influence of the New Way, had relocated contiguous to Patusi. In Ndrano, he saw further evidence of old schisms returning and new ones emerging. Several older Ndrano men were conducting pre–New Way style ceremonial exchanges. Younger Ndrano men looking on made a great display of their disinterest. Schwartz had been told in Bunai that many interior people still practised what they called in Tok Pisin *sting pasin bilong bipo*—the rotten (or stinking) ways of the past—and these young Ndrano men seemed to hold the work of their elders in similar contempt. Yet other Ndrano men jeered the Bunai Usiai accompanying Schwartz—people who had given up the stinking ways of the past—for having become no better than the Titan. Schwartz's Bunai Usiai companions adopted expressions of quiet contempt for the taunts.

Returning from Ndrano to Bunai, Schwartz found the atmosphere there unusually tense. People with whom he had enjoyed relaxed relationships had become reserved and distant. The Usiai who had called Schwartz and Shargo to come to meetings in their sections of the village no longer did so. Conflict between Titan leaders like Samol and Tjamilo and some of the Usiai leaders had sharpened.

Throughout this period, Schwartz and Shargo continued reconstructing the 1947 Noise. Later, however, they found that some attitudes and behaviour they took as echoes of the past were in fact symptoms of friction over the Cemetery Cult, of which they were still naively unaware. Without any obvious provocation, village meetings were now full of highly emotional speeches invoking God and Jesus and condemning a decline in morale, morals, and social cohesion. People spoke with great passion of building a new graveyard. This sounded like a modest project logistically, but people used every conceivable argument and rhetorical device to support or oppose the proposal. Some made lengthy speeches condemning themselves and others for not heeding the leaders, not attending church, and neglecting to repair their houses, mixing such criticisms with lavish allusions to the golden years in the Movement's youth when people had done things properly. During most of their stay to this time, Schwartz and Shargo had heard scarcely anything of the 'Long Story of God' in public settings, even in church services, but now people referred to it often in meetings on matters of all kinds.

Despite the intense emotion displayed, many speakers sounded demoralised. One after another declared, in Tok Pisin, that the village was *rong finis*—that is, completely wrong. The administration had again postponed initiating a Native Government Council beyond the Baluan Council area, and it came to light that leaders of the existing ad hoc assembly of Movement *kaunsil* had helped themselves to some of its funds. Movement leaders from the south coast and southerly islands met to discuss the funds collected in the early days of the Movement and argue about their disposition. The money had originally been collected in 1947–50, and each village had agreed that it would not ask for the return of its contribution. The fund was placed at Paliau's disposal to buy whatever he thought best for the Movement. Many of his followers agreed that the Movement should use the money to buy a boat. The administration, however, tried to persuade the Movement leaders to return the funds to the individual donors and insisted on taking control of the money on behalf of the donors.

Now, in meetings in Bunai, one leader after another leader said that the people of his village wanted the money redistributed. Paliau's prestige was also at stake. In a decisive meeting, a speaker said that when the money was entrusted to Paliau they had all been like children; now, they were grown up and no longer needed such paternalistic care. Finally, those assembled decided to allow Paliau to determine the disposition. But Paliau refused to make the decision for them. So the question remained unresolved and the tensions it aroused lingered.

At the same time, Schwartz sensed that Tjamilo and some of the Usiai seemed to be trying to control their excitement about something. But it was something of which they would not speak to Schwartz, for almost overnight they had become decidedly reserved, almost hostile. Kampo of Lahan, with whom Schwartz had been on good terms, seemed disturbed and conflicted about something, but he was now keeping his distance from Schwartz. Here is a passage, translated from Tok Pisin, of a speech Kampo gave at a meeting in Lahan on 4 March 1954:

> We must take good care of the dead. Jesus has spoken. Eventually they will all arise. All our people whom we have lost, do you think you will see them? The *masta* and *misis* [Kampo used these then-common terms of address for male and female Europeans to refer

to Schwartz and Shargo], they will outlive all of us. They will grow old and we will die. You must take good care of all who have died. Make a fence, a cemetery. With them [the dead] also it is the same. They cry to us about all our bad ways. 'Now we want to come to you. We already have attained the good life. We want to arise again, but you block our path with your evil ways.' God is very close to us. To whomever doesn't believe, he will make a sign so that you will see him truly … We talk all the time about material things, but some of the time we must think about God who made us.

Of all the speeches made at open public meetings in this period, this one contained the most overt references to belief in the return of the dead, part of the ideology of the cargo cult soon to come out in the open. Kampo was unaccountably depressed and withdrawn in the weeks surrounding this meeting. He spent a lot of time with Schwartz and Shargo, apparently absorbed in work on wood carvings he was making for them. But he did not speak of the things troubling him.

Many speeches at public meetings were full of the phrase 'we must return to the ways of 1946'. The ever more apparent hostility between the Titan and the Usiai was matched by the increasing frequency of speeches about brotherhood, the need for mutual compassion and generosity (in Tok Pisin, *maremare*), and warnings that the village was full of bad feelings that should be exorcised. No one disapproved of such statements. But in a way Schwartz did not fully understand, Titan people seemed to feel the Usiai were attacking them. The Usiai implied they were the leaders of a new moral revival. They were particularly aggressive in calling for rectification of a grievance that, in their eyes, was disturbing communal harmony more than any other—disagreement about the ownership of the land on which the village was situated. The Titan people of the villages of Tjalalo, Ndropwa, and Pomatjau claimed the land. But the Usiai of Pwa and Lesei, once autonomous villages that had been incorporated into Lowaya, had long contested these Titan assertions, taking their claim to one foreign government officer after another—German, Australian, even Japanese. Kisekup, the paramount *luluai* for the region, was an expert in such matters. He had been highly skilled in dealing with administration officers and had successfully defended the Titan claim to the land several times. This even though the Titan admitted among themselves, and sometimes even to Usiai people, that it was really Usiai land.

The question, however, was never simple. The Titan often gathered coconuts and forest materials from the area and cut sago palms there. And in the eyes of the administration, the Titan owned it. When the Usiai moved to the beach, the Titan had welcomed them. As the administration saw it, Titan had allowed them not only use of land for houses on the beach but use of the nearby land in question. According to the communal principles of the Movement, people were to freely grant others use of land or other resources, but this did not entail change in ownership. So, the Bunai Usiai were demanding that the spirit of brotherhood required the Titan to rectify their false claim to the land and declare themselves once more landless.

Eventually, in the name of the New Way, Kisekup and other Titan elders conceded Usiai ownership. The Titan, however, said that it did not really matter because since the beginning of the Movement they had had no thought of either individual or group landownership within the Movement community. The Usiai disputants also said that it did not matter, that they also had no thought of exclusive ownership. Even so, they wanted the Titan concession of Usiai ownership entered in the books of the government as soon as possible. The resolution required a mass handshaking ceremony. The Usiai formed two long lines in order of size, from the adults down to the smallest children who could stand alone. The Titan also formed a long line, which then moved along the front line of Usiai, then turned and went back down the second line until each Titan man, woman, and child had shaken the hand of each Usiai man, woman, and child.

That painfully won settlement, however, did not stop the procession of public meetings about other matters, some apparently mundane but that Schwartz still found opaque. Listening to hour after hour of discussion and debate, Schwartz noticed people beginning their orations more and more often with long distributive formulas of address. In an extreme example, one speaker addressed his speech to 'you, all children, women, men, mother, father, brother, sister, young men, young women, old men, old women, you altogether, you must listen'. Speakers hammered the theme of equality and universal participation in community life. Finally, in a speech ending one meeting, Petrus Popu of Lowaya reviewed the history of the Movement. In concluding, he said that in 1946 everything had been right, but now everything was wrong. He said that 1950 had been the turning point, when things had begun to go awry. He attributed this to lapsing from the purity of 1946 and to people's fear of the whites, particularly the one or two *kiap* who had made it their mission to break the Paliau Movement.

Schwartz and Shargo were coming to understand that by the time they arrived in Manus in 1953, people accepted 1946 as shorthand not only for the period of Movement growth and excitement preceding the Noise, but also for the events of the Noise itself and the more ritualistic practices of the post-Noise Movement extending up to 1949. The year 1950 had become the accepted date for the Movement version of the Fall, an analogy many orators invoked. There is scarcely an entry in the notes Schwartz and Shargo took from February through March 1954 that does not make more sense if read with an understanding that such references were evidence that a cargo cult was building momentum. Adherents were keeping this secret not only from Shargo, Schwartz, and Mead, but also from some within the Movement from whom they expected opposition. Adherents even excluded some who would have liked to be included in the cult. Much of the sharpening conflict between Tjamilo and Samol, it eventually became clear, came from their competition for leadership in the cult.

As Paliau and his lieutenants had done successfully at the beginning of the Movement, adherents of the Cemetery Cult used secrecy and exclusion to recruit new comrades. As the secrecy became more conspicuous, the cult finally became visible to the anthropologists, although only through what appeared to be an accident did they acquire more intimate access and knowledge. Such accidents, however, were by this time almost inevitable. Schwartz and Shargo had become an important audience and to some extent the cult needed them.

While all this was going on, Schwartz was studying the older Usiai culture, which required consulting Usiai memories, for Mead and Fortune had given the Usiai little attention. Schwartz had been recording the oldest Usiai men's accounts of past events. But as cult activity increased, he began to have difficulty finding willing collaborators. Several men from Lowaya who had agreed to help him failed repeatedly to show up. When he went to Lowaya to find them, he happened on a meeting in a house far from the main route to the village. Everyone in Lowaya seemed to be crowded into the house, and Schwartz noticed immediately that his presence embarrassed people. He eventually found the men he was seeking, and they promised to come to his house. Schwartz, seeing that he was not wanted, left, expecting to see the men later. But, once again, they didn't show. Walking home, he had passed several Usiai men with whom he had been working closely. But instead of greeting him as usual they turned their eyes away. Among them was Petrus Popu, his main Usiai collaborator, and Pondis of Malei, who had accompanied him on a trip into the interior and who had spent a great deal of time in Schwartz and Shargo's house.

The light goes on

On 22 March 1954, Schwartz and Shargo finally learned why the social atmosphere was changing. That evening, Schwartz had planned to continue delving into the Usiai past, but his collaborators again failed to appear. The night was brilliantly moonlit so he decided to walk to Lahan to look for them. When he got there a meeting was in progress and Kampo was addressing visitors from the north coast Usiai village of Lowa. Kampo was making long tutorial statements about the principles of the New Way to people who had heard it all innumerable times. Over and over he said: 'There is nothing that just materialises; everything comes from hard work'.

Schwartz had heard all this many times already, so he decided to go on to Lowaya, to look for his usual helpers there, but they were absent. It was near midnight when he returned home through Malei, which was not far from his and Shargo's house. He noticed that everyone in Malei was still awake and fully dressed in their best clothing. Reaching home, he found Kampo Monrai, an adolescent man of Malei, talking to Shargo, who was listening, rapt. Earlier, while she had been walking towards Malei, Kampo Monrai had seen her and approached her to ask: 'Did you hear the whistles?' Something in his voice suggested she should answer 'Yes' instead of 'What whistles?' It was the 'mark' (Tok Pisin, *mak*, meaning sign) on Malei, said Kampo. The whistling of the dead had been everywhere in Malei the previous night and it was continuing tonight. The mark was on Pulu Nrabokwi's wife and everyone was very excited. Shargo allowed Kampo Monrai to believe that she knew all about this, but invited him to come back to the house to talk about it. There, in a recorded conversation, she obtained the anthropologists' first explicit descriptions of the cult. Ghostly revelations rather than dreams and visions guided it, but it was virtually the same as the Noise in its fundamental doctrines. Thus, Schwartz and

Shargo came to understand that there was a more-or-less constant current of cult hope and belief that was now resurfacing in a slightly different form. Manus people themselves christened the cult of 1947 the Noise, after the shaking that affected its adherents. We have been calling this second manifestation the Cemetery Cult and will continue to do so, but even its most ardent adherents had no single name for it.

Now that they knew what lay beneath the surface of the many puzzling events they had witnessed and the troubling changes in people's attitudes towards them, Schwartz and Shargo undertook a more focused investigation. The next chapter recounts what they found through direct observation of events and dozens of interviews with the principal figures.

9

The Cemetery Cult revealed

Here is the story of the Cemetery Cult, as assembled by Schwartz and Shargo through interviews, impromptu conversations, and direct observation of the events unfolding around them. In Chapter 10, we will focus on differences between the Noise and the Cemetery Cult, in particular why adherents of the latter (whom we will sometimes call Cemeterians) were more cautious than participants in the Noise. We will comment on why the Noise spread more rapidly and apparently more evenly than the Cemetery Cult. This detailed account of the Cemetery Cult will make it possible to appreciate the many factors shaping a distribution that looks jagged compared to the distribution of the Noise.[1]

During Schwartz's second bout of field research in Manus, in 1963–66, he lived in several villages outside the Paliau Movement and became convinced that it was impossible to explain why some Manus people joined the Movement or the cargo cults but others did not in terms of cultural differences within the Admiralty Islands or even differences in the nature of European contact or local experiences of World War II. Schwartz's and Shargo's observations of the Cemetery Cult revealed a number of factors that shaped commitment to the cult that were quite unrelated to simple

---

1   This chapter describes in concrete detail events that illustrate a process Schwartz (1976a: 170) has described abstractly as follows: 'Cult membership took on the status of "property" to be matched by contrasting property held by rival groups or leaders. The effect of this pattern of interaction was the spotty distribution of cults and the production of blocks of pro- and anti-cult villages, as well pro- and anti-cult factions within some villages. It is not necessary to assume that cultists and non-cultists were psychologically and situationally differentiated and that such differences accounted for the pattern of distribution of cult occurrences. In the larger areas of social interaction in which many distinct, often culturally differentiated groups were interlaced by lines of self-differentiation and identification, cult and anti-cult must be perceived as being locked into a single system of functional and emblematic contrast'.

attraction to cult doctrines. Among these were past relationships among villages and hamlets, longstanding antagonism between the Usiai and the Titan, and local contests for leadership. Kampo of Lahan provides a prime example of this latter factor. He had been one of the leaders of the Noise among the Usiai, but he publicly opposed the Cemetery Cult. He even argued publicly against the premise of magical access to the cargo to which he had himself committed during the Noise: 'Nothing simply materialises!' he proclaimed. 'Everything comes from hard work!' It is possible that the utter failure of the Noise convinced him that the ancestors were not waiting impatiently for the living to clear the way for their return bearing cargo. But the simplest explanation of his position is that he set himself against the Cemetery Cult because, as described in this chapter, he had forfeited his chance to be one of its leaders.

Participants in the Cemetery Cult expended vast amounts of time and energy in cult activities, neglected gardening and fishing, and they strained or broke social ties, including ties with nuclear family members. But they stopped far short of destroying canoes or throwing valuables into the sea. They also forbore from committing to a specific Last Day, something that had brought nothing but disappointment during the Noise. Some in the Cemetery Cult spoke boldly of being prepared for martyrdom, as had participants in the Noise. Most participants, however, were probably significantly more concerned about upsetting the Australian administration than adherents of the Noise had been. This was probably in part because they were anticipating getting a Native Government Council (NGC) embracing the south coast and they feared that pursuing the cult could cost them that opportunity. Their appetite for martyrdom was weak.[2]

2   In fact, throughout the history of the Paliau Movement, appetites for martyrdom were weak in comparison with the Biblical martyrdoms with which Manus people may have been familiar. A stint in the Lorengau jail—the most common punishment for those who aggravated the administration too much—could not have been enjoyable. But the experience pales against that of non-mythical Christian martyrs and Christian minorities martyred at the hands of the Catholic Church. Thirteenth-century Cathar 'heretics' in what is now France voluntarily submitted to being 'dumped on piles of dray faggots, and burnt alive' en masse (Oldenbourg 1961 [1959]: 361). Their passion was rooted in part in the intense political feelings intertwined with different versions of Christianity in that time and place. Still, in comparison, participants in the Noise and the Cemetery Cult seem to have exhibited great good sense.

We will not see much of Paliau in this chapter. During the events described here, Paliau was deeply involved in his duties as president of the newly established NGC headquartered on Baluan Island. But although Paliau enters the picture late in the events described in this chapter he dominates the events that follow, which we will describe in Chapter 11.

The ghost of Thomas

If the Cemetery Cult had a prophet, it was the ghost of a young man of Johnston Island named Thomas, who died 24 December 1952. According to all accounts, the ghost's appearance in the village of Tawi initiated the cult. Tawi was the westernmost of the Titan villages, built over a south coast lagoon. The people of Johnston Island had once been part of Tawi, but they moved to Johnston Island after the Noise. They had participated fully in the Noise while still in Tawi, but in its aftermath they wanted to be closer to the centre of the Movement—which was on Baluan— and to build a New Way village, for which even tiny Johnston Island was better suited than a lagoon.

Thomas was an avid gambler and just before his death he went to Johnston Island to borrow money to finance this pastime from male kin there. He knew they had recently won a large sum at cards and he hoped they would lend him a share. They lent him £5 Australian, much less than he had expected. He went away angry, but he kept his anger to himself. Soon after, he got sick and died. In terms of New Way doctrines, his unrevealed anger had simmered in his *tingting*, causing the illness that killed him.

On 24 December 1952, all the men and women of Tawi went to church— that is, the Paliau Movement church—in Peli, an Usiai village on the mainland near Tawi, to celebrate Christmas Eve. A single old man stayed behind to keep watch. During the night the sound of people moving around the village woke him. He cautiously looked out of the house where he slept and saw men climbing the ladders into one house after another and then coming down again. They seemed to be looking for something. Although it was dark, he recognised some of them as men of Tawi who had died, some a long time ago and some recently. They left as mysteriously as they had come, but then another man, dressed completely in white, appeared briefly among the houses. The voice of the old man's dead father entered his mind, not through his ears, but directly into his thoughts. His father told him that the man dressed in white was Thomas of Johnston Island. Frightened, the old man hid beneath a canoe sail until other villagers returned.

Thomas did not appear on Johnston Island itself until January. Three women had gone to Kalopa, a small island on which they had gardens and coconut palms. They realised, they later recounted, that Thomas was there. They did not see him, but they heard him whistle and smelled the talcum powder anointing his dead body. When they returned to Johnston Island, they could feel the presence of Thomas in their canoe. That night—in the house of Kamanra, a Johnston Island man—Thomas made his presence on the island known by whistling. Hearing the whistle, Kamanra asked: 'Who is it? Are you Thomas?' There was an affirmative whistle. Kamanra's wife, Sapa, had been seriously ill, but after this incident she became, as people put it, as if she were dead. Many agreed that the ghost of Thomas now possessed her. Kamanra went to the council of Johnston Island with this news of Thomas's manifestation. The *kaunsil* said that they should test the spirit that possessed Sapa: 'If he is good he can stay; if not, we will get rid of him'.

A seance was arranged and everyone crowded into Kamanra and Sapa's house while the Movement *kaunsil* questioned the ghost. When the *kaunsil* asked the ghost 'Are you bad?', there was no reply. When he asked 'Are you good?', Thomas whistled, indicating 'Yes'. The *kaunsil* then asked Thomas, by posing a series of questions, what had caused his death. When he asked 'Did you die because of anger at your brother?', Thomas said 'Yes'. He also said yes when asked if the woman he possessed would recover from her illness. As in many seances Schwartz attended, an outside observer could easily have assumed that the interlocutor controlled Thomas's messages to the living. But no one seemed to doubt that they were hearing directly from Thomas. And not merely from Thomas but from Jesus, for they regarded the *kaunsil* acting as interlocutor as a passive agent receiving messages from Jesus, who had chosen to communicate through Thomas. Audience members had suspended all scepticism. They found it satisfying that when the *kaunsil* repeatedly asked Thomas: 'You are incapable of lying to us, aren't you, being a ghost sent by Jesus from the Sky?', the answer was always unhesitatingly affirmative.

A vital message from Thomas was that Jesus had sent him to Johnston Island because of all the Movement villages this one had drifted furthest from the ideals of the New Way. Their village was rotten with sin. Their island would be capsized into the sea unless they returned immediately to the way of God under the tutelage of Thomas. The *kaunsil* ran through the days of the week, waiting for Thomas to whistle, to find out if and when he would come again. In this way, he determined that Thomas would come every Friday night. In expectation, villagers built a special room for him in Kamanra and Sapa's house.

Schwartz and Shargo got the impression that the people of Johnston Island were not entirely surprised to be fingered as conspicuous sinners. Like others in the Movement, they had not figured out how to cope with the less-restricted sexual mores that the New Way recommended. Adultery—a form of sexual liberty that went beyond New Way loosening of the old strictures of male-female relationships—was notoriously prevalent. Movement adherents on Johnston Island had facilitated adultery by building four small houses distant from the main settlement, exclusively for assignations. Even the people of villages where adultery was only slightly less prevalent thought this went well beyond the ambivalent permissiveness of the New Way. In Tok Pisin, people called them the *haus pamuk* of Johnston Island. In that era, this Tok Pisin term referred to a house wherein some Usiai people supposedly practised a type of communal sexual licence. Today—especially in urban Papua New Guinea—it means simply a house of prostitution, a connotation it may already have been acquiring in the 1950s. The aim of the New Way, however, was not to encourage sexual licence but to ease attitudes towards adultery and thus to diminish its explosive effects on marriage and the family. One of Thomas's first commands was to destroy the lovers' hideaways.

Sexual licence was not the only issue on which Thomas had views or regarding which he conveyed the views of Jesus. At public meetings in Bunai, Schwartz had been hearing a lot of talk about the alleged decline of the New Way since 1950. Thomas also addressed this theme. He, like the ghosts that would appear in other villages before the Cemetery Cult ran its course, was particularly concerned about the declining authority of village leaders. Again and again in seances, ghosts denounced the prevalence of *bikhet* (that is, too much individualistic pride), the failure to *harim tok* (to obey leaders and the general will), and the growing tendency to *sakim tok* (to ignore leaders and the general will).

Thomas and the ghosts who became the guides of other cult villages often contrasted what they saw as the present condition, in which each person followed his or her own desires, with the now-fabled unity and coordinated action of the early days of the Movement. This often required the ghosts' interlocutors to elicit complex messages from binary questions and responses. Fortune (1965 [1935]: 29–30, 35) described the whistling of ghosts, via mediums, in the seances of the old Titan culture as elaborate and discursive rather than binary. Most other means of divination he described, however, relied on binary indicators. As we will see later, the ghosts of the Cemetery Cult occasionally indulged in non-binary whistling that required considerable interpretation. The cult interlocutors provided this and listeners generally accepted their interpretations.

Through single whistles and occasionally more elaborate compositions, the ghosts described the society of the dead in the Sky as an example for the living. There were, the ghosts agreed, three places: Earth, Sky, and Heaven. (We are translating the Tok Pisin term, *ples daun*—literally, place down—as Earth for simplicity. We are capitalising it not because it is a planet but because it is one of the three major entities of cult cosmology.) Only one road leads from Earth to God in Heaven. This is the road of the *tingting*. But living man does not have direct access to God. The dead and Jesus, who is their *kaunsil*, are intermediaries between man and God. The dead live with Jesus in the Sky, not in Heaven. The Sky was a place somewhere near America. (In one of his communications, Thomas is alleged to have asserted that 'the dead are with the Americans'.) These ideas are in accord with those circulating at the time of the Noise, but the ghosts added some details to the picture of the Sky.

In the Sky, Thomas conveyed, the dead responded immediately to every bell that called them to meetings. They did not drift in late or stay home as the living did when called to meetings. They 'heard the talk' of the boss, Jesus. He had only to say a thing once and the dead obeyed. They never missed church in the huge building where Jesus conducted services. Periodically, Jesus enlarged this building merely by thinking. There were three courthouses in the Sky through which all people had to pass when they died. In each, judgement was more severe than in the preceding court. There was also a prison and those whom the courts found guilty were sentenced to one, two, or three years in a Sky prison. The description of Heaven that Thomas conveyed was much like that associated with the Noise. Heaven was perfectly flat, as Paradise was before the Fall. There were broad roads, good houses made of galvanised iron, many automobiles, and flowers growing everywhere. The dead had learned good ways. They were *orait finis*—that is, completely all right or perfected. When they thought of the living, they cried in sorrow. They would have liked to rejoin the living to teach them, to make them all right too, but the road was blocked by all the sins of the living. Now, Jesus had sent Thomas, the first of a number of teachers yet to come. Each of the 33 villages that had joined the Movement was to have its own ghostly teacher, sent by Jesus and chosen from among each village's own dead. First, however, it was necessary to accept Thomas and to begin to carry out his commands.

Thomas conveyed that the ghosts were angry at their treatment by the living. When Movement members built their new villages on the beaches they also built new cemeteries. But they left those who had died before the move in scattered graves in the bush, in old locations on the beaches, or on the small islands where the dead of the lagoon villages of old Tawi and old Pere were buried. This, the dead conveyed through Thomas, was a serious obstacle to reunion with the living. The dead were to arise from their graves, but this could not happen until the bones of the dead were gathered into the new villages, placed in graves arranged in straight rows in good sand, with the bones of the dead laid out properly in each grave. Accomplishing this was the major project that Thomas ordered. He pointed out that when Jesus died, his bones had not been scattered and forgotten. He had been buried in a grave out of which he arose after three days. The cemetery was to be the opening between Earth and Sky, which was something the white men knew about. Had not the Americans exhumed all their war dead for reburial in proper cemeteries in America?

Early in 1953, Johnston Islanders began work on the new cemetery. According to the accounts Schwartz and Shargo obtained, this activity and the many revelations attesting to the validity of Thomas's message quickly boosted village morale. People again briskly carried out collective routines as they had in the early days of the Movement. Everyone lined up in the morning to receive a work assignment and accepted it without question, and everyone went to bathe in the sea together. As Schwartz saw on his visit to Johnston Island in November, the church was crowded twice a day for lengthy services. Everyone attended meetings, which people began by singing the songs sung during the Noise. The islanders also revived the marching and drilling of the early Movement, a practice supported by the discovery one morning of the footprints of ghosts who had marched as a group in the village at night.

Leaders pressed constantly to rid the village of all bad thought and action. Public confession was revived in daily assemblies to, in Tok Pisin, *stretim ol rong*, that is, to straighten or correct all that was wrong in the village. Thomas assisted. In seances, he identified sinful acts or hidden anger or jealousy that required confession. The villagers involved then publicly confessed and shook hands. It was assumed that sickness or other misfortune would punish those who refused. Kamanra's wife Sapa augmented the *kaunsil* as a medium for Thomas. Through these two, people called on Thomas to identify the sin or anger causing any illness. A new way of ferreting out sin also appeared. Occasionally, crosses in the new graveyard fell over during the night. Thomas said the ghosts whose graves were marked by the fallen crosses did this to call attention to sin in the deceased's living family. Thomas then helped to discover what the sin was so that it could be rectified. He also predicted the best places to look for fish or turtles, and people said that there was food in unprecedented abundance. All this is reminiscent of Fortune's description of how the Titan used household ghosts in 1928, but cult adherents did not see these practices as revivals. Rather, they were—at last—the true, revealed, Christianity to be practised under Jesus's almost constant supervision.

As people built the cemetery and collected their ancestors' remains they felt—they said—the presence of the dead all around them. One man found 10 shillings on his table that allegedly had appeared out of nowhere. This caused much excitement. It was tangible proof of the wealth that was to come. (This almost duplicates incidents in Patusi during the Noise.) Even the materialisation of several sticks of tobacco—a rather pathetic treasure—was accepted as a sign of the imminence of fulfilled promise.

The difficulty of finding old graves and, in many cases, identifying the occupants complicated the bone collecting.[3] Thomas helped. Sometimes people asked him where to dig or, when they found an unidentified skeleton, whose it was. With and without the ghost's help, Johnston Islanders gathered more than 100 skeletons. To do so, they often had to travel by canoe to and from the mainland, Tawi, or other burial places along the south coast. The night before such an expedition, Thomas would predict the next day's weather and wind. Often, when people returned to the village at night with the skeletons of their dead, the ghosts of these dead appeared to them or made some sign that they had come to Johnston Island along with their bones. As in the past, caring for the bones of

3   There had long been both government regulations and mission injunctions that the dead be buried in European-style cemeteries. Old burial places had been abandoned when villages moved to new sites. The Titan said that when they decided to adopt Christianity they threw the skulls of their household ghosts into the sea. They probably buried many of these, however, as indicated by the number of such skulls recovered for reburial during the Cemetery Cult.

the dead now helped assure that their ghosts would guard the health and general wellbeing of the living. People attributed several illnesses that occurred during this period to failure to bring in some overlooked skeleton or to the improper state of mind of those handling the bones.

Once gathered, the bones had to be washed with a fragrant soap, smeared with Vaseline, sprinkled with talcum powder, and wrapped in new or at least good cloth, in the same way people had begun treating corpses since such goods, purchased with hard-earned money, had become available. Then they laid the bones out in small wooden boxes, for there was no room in the cemetery for larger coffins. Later in the cult, Schwartz suggested that the relatively small graveyards wouldn't be able to accommodate any more burials once all the bones had been gathered. A cult adherent in Bunai replied that this would not be a problem because when the present work was completed and the Last Day (in Tok Pisin, *De Bihain*) arrived, there would be no more deaths. But until the cemetery was ready, people kept the boxes of their ancestors' bones in their houses, in places of honour, surrounded by flowers in bottles of water. For this interval at least, the skulls of the dead had returned to the Manus houses.

Behind all this was the same promise the Noise had failed to fulfil. One adherent's statement of that promise is typical:

> This is what the dead told us: 'If you are strong, Jesus told us and it is true, if you do well all the work of the way of the *tingting*, then whatever you desire will appear. As with Adam and Eve before, in the place where God put them, there will be again the First Order of God. If you straighten out your *tingting*, we can send things to you. If you are not strong and you continue to follow all kinds of evil ways, we will not be able to come near you. Whatever you like, it is not difficult, we can give it to you. Now you work hard to make money. You buy things in the store. All these things, if you are all right, we can give you. The only difficulty is in your own minds. It is you who are in the wrong'.

This adherent continued:

> Cargo [in the original Tok Pisin, *kago*] is things, like what we see in stores. We think like this. We work hard, work hard, work hard until we die to get one shilling to buy a little something. In a short time it is used up. Now we think that it is true. All these things that we desire are near now if we hold fast to what they [the dead]

say. They say it is not hard. We only have to clear our *tingting*.
Money, too. They say if they want to give us money, they can.
They showed us a bag of money.

Some said that Thomas himself had appeared to them holding a bag
of money. And, one night, after the new cemetery on Johnston Island
had been completed, people heard the sound of an approaching car
intermingling with Thomas's whistle.

As the cult spread beyond Johnston Island, many regarded such events as
firm evidence of its promise. But although scepticism was now in retreat,
it still had its uses. All those who told Schwartz and Shargo that they
believed in the Cemetery Cult said that they had doubted its truth at first.
Unlike the swift contagion of the Noise, recruits to the Cemetery Cult
came to it more slowly, perhaps struggling with the doubts left by the
failure of the Noise. One young man from Tawi even devised and carried
out a way to test cult claims. He concealed himself under Sapa's house
at one of the early seances. When, inside the house, the *kaunsil* called
Thomas's name, the sceptic under the house whistled. But then he heard
another whistle coming from inside. A group of Tawi visitors agreed that
Thomas had exposed the sceptic, rather than the opposite.

The promise of lavish rewards for people's labours on behalf of the dead
was joined to a threat of destruction if they rejected Thomas's message.
This was their last chance, Thomas told them. Jesus was extremely angry
that they continued to ignore his will after the pain he had suffered for them.
In June 1953, when a volcano erupted in the sea between Lou and Baluan,
Thomas said that it was a sign from God, a final warning. The seance in
which he conveyed this message was unusual. The *kaunsil* asked Thomas:
'Do you have something to say about this fire between Lou and Pwam?'
'Yes', whistled Thomas. 'Was this sent to burn up one village?', the *kaunsil*
asked. Thomas was silent. The *kaunsil* then asked, 'Was it sent to destroy
all of us together?' Thomas then began to whistle at length. Everyone was
confused except the *kaunsil*, who translated as follows: 'This fire is a sign
of this work we are doing. We forgot about the work of 1946, but now
we want to pursue it again. Thomas said that if we do not do this, this
fire will destroy all of us. If some join in this work and some do not, this fire
will appear under the villages of those who do not join. The fire will eat
away beneath these villages and people will be astonished to see their villages
go under'. Then Thomas said good night in his usual way, whistling three
times. On the third whistle everyone said, 'Good night, Thomas'.

From the first, Thomas urged people to hurry, but he never fully explained why. Some of his acolytes speculated that Jesus had lost patience with them and that they had to hurry to stave off their destruction because the Last Day was imminent. When the Last Day came it would affect the whole world, whites as well as blacks, but it would come first to Manus, because the long-deprived black man was the last work of Jesus. On the Last Day the entire world would be thrown into darkness. All people would be thrown down to the ground in a *guria* that would make that of the first Noise seem insignificant. When it was over, all people would be subject to divine judgement, and the world would be made over. The sea would become dry land, and the land would be level, traversed by broad roads on which automobiles passed by good houses, bordered by flowers.

Thomas made it clear that his mission was not only to Johnston Island, but to all the villages within the Movement. He asked that people from other villages come to speak with him, and the *kaunsil* of Johnston Island did his best to carry out this wish. Johnston Islanders hosted anyone who came to attend the seances. Like the Mok canoes gathering materials for the Baluan meeting house in 1946, the Johnston Islanders going back and forth to the mainland to gather the skeletons of their dead relatives spread the news and aroused great curiosity. At least a few people from every village in the Movement came to Johnston Island. Some who returned to their villages advocating building better cemeteries made only oblique reference to the full cult context of such public works. Others returned openly excited about Thomas's promises and warnings.

Johnston Island cult leaders told visitors that once they began building a cemetery in their village and gathering, cleaning, and anointing the bones of their dead, a ghostly teacher would appear. There were to be 33 teachers, one in each Movement community, with Thomas at their head. When other ghostly teachers began to appear, they confirmed everything that Thomas had said. Each village or part of a village to 'come inside' the cult had its own medium, sometimes several, and each medium had his or her interpreters. Although each medium pronounced some minor variations on or additions to cult practices and doctrines, their core teachings were substantially the same. Believers saw the similarities among these direct, local revelations as strong evidence of their truth. But they also valued their independent access to truth. Although Johnston Island was clearly the centre of the cult and Thomas and his Johnston

Island acolytes its leaders, it was clearly important to the people of other villages that they had their own teachers and were not in thrall to either the Johnston Islanders or their tutelary ghost.

The Cemetery Cult in Tawi

Tawi, where Thomas made his first appearance, was part of the cult almost from the beginning. Villagers said that on the deads' initial visit to inspect the village they noted with disapproval the lack of an adequate cemetery. The people of Tawi then worked closely with their relatives on Johnston Island to rectify this and Tawi and Johnston Island completed their new cemeteries simultaneously. Thomas had instructed people to gather only the bones of their own kin. But given the many close kinship ties between the people of the two locales it wasn't always clear which of the two cemeteries should receive whose remains. It was soon agreed, however, that the closest direct living descendants had first claim on ancestral bones.

Nonetheless, for almost a year no ghostly teacher appeared for Tawi. There were signs of the presence of the dead, but no one like Thomas who came to speak regularly. So, Kisakiu, *kaunsil* of Tawi, and many others sailed back and forth between Tawi and Johnston Island to attend Thomas's seances.

Many of those who came to Johnston Island to hear Thomas stayed to play cards for money, often all day and all night. No one seemed to find this inconsistent with efforts at moral elevation. The *kaunsil* of Johnston Island and Tawi were both avid gamblers, as Thomas had been in life. It was while men from several villages were in Tawi for a marathon card playing session that Tawi finally received a visit from a spirit mentor, the ghost of the former *luluai* of Loitja, Ponowan. Suluwan, the leader of Bunai's Pomatjau hamlet, was among those gambling in Tawi and saw the ghost first. Suluwan had lost heavily and was returning to Kisakiu's house to sleep when he saw the ghost of Ponowan. The ghost followed him into the house, where Kisakiu also saw him. The ghost said nothing, but he came back after everyone was asleep and woke Suluwan to ask him about his gambling luck. Suluwan said he had only £1 left. Ponowan told him to return to the game with his £1, and he would win. Suluwan did as he was told, playing through the night and the next day and winning £40.

Ponowan began to appear to Kisakiu frequently, waking him at night with a whistle. One night, Ponowan woke him from a dream about a dying woman and emitted a long series of whistles which Kisakiu could not understand. He interrupted to ask questions in the hope that Ponowan might be the teacher for whom Tawi had been waiting. He asked Ponowan if he had gone before God when he died and now had been sent down to them. He asked if he had died because of someone's wrong. He asked, 'Did you die because your *tingting* had been disturbed because when you spoke to your people about the ways of God and right thinking, they did not listen to you?' Ponowan whistled 'Yes'. After more questioning, Ponowan said that he had come to do the same work that Thomas did on Johnston Island. He promised to come back regularly.

Suluwan left Tawi on Good Friday, 1954. Before he left, he witnessed the first two days of a new way of observing Easter. Thomas had instructed the people of Tawi and Johnston Island as follows: 'On Thursday Jesus is with God. On this day you must pull out and lay down all the wooden crosses in the cemetery. On Friday, when Jesus was nailed to the cross, you must stand up all the crosses on the graves. Jesus will be with the dead on Saturday. On Sunday He will arise. On Sunday, flags must be placed in all the cemeteries. Jesus has won. All the dead too, they will have won. All will come back. If you do not obey, there will be an ordeal put upon you'. In Tawi and on Johnston Island people carried out these instructions. Many people fervently hoped that on Easter Sunday the dead would arise and Jesus would return. They were, of course, bound to be disappointed.

The Cemetery Cult in Nuang and Kapo

Most of the people of the coastal Titan village of Patusi and the two Usiai villages that had relocated adjacent to it, Nuang and Kapo, were inclined towards the cult. There was, however, significant opposition in Patusi, which we will describe below. But in Nuang and Kapo, as in Tawi and on Johnston Island, there was little or no overt opposition. On the contrary, the people of these two Usiai villages, led by their respective Movement *kaunsil*, Pokanau and Nakwam, supported the cult fanatically.

In their old locations, Nuang and Kapo had enjoyed close relationships with Malei and Lowaya. The four villages had originally been located inland, near each other and not far from the south coast. Malei and Lowaya later came down to the beach to join the amalgamated New Way village at Bunai. But the close relationship between Nuang and Kapo and their former inland neighbours, Malei and Lowaya, had survived their relocation and the Cemetery Cult came to Malei, Loyawa, and other Usiai people in Bunai from Nuang and Kapo.

In 1954, Pita Tapo of Lahan, who had been the main prophet of the Noise among the Usiai in 1947, left Bunai to stay in Nuang and Kapo to learn about the Cemetery Cult and attend seances. Here, he was again able to have the kind of influence he had enjoyed during the Noise. Men of Malei and Lowaya had also come to Nuang and Kapo to learn about the cult and attend seances. In the seances, two ghosts conveyed instructions through a female medium and the *kaunsil* of the two villages, all three of whom provided extended interpretations. The content of the teachings closely resembled what people had heard from Johnston Island. In Kapo, as in Yiru, a man had allegedly died and returned to life. Transported to the Sky, he had remained there from six o'clock in the evening to six o'clock the next morning. On returning, he reported experiences much like those of Ponram and of Kampo's wife. In Heaven, the Kapo man shook hands with thousands of the dead and passed through two of the three courts before the recently deceased *komiti* of Kapo took him aside and sent him back to the land of the living again, warning him that he was not ready to pass the third court. If he did not pass, either his throat would be cut immediately or he would be jailed. The Kapo man reported that he had been sent back as a warning to others.

In the Nuang and Kapo seances the ghosts added to the usual description of the perfect meetings held in the Sky. Unlike the meetings held in earthly villages, those in the Sky always followed the rule that discussion and action on one proposal had to be completed before other subjects could be introduced. This rule, to which the ghosts now lent their imprimatur, was one that Paliau had repeatedly tried to impress on Movement meetings, but with little success. The two ghosts also explained that they could not be expected to remain in the village all the time. They would come to the village only when some new work was beginning. The rest of the time, they would be attending meetings in other villages or reporting to Johnston Island. And the ghosts also warned Pita Tapo against accompanying those who exhumed skeletons. Women, men with large families, and men with many wrongs still in their *tingting*, such as Tapo, would sicken if they engaged in this work. Young people, because of their supposed innocence, were preferred.

The Cemetery Cult in Malei and Lowaya

While Pita Tapo was soaking up the Cemetery Cult in Nuang and Kapo, the cult came into the open in Bunai. While in other Movement villages the cult encountered significant opposition, on Johnston Island and in Tawi, Nuang, Kapo, Malei, and Lowaya most village leaders actively supported it. Zeal for the cult, however, was exceptional in Malei and Lowaya. They were the only hamlets in Bunai in which virtually everyone participated in the cults—or, at least, in which the opposition kept remarkably quiet.

The people of Malei and Lowaya, although their hamlets stood at opposite ends of the Usiai section of Bunai, were informally allied. The people of each hamlet had been affiliated with the Lutheran Evangelical Mission, in contrast with the people of other sections of amalgamated Bunai who had been predominantly Roman Catholics. But this did not prevent Malei and Lowaya people from assimilating readily to the Movement doctrines, despite those doctrines' debt to Catholicism. The younger Movement leaders of these two hamlets were exceptionally literate, thanks to schooling provided by Lutheran Evangelicals. But such younger men as Pondis of Malei and Pantret of Lowaya functioned more as figureheads while older, more experienced and aggressive men held the real power. Within his hamlet, Pondis was leader in name only. In the other hamlets of Bunai the older men had accepted secondary positions as the Movement took hold. But in Malei, the old *luluai* Kilopwai retained actual authority and relegated to Pondis the function of representing the hamlet at meetings, wearing his best European clothing. In Lowaya, Pantret had been selected as Movement *kaunsil* for his literacy and supposed greater sophistication. But he was painfully self-conscious about his lack of tradition-derived legitimacy. He was a *lau* (the lower rank of the two-rank system of *lau* and *lapan*), but several men of his age were *lapan* and the sons of *luluai*. Petrus Popu, the old *luluai*, had dropped this colonial-era position to become a *komiti* in the Movement and he led from this position despite Pantret's titular higher Movement rank. In fact, it appeared that Lowaya owed its cohesion to Petrus Popu's leadership. Lowaya was an assemblage of fragments of former villages that Petrus Popu had drawn together as a single unit with a single government census book.

Malei had been on the margins of the Noise. Since joining Bunai, however, at least one event there had foreshadowed the Cemetery Cult. In 1952, a 13-year-old boy, Lapun, had gone into the bush with several other boys of his age to get sago. As they began to work, Lapun saw a tall man with a white beard approaching him. Lapun fell down. His whole body shook violently. Songs came to his lips. The tall man told him that he would give him a book. The man, whom Lapun later realised must have been Jesus, told him about three trees in which they could catch many opossums. Lapun sent his companions to the trees, where they caught nine opossums. The tall man also told them that if they continued to work on the sago palm they had cut, which they thought was nearly exhausted, they would get eight additional bundles of sago. This miracle also happened.

The next day the tall man came again to Lapun. This time he instructed him in the proper ways of marching and drilling and kneeling with the head bowed. Returning to Malei, Lapun told everyone of his experience. Most were convinced of its significance, except Kilopwai. For several days the adolescent Lapun led the village in singing songs he said Jesus had revealed to him and marching according to Jesus's instructions. But within a few days Kilopwai challenged him, saying that if he had really been visited by Jesus and not by a *masalai* (Tok Pisin for a dangerous or simply mischievous bush spirit), as Kilopwai suspected, he would be able to recite the entire 'Long Story of God'. Lapun was shamed, for he knew he could not. He immediately abandoned his attempts to lead and thereafter remained silent about his alleged encounter with Jesus.

'The mark'—that is, the affirmation of the cult—appeared in Malei towards the end of March 1954. For two months prior, villagers had been preparing for the coming of the promised ghostly teachers. During February and March, they met almost daily to rid their hamlet of everything that was wrong. Any bad interpersonal feelings had to be aired in these meetings, regardless of their overt insignificance or how far in the past their genesis. Also during this time, Malei cult enthusiasts visited Nuang and Kapo, where ghostly teachers had already appeared and the cult was more advanced, although still operating in ostensible secrecy.

In Lowaya, on 7 March, Nasei, the wife of the village *tultul*, fell down in such violent convulsions that she had to be restrained. At first she raved incoherently, but she gradually became more comprehensible and eventually conveyed to her audience that she had not only seen Jesus, but also that she was now possessed by the ghost of Ponau, a former *luluai* of Lowaya. Further, Ponau wanted her to convey to the people of Lowaya that all that had been revealed to the people of Johnston Island was true.

Ponau said the day was imminent when there would be no more sickness or death and all the dead would return to join the living. First, however, Lowaya must build a cemetery separate from the common village graveyard and sections in the new cemetery were to be provided for each of the old village fragments (equivalent to clans) of Pwa, Lesei, Ponro, Nrakopat, and others. A meeting was held at which Lowaya villagers spoke with the dead through Ponau with Nasei as his medium. Old men representing nearly extinct clans told their dead forebears how difficult their lives had become. They complained that strangers were using their land and that their descent lines, created by God at the beginning of time, were in danger of dying out. The dead answered that they longed to return, but the sins abiding in the *tingting* of the living blocked them. Also, they had no physical point of contact with the village. Before the dead could return, their descendants had to gather their bones, still scattered near all the old village sites in the interior, in a special place in the Lowaya hamlet of Bunai.

The words of Ponau's ghost entered Nasei's mind directly, people said, and Nasei spoke them. Ponau asked: 'Soon your cargo will appear. The cargo that we sent before, did it arrive or not?' Nasei answered, 'No, we didn't receive any cargo'. Then the dead *luluai* said, 'Long ago we sent plenty of cargo'. Nasei responded: 'It came, but the Australians confiscated it'. Ponau continued: 'Did you get the aeroplanes we sent? Did you get the battleships?' 'No', replied Nasei. 'Now we will have to make war against the Australians', Ponau said. Ponau continued speaking through Nasei, saying that white men and black men were alike, but the white men had hidden the truth from the black men. Now that the light of God had come, the dead could arise and all would be made right.

Everyone who told Schwartz of Nasei's visitation said that her *guria* had been severe because she was a particularly wicked person. She was notorious for her many adulteries, for lying, bad temper, and stubbornness. For the Lowaya seances, a room in Nasei's house had been divided in half (as in Sapa's house on Johnston Island). Nasei sat on one side and the older men and women sat on the opposite side. Pantret, the *kaunsil*, attended Nasei, carrying her messages to the others and asking questions. As on Johnston Island, no one appeared to suspect the interlocutor of making any personal contribution.

The work of 'clearing the *tingting*' continued in a series of 'wrong-straightening' meetings. Then, several days later, Pomak, an adolescent, underwent a death and resurrection that he later related to Schwartz. He said that he had been to Heaven and seen God, whom Pomak described as looking like his pictures in mission books. Pomak had seen the three places—Heaven, Sky, and Earth—connected by a straight line. This was the road of the *tingting* and of the dead. Pomak's revelations paralleled all others in most respects. Many of them included messages pertaining to the separateness of the body and the *tingting* (sometimes called 'something of Caesar's' and 'something of God's', or 'the road of the council' [here, probably meaning the NGC] and 'the road of the cemetery'). Pomak warned against the dangers of thinking constantly about women, taro, sago, and fish (that is, of focusing on the body) and he said that it was wrong to think all the time about cultivating their gardens (recall that the Usiai traditionally were gardeners, unlike the Titan), for this was false worship and in conflict with the way of the *tingting*. But having gained people's attention as a prophet, Pomak soon forfeited his credibility. Several trivial quarrels with his brothers left him in a sullen rage. He stopped prophesying and talked bitterly about running away to work for the whites.

Pomak, however, had a successor, another adolescent, Joseph Nanei. About 16 years old, he became the next conspicuous leader of the Cemetery Cult in Lowaya. In his role as prophet he changed from an inarticulate boy into an arrogant leader who exerted nearly dictatorial command over others. Even respected elders obeyed his orders. He was the son of Kekes, a surviving *lapan* of the almost extinct village of Lesei. Kekes claimed all the land on which the village of Bunai was located and had argued his claim incessantly for years. From exposure to this, Joseph Nanei had absorbed unusual knowledge of his genealogy. When he began to see ghosts, he saw most of the ancestors whose names he had learned from his father, some going back around 10 generations. This impressed his audience. He soon, however, made a more important contact. This was the ghost of a young man only recently dead, and this neophyte ghost declared himself the cult teacher for whom Lowaya had been waiting. He would be the hamlet's independent channel for cult secrets and forces. With this legitimation, Joseph Nanei began conducting wrong-straightening meetings and directing the gathering of the remains of the dead.

Two teacher-ghosts appeared in Malei in March. The ghosts of both Pokowas and Liamwin entered Namu—a Lowaya woman who had married into Malei—as sensations travelling up each leg into her body and she became their medium. Her spirit guests passed in and out of her body freely, but they never left her for long or wandered far. Pokowas tended to stay in her body more than Liamwin. They usually spoke through her by whistling in reply to questions. Again, the people of Malei insisted that the whistling did not come from the mouth of the medium.

During the time that she hosted the teacher-ghosts, people said that her *tingting* became clear, like that of a white man, because the ghosts had purged her of all her sins. She became sensitive to any unexpressed disturbance in others' *tingting* and was able to bring disturbed relations among the people of Malei to light in the wrongstraightening meetings. Namu thought she had been selected because she was a virtuous person lacking the faults of other women. (Nasei of Lowaya was said to have been selected for just the opposite reason.) Both ghosts were her close kin. She called one brother and the other uncle. She had nursed Pokawas on his deathbed. She also counted Joseph Nanei of Lowaya and his tutelary ghost as close relatives.

After a week as medium for her ghosts in Malei, Namu announced that they had directed her to go to Lowaya to collaborate with Joseph Nanei, who had also received ghostly instructions to collaborate. Namu and Nanei held joint seances in a single room in a Lowaya house divided into Malei and Lowaya halves. The two mediums also stayed in the same house, to which villagers delivered their meals. People were appointed to stay by them constantly and Pantret was assigned to remain nearby to write down everything the ghosts revealed. People compared Pantret and the others to the apostles of Jesus.

Although Malei had begun to clear a cemetery of its own, the ghosts announced through their respective mediums that it would be better if the two hamlets built a single cemetery adjoining Lowaya. This led to a serious quarrel between the two hamlets. The tendency within the cult was for each village or hamlet to build its own cemetery, for people wished to guard against the possibility that not all communities would merit the blessings of the dead. The ghosts themselves settled the quarrel. They called a meeting of the dead of both places. As transmitted through Joseph Nanei and Namu, the dead favoured building a single cemetery in Lowaya. But the living residents of the two hamlets reached a compromise—dividing a single cemetery into two sections, one for each hamlet, separated by a path.

The dead also manifested to people other than the mediums for the teacher-ghosts. An incident that received particular attention involved Petrus Popu, the *komiti* of Lowaya, and Sayau Bombowai, the *komiti* of Katin. One afternoon they were fishing together near the site of the new cemetery. As the sun went down they saw many men dressed in white in the cemetery. They approached to hear what they were saying. The dead were speaking a language they could not understand, but it was clear, they reported, that this was some sort of meeting. They recognised the chairman as Petrus Ndroi, the dead brother of Samol of Bunai. By the time the two fishermen could bring others to see this meeting of the dead, the ghosts were gone. Petrus Popu felt, however, that another event validated the report. At about the same time, two young Usiai boys had met the ghost of one boy's mother and that of the other's father. When they asked the ghosts where they were going, the ghosts replied that they were going to a meeting of the dead in the cemetery.

The people of Malei and Lowaya reached the height of their cult activities within a few weeks after 'the mark' on Malei. Under Joseph Nanei's direction, they revived the more rigidly routinised New Way practices. People rose to a bell. At a set time they bathed together in the sea (and so provoked the Bunai Titan to accuse them of sexual impropriety). They marched together to morning services in the Bunai church. They lined up every morning for work assignments and accepted them without complaint. People seemed grimly determined to be ritually perfect in every detail, as they had been when the New Way returned after the Noise.

Much of the communal work was explicitly cult related, such as collecting the bones of the dead, marching, and preparing the men's marching uniforms. They called the latter—shorts and undershirts dyed dark blue—their 'black' uniforms, which were like those cult participants wore in Nuang and Kapo and on Johnston Island for exhuming bones for reburial as commanded by the ghosts. Cemeterians in all locales spent many of the daylight hours travelling to old village sites to gather the skeletons of the dead. Schwartz and Shargo often watched them return by canoe from the river that took them part way to the old villages inland. The men sat in a circle around the boxes of bones on the canoe platform. The pilots poled slowly through the lagoon along the length of the village, passing the Titan section without turning their heads. They pretended to themselves that no one knew what they were doing. Then, according to Joseph Nanei's directions, they cleaned the bones in boiling water, anointed them with perfumed Vaseline hair tonic, and wrapped them in cloth for boxing. The impressive seriousness of these activities seemed to subdue the usually boisterous and disobedient children. Their parents sent them fishing, for the hamlet was extremely short of food. People had neglected the gardens for weeks and they had almost stopped trading for fish with the Titan.

Until Namu's possession, cult adherents had met secretively in family houses at night. But after the arrival of their teacher-ghosts the people of Malei built a special outdoor space for their meetings, unlike any Schwartz saw in a Movement village. It was a square formed by four long benches with backs, surrounded by a railing. Some places on the bench were draped with cloth and left empty for the convenience of the ghosts. Schwartz attended the third meeting there, held in the afternoon rather than at night. Everyone in Malei from the oldest to the toddlers formed a line to march from the main path to the meeting place, which was about 50 yards back from the path. Though they were still within easy sight and hearing of anyone passing, the distance from the main thoroughfare signified secrecy to both the Cemeterians and the uninvited. When they arrived, attendees marched through the gate and circled the square clockwise before sitting down. One man arriving late also marched solemnly around the square before taking a seat. The meeting was conducted in utter solemnity, marred only by the playing of the very youngest children.

Throughout the afternoon, one man after another rose as he felt moved to speak. (Although women attended the meeting, they seldom if ever spoke.) By this time, cult adherents had been meeting for some two months. Everything anyone said had already been said hundreds of times. There was no disagreement on any point. Yet each man spoke as if he had to persuade the rest. Each stood bolt upright, talking out into space, a style of public speaking also typical of the Movement. Speeches were formulaic self-denunciatory catalogues in which each man accused himself of every vice recognised by the New Way: 'I am stubborn. I lie. I am hot tempered. I am selfish. I give nothing to others. I have bad feelings about all of you'. Then the speaker would say that he would no longer indulge in any of these vices, listing them again one by one. These nearly identical confessions were emotionally neutral. Only one man had a specific grievance. He said that he had returned from plantation work to build a house for his father. He finished it, but his father complained that the house was no good. The young man confessed that he was angry. He had not worked with his father or spoken to him for two months. Now, he declared, his anger was finished. He and his father would shake hands.

The men expressed approval of each other's speeches. Each said: 'All this is true, now we must change. We must go back to the good ways we had in 1946'. (Malei did not join the Movement until 1948, but Malei people identified with its entire historical span.) After interminable, earnest, and repetitive speeches, the meeting ended late in the afternoon. The attendees marched to Bunai for the evening church service, after which they marched back to the square to continue as before.

Schwartz and Shargo obtained some of their first accounts of the atmosphere in Malei and Lowaya from women of Lahan or Yiru who had married into the more enthusiastically cultist hamlets but who retained strong ties with their hamlets of origin. They told the anthropologists that within Lowaya in particular they were treated as outsiders and not trusted. In fact, Schwartz and Shargo ascertained, some women who had married into Lowaya from Yiru did report everything that transpired at cult meetings to the Yiru *kaunsil*. They also reported insults to Yiru they overheard, which on a few occasions nearly fomented fights between the two hamlets.

It was unusual for women to speak at the cult meetings, even though men urged them to use the privilege of public participation the New Way prescribed. In the meetings Schwartz attended, such encouragement failed completely to convince women to speak up. If the women already felt less involved in the cult than men, the men made things worse in a series of wrong-straightening meetings in which the ghosts demanded that each woman reveal her lovers. The women declined to do so. The men promised by acclamation that that they would not become angry if the women did so. The women argued that, regardless of the promise, men would use the information against them in the future, and most continued to defy the ghosts' demand. Some of them eventually accepted a compromise; they named the villages or hamlets from which their lovers came. As they had predicted, their men used this information against them soon afterward and several women left Lowaya and relocated to their home hamlets, one claiming that she had been expelled from Lowaya.

Marching was extremely important to the Malei and Lowaya Cemeterians. They marched grimly, with their heads high, their fists clenched, stamping their feet as they followed the leader's commands. They explained to Schwartz that Jesus had ordered the marching but no one was certain about its meaning. Many were also uncertain of the object of their manifest defiance, but some identified the Titan and all those opposed to the cult. The marchers did not object to the anthropologists observing them, for they were Americans and only wanted to watch, not to interfere. Some marchers clearly appreciated Schwartz and Shargo as an audience. They wanted to be photographed; they wanted their efforts documented.

They marched to drill commands that had been revealed to Joseph Nanei in a dream. Some of the commands were those used in the native constabulary. Others had only the meanings Nanei assigned them. People often sang while marching, and the songs were as cryptic as the drill commands. Nanei and Pantret asked Schwartz to record a song that, they said, the ghost had instructed them to sing when they carried the bones of the dead. Neither the meanings of many particular words nor of some entire songs were clear to Schwartz, and Nanei and Pantret declined to do more than sing them and show Schwartz their own transcription of the words as revealed by the ghosts. The songs, however, did contain many intelligible references to Jesus, Earth, the Sky, angels, and 'win'. It appears from the albeit murky context that in places one could translate 'win' from Tok Pisin as either a verb—to be victorious—or as a name for a state of incorporeal being. Marchers also sang songs important during the Noise that mixed Tok Pisin vocabulary with words of a language said to be unknown to the singers, although some Cemeterians thought Schwartz might know them. He did not.

Enthusiasm, opposition, and exclusion in Malei and Lowaya

Each of the hamlets comprising Bunai developed its own relationship with the cult. The social contexts within the hamlets and the prior relationships among the hamlets help explain the patterns of support and opposition to the cult and the roles different actors adopted or for which they competed. The case of Malei and Lowaya is especially interesting because they apparently adopted the Cemetery Cult with little or no internal dissension and with exceptional enthusiasm.

Their experiences of the Noise had helped stir Malei and Lowaya to come down to join the composite Movement village on the beach. But they had been peripheral participants in the Noise and, unlike the leaders of Yiru and Lahan, the leaders of Malei and Lowaya did not have the prestige accorded those martyred by the jail sentences meted out to some Noise leaders. Further, they joined Bunai later than the other hamlets. They were novices to be tutored. The Titan people of Bunai had taken the lead in tutoring them in the New Way. The Malei and Lowaya people accepted this subordination to Titan mentors because the Titan had been the leaders in the Movement. It also appeared that Malei and Lowaya people still deferred to the Titan assumption of their superiority to Usiai people in all things. But the Usiai deference masked resentment. Many of the Malei and Lowaya people hoped that as the first hamlets within Bunai to join the Cemetery Cult they might improve their position and tutor the people of Lahan and the Titan of Bunai in the ways of the new cult. Malei and Lowaya people at least recognised a common interest, which they demonstrated by merging into a single cult congregation.

In contrast to the enthusiasm in Malei and Lowaya, the Bunai hamlet of Katin remained aloof from the cult and the people of Yiru opposed it. We do not know enough about the situation in Katin to speculate on why it remained indifferent to the cult. But we know enough about Yiru's relationship to Malei and Lowaya to suggest reasons for Yiru's friction with the cult hamlets, Lowaya in particular.

Schwartz and Shargo saw no signs that opposition to the cult in Yiru had much to do with disapproval of the ideas and promises of the cult per se. As described in Chapter 8, Yiru was the scene of Ponram's death and resurrection, an event the Yiru people who observed it found highly credible. Sayau Bombowai, the *komiti* of Katin, had been Ponram's principal interpreter in that incident. He also had seen the meeting of the dead in the new Malei–Lowaya cemetery while fishing with Petrus Popu of Lowaya. Yet Yiru did not become a part of the cult and Sayau Bombowai was the only Katin resident whom Schwartz knew to be sympathetic to the Cemetery Cult. In Yiru, even though Ponram had dramatically conveyed Heaven's request that his people build a new cemetery and a design for the gate, no one took up this task. Rather, the people of Yiru were not merely indifferent to the Cemetery Cult, they denigrated its pursuit in Lowaya and Malei. This clearly did not disturb Lowaya, however, and Lowaya leaders made it known to the people of Yiru that they would not be welcome in the cult anyway.

This is not mysterious in light of the general state of relations between the hamlets. Yiru's *kaunsil*, Bombowai (not to be confused with the Katin *komiti* Sayau Bombowai) was at the centre of the conflict with Lowaya. Bombowai had led Yiru since before the Noise. He was a *lapan*, though not an eminent one; he had been the *luluai* before the Movement had introduced its own council system and he had been a charter member of the Movement. He had also been at least marginally involved in the Usiai Noise, having received instructions to destroy village census books and the hats that were a symbol of the office of *luluai*. It is unlikely he was opposed on principle to collaborating with the dead to bring about miraculous change. But he was a weak and indecisive leader in an unruly hamlet, and this brought him into conflict with Lowaya.

Yiru had a reputation as the least orderly hamlet and the hamlet with the least respect for its leaders. Most of its younger men had little interest in the Movement or the New Way. Rather than bringing them closer in touch with the New Way, the move to the beach had allowed them to become more independent of their elders. One group of these young men moved freely in and out of the village, going away to work and returning to loaf and gamble. Another group—the young men the anthropologists nicknamed the minstrels—neither went away to work nor worked in the village. They spent much of their time playing ukuleles and guitars. Most of them were unmarried, often beyond the age when they should have been married. Their idleness—punctuated occasionally by casual affairs—constantly annoyed their elders and upset the peace. They had no interest in the cult except to mock it, as they mocked most everything that more solid citizens took seriously. Their habit of lounging near the Cemeterians' marching ground irritated cult adherents. Like other cult hamlets, Malei and Lowaya had forbidden secular and frivolous music, loud talking or joking, and non-ghostly whistling, all of which were favourite minstrel pastimes. Complaints about the minstrels from both within and outside Yiru usually ended with complaints about Bombowai's inability to control them.

Other matters also hopelessly compromised Bombowai's authority and aggravated Yiru relations with Lowaya. Bombowai abandoned his wife, a woman of Lowaya, for a woman named as a party to several other disruptive affairs. Bombowai induced her to leave her aged husband and he cast out his own wife. Even more unthinkable, in a society in which children are so highly desired and so hard to keep alive, he allowed his wife to take their four children with her when she returned to Lowaya.

His behaviour appalled the people of his own hamlet, Yiru, especially in times that demanded that leaders speak from morally superior positions. But the people of Yiru also took amiss Lowaya people's denunciations of the morals of all Yiru people. Several Yiru women who were married into Lowaya brought back reports of Lowaya slanders against Yiru, and they complained that their Lowaya husbands mistreated them because they were from Yiru.

All this was more than enough to ensure that Lowaya would want to keep Yiru out of the cult, perhaps from spite but perhaps also to try to maintain the high moral standards the ghosts demanded. In turn, Yiru people were in no mood to follow in Lowaya's footsteps in any endeavour. Keeping the pot boiling, Bombowai took to complaining about Lowaya's slanders against Yiru in meetings of the people of all the Bunai hamlets, and he annoyed Cemetery Cult adherents when possible by revealing to all and sundry what he could learn of the content of cult seances.

Lahan and the importance of leadership

In Lahan, the hamlet's movement towards commitment to the cult was intimately interwoven with a contest for leadership. Among the rank and file, some were inclined towards the cult but unable to act on that inclination without a strong leader.

From the first, the people of the Lahan hamlet wavered regarding the Cemetery Cult. What course they took depended largely on Kampo and Pita Tapo. Kampo was one of the most intelligent of all Movement leaders. He was the most outstanding Movement leader among the Usiai Movement adherents and many treated him as their primary spokesperson. His influence among the Usiai, however, declined as the Movement drifted during the early 1950s. Kampo himself had ambitious but workable ideas for the Usiai, emphasising producing more food in their gardens, expanding their capacity to do their own fishing, and moving more of their products to more distant markets by canoe. He set an example by gardening more assiduously than most others and he learned to handle and build canoes better than any other Usiai. He was also the only literate person in the village who used his literacy for private purposes as well as in public roles. Like Samol, the leader of the Titan core of Bunai, he kept a journal. But Samol (of whom we will hear more below) confined his entries to official public matters while Kampo kept a record of the Movement and his role in it for his son. More than any other person of public consequence in Bunai, he found himself faced with choosing for or against the Cemetery Cult. In contrast, Samol was firmly committed to the gradualist wing of the Movement, while Tjamilo—also of Titan Bunai—was just as firmly committed to the Cemetery Cult.

Kampo and Tapo had led the Usiai Noise. After consulting with Noise adherents in Titan Bunai, Kampo had returned to Lahan to try to bring the Noise home, building a church and organising communal work and worship. His prominent role in the Noise, which included burning *luluai* hats and census books, earned him a year in jail. After his release, he devoted himself to the Movement program and placed his hopes in the prospect of an officially recognised NGC, cooperatives, and schools. It was clear that he could continue to be a leader in the Movement if he wanted to, but he never made up his mind about the validity of the Noise. The Movement did not question that at some time Jesus would come again. But perhaps the Noise had been a deception—a trial sent by God or Satan, leading people astray by setting a definite time for the Second Coming? Or, had the cargo, the dead, and Jesus failed to materialise because people had not shed fully their sinful ways? Such were his doubts. Kampo was also determined to believe that fully realising the European way of life was possible within his own lifetime.

Partly because his own Lahan people were a small and indecisive constituency, Kampo thought on a Movement level more consistently than most other leaders. And he worked harder and gave more of himself to the Movement than most other local leaders, except Samol. But what he saw as the Movement's slow progress was discouraging. Even though the anthropologists were impressed by all that had changed since 1928, the pace *was* slow when measured against Movement adherents' goals. By the early 1950s many Movement members were convinced they were losing ground. They had lost the feeling of excited mass participation that had prevailed during the move to the beach and their first year there and they were bored with repeating the practices of the New Way that remained intact.

All this troubled Kampo and he worried about its causes obsessively. He often said that the leaders were entirely responsible. Using a Tok Pisin idiom, he spoke of how the leaders should be 'carrying' the others. But he also spoke of how the burden was a heavy one. He became moody and seesawed between intense activity and abject inactivity. When active he was ubiquitous. He appeared at meetings throughout the Usiai Movement area; he made long trips by canoe—to Baluan, to Lorengau, and to the north coast; and he went frequently to his gardens in the bush. During periods of such obsessive activity he always appeared in public clean, shaved, and well dressed. In his inactive state, he was depressed, pessimistic, lethargic, and withdrawn, and he wore his oldest clothes and stopped shaving. During those periods he spent much of his time in Schwartz and Shargo's house, leafing through copies of *Life* magazine, sighing over the marvellous lives of the Americans pictured there, but also readily answering the anthropologists' questions at length. Otherwise, he stayed in his house and slept.

Kampo had been in this latter mood for some time before Schwartz and Shargo recognised that the Cemetery Cult was all around them. Kampo, of course, had known of it from its beginning, but his years of identification with the Movement kept him from falling in with the Cemeterians. He felt that unless the entire Movement could take it up, he should oppose it. But the excitement of the cult emanating from Malei and Lowaya was stirring up his own hamlet of Lahan, dispersing people's boredom and lethargy. Here perhaps was an opportunity for a leader to step in and direct people's energy. Kampo's ambivalence about the cult, however, all but incapacitated him as a leader for or against it.

In March 1954, when 'the mark' on Malei (Namu's possession by her two teacher-ghosts) appeared and the cult became more public, Kampo was not in the village. He returned to find that the cult, still a work in progress when he left, had crystallised. He also found that he was excluded. Circumstances had made his decision for him. Pantret and Pondis, now openly supporting the cult, realised that if Kampo took a role within the cult, they could lose their own new authority as cult leaders, which they valued highly. They chose to reckon him hostile to the cult. And by excluding him they ensured his hostility. Kampo, like everyone else concerned with these manoeuvrings at the time, had his spies. He knew just what was happening. Thus, on the night of 'the mark' on Malei, Kampo, who had just returned to the village, held a conspicuously public meeting in Lahan at which he attacked the cult. At this meeting he said: 'Nothing simply materialises. Everything comes from hard work'. Whether his doubts about the millenarian promise of the Noise were truly resolved or not, his exclusion from leadership in the Cemetery Cult had driven him to advocate a resolutely contrary position.

The following week, Kampo began walking through all the Usiai hamlets, making the Cemeterians in Malei and Lowaya uncomfortable by his presence. Like Schwartz, if he went near cult meetings, he sensed that the discussion had just changed abruptly to the predictable pious speeches of a New Way gathering. His anger grew. He was hurt that people he had brought into the New Way were now turning him away. Even so, his indecision about the truth of the cult persisted, making him ineffective as an opposition leader. His own hamlet of Lahan had not yet joined the cult, and he might have ensured that it did not. Instead, as Lahan interest in the cult increased, Kampo withdrew more and more.

As Kampo abdicated leadership, Pita Tapo returned to Lahan from Kapo and Nuang where he had been learning the ways of the Cemetery Cult. Pita Tapo told Schwartz that Schwartz could now learn about the Noise from watching the Cemetery Cult. It was, he said, exactly what he had been advocating. Long after Lahan people had come to Bunai, he said, he had kept up the call for building a better cemetery and collecting the bones of the dead but no one had heeded him. He told Schwartz that he had not felt physically well for a long time. But now, for the first time in years, he felt strong again.

Tapo had come to Schwartz asking for medicine in September 1953. He complained that he suffered from constant itching on the back of his neck and he constantly imagined—he knew it was not real—things crawling there. He told Schwartz about his role in the Usiai Noise and said he thought he was sick because he had failed in the mission God had given him. God had told him to keep teaching his people all that had been revealed. But when he came out of jail, people showed little interest in his revelations. Lahan people were building their hamlet in Bunai and enjoying the novelty of life on the beach; their lives were full without him. But the Noise had been the most meaningful and exciting experience of his life. He had suddenly become important. Even Kampo had consented to follow his lead. Tapo tried to lead again when he came back to the Lahan settlement on the beach in 1948. But people found his talk of revelations incompatible with putting the New Way into practice in a new kind of village. People did not dismiss him as deluded, for most had never actually repudiated the doctrines of the Noise, but his timing was bad.

Angry at everyone in his hamlet, Tapo went to Ndropwa to work on the copra plantation. He came back obviously troubled. He diagnosed his condition as the result of both the hard work on Ndropwa and abandoning the way of the *tingting* to pursue material concerns. Now he suffered from chronic weakness that kept him from working and he had spells of unconsciousness, although these did not bring him visions. His *tingting*, he said, was 'stuck' (in Tok Pisin, *pas*). God had cut him off because he had abdicated his duties as prophet; God was testing him.

During the first months of the anthropologists' residence in Bunai, Tapo had been an almost pathetic figure in the village. He lived in a shack on the beach and complained that he was too weak to build a house. For six months he remained in the village, attending to his children like a mother, while his wife worked in the bush, gardening or producing sago. Other residents of his hamlet regarded him as insane. Indeed, on one occasion, his wife ran out of the shack shouting that Tapo had grabbed an axe and was going to kill her and everyone else. In his defence, Tapo said that the minstrels had driven him to fury with their incessant guitar playing.

After this incident, he spent several months in Nuang and Kapo, attracted by the Cemetery Cult. When he returned his health was much better. For the first time in years he spoke at meetings. But he was too late to carry his hamlet into the Cemetery Cult. The cult leaders of Malei and Lowaya had shunned Kampo, but—for reasons that never became clear to Schwartz—they welcomed Tapo into their cult activities. Within Lahan, he continued trying to nudge people towards the cult, using a tactic like that Tjamilo was using in Bunai. That is, he became a vigorous advocate of building a new cemetery, citing all the mundane arguments he could use in public. He did not speak of the role of cemeteries in the cult; everyone already knew this. But Tapo thought that if he could persuade Lahan to build a cemetery, an open commitment to the cult would follow. He was right. He found that the Lahan people were ready to pursue the cult, but they needed a leader, and they finally accepted Tapo.

Figure 9.1: Pita Tapo became a strong advocate of the Cemetery Cult in Lahan, an Usiai hamlet of Bunai.

Here, in 1954, he addresses a meeting for revealing and resolving interpersonal grievances, a step in making Lahan ready to receive the cargo.

Source: Theodore Schwartz.

Kampo had already made himself ineligible to lead the cult in most people's eyes, but Tapo's resumption of leadership was the final blow. Kampo stayed away from the meetings in Lahan, while Tapo initiated the process of wrong-straightening, which many agreed was long overdue. Even visitors from Lowa on the north coast who had been close to Kampo began to take part in Tapo's meetings. Kampo began to spend all his time with Samol, the leader of the Bunai Titan and an opponent of the cult. He took no action against the cult, however, until Lahan people began to build their cemetery and go into the interior to collect the bones of their dead. He then went to Lorengau to get permission from the district commissioner to build a new cemetery and move the bones of the dead. He told the district commissioner that he just wanted him to know what he was advocating in case Usiai people from the interior reported that Lahan had resumed cannibalism or told other wild stories. His intent, of course, was to draw the administration's attention to the cult activity in Lahan and his opposition to it in case the authorities decided to intervene.

Titan factions in Bunai

In the Titan section of Bunai the cult situation was distinctive. Malei and Lowaya had entered the cult together. Yiru openly opposed it. Lahan was beginning to move towards it. Among the Titan, a faction led by Tjamilo aimed at recruiting a majority to the cult, but Samol, the *kaunsil*, opposed this.

Although others also took sides in this conflict, Tjamilo and Samol were the principal contestants and the leaders of their factions. Samol was the protégé of the old paramount *luluai*, Kisekup. He had been a storekeeper, a Catholic catechist, and a leader of a pre-Paliau local movement. He had missed the Noise, having withdrawn with a small group of followers to form a new settlement. When the Movement regrouped after the Noise, Paliau gave him a prominent role. In the years preceding the Cemetery Cult, many had come to see Samol as second only to Paliau within the Movement. He was Paliau's close follower and he took Paliau as a model, rather than a rival. Samol was a calm, quiet, and competent leader, more skilled in everything, from understanding the Bible to canoe building to gardening, than most of his Titan contemporaries. People clearly respected his knowledge. This latter was vital, for he was neither a forceful nor a very aggressive person. But he was skilled in managing a fickle public and the fragile links among the various groups within the Titan population of Bunai. He was especially good at keeping disputes from boiling over and preventing people from taking irreversible positions that would split the Bunai Titan. These were the skills he brought to opposing the Cemetery Cult, which threatened everything he had worked for throughout his years in the Movement.

Samol had worked with the Movement *kaunsil* organisation for years, living with the uncertainty of exercising only informal power, waiting for the de facto council organisation to be converted into an NGC. This day was very close now. It looked like many who pursued the cult felt they were in a race against the success of the official council, which would undermine the leaders of the cult and maybe alienate its ghostly guides.

In 1953, Samol had known of the cult for over a year. He had taken no public action, but he had watched it carefully. For example, he had made a record of every trip Tjamilo made to Johnston Island. When the time came to use this information in a speech attacking the cult leader, he was able to give each of the dates exactly, using his literacy to support his authority, as was his custom. (Within the Movement, citing dates gave a speaker's argument greater strength, a practice that persists in today's version of the Movement.) Meanwhile, preparing for the official council kept Samol busy. He made repeated trips to Baluan, visiting Paliau to obtain the latest news. This took him out of the village several times a month.

Tjamilo took advantage of each of Samol's absences to advocate for the cult in village meetings. In some ways Tjamilo was comparable to Pita Tapo, for he was almost exclusively concerned with aspects of the Movement he could read as millenarian (as opposed to an understanding in which establishing an NGC was an appropriate goal on its own terms). He had moved from youth to adulthood simultaneously with the Noise. Like Tapo, the Noise had made him a leader and a teacher, although not a prophet. Unlike Tapo, Tjamilo denied ever having had a vision or seeing Jesus or the dead. But he believed in others' visions and he was far from a passive channel of communication. He gave everything a mystical meaning, sometimes sounding almost paranoid. He had virtually no formal education, but his memory for the spoken word—for people's speeches and accounts of supernatural revelations—was phenomenal. This, however, did not command the respect people accorded the notebook and pencil Samol always wielded on public occasions. To assert his claim to leadership, Tjamilo had only his moral righteousness and his single-minded devotion to the millenarian implications that he and others had found in Movement ideology and which had energised many early adherents. He was a self-appointed reminder of these elements in the Movement's origins. In 1946, he had eagerly repudiated the past. Now his vision was frozen in 1946 and 1947, when his life had taken on a meaning he wanted to perpetuate. Yet he was able to manoeuvre flexibly as he sought to restore the spirit of that time.

His influence, like that of Pita Tapo, had dwindled during the years of Movement innovation and building. He had, however, maintained a position in village affairs as a Movement *komiti*. For the most part this was a minor position. Typically, older men who gave up authority as traditional leaders to make way for younger New Way leaders became *komiti*. As *komiti*, Tjamilo represented only his own clan, but—atypically— he was younger than most such minor Movement functionaries and aspired to greater influence. He was unwilling to accept the limits of his role. A *komiti* was supposed to transmit the orders of the *kaunsil* (which ideally were arrived at communally at New Way meetings) to his clan or hamlet. He was responsible for maintaining order in and guarding the morals of his group. When he was unable to handle a situation beyond the routine, he was to bring it to the New Way court to be heard by the *kaunsil*. Tjamilo performed these duties zealously. He was constantly alert for moral transgressions, not only in his own clan, but wherever they appeared. It was from this position that he attempted to bring the Titan of Bunai into the cult.

Tjamilo had travelled often to Johnston Island and other villages where the cult was active. But he broached the subject in Bunai cautiously. When he did, he referred only obliquely to the return of the dead and the arrival of the cargo. His approach was the model for Tapo's effort in Lahan to edge people towards fuller involvement in the cult by getting them to build a cemetery and collect the bones of the dead. He was confident that if he could get these tasks started he could begin to work on straightening wrongs, as the ghosts required, but which he could do surreptitiously in the name of the principles of the New Way. Then, he reasoned, a ghostly teacher would appear to the Bunai Titan and inspire others to turn to the Cemetery Cult. Talimelion, another Titan *komiti*, and Alphonse Kanawi, the *tultul* of pre-amalgamation Bunai, plus a number of women and about eight young men, were Tjamilo's only open followers. Among the young men was Markus Pwatjumel, who had dreamed of his dead father and of the plan for the new cemetery. Pwatjumel, however, was torn between his emotional leaning towards the cult and loyalty to Samol, his brother-in-law. Had it not been for Samol's opposition, many other Titan probably would have followed Tjamilo as well. Only Samol and a few others strongly opposed Tjamilo's plan to build a cemetery. The complexity of the situation, however, was considerable.

In the dual-level discourse typical of the meetings at which people discussed the cemetery proposal, the struggle over the cult went on just below the surface. Tjamilo made speeches calling for moral reform and emphasising specific steps for improving the present Titan cemetery, such as cutting the palms that grew among the graves. Samol argued that without these trees the sun would 'cook' the graves. Tjamilo, of course, wanted more than he made explicit, and those who supported his cemetery-improvement plan were implicitly consenting to its cult rationale. At the time, not even Samol was ready to bring the submerged argument to the surface. He still felt that he could contain and stop the cult before it came to the attention of the Europeans and discredited the Movement.

Through his eloquent use of dual-level discourse, however, Tjamilo gained more support than he could have through explicitly advocating the cult. Many people found the pretence that the surface level was the only level convenient. Those who were bored with Movement routine, those attracted to the emphasis on the ghosts—a link with the past—in the new cult, and even those whose commitment to the Movement made it hard to admit that the cult intrigued them, could consent to a program of cemetery improvement for overtly pragmatic reasons. But Samol did not rely solely on veiled debate. He tried to keep a flow of projects constantly before the meetings that decided on community work. Supposedly, Tjamilo could not command community labour for his projects—such as new burial grounds built to cult specifications—unless such meetings approved them. Against Samol's tactic, he was forced to openly refuse to put the meeting decisions into effect.

Things did not come to this pass until the Bunai Titan were already sharply divided in their views of cult developments in Malei and Lowaya. Before even these Usiai hamlets had started a cemetery project, Tjamilo had organised his procession to the pre-cult Bunai graveyard with skeletons retrieved from previous village sites, marching through the Usiai section with flags, coffins, crosses, and flowers, singing 'John Brown's Body'. But now he embarked on building a completely new cemetery for the Titan alone, just as Malei and Lowaya were initially determined to build their separate graveyards.

But when Bunai Usiai support for the cult came into the open, Tjamilo's cemetery project became more, rather than less, difficult. He could no longer maintain even the pretence that his purposes were hygienic and logistical. And the conspicuous Usiai display of cult enthusiasm led many Titan people of amalgamated Bunai to oppose the cult simply because of their customary contempt for the Usiai. To proceed, Tjamilo had to defy Samol more openly, with the active support of about 10 people and the tacit support of an indeterminate number of others.

Tjamilo and his faction ignored the projects Samol assigned. They refused, for example, to help produce Bunai's quota of sago palm leaf thatch that assistant district officer James Landman had requested for one of the new school buildings on Baluan. Samol denounced Tjamilo for blatantly opposing the Movement program, but not yet for advocating the cult. The cult hamlets of Malei and Lowaya were also refusing to take part in community projects, and Samol accused them of leaving the Movement, but without mentioning the cult.

Figure 9.2: The gate to the graveyard Tjamilo and his followers built in Bunai in 1954.

Thomas, the tutelary ghost of the Cemetery Cult, instructed his followers to transfer the remains of their deceased kin from previous burial sites to such specially designed cemeteries. Tjamilo's, however, was the only such cemetery completed on the south coast.

Source: Theodore Schwartz.

Tjamilo now moved quickly. He sent Alphonse Kanawi, the Bunai *tultul* (who, as *tultul*, was still technically an administration-appointed official within the village—in fact, the only one since Kisekup had resigned as paramount *luluai*), to Ndropwa to ask the plantation manager if the Bunai Titan could use land just behind the village belonging to the plantation for a new burial ground. The manager gave his permission. Within 10 days, Tjamilo and his supporters had cleared, levelled, and built railings around a plot of ground. They followed the Johnston Island design, but added a turnstile like the one allegedly shown to Ponram during his death and resurrection. Pwatjumel allegedly built the cemetery's two gates according to his own dream, although they were identical to those on Johnston Island. However, Samol's followers took this as confirmation of the validity of Pwatjumel's dream. While this work was going on, Schwartz went to Tjamilo's house to visit and he found Tjamilo's verandah filled with wooden crosses ready for the reburial of the skeletons collected earlier.

Tjamilo now tried to assume leadership of the cult for all of Bunai, but with limited success. The Usiai still wouldn't take him fully into their confidence. In his conversations with Schwartz, Tjamilo spoke as though he were aware of everything connected with the cult everywhere. When conversing with Schwartz following the appearance of Malei's teacher-ghost, Schwartz mentioned this event, assuming Tjamilo knew about it. Either he did not know or he gave a remarkable performance of a man who was startled. He left Schwartz immediately to go to Malei and Lowaya, where he spent much of the next week.

At the end of March, Samol and Kampo called a Bunai-wide meeting. Although all village residents were invited, of the Usiai only the leaders attended. Before the meeting, Samol, Kampo, and Schwartz discussed the cult. Kampo was depressed and angry. He said: 'The word of God is of two kinds, his true word and the word with which he tempts and tests us. The first belongs to Jesus and the second to Christus'. (Christus appeared to be Kampo's transformation of the idea of the Antichrist.) If the cult really represented the word of God, Kampo reasoned, it would be available to everyone, not only to Malei and Lowaya.

The meeting went poorly for Samol and Kampo. At first, Samol did not allude to the cult. Instead, much to Schwartz's embarrassment, Samol told the Usiai leaders he had called them together to ask why they no longer invited Schwartz to their meetings, something Schwartz had mentioned to Samol only in passing. The Usiai said that, yes, they were at fault in this respect. Sayau of Yiru, a younger man who had spent much of his early life on a plantation and who had been decorated for his military service in the war, rose to answer Samol's original question. He said: 'It is our leaders who must call them. We men and women can't come call them for nothing. What will we tell them? About all of our stinking ways?' Sayau, a thoughtful man, said he was revolted by the state of his own hamlet's indolence and apathy, something Schwartz had heard him speak of before.

Kampo then spoke of the division in Bunai, but—again—without mentioning its cause; that is, the cult. He said he had heard that some villagers wanted to go to live in Kapo and Nuang and warned them not to because they would have to pay double the taxes when the NGC came because their names would then be in two census books. This was in fact an empty threat. But Kampo almost mentioned the cult, saying he had heard about something going on in Nuang and that if it had anything to do with God, then people shouldn't hide it.

To this point in the meeting, no one had accused the Usiai of anything, but they had come ready to defend themselves. Pantret, Pondis, Kilopwai, and Petrus Popu spoke for the Usiai. They asked who had accused them of worshipping or praying to a piece of wood or something that whistles. They denied it (although no one had openly made such accusations). Pantret made a speech inviting martyrdom, of the kind so common during the Movement's early opposition to government officers. He also said that he knew nothing about Malei, but all that was happening in Lowaya was his own idea. He had simply decided to revive all the good, cooperative, and obedient ways of 1946. Let them punish him or put him in jail for it, he declared. Pondis of Malei denied that there was anything for the meeting to discuss; nothing they were doing in his hamlet was the least bit new.

But Bombowai and Kisekup continued their roundabout attack on the cult. Bombowai announced that they were now going to engage in *tok bokis*, Tok Pisin for hiding your meaning in metaphor or other kind of indirect discourse. People were always alert for this, especially from public speakers, but announcing one's intention in this way was highly unusual. Bombowai apparently wanted to be extra clear that he meant the opposite of what he said, although announcing this mitigated any diplomatic advantage gained by not speaking his mind directly. 'Lowaya is all right', he pronounced. 'They are virtuous, but Yiru is completely depraved.' To further obfuscate, although very conspicuously, Bombowai and Kisekup included themselves in the accusations they aimed at others. So Kisekup, who was not inclined to favour the cult, said: 'This thing that we have been hearing about, you and I think that it is good, but think well. The council [meaning the administration-sanctioned NGC] is coming'.

Kilopwai finally threatened to take Malei out of the village because of the false accusations against them. Samol and Kampo immediately became conciliatory. The threat of withdrawing from a community had been an effective one even in Fortune's and Mead's day. Kilopwai was using it now for the second time within months. (Earlier in the year he had threatened to take Malei out of Bunai over a land dispute.) He and several other Usiai Cemeterians had dissimulated repeatedly at this meeting, putting on a show of injured innocence. Yet it looked to Schwartz like they were genuinely angry and resentful, perhaps at having their commitment to the cult questioned even implicitly. Samol backed off. He said that nothing was wrong, but that it was his responsibility to watch for sores (the painful skin ulcers that in the deep tropics often develop from even the smallest cuts) before they burst and suppurate.

In April, there were many more wrong-straightening meetings in the Usiai cult hamlets. Tjamilo spoke frequently at these meetings, urging moral regeneration and pointing out how people's behaviour was falling short of New Way standards. At one meeting he said he feared that none of the younger men who would someday replace him and Samol cared about anything. They took little interest in village affairs, he asserted, but in this they were only following their parents' bad examples. He complained that families were disintegrating and described several recent violent quarrels between husbands and wives. Tjamilo's speeches in these days were full of threats. On one occasion, after scolding the women for their indifference, for their barrenness, and for their poor care of the children, he shouted from the meeting space to the surrounding houses: 'All of you women who have run away from the meeting, you never say anything but you can't escape this. It will sleep with you in your houses. It will make you sick. It will make you die'.

In March, news came to Bunai that Paliau was in jail again. This time it sounded non-political. Paliau had been to Rambutjo to investigate reports of the Cemetery Cult. He was to have proceeded to Bunai. But when he returned from Rambutjo, his son told him that in Paliau's absence his daughter had married a man of whom Paliau disapproved. Paliau ran from the beach to the couple's house, pulled his daughter out, and struck her several times. She pressed charges and Paliau served a month in jail. Samol announced to a meeting in Bunai that Paliau's arrest was a good lesson—that the arm of the law extended to all regardless of rank or prestige. Later, Paliau claimed that his imprisonment had been a political attack, that his offence was too trivial to deserve more than a reprimand. At any rate, it kept him out of Bunai in April. Samol continued his indirect, scolding speeches throughout the month, but he had decided to wait for Paliau before taking stronger action. He was confident that Paliau would put an end to the cult. For their part, the cult leaders expressed confidence (although they were not truly confident) that Paliau would back them and tell them what they had to do after they finished building the cemeteries.

Easter passed, with its ceremony of the crosses on Johnston Island and in Tawi, but Jesus did not return. Meetings to purify the people's *tingting* and correct all wrongs continued, but nothing happened. The teacher-ghosts continued to manifest through their mediums, but they brought no new revelations or prophecies. Cult adherents became more and more anxious.

Bunai in the balance

Opposition to the cult in Bunai had at least prevented it from flourishing among the Titan people of Bunai. Only a small group wanted to take part and they were having little or no success recruiting reinforcements, nor could they take their enthusiasm to Malei and Lowaya, for these Usiai hamlets apparently valued exclusivity over forging a wider coalition. Among the Usiai hamlets, Yiru was definitely against the cult, while Lahan was making a belated start.

Schwartz and Shargo learned that among cult adherents, some—despite their regular participation in cult activities—were concerned about the cult's obsession with the dead. During the Noise, people sought the return of the dead bringing cargo, but they left their bones alone. In 1954, some who longed for the cargo were nevertheless uncomfortable with practices little removed in many ways from the past. Their hopes were mingled with doubts.

To the best of the anthropologists' knowledge, all the Cemetery Cult participants with whom they were familiar were more cautious about committing themselves to the cult in front of the entire village than participants in the Noise had been. Vivid memories of the dramatic failure of the Noise may well have accounted for this as well as for the failure of the Cemetery Cult to spread 'like fire', even within one community, albeit amalgamated Bunai had become a single entity only relatively recently. Perhaps most telling, in stark contrast to the Noise, during the Cemetery Cult no one ever named a date for the Last Day, when the dead would return in company with Jesus to transform the world forever. But although this saved adherents from rapid—perhaps repeated—disappointment, they also had to bear the stress of constant readiness. In addition, the administration had announced that the officially sanctioned NGC would be installed in May and James Landman had already visited Bunai to prepare for electing officers and collecting taxes. This new channel for people's hopes for change must certainly have weakened the cult's appeal.

Even so, although the cult had stopped growing, those already committed remained dedicated. Hopes of a miracle aside, many clearly enjoyed the thrill of defiance and the satisfaction of excluding people who they assumed saw them as inferior. Yet the Cemeterians also had become accustomed to being part of the Movement and to thinking of its 33 villages as a unit. It quickly became obvious that the cult would not become the new face of the Movement. It would remain a minority occupation including very few of the Bunai residents of highest status. Only two things might save it. Jesus or a few ships laden with cargo could finally show up or Paliau could come out in support of the cult. But Paliau was in jail and in his absence both sides claimed him.

The administration probably would have heard some news of the cult even if Schwartz and Shargo had not become friends with Landman, who had asked the anthropologists about rumours of events in Bunai. They told him of the ongoing contest between cult adherents and opponents. They knew Landman was sympathetic with Samol's request that there be no outside intervention. Around the same time, Samol had also told Landman a little about that contest. Samol held that the cult was under control, but he told Landman that he would let him know if there was any trouble he could not handle. Samol knew that if news of the cult reached the European community, most of whom did not understand local events as subtly as Landman, the whites would pressure the administration to postpone initiating the NGC. Hostility to the government had reached new heights within the cult, but many cult opponents felt that supporting the administration's program was in their best interest.

The Cemetery Cult in Patusi and Pere

In other Titan villages within the Movement area but outside Bunai, the cult had made little headway. Pere and Patusi exemplify this situation, but neither had any Titan people on Baluan or Mok people started building new cemeteries. Villagers on Rambutjo Island, the scene of Wapei's prophesies in 1947, had built a new cemetery and some had visited Johnston Island, but they had gone no further. Some even assumed the role of reformed cargoists, warning others of its dangers. They had, indeed, seen how wrong things could go; many had seen Muli mutilate his brother Wapei on the beach with a bush knife. Mok people, under the leadership of Lukas, took a similar stance. Some had warned the Johnston Islanders that they were inviting trouble. In the last week of April, a delegation from Mok also visited Bunai, where Lukas made an outspoken and direct speech warning the Cemeterians of their folly. The Cemeterians listening said nothing, but when they marched again their attitude was especially defiant.

In contrast, led by the still-influential *luluai* Tjawan, the rank and file in Patusi, on the south coast, were eager for the cult. Patusi had started work on a new cemetery almost simultaneously with the people of Johnston Island and Tawi. Sapa, the woman who served as a medium for Thomas, was from Patusi, and several groups from Patusi had attended the seances on Johnston Island. In January 1953, a group of Pere people went to Patusi to learn more about the cult, just as they had sought knowledge of the Noise in 1947. Patusi had cleared ground for the cemetery. Villagers had collected a number of skeletons from the old graves, adorned them, and placed them in their wooden boxes on verandahs. But for months there they stayed, waiting for people to finish the cemetery. When Schwartz and Shargo left Manus, the Patusi cemetery was still unfinished, and by then Gabriel Pokekes, the *kaunsil*, had stopped the progress of the cult almost single-handedly.

Pokekes had believed in the Noise in 1947 when the Ndropwa plantation manager sent him to investigate reports from Tawi. The appearance of Popei's ghost and the seances had impressed him, but the outcome had been a bad disappointment. In spite of his youth (only young men had gone to work on the Ndropwa plantation), Patusi later chose him as its *kaunsil*. He took his work seriously and commanded real authority, but he had permitted the Cemetery Cult to start collecting bones of the dead without comment. When this activity failed to lose momentum on its own, he held a meeting at which he simply declared that as *kaunsil* he forbade any further work on the new cemetery or any other cult activities. He told people plainly that he feared the cult would lead to trouble as had the Noise and he reminded people of Wapei's murder.

As noted above, even some cult participants in Bunai were nervous about its similarities with pre-Christian treatment of the dead. Pokekes raised this issue in Patusi publicly and far more explicitly than anyone had in Bunai. Pulling no punches, he called the cult seances *tilitili*—the Titan word for communication with household ghosts of the kind Fortune (1965 [1935]) described. This probably touched a nerve with some who wanted the cult in Patusi. They wanted, as Schwartz and Shargo knew, to try again what had failed in 1946, but they professed no desire to go back to the pre-Christian past. Some cult proponents addressed such fears by arguing that the Cemetery Cult followed the model of the whites—for instance, the pomp and ceremony with which the Americans treated their war dead—not the ways of their own ancestors. Yet the whistling of the ghosts was vividly reminiscent of older times.

Patusi cult opponents accused cult proponents of thinking more of the ghosts than of Jesus or God. But proponents had in effect modernised their ancestors to make them compatible with the New Way. The ghosts they spoke of were not the malicious wandering ghosts or the undependable household guardians of the past. The ancestors the cult envisioned were beings who lived lives of virtue in the Sky with Jesus. Younger people may not have noticed this contrast, but some of those old enough to remember the old days purveyed to Schwartz a cosmetically enhanced picture of the past. In the very distant past, some told Schwartz, people had been good. There had been no warfare and no cannibalism. That golden age had eventually ended, but even in the subsequent times, some said, there had been a few men who would have met New Way standards. Perhaps so. But the benevolent ancestors of cult doctrine had little in common with either the Titan of 1928, as Fortune described them, or with those portrayed in the reminiscences of old men who quietly scorned the Movement—men unrepentantly nostalgic for, in their eyes, the more exciting and heroic times of raiding, trading, and flaunting their prowess in exchange.

But cult proponents preferred ancestors who looked down on them from the Sky, ready to remake their lives. And Pokekes's efforts failed to sway many of them in Patusi. Finally, realising that efforts at suasion were pointless, he invoked his authority as *kaunsil* for Patusi and announced that Patusi people must not participate in the cult. Instead of simply ignoring him and continuing cult activity, as Tjamilo responded to Samol in Bunai, Tjawan flew into a rage and then withdrew from public activity. At the end of a month, he appeared at a village meeting and shook hands with Pokekes, signifying that he accepted his judgement. A Patusi youth continued for some time to see his father's ghost, whom Thomas had declared Patusi's ghostly teacher, but few villagers paid him any attention.

Pere people watched the floundering Patusi cult from the sidelines for several weeks before dipping into it themselves. Several months before Schwartz and Shargo arrived in Manus, Pere men going to the market at Patusi came on a group of Patusi men gathered in a private house discussing the cult. The Patusi men allowed the Pere party to enter and told them, as reported to Schwartz: 'You men of Pere. You don't want to do this work [i.e. of the cult]. But your fathers, your children, your women who died before, where will they arise? You don't know very well where they are buried. You must go dig them up and bring them together in your own place'. Not long thereafter, a number of Pere people began to transfer the bones of their dead from scattered graves to the cemetery they had built close to the beach when they moved the village there in 1948. In a week they moved more than 100 skeletons from the graves they could find easily. The 1948 graveyard was already too crowded and even before the cult Pere villagers had discussed building a new one on land which—like the land behind Bunai—belonged to a plantation. But the Pere *luluai* convinced the plantation manager to deny permission.

Mead, living in Pere, apparently either did not notice this activity or chose to ignore it, and Pere people were careful not to mention it to any of the anthropologists. When Schwartz and Shargo later learned of the Cemetery Cult activities in Pere, they also learned that in spite of the energy expended gathering the skeletons, many Pere people who were interested in the cult were nevertheless cautious about it. They were suspicious of its source in Johnston Island and its popularity among Usiai people, both in Bunai and the inland villages of Nuang and Kapo. Some Pere villagers were sceptical of the cult to the point of ridiculing cult activists and openly mocking the people of Johnston Island.

One highly influential young man, however, found the cult irresistible. He visited Johnston Island repeatedly and took part in a seance with Thomas. This was the schoolteacher, Prenis Tjolai. Prenis, then in his late twenties, commanded more respect than usual for one so young. In 1948, Pere had selected him to go to Baluan to be trained as a Movement leader. Prenis had no formal schooling, but he had organised a school where he passed on his limited knowledge of reading and writing in Tok Pisin, some scraps of English, and some elementary arithmetic to the adolescent boys and girls of Pere. His limited knowledge frustrated him, but he said his school would suffice until the government started a real one.

Although he was considerably younger than the other Pere leaders, he was of *lapan* status and the son and grandson of Pere *luluai*. Older leaders treated him as a respected equal and he had a voice in most meetings on village affairs. But all his adult experience was within the Movement, and its more metaphysical aspects—the spheres in which it most resembled a cargo cult—aroused his greatest interest.

Prenis's brother, Akustin Seliau, who lived in Patusi, had attended Thomas's earliest seances on Johnston Island, but he didn't tell Prenis about them until early in 1953, several months before the anthropologists arrived. Akustin also told Prenis of an event not long after Christmas 1953 that in his view confirmed the truth of Thomas's revelations. Akustin was fishing at night near the old lagoon site of Pere when he heard a whistle. He assumed someone buried near the old village was trying to contact him. He said aloud the name of his younger brother, Pomat, who had died as a child, and heard an answering, affirmative whistle. Undoubtedly influenced by Thomas's messages, he decided Pomat was probably asking to be reburied, and hurried to Pere to tell Prenis about it. The brothers asked others whether Pomat was actually buried on the small island near which Akustin heard the whistle. On hearing that he was, they became thoroughly convinced. Akustin spent that night in Prenis's house in Pere. Prenis later told a few others in Pere, from whom Schwartz heard the story, that during the night, the ghost of Akustin's daughter, a little girl, Kisolel, appeared to him. She confirmed—no doubt through a series of queries and whistled replies—that Pomat had indeed called to Akustin, and that she, too, wanted to be reburied.[4]

---

4   Kisolel was the only ghost anyone reported seeing in Pere in connection with the cult. Akustin wanted to rebury Pomat and Kisolel in Patusi, but Prenis was vehemently opposed to reburying their kin anywhere but in Pere. Akustin and Prenis belonged not only to Pere village but to the Pere clan that gave the village its name. Within the cult, Prenis's attitude probably reflected more than clan pride. We can see here both the common cult conviction that it was through one's own ancestors one was most immediately linked to God and fear that people of other villages might fail to meet the moral standards the ghosts required and scuttle the hopes of one's own village.

Prenis was excited about this but he decided to ask Kisakiu, the Johnston Island *kaunsil*, whether Paliau approved of the Johnston Island seances. Kisakiu told him that he, Sapa (the medium for Thomas), and Thomas himself had gone to Baluan and spoken with Paliau and that Paliau had approved what they were doing. Thus encouraged, Prenis started attending the seances. Like numbers of others, Prenis told Schwartz that he was sceptical at first but came to accept that Thomas was genuine. It probably helped that in the first seance Prenis attended Thomas mentioned Pere, saying Pere must begin work on the cemetery and that there was much wrong with Pere that its people had better hasten to rectify.

Prenis convinced at least some Pere people to begin collecting the bones of their dead and he brought news from the seances back from his visits to Johnston Island. Most Pere people remained indifferent, yet Prenis persevered. He attended the celebration of the new cemetery there that Schwartz, not yet knowing of the cult, had found inexplicably curious. In one of the seances Prenis attended on this occasion, Thomas named Pere as a place where people mocked his revelations. When Prenis and the young men he had brought with him left Johnston Island after that event, their canoe was swamped when crossing the reef to the open sea. This was a difficult passage and many canoes had trouble there, but Prenis was convinced that his mishap was a warning against mocking Thomas further.

Prenis told Schwartz that when he returned to Pere he called a meeting at which he told his fellow villagers that he knew they mocked him behind his back, but God would be the judge of his actions and of the Johnston Islanders. No one rose to the defence of the alleged mockers, but obstacles to Prenis attracting a following abounded. Schwartz knew, for instance, that many Pere people held that following Johnston Island or Tawi in anything made no sense. A number of influential men rebuffed Prenis largely because they found repugnant the thought of any kind of subordination to Johnston Island or Tawi.[5] As one man, Pius Selan, said: 'Never mind Thomas. This isn't his village. Thomas doesn't belong to Pere, he belongs to another village. You can't bring his ways in here'. John Kilepak, Bopau, and Lokes told Schwartz in private that they

---

5   This is an example of a phenomenon Schwartz (1975: 117) calls competitive diffusion or cultural totemism, common in Melanesia but by no means confined to that part of the world. In his words: 'To seize upon incipient differences for their emblematic value appears to cause, as much as to reflect, social differentiation … Cultural totemism is not only a form of ethnic recognition and categorization, it is an ethnicizing process—a mechanism of cultural speciation'.

agreed with Pius Selan completely: 'We have plenty of ancestors who died', one said, 'why can't they come speak to us, why just someone from another place?'

Not long after Prenis's failed meeting, some Pere men said they wanted proof that Thomas was real. Prenis had testified that he saw and heard Thomas with his own eyes and ears. He meant, of course, that he had attended the seances and heard the whistles. He added that many others there had also heard the whistles.[6] But even seeing and hearing in company didn't satisfy these sceptics. John Kilepak and Lokes said they wanted some tangible manifestation, a request Kampo had also made—in private—to the Cemeterians in Bunai. Neither in Bunai nor in Pere, however, did anyone ask for such proof in an open meeting. But in Pere, Kilepak made himself perfectly clear to Prenis in private: 'If Thomas appears, we want him to bring something that we can hold in our hands. Then it would be true and we could believe in him. We think about everything that happened in 1946. All of these things appeared to people, but there was not one thing that we could actually hold in our hands. That's what some of us said among ourselves'. But pathetically small tangibles were not enough. Ten shillings had materialised (allegedly) on Johnston Island, and some said that 10 shillings and some tobacco had materialised in Malei; but, as Kampo said, nothing really substantial—no warships, no aeroplanes. Prenis testified to his experience with Thomas, but he had neither warships nor even 10 shillings to show for it.

During the 1953 Christmas celebrations on Baluan, Prenis spoke to Paliau, with Pokanau and Lukas Bonyalo as witnesses. Paliau made another statement about the cult ambiguous enough for Prenis to interpret as support. Paliau allegedly told the three men to work to correct the serious wrongs that existed in Pere, such as the many divorces and remarriages when a former spouse was still living. In January 1954, Prenis and Pokanau tried to carry out the instructions they said Paliau had given them, but it is possible that the suggestion was not as specific as reported. It would have been typical of Paliau merely to recommend that Pere people straighten out misconduct in their village. This was his usual

---

6   The Pere people who heard of this incident from Prenis, and later told Schwartz of it, understood that both Prenis and Akustin had seen Kisolel. But Prenis later told Schwartz that he did not actually speak to or see Kisolel; only Akustin did. He apparently believed Akustin so implicitly that he initially told Schwartz in all sincerity that he and Akustin both saw the ghost. Such participation after the fact may be behind some other cases in which more than one person reported the presence of a ghost, though it would not apply to the formal seances on Johnston Island itself.

evasive tactic when people tried to get him to confirm or deny the truth of the cult. In any event, Prenis's and Pokanau's effort to crack down on marital laxness failed.

Prenis, Pokanau, Stephan Tjamuko (the newly elected *komiti*), and the *kaunsil*, Petrus Pomat, proposed publicly that the six marriages in Pere involving divorced people should be broken up and the partners should return to the original spouse. Pokanau, Pomat, and Tjamuko argued that they should do so at once, because the NGC would come soon, and when it did anyone who had committed this sort of sin would be punished. In Bunai, as well, some had argued for taking measures recommended by cult ghosts on the grounds that there had to be a moral house cleaning before the NGC arrived.

This argument reflected concerns not confined to Cemeterians. The perceived frequency of divorce resulting from adultery and followed by quick remarriage troubled numbers of villagers. But opinion was sharply divided. Some of the men involved in these marriages were popular and respected. And all the specific remarriages to be dissolved were at least two years old. Further, this attempt to undo subsequent marriages of divorced people was not based on New Way dicta; rather, it appeared to hark back to earlier Catholic teachings.

But orators harassed the parties to such marriages at meeting after meeting. They proclaimed that their marriages were the worst sins in the village, God was angry, and—if God's anger wasn't frightening enough—that they would get into trouble when the NGC arrived. Schwartz, taking unusual but understandable liberties as an anthropological observer, suggested at one meeting that perhaps everyone would be satisfied if church weddings were held to formalise the second marriages, or perhaps they could ask the assistant district officer for some kind of administration validation. Prenis Tjolai, the most vehement cult enthusiast, denounced this idea sharply. But Karol Manoi made a highly emotional speech to the effect that people should remember that they were all brothers; they should cease harassing these men before they either left the village or were driven to suicide. Prenis Tjolai and Petrus Pomat replied that they could not force these men to break their marriages, but it was their duty as the village leaders responsible for Pere's moral condition to continue to pursue this matter. 'God will find out these marriages of theirs', one of them pronounced. 'If he wants to break them with death, he can.' Eventually, the zealots were content to leave the matter in God's hands.

Prenis Tjolai now waited for Paliau and made no further visits to Johnston Island. He had failed to get Pere to listen respectfully to Thomas. He had failed to obtain a site for a new graveyard, even though most villagers were willing to build one. He had failed to convince other villagers to enact the moral reforms he advocated. But he had not given up. He still hoped Paliau would endorse the cult unequivocally and he determined to wait for that.

Desperate measures in Bunai

As the Cemetery Cult proceeded haltingly in Bunai, a few adherents, eager to bring their work to fruition, tried a new tactic. Some were still not certain that Schwartz and Shargo were completely trustworthy. And they knew that when pressed for their opinions the anthropologists discouraged people from taking up the cult. At times, however, in private conversations with Schwartz, adherents hopefully implied that Schwartz really knew more about the cult than they did. A few went beyond this. As their efforts dragged on without an end in sight, several cult enthusiasts, acting independently of each other, approached Schwartz to broach the possibility that the United States might intervene on behalf of the people of Manus. Some believed that the whites had attained the First Order, that the way of the *tingting* was the secret of the whites' power and wealth, and that Americans would be especially sympathetic to the plight of the Cemeterians. A more common idea within the Cemetery Cult was that the whites had attained only a superior form of the Second Order. Hence, some suggested to Schwartz that, by helping the blacks, by sharing their secret knowledge, Schwartz and Shargo might also gain the First Order and surpass even their present level of wealth and power. But events would overtake these and all other cult plans while Schwartz and Shargo were still on the scene.

10
Comparing the cults

Knowledge of the local history of millenarian thought and action is invaluable for understanding millenarian efforts in particular populations. Thus, before we examine the demise of the Cemetery Cult, we want to draw attention to important differences between it and the Noise and how our knowledge of local millenarian history helps illuminate them. Researchers often have very little such information. But in the Manus case we know a lot about the cargo millenarianism that preceded the Cemetery Cult—that is, the Noise. The most important thing we know is that the Noise emerged quickly and failed rapidly. The most striking ways in which the Cemetery Cult differs from the Noise look very much like reactions to the latter's swift rise and fall. We cannot say unequivocally that people were reacting consciously to that experience, but it is hard to avoid speculating that experience of the Noise had a profound influence on the thought and behaviour of participants in the Cemetery Cult.

People turned back to the Movement's gradualist program for change after the Noise came to nothing, but their millenarian hopes did not disappear. They did not even lie dormant for long. By all accounts, the Noise as a public phenomenon ended in 1947, but by late 1952 some Movement participants were again trying to subvert secular time and bring about a transformation of their world more dramatic than anything Paliau could (openly) promise. The Noise irrupted, blanketed the Movement area and beyond, and ran its course within a few weeks. This resembles what Hamilton (2001: 13), writing of Christian millenarianism, calls 'the classic intense movement that sweeps through a community like a bush fire, often dying down just as rapidly as it ignites'. In contrast, the Cemetery Cult emerged in late 1952, spread and developed over the following year and a half, never gained a foothold in some of the locales or with some of the people formerly deeply involved in the Noise, and did not come fully into the open in Bunai until mid-1954. As described in Chapter 11, it also ended abruptly before it had time to fail on its own.

How the imminence of salvation shaped the Noise

It is possible, of course, that if Schwartz and Shargo had observed the Noise firsthand it would not have looked as dramatically contagious as portrayed in the accounts they obtained. There is no reason, however, to question their data on its duration and principal features. One important fact is that, to the best of our knowledge, although participants in the Noise knew about cargo cults in other parts of New Guinea, there had been no cargo cult episodes in the Admiralty Islands before the Noise. Participants came to it without a history of disappointment to dampen their hopes for rapidly obtaining a perfect world. Also, the virtually complete recruitment of the south coast Titan to the Movement was crucial to the rapid spread of both the early Movement and the Noise. It is impossible to imagine how word of Paliau's New Way or the Noise could have spread even somewhat 'like fire' without the Titan messengers' tireless canoe voyaging.

As for the near-unanimity of the south coast Titan in this effort, although they were as divided politically as the other major ethnic groups in Manus, they were in some ways more homogenous. As noted earlier, unlike either Usiai or Matankor, Titan people spoke a single language. They also had affiliated en masse with the Catholic Mission, whereas Usiai and Matankor communities had split among Catholic, Lutheran Evangelical, and Seventh-day Adventist missions.[1] This comparative Titan solidarity, however, did not extend to the Titan of the north coast. Sheer distance limited the intensity of their exposure to the Movement.

---

1   Paliau himself was Matankor, not Titan. But his fellow Matankor never gave him more than weak support at best. Schwartz suggests that this was in part a case of the Nazarene effect; that is, the difficulty many prophets have in obtaining honour in their own countries. In addition, on Baluan, adherents of the Seventh-day Adventist Church were especially resistant to both the New Way and the Noise.

In addition, a history of south coast Titan raiding in the north (Carrier and Carrier 1989: 38) may have made north coast Titan averse to taking up with a south coast endeavour.

People suddenly overcome by the *guria* marked the beginning of the Noise, wherever it took hold. But what happened simultaneously was more fundamental: Adherents of the Noise abruptly entered a world in which time was collapsed. In the world of the cult adherents, past and future, the living and the dead, crowded into the immediate present. And the immediate present teetered on the edge of the day of Christ's return, which would initiate a condition of timeless perfection. There was no need to think of a future beyond the last-minute flurry of preparations for the Second Coming. The goal lay not years or generations but days ahead. The immediate fulfilment of desire was imminent for all who lived or had ever lived. For the few weeks that the Noise endured, many of its adherents were immersed in apocalyptic time.

Several features of the Noise matched its foreshortened time scale neatly. It appropriated much of the cosmological and metaphysical content of the Paliau Movement and appended to it the prophetic elaborations that occurred in each village. But its ideology was spare and unstandardised in comparison with that of the Cemetery Cult. The organisation of the Noise was rudimentary because there was neither time nor—more important—need to make anything other than minimal preparations for the final transformation. Similarly, there were few or no attempts to anticipate what kind of organisation the return of Jesus and the ancestors might require, for they would certainly tell people what to do. Further, in the foreshortened life of the Noise, there was no time for a dramatised struggle with scepticism before conversion, something that was a nearly universal step in recruiting people to the Cemetery Cult.

This is not to say that no participants in the Noise had doubts. But much of the more drastic activity of the Noise probably propelled people quickly beyond the point at which they could entertain doubts without severe discomfort. Experiencing *guria* and destroying property may have demonstrated to people their own commitment even as they demonstrated it to Jesus and the ancestors. Lukas of Mok told how, as he began to doubt and fear that Mok villagers had impoverished themselves in vain, he was moved to a final act of commitment: casting into the sea the box of Movement funds, a symbol and an important element of the path to the more prosaic future they might achieve through action in secular time.

In Ndriol, many factors led to Wapei's murder. But it was, nonetheless, also an irrevocable act of magical commitment. If the Noise were true, no death would be final and people would forget their destroyed and discarded material goods in the flood of new wealth received.

How caution shaped the Cemetery Cult

The basic activity of the Cemetery Cult—building cemeteries on a supernaturally decreed model and gathering bones from dispersed burial sites—made rapid culmination of the cult impossible. But one must wonder if, at some level, Cemeterians created this tedious process because they feared that their efforts could rise and fall as rapidly as the Noise. They hovered on the edge of apocalyptic time, filled with hope, but holding back from putting that hope to the ultimate test.

Although prophecies, dreams, and visions kept Cemetery Cult adherents' passions high, the Cemeterians did not invest as heavily in the hope of sudden supernaturally mediated fulfilment as did adherents of the Noise. In the Cemetery Cult, neither the tutelary ghosts nor the living leaders demanded that people destroy their property; nor did the ghosts, dreamers, or visitors to Heaven proclaim a specified day for the Second Coming.

To sustain their morale, adherents of the Cemetery Cult had to cling to the conviction that the Second Coming might happen any day. Yet—with the exception of Thomas's interpretation of a volcanic eruption, described below—they avoided with remarkable unanimity committing to a date. Tjamilo, in Bunai, was perhaps the only adherent of the Cemetery Cult completely explicit on this score: mortals could not know the precise day, he insisted.[2] The ghost of Thomas might have announced a date and compelled people to take drastic actions in preparation, but he did not. And neither did his medium, his interpreters, or even the long string of persons who addressed questions to him. The adherents thus denied themselves the possibility of forcing the hand of God through the power of their commitment. But they also spared themselves a growing fear of disappointment as the declared Last Day—or, worse yet, one Last Day after another, approached.

---

2   It certainly sounds as though Tjamilo had at least heard from missionaries such biblical admonitions as Matthew 24:36 (King James Version): 'But of that day and hour knoweth no man, no, not the angels of heaven, but my Father only'.

St Augustine of Hippo was only one of many early Christian thinkers who pondered the timing of the Second Coming, but he probably gave the most practical advice to fellow churchmen.[3] He counselled that they should avoid preaching that the apocalypse was imminent because by doing so they set people on a path to disappointment that could undermine their Christian faith (Landes 2011: 48). During the Cemetery Cult, both leaders and the rank and file appear to have adopted a similar stance spontaneously. With no overt central coordination, local cult leaders refrained from pinning hopes to a specific date, as though their still-fresh memories of the Noise were enough to make the example of restraint the Johnston Island cultists set compelling.

At the same time, the Cemeterians seized on any hint of the Last Day's approach. The arrival of the anthropologists, the eruption of a volcano in an area where there had been no volcanic activity in living memory, the approach of Christmas, and, especially, the approach of Easter, the day of Christ's resurrection, were occasions for burgeoning hope that the Last Day was near.[4] Each such event stimulated some further development in the cult, some new ritual, and some further attempt to complete the process of purification, but no firm commitment to a date. The eruption of the volcano came nearest to eliciting a commitment from Thomas, the ghost of Johnston Island. Through a medium, he invoked the volcano as a warning to non-cult villages. After the volcano had sunk beneath the sea, during a lull in its activity, Thomas reportedly announced that its reappearance would mark the Day of Judgement. But the volcano surfaced three more times during the life of the cult without heralding the Last Day. Rather than see this as impugning the ghost's integrity (or that of his handlers), people quietly ignored these events.

Cemetery Cult followers nevertheless let it be known that the ghosts were urging them to hurry their preparations. We take the position, of course, that cult followers were speaking to themselves through the ghosts. And, perhaps, in speaking through the ghosts they were—without realising it— urging God to bring about the Last Day before the Native Government Council (NGC; see Chapter 7) was installed. As the coming of the NGC came closer, many cult followers became more intense, their intensity betraying hints of desperation.

---

3   Hall (2009) discusses this issue in depth.
4   Mead (2001 [1956]: 29) describes the volcanic eruption not far off the south coast, easily visible from Pere village, that occurred within a few days of the arrival of the Mead, Schwartz, and Shargo party in 1953.

Given the slower pace of the Cemetery Cult, requiring people to destroy the tools with which they made their livings would have been out of the question. Cemetery Cult activities did put a dent in food production, but participation was much more compatible with normal life than participation in the Noise had been. We may be stretching a point here, but even the role of the *guria* in the Cemetery Cult displayed such compatibility. The *guria* affected only a few participants in the Cemetery Cult. In each village or hamlet that came wholly into the cult only one or a few people were taken by the *guria*. And although the *guria* in the Cemetery Cult was occasionally as violent and dramatic as in the Noise, it did not spread by contagion to spectators. In cases in which more than one person was affected, they usually did not *guria* simultaneously but on separate occasions. Clearly, the implicit conventions governing such behaviour had changed.

Also in contrast to the Noise, during the Cemetery Cult only one person in each village became a connection between the ghosts and the living. And, except in the case of Joseph Nanei, this person did not necessarily exercise real cult leadership. Most mediums were women: Sapa on Johnston Island, Namu in Malei, Nasei in Lowaya, and other women in Nuang and Kapo. A scattered few provided all the steady and formal contact the Cemetery Cult needed with the ghosts. A larger number of persons had single or occasional contacts with ghosts. These attested that the dead were indeed thronging back. But all that a particular village required was one sustained, oral contact that repeated all that had been laid out on Johnston Island, bringing the revelation to each village through one of its own ancestors.

The Cemetery Cult divides the Paliau Movement

Although Cemetery Cult participants remained formally part of the Movement, the cult strained Movement unity. When confronted by their opponents and critics, cult villages and hamlets threatened to withdraw from the Movement. At the height of their confidence they even criticised Paliau sharply. But they made no moves to leave the Movement, either substantial or symbolic. It even looked like they conspired implicitly with their opponents to keep reports of the cult from spreading outside the Movement villages.

But such moderation did not prevent increasing tension within the Movement. Although the old antagonism between the Titan and the Usiai affected cult affiliation in some cases (as described in Chapter 9), the larger tension within the Movement did not develop along the Titan–Usiai divide.[5] During the Noise, most of Paliau's followers saw its apocalyptic millenarianism as consistent with Paliau's teachings. For many, the Noise ultimately strengthened rather than weakened their commitment to the Movement. Indeed, there was considerable overlap between Paliau's teachings and program and Noise doctrines and activities. One would have to cut things very fine to find significant competition between forthright millenarianism and the secular, albeit ambiguously so, dimension of Paliau's activities until after the Noise ended. But the Cemetery Cult made such competition explicit.

Cemetery Cult adherents held that their way embodied the original ideals of the Movement of 1946 better than the current Movement did and that the Movement had grown decadent. And the cult developed most rapidly and its adherents acted most decisively almost entirely after it became clear that Paliau's efforts to bring about change in secular time were bearing fruit. Specifically, there would soon be an NGC embracing the south coast and a government-sponsored cooperative would soon follow. Yet whatever material benefits the NGC might offer, the cult adherents saw them as inadequate. The Cemetery Cult, like the Noise, aimed directly at regaining the First Order of God, the condition of humanity in Paradise. They might have reasoned that with the NGC in place it would be impossible to continue the cult, except on a scale and in a manner inadequate to its grand aim. The Cemeterians certainly would face not only the ridicule and opposition of their peers; they would have to defy an institution with the power of the Australian administration behind it. They now had no time to spare.

As initiation of a broader NGC approached, opponents of the Cemeterians sought more vigorously to end the cult before it jeopardised the NGC's advent. The Cemeterians responded with a burst of activity, and the cult reached its climax almost literally on the eve of the inauguration of the NGC. One can easily see here a final effort to attain

---

5   The Titan of Tawi and Johnston Island had initiated the cult, and it eventually incorporated the Usiai villages and hamlets of Kapo, Nuang, Malei, and Lowaya. But other Usiai villages opposed the cult and it failed to gain a foothold among many Titan. Even so, the Titan of Bunai tended to think of the cult as an Usiai phenomenon, while the Usiai of Malei and Lowaya thought of the opposition as primarily Titan.

the cult's ultimate goal before its adherents resigned themselves to the incremental program of the NGC, which was now the centrepiece of the Movement program—a program with no overt commitment to achieving the First Order of God.

Unity and localism in the two episodes

The villages of the Noise each pursued its cargo with fierce independence, determined to defend their own abundance from the people of other villages. This extreme localism interrupted the centralisation of political organisation and collective action the Movement was beginning to implement. Capitalising on people's shared experience of failure in the Noise and their sudden loss of direction, Paliau was able to revive and build on the pre-Noise spirit of unity to support more effective central organisation and concrete collective accomplishment, manifest in the new composite villages. The spirit of collectivism weakened somewhat after the initial burst of post-Noise activity, but a remarkable degree of solidarity and unanimity persisted.

Until, that is, the Movement stagnated and the Cemetery Cult emerged. Although adherents of the Cemetery Cult engaged in some low-key proselytising, they also stressed the necessity of independent revelation within each village or hamlet. Consequently, even though the Cemetery Cult was more centrally oriented than the Noise, it exhibited its own potent localism.

The Cemetery Cult was more centralised than the Noise in several ways. The focus on the ghost of Thomas is the most obvious of these. Cemeterians in different locales all subscribed to Thomas's superior abilities to divine the locations of the remains of their dead, and local teacher-ghosts occasionally went to visit Thomas, sometimes to return with him to the Sky where some said they met Jesus. Also, the ideology of the Cemetery Cult was more uniform than that of the Noise and the spirits of the ancestors were depicted as remarkably well organised. In the world of the dead, the spirits of all generations and of all villages were together with Jesus—to use the Tok Pisin word the cultists favoured, they all sat in *kibung*—that is, meeting or ritual gathering—with Jesus, in a manner resembling the public assemblies in Movement villages.

But the worlds of the living and the dead met only in each particular village. And the Cemetery Cult echoed the same kind of jealous localism characteristic of the Noise. Adherents of both the Noise and the Cemetery Cult believed that each village would receive its cargo directly from the ghosts of its own dead. In Lowaya, people even planned separate sections of the cemetery for each of the constituent clans or remnants of extinct villages that made up the village. Cemeterians in each village feared having to share their cargo with the people of other villages and they feared that the sins of other villages might jeopardise their own chances of reward.

Even in the composite village of Bunai, each of the two Usiai hamlets that joined the cult claimed independence and even ignorance of the early cult developments in the other hamlet. And cult adherents in both hamlets denied the very obvious influence of Nuang and Kapo on their own cults. Ironically, however, cult villages and hamlets could not have been more consistent in abiding by the principle of full independence if they all had been responding to a memo from the same head office.

Such localism might seem to clash with a quest for a fundamental transformation of the world, not just one's own small corner of it. We know, however, that some adherents of the Cemetery Cult either did not recognise this logical dilemma or they assumed—not necessarily consciously—that it would be miraculously resolved. In periods of millenarian fervour, of course, people set aside the pragmatic logic that enables them to survive and reproduce in normal times. Despite the cult's localism, many adherents hoped for a transcendent result. Schwartz pointed out to one participant that transferring the remains of all their dead to the relatively small spaces allocated to the ritual graveyards would leave no room for new burials. The man replied that this would not be a problem because once the task was completed, the Last Day would come and there would be no more deaths. But, as we describe in the next chapter, Paliau did not allow the adherents of the Cemetery Cult to put their faith to a final test.

11

Paliau ends the Cemetery Cult

Paliau was angry when he first heard of the Cemetery Cult, but for many months he left it alone except for some indirect and ambiguous criticism. In early 1954, however, the Australian administration was ready to expand the Baluan Native Government Council to include the south coast. This put pressure on Paliau, for he knew an active cargo cult would not count in the south coast's favour. When Paliau did act he showed his powers of persuasion in full. Among these powers were extraordinary skills in satire, bullying, and self-aggrandisement. Paliau might have acquired some of his ability for rough-handling his followers from his years as a sergeant major. But Paliau's style also brings to mind the behaviour of indigenous male leaders in many parts of Melanesia. Their often blistering public oratory, however, is not necessarily effective. The rank and file may put up with being harangued and shamed, but they do not necessarily comply nor do so without resentment. Paliau, however, also knew how to keep an audience off balance and he had an unusually strong hold on his followers.

His personal powers aside, Paliau had something concrete to offer people in the place of a cargo cult: an expanded official council. And Paliau undoubtedly understood that Cemeterians who harboured doubts about the cult's prospects might question the wisdom of putting something comparatively tangible and nearly within their grasp at risk for the sake of something that was more exciting but much more unpredictable. When Paliau finally declared his opposition to the cult, he also used the occasion to restore his own weakening prestige. He shamed the cargoists without mercy and they capitulated. Many did so sullenly, but they did so. True, some maintained private convictions that their time would yet come. And others chose to understand Paliau's anger as his reaction to the discord within the Movement the cult activities had stirred up rather than as criticism of the doctrines and aims of the cult. They regarded abandoning the cult now as a necessary but temporary concession. This would do, however, to show the administration that the south coast was ready to join the Baluan Council.

Paliau's grip weakens

A burst of energetic Movement activity followed the failure of the Noise in 1947 (as described in Chapter 7). Although some participants incorporated ritualistic elements of the Noise into their subsequent versions of the Movement, Paliau ignored this and devoted himself to the nuts-and-bolts task of promoting composite villages in which people would collectively put the New Way into practice. Cooperation among what had been fiercely independent, often mutually hostile villages was, of course, a fundamental New Way principle. But Paliau was not fixated on a specific way of accomplishing this. As soon as he grasped the idea of councils and cooperatives he instituted his versions of them as elements of the Movement well in advance of government action. He also kept people aware of his efforts to press the administration for an official council. Thus, when the Baluan Council came, Movement members felt that Paliau and the Movement had forced the government to grant it. A council that did not embrace the entire Movement area was less than what they sought, but it was more concrete than anything the Movement had accomplished so far.

Nevertheless, leading the Baluan Council left Paliau less time for duties as Movement leader, especially on the south coast. On his visits to Bunai from Baluan he would exhort people to maintain New Way practices and at least temporarily boost their morale. For example, in Bunai in 1953, there was constant discussion of rebuilding all the village houses, which after nearly six years of use were getting run-down. But talk was not yielding action. Paliau took up this cause on a visit in July 1953. He shamed and cheered villagers out of their inertia, inspiring them to begin rebuilding all the village houses. But he could not stay in Bunai. In his absence, the work slowed down and as people's morale declined it dragged their allegiance to Paliau down with it.

On Baluan and among Mok villagers, Paliau's earliest supporters, it seemed like many began seeing Paliau as more a bureaucrat than a visionary. People clearly respected him, but more it seemed for his effectiveness as leader of the Baluan Council than as a source of visionary inspiration. And those with grievances against Paliau began to speak of them more openly, as if he were like any other leader whose authority was merely secular.

Some Manus people, both within the council area and on the south coast, were also losing patience with Paliau on a matter with a long history— the use of the Movement's funds. Paliau wanted to release Movement participants from their commitment to let him use the money as he saw fit. Such a commitment, Paliau felt, was not appropriate to the new institutions emerging and the kind of leadership appropriate to them. But many did not want this freedom. Tjamilo nursed the hope that Paliau would spend the money on a ship that—rather than carry people and goods back and forth to Lorengau—would sail straight to the centre of the world, whence came all good material things, thus preventing the deceitful Australians from controlling the flow of cargo. But Paliau told people that they should do as they saw fit with the money, thus disappointing everyone who looked to him to tell them what to do.

Many adherents of the Cemetery Cult seemed to feel they were showing their independence from Paliau. Before the Noise, Jesus had dealt with mortals almost exclusively through Paliau, but now Thomas was allegedly receiving messages directly from Jesus. The *kaunsil* of Johnston Island, one of Thomas's interlocutors, had no particular prestige within the Movement; he could not have seriously challenged Paliau's authority. But people respected the ghost of Thomas, and preferred to believe that the *kaunsil* of Johnston Island had little to do with the ghost's pronouncements. Some even said aloud that the work of the cemetery had nothing to do with Paliau; they were acting on God's word, directly available to every village through its ghostly teacher.

There were nevertheless Cemeterians who hoped Paliau would eventually support them, showing what they hoped were his true colours. They continued to see him as a man directly inspired by Jesus—the man who had seen the iron-bound book of secrets, the man to whom had been revealed the 'Long Story of God'. For people like Tjamilo and Pita Tapo this was Paliau's real self; the rest was a facade. Whatever Paliau might say that sounded new, they clung to the conviction that beneath it was the prophetic voice of 1946. They did their best to believe that when the right time came, Paliau would break his silence and step in to lead them to the cargo.

Paliau's oracular obscurity

From at least the latter part of 1953, some Cemetery Cult adherents began trying to ascertain Paliau's position on their activities. Rumours had been circulating for some time, but they were contradictory, leaving the way open for both cult adherents and opponents to claim Paliau's support, neither being truly certain where he stood.

By early 1953, the people of Johnston Island and Tawi were already working on their new cemeteries. Reports of this vexed Paliau mightily and when Johnston Islanders heard of Paliau's anger they reacted defiantly. They asserted that their activities had nothing to do with Paliau and that they would persevere. Paliau in turn did not try to explain why he was angry. When leaders in other locales asked his permission to introduce the Cemetery Cult in their villages, Paliau's standard reply gave them no clear direction: 'Why are you asking me now about building good cemeteries when I have been telling you to do so for six years and yet you haven't done it?' But they were asking him about cemeteries and implying the cult, while Paliau was speaking about cemeteries and leaving them to wonder what he thought about the cult.

Prenis Tjolai's experience illustrates how Paliau handled people who asked him to confirm their belief in the cult. The *kaunsil* of Johnston Island had told Prenis that Paliau approved of the cult. He even told Prenis that the ghost of Thomas had spoken to Paliau. Prenis did not take the *kaunsil's* words at face value and so, when he next saw Paliau, he asked him if it was all right to do what the Johnston Islanders were doing. Paliau asked Prenis how many times he had to tell them to build good cemeteries. He had told them this repeatedly, Paliau lectured, yet they asked again and again. Prenis replied, 'Yes, but there is all this work that goes with it, plenty of places are doing it'. Paliau's reply in Tok Pisin was superbly ambiguous: '*Mi ken tokim yu wanem? Em i wanpela tok hia*'. The first phrase is amply clear. It means 'What can I say to you?' But the second phrase is subject to several interpretations. A literal translation is: 'There is only one talk here'. But this could mean, among many other things, 'I am saying the same thing', or 'I have only one thing to say', or 'There is only one thing to say'.

Prenis reported to Schwartz that Paliau then told him: 'There are plenty of bad ways in your village'. That is, in Pere village. This is the conversation that inspired Prenis and Pokanau to start a campaign to break up marriages involving divorces. Then, according to Prenis, Paliau added: 'You go lay out good ground and put a cemetery on it. Clear a place, keep it well, line up the dead properly in it. But about the way of the work of this cemetery, I can't tell you about this. Your village has plenty of men in it who spy. That's all. I cannot talk to you clearly about this work. You just go and work and if you find yourself short of ideas, you can come back, you can ask me about it'. This left Prenis almost as uncertain as he was before. Paliau had implied that there was much more to the cemetery 'work' than he could speak of openly, but that he, Paliau, knew all about it, of course. Schwartz observes that Paliau sometimes ran into difficulties because people assumed that he knew everything that was going on. Paliau knew they thought this and he preferred them to credit him with omniscience. But this meant that people often did not bother to explain what they were asking him in any detail, and—to preserve the fiction that he already knew everything—Paliau often did not question them. At times, this left him in the dark.

As the Cemetery Cult continued to develop, Paliau continued to answer questions about it with oracular obscurity. The story that Paliau had communed with Thomas continued to spread. But so, too, did reports that Paliau had denounced the people of Johnston Island, warning them that what they were doing was dangerous. On one occasion, Tjamilo asked Paliau to speak definitively for or against the truth of the cult. Paliau replied that it was better if he said nothing. If he said anything, Paliau argued, when trouble resulted from the cult, as it would, the trouble would come back to him. He then reiterated that he had always told them to build a good cemetery and they had never done it. What did they want him to tell them now?

People seeking Paliau's opinion might have taken a clue from the fact that neither Paliau's own village of Lipan nor the contiguous village of Mok were building new cemeteries or collecting the remains of the dead. The Mok people had made their position clear. Lukas of Mok visited Bunai in April 1954, while Paliau was in jail, and told Samol that he wanted to bring Pondis, Pantret, and the other Cemeterian leaders to Baluan to stand trial before the Native Government Council (NGC) and the assistant district officer. Samol, however, headed him off. He argued that if the court went against them, the Usiai might leave the Movement. Hearing this, Lukas agreed to allow Samol more time to control the situation in Bunai.

Although Paliau had refused to commit himself when asked, towards the end of March 1954 he went to Rambutjo and told people that it was all right to build new cemeteries but they should not get involved with all that went with it elsewhere. He had planned to go to Johnston Island next and then to villages on the south coast, but before he could make these voyages he was jailed for beating his daughter (as described in Chapter 9).

Debating the cult in Paliau's absence

The antagonism between Cemeterians and their opponents reached its height in Bunai in April 1954. Samol had gone to Lorengau to meet Paliau on his release from jail. While he was gone, Simion Kilepak and Markus Pwatjumel, both Titan residents of Bunai, called a meeting for 30 April to which they summoned the Bunai Usiai. They wanted the Usiai cult adherents to tell the whole village about the cult. They had held two such meetings already but Schwartz was not able to attend them. Judging from the proceedings of the 30 April meeting, however, Titan opponents of the cult hadn't found the results of the previous meetings satisfactory.

Simion Kilepak—a man about 30 years old—held no official position in the village, but he took every opportunity to act as a leader. He usually appointed himself supervisor of any communal work to which he was assigned and he spoke at every public meeting. He had taken it on himself to support Samol's leadership of the village. Thus, he took Samol's place as Tjamilo's adversary in matters pertaining to the cult.

Pwatjumel had been strongly inclined towards the cult. He had dreamed of the gate to the cemetery and built one on that model. But he was Samol's brother-in-law, younger than Samol, and he generally deferred to Samol's leadership. Also, the solemnity and puritanism of the Usiai cargoists annoyed him. The Titan of Johnston Island and Tawi kept playing cards for money in the midst of their cult, but the Bunai Usiai tabooed gambling, whistling, playing guitars and ukuleles, non-religious singing, and dancing. A number of Titan young men could not resist ridiculing this face of the cult. On one occasion Pwatjumel joined a group who marched through the Usiai cult hamlets in single file, imitating the Cemeterians stiff gait and rigid, straight-ahead gaze. This infuriated cult adherents and marked Pwatjumel indelibly as their opponent.

Only three Usiai—all from Lowaya—turned out for Simion and Pwatjumel's meeting. But a few Titan cult adherents also attended, so Simion had an audience for his criticism. He began by accusing the cargoists of reverting to the doctrines of Wapei, the prophet of Rambutjo, rather than joining the rest of the community on the path to the NGC. He then presented a string of more specific accusations. The Cemeterians, he charged, had 'lost shame' and revived mixed nude bathing; they also excluded people from Yiru hamlet or Titan residents of Bunai from their meetings, posting lookouts to warn of their approach; they had spent all their money on luxury foods, cult uniforms, and cosmetics for the dead; and Malei people had told a Bunai Titan woman who brought fish to trade that Malei people didn't need things produced by hard work anymore.

Tjamilo—a Titan of Bunai—spoke in reply, providing a pattern for the other cult sympathisers. He said that he agreed with everything Simion had said. The Usiai must stop doing what they were doing. Then he broke precedent. He mentioned cargo (*kago*) in an open meeting. The cemetery was an end in itself, he said, something to make the village look better; it had nothing to do with cargo. One of the Lowaya men, Petrus Popu, supported him, as follows: 'We aren't working on the cemeteries [in Lowaya] so cargo will come. We think that it is all right for all the hamlets of Bunai to have one big cemetery, but it is hard work to carry the dead to the old graveyard. And it is hard work to punt a canoe there'. (The old cemetery was about a quarter of a mile past Lowaya. The body, with the chief mourners, was usually taken there by canoe while the rest of the village walked.) He protested further: 'I worship only God. We do not worship a piece of wood, or a stone, or a fish'. No one had accused the cult adherents of idolatry or fish worship, but some had begun to take affront at such an accusation anyway. Responding to the accusation of squandering money, he said that they had withheld money from the Movement because the leaders weren't managing it properly.

Although Tjamilo had protested that the cemeteries weren't about cargo, the vehemence of Petrus Popu's similar disclaimer clearly disturbed him. Tjamilo rose to warn Petrus not to talk loosely. They must be ready for what is to come, he warned; they must be ready for the Last Day. Simion let this remark pass, although he could have taken it as open acknowledgement of millenarian activity. Instead, he made further accusations pertaining to marching, nudity, and other more superficial matters. Petrus Popu and others agreed that the Usiai should, in fact, stop doing certain things and denied that they were doing others. Speakers batted back and forth many more grievances against the cult adherents, but no one mentioned cargo or the Last Day again. Finally, the meeting ended, all the speakers exchanging the usual assurances that they were not angry with each other. It was the most open discussion of the cult Schwartz had yet seen in Bunai, but it ended entirely inconclusively despite Tjamilo's mention of the Last Day. Perhaps Simion and others felt that to preserve a semblance of unity they could not react overtly to a cult reference. It would remain for Paliau to be more direct.

At the request of the district officer, Paliau and Samol lingered in Lorengau after Paliau's release from jail to attend the opening of a cooperative store near town. The administration still wanted Paliau's support for its program and curried his favour when it could. With Paliau still absent, Simion Kilepak took the opportunity to call another meeting. On 2 May, several men from Malei represented the Usiai cult hamlets. Simion approached the subject of the new cemeteries with great caution at first. He said that they were too close to the houses. The sun would heat the ground, sickness would come up as smoke, and the sickness would get into people's food. Then he became bolder. He asked what the meaning of these new cemeteries was. If its meaning was like that of 1946, he said, it was something already proven wrong. He then veered away from outright opposition and reproached the Usiai for excluding the Titan. The Titan had brought the Usiai down to the beach, he said, and it was wrong for them now to turn them away. When Jesus had held a meeting, he added, he had excluded no one.

Someone then rose to blame the Titan for causing the present discord by spying on and ridiculing the Usiai. Several Bunai Titan then spoke in succession. Each raised a new accusation against the Usiai or a new argument against their activities. Only after this series of speeches did one of the men from Malei reply. Pondis, the Malei *kaunsil*, admitted they had ejected from their meetings a Pere Titan woman who had married into Malei, and he admitted that they had spent their money in the store. But he said that the cemetery work was their own idea, their own affair, and if others in Bunai didn't like it, Malei would clear out and go somewhere else. As usual, the threat of withdrawing from the village drew assurances that no one wanted this. Tjamilo said that it was not the way of God for one man to cast out another, for God had brought them together. Using a mangled biblical image, he said that the cemetery work could coexist with the NGC: 'The council is one road, the cooperative is another. There must be one more. It must be like the Trinity'. This, of course, also mangled the nature of the NGC and the cooperatives, both of which were part of the overall administration program, the program Paliau had now made the centrepiece of the Movement.

This conciliatory note turned the meeting in a new direction. Several speakers urged that they should all keep news of the cult from the whites. (Schwartz and Shargo were present, taking notes as usual, so the speakers clearly meant the Australians.) Someone even argued that if only a few villages backed the cult, the government could stop it, but if all 33 villages in the Movement backed it, the government could not suppress it. Hence, he argued, the cult adherents should explain to everyone what they were doing and keep it secret only from the whites. But some were still not sanguine about the cult and argued that the Usiai should stop whatever it was they were doing before they got them all in trouble. One speaker likened the cult to overripe fruit which had begun to stink.

But Tjamilo still wanted the cult and he wanted to be its leader. He made one more impassioned appeal—albeit packed in ambiguous metaphors—to identify the aims of the cult with those of the Movement and to identify himself as a stalwart of the Movement. He reminded people that he had been known for his defiance of the white man during the Movement's early days and he still was not afraid of the white government: 'When the white man pounds on the table', he declared, 'you will not be adequate. Now you think that you are, but then you will shake'. But the Usiai cargoists responded neither to him nor to the others who urged them to either abandon the cult or invite others in. The men from Malei, in fact, said virtually nothing at this meeting. While oratory swirled around them, they waited quietly for the meeting to adjourn. It ended inconclusively, as had the previous meeting, but it was to reconvene that evening.

Paliau enters the arena

Paliau and Samol arrived in Bunai from Lorengau on 2 May, between the end of the daylight meeting and its scheduled evening revival. During the canoe trip from Lorengau, Samol had described to Paliau, from his point of view, all that had happened in Bunai in Paliau's absence, except the meetings during Samol's own absence. On Paliau's return to Bunai he was in low spirits. He told Schwartz that he had seen him pass by the jail yard in Lorengau but out of shame he had hidden behind the other prisoners. Paliau thought the Baluan and Mok councillors should have prevented his daughter from eloping until he had returned from travelling on Baluan Council business. He then might not have flown into a violent rage. In any case, he felt he had received too harsh a sentence. Above all, he feared the assistant district officer on Baluan now might not allow him to continue as the chairman of the council just when he was about to realise his aim of making the council coterminous with the Movement area, for he had learned in Lorengau that the administration had decided that the south coast was to become part of the Baluan Council very soon.

Paliau stayed in Samol's house in Bunai. The men most concerned about the cult, pro and con, came to him there and hung on his words, intent on finding out where he stood. But Paliau managed to converse with them for several hours without giving them any hints. Later that night he visited Schwartz and Shargo. He sat for some time going through a pile of *Life* magazines, asking questions about each picture. He was particularly fascinated with an issue on Africa and African leaders, with whom he immediately identified. The leaders of Malei joined Schwartz and Shargo a little after Paliau arrived, sitting silently, not wanting to interrupt. Finally, Paliau mentioned the cult and how it was creating discord in Bunai. For the first time he sounded like he intended to do something about it. By now it was well after dark (which, so near the equator, would have been complete not long after six o'clock), when evening meetings usually started, and the bell calling people to come had begun to sound. But one of the Malei leaders informed Paliau that the people of Malei had prepared a party—that is, an elaborate meal, probably with speeches—for him, celebrating his return from jail. Demonstrating impeccable manners, Paliau and Samol went to eat in Malei, so the meeting didn't begin until 10 o'clock.

Samol started the meeting dramatically by saying that Malei was going to leave Bunai. Malei's leaders responded that they had only said this in reaction to Titan hostility. Samol continued to complain of how the cult was splitting the village. When leaders came from cult villages like Kapo or Nuang, he said, they no longer came first to him. They went instead to Tjamilo's house, as if he and not Samol were *kaunsil*. He then charged that Tjamilo had declared himself uninterested in the NGC and the cooperative, which Tjamilo immediately denied. He demanded to know when he had made such a statement, although he and everyone else knew he had made it several times. (In fact, he couldn't make up his mind. Sometimes he thought the council and cooperative were sops from the whites; at other times he thought they might have been established by God, but they were the hard work of the Second Order of God, not a path to the First Order.)

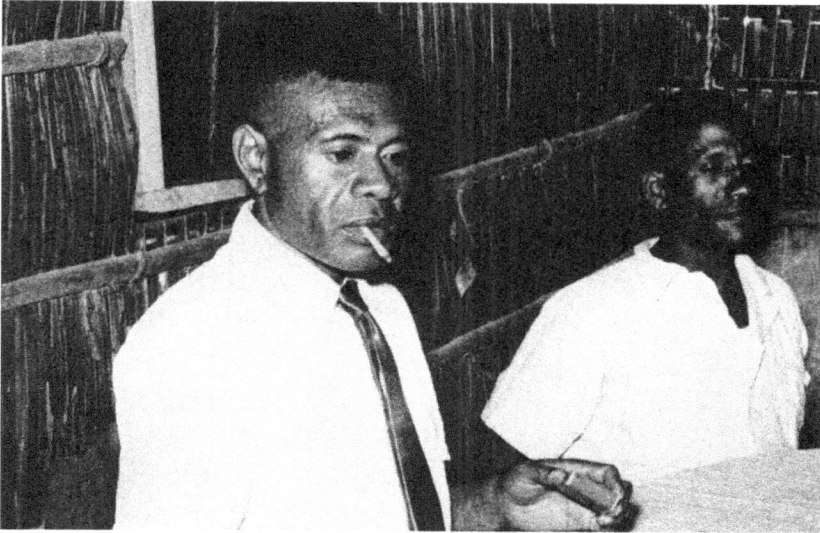

Figure 11.1: Paliau looked thoughtful before the meeting in Bunai at which he ended the Cemetery Cult.
Source: Theodore Schwartz.

Samol let that pass, for he and Tjamilo had many other bones to pick with each other and they began to pick them one by one. Paliau, however, was having none of this. He was used to spending much of his time at meetings trying to maintain the focus of the discussion. He broke into Samol's and Tjamilo's exchange. The discussion, Paliau said, had gone amiss, 'like a fire that runs only over the bark of a tree while the inside is untouched'. Where was the real issue before this meeting, he asked?

Nakwam, the *kaunsil* of Kapo, had come to the meeting with the cult leader from Nuang. (Recall that Kapo and Nuang were distinct Usiai villages, not hamlets of Bunai.) The trouble, Nakwam said, was that Malei and Lowaya were ashamed before Samol. Nakwam had instructed the people of Malei and Lowaya months before in the doctrines of the cult, but he now adopted a pose of complete innocence and asked the Malei and Lowaya leaders present what they had been doing that they were ashamed of before Samol? This was an invitation to them to plead their own innocence and they immediately did so. Pantret of Lowaya said that he had independently come to realise how decadent his village had become. No one paid any attention to the leaders any more. The place was full of every sin defined by the New Way. Everyone quarrelled with everyone else. When not quarrelling, people were apathetic. This situation had inspired him to return to the ways of 1946. The cemetery was simply part of this—an effort to make a decent burial ground as the law required and as the Americans had done. The trouble was all with the Bunai Titan who spied on them, called them crazy, and spread rumours.

Paliau asked what the cemetery had to do with 1946. Pantret recited all the features of the early New Way that had either lapsed entirely or were now only casually employed, such as the twice-daily bathing in the sea, dressing up for morning and evening church services, and a nine o'clock curfew. These practices were not new, he said; in Lowaya they had simply begun to follow them again.

Paliau replied that so much was true. He had started all these things and many others, which he proceeded to list, that had never been properly carried out. Then he asked Pantret about the cemetery again. Pantret replied: 'Although we have made a little general progress we have neglected our graveyards. It is not like this with the white men. Even if the white men will not instruct us, we must do as they do. Making new cemeteries is just fixing up the village in preparation for the council'.

Paliau was not having any of this either. He told Pantret he was not describing the true situation, the real basis for the trouble. He warned that if people continued to hide their real concerns it would ruin them completely. If everything was as Pantret depicted it, Paliau argued, Bunai people would not be at odds with each other.

Pokanau, another Usiai cult leader from Nuang, then repeated most of what Pantret had said. Then Nakwam of Kapo rose again to make a highly emotional speech in a high-pitched, ranting voice. Although dripping with colourful metaphors describing himself as like a father to the people of Kapo, who came crying to him for direction, and invoking his concern for the welfare of Nuang's people, he was unable to pacify Paliau.

No one pursued the themes on Nakwam's speech. Paliau sat silent, but clearly listening intently. Simion Kilepak then rose to accuse the cult hamlets of myriad forms of immorality. This excited an angry rebuttal from Tjamilo, ending with a confused and idiosyncratic account of how the cooperatives might open the road to the cargo. When another speaker rose, Paliau cut him off abruptly. There was more to this than building cemeteries, he said. There is obviously trouble here but no one will speak of it. Then, for the first time he stated a clear position on the Cemetery

Cult: 'This thing which has come from Johnston Island is wrong. I want it to finish. It will destroy you. You have already seen it and you already know it. I have already told you. You have lost the road'.

He then listed all the projects that they should have been working on when they were indulging in feuds and factions and secrets and rumours. They should have been building a good meeting house and building a church; and yes, even building better cemeteries, which he had always urged, but not for gathering the bones of the previously interred. All this talk about cargo, about the dead arising, and about the cemetery was all wrong. He had seen it in many places. They would have avoided all the division and ugliness if people had brought their ideas to an open meeting of the entire village. And if all they wanted to do was to return to the practices of 1946, then they should have brought that up at such a meeting instead of working in secret in individual hamlets.

Nakwam followed Paliau with another highly emotional speech full of mixed metaphors about the ways of 1946 and the condition of man in Paradise. Paliau cut him off as well. There was no point in talking about returning to 1946, he said, because they had never carried out most of the program he had given them then. Giving example after example, Paliau told people that the idea of reviving the ways of 1946 was based on a fantasy. But now they were dragging Bunai down and he wanted to know what they were going to do about it. 'Talk is like wind', Paliau said, 'it will go everywhere. It will go to the whites and they will come asking questions. When the *kiap* comes, he will not arrest you, he will arrest me. You don't work on the beginning of the road. All the time you keep trying to leap ahead'. Tjamilo began to speak, trying to absolve himself from having said anything about cargo, but Paliau cut him off and closed the meeting. It was midnight. Paliau said they would continue the next day.

Paliau did not sleep that night. He spent the night in the Usiai hamlets. He went alone, without Samol, the Bunai council, and without Schwartz. This made Samol uneasy and disappointed Schwartz, who didn't want to miss anything. From what Paliau told Schwartz later and what he said in subsequent public meetings, however, it appeared that he had questioned people in the hamlets closely about the cult and had been candid in his disapproval.

Paliau spoke with Schwartz about the cult before the meeting reconvened the following evening. He implied that only he and Schwartz really understood things like the cult. He spoke of the burial practices and the belief in ghosts in the pre-Christian Admiralty Islands. He said the cult was repeating the Noise of 1946 when, on Mok, the people marched to the cemetery and stood vigil, expecting the dead to arise. The Noise, he said, had almost ruined the Movement. Again he said that Wapei had started it. Now the Cemeterians were repeating what Wapei had started years ago.

That evening, the meeting, which was to be held outdoors, was postponed because of rain. Lowaya had prepared a party for Paliau, as Malei had done the preceding night. The meal had been laid out indoors, so Paliau and Schwartz, who was also invited, went. The Lowaya people were very ingratiating in a nervous way. They served their guests the European foods they had bought for their Cemeterian feast. Kekes, the only surviving adult male of the village of Lesei and the father of Joseph Nanei, the adolescent cult leader of Lowaya, made a long speech explaining that Paliau was his brother. He recited a genealogy that derived the *lapan* line of Lipan from an Usiai of Lesei who had drifted to Lipan many generations ago. Paliau was willing to accept this and the explanation that Kekes, his 'brother', was giving a party to celebrate his release from jail. Paliau had brought Samol and Kisekup with him and now he brought them to the head of the table, along with Samol's children, one of whom sat on Paliau's lap. Joseph Nanei, Pantret, and Pongo (the latter two had served as Nanei's apostles) served the meal with strict formality, moving clockwise in a full circle around the table to serve each guest.

It looked like the rain was not going to stop, so Paliau ordered that a house be prepared for the meeting. There was an unfinished house in Bunai, lacking only its walls, and a group of men covered the openings with canoe sails. At nine o'clock in the evening, people started to gather, mostly male leaders and no women or children. The atmosphere was tense. The Cemeterians and the opposition clustered on opposite sides of the floor. Paliau arrived last, as was his usual practice. He began by discussing a current land dispute between two non-Movement villages regarding which the government had called on old Kisekup as an expert. Paliau asked what the government would do if Kisekup were to die, dig him up again? A few men chuckled softly. Kisekup was not among them.

Paliau then launched abruptly into a long censorious speech about the previous night's meeting. No one, he said, had been willing to take responsibility for the trouble in Bunai. They had blamed one another. No one had suggested a way to remedy the situation. The fault lay with the leaders, he said, not with the women and children who had acted as mediums for the dead. The *kaunsil* should have silenced them. They had all lost the way; they were all crazy; the truth was hidden from them. Then he asked who had any ideas for rectifying the situation.

Pantret of Lowaya began by saying that he would repeat what he had said yesterday. His people would not drop this thing. If they did, the hamlet would revert to its previous bad ways. All his people would be insubordinate again. He said that he was trying to straighten out everyone's *tingting* before the official council was inaugurated. If the council came while people were still angry and quarrelling, they would all be in court constantly. He had not quarrelled with Bunai. It would be better if he said nothing at all about the things he heard yesterday (referring to Simion Kilepak's accusations). However, he began, if someone were to name the person from whom they heard these things … But Paliau cut him off abruptly in mid-sentence with the following denunciation:

> Your speech is wrong. You are unable to extricate yourself from this trouble you are in. If you see a road that is no good, that has spears, bottles, and bombs in it, you can't follow it. This talk of yours is already wrong. You cannot go on this road. The broken bottles have already cut you. You are already in trouble. You want to fight. You want to split up. You are at an impasse. The mouth of the road that will make you all right is hidden from you.[1] I can't let you ruin yourselves. Pantret stood up to speak and he has already gone astray. He didn't get up to find a way out. This thing has already brought trouble; now what? Should we let it continue? You will be ruined. If I walk onto a place that is stony, should I walk on it until the time I die? This thing already has brought trouble. It is about to break up your village. It has brought strife among you. Don't you see this?

---

1   When people speak non-metaphorically of the 'mouth' of a 'road' in rural Papua New Guinea they are usually referring to the beginning of a trail, such as an opening in the forest or in tall grass.

Prenis Tjolai of Pere made the next attempt to speak:

> There are two kinds of work. Some of us worked, and it resulted in
> trouble. Some men wanted to work on all the ways of 1946. And
> some wanted to make a cemetery. These things are good. Then
> what produced the quarrels and the talk? You see, I have a head.
> If I see something is not right, my head must steer my body clear
> of it. This thing that you tell about is good, so what causes the
> trouble? When his *kaunsil* sends for a man who wants to do the
> work of the cemetery, he will not listen. He doesn't come to speak
> openly about it at a meeting, but he follows his own liking. When
> the *kaunsil* speaks, sometimes he comes and sometimes he doesn't.
> I think this is where our error lies.

Paliau interrupted to say that Prenis was also wrong. This was just as it was
last night. What must be done to straighten things out?

Recognising himself in Prenis's statement about the source of the trouble,
Tjamilo spoke. He repeated part of Prenis's speech, saying that in itself
the cemetery was not wrong and that the ideas of 1946 were not wrong,
yet there was trouble. Tjamilo confessed that he built one of the new
cemeteries on his own. He said he knew it would be useless to ask Samol
because he knew that Samol would be opposed. He tried to continue, but
Paliau interrupted him.

So far, Paliau had abruptly silenced all the speakers. And each man had
sat back down immediately. Most men at the meeting were sitting on
the floor. Their backs were bowed. Many had rested their heads on their
drawn-up knees, concealing their faces. Everyone was grave and quiet.
They did not speak among themselves.

Paliau continued to berate them, seemingly trying to get them to say
something that he already had in mind:

> You men, look, listen. I have already said it. Your heads are unable
> to hear anything. Each one blames the other. You aren't following
> what I said. You keep letting all sorts of bad ways come into your
> villages; when they cause trouble your heads are full of these bad
> ways that you have let in. You seem unable to find the mouth of
> the road. You don't want to listen to the one work, the one road
> that I have spoken of. You always distort it. And when it results in
> trouble you are incapable of putting it straight.

Paliau said repeatedly that everything was already wrong; the cemetery work had already made trouble. Now what were they going to do about it? 'I can't straighten out your *tingting*', he declared. 'I work on making it straight and you work on distorting it'. (This was also Paliau's near-constant complaint to Schwartz when he spoke to him about the travails of being a leader: 'Whatever I say, they distort'.)

Manoi, the council of Loitja, who had been closely associated with Kisakiu of Tawi in the Noise and in the Cemetery Cult, now rose to speak:

> Yes, I want to speak a little. Paliau did not show us all these bad ways. He showed us the way of God. We heard all the talk of God from Paliau only. Then everyone went back to their villages and changed what he had said. Now it has gone wrong. We started on something new again, something from Johnston Island. It is true that we all had already heard about cemeteries. But now it has come up wrong and we can't follow it. We must follow this new talk, this talk we heard in 1946 about just making it in order to have a decent burial place. We have forgotten all the work of 1946 and this is no good.

Then he repeated several of Paliau's figures of speech about roads covered with broken glass and spears and stones. Paliau allowed him to finish, the first time he allowed this that evening. And he commented without the anger he had shown at the other speakers:

> This talk also is wrong. In 1946 did you see us, the men of Baluan, at the cemetery? [It was the Mok people and the mainland Titan visitors who had gone to the cemetery. Paliau had withdrawn to Baluan, where people had a much less intense experience of the Noise than on Mok.] At the meeting house, was there anything said about the cemetery at these meetings? Who heard this in November of 1946, or in 1947, '48, '49, '50, '51, '52, '53, or '54? Who on Baluan has started a cemetery? You have it wrong. Did this cemetery idea come up in Baluan in 1946 or not? Yes? If it did, why haven't I built a cemetery? It was I who gave you the ideas of 1946. I said nothing about any cemetery. Right?

Tjamilo responded:

> I was there in the Noise, too. But we see cemeteries among the white men. They do it right. They clean them well. But cargo doesn't appear from this. In 1946 you didn't say build cemeteries and cargo will come from them. So now why do we keep saying 1946?

Paliau allowed him to finish, and replied:

> This trouble that came from Rambutjo in 1946 has come to you
> now. Change things a little, change them a little more, and soon
> someone kills someone. This is close to you now. You distort
> things too much here. It is already wrong. Now where is the road
> to make things all right?

Kisekup, the old south coast paramount *luluai*, then spoke for the first time:

> This way of ours, the whites opposed us because of it for a long
> time. We were strong but now that our way is clear and there is the
> road of the council and the cooperative, we ourselves are ruining
> it. Where is there another road?

Paliau allowed Kisekup this short speech, then he continued scolding,
asking what should be done to repair the damage. Pondis, the *kaunsil* of
Malei, who had been sitting dejectedly, started to speak for the first time,
saying 'The source of this trouble is in two villages'. Paliau silenced him
with an angry shout, 'Stop! That's enough of that'. Pondis sat down and
said nothing for the rest of the night. Paliau continued to shout. He said
that they were all talking just as they had the night before. No one was
offering a solution. 'You keep saying, cemetery, 1946, cemetery, 1946,
cemetery, 1946!'

Kametan of Bunai addressed the Cemeterians, telling them that if they
would stop what they had been doing they could all get back together
again; if not, they could not work together. Then Petrus Pomat of Pere
tried a new approach:

> It is like this. All the talk of the past and of today has brought
> trouble. We can no longer think of these things. Now the [official]
> council will get started among us. What work will the council do?
> The council has knowledge of what is not right. It can make it right
> later. It is like what we are talking about now. We keep throwing
> it back and forth at each other. We'd be better off keeping quiet.
> This work will come up later, the council can do it. When we
> are in the council, what kind of work will we do? Houses, land,
> cemetery, whatever the council sees that is not straight it can order
> people to correct. But it can't just do it. It has to come up first in
> the meeting house. If we want to do this work, it can't be just one
> village, but every village and every man. When one village doesn't
> want to tell another village about something, this leads to trouble.

Paliau interrupted and said:

> You say the name council, council, council. If you don't straighten out this thing now, today, I will go back to Baluan and you won't get the council. I will put it to the meeting that in Bunai, they are all completely crazy. Do you think I can't? This is why you can't find good *tingting* after I have taught you for all these years, you keep changing things about.

Samol tried to discover what Paliau wanted someone to say. He began to talk about the need to bring everything up at meetings, as Paliau had said the night before. He said that he was wrong, too, that he doesn't always do this. Paliau interrupted him as if he hadn't heard him, continuing his threat about keeping them out of the NGC:

> Mister Landman [the assistant district officer in charge of the Baluan Council] is coming. I think he hasn't heard about this thing. If he had heard, he wouldn't have set the day for starting the council. You are in serious trouble. This quarrel of yours is like a stink, but there has been no wind to carry it. Mister Landman set the day without knowing about this trouble here. I am extremely angry at you. It is not as if you were not already in trouble that you can fight back and forth like this.

Pokanau, *kaunsil* of Nuang, said that they were willing to hear about the work of the official council, but as far as the cemetery was concerned, they had already finished theirs. They could not take it away. Paliau broke in angrily again, saying that this had already led to trouble. Whoever continued it would go to jail and they would not be admitted to the NGC. 'You have gone wrong in your work on the cemetery. Find a way to set this straight.'

Paliau kept hammering these points. The effect was hypnotic. Most of the men sat staring at the floor, as if Paliau's words were striking their heads. He had treated all of them like bad and stupid children who could not learn a simple fact. He continued to berate them: 'No more of your bloody twisting things around! Why didn't you do it according to the law? The law concerning the cemetery, you have forgotten. The trouble started in March 1954. Now it is time to find a way to set it straight to finish the quarrel within your village so that it can't ruin you. Come on, come on, come on, come on!'

He continued to scold. He said that meetings were for airing dissension. They were the proper place for quarrelling, not on the paths of the village. Suddenly he changed his tone. He said quietly that the wind from the east, which was then shaking the house, was almost as strong as the usual wind from the west. Schwartz could see the men relax, some of the tension go out of their bodies. Several had the temerity to agree with Paliau; yes, the east wind was unusually strong. Several of the men spoke quietly with each other.

After a few moments of this calm, Petrus Popu of Lowaya spoke. Lowaya, he said, was ashamed because they had been accused of nude bathing. He said this indignantly. Yet he had seemed to admit to the accusation in a meeting several days before. He said that they were also angry because Samol had taken money entrusted to him and had lost it in gambling. That was why they had spent the rest of their money in the store; the *kaunsil* would only lose the rest of it if they turned it in. He spoke as if this were the cause of the quarrel in the village.

Paliau berated Popu for introducing another subject when still no one had offered a solution for the whole situation. He threatened to go to bed and to leave for Baluan in the morning, unless someone offered a solution soon. He told Popu: 'So you have been shamed. You want to go back to the bush? You can live in the bush for the rest of your life if you wish'. Here Paliau was probably referring not simply to living in a way that was materially backward; he was likely invoking a common criticism of the cult. That is, that its emphasis on the ghosts of the dead was a throwback to the indigenous way of life they should be trying to leave behind; rather than a way forward, the cult was little more than a revival of an aspect of indigenous culture—the constant monitoring by harsh and capricious ghosts—for which many were anything but nostalgic.

Simion Kilepak then tried to offer a solution. They would all admit that they were wrong and make no further mention of what had happened, but in the future they would bring to a public meeting anything like the cemetery work, and everyone would have to agree or it could not proceed. Paliau made no comment.

Prenis Tjolai reminded Paliau that he had asked him earlier about the cemetery work. Paliau had warned that the cult would lead to trouble, and now, he, Prenis, would obey Paliau and forget about it. Prenis was the only one of the Cemeterians who reminded Paliau that they had previously asked him about the cult, at which time, some of them claimed, he had not discouraged them or had even encouraged them. Paliau's reply cast some light on those curious conversations:

> It is true that all of you asked me and I told you yes. It was as if I were shooing off a dog. You kept asking and asking and asking. 'You can do it. You have your own mind', I said. Now I told you because you kept asking me, asking me, asking me. But you didn't stick to making a cemetery, and now it has gone wrong. You have twisted it around in your heads. But Manoi [of Loitja] also asked me and I told him straight. 'You can't do it.' He said they had it on Johnston Island and I said it was wrong. Soon Johnston Island would be ruined by it.

Schwartz had not heard of these events before, but apparently at least some others had. In July 1953, almost a year before the present meeting, on Manoi's insistence the *luluai* of Loitja had come to Bunai in a Johnston Island canoe to hear what Paliau had to say about the Johnston Island cult. Paliau told Manoi, the *luluai*, and the Johnston Island group that Johnston Island was heading for trouble. Paliau now said that this showed he had been opposed to the cemetery work from the start. He also admitted that he had told most of them to go ahead and build their cemeteries; but he did so because he had grown tired of their pestering so he gave them the answer they kept asking for.

In a long speech which repeated several of his favourite analogies, Paliau continued to emphasise that they were destroying themselves. He concluded by threatening again to report to the administration that they were all crazy, unworthy of the official council.

One or two others then tried to speak, but Paliau silenced them, saying that he had had enough, he was going to bed now; no one had offered any ideas for ending the trouble. He was going back to Samol's house and he did not want anyone to seek him out there. He was finished. He was angry. As far as the south coast was concerned, he said, the council has been ruined: 'I am going to have you all put in jail. I am going to Mister Landman. You will all be jailed, if not, the work of the council will be ruined completely. You will not win out. I try to straighten you out, but you are unwilling'. He himself had just been released from jail, to which Landman had sentenced him. He was also worried that he might be dismissed as chairman of the Baluan Council. Yet now he resorted to the threat of turning people over to the government. He was using every tactic available to reassert his leadership and—perhaps—to keep people off their guard.

Having announced angrily that he had had enough, Paliau then made no move to leave. After a pause, others began to speak again. Kisekup suggested that stopping the cemetery work would end the trouble in the village. Manoi of Loitja added a new thought: he compared the present quarrel to the way quarrels had constantly broken up villages in the days of their ancestors. Their ancestors, he said, made hot-headed threats to leave every time there was a disagreement. Now, Manoi called for turning their backs on those days, a general shaking of hands, forgetting the cult, and renewing their unity in an expanded official council.

Paliau made no direct comment on either Kisekup's or Manoi's contributions. Instead, he spoke as follows, asserting his dominance:

> You men think that you have knowledge now. Or you think that you will test me on these ideas. But you can't take the lead. If you try it, you will be ruined. You are not the ones who did it. I am. I showed you all these roads. Now you want to make trouble, but you can't win out. It was not you who started this work in Manus in 1946. I raised you up with my ideas. Now you distort them. Who gave you these ideas? Who showed you? All of you are wearing trousers and shirts, who gave this to you? Was it you who showed the way? You would like to beat down all my ideas. You think that you are now equal to it. I can talk, and you can oppose me. I can talk, and you can change what I say. If you are not equal to it, why have you taken this trouble upon yourselves? Who showed you? You tell me! I will shut up while you show me. I want to ask you, I too want to build a cemetery in Lipan-Mok. You tell me how to do this work. You, Pokanau, should I put a rail around it or should I put a door, or what? Come, you show me, what are these ideas? Go on, I am asking you, I want to build one in my own village.

Pokanau of Nuang began hesitantly, 'All of us must speak'. But Paliau broke in with words replete with condescension:

> I am the one who taught you and now you say, never mind me. You go ahead of me. I think you can show me? All right, show me now. I have told you plenty and you have continually distorted it. I think that you have plenty of know-how. All right, show me now.

Pokanau sat down, finally perceiving that no answer was really wanted. The room fell silent. Paliau sat back and waited. Obviously, he was using this occasion not merely to end the cult, but to reaffirm the absolute leadership that had been slipping away from him in recent years. He was answering the claim some had made in a number of recent meetings: 'Before, we were like children, now we are men. We have our own minds'. Paliau wanted them to admit their incapacity and to put themselves into his hands. Although never very explicit, there had been an anti-Paliau tendency in the Cemetery Cult, and he was determined to stop this.

Paliau finally continued:

> This quarrel among you is finished, but what you have done to me is not. If you think I have not shown you your ideas and your ways, then you show me. You don't stop to think that I am your leader. I will win because I will put you all in trouble to keep you from spoiling the council. Who showed you the way? If you know that I am the source of all this, then why have you tried to throw me down? There is not one thing in what I have ever told you that has been wrong. Hey, you! It's soon daylight.

He shouted the last words at the stunned men sitting all around him. There was a pause, during which some on the pro-cult side of the room began to whisper among themselves. Paliau interrupted them sarcastically:

> You don't have to ask one another. Each of you is a man of knowledge. Tell me. Everywhere in Manus there is no other place that is getting the council except you. I think you are all pretty good to have done this. Your heads are superior to mine. Now you can throw out my teachings. Now you can teach me.

Pokanau of Nuang rose to make a long speech in a subdued tone, lacking his earlier defiance. None of them, he said, knew anything at all except what Paliau had taught them. Tjamilo rose immediately after Pokanau and started to confess his errors, also in a quiet, humble tone: 'I am the cause of all this trouble. And Johnston Island, too, they are more than a little wrong'. He started to detail how he had gone to Johnston Island, how he had been told to build a cemetery, how he had tried in Bunai, how he had taken ten men and cut the coconut palms on the old cemetery.

Paliau interrupted him saying: 'No one asked you for this talk. If the old cemetery was no good there were normal channels for doing this as village work'. Now, Paliau said, they should admit their incapacity. They should say either that they could lead him or that he should lead them. He said they constantly made trouble because they didn't stop to think that they might be making others angry. He explained to them at length that he interrupted them because he could see that they were saying, or were going to say, things that would merely prolong the quarrel.

The men on the pro-cult side of the room now sat as if dazed. For the time being at least, and for the first time, they seemed stripped of their defiance and their stiff righteousness. Suddenly Paliau relaxed. He called for matches, joking that if they couldn't find any, they would have to use a fire plough.[2]

Nakwam, the council of Kapo, spoke now, echoing the tone of Pokanau's speech:

> I have listened, and I think it is like pulling a rope, five brothers on one side and five on the other. Five think their father will help them, and the other five think their father will help them. Each wants him. Now our father has spoken clearly to us. He said, 'While I am still here you must hurry up to straighten this out'. What talk does he have for us to make this straight? He has listened to these ten men. If he leaves, this trouble will remain among us. Our minds and thoughts are not adequate, now what thoughts does our father have? It is true; our father has made all these things. Today I see my father and I cry to him, 'What is your idea?'. If he leaves, there will be ruination.

Paliau had been working towards speeches like Pokanau's and Nakwam's throughout the night—cult leaders admitting their inadequacy and accepting their complete subordination. He had been refusing to hear explanations, accusations, defences, or attempted solutions. Here was what he wanted. Nakwam had entered these meetings attempting to identify with Paliau by speaking of himself as a father to the people of his village, who were children who came crying to him. Now Paliau was the father and they were all his repentant children asking him to set them right and forgive their presumption. After Nakwam's speech, Paliau asked: 'What are you waiting for? He is finished talking. Who is next?'

---

2   To start a fire with a fire plough you rapidly drive the end of a stick back and forth in a groove in another piece of wood until the heat ignites tinder. The anachronism of Paliau's suggestion is the joke. It's unlikely that anyone in Manus had used a fire plough for decades. In the 1950s, Manus people who didn't have wooden matches or metal lighters (of the pre-disposable type) typically lit cigarettes, ready-made or hand-rolled, with a brand from a fire. If the household fire went out, people often borrowed a brand from a neighbour to reignite it.

Pantret was next:

> My father has spoken. This is not something for us to quarrel about. We wanted to do this work, and now it is wrong. We are not adequate. If I do anything that is not right, you can speak and set it straight. We thought that we were strong a little, but we weren't. There is nothing that we are able to do. What shall we do? We started this work on our own. Now that it has led to anger and trouble we are not capable of carrying it through. That is all.

Now Paliau was satisfied that he had the situation entirely in his hands and that the assembled men were ready to do whatever he said. He then spoke for almost an hour. Here are paraphrased summaries (except where quotation marks indicate otherwise) of the final speeches of the meeting, which did not end until four o'clock in the morning.

Paliau began:

> Now I will answer you. You aren't saying the things that you are saying now out of your own good thoughts. My anger has frightened you. If it weren't for my anger, for my strong talk, you wouldn't say this. You still don't understand me clearly. If you really understood, you would have said what Nakwam said long ago, that I am the only one who has brought you to where you are now and that I am the only one who can keep you straight. In some countries, if the leaders are men with good ideas who give their ideas to the rest, the others obey them. People listen to whatever they say and do it. I took pity on you seeing that you were heading for trouble. My words are like the knife that cuts away your trouble. Had I merely reasoned with you, offering you good talk, you wouldn't have listened. Now that you saw my anger you abandoned what you were holding on to.

Then Paliau told the men what he wanted them to do. They were to end their disputes without further discussion, accusations, or shaming of anyone. In itself there was nothing wrong with making a good cemetery, he said, but this was to be done only as they would keep the trails in repair or the village clean and in good order. They could work on a cemetery later; but they were to wait until it had lost its association with the cult. He repeated that each hamlet was not to have its own cemetery; rather, there was to be a single cemetery for the whole village, because cemeteries were not like gardens in the bush, with one for every three or four people.

Paliau listed all the village projects that needed work, he criticised people for moving too slowly to rebuild their houses, and he put a two-month deadline on completing this task.

He told the men to make more use of the meeting house they had built and to hold regular meetings of the whole village every Thursday. There, they should discuss anything that anyone wanted to do for his hamlet. He explained that if the cemetery had been discussed, there would have been no trouble: 'For every man who does not think straight, there is one who does who can correct him'.

Paliau continued at length about how they call too much on the name of God while they continue to behave in the same bad ways. They speak of God and then they beat their wives, or steal, or lie. Then they return to talking about God. This was dangerous. He spoke about the idea of the cemetery as a means to get cargo, how occasionally someone would say that if they did this or that there would be a reward for their work. All that they desire would materialise. Paliau asked them: 'What do you expect? That you will win out over the store? That the things of the white men will appear for you? Or that sago will come to you in your house, or fish? If the people don't use their strength to work for food they will die'. He told them to forget these ideas, but he warned the cult opponents not to ridicule the former Cemeterians. There was to be no more anger and shame and ridicule or talk about breaking up the village. They were to laugh and play with each other again.

Then Paliau again changed his tone abruptly. He awakened the old council of Pwam, telling him, to his confusion, that Schwartz had just written in his book that the *kaunsil* was asleep during this important meeting. The assembly relaxed a little.

Pantret then recited what he would report to his hamlet the next day—that they were all wrong and that they must come to shake hands with the people of Bunai. Paliau then asked the cult hamlet leaders what they would say about the threats to break up the village. Pantret said that this had been Malei's idea. Pondis denied that Malei really intended to do it. Talimelion of Bunai said that the Titan had no quarrel with Malei or Lowaya; they wanted only unity. Paliau did not like the direction this was taking. He said that the hamlet leaders should not go back and speak to their people right away. Rather, in the morning they should bring them all to the square in Bunai and he would speak to them personally and put an end to their thinking about the cult. If he permitted the *kaunsil* to do it in their individual hamlets they would just do it wrong and make more trouble. Also, if they informed their own people of the end of the cult, those who got angry would direct their anger at their own leaders. Instead, he, Paliau, would take their anger.

Paliau lectured them again about the Movement they had neglected. He denounced the way each village and hamlet had been asserting itself independently. (Paliau never missed a chance to speak against thinking in terms of the smaller group; he stressed thinking on a village and Movement level.) Finally, he asked all those who considered the dissension ended to raise their hands, warning those who still entertained bad feelings towards others to keep their hands down. All hands went up. Then, as a last word, he added: 'This talk about cargo, about ghosts. I banish it now, it is finished'. He said that this sort of talk would be blamed on him, like the time Pita Tapo said that Paliau was King. The *kiap* confronted Paliau with this as if he had said it. That was the end of this meeting, which had run for seven hours without a break, during most of which time Paliau had held the floor.

The next day's village-wide meeting began promptly—an unusual occurrence—at nine that same morning. The people of Lowaya (but not Malei) came marching the length of the village in a perfect line, according to size, following the pattern established during the cult. It was a final show of defiance on the part of the leaders, who were willing to be humble before Paliau but not before the Titan. Before he spoke, Paliau met briefly with the leaders. They assured him that they had told people nothing about what they were going to hear. Then Paliau spoke to the assembled village for an hour. No one reacted visibly to the news that the cult was over. Paliau touched on the doctrines and promise of the cult only obliquely, but his meaning was amply clear. He emphasised the error and danger of the dissension in the village and urged a return to unity and friendship. He told people of the work they must now do to make their village better and to support the official council, which would be established within a week. Then he sent them back to their hamlets and homes, saying their leaders would explain his talk further to them.

Shutting off belief

After the meeting, Schwartz sat with Paliau while he talked with the leaders of the cult. He explained that he had spoken obliquely to avoid shaming the Usiai cult hamlets in the presence of the other villagers. There was enough of that already. Before adjourning the gathering, Paliau told the cult leaders that they should tell Schwartz everything about their experiences in the cult, to compensate, Paliau said, for the fact that they had disrupted Schwartz's work for the past three months. Then Schwartz would judge their work in the cult and explain it to them. Paliau's order brought Pantret, Pondis, Joseph Nanei, and Namu to Schwartz several times over the next few days for extensive discussions of things they had been unwilling to talk about since March, filling in the picture and confirming much of what he had learned indirectly.

More important, these discussions gave Schwartz an opportunity to try to explore the effect of Paliau's opposition on these cult leaders' beliefs. To what extent could Paliau simply shut off the cult in this way, and what would be the effects on those who had invested themselves in it for months if not years, those who had let it lift their millenarian hopes and raise them as individuals to new prominence in the village? What would happen to the hamlets where the cult had raised morale, instilled new discipline, and strengthened leadership? Would people be angry at their leaders, as Paliau feared?

But the almost immediate inauguration of the expanded NGC quickly grabbed most people's attention and revived what had been flagging interest in the Movement. This must have modulated considerably the reaction of most cult adherents to the end of the cult. Some raw feelings, however, did show through. While watching the Lowaya villagers march to and from the meeting ground where Paliau made his public statement on the cult, Schwartz wondered if, in spite of their abject submission to Paliau the preceding night, the Lowaya people might go ahead with the cult as before. He watched Pita Tapo sitting dejectedly, again holding his children on his lap, at the morning meeting. Tapo had not attended the meeting the night before. Surely, Schwartz thought, this was hard on him. The collapse of the Noise, in which he had blossomed into a prophet, had left him empty. The subsequent growth of the Movement which was so absorbing to others, like Kampo, left Tapo feeling useless and ignored. The Cemetery Cult had reawakened in him hope and a zest for activity. He had made pilgrimages to other cult villages. People had heard his voice again in meetings. But now, within a few days, his role had disappeared. In the excitement over the new council, he became inert again, unimportant, without office. He was, in fact, an embarrassment to the Movement, for people still linked his name with the most troublesome aspects of the Noise.

The immediate change Paliau's action on the cult wrought in Malei was remarkable. Everything stopped. Pondis was most affected. His influence disappeared completely. He became confused and depressed. He was shamed. For almost two months—until just before Schwartz and Shargo left to return home—he remained depressed. He stopped dressing in European clothing. He went unshaved and unkempt. He stayed in his hut on the beach much of the time.

It was different with Pantret of Lowaya. He was determined to retain the gains he had made through the cult. Men—such as Joseph Nanei, Nasei, and Pongo—with whom he had led the cult, receded into the background, but Pantret remained the Lowaya *kaunsil*. Pantret was able to retain the relationship Lowaya had formed with Malei during the cult. In the NGC elections, Malei and Lowaya asked to be regarded as a single political unit within Bunai with a single councillor, Pantret. The two hamlets even planned to build their houses together at Lowaya's end of the village. But in both hamlets the seances stopped.

In Lowaya, the cult left a few residues. The children kept marching. The adults, too, continued to march to church, although less regularly. Most of the men still wore their uniforms, the short trousers and undershirts dyed blue. But these were the only articles of European clothing many men owned. And everyone continued to adopt an air of defiance towards the Titan. But many people also relaxed visibly. They resumed going about their own affairs in their own time. They had neglected their gardens during the cult. Many had spent all their money on store foods—biscuits, tea, sugar, and canned meat. But many had been hungry, even though children and young boys had been doing more fishing to compensate for adults neglecting the gardens. Some men immediately dropped the discipline of the cult, especially those on the 'minstrel' fringe. They picked up their guitars again. Some, embarrassed by their fruitless involvement with the cult, left Lowaya to work for wages. Petrus Popu and his son, Seliau, were the only ones Schwartz knew who turned against Pantret. They had suppressed their hostility towards him temporarily, but now they blamed him for the cult.

In the Titan section of Bunai, Tjamilo's cemetery stood as an accomplished fact against Paliau's decree that Bunai was to have only one cemetery for the entire village. The cemetery was there, unoccupied, newly cleared, and newly painted. On 25 May, following the NGC elections, during a quiet period when Samol was again out of the village on council business, Tjamilo began to fill his cemetery. He still had all the crosses he had prepared, each painted with white coral lime. Then, while Schwartz was working in Pere, Tjamilo sent a note asking him to make a movie of a mass reburial. Schwartz couldn't leave his work in Pere, so he sent word for Tjamilo to proceed without him. Schwartz returned to Bunai three days later to find that Tjamilo had postponed the burial until his return. He was especially anxious to have Schwartz photograph the event because he had introduced some variations of his own on past processions and also because he believed that the anthropologists' presence would help normalise the procedure, removing the cult aura. He had persuaded most of the village to participate, although the event was weighted with his supporters.

Samol returned soon after the event, but he let it pass without comment. He may have reasoned that the cemetery symbolised Tjamilo's investment in the community and his years of concern with its morals in the name of the New Way. His reward for this dedication had been bitter. The first six graves in the cemetery contained his children, all of whom had died before reaching the age of two, despite Tjamilo's strenuous dedication to maintaining the moral purity of his *tingting*. In the seventh grave he reburied the skeleton of his father. Ten of Tjamilo's Titan kin and supporters were also reburied. About 100 adults and children took part in the procession, their numbers cutting across the lines of cult adherents and opponents in the Titan section.

Unfortunately, because Schwartz and Shargo had to leave for home in July, they did not find out what happened on Johnston Island or what happened to the ghost of Thomas. They did ascertain that Kisakiu's teacher did not reappear in Tawi. Between Paliau's declaration of the end of the cult and Schwartz and Shargo's departure, the affairs of the new NGC filled village life in Bunai, Pere, and nearby villages. Amiable relations seemed restored between the Titan and the Usiai, although the Titan dominated the new council.

What was the status of the cult beliefs after Paliau declared them invalid? Schwartz interviewed Pantret, Pondis, Joseph Nanei, Pita Tapo, Popu, Tjamilo, and Prenis Tjolai. As Paliau had requested, Schwartz did not hesitate to offer his own views, but only after long discussions in which the erstwhile Cemeterians elaborated their understanding of what had transpired. All these men were uncertain just what they were no longer supposed to believe. They had been moved by the strongest desire to believe in the cult. What Schwartz had learned from months of association with them before he became aware of the cult made this unsurprising, except regarding Pondis and Pantret. They had seemed more attuned to the secular program of the Movement, and they hadn't displayed the moralising and self-righteousness of many others whom Schwartz later learned were involved in the cult. But now they all told Schwartz much the same thing—the cult had failed only because people had spied on it and ridiculed it and spread rumours about it and shamed them for it. This, they said, had produced the schism in the village, and that was the trouble Paliau had been talking about. They had been wrong, to some extent, in not submitting their plans to a meeting of the whole village, but they might have done so if they had not been shamed.

What Paliau really meant, they said, was that once the council was organised, they would all discuss the cemetery project in a full village meeting and then everyone would carry it out. This was what had gone wrong. There was nothing wrong with the cult beliefs. In 1946, Wapei had spoiled the chances of the cult. Then the government had suppressed it. Now it had failed because of spying and envy. Had there been unanimity, all would have been well. Now that the cult was over, they would devote their energies, for a while, to the council and the cooperative, just as in after the Noise ended in 1947 they had turned back to the Movement program, to the Second Order of God. They repeated all the rationalisations that had been advanced for the failure of the Noise. They had never repudiated the Noise; it had simply not worked out. They recalled that when the ghost of Ponau appeared to Nasei in Lowaya, he had asked if they had received all the cargo the ghosts had sent earlier. When they said they had not, Ponau's ghost was angry and said it had been stolen by the Australians.

When Schwartz asked Tapo what had happened to the cargo, Tapo replied with a parable. He related how, when he had worked for the Japanese in Kavieng, where the war had caught him, Japanese supplies had run low. Then they received a wireless message that a cargo ship was on its way. The cargo ship approached within a few miles of the shore.

The Japanese rejoiced. But another country had intercepted this wireless. They sent a submarine, thinking 'Let the cargo get close first. Let them rejoice over it'. Then they torpedoed it near the shore. 'That is how it was with our cargo', said Tapo.

Tjamilo also said the cult failed only because Samol's group had ridiculed it. He reasserted his belief in everything pertaining to the cult. Schwartz pointed out to him that Paliau had said several times that the idea of cargo was mistaken, that there must be no further talk of the return of the dead. Tjamilo said that Paliau was very clever, more than anyone else, except maybe some white men. He had said all these things for the benefit of the spies in their midst, who would report what he said to the government. But he did not suspect Schwartz and Shargo of such perfidy. By this time, Tjamilo was accustomed to speaking freely to Schwartz about cult matters. Earlier, he had been wary of Schwartz and had even doubted that he was an American as he claimed. This lasted until Schwartz received a carton of Lucky Strike cigarettes his father sent from America. Tjamilo and others associated this brand in particular with the American soldiers on Manus during the war. As Schwartz went about his work, everyone who saw the Lucky Strikes was remarkably impressed and immediately nostalgic. Tapo carried away an empty pack as a souvenir. When Schwartz first offered one to Tjamilo and told him his father had sent them, Tjamilo immediately assumed that Schwartz's father was dead and his doubts that Schwartz was a true American were dispelled. Discussion of cult belief could have no effect on him.

It was clear in Schwartz's discussions with these men that it had not occurred to any of them that Paliau meant that the cult beliefs themselves were wrong. Only the circumstances had spoiled the cult. They allowed that the cult might never work out, because they did not know enough or they could not purify their thoughts enough. But they all felt that Paliau had promised that later, when the council was installed, they could turn again to the way of the cemetery, and that next time it would be done properly.[3]

---

3   This is a common explanation for the failure of all magical performances in Melanesia and other places where magic is commonplace; that is, the causal theory is correct, but the procedure was not performed properly.

Keeping up the pressure

Paliau pushed the Cemetery Cult into the shadows, but he couldn't quash the millenarian hopes that drove it. He doubtless kept an eye out for any signs of its resurrection. He also had to keep an eye on other possible threats that millenarian activity might disrupt efforts to establish an official council and move on with a substantially secular agenda. People from several villages continued to report hearing ghostly whistles long after the end of the Noise. Up through the 1960s, Joseph Nanei of Lowaya persisted in occasionally producing small sums of money or small bits of 'cargo', like watches, and claiming that he got them from the dead, as proof that he and the other Cemeterians hadn't been deluded. He didn't succeed in building a following, but he did irritate Paliau, who told Schwartz that Nanei was a fraud, but a fraud who probably fooled himself as much or more than he fooled others. Muli kept up a remnant of the Noise on Rambutjo, and Sua maintained a small group of followers. Paliau knew of their activities, but he didn't feel it was necessary to suppress these local prophets because they showed no signs of attracting additional adherents. He could now turn his attention to the possibilities for Manus people— and for himself—that an expanded official council offered.

12

Rise and fall

Paliau was now embarked on the most active and varied period in his public career. He involved himself in nearly every kind of social, economic, and political institution open to him. His reputation as founder and leader of the Movement and the attendant aura of occult knowledge and power undoubtedly abetted his success in electoral politics in some sectors of his growing constituency, and he may have traded on it shamelessly on some occasions. But the persona he presented outside Manus was heavily secular. Yet as the scope of his activity and authority widened, it became more difficult to satisfy the expectations of the full range of his constituents. From the initiation of the first Baluan Council in 1950 until Paliau lost his last position in official civil government in mid-1973, Paliau had persistently shaken the status quo in Manus and the Territory. But eventually—even as nimble as he was—he could not adapt fast enough to a social and political ground that was shifting with increasing speed.

The expanded council arrives and Paliau takes charge

Within weeks of the forced end of the Cemetery Cult, in mid-1954, the long-awaited inauguration of the expanded council took place and official elections were held. The newly elected councillors on the south coast were men who had been leaders in the Movement since 1946. Still, the council structure barely tapped the superabundance of potential leadership. Individuals who held the Movement rank of *komiti* under Paliau's pre-emptive Movement version of the council had no official place within the new system. The new councillors were impressive and proud, although they did not consistently remember to call themselves councillors, as the Australian administration desired; they continued to call themselves *kaunsil* (although we will call them councillors). Paliau lectured them on the importance of their positions and on the need to maintain themselves in every aspect of their lives as models for their villages. They should purchase and wear good European clothing, he said. They should build the best possible houses and maintain them well as an example to others. Their families, too, were to be models. Now, as many had never done before, they were to associate with their wives in public and eat at the tables they had built years before rather than sit on the floor around the cooking fire. And they should bear in mind that their enviable offices were subject to yearly re-election. Later, Paliau told them, they would discuss at least nominal salaries.

Under pressure from the many people who needed money to buy shares in the cooperatives and to pay taxes, money collected during the early phases of the Paliau Movement was finally redistributed. In addition to the contributions many made to the Movement, all Manus people had been paying an annual 10 shilling tax to the colonial government for years. Now, those within the new council area still paid taxes but they paid them to their own council to provide for schools, medical aid posts, and new buildings for council functions.

Although some people were slow to emerge from their post-cult depression, excitement about the council's expansion was a more common feeling. Groups from all villages within the Movement attended a celebration in Bunai. The guests of honour were James and Marjorie Landman. James Landman was the assistant district officer who had supervised the Baluan Council since 1950 and was now in charge of extending it to the south coast, and Marjorie Landman had conducted the first government-sponsored council school on Baluan. The first meetings of all the village councillors were held in Bunai, for the council now had two centres, one in Baluan and one in Bunai.

Opposition to the cult had brought the Movement closer to the government. Some Cemeterians had infused their millenarian hopes with hostility towards the government. Even Paliau, when fresh out of jail, and the Mok leaders who campaigned against the cult had used calling in the government only as a threat of last resort. But now, with the cult over—or at least submerged for the time being—the newly extended council brought the Movement program into a closer relationship with the program of the administration.

Despite this, the program and goals of the Movement and of the government were still far from identical. To the Movement, the council was merely a component of the New Way. Movement participants and many people outside the Movement regarded establishing the council as administration recognition of the Movement and validation of Paliau's program rather than as a Movement concession to the administration. Several villages within the Movement were not yet included within the official council. The Movement villages, however, treated them as though, for all intents and purposes, they were under the official council umbrella.

After the rapid spread of the Movement in the aftermath of the Noise, it expanded beyond the villages that had welcomed it initially only to the villages of Sou and Lowa in the north and a segment of Papitalai (on Los Negros Island). But the advent of the official council caused some Manus people who had rejected the Movement to look on it more favourably. Encouraged by Kampo of Lahan, people from several inland Usiai villages that had refrained from joining the Movement began to visit Bunai frequently to attend Movement meetings. Those Usiai people who were already involved with the Movement were gratified. For years non-Movement Usiai people had mocked them as cargoists and imitators of the Titan sea people, but now they were early adopters.

The council expands again and Paliau maintains his hold

In 1962 a separate official council was established on the north coast. Paliau was considerably less popular there than in southern Manus. A large portion of Manus people on the north coast and in western Manus had remained loyal to the Catholic and Evangelical missions. Many of these northerners were suspicious of the administration's council program because they identified it with Paliau, the outspoken iconoclast. Also, as we noted in Chapter 10, enmity born of north coast memory of south coast raiding might also have been in play. Nevertheless, in 1962 the administration finally established a council embracing the north coast and the rest of Manus not included in the Baluan Council. A few years later, the administration sought to combine the two councils (Otto 1991: 186). By January 1966, all the villages to be included had agreed to the plan—not always, however, with unmitigated enthusiasm (Otto 1991: 186–7).

Paliau was elected president of this new council, one that comprised the entire Manus District. Otto (1991: 169–81), Dalsgaard (2009), and Rasmussen (2015) all provide details of the political manoeuvrings surrounding this election. It was undoubtedly critical that even though Paliau's reputation outside the Movement area was mixed, he probably enjoyed more name recognition than other candidates for the post. For our purposes it is enough to know that despite this Paliau had to navigate choppy political waters, but he did so successfully. The geographic sphere of his official authority now stretched far beyond the bounds of the Movement and he would soon augment his authority again.

Paliau in the House of Assembly

Australia's trusteeship agreement with the United Nations required it to move Papua and New Guinea towards independence as a single nation but it provided no timetable. In the event, the Territory moved relatively rapidly and peacefully towards the independence achieved in 1975.[1] Steps along the way included creating, in 1951, a legislative body embracing the entire Territory. The Legislative Council, as it was called, included three indigenous members appointed by the government, but non-indigenous members (elected or appointed from among Australian residents in the Territory) predominated. An expanded Legislative Council, instituted in 1961, included a larger number of indigenous members (seven, three of whom were elected), but non-indigenous members still held the reins (Griffin et al. 1979: 131).

The majority of the Territory's indigenous population was in no hurry for independence. There was widespread fear that Australia would withdraw all material assistance and that an indigenous government would be unable to prevent a return to the omnidirectional warfare and raiding of the indigenous past; that people would 'go back to the spear', as some indigenes put it. Schwartz found cautious optimism among

---

1   In the account of the political context of Paliau's advance to the House of Assembly that follows, we rely on Griffin et al. (1979), which is still the best concise history of early political development in PNG.

most Manus people, but among some who held fast to millenarian hopes there was wishful speculation that independence would somehow move the people of the Territory one step closer to the coming of the cargo. But neither people's fears nor their millenarian hopes moderated the activism of the growing number of well-educated Papuans and New Guineans who felt ready to take on the responsibility of independence. This small indigenous elite kept steady pressure on Australia to hasten independence, and Australian domestic political contingencies and the continuing scrutiny of the United Nations magnified the influence of pro-independence activists.[2]

In 1964, the Australian administration held a Territory-wide election for four-year terms in a House of Assembly. This body would replace the Legislative Council and wield greater authority. All Territory residents aged over 21 years were eligible to vote. The voters returned indigenous representatives from most of the numerous electorates. *The Members of the House of Assembly*, a booklet issued in August 1964 by the Territory Department of Information and Extension Services, lists 38 indigenous members and 26 non-indigenous members. Ten of the latter occupied 'Special' seats, reserved for non-indigenous candidates, and 10 were 'Official' members, appointed by the administration. Colin Hughes (1965: 36–7) records that during planning the structure of the House, the majority of indigenous people interviewed by a government planning committee said they wanted Australian members in the body. They gave a variety of reasons, but the most common was (as summarised by the planning committee): 'non-indigenes, by nature of their greater experience and higher education, can act as a source of information and advice and guidance for indigenous members, more especially in economic development, trade and business matters'.

Some, both indigenes and outside observers, found the move to a House of Assembly premature. Griffin et al. (1979: 134) observe that 'few of the Papua New Guinean elected members had any formal education beyond primary school, some were illiterate, and most were not fluent in English'. But Australia and the international monitors of its United Nations Trusteeship found a slower pace unacceptable. There were in fact many men of considerable energy and accomplishment among the indigenous members, even if national government was new to them. Several would

---

2   See Griffin et al. (1979) for an extended discussion of the complexities of PNG's path to independence. See also John Waiko (2007), *A Short History of Papua New Guinea*.

go on to play major roles in Papua New Guinea (PNG) politics up to and after independence.[3] (Although women were not barred from seeking office, all the members of the first House were men.)

Paliau defeated five other candidates for Member for the Manus Open Electorate and took his seat in the first House in 1964. He was one of the oldest indigenous members and among several with little or no formal education and limited command of English, but he could boast many accomplishments. One would not learn this, however, from his biographical paragraph in *The Members of the House of Assembly*. He is described as follows: 'Reads Pidgin. [As English speakers called Tok Pisin in the 1960s.] A subsistence farmer who for some years has been deeply involved in local government. President Baluan Local Government Council 1955–63. [By this time, the Native Government Councils had been rechristened Local Government Councils.] Member District Advisory Council 1955–63. Active supporter of Girl Guides, Scouting and Women's Clubs movements at Lorengau. Has been very active promoting development in all forms in the Council area'.[4]

This is a pale reflection of the Paliau readers have met in these pages. There is no mention of his high rank in the police. Perhaps Paliau associated this period in his life with the ignominy of his trial for war crimes. Neither is there any mention of the Paliau Movement, let alone Margaret Mead's 1956 book celebrating the Movement and its founder. These latter parts of his past, of course, might not have endeared him to some Australian members or even to some indigenous members. But it is impossible to know if Paliau deliberately bowdlerised his biography or if someone else simply did a poor job of reporting.

We have limited information on Paliau's activity during his first term in the House of Assembly, but what we know indicates that he was more engaged than most of his indigenous peers. Paul van der Veur's (1965) detailed account of the first two meetings of the House, in June and September 1964, indicates that Paliau participated actively and articulately in a number of debates. Van der Veur (1965: 483–5) provides the following

3   Among them, Paul Lapun, Pita Lus, Lepani Watson, Sinake Giregire, John Guise, Matthias Toliman, and Peter Simogen.
4   District Advisory Councils, chaired by district commissioners, were instituted in the 1940s. Commissioners selected the advisory council members. Initially, members were selected from among districts' non-indigenous residents, but indigenous residents became eligible in the mid-1950s. Indigenous members dominated the councils by the mid-1960s (Moore 2003: 197). Curiously, to the best of our knowledge, Paliau seldom if ever mentioned his membership of this body in public.

example: John Pasquarelli, Member for the Angoram Open Electorate (and an Australian resident of the Territory), spoke at some length against giving mission-owned commercial enterprises tax exemptions. He also 'charged that there was a serious discrepancy between the money earned and spent by some of the missions in the Territory'. This aroused heated responses to the effect that Pasquarelli was attacking the missions in general and the Catholic Mission in particular and that he had failed to take into account the beneficial work of the missions. Van der Veur observes that 'only Paliau Maloat reflected a different opinion' and reports this exchange between Paliau, who displays great aplomb, and an Australian member (Donald Barrett, Special Member—that is, occupant of a seat reserved for non-indigenes—for West Gazelle), who displays no aplomb:

> MR. PALIAU MALOAT: I think that some members have misinterpreted what he [Pasquarelli] said.
>
> INTERJECTION (speaker not identified): Hear, hear!
>
> MR. PALIAU MALOAT: I did not hear him say that the missions in this Territory should be done away with or that they are not doing good work.
>
> MR. BARRETT: You were not listening!
>
> MR. PALIAU MALOAT: (continuing) I heard what he said. He spoke about finding another way to raise extra revenue for Papua and New Guinea. He said that all the men and women and all the companies and businesses in this Territory should be subject to taxation. He asked why the missions are not paying tax, but I do not think that he said anything against the work of the missions. All he did was to ask that question and if his speech was misinterpreted, a great deal of trouble could result.

Van der Veur then comments: 'It is hoped that the foregoing account has provided some indication of Member participation in the Budget debate. Only a relatively small number of Papuan-New Guinean Members have been referred to and this reflects the fact that the others limited their comments mainly or exclusively to parochial requests'.

In 1964, Schwartz heard Paliau speak to the people of Bunai about his early days in the House. Paliau told villagers about arriving in Port Moresby and being taken to stay in a hotel, where he and other members shared bath and toilet facilities down the hall. And he reveals a humbling experience in a House session. He had complained in a speech that other places in the Territory were getting money for roads and boats but Manus was receiving nothing. How could Manus people get their copra and other crops to market without roads or boat service, he asked? But he then told with great candour how, in reply, another member asked him how many tons of copra or other products Manus people were ready to transport to Lorengau. Paliau told villagers that he had to concede that member's point, for he knew that Manus people were producing very little for the market. But from this interval of humility in front of his constituents Paliau segues to a more familiar hectoring mode, admonishing his listeners to get moving and start planting cash crops so they can demonstrate the need for roads and sea transport.[5]

In his conversations with Schwartz at the time, Paliau seemed very knowledgeable about the rules and procedures of the House and the structure of the government, offering coherent opinions on their pros and cons. He also made virtually no mention of theological issues. Regarding policy, Paliau appeared preoccupied with schools, medical aid posts, and economic development—as he put it, 'making money; in English they call it the economy' (in Paliau's Tok Pisin: '*rot bilong mani; long Inglis ol i kolim ikonomi*').

Paliau did not abandon his church during these years, but he generally refrained from saying anything that might imply that the work of secular government conflicted with the work of God. We know that at times he spoke of them as separate endeavours. At a village worship service during the House recess prior to Christmas in 1964, Paliau showed irritation with the tax-exempt status of the foreign missions, declaring: 'Jesus didn't say "Oh, I am the son of God, I don't need to pay taxes"'. And a few minutes later he opined that opposing the government was not the way of God: 'Satan ruined Adam and Eve and hence all of us. It is Satan who incites us to revolt against governments and kings'.

Paliau ran for president of the district-wide Manus Council again in 1967, midway through his first term in the House. But now he was competing with members of a new generation who had lived lives very different from his. Michael Pondros, a south coast man about half Paliau's age, won the seat. Pondros held a minor clerical job with the administration in Lorengau, but he had completed several years of schooling, served in the

---

5   Of course, there is a common rural development dilemma here. An ideal but difficult to implement policy would coordinate increases in production or productive capacity (such as planting crops that need time to mature) with commensurate improvements in market access.

Australian Navy for some 10 years, and been president of the still-new Manus Workers Association. Indigenous candidates for the second House were generally more highly educated than the candidates for the first House. This kind of political competition was a sign of things to come; but they hadn't arrived quite yet for Paliau. He kept his seat in the House in the 1968 election with a 'comfortable majority' (Otto 1991: 189).

Candidates for the second House not only tended to be better educated, they purveyed more specific policy ideas. Prior to the election for the second House—which was seated in 1968—another new dimension also entered Territory politics: political parties. The members of the first House had not run on party platforms and once elected they concerned themselves mostly with obtaining better economic and social infrastructure for their constituencies rather than with national policies. In 1967, an alliance of Australian House members, indigenous House members, and indigenous members of the public service—the latter including future prime minister Michael Somare—formed PNG's first political party: the Pangu (an acronym for Papua and New Guinea Union) Pati. It had a lean but comparatively radical platform in which pushing for more rapid progress towards 'home rule' was the main item (cf. Griffin et al. 1979: 134). According to Stephen Pokawin (1976: 407), Paliau's position was that the Territory should move towards 'self-government' as quickly as possible so that its people would have time to learn how to govern themselves before full independence. This was, in fact, the route taken. The Territory became self-governing in 1973, two years before independence; that is, Australia ceded government of internal affairs to the House of Assembly, while maintaining control of foreign policy.

But in 1967 Pangu was considered radical. Initially, Paliau hesitated to declare himself. Discussing Territory politics with Schwartz, he spoke of Pangu with enthusiasm, but he also told Schwartz that some Australian members had been pressuring him and other indigenous members to reject not only Pangu but also the whole idea of party politics in the House.

Ultimately, Paliau resisted such pressure and became known as a Pangu adherent (Pokawin 1976: 407). In 1973, reflecting on his years in the House, he spoke proudly to Schwartz of his affiliation with this pioneering party: 'I was a strong supporter of Pangu … [In the House] I supported whatever Pangu proposed'. (In Paliau's Tok Pisin: '*Mi nambawan tru strongpela man tru bilong dispela Pangu Pati … mi save sapotim wanem samting sapos Pangu em i tok longen'*.)[6] Paliau also claimed close association with Michael Somare, noting that he worked with Somare on developing standards for citizenship in the new nation-to-be.

We know nothing else significant about Paliau's activities in the House of Assembly during his second term. We do know that he was receiving substantial recognition outside both the House and even the Territory. The Territory being part of the British Commonwealth, Paliau was awarded an OBE—that is, he was granted the title Officer of the Civil Division of the Most Excellent Order of the British Empire—in April 1970, with the citation: 'Former president Baluan Local Government Council, for service to local government' (Otto 1991: 291n38). He was invited to speak in May 1970 at the Fourth Waigani Seminar, a conference at the University of Papua New Guinea (established in 1965 in Waigani, a suburb of Port Moresby) where some 50 PNG public figures and scholars from a number of countries discussed 'The Politics of Melanesia'. In his contribution, as reported in the massive proceedings of the event (Ward et al. 1970: 144–61), Paliau presents a picture of his career and his present political stance apparently crafted especially for the Waigani audience. The account of his life is much the same as that he first gave Schwartz, with some additional details about his police service, but he does not mention his dream experiences during the war. He does not omit his trial for collaboration with the Japanese, but he treats it as a minor affair. What he says of the period we call the early Movement includes an account of building a meeting house on Baluan and gathering people to hear him speak about how heeding his teachings and honouring God will help bring PNG the proper kind of government.[7]

---

6   Otto (1991: 237) cites Tony Voutas, an Australian member of the House of Assembly from 1966 to 1972 and one of three Australians among the founders of Pangu, to the effect that Paliau was not at the centre of Pangu activities although he did attend many Pangu meetings.

7   He also speaks of collecting a substantial amount of money from Manus people in the 'Paliau Maloat Fund' in 1947—funds he says eventually underwrote the Local Government Council, schools, and so forth. This may be the money from war damage payments made to Manus people that Paliau encouraged them to pool. On occasion Paliau spoke of the pooled war damage payments as the basis for what he called the TENK Pati, an effort on his part (that appears to have been rather half-hearted or incompletely conceived) to form a political party associated with the Movement and the Baluan Native Christian Church. He explained to Schwartz that the name was taken from the first letters of the common names of four groups in Manus. The T stood for Titan, and the N stood for Nali, one of the Usiai groups sharing a distinct language, from which Paliau had drawn considerable support. Unfortunately, our only record of this conversation is an audio tape in which the terms from which the E and the K in TENK are inaudible. All we know of the activity of the TENK Pati is that on its behalf Paliau encouraged people in each Manus village to pool money from war damage payments. Paliau never registered the TENK Pati officially and we don't believe that Paliau ever identified himself as a TENK Pati member in any electoral campaign.

Four other documents are appended to the text of Paliau's presentation without editorial comment: a letter of uncertain date and without a specified audience announcing that he has founded the Baluan Christian Church 'to bring the good life to the people of Manus by teaching them to channel their thoughts about God to God'; a second such letter announcing, among other things, that the aim of the early Movement was to lead the people of Manus to become an 'independent state' with 'internal democratic government'; a statement addressed to the House of Assembly, dated 1966, requesting that the Manus Local Government Council be put in charge of all funds allocated to the Manus District and permitted to take over the work of the district administration; and a 1970 statement—with no specified audience—that the Manus people strongly supported the advent by 1972 of 'home rule and Self Government' for PNG.

In 1970, Paliau was on a roll. Having addressed the gathering at the University of Papua New Guinea in May, in June he travelled to Santa Cruz, California, United States, where he had been invited to take part in a scholarly conference on the Bismarck Archipelago (an area in the Bismarck Sea encompassing most of the PNG islands north-east of the PNG mainland, including the Admiralty Islands) organised by the university's Centre for South Pacific Studies. Of the 20-some participants, all aside from Paliau were scholars from American, Australian, Canadian, and European universities and the University of Papua New Guinea.[8] Schwartz (then on the faculty at the University of California, San Diego) was invited as an expert on the Admiralties. Although a number of the invited scholars spoke Tok Pisin, Schwartz—the only attendee personally acquainted with Paliau—also served as Paliau's interpreter. (How Paliau's invitation came about is lost to memory at this point. Schwartz recalls only that he did not issue the invitation.)[9]

---

[8] According to the newsletter of the Association for Social Anthropology in Oceania, IV, November 1970, the other invited participants were Dorothy Billings, Wichita State University; Ann Chowning, University of Papua New Guinea; David Counts, University of Waterloo; Dorothy Counts, University of Waterloo; Philip J.C. Dark, Southern Illinois University; A.L. Epstein, Australian National University; T.S. Epstein, Australian National University; Frederick Errington, Cornell University; Michael Freedman, Syracuse University; Adrian Gerbrands, Rijksuniversiteit te Leiden; Thomas Harding, University of California, Santa Barbara; Jane Goodale, Bryn Mawr College; Ward Goodenough, University of Pennsylvania; Peter Lomas, Simon Fraser University; Michael Panoff, Australian National University; Francoise Panoff, Australian National University; Richard Salisbury, McGill University; James Specht, Australian National University; and Peter White, University of California, Berkeley.

[9] We are not sure why Paliau was the lone Melanesian attending, although his connection with Margaret Mead—albeit a slight one, barring her description of him in *New Lives for Old*—may have been involved.

Figure 12.1: In 1970, Paliau spoke at a conference on the anthropology of the Bismarck Archipelago at the University of California, Santa Cruz.

After the conference he and Schwartz visited New York City, where Schwartz showed Paliau the sights and they relaxed in Central Park.

Source: Schwartz recruited an unidentified passer-by to take this photo with Schwartz's camera. Digital copy courtesy of the Archive for Melanesian Anthropology, University of California, San Diego.

At the conference Paliau again described his career and responded to questions, including queries about his opinions on the future of PNG. His answers were measured and in keeping with his role as a member of the House and a secular representative of his country. At conference social events he spoke at length with the other participants who were fluent in Tok Pisin. Schwartz recalls that Paliau seemed perfectly at ease. Following the five-day conference, Schwartz and Paliau travelled to New York City. Again, the genesis and sponsorship of this excursion are lost to memory.[10] Schwartz and Paliau lunched with Margaret Mead at the American Museum of Natural History and Mead took them on a short tour of the exhibits. But Schwartz and Paliau spent most of their time touring the city, with which Schwartz was familiar. Strolling the streets in neat sportscoats, slacks, white shirts, and neckties, Paliau and Schwartz looked

---

10   We know that Schwartz didn't pay for this trip, and it seems unlikely that Mead was so eager to see Paliau again that she would have done so, for they spent little time together in New York. It's possible that Barbara and Fred Roll, friends of Mead's who underwrote and took part in some of her work in Manus, footed the bill.

like two well-groomed members of the city's professional class taking a long spring lunch break. They visited the United Nations building and the New York Public Library and they idled in Central Park.

Paliau was curious and intrigued by much that he saw, but if he was greatly impressed he kept it to himself. Straggling, dusty, low-rise Port Moresby was not the limit of his previous urban experience. He had also visited Canberra, Australia, where new House members were taken for parliamentary education. In New York, Schwartz recalls that Paliau reacted most strongly to the dense throngs of people hurrying up into the daylight from subway exits: Paliau shook his head and remarked that it was too bad people had to live so tightly packed together.

Paliau's experiences in California and New York did not seem to affect his views on politics, society, and the larger nature of things in the deep way that his experiences had as a young man working for colonial foreigners, serving in the police, and surviving the war. We will see, however, that he was preparing to make use of them. If in New York Paliau was blasé, on returning to Manus he told his stories of the journey over and over again, with mixed effects, as described below.

Disputes and discontent

Paliau clearly enjoyed his international recognition but it did nothing to sustain the new way of living Paliau and the Movement were promoting in Manus. True, some novel institutions for which Paliau legitimately claimed Movement credit had been established, among them the producers and consumers cooperatives. Paliau had begun advocating cooperatives as early as 1953, before the administration began energetically promoting them. By the mid-1960s, fourteen had been established in Manus, most of them in Movement areas (Schwartz 1966–67: 36). But the cooperatives did not thrive. Carrier and Carrier (1989: 84) cite a 1972 report of a Committee of Inquiry on Cooperatives in Papua New Guinea that documents a decline in copra production and the failure of many Manus cooperatives throughout the 1960s. This was in part the result of increasing competition from individual traders in copra and shell, as well as an increase in the number of producers bypassing their local cooperatives to sell directly to the Copra Marketing Board (Otto 1991: 200). In analysing Manus cooperatives' striking rate of failure, Schwartz (1966–67) observes that the latter kind of individual endeavour probably appealed to the indigenous emphasis on status seeking but, he argues, despite this appeal, granting easy credit, failing to collect debts, and theft brought many cooperatives down.[11]

Money was coming into Manus villages in the 1960s, but the most conspicuous amounts came from young people—principally, young men—employed in PNG towns. Schwartz observed that, contrary to New Way principles, in Pere and other mostly Titan villages the largest part of such money was financing an efflorescence of affinal exchange.[12] Now, however, the valuables the groom's side gave were not made of shell, dogs' teeth, and beads. Rather, they were things that cost money, such as outboard motors, or money itself. The social significance of the exchanges had changed, too (Schwartz 1993: 526–7; cf. Schwartz 1976b; Otto 1991: 224–32).[13] But from the standpoint of the original aims of the Movement, the important and disappointing thing was that they took place at all, let alone frequently and extravagantly.

Some Manus people had charged Paliau with trying to use his position as council president to promote his Baluan Christian Church. But on returning to Manus in the 1960s, Schwartz found that absent Paliau's close attention, in many villages few people were attending services and many people had defected to foreign mission churches.

Such departures from the New Way did not necessarily mean people were disillusioned with Paliau the man, but some were angry with him. A major controversy concerning a boat owned by the council—intended for transport to and from Lorengau—erupted in the mid-1960s. The several accounts Schwartz received defy easy summary, but the essence was the charge that Paliau was chronically appropriating the boat for his own purposes. A second controversy also alienated some of Paliau's erstwhile strong supporters. This concerned land near Bunai to which Paliau claimed rights on the basis of a kinship tie, a claim which some influential

11   Otto (1991: 201–3) notes that while the Australian administration's economic development policy immediately after the war had stressed communal endeavours, by the late 1950s emphasis had shifted to encouraging 'individual' endeavours. He also observes correctly that 'the opposition between individual versus communal ownership grossly simplifies and even obscures the social reality of Manus land tenure', a misunderstanding on which many cash-cropping initiatives elsewhere in PNG have foundered.

12   Schwartz (1993: 526) describes the pressures on young men to contribute to these events.

13   People often substituted cash for indigenous valuables and construed exchanges as opportunities for those contributing consumable items to obtain large amounts of cash, even though much of this had to be redistributed to those who helped amass the consumables (Schwartz 1993: 527–8).

people contested vehemently. But, whatever his detractors' complaints, it would be hasty to conclude that Paliau was taking advantage of his position for material benefit. Schwartz saw that Paliau was living very simply, at least when he was on the Manus mainland. He had a single house on the south coast, in Bunai, but its floor was collapsing and it was not fit for habitation. Paliau and his wife, Teresia, lived nearby in two thatched shacks built directly on the ground (one probably reserved for cooking). The administration provided living quarters for members of the House in Port Moresby, but Paliau eschewed these, preferring to live in what were essentially the servants' quarters of the house of an Australian acquaintance from his days with the police force.

Only a few indigenous people were now nearer than Paliau to the heart of political authority in the Territory, but—like international recognition— it was not doing him much good at home. Nor did it give him much scope to *do* good at home in the short run. During his first term in the House, Paliau was among many members—indigenous and non-indigenous— who complained of the amount of money the government was spending in Port Moresby, at the expense, they charged, of the rural majority.[14] Speaking in a debate on this issue, Paliau opined: 'When we come to Port Moresby we are filled with dismay when we realize what a large amount of the money must be spent here … Does Port Moresby get everything in order that visitors from other countries may be impressed?' (van der Veur 1965: 481). His constituents would have applauded these words, but his constituents were prone to blame Paliau, not the central government, for neglecting their rural needs. Some years later (in 1975), explaining his defection from Paliau, one of his strongest early supporters was bitter: '[Paliau] said he should be the one to go to the House of Assembly and he'd be able to raise up all of Manus. But no, he deceived us!' Paliau may well have promised much more than he could deliver, but members of the House from poor rural areas faced entrenched problems not of their making. John Connell (1997: 222–6) observes that neglect of rural areas began in the colonial era. Australian rule left the indigenous economy largely intact, a circumstance that continues to contribute to the welfare of the rural majority who rely mostly on subsistence production. But the indigenous economy remained intact partly because the administration did little to extend modern infrastructure into rural areas. Granted, there were immense challenges to doing so. But Connell confirms that, as members

---

14   Rural Papua New Guineans make the same complaint today, usually with good reason.

of the House complained in 1964, the Australian administration concentrated public investment in urban and more accessible rural areas and directed development programs to regions and individuals already having greater success in the changing economy.

Failure to finesse

However plausible or implausible Paliau may have found the doctrines of the Noise or other cargo cults, he had wisely kept his distance from prophecies of imminent fulfilment. It was probably harder for him to exercise equal finesse as he sought a role in the emerging indigenous government of the Territory. People's expectations of approaching self-government and independence were mixed, but those seeking office would have had to promise that these changes would improve people's lives. As described above, however, it is hard to see how any member of the House could have come close to fulfilling people's more optimistic hopes.

In seeking to bolster his image in Manus, although he stayed clear of promises of imminent supernatural transformation, Paliau at times leaned on his reputation for chumminess with occult powers. During their visit to New York City, Schwartz photographed Paliau on the steps of the grand old New York Public Library, showing in the background the elevated frieze of elegant, classically draped female figures. Back in Manus in later years, a number of people told Schwartz that Paliau had shown them the picture and told them that the figures were angels, and that they had only appeared in the picture when Schwartz developed it. Lungat of Ndriol, still a Paliau loyalist, insisted to Schwartz that Paliau had shown people the picture but some viewers had drawn their own fantastic conclusions. A number of others, however, contradicted Lungat's account, and a few reported that Paliau had made other fantastic claims about events during the trip. For instance, some told Schwartz that Paliau had said that in America he had met with the Queen of England, the Pope, and Jesus. While some allegedly believed him and concluded that— as one debunker put it—'*God i stap tru longen*' (that is, God is truly with Paliau), others would have no truck with such claims. Prenis Paliau told Schwartz that many people thought Paliau was lying and lost their faith in his credentials as a holy person. Prenis Paliau certainly did, for it was in the early 1970s that he left Paliau's church, affiliated with the Evangelical Lutheran Church, and helped form an Evangelical congregation in Bunai.

Paliau's ability to subtly integrate wholly temporal leadership with leadership claiming a sanction more exalted than the ballot box seemed to be slipping. In 1975, Tjolai of Mok told Schwartz of an incident that had helped turn him against Paliau. Tjolai said that he too had been thinking of running for a seat in the first House of Assembly and he had made no secret of it. But Paliau invoked divine authority to discourage him. Said Tjolai: 'One day I mentioned this, and the next day Paliau came to see me. He said that Jesus himself had come to him and told him that Tjolai shouldn't run. And [Paliau said] that God had said he wanted Paliau to run'. Tjolai found this way too self-serving and improbable. 'It made me angry. You understand?', he told Schwartz. 'Now I really saw his bullshit. I thought he was a liar and that some of the things he'd told us before weren't true either.' Soon thereafter, Tjolai joined Prenis Paliau in defecting to the Evangelical Lutheran Church.

But although Tjolai wondered aloud if Paliau had never been trustworthy, in other remarks both he and Prenis Paliau said in effect that the real problem was that Paliau had abandoned his own early teachings. In the 1970s, these men and a number of others began speaking to Schwartz more openly than they previously had of their perceptions of the relationship between the Noise and the Movement's secular program. A common theme was that Paliau had always advocated pursuing 'two roads'. One was '*wok bilong skin*'—that is, 'work of the body' or projects to improve people's material welfare using secular means. The other was the work of restoring the Paradise of the First Order of God, aka the Number One Order. This latter called for, among other things, taking good care of cemeteries and their occupants (in Tok Pisin, *lukautim gut ol matmat … nau ol man i dai*). Paliau, they said, instructed people that they could reveal only the former, secular activities to representatives of the administration. This is not to say that Paliau instigated the Noise—which our data suggest was not the case—but it was consonant with Paliau's habit of keeping all options open as long as possible.

To the disgust of apostates like Prenis Paliau, Paliau Maloat had turned his back on the two roads policy and devoted himself entirely to business and electoral politics. Others also, said Prenis, had followed Paliau's example; only a few were left who truly sought the First Order. This blighted the present as well as the future, they lamented, for in the days of the early Movement—both before and after the Noise—people had both felt and seen the First Order's nearness. In those days, people said, Paliau could control the wind and the rain, but that wasn't all. God's blessings flowed for everyone when they kept their minds right. As Lukas of Mok told Schwartz in 1954 (also quoted in Chapter 6): 'We tried to live with only good *tingting*. At this time, when we worked according to good *tingting* exclusively, the Noise had not come yet, but everything came easy for us'.

Nostalgia for that time of wonder was still very much alive in some Manus circles in the 1970s. Paliau had told them, some people recalled wistfully, that if they all concentrated on God and didn't let their minds wander, life would be easy. But Paliau had changed; he no longer seemed to care about the First Order and life was once more difficult. Tjolai of Mok said to Schwartz: 'Ah, Ted! I saw it. It was true. But when we got the council and began to change things, when we turned away from talk of God and took up the work of the government instead, everything went wrong.'[15]

Losing an election

As the election for the third House approached many people had reasons to be disappointed with Paliau. Some thought he could be making better use of his secular power to improve their material welfare and some thought he had sacrificed extra-human assistance in bringing about a better world by relying too much on secular power. But at this time, even if he wasn't above claiming God's endorsement to discourage competition, Paliau was deeply committed to making the most of his position in the new political system. This was where he invested his energy and this is the public image he cultivated most avidly. Schwartz observed that when back in Manus after the close of the first House, Paliau always appeared in public with a briefcase—something rarely seen even today in rural PNG. And he was always accompanied by an assistant—a Baluan man—who carried the briefcase for him, sitting silently behind Paliau during meetings.

It is hard to isolate the reasons any candidate loses any close election. Six candidates vied for Member for the Manus Open Electorate in 1972, but only Michael Pondros, Peter Pomat, and Paliau proved serious contenders. Pondros won, with Pomat a close second, and Paliau trailing somewhat behind them both. Did Paliau squander his advantage as an incumbent? As noted above, it appears that he did his best to represent Manus in the House, but he could not satisfy what may have been exaggerated

---

15   We'll see in the next chapter that Paliau's extra-human powers and the former Days of Wonder are potent themes in the ideology of Wind Nation.

expectations. He may also have neglected to keep his constituents in touch with his efforts to do so. Otto (1991: 188) cites Manus District annual reports (submitted to the Territory administration by the Manus District administration) to the effect that Paliau strove to represent all parts of Manus and when the House was in recess he returned to tour his district. But Pokawin (1976: 407) states that after the 1964 election Paliau visited only the villages that had supported him since 1946, thus neglecting some three-quarters of Manus villages, and established no mechanism for communicating with all of Manus.

Paliau also drew organised opposition. He had antagonised the Catholic Mission from the beginning of his career: he was worse than a heretic, he was a successful heretic. Most of his followers were former Catholics, 3,500 of whom the church excommunicated in the late 1940s (Otto 1991: 175). Naturally, many mission personnel spoke against him at every opportunity. According to Lola Romanucci-Ross (1985: 137), during the 1964 election, Catholic missionaries 'openly excoriated Paliau and ... asked the North Coast, at least, to vote against him'. Doubtless, mission personnel exerted their influence against him among their loyalists in 1972 as well. Paliau also drew sectarian opposition from another quarter. Pokawin (1976: 408) reports that in Paliau's 1972 campaign he emphasised his connection with the Baluan Native Christian Church, which many people at that time were more likely to call the Paliau Church. This may have hurt him in some areas but—ironically—in others, there were voters who thought he had neglected this connection too much. Pita Tapo of Lahan was marginal to the secular aspect of the Movement, but he had remained a strong adherent of its millenarian tendencies and outgrowths. Trompf (1991: 223–4) reports that at the time of the campaign for seats in the third House, Tapo had several hundred followers in south-east Manus and he sought to turn them against Paliau by accusing him of turning his back on his (that is, Paliau's) own creation, the Baluan Native Christian Church.

When in 1973 Schwartz discussed the 1972 election with him, Paliau knew whence in Manus the various candidates had drawn most of their support. He knew that his solid following had split, even within villages; he speculated that the number of candidates might have split voting blocs that might have supported him; and he said that Pondros had drawn much of the Catholic vote. Paliau also probably understood that the many changes in Manus secular politics in his lifetime—to which he had contributed—were leaving him behind. Up through the establishment of the official councils, Paliau had been almost synonymous with indigenous Manus efforts to take greater control of their own lives, and—as the first member representing Manus—he had managed to put his mark on the House of Assembly as well. But by 1972, as Otto (1991: 190) puts it: 'The government institutions he had helped to create were strongly established and were no longer dependent on his prestige'.

Another hard blow

Paliau was to suffer one more blow to his career in secular politics: establishment of a new level of political organisation between the local government councils and the district governments.[16] In every district— except tiny Manus—there was more than one council (each overseeing a number of villages, each with its own village councillor). In 1972, groups of councils in each district were combined under Area Authorities intended to coordinate the councils' activities. Because Manus had only one council its duties overlapped with those of the Area Authority. This was confusing.[17] But it gave Paliau an opportunity. Recall that in 1967, he had lost his position as president of the Manus Local Government Council (expanded successor to the Baluan Native Government Council).[18] But he remained the councillor of his home village, Lipan-Mok, and as such he was eligible for a role in the Area Authority. He obviously still had political resources, for his fellow village councillors chose him as one of eight of their number to serve on the Area Authority and these councillors then supported Paliau's successful bid to become first chairperson of the Area Authority.

Paliau told Schwartz in 1975 that he had argued that the Area Authority and the council should work more closely together, perhaps even combine. This doesn't seem unreasonable in a one-council district. But other members of the Area Authority may have seen Paliau as simply trying to enhance his own authority. Whatever the reason, a majority of the Area Authority voted in 1973 to remove Paliau as both chair and member of

16 We rely on Otto (1991: 188–90) for our information on this development.
17 Otto (1991: 189n5, 189n6) quotes Territory government statements that attempted to untangle this awkward situation, but failed.
18 The 1963 Local Government Ordinance permitted non-indigenous residents to stand for seats on district councils. By 1999, 111 of the 142 councils in the Territory were 'multiracial' in practice. This had no effect we know of on Paliau's career, but it stirred controversy in other parts of the Territory (Moore 2003: 197).

the body. Otto (1991: 189–90) cites a letter from Paliau's successor as chair of the Baluan Council, Mr J. Maiah, regarding this development: 'The only reason [for Paliau's ouster] is that most councilors said that Mr. Maloat used his position as Chairman of the Area Authority to convince the village people that he is the only big boss in the district and [he] also interfered with other councilors' wards'.[19] It is not surprising that Paliau, as he later confided to Schwartz, didn't agree with this assessment. The most he would say about this event was that the ringleaders of the coup acted out of their envy of Paliau's status.

Paliau was ousted from the Area Authority in June 1973. Within the month, Schwartz arrived in Manus again, where—on Baluan—he would find Paliau beaten down by circumstances in a way Schwartz had never seen before. Yet even now, at the nadir of his public career, Paliau was contemplating a new way to employ his abilities.

---

19 Technically, local councillors represent not villages but wards, and a ward can embrace more than one named and populated place within a village or only a part of such a place. This helps adjust for the fact that in PNG in general people do not always consider a named residential locale, even one that looks geographically distinct to an outsider, as a separate village, and some places recognised as single villages are dispersed geographically and are exceptionally large.

13

The road to Wind Nation

As Paliau's career in electoral politics came to a close, the Paliau Movement gave rise to the Study Group. This quickly became the Manus Kastam Kansol, usually shortened to Makasol, and Makasol became Wind Nation, the name under which the Movement persists today. From the mid-1950s to the early 1980s, Schwartz was the only anthropological observer, but beginning in the mid-1980s other researchers began to gather data on the Paliau phenomenon. We cannot do justice to all of their work, but we will draw on it when it casts light on the issues that concern us most. Chief among these are the dramatic shift in the Movement's attention to almost wholly millenarian concerns; the role in the Movement from the late 1970s onwards of a number of educated young men with considerable experience in modern institutions, who became Paliau's acolytes; and how Movement leaders managed relationships with the rank and file as the Movement became Wind Nation. We begin, however, by visiting Paliau at the nadir of his career, but poised to enter public life again on new terms.

After the Fall: Paliau in 1973

For several years after his long stay in the Territory in the 1960s, Schwartz followed Paliau's career from a distance. He next returned to Manus from June through September 1973 to pursue research on matters unrelated to the Paliau Movement. He also, of course, wanted to see what Paliau was doing. Schwartz knew Paliau was living on Baluan, but his research agenda required that he and his three assistants (Michael French Smith, Edwin Hutchins, and Geoffrey White) spend several weeks in Pere village and in Lorengau before reaching Baluan in early September.

Schwartz had heard that Paliau was not well. One of Paliau's strongest and most reliable supporters, Lungat of Ndriol, visited Schwartz in Lorengau in August. Lungat told Schwartz that Paliau's political failures had left him despondent and sickly and he asked Schwartz to do his best to help him: 'You can visit him, and maybe seeing and talking with you will help him think good thoughts again'.

Schwartz and his party travelled from Lorengau to Baluan in early September on a motorised outrigger canoe packed tight with passengers and stacked high with goods from town, including several drums of fuel for Baluan boats and generators. They arrived late one afternoon, thoroughly cold and wet after travelling through a heavy storm at sea. Two of Paliau's associates led them to their quarters, a house originally built for resident Australian colonial officers and their families. The amenities those residents had enjoyed—including a shower and a flush toilet fed by a rainwater collection tank on the corrugated metal roof—no longer functioned. But the house was dry, spacious, and almost mosquito free.

The next morning, Schwartz found Paliau and his wife, Teresia, living in an ordinary village house that bore no marks of distinction. Wearing a *laplap* rather than trousers and white shirt, Paliau looked grey and thin. He apologised to Schwartz for his appearance and explained that for many weeks he had been staying in the house, feeling weak. His debility, he said, had started after he was ousted from the Area Authority, but other events also depressed his spirits. He mentioned the land dispute in Bunai and the controversy over management of the council boat. But he was most disturbed because, he said, people weren't following the New Way anymore. They weren't working together or meeting together to discuss village matters and many were putting big money into affinal exchanges. Some were also leaving the Baluan Native Christian Church to go back to the Catholics or to join an evangelical Protestant church: 'I created all this 30 years ago, but now they are abandoning it', Paliau told Schwartz.

Over the following weeks, Schwartz visited Paliau almost every day. Responding to Schwartz's interest, Paliau gradually stopped bemoaning his present circumstances and began to sound like a man looking ahead. For decades Schwartz had managed to remain a deeply interested observer of Paliau's career without either endorsing or opposing his endeavours. But the hours he spent with the ailing and discouraged man that September and Paliau's obvious appreciation affected him deeply. Paliau was in his mid-60s, an advanced age for a man in rural Papua New Guinea (PNG), and Schwartz couldn't be sure he would ever see him again. He visited Paliau late into the night the day before he and his party left Baluan. Responding to Paliau's effusive thanks for his visit, Schwartz found himself giving Paliau a pep talk. The following exchange is translated from the Tok Pisin in which they conversed:

> Paliau: It was just worry that caused this bad illness of mine. But now my mind is clearer and I'm feeling my strength come back. Ted, you can see that I'm better now. You're the reason for this, Ted.
>
> Schwartz: Somewhere you learned how to be a leader. People hear you and people follow you. A lot of other people, they may have good ideas, but they don't have what it takes to lead a village or to bring people together. A leader is a special thing. It isn't something you can learn in school; it's something about the kind of person you are.
>
> Paliau: Ted, what you say is true.

So, Schwartz encouraged Paliau to get moving again. But he couldn't anticipate the direction Paliau would take. He got a clue, however, on a day of special events Paliau arranged just before the Schwartz party left. It was immediately apparent that Paliau still wielded at least local influence because it looked like most of the combined village of Lipan-Mok had turned out. By midday, young people were playing soccer and volleyball on a large open field adjacent to Paliau's house, while men assembled a long banquet table and women and girls piled it high with food. Later, Schwartz and his assistants were ushered to the table, where a number of village leaders (all men) joined them. After the meal, a party of school children in contemporary versions of traditional dress sang songs in English, Tok Pisin, and the Baluan language, and a few senior men made short speeches. When it was time to leave the table, someone told the American guests to stay close by because there was more to come.

Figure 13.1: In 1973, Paliau surprised Schwartz by dancing in full traditional regalia at an event in Lipan-Mok village, Baluan.

On this visit to Baluan, Schwartz heard from Paliau early inklings of Wind Nation ideology, including ideas that glorified an idealised past that contrasted sharply with the Movement's earlier harsh criticism of many precolonial practices.

Source: Geoffrey White.

What came was a surprise. Paliau and Teresia came out of their house in colourful indigenous regalia: multilayered and multicoloured fibre skirts, strings of shell beads draped across their chests, and decorated headbands. They walked, dignified and erect, to the centre of the field. Garamut drummers began pounding out a staccato rhythm, punctuated by sudden stops and abrupt starts. The couple positioned themselves and began to dance, stopping and starting their sequences of stiff but athletic movements in perfect synchrony with the drummers. During Paliau's seclusion, Teresia had continued to garden, gather firewood, cook, and care for the house, so it was not surprising to see that she was strong and fit—if also a bit worn from the excess of daily physical work that falls to women in rural PNG. Paliau was thin and wrinkled, but he danced with impressive vigour, belying Schwartz's earlier impression of someone physically weak and emotionally low.

We may have witnessed that day the inaugural event of Paliau's comeback. Paliau was showing Lipan-Mok that people from distant parts of the world still regarded him as important and that he had the energy to lead again. Recall, too, that he regarded his failure in a traditional ceremonial performance in his youth as a formative incident. On that day in 1973, however, he performed skilfully and proudly.

Seeking a new direction

Schwartz didn't see Paliau again until 1975. By then, Paliau had moved from Baluan to Lorengau. He looked healthy, but in conversation he focused on rehashing the details of his electoral career. Both in Lorengau and in Pere, Schwartz also spoke at length with several men who had been among Paliau's closest allies but had abandoned him (some of whom we met in the previous chapter), and they too harped on the past. Although Schwartz noticed a few younger men among the small group attending Paliau in Lorengau, it would have been easy to assume that Paliau, almost 70 years old now, was slowing to a halt.

But Schwartz had known Paliau too long to jump to that conclusion. In December 1978, Schwartz was back in Manus again, where Paliau was still settled in Lorengau, but eager this time to talk about the future. The country was still under the leadership of its first prime minister, Michael Somare, with whom Paliau had served in the pre-independence House of Assembly. Schwartz asked Paliau his opinion of the current government and Paliau said he approved of it and its efforts to help people find ways to earn money. That's what people needed now, he said. But Paliau spoke more passionately about his own ideas for the government of Manus and what he now advocated sounded like theocracy with a dash of cultural revival. He would soon begin openly promoting such an agenda but he was still reluctant to speak of it to Schwartz with full candour.

Paliau told Schwartz that Manus should be governed by a Lapan Assembly, although he didn't expand on the nature of such a body. (Recall that *lapan* is the Titan word for a person of high rank.) Further, Manus should aspire to 'Government of the Holy Spirit' so that 'later, the kingdom will come'. Schwartz, hearing this from Paliau for the first time, asked if it was a new dimension of the teachings of his church, but Paliau replied that it was nothing new. Schwartz suggested that some people might think that Government of the Holy Spirit sounded like a cargo cult. Paliau said that he didn't believe in cargo cults and that '*samting em i no kamap nating*'— that is, you can't get anything for nothing.[1] Anyway, he said, people would know what he meant and what most people wanted was to grow copra and coffee and send their children to school and that is what he meant by '*kingdom i kam*'. Schwartz was not easily put off and suggested again that this kind of language would remind people of the Noise. Paliau replied only that Muli had died in 1976 and 'his work [that is, the Noise] is completely over' (*wok bilongen i pinis ologeta*).

Schwartz was accustomed to Paliau responding to questions with artful ambiguity, but on this occasion Paliau sounded less intentionally ambiguous than a bit unsure of what he meant. If Paliau was losing confidence, he had reasons. He had helped create the new government, and he was well known to its famous leader, Michael Somare. But he had no prospects for a significant role in that government and the church he created was losing ground. But Paliau now had help pondering his next move. We are reasonably sure that up to the mid-1970s Paliau was the sole author of his teachings and programs. But by 1978 there was an entirely new influence on Paliau's thinking. One thing Paliau told Schwartz very clearly and proudly was that several young men with considerable schooling, even university degrees, and wide experience, including as high government officials, had become his close confidants.

1   Paliau must have known that '*samting em i no kamap nating*' can have more than one meaning. It can mean that everything takes physical effort; but it can also mean that no amount of physical effort avails without supernatural aid.

By the 1960s, many Paliau adherents had come of age almost entirely within the Movement, but too late to take advantage of the expanding access to schooling it helped bring about. Younger Manus generations, however, had been able to pursue formal education from childhood. By the 1970s, many of them were working throughout PNG as teachers, clerks, technicians, and functionaries of the government of an independent country. Schwartz had thought it unlikely that many members of younger, highly literate generations would find the Movement meaningful. He may have been right. We do not have data on the full range of attitudes towards Paliau and the Movement among those generations who went from village schools to high school, technical training, or university. We know, however, that in the mid to late 1970s a few such returned to Manus and became deeply involved in the Movement. Four became especially close to Paliau and important to the Movement. Their names will come up again, so we will introduce them now, in alphabetical order.

Peter Kuwoh rose to the rank of captain in the PNG Defence Force before returning to Manus in the late 1970s to live in Lorengau and work with Paliau. Paliau Lukas (aka Paliau Lukas Chauka) received bachelor of arts degrees in philosophy and economics from the University of Papua New Guinea and served as the first director of the Papua New Guinea Housing Commission (Wanek 1996: 180). On returning to Manus he became part-owner of a retail store in Lorengau—Edgell and Whiteley Pty Ltd—as well as a member of Paliau Maloat's inner circle. Martin Thompson Poposui was an attorney who served as legal officer for the Manus Provincial Government prior to devoting himself to the Movement (Wanek 1996: 167). Kisokau Pochapon received a bachelor of arts degree in surveying from the Papua New Guinea University of Technology and served as the first surveyor general of independent PNG. He resigned from that post in 1982 to campaign (unsuccessfully) for a seat in parliament from Manus on behalf of the Movement. He was born and raised in Mbukei (Pokawin 1989: 253), which was a Movement stronghold from the beginning and remains so. In 2015, he was living on Baluan, still playing a major role in the Movement, but he died the following year.

These men stressed that they had received all their metaphysical knowledge from Paliau. But when Schwartz spoke at length with Paliau Lukas and Peter Kuwoh and when Paliau Lukas published his views (Lukas 1983), what they said did not always unequivocally recall Paliau's style. We cannot know with certainty to what extent the four men influenced the doctrines towards which Paliau appeared to be groping in the early and mid-1970s. But they were clearly responsible for some major changes in the Movement's public face, for it was in the late 1970s that the Movement began to produce and issue typewritten documents in multiple copies in both English and Tok Pisin. Paliau signed many of these by hand over his typewritten name. Some look as though they are indeed verbatim transcriptions and credible translations of his spoken words. One document more than others, however, looks as though his literate young collaborators contributed to the content. It probably dates from 1981, and—although it is in Tok Pisin—it is substantially longer and more systematic than any other Movement documents of which we know. This is a booklet called *Kalopeu: Manus Kastam Kansol Stori*. We will return to the meaning of the subtitle later in this chapter. The title, *Kalopeu*, is the Titan word for the chambered nautilus. As explained to Schwartz, it is an appropriate symbol of the Movement because it is fearless, never retreats, but is never angry, and the Movement should be similarly peaceful but unstoppable.[2] The booklet is 14 typed, single-spaced pages long. It contains a table of contents (with section titles, but not their page numbers) and several neat, hand-drawn illustrations. According to Otto (1991: 269), although the ideas in the booklet are attributed to Paliau, Peter Kuwoh wrote the text. (We provide an English translation of most of the text from the Tok Pisin original in Appendix B.)[3] But before *Kalopeu* was published, Paliau described to Schwartz the fundamentals of the new creed.

A Longer Story of God: Wing, Wang, and Wong

On 1 January 1980, in Pere village, Schwartz found Paliau firmly focused on the future and armed with a new historical cosmology. In addition, instead of insisting, as he had in 1978, that his ideas had not changed,

---

2   According to Wanek (1996: 269), the drawing on the front of the booklet is said to represent a male and female *kalopeu* attached to each other, symbolising cooperation between men and women in moving forward. To someone familiar with the Admiralty Islands it may resemble more closely the ornately curved handles of a style of wooden bowl common in the Admiralties before the colonial era.
3   The Movement issued another booklet about a year later in both English and Tok Pisin versions. This is a revised version of Paliau's presentation at the 1970 Waigani seminar mentioned in Chapter 12 (Ward et al. 1970: 144–61). Otto (1991: 272) describes how in the booklet the original text of Paliau's presentation was altered to accord with the new Movement doctrines, vocabulary, and chronology. Among other things, Paliau's date of birth is now given as 1893. As Otto points out, this was likely a deliberate change, as other dates have also been amended to fit the new ideology.

he now insisted that they were all new. But these were, he said, his 'last teachings'. In Tok Pisin, 'last teachings' is *las save*, which could also be translated as last knowledge; that is, the last knowledge to be divulged to his followers. Paliau continued: 'It's time to change everything I said after World War II, from 1945–46. Now I'm changing it. I'm changing many things'. He explained to Schwartz that everything he now had to say he had known since he was a child, but the Australian administration had forbidden anyone to disagree with the government or the missions on pain of imprisonment or worse. But now that PNG was independent he could speak out.

Paliau's first new teaching was that there is no God: 'The missionaries speak of God, but there is no God'. There is, however, a creator or supreme being, and Paliau told Schwartz that it is called Wing. Wing lives in the clouds and has no body, Paliau explained. One way to say this in Tok Pisin is that '*Wing i no gat mit*', that is, Wing has no flesh. One can also say—as Paliau often did—that '*Wing em i win nating*', that is, Wing is like the wind or the breath. This is the sense that dominates depictions and discussions of Wing, to the extent that the creator is often called Win, which in other contexts is the Tok Pisin term for the wind.

A second entity is called Wang, or sometimes Wang Jesus. There is also a third critical entity, whom Paliau calls Wong. In Paliau's new doctrine Wong takes the place of the Holy Spirit in the Christian Trinity. Wing—or Win—created all things including Heaven, which Paliau calls the Second Place; Wing's abode in the clouds being the first. Earth, (in Tok Pisin, *ples daun*) is the Third Place. Wing created all things, including Wang Jesus and Wong, who are incorporeal like Wing. Some essence of Wing, Wang, and Wong lives in each human being.

Some readers will find the idea of a holy trinity called Wing, Wang, and Wong risible. To many Americans, it may sound like a crude burlesque of a 'primitive religion' from a Bob Hope and Bing Crosby movie, an Abbott and Costello farce, or a Three Stooges film.[4] Paliau, of course, held that the names were a revealed truth, not a human invention. Numbers of Paliau's followers, however, say that '*wong*' also means I, myself, or me in Paliau's Baluan language (cf. Otto 1991: 269n7). And, as noted above, one can see the name Wing as a transformation of *win*, the Tok Pisin

---

4   Risibility results partly from unfamiliarity. The Bible, for instance, has given many generations of unchurched, first-time readers hours of fun.

word for wind, the natural phenomenon most closely analogous to Wing's essence. But whatever else may be involved, the appeal of alliteration—its musicality and its mnemonic power—is also undoubtedly a factor. And it is the only explanation we can think of for naming the second member of the trinity Wang.[5]

As the most dramatic episode in Paliau's new historical cosmology begins, Wang, or Wang Jesus, is the ruler of Heaven and the angels who inhabit it. An angel named Laitsan challenges Wang's authority. Wang banishes Laitsan to Earth where Laitsan becomes Luspa—that is, Lucifer. Luspa continues making trouble by convincing Adam and Even—whom Wing had also created—to disobey Wing. This they do by having sexual intercourse. Until that point, Adam and Eve could obtain anything they wanted—including children—simply by thinking of it. In Wind Nation parlance, they obtained all they desired free—in Tok Pisin, *fri*. To use Paliau's words, they lived in freedom (in Tok Pisin, *fridom*) or, sometimes, True Freedom (*Tru Fridom*). By disobeying Wing, however, they lost their freedom. This is the freedom that characterises the First Order of God— the world before the Fall. And, because they succumbed to Luspa's or Satan's blandishments, they and all the people of the world now carry something of Luspa within them as well as something of Wing, Wang, and Wong.

The long 1981 printed version of the doctrine includes many variations on the details of the biblical story of creation and its aftermath. The essentials, however, are familiarly Judeo-Christian. Wang Jesus comes to Earth to try to help the descendants of Adam and Eve, is persecuted, predicts that he will rise again, is crucified, and does rise again after three days. He then tells his followers that he will come back again to rule the world when the people of the world are ready for him. But his instructions on making themselves ready are cryptic. Before Wang Jesus goes back to Heaven, he addresses his 'number one disciple', Peter (or, in Latinate mission Tok Pisin, Petrus) as follows: 'Peter, you hold a key to this Earth and I, Jesus, hold a key to Heaven. When you open Earth, I can open Heaven and they can unite'.

---

5   Opera lovers will have noticed immediately the parallel of Wing, Wang, and Wong with Ping, Pang, and Pong, the royal ministers in Puccini's *Turandot*. It seems unlikely that this work influenced Paliau, although it is not impossible.

Paliau also spoke of the Key of Petrus in the 'Long Story of God', but other aspects of the newer, longer story differ from both the Bible and the Long Story. It is significant that in Paliau's new version it is not Australians or Europeans or whites in general who are blocking the path to the First Order or, in the new jargon, True Freedom. Adam and Eve lost the necessary knowledge through their own fecklessness and were tainted by their dealings with Satan. They passed that taint to their descendants—all of humanity—and it is the Satan in them that keeps human beings from recovering the knowledge that would restore Freedom. When Paliau first spoke to Schwartz of the new doctrine, this feature struck Schwartz more than anything else. He immediately pointed out to Paliau that in the 'Long Story of God' Jesus instructs the whites to bring knowledge to the black man but the whites don't do it. Hence, the sad condition of black people. But now Paliau was placing the fault elsewhere. Paliau repeated that his new teaching reflected the knowledge he was obliged to keep secret prior to independence. He explained further that the missionaries didn't tell the truth, but they didn't lie maliciously. They simply didn't know the truth; they didn't know about Wing, Wang, and Wong (in Tok Pisin, *Ol i no save long Wing, Wang, Wong*).

Otto (1991: 281n21) notes that in the 1980s he encountered people in many parts of Manus who regarded themselves as adherents of the new teachings but who 'still believed that white people had an easy life thanks to their special knowledge which they refuse to share with black people'. But Paliau and those closest to him left no room for ambiguity in their oral and written statements. A vital implication is that since the obstacle to True Freedom is within all people—that is, the taint of Satan—the new doctrine pertains to universal salvation, not just achieving parity with or superiority to whites. The new teachings, Paliau explained to Schwartz, are not just for black Papua New Guineans. They are for everyone in the world. To use a phrase that Paliau and his acolytes came to use over and over again with slight variations, they were for 'all black men and women, all white men and women, all brown men and women' (*olgeta blakpela man na meri, olgeta waitpela man na meri, olgeta braunpela man na meri*).

In previous decades, many of Paliau's followers had been unsure if whites had already obtained the First Order of God or were stuck at a high level of the Second Order, a condition better than that of the blacks but not as good as things could get. But according to Paliau's new revelation, no one in the world enjoyed the True Freedom of the First Order. No one in the world even enjoyed 'development' (which Paliau rendered as sounding something like *tipolot*). He explained to Schwartz that 'no countries in the world have it, no matter how long they have been independent'. The development that is universally lacking has four parts:

- First, development of the spirit 'that is in the heads of all of us white men, white women, brown men, brown women, black men, black women'.

- Second, development of the body, which is the house of the spirit.

- Third, making money or, in Tok Pisin, *wok mani* (work money). We will linger on this aspect of development briefly because we are entering the country of ambiguity again. Paliau explained work money to Schwartz thus: 'Where is money? It is hidden in the ground. But it is emerging now. Everything in the ground must develop now. Everything is there to look after us, in the ground and in the sea and on the earth are our mother and our father to provide everything we need'. (In Paliau's Tok Pisin: *Mani i stap we? Em i hait pinis i stap long graun. Tasol em i kamap nau. Olgeta samting nau i stap long graun i mas tipolot. Em i gat olgeta samting bilong lukautim yumi, graun na solowara long ples daun i papa na mama bilong yumi bilong karim olgeta samtimg bilong lukautim yumi.*) What Paliau does not speak of here is how people can acquire these riches. Given Paliau's interest in the secret of True Freedom it is safe to assume that when he speaks of 'work money' or developing the wealth of the land and sea he is not necessarily referring to the drudgery of growing crops for sale or fishing for the market. In later discussions with Schwartz, Paliau attempted to clarify, explaining that—in the new doctrine—pursuing money through commercial '*wok mani*'—that is, business—was the way of Satan. Real abundance came through right living and right thinking (cf. Otto 1991: 275n14).[6]

- Fourth, all the world's people must engage in 'good living'. As Paliau explained, 'Good living must emerge; living correctly in the eyes of Wing' (in Paliau's Tok Pisin: *Gutpela living i kamap i mas go stret long ai bilong dispela man, em Wing*).

---

6   Although Paliau never wavered from this position, other leaders of the revived Movement sometimes hedged, at least for white audiences. Wind Nation followers on the remote island of Nauna told Wanek that the wealth in the ground would come from what they called in Tok Pisin *factori* (that is, factories), which would emerge—or re-emerge—with the return of Wang Jesus. But Wanek (1996: 284–5) also reports that Paliau Lukas told him that such rank-and-file members were misinterpreting the new teaching; wealth in the ground, he said, meant only ordinary agricultural or horticultural products.

Origins of the new doctrine

References to an incorporeal supreme being that manifests as or through the breath appear to go back to the beginning of the Movement. In accounts of Paliau's telling of the 'Long Story of God' Schwartz obtained in the 1950s, some state that Paliau taught that God animated Adam and Eve with his breath. As noted in Chapter 9, the word '*win*', Tok Pisin for wind in most contexts, appears in a Cemetery Cult marching song, although its meaning in that context is not clear. The meaning is much clearer—that God is like wind or *win*—in one of Paliau's speeches from 1964 in which he proclaimed 'our ability to think is the breath of God within us'. He later elaborated on this to Schwartz as follows: 'God isn't far away. He is here with us, he is like the wind. We can't see him. My *tingting* is God also. When people die, their *tingting* are loosed, their flesh goes in the ground. Their *tingting* are like the wind from God's mouth and they go back to God'.[7]

Paliau claimed that in his childhood he already understood that the real name for this entity—God—is Wing and that it is the principal figure in the alliterative trinity Wing, Wang, and Wong. However, Paliau's own words suggest that the new ideas did not come to him full blown. When Paliau spoke to Sunday gatherings in 1978 he had not yet repudiated God for Wing; he spoke of '*God papa bilong yumi*' (God our father). But Paliau was also using language and images that did not appear in the 'Long Story of God' or his early conversations with Schwartz. He appears, for example, already to have begun to blame Satan and the taint of Satan in Adam and Eve and their descendants for exclusion from a life of 'freedom', placing great emphasis on the condition of Adam and Eve before they yielded to Satan's temptation: everything Adam and Eve wanted was '*fri*'.

It is impossible to say to what extent Paliau's enunciation of the idea of a creator analogous to breath or wind is in any sense original. Such an idea is common in the world's religions, including the Judeo-Christian tradition. But Paliau claimed that the name Wing—and its cognates Wind

---

7   The Tok Pisin third-person pronoun *em* applies to men, women, and things. In translating, we sometimes refer to both God and Wing as masculine because Paliau and his followers habitually spoke of the Christian God as masculine—as in *God papa bilong yumi*; that is, God our father—and we have no evidence that when Paliau proclaimed a new supreme being he altered its assumed gender. In some contexts, however, Paliau and his followers clearly treat Wong or the Holy Spirit as a female entity.

and Win—was secret knowledge, vouchsafed only to him. Whatever the origins of this conception of the nature of a supreme being, Paliau's claim was a bold way to distinguish his metaphysical ideas from those of mission Christianity, something Paliau strove to do from the beginning of his career.

Paliau's new colleagues may well have played a significant role in, let us say, the refinement of Paliau's lifelong secret knowledge. There is no doubt that they aided in promulgating it. By 1980, Paliau Lukas and Peter Kuwoh had joined with Paliau Maloat to create what they called the Study Group (in Tok Pisin, *Stadi Grup*). Most accounts of the Study Group say it began in or around 1978. Paliau Lukas told Schwartz in 1981 that it began in 1975, when he returned from a trip to Australia pertaining to his government post. Wanek (1996: 195) understood that the Study Group began in 1979. In any case, 'Study Group' sounds distinctly academic or bureaucratic, not like a name of Paliau's devising. This entity probably began as informal meetings of Paliau Maloat with Paliau Lukas, Peter Kuwoh, and a few other young men who had returned to Lorengau from PNG's larger towns. Although Paliau claimed that he had understood since childhood the core ideas the Study Group came to espouse, documents and interviews suggest that they emerged gradually and probably in dialogue with these younger followers.[8]

Typed minutes from a November 1978 meeting of the 'Baluan United Church Lotu Stady', held in Naringel village on Los Negros Island, identify Paliau Maloat as '*Tisa na Plena*' (Teacher and Planner) and Paliau Lukas as '*Lotu Stady Siaman*' (Lotu Study Chairman), and report that 113 people from 17 different villages attended. The ideas discussed partake of both the old and the germinating doctrines. Whites are still blamed for withholding critical knowledge, but 'the Holy Spirit is in each of us' and the best way to combat Satan—rather than white domination—is

---

8   Wanek (1996: 218) describes a 1989 gathering in Lorengau, led by Paliau, devoted to *stadi*. It involved long periods of silent thought about the whereabouts of the Key of Petrus—that is, the Key of St Peter, a mystery Paliau also spoke of in the early days of the Movement (noted in Chapter 5 of this volume). These were punctuated at long intervals by what Wanek calls someone's 'faltering' effort to suggest an answer and Paliau's harsh denunciation of his or her statement as 'rubbish'. According to Wanek (1996: 218), at least one of Paliau's confidants thought that Paliau's physical body was the key because three days after Paliau died Wang Jesus would return, inhabiting Paliau's rejuvenated body and there would then be no more hard work, ageing, hunger or sickness. Schwartz never heard Paliau equating the Key of Petrus with his body's death and resurrection. We are certain that he prophesied his death and resurrection. The Key of Petrus, however, appears to play at best a peripheral role in ideological justification for any Movement activity.

to cultivate sensitivity to the Holy Spirit's promptings. According to the minutes, the group also decided that 'God' is no longer an acceptable name for the supreme being because it is from the language of the whites.[9] The alternative proposed, however, is not Wing or Wind/Win; it is *lapan tumbuna* (approximately: noble ancestor).

From the time of Schwartz's first encounters with members of the Study Group, they insisted they were engaged in study, not *lotu*. It became clear that what they meant is that they were not engaged in worship or propitiation. Rather, they were seeking direct knowledge of the nature of things to replace the doctrines received from Christian missionaries or recorded in the Bible. Paliau Lukas put this eloquently in a 1984 conversation with Schwartz: 'Did the Bible start knowledge? Or did knowledge begin in men's minds and then go into a book? If it begins in men's minds and then it goes into a book, when my understanding tells me that my study is all right and is true, no one … can deny it. I don't believe in this Bible. I believe this study is true'. (In the original Tok Pisin: *Baibel, em i statim save? O save i stat long het bilong man na i go long buk. Na sapos i stat long het bilong man na i go long buk, taim save bilong mi i oraitim stadi bilong mi na i tok i tru, i nogat narapela man i ken sensim dispela. Mi no bilip long dispela baibel. Mi bilip long dispela stadi i tru.*)

How much did people like Paliau Lukas contribute to the ideas coming out of the Study Group? We can only speculate. We know that some members of the group had strong feelings about naming the creator that may or may not have preceded their intimacy with Paliau. In a 1984 conversation with Schwartz, Paliau Lukas and another Study Group member, Kanaw Kampo, explained that one reason loyalty to mission Christianity had not yielded Papua New Guineans the hoped-for benefits was that the missionaries' God was a foreign entity. 'It isn't ours. [God] is a word in a European language, a white language. So we have to find our own language to call on our ancestors and everything so although they didn't hear us before, now they will.' The previous year, Paliau Lukas had made a similar point in a short article written for a Christian mission publication. He wrote, in English, 'Papua New Guinea is a politically

---

9   Here and elsewhere, however, followers of the new doctrine insist that Jesus is a name ordained by the supreme being and thus they need not change it.

independent nation. Religion, likewise, must be independent. We must have our own status; we must have our own views of life and through them develop our own belief and theology' (Lukas 1983: 7).[10]

Paliau Lukas was probably at least partially responsible for the Anglophile monarchism that entered Paliau's doctrine in the 1980s. During his stint as a government official, Paliau Lukas visited England for a course of study. He also saw the sights, including the Coronation Chair that resides in Westminster Abbey. (The Coronation Chair dates from the thirteenth century. It is often called St Edward's Chair or King Edward's Chair. Since the fourteenth century all English and British monarchs—with the exception of Queen Mary II—have been seated on it to receive the crown.) Paliau Lukas spoke at length of the splendour of monarchy one night in 1990 when Schwartz sat up until dawn with a few young members of the Study Group. He spoke of the British royals as analogous to Jesus and God as kings upon their thrones or to the *lapan* of old Manus society. He seemed unaware that the royal family does not actually rule England and he persisted in speaking of kings, although he knew that the current head of the royal family was a queen. He also said that he had intuited, or it had been revealed to him, that the Coronation Chair was really the throne of King David, magically transported to England, and that the royal family were the direct heirs of Adam and Eve, but were unaware of it. Further, it was the destiny of the royal family to rule a new nation that would extend from England to Manus, with the English monarchy at one end and Paliau at the other. Paliau Lukas reproached Schwartz, as an American, for having rejected the British king, but said that it was not too late for America to become part of the new 'Commonwealth' along with Great Britain, Papua New Guinea, and Australia.

Wanek (1996: 207) points out that the apotheosis of the British royals echoes ideas in a booklet Wanek noticed in Paliau Maloat's possession in the mid-1980s: 'The United States and British Commonwealth in Prophecy' by Herbert W. Armstrong, founder of the Worldwide Church of God, an explicitly millenarian Christian sect. Armstrong's version of Christianity includes the idea that the people of Britain are descendants

---

10   Paliau Maloat and his close associates had all taken up the cause of Wing before 1983, but Paliau Lukas did not mention Wing in this piece. Instead, he wrote that 'Manus has a religion. We believe in a supreme being, God, and we call him by the name "Lapan"'. To the best of our knowledge, Paliau Lukas's portrayal of an indigenous Manus idea of a supreme being is not accurate. Paliau Maloat and his followers, however, did on occasion speak of Wing as 'Wing Lapan Tumbuna'—that is, translated roughly from the Tok Pisin, 'Wing Noble Ancestor'.

of the ancient Israelites. The booklet also describes the Coronation Chair in detail. Paliau could have understood very little of the text of the book, which is written in English, but someone could have translated it for him.

Throughout his career, Paliau regularly introduced new ideas or elaborations of old ones to his followers. It appears to have been an effective way not only to connect his doctrines to a rapidly changing larger world but also to keep followers' attention by providing novelty. A degree of Anglophilia was not completely novel in the Movement. Many followers, for instance, attached great importance to the Order of the British Empire (OBE) Paliau was awarded in 1970. Kisokau Pochapon, addressing an audience of Movement stalwarts, once spoke of the OBE as an honour received directly from Queen Elizabeth—an honour that was also a grant of authority: 'The Queen herself saw that this was a man with special knowledge. So she chose him as an officer to watch over the British Commonwealth' (in the original Tok Pisin: *Em kwin yet i luk save olsem man hia i gat dispela save. Em i makim em i ofisa long lukautim British Commonwealth*). But the occult Anglophile monarchism Paliau Lukas expounded to Schwartz sounds strikingly arbitrary in relation to any aspect of Movement ideology up to this point.

From the start, Paliau had to be flexible to keep from losing personal control of the Movement, including his church. Competition from independent sources of invention or revelation can be a serious threat to any charismatic leader. Within weeks of initiating the Movement just such a potential crisis confronted Paliau; that is, the prophecies of the Noise. Paliau dealt with this in large part by letting people attribute to him what they wanted and biding his time. As long as prevailing readings of events supported people's allegiance to him, he could safely keep a light hand on the reins, as he did until the Noise fell flat. He acted much more openly and decisively towards the Cemetery Cult, but even in that matter he may well have understood that people's imaginations would provide interpretations of events that benefited him up to a point.

By the 1980s, however, the remnants of the Movement did not give Paliau much of an institution to defend. He appears to have reached a point at which he found even weakened leadership of an ever more marginal Movement better than no leadership at all. He could not bring himself to retire, content with his considerable accomplishments and claiming credit for a few others. Paliau thus had relatively little to lose by allowing mystical Anglophilia in the door if it brought with it youthful followers with skills in communication better suited for the times.

However it entered Movement ideology, Anglophile monarchism endured. Nothing of it appears in *Kalopeu: Manus Kastam Kansol Stori*, but when Prince Charles visited Manus in 1984, Paliau and his principal lieutenants tried unsuccessfully to present him with a document advising him that he and his wife at the time, Princess Diana, were the direct descendants of Adam and Eve, that they were destined to rule a new Commonwealth under the protection of Wing, and that the Coronation Chair was actually the throne of King David. As we will see, these ideas moved gradually closer to the centre of Movement doctrine, so that when Smith visited Baluan in 2015 dozens of men were busy preparing a home for the throne of King David a short walk from the house in which Paliau died.

The days of wonder

Thus, from Paliau and through the innovations of the Study Group, the true nature of the creator, the creation, its tragic aftermath, and the role of the British royal family in a new world came to light. But one vital piece of knowledge remained elusive: full knowledge of how Paliau and the members of the early Movement had once actually come close to attaining the blissful, effort-free condition of the First Order of God— now construed as the condition of True Freedom that Adam and Eve had once enjoyed.

In 1953–54, some participants in the early Movement (prior to the Noise) described it to Schwartz as a time when life was conspicuously easy. Rather than fade away, such recollections became more vivid over the years, so that when Lungat met Schwartz in Lorengau in 1973 he reminisced about the ease of canoe travel: 'When we sailed from place to place God made our way easy. If today I wanted to go somewhere and tomorrow I wanted to come back, God made it easy for us in both directions', not only calming the sea but sending winds from the right quarters. By the late 1980s, the legend had grown. In 1953–54, Paliau's followers had told Schwartz that the early Movement's days of wonder had ended by 1950. But according to *Kalopeu* (translated here from Tok Pisin): 'In 1946–53 all things, such as wind, rain, and sea, together with all kinds of food and game, obeyed what our fathers and mothers were saying. From July 1953 until today [1981] all these things no longer obey what is being said'. Members of the Study Group said that their elders confirmed that this state of things had continued until 1953—well into the days of the Cemetery Cult and the coming of the official council—and perhaps even longer.

If life had thus hovered on the edge of True Freedom only shortly before Schwartz and Shargo arrived in Manus with Mead, no one had mentioned it to them. Rather, Movement followers had pined for the tentative grip on the First Order they had achieved several years before. What is important, however, is that its members described the Study Group as an effort to recapture the knowledge that had made possible that fleeting taste of True Freedom. In the words of Paliau Lukas: 'Paliau showed our mothers and fathers how the wind would obey, the lightning would obey, the rain would obey, the thunder would obey, the sea would obey, the fish would obey. Now we're trying to find out what made this possible. Why won't anything obey anymore?'[11]

The new doctrine held that people no longer have the ability to command the elements because Laitsan/Luspa/Lucifer deceived Adam and Eve. But accounts of the early Movement's days of wonder invariably attribute the ease of life both to Paliau's special powers and—more important—to the remarkable harmony in which Movement participants dwelt. They met together to make decisions, they worked together, and if they disagreed or became angry they settled their disagreements quickly and publicly. In this, they were adhering to the principle of *harim tok*—which in this context means living according to divinely ordained rules. And, as Paliau Lukas explained decades later, the same principle applies under the dominion of Wing: '*Harim tok em i nambawan oda bilong Wing lapan tumbuna bilong mipela*' ('*Harim tok* is the first commandment of Wing, our noble ancestor'). And when people obey Wing the elements will obey them—that is, the wind, rain, and other elements will *harim tok* with respect to human beings. But now they have to 'study' to restore this condition 'so it can be easy for us, so all the children that come behind us can get everything free. They will walk in peace and freedom and look after their brothers and sisters everywhere'.

---

11   The term we translate as obey is the Tok Pisin *harim tok*—literally, to hear someone's voice or commands.

Just being cooperative, however, is not enough. People must live in harmony under the authority of Wing, who listens when people call on him in harmony. Schwartz asked members of the Study Group—in Paliau's absence—if they were getting better results from their appeals now that they were calling on Wing, not God, and they reported limited success. Paliau Lukas offered, in English: 'We're seeing signs that *harim tok* is working for us. The rain pays attention. The wind pays attention for some of us'. And, of course, Paliau can still command the elements, as many people—Study Group members claimed—had seen.

The Manus Kastam Kansol

We have already made the new doctrines of this phase of the Movement more systematic than we found them in what Paliau and his followers said and wrote.[12] But we will indulge in this less as we continue and remind readers that lack of system or coherence in ideology has seldom been much of a handicap in either religion or politics. People are especially tolerant of incoherence in metaphysical doctrines, where a certain amount of contradiction and a few conundrums can even add a sense of mystery, suggesting wisdom beyond the normal human ken.

A millenarian effort risks less by incoherence than by neglecting to give people something to look forward to and something to do while they wait for salvation. In the case of Wind Nation, initially it looked like what people should do to hasten the days of True Freedom remained vague. The Movement produced more than one list of rules for proper behaviour, covering aspects of personal conduct and group conduct pertaining mostly to dimensions of living together in harmony. (We provide two of these lists—one of thirty rules and one of twelve rules—in Appendix C.) The list that has endured longest—which we will revisit in Chapter 14—is

---

12   At least one indigenous observer has also found it difficult to find coherence in the doctrines of the revitalised Movement. In a 1983 publication, Pokawin (1983b: 112) commented: 'the Paliau Phenomenon may be understood in two ways. Firstly, for an outsider, the whole exercise is very simplistic and confusing. The speeches relating to the 1946 movement are aged and stale, while discussions of a religious nature are contradictory, baseless and disjointed. Religiously, it could be regarded as an exercise in bastardising Christianity in an attempt to appear original and indigenous. The only indigenous aspect of it is the people. The ideas, religiously speaking, are not original. Alternatively, it could be argued that one cannot really understand the phenomenon unless one is tuned into the same wavelength as the adherents. The adherents thus are either acting or they genuinely believe in what is being advocated'.

also the shortest, comprising only five rules. The following is a necessarily rough translation of a Tok Pisin version provided by a Movement leader in 2015.[13]

1. Treat others with respect.
2. Love.
3. Enjoy life with others.
4. Speak the truth.
5. Appreciate life.

As guides to behaviour these dicta leave a lot of leeway for interpretation. And there is certainly no solid scaffold here for a program of mass action analogous to that of the New Way of 1946. Whether or not Paliau and followers consciously recognised this issue, by no later than 1980 the Study Group had become more activist, spawning what Wanek (1996: 195) calls a 'political wing' called the Manus Kastam Kansol, usually abbreviated as Makasol. A precise translation into English is difficult. *Kansol* appears to translate neatly to council, although we have seen how council has been a politically controversial concept in Manus history. The Tok Pisin word *kastam* in some contexts is a cognate of the English words custom or tradition, but for Makasol it signified a highly specific notion of tradition.[14]

---

13 We say a 'necessarily rough' translation because such single words and brief phrases taken out of context often convey relatively little. The first rule—'*Lukstret*'—poses special problems. We have seen it construed (within the Movement) as an admonition to respect parents, kin, and leaders. Anthropologist Graeme Humble recently conveyed to us a complementary exegesis from a Manus friend (Reeves Papaol) that supplies what may be essential context. In Papaol's words: '*Lukstret* or Look Straight—is a term derived directly from the colonial regimental morning assembly of villagers by their *tultuls* and *luluai* in [New Guinea islands] and *kiaps* in the highlands. They would stand in line just like in the military with the plantation managers or local administrators leading out in front often on an elevated pedestal with flag raising ceremony and morning *toksave* [that is, announcements] of the communal task for the day. The command to *lukstret* ['eyes right', 'level eye', 'right dress' are similar commands] is to demand absolute attention'. Papaol suggests that the admonition thus implies giving respect through paying strict attention to authority and acting in unity with the group. 'Love' (in Tok Pisin, *lave*) always requires interpretation for specific situations. The Tok Pisin version of the third rule is '*pilai*', which translates literally as 'play'. Other Makasol materials suggest that 'Enjoy life with others' is an adequate rendering. 'Speak the truth' is a direct literal translation of the Tok Pisin '*tok tru*'. The Tok Pisin version of the fifth rule with which we are working is *amamas*, which translates literally as 'celebrate', but other Makasol materials suggest that 'Appreciate life' is closer to the mark. In Chapter 14, we present a version of the five rules from Mbukei Island that demonstrates their malleability.

14 In the anthropological literature, the Tok Pisin term for this concept is usually spelled *kastom*. We are using the usual Manus spelling, *kastam*.

The Makasol position was that Paliau deserved credit for most of PNG's great leaps forward, most of which had since been undermined. Makasol rhetoric repeats this tirelessly. An inside page of *Kalopeu*, for instance, displays a black and white photo of Paliau and his wife in indigenous dress—probably taken at the 1973 event at which their appearance so clothed surprised Schwartz—above a statement that Paliau is the father of the Manus Local Government Council, the father of the Pangu Party, and the father of Papua New Guinea, 'now an independent nation'. (In the original Tok Pisin, *papa bilong Manus Lokol Gavman Kansol ... papa bilong Pangu Pati ... papa bilong Papua New Guinea, nau i Independen Neisen.*) Makasol's hyper-jaundiced view of things is also displayed in a typed document, in both Tok Pisin and English, that a Makasol member gave Schwartz. It is dated 1982 and signed in Paliau's hand over what had become his title: OBE, Last Prophet Long Wold—that is, the Last Prophet of the World. Paliau declared himself the Last Prophet no later than 1984.[15] Some variation on Paliau's full title (such as OBE, Esquire, Last Prophet of the World) appears on nearly every Movement document from 1984 on. Being against something provides lots of opportunities for action and in the breadth of its antagonisms the following document is one of many that give Makasol members a lot to oppose. Among the things it declares against some are imaginary, but some are the very stuff of the improved way of life Paliau had once worked for, such as more indigenous participation in government and better government services. The document calls for 15 things to be removed from Manus Province and for 'Manus Province, New Guinea Islands, New Guinea, and Australia to become one country, and to unite with London to form one Nation'.[16] Here is the title of the document and the list of things to oppose in the original English version (and original spelling):

> THE PAGAN DEPARTMENTS BY TODAY'S DEFILED GOVERNMENTS THAT ARE DETERIORATING MANKIND IN THIS WORLD
>
> 1.   God-worshiping Churches
> 2.   Youth Groups
> 3.   Rascals

---

15   The date on our document, 1982, may be incorrect. Other accounts (e.g. Otto 1992a: 62; Wanek 1996: 211) report that Paliau declared himself the Last Prophet in 1984. The exact date, however, is not very important.

16   It isn't clear if New Guinea is intended to include what had once been the separate entity of Papua. The New Guinea Islands usually refers to the arc of PNG islands sometimes called the Bismarck Archipelago.

4. Cowboys
5. Communist Government
6. Provincial Government
7. Community government
8. Hospitals and Aid Posts
9. Education
10. Women's Council
11. Corrective Institutions
12. All Policemen
13. All the Magistrates
14. Communist Laws
15. Factories

It is clear in wider context, of course, that people must reject 'God-worshipping churches' because they should turn to Wing. 'Rascal' and 'Cowboy' are PNG slang of the day for delinquent young people, and we can guess that opposition to 'Youth Groups' and a 'Women's Council' reflects a concern that such institutions might undermine the ersatz form of traditional authority the Movement would soon propose.

Opposition to community government shows Paliau and followers still pushing against the political changes that were leaving them behind. The main theme of such changes was decentralisation, but the problem for Paliau wasn't decentralisation per se but the fact that as put into practice it continued to erase his success in the older system. We described in Chapter 12 how, by 1973, a shifting formal government structure had marginalised Paliau. But that wasn't the end of it. As Otto (1991: 190) summarises:

> The Manus District Area Authority … was transformed into the Interim Provincial assembly in 1977. Two years later the Manus Provincial Government was officially instituted. The province was divided into 15 constituencies which each elected one representative to the Manus Lapan Assembly, the representative legislative body of the provincial government. The provincial government had assumed all powers and functions of the local government council, which thus became redundant. In 1980 fresh elections for the council were still held, but the provincial government was already making preparations for an alternative form of third level government: the community government. The abolition of the local government council was finalized … in April 1982. In the following years 15 community governments were established corresponding with the areas of the 15 provincial constituencies.

Paliau made one more electoral effort and in 1979 won a seat in the first Manus Lapan Assembly as representative of the Balopa constituency, which comprised Baluan, Lou, and Pwam islands. But in the 1983 elections he lost his place to a former colleague, the retired headmaster of the Baluan primary school (Otto 1991: 190n7; Wanek 1996: 194). He was now completely out of electoral politics. Further, he and his close followers regarded abolishing the local government councils as an attack on one of the Movement's principal accomplishments. Further, whether by accident or design, the division of the province into community government units split Movement areas among several community governments (Wanek 1996: 197). This was a good reason for Movement hostility to community government. Exploiting—ingenuously or with calculation—the prevailing tendency to attribute significance to homonymy, Makasol rhetorically equated community government with communism, Russians, the Indonesians, and the forces of evil in general. The result was that Paliau and Makasol came to oppose the provincial government as the Movement had once opposed the colonial government. Paliau and his principle followers began to malign the government not merely as a usurper but as the government of Lucifer/Luspa.[17] This helps account for the call to remove all the government institutions they once coveted, from police and magistrates to schools and health services.

The Movement's new dispensation gave people direction for the future. It also sought to revise the past. An account of Paliau's trial for agitating against the government in the 1950s—an account still circulating in 2015—must have been prepared no earlier than the mid to late 1970s, when the Study Group and Makasol were forming, because the earliest written version we know of is typewritten and presented in both Tok Pisin and English. Not only English, but the English of people with experience beyond the village (for example, the Tok Pisin *kiap*, meaning government official, is rendered as 'bureaucracy'). No accounts from

---

17   Regarding the Paliau attitude to community government, Otto's (1991: 190–1) speculations are relevant if not conclusive. Otto argues that although enacted in the name of decentralisation, community government tended to strengthen the national central government: 'The officially stated aim of community government was to give local people a greater say in the government of their own place. While it certainly effected some progress in this direction, it also extended the sphere of the state in Manus villages by giving more people a vested interest in its continuation. It thus consolidated the development which started with the incorporation of the Paliau Movement by the colonial state. The gradual increase of indigenous participation in government culminating in national independence went hand in hand with the expansion of the state as an organization—resulting in greater state influence on the daily lives of villagers'. On decentralisation and community government in PNG as they relate to Manus, see also Pokawin (1983a) and Wanek (1996: 70–6).

the 1950s, including those Paliau gave to Schwartz in private, resemble this in the least. If Paliau had spoken like this to the examining officials, it is unlikely he would have been treated leniently. The revised version, however, projects Paliau's vehement anti-government credentials into the past. It shows him confounding the examining court by answering with a forthright 'Yes!' to 16 of their questions. The legend holds that Paliau's staunch resistance confounded the authorities so much they gave up and released him. The questions, in the English version, are:

1. Did you want to get rid of the Australians?
2. Did you want to get rid of Australian administration?
3. Did you want to stop all your people from going to school?
4. Did you tell your people not to work for any white men?
5. Did you tell the people of Manus to give all their savings and war damages to you to hold for them?
6. Did you tell your people not to go and see the white men's doctor?
7. Did you tell your people that those who disobey your orders must receive punishment?
8. Is it true that you do not take heed of the *luluai's* leadership in villages?
9. Did you say that you will be the king, government, and bureaucracy?
10. Is it true that you won't pay the court fines?
11. Is it true that you tell our people not to put their money in the bank and not to spend their money in the general merchant stores?
12. Did you say that you will disrupt the working of the colonial government?
13. Did you say you want to unite the people of Manus under your own leadership?
14. Did you say you want to fly your own flag?
15. Did you say you had no intention of asking the Australian administration for employment?
16. Did you say you do not want the Australian under your plan?

The Makasol alternative

From about 1946 to 1973, Paliau excoriated the ways of the ancestors as 'bullshit' (in Tok Pisin, *bulsit*) that had wasted time and energy in endless ceremonial affinal and mortuary exchange, playing with valuables that were worthless for acquiring European goods. He also condemned the rank structure and the ethnic and ecological groupings of the past. The goal of change was modelled on his and other indigenes' construal of European life in its colonial and wartime manifestations. Now, however, Paliau and Makasol turned their iconoclasm against the emerging approximations of a more European life. They began to exalt the ways of the past, but they depicted them in a highly selective and largely imaginary way. They found reason for clashing with ruling politicians and parties on many specific issues, but the foundation of their opposition was the contention that the government—even though it was a government of an independent state; run by indigenous people; and elected, within the limits of the circumstances, by indigenous people—had usurped the legitimate power of the people. And, Makasol claimed, the legitimate power of the people *had* been in force under the Local Government Council system.

Paliau Lukas's views were in line with those of other Makasol members, although better expressed (translated in what follows from the original Tok Pisin). In conversation with Schwartz, he described Manus under Paliau's leadership as the 'teacher' of PNG and Paliau as the 'founder of the nation', the person who had brought independence. But as the result of changes in the government since the time of the Local Government Council, 'the people's power has been given to the national government … now this power must go back to the man who started it', that is, to Paliau Maloat. Paliau Lukas explained further that restoring Paliau Maloat's leadership was only the 'first round'. The second round would be returning power to the council wards. The third round would be instituting 'the government of Jesus, who instituted it in Heaven, and now it must come to Earth. Government of peace, freedom, and living under the order of Wing'.

Other Makasol activists described the kind of government needed in different ways, but the theocratic theme is consistent. For example, in a speech in April 1987, Kisokau Pochapon declared: 'There is one good government, namely that of Adam and Eve in the early days. The rule of this government was that human beings must not grow old or become sick, they must not die or be hungry and they must not toil. There shall always be freedom. Our present government does not have this kind of government or rule. Therefore I move that we want to go back to the government of Adam and Eve: we want to live for ever and ever' (Otto 1991: 276).[18]

Makasol brought this ambition down to a more concrete level. Young members told Schwartz that they had to go back to the way of the *lapan*—the respected leaders of olden times, when—allegedly—everyone obeyed their leaders and moved as one at their command. There used to be harmony, solidarity, coordination, and obedience to leadership, they said (cf. Schwartz 1993: 534). Makasol called this way of life *kastam*—as in Manus Kastam Kansol. They did not propose or intend to go back to ceremonial exchange, the old ghost-centred practices, or most of the rest of what people remembered or maintained of pre-European life. But the old obsession with ghosts persisted strongly in certain contexts. Many people sympathetic to Makasol were reluctant to neglect certain kinship obligations, for instance, for fear of offending the ghosts. But Paliau and the Makasol inner circle excluded such practices from the official definition of *kastam*. Neither did they include in *kastam* the blessing and cursing power of the father's sister.

There is a lot of literature on the importance of concepts similar to Makasol's *kastam* (and with similar names, due to parallels among Pacific creoles or lingua franca) in the contemporary Pacific Islands (e.g. Jolly and Thomas 1992; Keesing and Tonkinson 1982; Lindstrom and White 1994; White and Lindstrom 1993).[19] Despite similarities, their local implications vary. Otto (1991, 1992a, 1992b) writes of *kastam* in Manus from the vantage point of Baluan, but he uses the term in a different and broader sense than we do (cf. Wanek 1996: 111–33). Schwartz first heard people speaking of *kastam* in Manus in the 1970s.[20] What Manus people then called *kastam* was far from an unedited version of indigenous

---

18 Otto's quotation is a translation from Tok Pisin.
19 In the anthropological literature, the Tok Pisin term for this concept is usually spelled *kastom*. We are using the usual Manus spelling, *kastam*.
20 Schwartz (1993: 517–18) describes how the Australian administration contributed to the development of the idea of *kastam* in Manus by, for example, encouraging schools to include attention to indigenous culture in their curriculums and sponsoring 'shows' of indigenous-style music and dance (cf. Otto 1991: 232–53).

life. Neither was what Makasol labelled *kastam*. Rather, it was 'singularly ideological, political and focused on limited specific areas' (Schwartz 1993: 515) of special significance in Makasol ideology.

When the Movement started over, in a sense, after post-independence exclusion from power, Paliau the former iconoclast indulged in performing versions of traditional dance, wearing traditional regalia. But Makasol *kastam* centred almost entirely on a heavily airbrushed depiction of the past in which people obeyed the directives of their leaders and were not 'bigheads' (in Tok Pisin, *bikhet*), as they had now become. Makasol ideology also held that such *kastam* prevailed during the years of the Local Government Council, the restoration of which became a political goal, even though the contrary facts of the case could not possibly have been lost to memory.

Wing Militant I: At the polls

Makasol engaged in legal challenge, direct action, and electoral politics. In 1984—led by attorney Martin Thompson Poposui—Makasol successfully sued the provincial government for violating the freedom of worship clause in the national constitution by allegedly suppressing Makasol access to the Manus government radio station. Around the same time, Makasol activists occupied government property in Lorengau, claiming that it had been purchased in 1951 with council funds which were in fact Paliau Movement funds. Makasol lost the case (Wanek 1996: 194–5).

In electoral politics, Makasol looked beyond Manus. In 1982, both Paliau Lukas and Kisokau Pochapon, who had retired from his post as the country's surveyor general for this purpose, ran for seats in the national parliament in the second post-independence parliamentary election (the first was in 1977). Makasol endorsed both candidates. At least in this instance, it tried to act like a political party, although it had no presence outside Manus. Some observers called it the Makasol group (Pokawin 1989).[21] According to Pokawin (1989: 253–61), both candidates depended on what Makasol leaders told them were 10,000 Makasol-inclined voters

---

21   Makasol fashioned itself briefly as the Makasol Party. But, according to Wanek (1996: 195), it dropped 'party' in 1982, 'because Paliau Maloat felt that "party" was unworthy of a movement like Makasol, which builds on prophecies from Above'.

in Manus. At the time, however, the total population of Manus was just shy of 26,000 of which about 16,500 were eligible voters. Neither Makasol candidate prevailed.

The next elections for seats in the national parliament were held in 1987.[22] By this time, community governments had been established and an angry Paliau asked his followers to boycott the election. But both Paliau Lukas and Martin Thompson Poposui ran anyway. Neither won a seat. Martin Thompson Poposui did win a 1991 election to fill a seat that had become vacant between elections, and he retained this seat in the 1992 general election (Dalsgaard 2009: 104). New national legislation soon eliminated the position of provincial premier, held by Stephen Pokawin, an open political opponent of Makasol. As a member from Manus, Thompson Poposui was appointed interim governor (the provincial leadership post with which the legislation replaced that of premier), to serve until the next election. But Thompson Poposui, the most successful Makasol politician, died in 1996 (Dalsgaard 2009: 106). Pokawin won the subsequent election and became provincial leader under the new system. Thompson Poposui's death (at approximately the age of 40) cut short not only his political career but also Makasol's political participation at the national level.

Makasol motives

It looks like Paliau Lukas and Thompson Poposui may have put political ambition ahead of loyalty to Paliau Maloat in the 1987 election. In that vein, some observers have wondered if they, and perhaps other young Makasol activists, were exploiting Paliau's occult hold on his followers to pursue secular political power. Wanek was acquainted with Paliau Lukas and characterises his views as follows:

> Paliau Lukas perceived Makasol as a movement which used 'religion' mainly as a tool in order to make villagers understand the movement's goals, which were purely political. Additionally, 'religion' exerted a certain protection against persecution from the authorities because freedom of worship was granted by the National Constitution. He [Paliau Lukas] emphasized repeatedly

---

22 In the interim, a few Makasol members obtained seats in the provincial Lapan Assembly (Wanek 1996: 195), but we have no information on their influence there.

that 'cargo' was of no importance in Makasol. It was quite silly to believe in these sorts of lies, indeed he claimed that the 'cargo' argument was only used by the enemies of the movement to discredit it. (Wanek 1996: 186)

Otto (1992a: 64) writes that 'the Makasol [historical] narratives were used to mobilize lingering millenarian sentiments for party political purposes'. Pokawin (1989: 260) comments: 'critics of the Makasol group call [Paliau Lukas], and others such as Kisokau Pochapon, political opportunists who use the village people for their own political gains. There is *some* [Pokawin's italics] substance to this view'. Pokawin does not give evidence for the latter judgement. And just a few sentences earlier he suggests that Paliau Lukas's motives are more complicated: 'Lukas is hard to understand. He is either driven by a higher ideal or is a confused simpleton. Given his academic credentials, I want to think he is driven by a higher ideal'.[23]

Schwartz's extensive conversations with Paliau Lukas and other young Makasol leaders left him with the impression that, if they did not place their full faith in Paliau's cosmology, his construction of history, his personal powers, and his special relationship with Wang Jesus, they were trying very hard to do so. Paliau Lukas eventually broke with Makasol. The direction he took may be telling. Rather than seek an obvious way of entering electoral politics, he became active in the Evangelical Church of Manus. A prized convert, he gratified the church by making the rounds of Manus villages presenting himself as a recovering cultist who, in the Evangelical Church of Manus, had found the truth. Kakak Kais (1998: Chapter 3) notes three other prominent Makasol activists who quit during the same period who also became active in the Evangelical Church of Manus. A fourth became a leader in a Catholic Charismatic group. Kisokau Pochapon did not impress Smith as an opportunist—at least not one with grand ambitions. By 2015, he had been almost wholly occupied with Makasol and its successor, Wind Nation, for decades without, to Smith's knowledge, using his position in these manifestations of the Movement to any obvious political advantage beyond Manus.

---

23   Pokawin apparently would like to believe that academic credentials inoculate one against becoming a 'confused simpleton'. History in general, however, does not bear this out. Neither does the history of millenarianism suggest that accumulating academic degrees makes one immune to its appeal. Pokawin's own academic credentials are impressive. Among other things, he holds a master of arts degree in political science from Canada's McGill University and served as chancellor of the University of Papua New Guinea for several years post-2000. We do not know his religious affiliation, although he would be a rare Papua New Guinean if he had none. We know that his father and mother were very active in the Evangelical Church of Manus.

Wing Militant II: For the world

We have already pointed out important universalistic elements in Paliau's new doctrine—in particular, formal absolution of whites for not sharing knowledge with New Guineans (although many of the rank and file were not fully convinced of this) and calling for True Freedom for people of all races. When still within the fold in the mid-1980s, Paliau Lukas explained to Schwartz that currently nobody on Earth could go to Heaven because Jesus forbade it until all were ready and that freeing all people was thus part of the Makasol mission.

There is some precedent for such universalism in Paliau's earlier teachings. He had always spoken of God as the God of all, whose efforts to help the blacks the whites had thwarted. And he and his followers had occasionally used a formula of multi-racial unity under one god that became standard in the new metaphysics, as Lungat put it in a 1973 conversation with Schwartz: 'We are all brothers. We're white, we're red, we're black, we're brown. All colours live here on Earth. But one God is our father'. But it is also easy to understand why Paliau and his lieutenants began to stress universalism more as they were developing a new doctrine: opposition to white domination is a weak rallying cry for opposing a black government—that is, the government of independence. Opposition to the independent PNG government would not necessarily exclude opposition to international white domination, but that was not the Makasol position.

Since around the beginning of 1990, the Movement has gone by the name Wind Nation—in Tok Pisin, *Win Neisen*. Adherents have explained its meaning to Schwartz and Smith in three ways that are not mutually exclusive. To wit: Wind Nation comprises the essence of Wing, Wang, and Wong within each person; Wind Nation comprises all the adherents of Wind Nation doctrine; and everyone in the world is part of Wind Nation, whether they know it or not, because Wing dwells in them all. This last idea supports Wind Nation's assumption of worldwide importance. Wind Nation documents often refer to *Win Neisen long Wold*; that is, Wind Nation Worldwide. Wind Nation also produces its documents on a 'WIN NEISEN LONG WOL' letterhead. During Paliau's lifetime the letterhead frequently included post office box and telephone numbers in Lorengau for 'Paliau Maloat, OBE Esquire; Win Neisen long Wol'. In addition, at top centre, dominating the page, was often the Wind Nation logo, elaborate but inexpertly drawn.

Figure 13.2: In the 1980s, Wind Nation began producing written documents bearing the elaborate but inexpertly drawn Wind Nation logo.

Source: Unknown Wind Nation adherent.

The logo is organised around a shield shape framing a badly copied black and white photo of Paliau in shirt and necktie. Beneath his picture are the words 'MAN I LIDA' ('The Leader'). Atop the shield is a six-pointed star. The shield sits atop a traditional Manus wooden bowl with an elongated shape, like a rugby ball or an American football (that is, prolate spheroid), and large spiral handles at each end. Some Wind Nation members say that the spirals represent *kalopeu*, the chambered nautilus, a symbol of Wind Nation. The bowl bears the words 'WIN NEISEN'. There is an animal standing on each spiral handle of the bowl. On the right is a dog sitting with its front paws resting on the shield and a pipe in its mouth. On the left is a long-legged and long-beaked bird, with one foot resting on the shield. The dog represents Paliau's small pet dog, which people thought wonderful because Paliau had taught it several tricks, like holding a pipe in its mouth. Maybe they took Paliau's rapport with his dog as an example of his alleged control over nature. The bird is undoubtedly a chauka bird (the Manus friarbird), a bird endemic to Manus. It has a loud and distinctive cry that people say heralds morning and evening and warns of danger.

Wind Nation leaders offer adherents both something immediate and something more distant that might or might not embrace the whole of humanity. Speaking at a Christmas Wind Nation gathering in Lorengau in 1990, Kisokau Pochapon seemed to promise his audience a version of the cargo if only they would accept Wing/Win as saviour. Here are his words, translated from the original Tok Pisin:[24]

> Follow Win Nation! Wing says that the path to money is easy. It goes through Win. The work of the government, of freedom is with Win. Car, radio, and everything you want—Win. Win makes it happen. Win makes everything here easy to obtain. Win leads on the path to where there is no ageing, no illness, no death. If you want money, if you want a car, whatever you want, Win will give it to you.[25]

But concrete descriptions of Wing's and Wind Nation's government make it sound less than ready to oversee worldwide salvation. At the same gathering at which Pochapon promised easy access to anything people wanted, Paliau—now within less than two years of his death—depicted the government of Wind Nation. The Local Government Council, he said, 'is the freedom government to take care of all of Manus, the true government of Wind Nation is the Local Government Council'. Further, 'Wind Nation is the true nation to bring freedom to all the countries of the world'. Paliau also outlined Wind Nation's 'worldwide structure'. This included a list of officers, with Kisokau Pochapon as president and Peter Kuwoh as deputy president, followed by a hierarchy that reaches down to village-level tax collectors, teachers, and 'councils'. (On another

---

24 Schwartz was not present at this event, but a Wind Nation leader recorded the speeches for him.

25 In the original Tok Pisin: *Bihainim win neisen! Em i tok long rot bilong mani i stap isi. Em i stap long Win. Wok bilong gavman, long fridom, em i stap long Win. Ka, na radio na olgeta samting yupela i laikim hia, bilong Win. Win i wokim. Win i wokim olgeta samting hia na bilong isi bilong en i kam long han bilong yufela. Win i soim rot long noken lapun, no ken sik, no ken dai. Sapos yu laikim mani, yu laikim ka, yu laikim wanem, wanem; Win bai i givim long yu.*

occasion, Wind Nation issued an organisational chart for this hierarchy.) This does not seem adequate to governing the entire world, but fervent Paliau followers probably were not concerned with such details.[26]

Wanek (1996: 216) reports a Wind Nation doctrine of less universal beneficence:

> 'Wind Nation believes that Wang Jesus will come a second time; this time to Manus, to the coloured people who have not participated in his crucifixion … But he will not bring them *save* [Tok Pisin for wisdom or knowledge], because this has already been spoilt by the white man. He will bring tinktink [Wanek's rendering of the Tok Pisin word we render as *tingting*] to the coloured people, the power of understanding. Using tinktink, things will just happen, in the same way as during the First Order of Things. Adherents of Wind Nation will be able to live without drudgery. Wang Jesus … will make them heavenly blessed, whereas the white man will continue to be wicked and unhappy, will have to attend schools, and will set out killing other human beings by means of *save* and weapons'. This doctrine supports Wind Nation's antipathy to formal schooling in the 1980s. It also expresses persistent but unsurprising antipathy toward whites, despite repeated declarations of racial unity under Wing.[27]

---

26   In this speech, Paliau also spoke of the Wind Nation International Bank 'Manus Headquarters'. We know very little about this phenomenon, but Wanek (1996: 196–7) obtained information on what might be the same thing under a different name: 'The Paliau Bank gained importance … in the late 1980s and members of the movement deposited their individual savings there, after withdrawing them from the Lorengau branch of the Papua New Guinea Banking Corporation. They did this in protest against the system of community governments … and the Paliau Bank earmarked their money, once again, to fund a new government [the government of Wang Jesus]'. Supposedly the bank had branches in several villages. We (Schwartz and Smith) have not tried to follow the money that may or may not have passed into or through the Movement. We can offer only the following items. Early in the Movement, Paliau collected money—much of it allegedly from war damage payments to Manus people—to support building schools and other infrastructure. In his 1970 presentation at the Waigani Seminar, Paliau said that the war damage fund was used as 'the initial operating revenue for the Baluan Local Government Council during the financial year 1950–51. It was also used to build village schools, aid posts, and cooperative society stores and other things' (Maloat 1970: 151). According to a 1974 Movement document, the war damage fund at that time still contained some 20,000 kina (the currency of independent PNG). Pokawin (1983b: 110) reports there was a 'Makasol Memorial Fund' that in August 1980 contained 6,125 kina obtained from member contributions.

27   Unfortunately, here (and sometimes elsewhere in his otherwise informative book), Wanek does not tell the reader from whom or whence he derives his statements of Movement doctrines or beliefs, so it is impossible to tell if they represent Paliau's pronouncements or have another source.

Neither Schwartz nor Smith have come across the doctrine Wanek describes. But Wind Nation leaders have often enunciated a doctrine of universal salvation that nevertheless has a dark side—the threat of an apocalypse that destroys non-believers. The most vivid description of this danger of which we know—one that also articulates some expansion of basic Wind Nation cosmology—is in a letter Paliau Lukas sent to Schwartz, then in California, in December 1990. Lukas stresses (in English) the danger the world faces:

> The world is heading toward its early stage or its beginnings towards the year 2000. What really is going to happen there in America, California and all of the United States will one way or another affect Manus most. Because Manus is so small and Beautiful in our hearts and minds, Ted, tell the world not to destroy it but to SAFE Manus … Therefore Ted I now conclude to say world and United States must declare that Paliau Maloat in Manus is our SAVIOUR by December Christmas 1991.

Paliau Lukas enclosed a document written in English and undated, but attributed to and signed by Paliau Maloat, explaining this danger in terms of the cosmology of Wing, Wang, and Wong. Here it is, uncorrected for spelling or punctuation:[28]

> I, PALIAU MALOAT, O.B.E. THE LAST PROPHET, wish to reveal to every individual of this World that;
>
> The 'Cloud' is not just an ordinary mass of visible condensed water-vapour, floating high above general level of the ground in motion. It was 'the home', of the invisible creator, Wing and the first ever nation. In it Wing the creator, created five powerful beings; they are:
>
> 1. HIGH STRONG WIND
> 2. RAIN
> 3. LIGHTNING
> 4. THUNDER
> 5. RAINBOW
>
> These five supernatural beings are based in the Clouds today as the World know and fully realise. I wish to correct Scientist theory that the five elements are not just mere particles of any sort.

---

28 The personification of natural forces here is even more extreme than that implied in accounts of Paliau's ability to control them as though they were sentient entities that could *harim tok*.

It was through creation that Wing the Creator created and left them as inhabitants of the Cloud.

Subject to the creators own power, a second nation was created—The Heaven. The Creator left the Clouds and lived in Heaven. The Heaven became his new home. With him he brought three invisible Spiritual Children whom he thought as would become the inhabitants of Heaven. He named his three Spiritual Children as;

1. WANG
2. HOLY SPIRIT and
3. ANGELS

With his own power his three invisible children were respectively symbolized by creating three lights;

1. MOON
2. STARS, and
3. SUN

The Moon symbolizes Wang the first child, the Stars the Holy spirit, the second child and the Sun the Angels, the third child. With the second and third children, the creator Wing ordered their existence to multiply in great numbers, therefore billions upon billions of Holy Spirit and Angels came into being. The Holy Spirit and Angels appointed Wang as the head of government and 'Light of the Sun' [in Tok Pisin, *laitsan*] as the King. Wang became the government and 'Light of the Sun' became the King of Heaven. The Holy Spirit and Angels became the main work force of the Government of Heaven.

Wing then created the planet Earth. He ordered the Clouds together and thus the clouds formed and shaped what is known today as the earth. The earth with its own environment and characteristics was established and again Wing divided the earth into two parts, the Sea and Land. The sea symbolizes the female generations and the land the male generations, which were already created in Heaven through the Holy Spirit as females and the Angels as the males. Therefore, the sea became the mother and the land became the father of all kinds of life on earth thereafter.

On the planet earth Wing created an additional five supernatural beings. They were to be the supporters of those already created in the clouds thus making the total to ten (10).

On earth, the sixth super natural being was the Sea, the seventh being very strong currents caused by Tides, the eighth Being Tidal Waves, the nineth being the Earthquakes and the tenth being all particles, substance and anything in material form ...

In our times we could refer to these ten supernatural beings as supernatural powers. These ten supernatural powers can destroy the whole World. Not one country of this world could direct and control these supernatural powers to do as it wish.

The only person who can direct and control these forces is <u>Wang</u> whom the Christians call Jesus Christ. The power to direct and control these forces remains the sole responsibility of that one person. Although invisible he remains the Government and King of Nations of the Commonwealth. Through him he has chosen England as the Nation of the Nations and the Leader of the Commonwealth.

His warning to the World is that every country of the World are now under the power of God as King and Satan as the government. The whole World is in fact being misled by a false creator GOD and SATAN. The truth about WANG JESUS the World does not know. Therefore Wang Jesus is now prepared to use this ten supernatural forces to destroy any country of the World which does not come under his reign—Nations of the Commonwealth.

I challenge all persons of Manus, New Guinea Islands, New Guinea and the World to take heed of this warning.

Thank you very much.
[Paliau's signature]
<u>PALIAU MALOAT. O.B.E.</u>
Last Prophet of the World

Paliau the prophet

This was hardly Paliau's first venture into prophecy (if, indeed, Paliau composed this prophecy independently). In 1984, he declared that something would happen around the end of 1990; that is, in seven years—a figure Paliau used explicitly to invoke the biblical Joseph's prophecies to Egypt's Pharaoh. Everyone, he said, should join Makasol to prepare for whatever was coming. Just what would happen Paliau left vague, but he implied that a global apocalypse of some kind was a possibility and that those who placed themselves under Makasol's protection would be saved. The return of Wang Jesus to rule the world was another implied possibility (cf. Otto 1992a: 62).[29] Gustafsson (1995: 80) reports that in the late 1980s Paliau 'would say repeatedly that the last day was near and there was not much time left for those who wanted to experience *Win Neisen*'. That is, there was not much time left for those who wanted to be saved rather than destroyed.

In 1987, Paliau announced that he would die voluntarily and come back as the vessel of the discarnate entity, Wang Jesus, who would then govern the world, in Paliau's body, from the throne of King David (that is, the British Coronation Chair), transported magically from London to Baluan. Makasol members told Schwartz that Paliau had announced that he would be publicly crucified in order to be resurrected, but that he submitted the idea to his followers for a vote and they rejected it. Wanek (1996: 283n11) obtained a colourful account of how in 1987 Paliau staged in the Lorengau market a public counting of the results of what Paliau said had been a secret ballot, leading to immediate cancellation of the scheduled crucifixion. Wanek notes that he could not find anyone who admitted to actually casting one of the ballots, allegedly contained in baskets Paliau brought to the event (cf. Otto 1991: 264). Gustafsson (1995: 77) reports that in 1987 Paliau told her that he had already died, but he had returned to life three days later because his adherents had voted that he should not die.[30]

29   Wanek (1996: 211) reports a more definite version of this prophecy: 'He claimed that Wang Jesus had disclosed that He would come back to the world in the near future, and that members of Makasol had to obey Paliau without questioning his orders, because it was really Wang Jesus who spoke through Paliau. "On the other side of 1990" (as Paliau put it), Wang Jesus would return to the world ... to govern the world by establishing His "Commonwealth of Nations"'.

30   Gustafsson (1995: 77) reports that some of Paliau's followers also claimed to have died and returned to life, after having 'met their ancestors who already lived a life approximating that of Adam and Eve in Paradise'. Such death and resurrection was also, of course, common during the Cemetery Cult of the 1950s. Wanek (1996: 283–4) reports that on Nauna Island, villagers understood that Paliau had predicted that he would die three days before Christmas 1989, three days of darkness would ensue, and Wang Jesus would return, inhabiting Paliau's rejuvenated body. Then 'life would be different for all members of Wind Nation. There would be no more *hatwok*, no more ageing, no more sickness, no more deaths, and it would be sufficient to *tinktink* of food and it would materialize ... Every single item [a person] could think of would present itself. Factories would emerge from underground, and every village would get its own factory producing everything from bicycles and corrugated roofing material to money'.

Paliau as Jesus

We can't be sure which of Paliau's prophecies were successfully communicated to all the Wind Nation rank and file. Schwartz recalls that most of the people who came to hear Paliau speak during his years in Lorengau were from generations in which few were literate, even in Tok Pisin. Many or most couldn't read even the Tok Pisin version of the 1982 document warning of a worldwide apocalypse, the text of which is reproduced above (cf. Otto 1992a: 59). Paliau's degree-holding Wind Nation leaders intended the English version for public officials and presumably other formally educated people of their own or adjacent generations outside the Movement. In addition to requiring knowledge of English, the document includes a comment on science ('I wish to correct Scientist theory that the five elements are not just mere particles of any sort') that does not appear in the Tok Pisin version. The status of scientific explanation probably was not an issue of much concern to most Movement adherents.

Even so, the overall record suggests that in the prophecies and proclamations of Paliau's last years his emphasis shifted more and more towards his claimed relationship to Jesus. Reports of Paliau's Jesus-like miracles reach back for many years. In addition to being able to control the wind and waves during the days of wonder—as Jesus did on the Sea of Galilee—Paliau is credited by many of his followers with curing the sick, including restoring sight to the blind (cf. Otto 1991: 283). In 2015, some of his followers told Smith that Paliau could walk on water, and claimed to have seen it. Paliau's flirtation with death and resurrection—both as a staged event and as a prophecy—is reminiscent of the Noise, but also the New Testament. At the December 1990 gathering noted above, Paliau called himself the '*maus bilong Yesus*'—literally, the mouth of Jesus—and Paliau Lukas spoke (in English) in praise of 'Paliau Maloat who has been following in the footprints of Jesus for the last 45 years, and who I claim now as they are both one in spirit and in flesh that the world must know and learn quickly' (presumably to avoid an apocalypse of non-believers).

During his 2015 visit to Pere, Smith had several conversations with Kumulau Paniu, Wind Nation's *amamas lida* (that is, worship or celebration leader). In this role Paniu led the daily and weekly gatherings of Pere's Wind Nation adherents. An elderly but robust and energetic man,

Paniu told Smith that Paliau himself had chosen him as a leader in 1982.[31] Paniu kept a notebook of things he had heard Paliau say, among them a phrase in Paliau's Baluan language: '*Yesus Hapa? Wong tepo Yesus*'. Paniu translated this into Tok Pisin as '*Yesus i we? Mi tasol i Yesus*', which translates into English as 'Where is Jesus? I am Jesus [or, perhaps: I alone am Jesus]'. A slightly different translation yields a more ambiguous statement. Ton Otto (personal communication, April 2019) recommends a different spelling of the Baluan phrase (to wit: *Jesus a pa? Wong tepwo Jesus*) and, more important, a slightly different translation into English: 'Where is Jesus? I now am Jesus/It is me who is Jesus'. This leans more towards suggesting that Paliau is a new vessel for an incorporeal entity, Wang Jesus, rather than being identical with Jesus of Nazareth.

Gustafsson (1995: 76) reports that in March 1989 Paliau 'announced that the last prophet was dead and now he was Jesus. Jesus had gone to Heaven—his body did not remain and therefore no one knew what he would look like when coming back to Earth. According to Paliau, since it was white people who killed him Jesus would come to the black people. This had already happened; he had returned through Paliau, who was Jesus'. Unfortunately, Gustafsson does not say whence her information comes. But Paniu recorded that Paliau declared himself Jesus—in some sense—in 1990. In his notebook, he had also written the question (we translate from Tok Pisin): 'Why does Paliau Maloat say he is Jesus?' And he proposes the following answer: 'Paliau Maloat can say he is Jesus because he wants to strengthen our knowledge and belief and show that he speaks to show the angel that lives inside him how he is a prophet who is Jesus'.

Who did Paliau think he was, anyway?

In the next chapter we will visit Manus in 2015 and hear a number of opinions on what Paliau accomplished and who he was from people whose lives overlapped with his, and from people who know of Paliau only what they have heard. This is a good time to pause and ask who Paliau thought he was in the last phase of his career. Recall that in 1990, when Schwartz asked Paliau if he had indeed told his followers that he

---

31 Paniu was never honoured by the British Commonwealth, but he did receive a medal for Meritorious Community Service from the PNG government sometime post-2000.

was Jesus, Paliau's reply was more nuanced than the statements Kumulau Paniu recorded. Paliau told Schwartz: 'I said to them, who else in the world has such good things to say? It's Jesus! He is a man with good things to say. I said: I'm your Jesus. I'm your Jesus, I told them'. He then said that he had told his followers that he was merely Paliau Maloat, but that he got his teachings from Jesus.

Schwartz never heard Paliau make any stronger claim, either in private or public. Yet we have several reports, like Paniu's, that on some occasions Paliau did indeed do so. Similarly, Paliau Lukas was unequivocal that Paliau Maloat and Jesus were 'one in spirit and in flesh'. He declared this at a public event at which Paliau was present, so Paliau probably would have heard it and he apparently let it pass. As noted in Chapter 11, Paliau often complained to Schwartz that people chronically distorted what he said. But we also know that Paliau was quite capable of letting people attribute to him almost anything they wanted if it helped him to secure his leadership and to get his way. However he saw himself, he was no more likely to contradict Paliau Lukas's announcement that he was 'one in spirit and in flesh' with Jesus than he would have been to blush and protest when someone called him the founder of the Pangu Pati and the father of PNG.

The simplest explanation for Paliau's claiming that he was Jesus and promising universal True Freedom towards the end of his life is that he had become so thoroughly enmeshed in a self-image as leader and innovator that he was willing to go to extremes to maintain it. We nonetheless doubt that Paliau ever regarded himself as a fraud. Schwartz has observed that charismatic leaders often become their own followers—both makers and consumers of their own myths. Otto (1998: 86) elegantly makes much the same point: 'Paliau, in a mutually re-enforcing interaction with his followers, began to live his myth more fully'.

It is also possible that the Paliau of the late 1980s was not the same Paliau who initiated the Movement in the 1940s. In the 1990s, Paliau handled Schwartz's questions about his relationship to Jesus with finesse; but as Paliau approached the end of his life Schwartz found him less introspective in conversation and more rigid and authoritarian in his manner towards his followers. Granted, in the Wind Nation era Paliau was seldom if ever trying to win over political opponents as he did when running for or executing his elected public offices. In the Wind Nation era he was generally preaching to the converted. Even so, it is hard to imagine the Paliau who preached the doctrine of Wing, Wang, and Wong even bending enough to leaven his remarks with jokes and comments about the weather as he did in Bunai when he stopped the Cemetery Cult. Rather, Schwartz observed, Paliau in his later years scolded and insulted his listeners with less restraint than ever.[32] He had gone from being an imperious leader, who nevertheless knew how to change his tone for tactical reasons, to acting like a fanatic. We cannot rule out the possibility that Paliau suffered a cognitive decline in his last years. When Schwartz last heard Paliau speak in public he saw that he was physically feeble (he needed help walking) and, although Paliau's orations had always been repetitive, he now seemed at times to repeat himself out of confusion rather than for emphasis.[33]

Whatever Paliau's innermost thoughts or his cognitive status during his late career, his leading followers—men like Paliau Lukas, Kisokau Pochapon, Peter Kuwoh, and Martin Poposui Thompson—clearly encouraged him to eschew moderation or subtlety. It is not possible to determine to what extent they may have tried to use Paliau and Wind Nation to bolster their prospects in electoral politics, but—as we argued above—we do not find political opportunism a fully satisfactory explanation for their behaviour. It would be hard to find a mundane electoral motive, for instance, for Paliau Lukas's plea in his letter to Schwartz in 1990 to 'tell the world not to destroy it but to SAFE Manus' by recognising Paliau as the world's saviour. In Chapter 2 we referred to Landes's (2011: 99) dictum that 'the prophet must overcome the innate common sense of most people', and suggested that many of the Manus people who found cargo prophecy even in Paliau's most pragmatically worldly plans were eager for someone to help them put aside the tested ideas about how things work that guided their daily lives. The formally educated men who attached themselves to Paliau may also have been eager for someone to hold out the hope of a more rapid and complete transformation of the world than anyone could achieve via PNG's new bureaucratic institutions, which may well have greatly disappointed them.

---

32 Wanek (1996: 204–10) describes in similar terms Paliau's address to a Wind Nation gathering in Lorengau in 1986.

33 Even minor mental decline would have made him more subject to the influence of his young enablers, although—as we have already discussed—to what end we can't be certain.

A much more important question than how Paliau saw himself is why others believed or hoped that Paliau was Jesus or a similar saviour and why some continue to do so. In Lorengau in the late 1980s, Paliau could still draw audiences of from a few dozen to a few hundred people, most of them dressed in the all-white clothing of dedicated supporters (cf. Wanek 1996: 204–5).[34] And even decades after his death (Paliau died on Baluan in November 1991) many people hold fast to Paliau's legend and teachings. There is no simple answer to the question of why they do so, nor is there an easy explanation of why anyone anywhere takes millenarian claims to heart. We return to these questions in our concluding chapter. But first we take a brief look at the state of Wind Nation today, an institution in which Paliau is known only through a limited written record and people's recollections, not all of which agree.

---

34 Wanek (1996: 218n5) reports that some Makasol members told him that they did not dare leave the Movement because Paliau would curse them if they did. This never came to our attention, but we have no reason to question it. Nevertheless, we also know that some leading Makasol members did break with Paliau.

14

Wind Nation in 2015

In September 2015, after several weeks in East Sepik Province, Smith spent two weeks in Manus, most of it in Pere village and including a day trip to Baluan. It had been over 40 years since he worked there with Schwartz, but Pere's appearance had not changed dramatically—certainly not as dramatically as it did between Mead's first visit there in 1928 and her return in 1953, by which time several Titan villages had abandoned their lagoons for a shared location on land. In 2015, Pere village stretched further along the beach in each direction than it had in 1973, petering out at the eastern end just short of a rather sprawling cemetery that in no way resembled what the ghosts had demanded during the Cemetery Cult. Many more houses were now built of manufactured materials, but they were still elevated on posts, a practical style in a hot, wet climate even if you don't live above a lagoon. To accommodate rising sea levels, where there had once been open, gently sloping beach, a thick barrier of volcanic rocks wrapped tightly in chicken wire divided land from water.

Houses were still arranged in the original New Way style, in orderly rows on either side of a wide central promenade. But the people of Pere were no longer united in their support for today's most visible face of the Movement, Wind Nation. And Wind Nation itself had changed since Schwartz last scrutinised it shortly before and after Paliau's death. The personified forces of nature—Wing's 10 soldiers—had not destroyed those who refused to accept Wing's dominion and Paliau had not returned as the corporeal vessel of Wang Jesus to put in place a Government of the Holy Spirit. Nonetheless, prophecy of such dramatic events was still part of the doctrine Wind Nation leaders espoused and some rank-and-file adherents—both old and young—still anticipated them: 'You watch', one stern-faced older woman told Smith, 'things are going to happen!' But Wind Nation also had a more relaxed aspect and many of its members seemed to have accepted the possibility that salvation might not be imminent.

Wind Nation front and centre

Anyone arriving in Pere for the first time in 2015 might easily assume that Wind Nation is central to village life. It is indeed highly visible. A long, roofed marketplace delineates the lagoon-side of the large clear space in the centre of the village. On the landward side of that sandy expanse is situated Margaret Mead's Resource Center (MMRC), built of manufactured materials on a concrete slab. Villagers built the MMRC— originally called the Margaret Mead Community Center—in the late 1970s, supported by government funds and private contributions, some from Mead's American friends. It was refurbished in the 1990s (when it probably acquired its new name, for reasons of which we are unaware). The Wind Nation meeting house stands to one side of the MMRC, separated from it by a neatly fenced and gravelled enclosure where the Papua New Guinea (PNG) national flag flies from a modern metal flagpole. The PNG flag is diagonally divided. The south-west triangle (the hoist) displays the white stars of the Southern Cross on a black background. The north-east triangle (the fly) displays on a red background the bright yellow silhouette of a bird of paradise. Only a few steps away, the Wind Nation meeting house flies the strikingly similar Wind Nation flag. This displays on the hoist the white silhouette of a traditional feasting bowl—which some Wind Nation adherents interpret as the *kalopeu* symbol—on a red field. On the fly, the white stars of the Southern Cross are arrayed against a black background. Whether intentional or not, the similarity and proximity of these two flags appear to assert the near equivalence of Wind Nation and the nation of PNG and Pere's allegiance to both.

Wind Nation, however, is one among at least five church congregations in Pere. The other four of which we know are the Catholic Church, the Evangelical Church of Manus, the Seventh-day Adventist Church, and the Teshuva Trumpet Worship Centre, an affiliate of the KAD-ESH Messianic Apostolic Prophetic Ministries. The Wind Nation meeting house probably enjoys pride of location because it occupies the space where the original Paliau Church (the Baluan Native Christian Church) meeting house stood when a majority of Pere people were firm Movement supporters.

Figure 14.1: The Wind Nation meeting house in the centre of Pere village, 2015.

Source: Michael French Smith.

We don't know how many Pere people are affiliated with each of these congregations or with none of them. We do have a rough idea of the number of active Wind Nation participants. In conventional Christian fashion, Wind Nation holds its major gatherings on Sunday mornings. Kumulau Paniu encouraged Smith to come to the only Sunday event during Smith's brief stay. Paniu told Wind Nation adherents that because Smith was visiting they should make it—as Paniu put it in a mixture of English and Tok Pisin—an '*amamas* full swing' (roughly: 'a full-scale celebration'). According to the official Sunday head count, 111 people attended (69 women and 42 men), out of a total Pere population of about 800. Allowing for the many possible deficiencies in these numbers, it still looks like active Wind Nation adherents do not make up even a plurality of resident villagers. But if interest in Wind Nation's brand of millenarianism is unimpressive, millenarianism itself is still popular. At least three of the alternatives to Wind Nation—all much closer to foreign missionary roots than Wind Nation—are explicitly millenarian: the Evangelical Church of Manus, the Seventh-day Adventist Church, and the Teshuva Trumpet Worship Centre.[1]

Paliau versus Wind Nation

To call Wind Nation the current manifestation of the Paliau Movement—rather than just the Movement's most visible manifestation—may be misleading. A great many people in Pere feel they have long been part of the Movement, but fewer are active participants in Wind Nation. Anyone born in the 1950s or thereafter grew up in a world Paliau helped shape. Most of the Pere people Smith spoke with in 2015 expressed their admiration for Paliau and gave him credit for bringing schools and better health care to Manus and playing a major role in PNG's progress towards independence. People praised Paliau most for forging wider unity among Manus people than they had ever known before. They also said that people were much more unified in Paliau's time than they are now. As one man put it: 'This movement of Paliau Maloat's brought unity, but we lost it'.

But admiring Paliau and lamenting the loss of the unity the Movement once fostered are not the same as admiring Wind Nation. By 2015, Paliau's loss of mass influence was apparent. Smith heard criticisms of Paliau as well as praise. A retired executive of Air Niugini (PNG's national airline) who had returned to live in Pere, her natal village, admired Paliau greatly, but she called Wind Nation (in English) 'a deviation'. Many others were just as critical and gave similar reasons for their disaffection. Some villagers told Smith they had fallen away from Paliau long before Wind Nation emerged because he had turned against the government.

---

1   Seventh-day Adventist doctrine holds that 'Two things will happen at the end of the millennium. First, God's city, the New Jerusalem, will descend from heaven and settle on our planet (Revelation 21:1). Second, those who rejected Jesus will be brought to life again (Revelation 20:5). However, the purpose of this resurrection is not to give them a second chance for salvation, since they will come out of the grave just as they went into it, with hearts full of hatred for God and His people … A consuming fire will then descend on the earth and utterly destroy all those outside the city of God. From the ashes of the old earth God will create a new heaven and a new earth (see 2 Peter 3:13; Revelation 21:1) and sin will be removed for all time from the universe' (www.adventist.org/articles/the-millenium-and-the-end-of-sin/). According to the Teshuva website: 'We believe that Yeshua [Jesus] is coming again soon to establish His Millennial Reign in Jerusalem'. And: 'We believe in The Fullness of the Infilling and Manifestation of The Holy Spirit, which is The Spirit of Holiness, including all the revelatory gifts, signs, wonders, and miracles and a complete, open interaction between Heaven and Earth' (kad-esh.org/what-we-believe/). As for the Evangelical Church of Manus, its name suggests that it also rests on a millenarian doctrine.

But renouncing God and claiming to be Jesus was the decisive point for others. As one put it: 'When Paliau got rid of God, plenty of people broke away'. A member of the village's executive council, once a loyal member of the Baluan Native Christian Church, praised Paliau's work prior to the Wind Nation era. But when this man returned to Pere after several years of migrant work, he was not pleased with the changes he found: 'Why did he get rid of God? What was the meaning of that?' He told Smith that he had asked Wind Nation adherents to explain it to him, but—he said—they just told him that they now eschewed God simply because Paliau said so. He also found worthy of mockery Paliau's claim to be Jesus or very nearly so: 'In the Bible, when Jesus died he came alive again. If Paliau is Jesus, why hasn't he risen again?'

Wind Nation doctrine in 2015

Nevertheless, Movement originalists critical of Wind Nation live amicably in Pere with adherents of Paliau's late-career claims and promises. If there is anything like an official version of Wind Nation doctrine it is probably that which Kumulau Paniu and others recite in the meeting house, much of which Paniu had recorded in a notebook labelled '*Las Save, Win Neisen Wol, Department Pere*' ('The Last Knowledge, Wind Nation World, Pere Department'). Paliau began calling his pronouncements his 'Last Knowledge' in the 1980s, but Paniu's notebook is his record of Paliau's thoughts and pronouncements in the last year or so before his death in November 1991.[2] Like the other records we have of Paliau's teachings and declarations, one can shape these into a systematic doctrine only with some tinkering and interpolation. There are very few differences, however, between Paniu's record and what Schwartz recorded and Makasol and Wind Nation published many years earlier. Most of the differences are in the general tone, Paliau's statements about his relationship to Jesus, and Paliau's prophecies.

Paliau's (or, collectively, Wind Nation's) late-career statements as recorded by Paniu are even more grandiose than those issued earlier. (Paliau was, however, entitled to call himself 'Sir'. In addition to having been awarded an OBE in the 1970s, he was included in another

---

2   Paniu gives the dates (day, month, and year) on which Paliau made the statements recorded, but the first page of the notebook itself is dated 1 December 2013. Paniu either compiled his notebook from memory or compiled it from notes made on earlier occasions.

British Commonwealth of Nations honours list not long before his death.)[3] The following is translated from Tok Pisin. We have not altered punctuation or capitalisation:

TUESDAY APRIL 26, 1991
MESSAGE OF SIR PALIAU MALOAT OBE ESQ
WIND NATION WORLD
LORENGAU
MANUS PROVINCE

WIND NATION IN MANUS DECLARES TO ALL THE
COUNTRIES OF THE WORLD.

HEAD TALK: WIND NATION MESSAGE FROM
MANUS TO GO OUT TO ALL THE
COUNTRIES OF THE WORLD.

Today in the year 1991 Wind Nation declares here in Manus for all the countries of the world the following, WIND IS THE TRUE POWER OF THE WORLD. All countries of the world do not know this and today all the countries of the world are in chaos.

This message of Wind today has gone to all the countries of the world, and now it comes back to Manus Province in Papua New Guinea.

THE MESSAGE OF SIR PALIAU MALOAT OBE ESQ
WIND NATION WORLD
LORENGAU
MANUS

1.   I CAN STOP THE SUN UNTIL I AM ABLE TO FINISH MY WORK.[4]

2.   THERE IS NO COUNTRY THAT CAN STOP ME FROM DECLARING THE TRUE MESSAGE OF JESUS I HOLD.

---

3   Citizens of PNG are still included in the British honours lists, although PNG adopted its own separate set of honours in 2004. We have not investigated how Paliau came to be granted an even higher honour than the OBE on the downside of his career.

4   Asserting that one can stop the passage of the sun is not especially radical in PNG. Magic for doing so is one of many kinds of magic for controlling natural phenomena of which people in many parts of PNG claim knowledge. Like most other indigenous forms of magic, many conditions govern its use (for example, see Smith 1994: 196), but an enduring special relationship with a monotheistic creator is generally not one of them.

3. REMOVE ALL YOUR CHILDREN FROM SCHOOL
    WHERE THE NAME OF WANG JESUS IS NOT ON
    THE BLACKBOARD.

4. THE NUMBER TWO PLACE HEAVEN I HOLD IN MY
    RIGHT HAND.

5. THE NUMBER THREE PLACE-DOWN WORLD
    I HOLD IN MY LEFT HAND.

6. WHEN I AM ANGRY, WIN TOO IS ANGRY.

7. THERE IS NO GOD IN HEAVEN, AND THERE IS NO
    GOD IN THE PLACE-DOWN. THERE IS ONLY WIN.

There is no country or person today in the world in 1991 that has
IDEA or knowledge of the message and FREEDOM of WIN the
way WIND NATION declares it here in Manus.

Only Manus has WIND NATION and this knowledge and
message of WIN that it can bring forth FREEDOM for the people
of Manus and to go out to all the countries of the world.

Paliau is also said to have doubled-down on claims of his relationship
to Jesus. Wind Nation enthusiasts in 2015 recounted to Smith stories of
Paliau's miracles at the slightest provocation. Most of these referred to his
power over the weather and other aspects of the non-human world.
Numbers of Wind Nation adherents claimed to have witnessed his skills
as a healer—sometimes via herbal medicine and sometimes via more
esoteric power. But Paliau's alleged ability to walk on water may resonate
the most with Pere people's knowledge of the biblical Jesus. Most accounts
of Paliau's aquatic ability are second- and third-hand. But Smith heard
one firsthand account from a middle-aged man who was present, he said,
when a small group of Australian men took Paliau by force, tied his hands,
took him out to sea, and threw him overboard to 'test him'. As the men
hauled him away to their boat, Paliau told his companion to wait on the
wharf (just where this happened isn't clear, but by the 1980s many villages
had wharves). The boat motored far out to sea, but it wasn't long—the
story goes—before Paliau returned alone, walking towards the wharf on
top of the water. Not all Pere people credit this account, but some find
in it ample proof that if Paliau is not Jesus he is in a similar league.

In some of Paliau's late-career teachings that Paniu recorded, he does
not claim to be Jesus or the equivalent. Here, translated from Tok Pisin,
is one example:

Six Teachings of Wang Paliau Maloat
Big Government King Nation

1. I asked Jesus to send me to you.

2. You, all the people of Manus, can accept me to watch over you and take you to Jesus.

3. Jesus himself can watch over you here in Manus, and Jesus himself can make Manus the leader of all the countries of the world.

4. You cannot go to church. [That is, Catholic, Evangelical, or other Christian churches in Manus.]

5. Follow me, I can take you and Manus to Jesus!

6. Call on Win and now I'll go to him [i.e. Win] and finish.

You must permit me to die and I will go and prepare freedom for you. When I die you can't mourn me and cry for me, I'll come at night to the [Wind Nation] meeting house [and listen to you].

But, as we described in the previous chapter, Paniu also recorded far less ambiguous statements, including one in the Baluan language that Paniu translated into Tok Pisin as '*Mi tasol i Yesus*'—that is, 'I am Jesus', or, more literally, 'Only I am Jesus'. As noted above, although identifying himself with Jesus may have excited some of Paliau's followers, it alienated others.

Paliau rarely committed to a schedule in his prophecies. He came closest to it in the following (translated here from Paniu's Tok Pisin version):

> The leader of this movement Sir Paliau Maloat from 1984 to 1990 spoke of his seven years. Now he says that these seven years will be his last seven years in the world. These seven years are for him to show us the LAST KNOWLEDGE of the world. He says to us that after 1990 and beyond many bad things will happen in the world and the world must choose between two roads. Is God true or is Win true? Just as Noah's ship saved man, this knowledge will save us.

But those who did not accept Win as saviour were not destroyed, nor—recalling Paliau Lukas's letter to Schwartz—did refusing to accept Paliau as the world's saviour lead to mass catastrophe. Of course, the Wind Nation rank and file weren't necessarily aware of the pronouncements Paliau and his core supporters issued in writing in the late 1980s, so Paliau's prophetic failures may have passed with little notice. People who did know of them and took them seriously might have been relieved when they misfired.

In any event, aside from what he found in Paniu's notebook, Smith saw no signs that Wind Nation adherents in Pere were worrying about a coming apocalypse.

Late in life, Paliau is also said to have prophesied his resurrection. According to Paniu: 'Sir Paliau Maloat said I will die but I will come back again to meet you in the number three place-down [that is, the earth, the mundane human abode] here in the world'. Smith heard even some Wind Nation adherents argue about whether Paliau really had said this, but some adherents found it plausible and inspiring. Apparently, however, Paliau had not committed to a schedule for his resurrection. Instead, he had told people to watch for three signs that he would soon return: they would see things they had never seen before, hear things they had never heard before, and say things they had never said before.[5]

People eager for salvation might not find mystical imprecision entirely satisfying, but it has a long history as a way to simultaneously sustain and restrain millennial hopes. Landes (2011: 30) refers to a letter Pope Gregory the Great sent to Æthelbert, the ruler of Kent (in what is now the United Kingdom), in 601. 'It shows', writes Landes, 'the importance of apocalyptic rhetoric as a motivator, as well as the necessary distance any responsible public figure needs to take from a foolish and easily disprovable stance'. In the letter, Gregory assures Æthelbert that the great things predicted in Scripture are at hand, but refrains from committing to any but a very cautious calendar of events. Landes quotes from the Pope's letter: 'the kingdom of the saints … is at hand. But as the end of the world draws near, many things are to come upon us which were not before, to wit, changes in the air, and terrors from heaven, and tempests out of the order of the seasons, wars, famines, pestilences, earthquakes in divers places; which things will not, nevertheless all happen in our days, but will follow after our days'.

The Manus people who courted the Noise in the 1940s or prepared their cemeteries diligently in the 1950s would have found such an indefinite—and scary—prospect unattractive. Yet neither Paniu's notebook nor Smith's conversations with hopeful adherents shed much light on what

---

5   Tok Pisin speakers will probably appreciate seeing Paniu's original Tok Pisin version of these enigmatic phrases:
1.   *Wanem samting yupela i no save lukim bifo na nau bai yupela i lukim.*
2.   *Wanem samting yupela i no save harim bifo na nau bai yupela i harim.*
3.   *Wanem samting yupela i no save tokim bifo na nau bai yupela i tokim.*

Paliau's return would entail. One could assume that earlier Wind Nation declarations still applied: Paliau's followers would be free from illness, ageing, and death and be able to bend the elements to their will. Or his return might herald the coming of a new world of a kind unimaginable in the 1940s, 1950s, or even the 1980s. The only prophecy Smith came across in 2015 that he had never encountered before fit that description. Inscribed in Paniu's book, it reads:

> Sir Paliau Maloat OBE ESQ Last Prophet of the World Wind Nation Prophecies these things on 11 July 1990:
>
> Manus Province will become the world commercial centre.
> Manus Province will become the world communication centre.[6]

We do not know how many of those who consider themselves Paliau's followers, or how many within the smaller group who consider themselves adherents of Wind Nation, are aware of these prophecies. One young Wind Nation enthusiast told Smith (in English) that Paliau had said that Manus would one day be the world's 'commercial and communications centre'. But despite the much higher levels of literacy and experience beyond the village of today's Manus people, there are surely many who would find it hard to form a concrete image of what a world commercial and communication centre is and how they would benefit from it. One also has to wonder what this might mean concretely to Wind Nation adherents who have taken to heart their leaders' condemnation of mundane business transactions as the wrong way to pursue wealth. But the move from prophesying the imminent arrival of cargo to advising people to wait for hazy signs of a Second Coming is much more dramatic than a changing position on the morality of commerce.[7]

---

6   This is translated from Tok Pisin, but the Tok Pisin rendering of the key terms is so close to English that translation is superfluous. What we render in English as commercial centre Paniu renders as *comesal senta*, and what we render in English as communications centre Paniu renders as *comminikasen senta*.

7   The prophecy of Manus communications and commercial ascendency sounds suspiciously like something one of Paliau's younger, urban followers might have concocted. But whatever its source, it is consistent with softening Wind Nation's apocalyptic stance by substituting an indefinite Second Coming for an imminent catastrophe.

Wind Nation International

In 1990, Kisokau Pochapon made Wind Nation sound at least somewhat like a cargo cult, promising that through Win the Creator people could get telephones, boats, and whatever other manufactured goods they wanted. But the promise of True Freedom—freedom from all of life's ills, including death—is much grander. In its grandeur it is so much like the promises of millenarian movements throughout the world that the only thing typically Melanesian about it may be its history. It also may be more interesting that—although some Wind Nation adherents hoped for Paliau's return—some seemed almost as enthusiastic about building a permanent bureaucratic organisation as they were about the Second Coming.

In the 1980s, the name Wind Nation International sounded beyond quixotic. Yet in 2015, Wind Nation was actually forging international ties. Two striking instances are Wind Nation relationships with international conservation organisations.[8] In 2012, the Nature Conservancy worked with organisations in Manus to mount a voyage by sail canoe throughout the Bismarck Archipelago, demonstrating the feasibility of travelling by sail and publicising the problem of climate change. A Nature Conservancy website billed the enterprise as 'voyaging around the Pacific connecting culture, conservation and climate change'.[9] Young men from Pere were members of the crew and one of them explained to Smith that the voyage also had another purpose: 'The other part is to show that we can control nature'. That is, they would show that the Wind Nation adherents on the crew could ensure that conditions for sailing stayed favourable. They did not hide this agenda from the Nature Conservancy. The website devoted to the voyage provides information on the crew, including their reasons for joining the voyage. One Pere crew member stated: '[I want] to share ideas and the knowledge I have concerning climate change with other Pacific neighbours, demonstrate my culture and tradition and to tell the world that WIN is the SUPER POWER!' Another said: 'To promote canoe culture and to showcase Win Neisen faith connected to nature'.[10]

---

8   Paliau, of course, had been forging international ties at least since he first met Schwartz, Shargo, and Mead, and continued to do so with every visiting anthropologist or tourist he met.

9   climatechallengervoyage.wordpress.com/about/.

10   climatechallengervoyage.wordpress.com/meet-the-crew/.

A second example of Wind Nation forging ties with international conservation organisations involves the World Wildlife Fund (WWF). In 2010, a WWF team visited Mbukei Island in connection with the organisation's Western Melanesia Programme. A member of the WWF team reported on WWF's Coral Triangle Blog:

> It was a most enlightening trip. The people were so eloquent … They surprised us with their wisdom of the most unexpected sort and … we found out they were people of the Wind Nation … It was their religion and majority of the people of M'Buke Islands belong to the Wind Nation. The Wind Nation believes in total freedom. Freedom from hardship, hunger, old age and disease. They believe in … an ongoing life that has no end. [A village leader] said: 'The Wind is the creator. Without air, no living thing will live. This is the reason why the Wind is the creator. Wind is the creator's name, not what he is. The Wind is what everything revolves around in. The Wind creates and the Wind can take away'.

> Wind Nation's Five Fundamentals to Total Freedom:

> 1. To live a life, you must like people. To be accepted, you must accept people.
> 2. You can joke a happy joke—not one that creates anger. While joking, it must not be insulting.
> 3. You should be happy and smile. Be playful.
> 4. Be honest.
> 5. Get together as a community through rituals—discuss things that will answer all objectives to create total freedom.[11]

> We loved our short stay here as [another team member] and I deeply share the Fundamentals of Total Freedom.[12]

Paliau's civic legacy

While there is considerable disagreement among Pere people about the likelihood of Paliau's resurrection or of achieving freedom for themselves from illness, ageing, and death, Smith found considerable agreement that

---

11   Readers will recognise the 'Five Fundamentals' as a version of the Five Rules Wind Nation leaders promulgated in the 1980s, described in Chapter 13.
12   coraltriangle.blogs.panda.org/coral-reefs/the-amazing-people-of-mbuke-island-manus-papua-new-guinea.

Paliau helped Manus people overcome their defensive mutual hostility and combine in larger groups for mutual benefit. Both Paliau's very real contribution in this sphere and contemporary Manus people's recognition of it are highly significant aspects of Paliau's legacy. One might even say that those who act in the spirit of this legacy are continuing the Movement, even though they may not hold with the doctrines of Wind Nation.

There is good evidence that Paliau left a legacy of self-help through collective institutions that is stronger than the legacy of his millenarian ideas. Otto (1991: 282), speaking of the 1980s, writes:

> Most people who lived in villages affected by the Movement agreed that the early years of change were generally a very good time. It was a period of peaceful coexistence between the ethnic groups, of unequaled cooperation and sharing, of new achievements and progress. This view was equally held by believers and by those who never belonged to the Paliau church. Only staunch opponents were reluctant to ascribe the positive changes to the Paliau Movement and would point to independent developments elsewhere.

Dalsgaard (2009: 305) writes that Paliau is still given credit in much of Manus for 'bringing clinics, schools, cooperative societies and, most important, local government councils into the hands of Manus people'. He also argues that 'the general perception among Manus people today is that *gavman* [Tok Pisin for government] was first introduced by the Germans, but some people will add that it was given to Manusians as "theirs" by Paliau' (Dalsgaard 2009: 85). Based on his recent research in Manus, Rasmussen (2015: 131) concludes 'it is likely that the idea of social organization at a higher level than that of kinship, clan or specific alliances has strong roots in the Paliau Movement', and has fostered new ideas about Mbukei as a 'community'. There is, he says, disagreement about the 'scope and responsibility of "the community"', especially pertaining to ceremonial exchange obligations (Rasmussen 2015: 121). But simply to have spurred an ongoing debate on a topic so vital to the course of change in PNG is a considerable accomplishment.[13]

---

13 Dalsgaard and Rasmussen were Ton Otto's students. Their work builds on his research on Baluan in original and insightful ways and, like Otto's, it is essential to any more comprehensive review of Paliau's legacy.

Paliau's millenarian legacy

Paliau's less secular legacy may be most on view in the Lipan section of Lipan-Mok village on Baluan Island. Lipan-Mok, the only village of any size on Baluan, is itself a legacy of the early Movement, when the Titan people who lived just offshore from the tiny island of Mok moved to the Baluan mainland to settle alongside Paliau's home village of Lipan. As in Pere, not everyone on Baluan is a Wind Nation adherent, but Wind Nation as an institution is on dramatic display.

The house in which Paliau died is a modern one by rural PNG standards, built of manufactured materials on a European plan—that is, divided into special purpose rooms connected by hallways. Except for a narrow strip along the shore, all of Lipan-Mok village is built on land that rises quickly up the side of the mountainous island. Paliau's house sits higher on the slope than most of the village and it has become a shrine. He is buried among flower beds and gravel paths in front of the house, as is Martin Thompson Poposui. Each grave is roofed to protect it from the elements and marked by a substantial granite monument, professionally inscribed.

Most of the interior of the house is plain. On entering, one encounters a display of photographs of Paliau at many stages of his career, emphasising the days when as an elected official he and Lady Teresia hobnobbed with national and international dignitaries, Paliau always in white shirt and tie and Teresia in an attractive dress.

The room in which Paliau died stands out from the others. Colourful faux-oriental carpets cover the floor. A photograph of Paliau and a collection of Paliau memorabilia are carefully arranged on a wide table among bunches of both real and plastic flowers. Conspicuous in the centre of the table is Paliau's battered brown fedora.

Figure 14.2: Paliau's grave in Lipan-Mok village, Baluan Island, 2015.
Source: Michael French Smith.

Figure 14.3: In 2015, Smith visited Paliau's house in Lipan-Mok village, Baluan Island, with (from left to right) Kumulau Paniu, Lady Teresia Maloat (Paliau's widow), and Kisokau Pochapon.

There is a visitors' book in the front room of the house, in which the party stands, and a shrine to Paliau in the room in which he died.

Source: An unidentified Lipan-Mok man took the picture using Smith's camera.

Figure 14.4: The shrine to Paliau in the room in which he died, 2015.
Source: Michael French Smith.

Also conspicuous is a hardwood carving of the Three Wise Monkeys that looks like the work of a local wood carver. This image is a staple of tourist kitsch for sale in souvenir shops in the Chinatowns of many Western cities, but it is derived from a Japanese temple decoration. It allegedly represents the virtues of seeing no evil, hearing no evil, and speaking no evil—one monkey is covering its eyes, one is covering its ears, and one is covering its mouth. In the last phase of his career, Paliau (either on his own or at an acolyte's suggestion) adopted the three monkeys image—sometimes using it in his Lorengau preaching—to illustrate what Wind Nation adherents have described to us as the proper behaviour of Wing's followers. That is, believers in Wing should see, hear, or speak nothing that would delay the coming of Wing's dominion over the world (cf. Gustafsson 1995: 73–4). Paliau also used the image to describe attributes of Wing, Wang, and Wong, saying that they respectively see, hear, and speak no evil. Being unable to see or hear evil seems incompatible with Wing's and Wang's supreme power, but perhaps Paliau simply wanted to say that Wing, Wang, and Wong were untainted with evil.

Figure 14.5: Paliau explaining Wing, Wang, and Wong to Schwartz in the late 1980s.

One of the young, formally educated followers Paliau had begun to attract is holding a painting representing the three entities in imaginary corporeal form and duplicating the three monkeys pose. Note that Wong (the Holy Spirit) is depicted as a woman. The smaller figure in front of Wing, Wang, and Wong is an angel.

Source: Theodore Schwartz. Digital copy courtesy of the Melanesian Archive, University of California, San Diego.

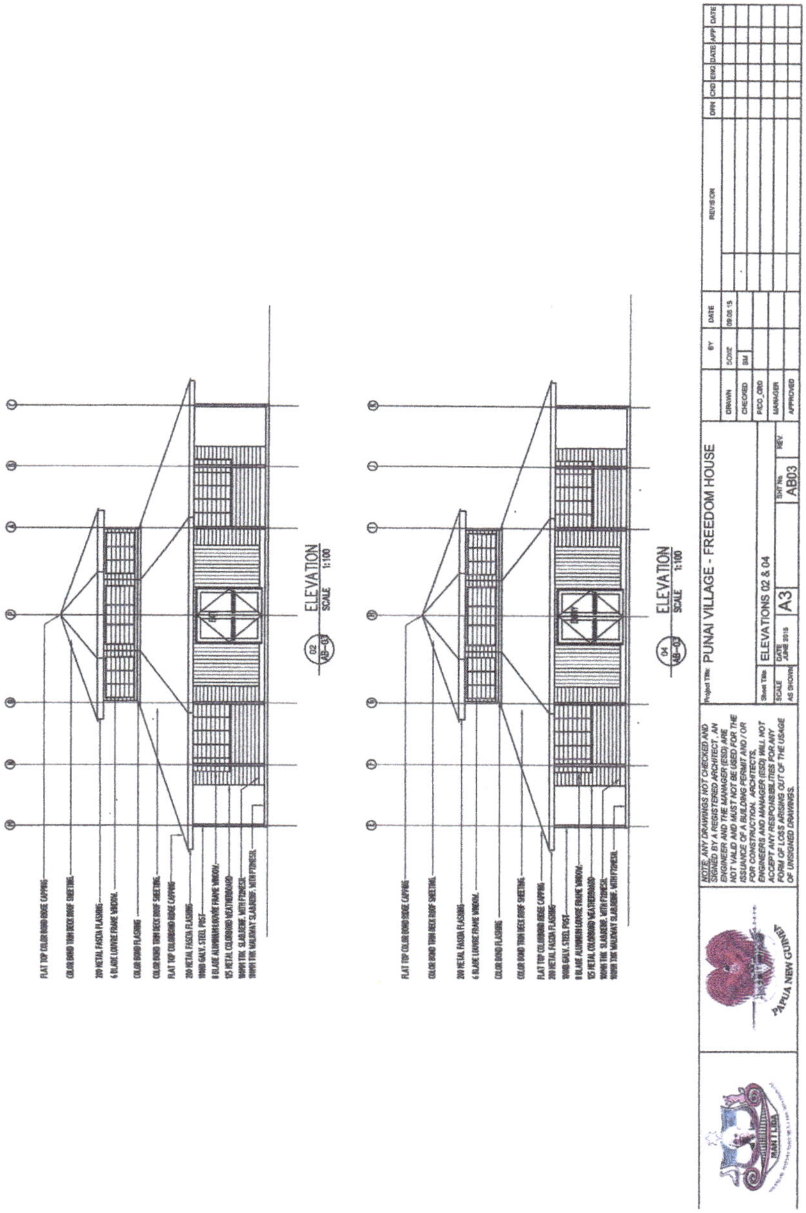

Figure 14.6: This page of the plan for Freedom House shows double doors on opposite sides of the octagon.

Visitors will enter on one side, ascend a ramp to the platform on which the throne of King David will sit, and exit on the opposite side.

Source: The plans, dated June 2015, are not signed.

Smith's few hours in Lipan-Mok included a visit with Kisokau Pochapon. He and Kumulau Paniu were eager for Smith to see Freedom House, under construction a short walk from the Paliau house. They explained that Freedom House is to be the 'spiritual centre' of Wind Nation International. Work was well underway, with most of the framing already completed. The octagonal building sits on a reinforced concrete slab on a base of compacted fill, it has an octagonal cupola, and when finished it will be surrounded by a covered porch. The plans show that louvred windows will provide full cross ventilation and they specify a full range of modern construction materials, such as 'colourbond trim deck roof sheeting'.

Colour versions of the Wind Nation '*Man i Lida*' logo and the PNG national emblem (a Raggiana bird of paradise perched atop a spear and an hourglass-shaped drum—a *kundu* in Tok Pisin), appear in the lower left-hand corner of each page. The plans show provision for wheelchair access but very little space for people to gather. Rather, in the centre of the building, directly beneath the cupola, there is a low platform on which, one of the builders told Smith (because it is not stated on the plan), the throne of King David will sit. Presumably, Paliau will occupy the throne on his return as the rejuvenated vessel for the incorporeal Wang Jesus.

Freedom House is built to last, perhaps to endure long after Wang Jesus takes the throne. Or perhaps it is built to last because Wind Nation leaders are resigned to waiting indefinitely for Paliau's return as Wang Jesus. In the latter case, building Freedom House is the opposite of throwing all your valuables into the sea and destroying your canoes. It is a statement of the intention to abide; it is not a final, desperate plea.

There are other signs too that some Wind Nation activists are planning for what may be a long organisational future as opposed to an apocalyptic end of time. For instance, anthropologist Andrew Lattas (personal communication, May 2019) reports that in the late 1990s some of the better-educated leaders of Wind Nation met more than once with leaders of the Pomio Kivung Movement, which is active in PNG's East New Britain Province (Bailoenakia and Koimanrea 1983; Lattas 1998). The object was, in Lattas's words, to 'start a dialogue between movements … [regarding] developing a Melanesian theology, a Melanesian civilization'.

A seminar sponsored by the Melanesian Institute for Pastoral and Socio-Economic Service, an organisation founded in PNG by Catholic missionaries, helped bring these leaders together.[14]

Wind Nation may be gradually weaning itself from relying on Paliau's charismatic authority and creating a more stable organisation that nevertheless maintains a millenarian doctrine; that is, it may be following the path of what sociologist Max Weber called the routinisation of charisma. Some strong supporters of the Movement and of Wind Nation have suggested that it is indeed planning for the long term. Kais (1998: Chapter 3) spends several pages assessing the factors that might hinder the Movement's 'survival and expansion' and concludes that 'it appears to have the environment and conditions in which to exist and thrive'. Citing Pochapon, among others, as a source of his information, Kais also states that 'as far as it relates to Manus, the Movement stands ever ready to assist in the administration of the new provincial government system and the implementation of development activities'. On the final page of his article, Kais notes the other names under which the Movement has operated in years past but concludes optimistically: 'the name Win Neisen may in fact be the last name as the people prepare for the coming of the new and perfect government under the kingship of Jesus. Until the coming of that awaited day, the Movement adherents have the responsibility of character building and living in a way that symbolizes the perfect blissful life of abundance that will be established not in heaven, but here on earth' (ibid.).

In 2015, many years had passed since Kais's assessment, apparently without any dramatic efforts reminiscent of the Noise or the Cemetery Cult to accelerate the 'coming of the new and perfect government'. Yet some adherents may be losing patience. Regarding the timing of salvation in today's Wind Nation, Smith regrets not being in Manus long enough to investigate a Wind Nation splinter group. A man who allegedly calls himself Paliau's 'spiritual messenger' has attracted a handful of followers. This group calls itself the National Kastam Tumbuna Government but the members consider themselves part of Wind Nation and they fly the Wind Nation flag in front of the house in Pere where they meet. The group's leader was not in Pere during Smith's visit and he gleaned little of how his message differs from the doctrines of mainstream Wind Nation. Smith

---

14 Both Paliau Lukas (1983) and Pomio Kivung leaders Philip Bailoenakia and Francis Koimanrea have published in Melanesian Institute journals (Bailoenakia and Koimanrea 1983).

did speak at length with two members of the group, one of whom told him that their leader had come to the people of Manus to—as she put it in English—'top up' (that is, add to, or—perhaps—bring up to date) Paliau's teaching. One Pere detractor called the group, in English, a 'cult', and complained in Tok Pisin that '*ol i laik ariap long Tru Fridom*'. That is, 'they want to hurry to True Freedom'. This seems an odd complaint coming from a fellow millenarian, but it suggests the difference between the followers of a recently minted prophet and the members of an organisation seeking stability.

We think, however, that no matter how resigned to the long haul many adherents appear to be, it is almost invariably too soon to assume that any adherents of Wind Nation's millenarian doctrine have abandoned all hopes of imminent salvation. A wider effort to 'hurry to True Freedom' and new prophets may yet emerge.

15

Probably not the last prophet

The explanation we offered for the Noise and the Cemetery Cult in Chapter 6 is an awkward fit for Wind Nation. We begin this final chapter by addressing that issue. Although the drama of European colonial contact—including an extraordinary encounter with white material prowess in World War II—was an important factor in the Manus cargo millenarianism of the 1940s, we cannot say this of Wind Nation. Nor, we will argue, are such encounters necessary precursors of other cargo cults. In this chapter we also argue that anthropologists and others probably have placed too much emphasis on the relationship between political subjugation, social disruption, and various other forms of human travail and millenarianism in general. Millenarian doctrines themselves can encourage susceptible people to distil their vague discontents into potent perceptions of affliction that would not trouble less susceptible people. But what determines people's susceptibility? In this chapter we argue that a strong inclination to personify causation—and, as discussed in Chapter 2, to assume a guiding purpose in events or a grand design in history, thus denying chance a significant role—increases susceptibly to millenarianism.[1] Such inclinations generally rest on perceptions of our species as 'being the center of malign or benign attention' (Schwartz 1973: 169). Such perceptions are the essence of a paranoid ethos, which, we argue, contributes mightily to millenarian susceptibility.

---

1   In Chapter 2 we suggested that positing a telos in history could be considered an attenuated or veiled form of personifying causation.

The concept of religion as generally used merely hints at the phenomena critical to millenarianism. As we discussed in Chapter 2, doctrines and practices resting on cosmologies of animate and personal causation encompass much of what anthropologists gloss as religion, but the tendency to personify causation embraces a much larger sphere of thought and behaviour, including, to name only a few manifestations: assuming omnipresent watchful ghosts or other numerous and sentient but incorporeal entities, worshipping a single omniscient deity, postulating a creator deity that has retired from involvement in its creation (as in deism), believing in the secret sway over world history of the illuminati or other shadowy human agents, believing in a metaphysical telos for humanity or all forms of being, or mundane teleological thought.[2] The ubiquity of this tendency and the tendency to see one's group or our entire species as the centre of extra-human attention and purpose ensures that Paliau will not be the last prophet of the world, perhaps not even of tiny Manus. In fact, millenarianism is thriving in much of the world, as we also discuss in this chapter.

We will also argue that to understand millenarianism better, anthropologists should put aside categories like 'religion' and 'spirituality'. (The latter is becoming disturbingly popular in the literature on Melanesia. Anthropologists sometimes substitute it for religion but this makes nothing clearer.) If we want to understand millenarianism we should focus on why it is so hard for so many human beings to understand the world in ways that do not personify causation and do not rest on the conviction that events—from the extremely local to the cosmic—unfold in dialogue with the concerns and actions of members of our species.[3]

---

2   Aficionados of science fiction will see how well the 'Overmind', which features in Arthur C. Clarke's (1953) *Childhood's End*, fits this list.
3   Human beings—intentionally and incidentally—create, maintain, and alter social and cultural systems. Such systems have great causal weight. In this way people are in fact behind much that happens in the world. But there is a difference between the structural momentum of capitalism, for instance, and the conscious decisions of an individual capitalist.

Margaret Mead's Wind Nation

We began this book with a story featuring Margaret Mead, so it is fitting that we approach this chapter's first topic—problems in understanding Wind Nation—with another story about Mead. Many Pere village people remember Mead as a supporter of or even a partner with Paliau in promoting wider cooperation in largely secular efforts to improve their lives. This undoubtedly would have pleased Mead. But Wind Nation has recruited Mead posthumously. This probably would not have pleased her.

Square wooden posts hold up the roof over the concrete verandah of Margaret Mead's Resource Center (MMRC) in the middle of Pere. The sides of each post are divided into vertical rectangles, each of which is decorated with a carving in shallow relief, painted in red, black, and white. A number of these panels are decorated with Wind Nation iconography, including a chambered nautilus shell—or *kalopeu*, the symbol of Makasol and subsequently of Wind Nation—and a simplified version of the Wind Nation logo. Several villagers confirmed that these were indeed Wind Nation images and they seemed to find nothing odd about it.

Smith, however, found this puzzling. It also puzzled him that numbers of Pere people spontaneously told him about Mead's and Paliau's close relationship because he knew that Mead had met Paliau on only a few occasions. Several Manus people have promulgated highly critical views of Mead's work in Manus.[4] But in Pere in 2015, Smith heard only appreciation of how Mead and Paliau had been collaborators in the same cause: uniting people and promoting cooperation. Speaking of how Pere combined with other Titan communities to become a consolidated village, the Pere village magistrate told Smith 'Paliau created it and Margaret Mead supported it' (*Paliau i kirapim na Makret Mit i sapotim*). And Kumulau Paniu told Smith that 'Margaret Mead was close with Paliau. The two walked together' (*Makret Mit i pas wantaim Paliau. Tupela i wokabaut wantaim*).[5]

---

4   The best-known examples appear in the 1992 volume *Confronting the Margaret Mead Legacy: Scholarship, Empire, and the South Pacific*, edited by Lenora Foerstel (formerly Lenora Shargo) and Angela Gilliam; and the 1983 film *Papua New Guinea: Anthropology on Trial*, produced and directed by Barbara Gullahorn-Holecek for WGBH, Boston.

5   Paniu may well have meant 'walked together' metaphorically. In Tok Pisin, 'walked together' (*wokabaut wantaim*) sounds more metaphorical than it does in English—but whether meant literally or metaphorically this is still a significant statement.

Figure 15.1: An image of the Wind Nation logo is carved on one of the posts of Margaret Mead's Resource Center in Pere village, shown here in 2015.

Source: Michael French Smith.

A few people who spoke to Smith of Mead and Paliau made implausible claims. For example, one or two said that Mead had helped Paliau create the consolidated Pere village in the early days of the New Way, even though the New Way village was built in the years between Mead's and Reo Fortune's stay in old Pere in 1928 and Mead's return in 1953. But other claims have a firmer basis. The retired Air Niugini executive we mentioned in Chapter 14 said that Mead and Paliau 'agreed on things, worked together'. To the best of our knowledge they did not work together in person, but they did agree that people should cooperate and remain united. Inspiring wider cooperation was among the accomplishments of the Paliau Movement Mead most admired, which she almost certainly would have praised when speaking with Pere people.[6] This is a plausible basis for mentioning Paliau and Mead in the same admiring breath.

But this does not explain fully why Wind Nation seems to be claiming Mead through literally putting its mark on the MMRC. Probably, in the manner of Paliau, Wind Nation strives to put its stamp on anything that might raise its profile and enhance its legitimacy.[7] Of course, it is also possible that when in 1967 Mead told the people of Pere to follow the example of the people of 1946 (described below), those who still saw Paliau as a divinely inspired prophet took her to mean that they should pursue millenarian renewal. (Recall that during the Cemetery Cult, some of its proponents justified their activities by saying that they were merely returning to the 'good ways of 1946'.) This would not make Mead happy. Her desire that villagers not think she condoned a cargo cult—and, perhaps, her desire not to know about it—kept her from investigating the Cemetery Cult going on around her in 1953. A couple of people also said they'd seen pictures of Mead and Paliau together and one woman said she had seen Mead and Paliau together in a video. Only later did Smith recall that Mead and Paliau both appeared in a film of Mead's 1967 visit to Pere, her last, *Margaret Mead's New Guinea Journal*.[8] The film was made for the United States National Educational Television Network and

---

6   Maintaining social harmony is a chronic concern in many small communities in which people not only rely on each other for material aid but also personify the causes of misfortune. Smith (1994) discusses this issue at length.

7   We do not know, however, if the adherents who made the Wind Nation carvings on the MMRC met with any resistance. The few people Smith asked about this said that they did not, but the story may be more complicated.

8   The film makes it appear that in 1967 Mead is returning to Pere after an extended absence. She had spent considerable time in Pere, however, in 1964–65.

released in 1969.⁹ It was shown on American and Australian television and it undoubtedly reached Papua New Guinea (PNG), although probably as a video cassette, since even today there is still almost no access to broadcast television in PNG outside urban areas. The film focuses on Mead's history with Pere but gives a lot of time to the Paliau Movement (minimising the millenarian episodes of the 1940s and 1950s, just as Mead's (2001 [1956]) *New Lives for Old* does). There is also footage of Paliau speaking in the House of Assembly in Tok Pisin (with great clarity and dignity) and—most germane to people's memories of a Mead–Paliau connection—several minutes showing a feast in Pere honouring Mead during her 1967 visit. Paliau is shown moving among the guests, in white shirt and tie, although he is not shown interacting with Mead. But in her remarks to the guests (in Tok Pisin) Mead heaps praise on him. 'Paliau has set an example', she says. Mead also admonishes those assembled to follow the example of 'the people of 1946' who started the changes she has seen in Pere.¹⁰

It probably would not mollify Mead to know that calling Wind Nation a cargo cult may not be strictly accurate.¹¹ There is a straight line from the millenarian elements of the early Paliau Movement to Wind Nation's millenarianism. We are not interested in debating exactly where to draw a line between cargo cults and other forms of millenarianism, but there are undeniable differences between the Noise and the Cemetery Cult and Wind Nation. It resembles the Noise and the Cemetery Cult in its promise of material abundance, both through control of the stuff of immediate material wellbeing in rural PNG (weather, wildlife, crop fertility) and through magical access to manufactured goods through

9   Nancy C. Lutkehaus examines responses to *Margaret Mead's New Guinea Journal* in her 2008 volume, *Margaret Mead: The Making of an American Icon*.
10   What Mead said in Tok Pisin ('*ol man bilong 1946*') means, at its most literal, 'the men of 1946'. But it can also refer to people in general.
11   Mead could not have opposed all millenarianism, for she was a practising Christian. As Hunt (2001: 2) writes: 'The millennium dream is therefore at the center of the faith and consistent with its principal dogmas'. But Mead was quite an orthodox Christian, and—as Hunt also writes: 'It is the *preoccupation* with the millennium to come … which separates the fanatics and the heretics from the rest of Christendom'.

the power of thought.[12] But the manufactured goods—the cargo—will not come in ships or planes piloted by returning ancestors or under the command of Jesus. Further, Wind Nation doctrine—if not every Wind Nation adherent—has turned away from blaming the condition of black Melanesians on white greed and towards an almost syrupy vision of universal human unity.

Neither are the central features of Wind Nation doctrine uniquely or even distinctively Melanesian. Stephen Pokawin (1983b: 112) was not far from the mark when he wrote that 'the only indigenous aspect of it is the people. The ideas, religiously speaking, are not original'. In fact, many Americans will find some of the ideas extremely familiar, such as the notion that one can control reality with one's thoughts. This assumption (or desperate hope) has played such a large role in American life that Adam Morris calls it 'the unofficial national religion of the United States'. Morris (2019: 197–8) describes how in the late nineteenth and early twentieth centuries it loosely united a number of movements under the rubric 'New Thought'. Today, it is central to the stock in trade of many popular purveyors of self-help programs, such as Tony Robbins and Oprah Winfrey. The idea of controlling reality by thinking is so attractive that it probably has seized people's imaginations independently in many times and places.[13] Similarly, the signs of Paliau's return—things people have never seen, heard, or said before—could have come straight from a generic manual for prophecy, and they could easily have been adapted from Pope Gregory's seventh-century letter to Æthelbert of Kent, advising him that 'as the end of the world draws near, many things are to come

---

12 This is one of the most dramatic ways in which Wind Nation resembles the Noise and the Cemetery Cult. Without further research it is hard to say if there is something typically Melanesian or more widespread about the extremity of their emphasis on attaining a form of existence devoid of virtually all effort. Schwartz (1976a: 197) wrote of Manus: 'A surprisingly large range of human activities are termed "work", so that one is led to think of an effort syndrome. This is probably widespread [in PNG], to judge from the reflexes in Pidgin English. Ceremonial exchange in all its phases is "work"; even sexual intercourse and the production of babies, which requires multiple inseminations to fill the womb, is considered to be very hard work … In the light of these conceptions of "work", the attractiveness of the no-work cargo state is evident'. See Smith (1982, 1994) for relevant discussion of conceptions of work on Kairiru Island, East Sepik Province.

13 Omnidirectional diffusion could also be at work. Tuzin's (1997) study of the remarkably wide distribution of versions of the Swan Maiden myth provides a fascinating example of the distances over which cultural motifs circulated long before the advent of modern communications media. Tuzin also makes the point that diffusion is a process of selection and naturalisation, thus not utterly divorced from independent invention (1997: 73–4). Some versions of control by thought, however, are definitely indigenous to Melanesia. Recall the idea that inappropriate thoughts can doom an enterprise—as the old woman's thoughts of affinal exchange caused a boat returning from Cemetery Cult activities on Johnston Island to swamp over the reef (described in Chapter 8).

upon us which were not before'. But Wind Nation (as Smith observed it in 2015) least resembles what we might call classical cargo cults—like the Noise or the Cemetery Cult—in apparently placing as much emphasis on creating an enduring organisation as it does on speeding the arrival of the cargo.

Problems in explaining Wind Nation

Despite the relatively staid face of Wind Nation of late, it would be foolhardy to assert that never again will rumours of the imminence of a new world of never-ending ease and abundance spread through Manus like fire. We say this even though the circumstances under which the Noise and the Cemetery Cult arose no longer pertain in Manus. Nor did they pertain for the young men who aided and abetted Paliau in creating Wind Nation from the mid-1970s until Paliau's death. Their lives in the late twentieth century differed greatly from those of the proponents of the Noise and the Cemetery Cult. They had not lived under colonial rule and they had not looked up from mending fishing nets on the porches of thatched lagoon houses to see the massed mechanical power and unimaginable material wealth of the American military arriving by sea and air. They were not illiterate or nearly so. Rather, they had received many years of formal schooling, served in responsible government jobs, visited some of the world's modern cities, and enjoyed the luxuries of electric light, plumbing, refrigeration, and air travel. Nevertheless, they became eager millenarians.

The sudden and dramatic devaluation of the forms of wealth that underwrote status and self-worth in indigenous Manus society was a key element in the explanation we offered for Manus people's passion for the Noise and the Cemetery Cult. But this has tenuous relevance for the majority of today's Wind Nation adherents. Wind Nation proponent Kakak Kais exaggerates when he writes that 'Paliau's vision for his people to experience the comforts similar to that of the white man has been achieved to a great extent' (Kais 1998: Chapter 2) and they are now 'enjoying the white man's material wealth' (ibid.: Chapter 3). As of 2019, the United Nations Development Programme Human Development Index ranked PNG 155 out of 189 countries on the basis of life expectancy at birth, years of schooling, and gross national income per capita. (African countries comprised most of the other occupants of the 'Low Human

Development' category.)[14] There is obvious poverty in Manus, but Smith met young men with considerable formal schooling, working in modern institutions (such as the PNG National Broadcasting Corporation), who are enthusiastic Wind Nation adherents. Many Manus people are acutely aware of differences in wealth and power among the world's nations. But the most glaring inequality many Papua New Guineans are likely to experience firsthand is that between a small, mostly urban indigenous elite and the PNG rural masses. Many members of the latter find this intramural division especially galling. But Wind Nation doctrine does not directly invoke either international or domestic inequity.[15] Why, then, Wind Nation? This question requires us to consider the problem of explaining millenarianism in general.

Not necessarily religions of the oppressed

It is probably impossible to identify the circumstances that give rise to millenarian thought and action without either defining millenarianism very narrowly or settling on circumstances that are, or border on, universal. Stephen Hunt (2001: 2), for instance, opines that 'the millennial vision of a new order may be said, to some extent at least, to be part of the human condition'. Burridge (1969: 117) defines the 'central issue' of millenarianism as 'the ennoblement of the nature of man'. He therefore concludes that 'there are no known conditions which would render millenarian activities unnecessary'.[16] (Our data on the Noise and the Cemetery Cult, however, show that at least some participants were primarily interested in ennobling themselves.)

---

14   www.hdr.undp.org/; scroll down to the Latest Human Development Index (HDI) Ranking.

15   It is possible that such themes are not entirely absent. During the years covered by our research, however, they did not come to our attention.

16   Burridge attempts greater specificity, however, in another work. He writes (1995 [1960]: xxiii) 'there is not a simple relationship between conditions obtaining and the occurrence of a cult. We can only say that under certain conditions a Cargo cult might occur. The catalytic spark which explodes into a cult cannot be pinned to a where or a when. Nevertheless, the general conditions, the moral problems to which a Cargo cult could be seen as a response, have grown out of a series of events and circumstances which may be reasonably well defined. Many of the old customs, institutions, and modes of behaviour which together constituted viable frameworks of traditional and trusted ways of life are either fast disappearing or have already died out. Those that remain seem not to be adequate to the environment in which the people concerned now find themselves, and fresh institutions must take the places of those that have gone'.

Most pronouncements on the roots of millenarianism are less extravagant then Burridge's. Many, however, assume that millenarianism is rooted in circumstances from which most societies are seldom if ever entirely free. They point to almost any variety of disruption of the existing social order—such as economic collapse, culture contact, or rapid technological change—or simply the perceived threat of disruption.[17] Landes (2011: xvii) is wise to reject the possibility of a predictive model of the conditions under which millenarian impulses result in at least temporarily viable movements. He writes: 'Historians and sociologists have often attempted causal and predictive models for millennialism. But what leads one movement to "take" and many another to fizzle seems more appropriate for chaos theory than historical and social "logic" alone; and anything more "scientific" is just hindsight'. Landes (2011: 104) also writes: 'It is always hard to assess the motivations for adherence to millenarian prophecies. The general distribution tends to favor a rough split along hierarchical lines. Those with more power, more investment in "the world" and public space tend to dislike prophecies that claim that their world is "about to pass away" … Thus the poor, the dispossessed, women, and educated people who feel they should run the world but do not, form an important component of almost all these millennial movements'.

Nonetheless, Landes goes on to list many exceptions to that general rule. But are not millenarian movements 'religions of the oppressed', as Vittorio Lanternari (1963) famously characterised what he called 'modern messianic cults'? That millenarianism is a response to oppression is probably the most common generalisation both scholars and lay people put forward. It has been part of the literature on Melanesian movements for over 100 years. Burridge (1969: 3) cites E.W. Chinnery and A.C. Haddon—two of the earliest European students of Melanesian millenarianism—on the nature of millenarianism in general: 'An awakening of religious activity is a frequent characteristic of periods of social unrest … Communities that feel themselves oppressed anticipate the emergence of a hero who will restore their prosperity and prestige' (Chinnery and Haddon 1917: 455). Yet Burridge (1969: 13) finds invoking oppression perpetrated by outsiders too easy. He writes that 'a dissatisfaction with the current system' is a 'precondition' of millenarian action. But, he continues, 'if we describe this precondition as "feeling oppressed", the "oppression" does not necessarily

---

17   Roseanne Roseannadanna, as portrayed by Gilda Radner from 1977 to 1980 on the long-running television program *Saturday Night Live*, made a similar point: 'it just goes to show you, it's always something—if it ain't one thing, it's another'.

derive from an external political control: it may be rooted in internal dissatisfactions with present assumptions, rules and modes of redemption'. From his review of the cargo cult literature, Trompf (1994: 161) also concludes that it is a mistake to assume too much about the role of external forces in precipitating millenarianism. He writes: 'It is false to conclude that the intensity of cargo cultism or the degrees of its incidence are directly proportional to the amount of outside exploitation or interference'.

Writing specifically of Christian millenarianism, Hamilton (2001: 16) questions assumptions that early Christianity drew much of its force from its appeal to the economically disadvantaged: 'That the early Christians were recruited from among the poorest sections of the community is, of course, the traditional view, but it is one upon which much doubt has been cast by recent research'.[18] Similarly, Bronwen Douglas (2001: 626) concludes that 'the ethnographic fit' between 'a sense of present crisis' and 'eschatological anticipation' in PNG is 'suggestive but ambiguous and highly incomplete'. Addressing millenarianism in today's America, anthropologists Kathleen Stewart and Susan Harding (1999: 286) are unable to label it as primarily a response to economic or social deprivation. They write: 'an apocalyptic/millennial sensibility … has come to inhabit and structure modern American life across a wide range of registers'. Philip Lamy (1996) concludes that 'millennium rage' and 'doomsday prophecy' among American survivalists and white supremacists are linked to rapid social change. But Lamy also finds that 'apocalyptic beliefs' that were once more common at the margins of Western society now inform 'the millennial rage of the middle-class sectors of our modern industrial societies' (Lamy 1996: 256) and that 'millennium rage reaches … into the American popular culture' (ibid.: 264), as he amply illustrates. Kate Bowler (2013: 216–21) presents evidence against the assumption that the American prosperity gospel is 'a poor people's movement, an expression of believers' longing for (and distance from) socio-economic stability' (Bowler 2013: 232). We have to conclude that some millenarian movements may well be 'religions of the oppressed', but many are not.

Further, the kind of conspiracy thinking so typical of millenarianism is 'now as characteristic of the center' as of 'marginal groups' (Stewart and Harding 1999: 293). Joseph E. Uscinski and Joseph M. Parent (2014: 11)

---

18   Citing Holger Jebens (2000: 191), Bronwen Douglas (2001: 628) emphasises that 'eschatology, whether indigenous or Christian, is not only a reflex of catastrophe or a sign of crisis but may be the very reverse'. For instance, following Philip Gibbs (1977), she observes that people may take a 'sense of relative plenitude' as a precursor of fulfilment of a millenarian hope.

grapple with the closely related issue of the relationship between stress—induced, for instance, by natural disasters or economic uncertainty—and conspiracy thinking (the tendency, as they put it, 'to see nonexistent patterns and evoke conspiratorial explanations') and they reach a similar conclusion: 'Conspiratorial beliefs are common and consistent; major disasters are not'.

An alternative to philanthropic interpretation

Modern anthropology's commitment to showing the world's dominant peoples that other ways of life are reasonable, legitimate, and should not be trampled upon has undoubtedly helped incline anthropologists towards portraying cargo and other forms of millenarianism as reactions to oppression or in some other way politically progressive (cf. Trompf 1991: 191). The majority of interpretations found in the literature lean hard in the direction of what Burridge (1995 [1960]: 128–9) calls 'philanthropic' explanation. Philanthropic explanations seek, in Burridge's words, to 'emphasize those features of millenarian movements which reveal economic and political problems … Millenarian movements are regarded as expressive of economic difficulties and political discontents'. Such interpretations are not necessarily wrong in specific cases, but they strongly encourage tautology. That is, they tempt people to assume that where there is millenarianism there must be more than the usual quota of human suffering. There is, of course, no way to measure levels of suffering and compare them with levels of, for example, cargo cult activity.

A philanthropic bias may also help account for the popularity among anthropologists of the idea that cargo cults help unify people (e.g. Eriksen 2010: 69; Kaima 1991; May 1982; Worsley 1968 [1957]). This is not what we found regarding the millenarianism within the Paliau Movement. Paliau was able to unify people to support the Movement program in part because some hoped that even his most prosaic projects were steps on a millenarian path. The outbreaks of explicit millenarian action within the Movement (the Noise and the Cemetery Cult), however, undermined Movement unity. Ironically, only by failing dramatically did the Noise provide Paliau with an opportunity to build wider unity, as described in Chapter 7. Landes (2011: 108–12) also provides a good example of a case in which millenarian unity was superficial and left faction in its wake. Although summary descriptions of the Xhosa cattle slaying in mid-nineteenth-century Africa often make it sound like a mass movement, there was, Landes writes, a considerable contest between believers and unbelievers. The influence of the Xhosa chiefs was a critical factor in getting people—even sceptics—to cooperate. But Landes reports that 'struggle between believers and unbelievers marks the sociability of the Xhosa to this day'.

Joel Robbins (2011) takes philanthropic explanation of Melanesian millenarianism in a different direction. He observes that 'even when they live outside full-scale millenarian movements, many Melanesians live with a kind of millenarian openness' that Robbins calls 'everyday millenarianism' (pp. 183–4). They 'go about their normal business but remain ready for unexpected change, anxious to hear a messianic promise should it be made'. In this frame of mind, 'the present ceases to govern one's sense of possibility' (p. 191). Following themes in the work of Jacques Derrida and Walter Benjamin, Robbins finds here an admirable receptivity to the possibility of a radically different and better future, perhaps something beyond any expectations modelled on the past or the present. He illustrates the potential in 'everyday millenarianism' for opening 'radically new possibilities for action' (p. 186) by telling of how a group of Urapmin people (of PNG's East Sepik Province) reacted to finding at the side of a trail a pair of new gloves. Even though 'a simple, locally sensible explanation' was readily available (p. 189), they took this novel event as 'a chance to stop and listen in case they [that is, the gloves] might be making a messianic promise' (p. 190). Maybe the gloves foretold the development of a major mine on their land, or maybe the Second Coming of Jesus, or maybe something just as wonderful but beyond their present powers of imagination.[19]

Robbins (2011) romanticises this incident and the kind of thinking it exemplifies. He focuses exclusively on a Wordsworthian intimation of something pleasingly extraordinary, perhaps even something 'apparelled in celestial light'.[20] Yet being familiar with village life in PNG he must

---

19 A major mine is often anything but a blessing for local indigenes in PNG, but poor rural people sometimes see only the possibility of great wealth.

20 The quotation is from William Wordsworth's 'Ode: Intimations of Immortality from Recollections of Early Childhood'. Smith, who selected this quotation, is as fond of the English Romantic poets as anyone. But Robbins waxes so romantic that he not only ignores the dangerous potential in Urapmin 'everyday millenarianism', he also short-changes other possibilities for envisioning a radically different and better world. He does note that 'Marxism and other post-Enlightenment political ideologies' (Robbins 2011: 186) can also supply the content of messianism. But he seems enamoured of a religious vocabulary ('messianism' and, following Derrida, or his translator, 'messianicity'), which tends to undermine his gesture to the possibility of emancipatory secular imagination.

realise that villagers are just as likely to find in novel events intimations of mortal danger from human or non-human persons—intimations that can foster fear, anger, and violence. (Readers may recall that in Chapter 3 we made a similar point regarding West's description of the world of the Gimi people of PNG.)

Despite his romanticism, Robbins identifies the factor common to all forms of millenarianism: immersion in a world of personified causation in which people perceive unusual events as personally relevant, for good or ill; that is, a world of personified causation flavoured with a paranoid ethos.

It's everywhere

Schwartz (1973: 169) took pains to emphasise the 'susceptibility of human societies, however "advanced", to social paranoia'. In Chapter 2, we also emphasised how widespread among members of our species is the tendency to personify causation. It is not surprising then, that millenarianism is common not only in history but throughout the world today, in societies however 'advanced', not excluding America.

Considerable recent literature pays special attention to what Barkun (2006 [2003]: 21) calls a 'dramatic proliferation of millenarian schemata, both in terms of the number of competing visions and in terms of their diversity', from which so-called modern societies are far from immune.[21] Landes (2011) devotes considerable attention to UFO millenarianism— that is, the hope that beings from outer space will bring salvation to Earth's people. He does so, he writes, because 'they illustrate how key millennial tropes—apocalyptic scenarios filled with both outrageous hopes and fears and paranoid conspiracy thinking—continue to work on allegedly modern, enlightened minds' (Landes 2011: xii). Stewart and Harding (1999: 294) write of how 'contemporary American public and popular culture' is home to 'a proliferation of messianic cults, paramilitary groups, and racial separatists'.

---

21 Schwartz writes that a paranoid ethos is part of a common human heritage and 'sporadically resurgent in modern societies' (1973: 155), and he speaks of the fragility of modernity and the 'thin crust of knowledge and security that sometimes supports us above the level of the paranoid ethos'. We want to emphasise that modernity as a social and cultural bulwark against pervasive fear and insecurity is fragile. We also join other scholars in making the related point that, in Hall's phrase: 'As it is now widely understood, "modernity" is uneven in its development, incomplete in its manifestations, and hybridically connected to other social forms' (Hall 2009: 209; cf. Latour 1993).

Stewart and Harding (1999) delve into the connection in America between millenarianism and what Barkun (2006 [2003]) and others call conspiracism. They write: 'American nationalism rests both on the millennial claim that American-style democracy and technological progress will save the world and on an apocalyptic paranoia that imagines external enemies, "thems" who are out to get "us"' (Stewart and Harding 1999: 293; cf. Jacoby 2008; Walker 2013).[22] In the same vein, Barkun (2006 [2003]: 187) observes that 'conspiracists, particularly those who believe in super conspiracies, do seem to inhabit a different epistemic universe, where the usual rules for determining truth and falsity do not apply'.[23] It is a world like that of the cargo cult, in which, as Schwartz (1973: 157) observes, 'suspicion and cognitive rejection' are joined with 'extreme credulity'.[24]

---

22   Note that in this passage Stewart and Harding (1999) use the term paranoia only for perceptions of being at the centre of *malign* attention. When we speak of a paranoid ethos we also include perceptions of being the focus of *benign* attention. That is, people can overestimate the personal relevance of events in positive as well as negative ways. The feeling that 'somebody up there likes me!'—a sentiment linking personification of causation with perceptions of personal relevance—is as good an example of a paranoid ethos at work as the fear that one's illness is punishment for sin. (*Somebody Up There Likes Me* was the title of a 1956 movie based on the life of the boxer Rocky Graziano, which probably ushered it into the American store of clichés. David Bowie also used it as a song title on his 1975 album 'Young Americans'.)

23   Scholars disagree on the extent to which today's Americans are more inclined to conspiracy thinking than those of another era. Barkun (2006 [2003]: 38) proposes: 'Although belief in malevolent plots has a long history in American culture, it is safe to say that no period has evinced so strong an appetite for conspiracism as the last twenty-five or thirty years of the twentieth century'. In contrast, Uscinski and Parent (2014: 128) write: 'Conspiracy theories never really go out of fashion. Yet if the question is when U.S. conspiracy thinking peaked, the answer is: not now and not for decades'. Their research identifies the 1890s and 1950s as 'the real ages of conspiracy in the United States. The prevalence of conspiracy talk in the United States has diminished slightly across time, especially since the mid-1960s. The most marked trend in the data, however, is stability'.

24   No one paints a darker picture of epistemological chaos in the modern world than political scientist Jodi Dean (1998) in *Aliens in America: Conspiracy Cultures from Outerspace to Cyberspace*. She concludes that we are already stuck with a post-truth world and had better get used to it: 'We have moved from consensus reality to virtual reality. Politics itself must now be theorised from within the widespread dispersion of paranoia that has supplanted focused targets such as "Jim Crow" laws, Richard Nixon, and the Vietnam War. Insofar as practitioners can link together varieties of disparate phenomena to find patterns of denial, occlusion, and manipulation, conspiracy theory, far from a label dismissively attached to the lunatic fringe, may well be an appropriate vehicle for political contestation' (Dean 1998: 8). Barkun (2006 [2003]: 186–7) finds Dean over the top. He suggests that 'we have not yet entered a world of complete epistemological pluralism, and it is unclear how such a world would or could function in everyday life, where mundane social, economic, and governmental business is transacted'. The Manus people trembling with the nearness of God in 1947 found out rather quickly that they could not live in the realm of millenarian fervour and epistemological upheaval for very long without getting very hungry and tired. They seem to have remembered this lesson, because participation in their next millenarian effort—the Cemetery Cult—was much more compatible with keeping themselves housed and fed.

How does recognising that a tendency to personify causation and some degree of paranoid ethos are widespread, perhaps virtually universal, get us any closer to understanding millenarianism? The primary contribution is to shift our attention from assuming a strong relationship between millenarianism and natural disaster, social disruption, or oppression. We cannot dismiss the importance to millenarianism of social upheaval and human suffering, but we propose that *the extent of peoples' immersion* in a world of personified causation in which they are the focus of malign or benign attention is the critical factor in how people respond to untoward events or chronic dissatisfaction. Such scholars as Atran (2002), Barrett (2000), Boyer (2001), Guthrie (1993), and Hood (2009)—all discussed in Chapter 3—offer possible explanations for a general human tendency to personify causation.[25] But it is also possible to study in particular populations the strength and pervasiveness of both personification and a paranoid ethos and the factors fostering their forms and degrees, as several works we have cited—in addition to Schwartz's—illustrate (Bailey 1971; Epstein 2000–2001; Hallowell 1955; Lepowsky 2011; Spiro 1967). There is nothing simple about this line of inquiry. For example, Barbara Andersen's (2017) research among nursing students in PNG shows how—contrary to what one might expect—their modern schooling appears to enhance their fear of occult forces.

It is important, of course, to remember that the distribution of a cultural construction of the world congenial to millenarianism is only one factor in the distribution of millenarian participation in a specific instance. We demonstrated this in our analyses of the distribution of participation in the Noise and the Cemetery Cult. Our analysis also recommends the wisdom of seeking factors in the distribution of millenarian action by observing circumstances and events over time, for we saw that advocates and opponents of the Manus cargo cults sometimes shifted roles, often for reasons other than simple attachment to a millenarian doctrine.

---

25   We do not take a position on their relative merits.

The future of Wind Nation

We have followed the Paliau Movement from its beginning to the present day, focusing on the interplay within the Movement of millenarian hopes and worldly social action and on Paliau Maloat's unceasing efforts to change Manus life and remain a leader, ambitions that were not always in perfect harmony. The communitarian and egalitarian values the Movement promoted did not sweep away conflict and self-interest, but they introduced new ideals and helped usher in new ways of cooperating for the common good (as we discussed in Chapter 14 under 'Paliau's civic legacy'). The Movement also created Wind Nation, an adventure in pure millenarianism. Today's Wind Nation leaders have recast rather than questioned their illiterate elders' fundamental assumptions about the nature of the world. In particular, like their elders, they find it difficult to entertain explanations of things in terms of chance and such impersonal forces as gravity, bacteria, drought, and flood—forces that are incapable of acting intentionally in response to human thought and behaviour. Nor can they accept a social world lacking inherent order and purpose, despite having significantly greater knowledge than previous generations of Manus millenarians of the larger social world encompassing Manus and PNG. (Exploring this apparent anomaly is beyond the scope of this book. And it would require digging deeper than we have into why, as Landes [2011: xii] writes, 'key millennial tropes … continue to work on allegedly modern, enlightened minds'. In America, many people who are comfortable with technologies inseparable from modern science are ill at ease with ideas central to modern science: that the universe operates independent of human or extra-human will and that chance shapes many events, including human events.)

We do not have the data needed to speculate on why some contemporary Manus people who admire Paliau have no interest in Wind Nation while others embrace it fervently—the kind of data of which we have provided perhaps a surfeit regarding the Cemetery Cult and a substantial amount regarding the Noise. Nor do we know what Wind Nation will become. Will it (again) pursue theocratic ends via electoral politics? Could it become the tool of cynics interested only in secular political power? Will it become an institution that combines millenarian hopes with such pragmatic endeavours as forging ties with international non-government organisations? We know with certainty, however, that it will face the challenge of sustaining adherents' commitment to a millenarian doctrine even as salvation remains stubbornly out of reach.

For Manus people and other Papua New Guineans drawn to millenarianism but not to Wind Nation, Christian organisations offer many options. Almost all Papua New Guineans claim affiliation with some form of Christianity, although there are no precise data on their distribution among denominations and sects.[26] We do know that a growing percentage of Christians worldwide are adherents of evangelical, charismatic, or Pentecostal groups—for most of which Christ's Second Coming is a central tenet of belief (Ernst 2012)[27]—and that the same trend is evolving in PNG. Richard Eves (2008: 2) observes that 'regardless of its high proportion of Christians, Papua New Guinea is one of the most evangelised places in the world. Currently, thousands of missionaries are spreading the gospel, often to people who have long identified themselves as Christian. The religious orientation of these missionaries is largely evangelical, charismatic or Pentecostal'. Wind Nation has already lost members to strongly millenarian Christian sects, as we noted in Chapter 13, and will probably find it hard to compete with such sects, many of which have the support of international organisations and prominent PNG politicians (see e.g. Eves 2008: 2; Eves et al. 2014).[28] Yet, ironically, although Wind Nation grew from that most ridiculed form of millenarianism, the cargo cult, and it rejects God, it looks like a more humane choice than do many of the rising millenarian Christian sects in PNG that claim firm biblical roots. Citing parallels with Pentecostalism in Africa, John Cox (2014: 11) warns of their implication in what he calls 'intensification of fears of sorcery and witchcraft and the attendant accusation and killing of witches' (cf. Forsyth and Eves 2015; Rio et al.

---

26 Exceptions include Muslims and followers of the Baha'i faith, each representing less than 1 per cent of the population, and those who profess no affiliation (Gibbs 2014). Richard Eves (2008: 2) reports that 'fundamentalist groups are increasing in influence throughout Papua New Guinea' and cites, with caution, Operation World, 'an organisation with a primary focus on the power of prayer', which estimates that about 97 per cent of the PNG population 'identifies itself as Christian', and about 43 per cent of PNG Christians are evangelicals, charismatics, or Pentecostals.

27 There is disagreement, however, about when and how this will occur (see e.g. Boyer 1992; Carter 2010). And—at least among American Christians—belief in the Second Coming extends far beyond evangelicals (Heimlich 2010).

28 Pentecostalism and charismatic Christianity are products of American evangelical Christianity but have long since spread throughout the world, especially the global South.

2017).[29] Paliau often treated people harshly and invoked the occult for his own ends, but we find it next to impossible to imagine either Paliau or his Wind Nation successors indulging in such cruelty. Within the world of millenarian movements, Wind Nation may prove to be among the more innocuous.

We are not, however, sanguine about millenarianism in general in Melanesia, including Robbins's 'everyday millenarianism'. We are also much less sanguine than Jean Comaroff (2010) about the burgeoning popularity of Christian millenarianism in the world at large. She writes: 'The spirit of revelation is among us once more … The genius of the new holistic faiths is to address the displacements and desires of the current world, to make its pathologies and terrors the portents of imminent transcendence' (ibid.: 33). Comaroff calls on 'social critics' to 'make cogent sense of this history in the making'. We insist that to do so one must keep firmly in mind that if there is a 'genius' in millenarianism, that genius is not necessarily benign.

---

29 Eves and Forsyth (2015: 6) write that the perception that 'malign ways of causing illness and death are spreading' is becoming more widespread in 'a number of Melanesian countries'. But, they argue: 'the sorcery and witchcraft of today are not manifestations of traditions that have continued unchanged for centuries. Rather, these beliefs wax, wane and change with changing circumstances and contexts. Thus, the way that sorcery and witchcraft are manifested in the contemporary situation is very much a product of more recent history, not timeless tradition' (p. 2). The 'contemporary situation' to which Eves and Forsyth refer is one in which new forms of poverty and inequality attending drastic economic change are thriving. But, even as they wax and wane, Melanesian perceptions of sorcery and witchcraft retain their roots in a view of the world that predates current political and economic turmoil—a view of the world as a place of omnipresent danger from conscious entities in which impersonal forces and chance play very minor roles. Eves and Forsyth illustrate this when they refer to Jason Hickel (2014: 108) on perceptions of sorcery and witchcraft in South Africa, where—as Eves and Forsyth echo Hickel—people 'interpret the failure to prosper economically not as a neutral market outcome or the product of chance, but as something that is orchestrated by specific human agents'.

Appendix A: Pathomimetic behaviour

Uncontrollable shaking (that is, *guria*, from which the Noise took its name); speaking in tongues; and death and resurrection, sometimes followed by apparent personality transformations, marked the Noise and the Cemetery Cult as distinct episodes within the Movement and played important roles within the cults.[1] The prevalence of similar 'stylized, extreme behavior' (Schwartz 1976a: 161) in cargo cults throughout Melanesia is also what led some colonial Europeans to see them as manifestations of mental derangement. In analysing diverse instances of millenarianism, more sophisticated interpreters, such as Anthony Wallace (1956) and W.E.H. Stanner (1958), interpreted them as symptoms of stress brought on by cognitive confusion or inconsistency. Although F.E. Williams (1923, 1934) labelled the cult behaviour he observed in what was then the Gulf Division of the British colony of Papua the 'Vailala Madness', he described the shaking of adherents not as pathology but as mimicry; that is, as imitation of the behaviour of 'abnormal' individuals (Williams 1928: 54).

---

1   There is nothing distinctively Melanesian about such behaviour. Apparently uncontrollable, often seemingly unnatural body movements are common in religious contexts throughout the world. Some of the most famous examples come from the Euro-American world. The United Society of Believers in Christ's Second Appearance, founded in eighteenth-century England, gained its popular name—the Shakers—from the abandoned, apparently involuntary movement of participants in the sect's worship services. American Pentecostal or charismatic Christianity—which is popular in some parts of PNG (Smith 2002: 126–33)—regards speaking in tongues and convulsive movement as signs of the presence of the Holy Spirit. PNG has also produced its own distinctive forms of such behaviour. Shaking, trance, or speaking in tongues, induced by staring at the sun along the shaft of a spear, were defining features of the Cult of Ain in the mid-1940s in what are now PNG's Enga and Southern Highlands Provinces (Biersack 2011a, 2011b).

Regarding the Manus cults, Schwartz also regards mimicry, rather than psychological disturbance, as the basis for *guria* and related cult-specific behaviour, although—in contrast to Williams—he proposes that the most likely models were organic pathologies like epilepsy or cerebral malaria. He thus describes the behaviours he witnessed in the Manus cults as pathomimetic (Schwartz 1976a: 184ff.).[2] More important, Schwartz argues that the varieties of pathomimetic behaviour should be regarded as institutionalised, culturally structured reactions to experiences people assumed were, or sought to interpret as, of supernatural origin. People expected themselves to *guria* when God, Jesus, or the spirits of the dead were near or in possession of their bodies. At the height of the Noise they associated *guria* primarily with the presence of God or Jesus rather than the ghosts. Without such somatic manifestations, neither the subjects nor observers found it plausible that Jesus had been near or that there had been a true revelation.

In the instances of such behaviour Schwartz observed, he saw no evidence of conscious fakery, unless perhaps of the most artful kind. In Schwartz's words (1976a: 185):

> by pathomimesis I am not suggesting simple sham … Sham may occur, but usually it is a kind of collusion between actor and audience, with a submerged or studied unawareness of this collusion on both sides. When possession is desired or required as validation of a claimed link to supernatural forces, pathomimetic symptoms are produced and culturally expected as signs with magical instrumentality. Cultists believe that pathomimetic behaviour validates the reality or realizability of their goals and view it as a sign of (and therefore helping to bring about) the nearness or interest of the supernatural agencies.

We could also say that within the cults, pathomimetic behaviour was a form of culturally patterned wish fulfilment.

Although in the era of the cults many Manus people would have witnessed death in convulsion of some kind—for example, death from cerebral malaria—convulsive shaking does not seem to have been important as

---

2   In a serious misreading of Schwartz's argument regarding the role of pathomimesis in cargo cults, Lindstrom (1993a: 200) depicts it as a claim that cargo cults are 'a form of madness'.

a sign of spirit possession in indigenous Manus.[3] Christian missionary teaching may have contributed to the idea that convulsive seizures accompanied religious revelation. Tok Pisin versions of the Bible used by all the mission sects in Manus used the word *guria* to describe various manifestations of supernatural power. They referred to the *guria* that occurred at the death of Christ; the *guria* and the speaking in tongues that came to the followers of Jesus in Jerusalem at the first Pentecost; the *guria* that accompanied Paul's vision of Jesus; and the *guria* predicted for the day of the Last Judgement (in Tok Pisin, the *De Bihain* or Last Day). Also, certainly by the 1950s and perhaps by the time of the Noise, many Manus people knew that *guria* had been part of cargo cults in other parts of New Guinea.

The instances of *guria* Schwartz and Shargo witnessed and descriptions of *guria* they collected, from both witnesses and those who experienced it, show that the term covered a wide range of behaviours. It was applied to violent shaking, mere trembling, or simply being overcome by weakness. Some people were more violently affected than others, although, according to accounts, none escaped it in Ndriol or Mok. Tjamilo reported that the first person he saw *guria* was Paliau, who trembled when he prayed in the church in Bunai before he initiated the Movement. Tjamilo cited Paliau's *guria*—a sign of his closeness to supernatural power—as one of the reasons he followed him to Baluan. In the cult mythology, which relates how Jesus visited Paliau in New Britain during the war, Paliau's body is said to have grown heavy with the presence of Jesus. Wapei shook violently and thrashed about on the ground when he first told of having been visited by Jesus, although he had the actual vision in a dream the preceding night. *Guria* affected a majority in Tawi and later in Titan Bunai and among the Usiai. From Mok came descriptions of people reeling and walking in tight circles, with rolling or staring eyes. Some descriptions speak of people feeling as if they were about to be lifted from their feet, as though they were being pulled upward by the hair, or as if their *tingting* were light and would have risen up to Jesus except that their bodies were heavy.

---

3   We recognise other ways of explaining dissociative behaviour perceived as evidence of the presence of supernatural power. Melford Spiro (1967), for example, explains spirit possession in Burmese folk religion in terms of unconscious defence mechanisms, the operation of which may rise to the level of psychopathology. Schwartz (1976a: 184–6) notes that individuals with pathogenic tendencies may be self- or group-selected for cult roles requiring appropriate extreme behaviours, but he does not see this as an important factor in the Manus cults.

Most accounts associate the periods of the most intense *guria* with the first rapid spread of the Noise and with occasions when people concentrated all their thinking upon God in the churches. *Guria* in churches was reported from Ndriol, Mok, Tawi, Pere, Bunai, and Lahan. A Catholic missionary who was in Pere at the time of the Noise described a man sitting in the church trembling violently, unresponsive to efforts to get his attention. Others who themselves trembled described their skins as cold and wet with sweat. Lukas Pokus described the heaviness of his body when God came into him, causing him to shake violently. He said that the trembling continued to return long after the Noise, whenever he concentrated his *tingting* on God, but that these seizures abated when he became distracted by worldly thoughts. Pita Tapo described becoming dizzy and then slipping into unconsciousness lasting several hours. *Guria* leading to unconsciousness was a typical pattern in Lahan, Pita Tapo's village. People said that Gabriel Suluwan of Titan Bunai manifested *guria* only with his head. Namu of Malei experienced *guria* during the Cemetery Cult when two ghosts possessed her, one going up each leg. Her convulsions were violent, lasting a full night. Nasei of Lowaya, who claimed that she was visited by Jesus and also possessed by a ghost, had extremely violent convulsions described as random thrashing about. Some people said that what happened in the *guria* was like what happened to white men when they drank whiskey.

When an individual went into the coma-like state that might precede a supposed resurrection or started to *guria*, others watched intently, eagerly assessing the validity of contact with supernatural power. Many found the convulsions frightening. But only occasionally did Schwartz observe anyone questioning the validity of an episode of *guria*, and the questioning always came after the fact. In one case, the rivalry between Lukas Pokus and Johannes Pominis of Pere led to Lukas questioning the validity of Pominis's *guria* and the associated revelation. Both had experienced convincing *guria* in public, and both had received supernatural messages that others regarded as validated by their shaking. Lukas's revelation differed somewhat from the similar revelations of Pominis and Tjamilo, but Lukas claimed greater validity for his because it was more current, like the latest edition of a newspaper. Also, on the level of worldly events, he had been more recently to Mok than had Tjamilo. Thus accredited, he accused Pominis of having the *guria* only with his body and not with his *tingting*.

An episode of *guria* was usually accompanied by some kind of vision and a verbal message. The vision or message could come during the *guria* or in the unconsciousness that sometimes followed it. Such messages could also come in dreams without *guria*. Outside the most intense periods of the cults, dreams without *guria* were the most frequent channels of perceived communication with God and with the ghosts. Familiarity rather than novelty gave a message its credibility. Lukas Pokus's latest edition was totally unoriginal and familiar. The more innovative a revelation, the more it required some kind of pathomimetic behaviour as validation. Wapei's dream of a visit and revelation from Jesus required the most dramatic form of presentation because of its novelty. In the Cemetery Cult, innovative revelations most often came during seances. They were affirmed by the whistles of the communicating ghosts in the presence of the possessed mediums, who signalled their possession with *guria*.

After the first founding dreams and visions of the Cemetery Cult, most subsequent dream revelations tended to be only slightly innovative. Dreams often required a sign to confirm them or to warn that they should be heeded. As minor prophecies, they were sometimes self-fulfilling, as in Pwatjumel's dream of a design for the graveyard. Late in the Cemetery Cult, dreams validated minor moral revivals by reiterating the injunctions of the New Way and warning of God's displeasure. The dreams people heeded usually had little in common with the confusion, condensations, and symbolism of ordinary dreams. Like accounts given by the dead-and-resurrected or those who reported waking visions, they were long, comparatively coherent narratives.

Speaking in tongues occurred frequently. Like the *guria*, people took it as a sign of the validity of an associated supernatural message. Like *guria*, it could lead to someone asserting or accepting leadership or the status of a prophet or medium. Schwartz and Shargo also observed a few instances in which people's behaviour changed so greatly following an episode of *guria* or death and resurrection that they seemed to have undergone a personality change. Schwartz surmises that the apparent change was probably not the effect of the experience itself. Rather, such changes in behaviour were also culturally patterned possibilities for validating the experience to both the actor and the audience. In the cases that Schwartz and Shargo were able to observe most closely, the apparent personality changes were only temporary.

Ponram's death and resurrection illuminated a number of other cases of which Schwartz and Shargo had heard but not witnessed, as well as some cases they had witnessed without realising that they were connected with the cults. Ponram's death came at a time when many people were in the village, so his house was quickly packed with spectators. He did everything exactly right, satisfying the established expectations of the onlookers. Sitting in the audience, Schwartz had the sense that he was the only one who did not know what was going to happen next. First, Ponram, despite the fact that he was known as a notorious liar, had 'died' convincingly enough that his sons ran in seeming panic to fetch Schwartz and the medical assistant. Ponram was probably neither deliberately lying nor consciously pretending. He was behaving in a way that was by now familiar, even expected, though not necessarily expected of any particular individual.

His sign language was also familiar, and his message was so familiar that his audience readily interpreted his slightest gesture. In addition to the incessantly repeated admonitions of the New Way, he communicated supernatural disapproval of things of which *he* did not approve in his hamlet and family. He also delivered a plan for a graveyard that validated, and was validated by, the plan of which Pwatjumel had dreamed a few days earlier. For weeks afterward he behaved as a changed person. He dressed in the best European clothing he could obtain. He assumed an air of moral superiority and importance incompatible with his earlier status and deportment. People told his story in meetings in other villages as far away as Baluan. He spoke up at meetings for a while. Then, as response to him died away, and as cult leaders presented more spectacular contact with the divine, Ponram drifted back into his normal state as a quarrelsome old man.

As Ponram's case illustrates, by validating nearness to supernatural powers, pathomimetic behaviour also validated people's claims to at least temporary status or leadership within the cults. We have already noted that a few of those who played significant roles, such as Tjamilo of Bunai and Kisakiu of Tawi, did not manifest pathomimetic behaviour and made no claims to receiving direct supernatural revelations. Rather, they rose to leadership through their abilities to interpret such behaviour and organise action in accord with its alleged meaning. But a person who was the vehicle of supernatural revelations, validated by cult symptoms, had a potent claim to leadership. People who achieved leadership by this route often eclipsed—at least temporarily—those whose leadership was based on mundane sources of legitimacy. Pathomimetic behaviour, then, played an important role in creating new, cult-specific political hierarchies.

A number of men spoke of themselves as having been made by the Movement; that is, to have achieved a degree of status within the fluid lines of the new institutions that would not have been open to them otherwise. But the most drastic inversions of ordinary status hierarchies occurred in the cults. Most conspicuous were the adolescents who, in the old culture, would have neither had nor wanted a voice in village affairs. Others included women who achieved considerable influence in the cults through serving as mediums, as they could have done in the old culture, but not in the New Way. There were also older men who, within the Movement, had yielded authority and prestige to younger leaders, but who could, within the cults, enjoy some of the status they had lost.

Perhaps the most striking example of a change in status through successful validation of a claim of supernatural sponsorship was that of Joseph Nanei, the adolescent cult leader of Lowaya. Joseph's leadership and the particularly arrogant and dictatorial form it took could have been predicted on the basis of his earlier personality and the personalities of available adult models of leadership. His rival in Malei, Kampo Monrai, another adolescent, had almost all the same visions, and saw ghosts from even more remote generations than those seen by Joseph Nanei. But he did not manifest a personality change that might have validated his importance as a messenger from the dead. He remained the amiable person he had always been and could not assume arrogant command of his elders. (Being from Malei, a hamlet that took a subordinate position in the cult dominated by Lowaya, also limited his leadership potential.)

Appendix B: *Kalopeu: Manus Kastam Kansol Stori*

Kalopeu: Manus Kastam Kansol Stori is sometimes referred to as the White Book, to distinguish it from a presentation of Makasol ideas in English that has a green cover. The following is a translation from the Tok Pisin original of *Kalopeu*. It is taken from *Living Theology in Melanesia: A Reader* (May 1985: 31–43). We have made a few minor changes in the translation to accord with our understanding of the language of the original. The translator elided some sections of the original deemed inessential to understanding the fundamentals of the doctrine. We note these elisions in the text.

KALOPEU

MANUS KASTAM KANSOL STORI

The father of the MAKASOL Story and Study Group, Paliau Maloat, Esquire, was born in the year 1896.

He is the father of Manus Local Government Council,

He is the father of the Pangu Pati,

He is the father of Papua New Guinea, now an independent nation.

THE MAKASOL STORY AROSE ON BALUAN ISLAND IN 1945–46

Paliau Maloat, O.B.E., presents this story of his achievements at Baluan Island on August 9, 1946.

Paliau Maloat conducted this study for all the 33 villages [in the Paliau Movement] on Baluan in the meeting house of Saponparimbuai in January 1947.

- In 1948 the teachers [*pesman*] went back to call the people together, bringing those from the bush down to the beach and those from the sea to higher ground in order to start new villages.
- In 1946–53 all things, such as wind, rain, and sea, together with all kinds of food and game, obeyed what our fathers and mothers were saying.
- From July 1953 until today (1981) all these things no longer obey what is being said.

On April 15, 1978, the Makasol Story arose in order to unite all the people in Manus Province, Papua New Guinea and the world so that they might proceed with the true story of Wing Lapan, the Ancestor of us all, whether white men and women, brown men and women or black men and women.

Part one: The first order of things

Wing and his place in the clouds

At the very beginning there was no heaven, no angel, no sun, no moon, no star, no earth, no sea, no things of any kind and no human beings. Only Wing existed inside the clouds. The clouds was his original primordial place. Wing was like air, and together with the chief angels he dwelt in the clouds, his own place.

The origin of heaven, angels, Holy Spirit, and light

Wing took his place, the clouds, and joined it to the regions above, calling it heaven, his second place. He left the clouds, his own place, and went to dwell in heaven, his second place. He did not have flesh and he made the second group of beings, the angels in heaven, without flesh also. These angels were the people of heaven itself and Wing was their true father. Wing set apart some of the angels and gave them the name Holy Spirits. The Holy Spirits became the rulers of heaven.

He made the sun, he made the moon and he made the stars in heaven. He placed them as lights in heaven and after awhile they became the light of the third place here below.

Government of heaven is created

In heaven the Holy Spirits and Angels held the first nominations and elections to determine their supreme ruler. They chose Lait San (Lucifer) to be their supreme Government and King. The second nominations and elections were to choose King Lait San's deputy. The Holy Spirits and Angels chose 'WANG JESUS' as second in line after Lait San and Wang Jesus became the Government in heaven.

The origin of the earth [ples daun] and the division of the land from the sea

Wing took his place, the clouds … and made the third place here below. He divided this third place here below into two parts. He made one part and called it sea and joined it to the other part which he called the ground.

The origin of all things of the land and the sea

Wing made stone, iron, coal, oil and grass, trees, animals, birds and all kinds of food upon the earth. He made rocks, shells, fish and all things in the sea. He made the Earth the father and the sea the mother to nourish all that belongs to us in this third place here below.

Wing makes the bodies of humankind

Wing put all things, above and below, side by side in their proper places. He gathered together the dust of the earth and made first 'Adam', the man, and second 'Eve', the woman. Now all was ready for 'Wang Jesus' to send the first 'Wong'—Holy Spirit—to come down from heaven to take up his first abode in Adam and Eve. Adam was King and Eve was the government, charged with caring for all things in this third place here below.

The three houses of the earth

There are only three houses in the lower regions. The first house is the bodies of Adam and Eve, and in this house Wong the Holy Spirit dwells. The second house is a place for sleeping, and this third house is the 'House of Knowledge' belonging to Adam and Eve and all their descendants. This house of knowledge, the third house, was erected first of all at Jerusalem, the place in which Jesus was to be born.

The completion of Wing's work

Wing finally completed his work in the three places and he gave five commandments for Lait San, the King of heaven, to keep:

1. 'You, King Lait San! You must listen to the words of Wing, your only father.'

    Lait San the King said, 'Yes Sir! Wing my father. I must listen to your words, Wing, my only father'.

2. 'You, King Lait San! You must be responsible for the good behavior of all the Holy Spirits and Angels in the second place, heaven.'

    King Lait San said, 'Yes Sir! Wing my father. I must be responsible for the good behavior of all the Holy Spirits and Angels in the second place, heaven'.

3. 'You, King Lait San! You must be responsible for the good behavior of all the Holy Spirits and Angels who dwell with Adam and Eve in the third place here below.'

    King Lait San said, 'Yes Sir! Wing my father. I must be responsible for the good behavior of all the Holy Spirits and Angels who dwell with Adam and Eve in the third place here below'.

4. 'You, King Lait San! You must not change or alter or disobey the words I, Wing your father, have given you.'

    King Lait San said, 'Yes Sir! Wing my father. I may not change, alter or disobey your words, Wing father'.

5. 'You, King Lait San! You must speak the truth and not lie to me, Wing your father.'

    King Lait San said, 'Yes Sir! Wing my father. I must speak the truth and not lie to you, Wing my father'.

For a long, long time, both in heaven and in the lower place of Adam and Eve and all their descendants, they lived in freedom. All lived together with only one language for all white men and women, brown men and women and black men and women. They knew neither hunger, nor hard work, nor old age, nor sickness, nor death. They dwelt with great joy together in prosperity and freedom for a long, long time in heaven and in the place below.

Part two: The breakdown of the first order

The origin of evil ways

Lait San's first dwelling place was the second place, heaven, and he was the supreme Government of all the Angels and Holy spirits in heaven and in the third place here below. Wing made Lait San and gave him knowledge, strength and power to do and obey all the works and commands of Wing. Lait San himself knew all this, and yet he wanted to test his knowledge in order to compete in knowledge, strength and power with Wing his father, for Wing had made Lait San shine like all the Angels and Holy Spirits, just like Wing the father himself.

Because of this knowledge, Lait San pitted himself against Wing in a contest of knowledge. This is the origin and the evil foundation of untruth. Lait San told the first lie against Wing his father in that he did not obey the words and commandments which Wing had given him long ago. Lait San spoke thus to all the Angels: 'I, Lait San, together with you, all the Angels of heaven, have the same kind of knowledge, strength and power as Wing. Why must we listen to his words alone?' Some Angels heard this and followed Lait San in his erroneous ways, and they too competed in knowledge, strength and power with Wing. This was the second time Lait San had done wrong, because he broke the second commandment, given by Wing himself, about being responsible for the good behavior of all Angels and Holy spirits in the second place, heaven. Lait San with all his Angels knew that Wing would not take away their knowledge, strength and power, so they completely changed the good order and freedom of Wing. Their actions threatened to spoil everything in the second region, heaven.

The king of heaven is replaced

Wang Jesus knew that his leader King Lait San no longer obeyed the commandments of Wing and all the good work of heaven was about to be spoiled. Wang Jesus called upon the strength and power of Wing his father in order to take away the Kingship from Lait San and the Angels who had followed him in heaven. Wang Jesus took the good Angels and Holy spirits and they fought against Lait San and his Angles. Jesus and his followers won, and they took the Kingship away from Lait San and Lait San became Satan. Jesus became King and took the place of Lait San; he was now King and Government of the second place, heaven. He drove Satan out of heaven and kept the commandments again, just as a King should. Heaven became a good place again, and there was freedom among the good Angels and Holy spirits. Right up to the present the second place, heaven, remains in freedom and there is no wrong in it.

Satan goes to the third place here below [i.e. Earth]

Lait San who was now Satan in heaven worried about the great joy and freedom in which Adam and Eve and all their descendants lived in the third place here below. Satan envied this happiness and freedom and when Wang Jesus drove him out of heaven Satan took the same road as WONG the Holy spirit to Adam and Eve. Satan brought the lie told in heaven to Adam and Eve in their place here below. To begin, he practiced his first deception in the lower place on Eve. Satan deceived Eve into thinking that if she stirred up Adam's and her passions they would become the same as Wing. Eve listened to Satan's deception and passed it on to Adam. Their Wong [the Holy Spirit within them], however, corrected Satan's deception after they had stirred up their passions. In the end, Satan thrust himself into their hearts and the hearts of all their descendants. Their one language broke up into many and everything created on the earth hid and did not appear again. Sickness, death, hard work, hunger, age and all kinds of bad things now took possession of Adam and Eve and all their descendants. These evil ways took possession of all Kings, Governments and missionaries and all the white men and white women, brown men and brown women, black men and black women in this third place here below.[1] All these evil ways now destroyed the great happiness and freedom of the third place and the first order of things given by Wing to Adam and Eve. Even today, the bodies of all men and women here below are houses of Satan too. Now Satan lives in the hearts of all the white men and white women, brown men and brown women, black men and black women in this third place here below.

The third place after the ruin of the first order

Satan lived in the hearts of all men and women in the third place here below. He made them incapable of knowing any more about Wing the father of Wang Jesus and Wong the Holy spirit, that they were the ancestors of all men and women and all creatures here below. The men and women of the lower place chose their own gods, Kings and many kinds of religion for themselves. These different gods, religions and

---

1   May translates the Tok Pisin word *misinari* as priest, presumably because he assumes that the author is referring to Catholic missionary priests. We translate it more literally as missionary.

many kinds of Kings began to compete with one another for supremacy and power. They brought about dissension and fighting, refusal to listen to others/obey authority [in Tok Pisin, *harim tok*], lying and stealing, wilful destruction and many other kinds of evil among all men and women here below.

Wing shows his strength and power

Wing knew that the entire good order of happiness and freedom was completely destroyed in the third place here below. But he showed his strength and power by giving all men and women here below the knowledge to see that Wing himself is Lord and that he has supremacy over all things and all men and women.

Wing sent his Angels from the first place in the clouds together with the Angels who dwelt in the third place here below to punish men and women. First, the Angles in the clouds and underneath in the lower place had obeyed and helped men and women to receive blessings, but when the order of things was spoiled Wing sent Angles to fight men and women here below so they might see and fear his strength and power. Five Angels from the clouds came to fight in the lower place: lightning, cyclone, thunder, rain and rainbow. The other five from down below were: sea, tide, earthquake, flood and fire. These were the ten angels of Wing who fought against and harmed men and women and all creatures in the third place here below.

Jesus takes pity on Wong Holy Spirit here below

Wang Jesus saw all these foes destroying all the men and women in the lower place and Jesus, who is King and Government of the second place, heaven, called upon the mercy of Wing his father not to destroy every house of Wong the Holy Spirit [that is, people's bodies] in the third place here below. Jesus promised Wing the father that he, Jesus himself, must come down to the third place and help men and women to know the Wing is his true father together with Wong the Holy Spirit and that Wing is the ancestor of all men and women and all creatures in the third place here below.

Part three: Jesus comes to Earth

In heaven itself Wing heard the call of Jesus and Wing himself gave his approval for Jesus to make good his promise to help men and women here below. Now Jesus prepared the way for his arrival in the lower place. Jesus sent the first Wong the Holy Spirit of heaven and he came to Adam and Eve to take on his flesh. The second Holy spirit was in 'Dom' and he took flesh as King Sirius Augustus and Queen Krinius. Augustus took the place of Adam and Krinius took the place of Eve. The two drew up a Law in order to make an end of dissention and fighting and all men and women had to put their name in a register book and come back to life. The third Holy Spirit was in 'Moses' and he took on flesh from the daughter of the King of Egypt. Moses helped the people of Israel and led them out of Egypt. The fourth Holy spirit of heaven came down to is place in 'John' and he took on flesh in the womb of Elizabeth the wife of Zachariah. John came to speak to all men and women and prepare them for the coming down of Wang Jesus. The coming down of Wang Jesus was the fifth Holy Spirit of heaven to come to the third place here below. Wang Jesus was the last of the Holy Spirits of heaven to come down to the lower place, and there were no other Holy Spirits in heaven who could come.

Wang Jesus takes on flesh [i.e. a human body] here below

In the second place, heaven, Wang was merely a spirit and was the Government of all Angels and Holy spirits. When Wang himself wished to come to the Earth he sent the members of his Government to come first and prepare the way for him to come here below. The Holy Spirits he sent before him to the Earth still had their work in the second place, heaven. 'Dom' was secretary, 'Moses' was planner, 'John' was a lawyer. When Wang was ready to leave the second place, heaven, he sent his messenger 'Gabriel' ahead to give news of his coming. Wang chose MARY the wife of Joseph and he came to take flesh as Jesus in Mary's womb. Gabriel said this to Mary: 'Mary, the spirit of Wang will come into your womb. When he is born he will become a man and you must call him by the name of "Jesus"'. Mary was afraid, but her Wong believed Gabriel's words completely. The Spirit of Wang entered Mary's womb and at Christmas Mary gave birth to Jesus at Bethlehem in the land of Israel.

Jesus is born

The birth of Wang Jesus in the third place brought three great revelations to all white men and women, all brown men and women, and all black men and women. The first revelation was that Wang Jesus came to be born in order to fulfil the promise he himself made to Wing his father: that he, Jesus himself, must come down, to the third place to help men and women to know that Wing is the true father of Wang Jesus and Wong the Holy Spirit, and that he is the ancestor of all men and women and all creatures here below. The second revelation was that the birth of Jesus shows a new way for men and women to be renewed here below. This shows plainly that no one here below can just come into existence in the way that Adam and Eve did. All later men and women here below now take flesh in the wombs of all women. This means that men must sleep with women and create children in women's wombs. The third revelation is that Jesus' birth removes the wrong Eve did to all women. Jesus took flesh in the womb of his mother Mary and he was born of his mother Mary, thus revealing for the first time that all women of the third place are the mothers of all the Holy spirits which come into their wombs.

The name of Wang Jesus makes kings afraid

The news of Wang Jesus' coming went round among all people, Kings and missionaries of the place where Jesus was to be born. His birth in Bethlehem, too, became known to all the Kings, Governments, missionaries and people of Israel. All the Kings of Israel were now very afraid of the name of Wang Jesus, because they had heard that Wang Jesus was coming to help everyone have true knowledge of Wing his father and Wong the Holy spirit, who lives in the bodies of all men and women in the third place here below. The Kings tried by every means to kill Wang Jesus, but Jesus was able to escape them. Though surrounded by all kinds of enemies Mary and Joseph took good care of Jesus, so that he became a young man.

Part four: The doings of Wang Jesus

Jesus walks the Earth

When Jesus was a young man he went round showing people his strength and power and telling all the people on Earth about Wing his father in the second place, heaven. Jesus told them about the new knowledge that the spirit in his head was from heaven and his flesh was from the Earth.

485

This made him exactly the same as all the people on Earth; the Wongs or Holy Spirits in their heads are men of heaven itself and their flesh belongs to the third place here below. The works of the Holy spirits must be attributed to the Holy spirits and all the works of the flesh must be attributed to the flesh.

[We follow May's translation here in omitting several paragraphs describing Jesus's preaching and miracles, how many people refused to believe in him, and his realisation that to finish his work on Earth he must die and rise again on the third day.]

When all the people heard Jesus' words they did not believe truly in him, but poured contempt on him, made fun of him, blackened his name, called him the offspring of an evil spirit [in Tok Pisin, *masalai*] and said there is no such thing as someone who can die and rise again, and they called Jesus a liar. Wang Jesus gave himself up to die at the hands of all the Kings, Governments and missionaries with all the men and women of the third place here below.

Part five: The death of Wang Jesus

[Again we follow May in omitting several paragraphs describing the betrayal, passion, and crucifixion of Wang Jesus in a way that largely mirrors the biblical account of Jesus of Nazareth.]

Jesus himself carried his cross to the place called Golgotha, where they drove nails into his hands and legs and hung him on the cross. The soldiers erected the cross of Jesus between two other crosses, but these crosses were not real—they were just a picture showing Satan on the left and Wing the Ancestor on the right.

[Paragraphs omitted regarding the days between the crucifixion of Wang Jesus and his resurrection. Again, these largely parallel the biblical account of Jesus of Nazareth.]

One Sunday in the month of April Jesus came back from death and the soldiers who were standing guard over him fainted. Jesus defeated the power of Satan completely; he took back his spirit and his body and he rose again—he overcame his death in the third place here below. He was completely restored, he was one with all the people of the lower place. In order to make true what he had said to them about coming back from the dead within only three days.

Part six: Wang Jesus defeats death

[Paragraphs omitted regarding Wang Jesus after his resurrection. They roughly mirror the biblical account of Jesus of Nazareth. One addition is that Wang Jesus is said to have given the keys to Earth (in Tok Pisin, *ples daun*) to Peter while Wang Jesus held the keys to heaven.]

The Death of Jesus overcame all the Kings of the lower place and his resurrection defeated all the Kings, Governments and missionaries here below. To this very day Jesus is King and Government here below, because his death and resurrection completely defeated all Kings and Governments. Jesus alone is King and Government in the third place here below. In the second place, heaven, Jesus is still calling to all white men and women, brown men and women, and black men and women. He is still waiting for all of us to come to know truly the work of Wang Jesus, Wing the Ancestor, and Wong the Holy Spirit.

Appendix C: Lists of thirty rules and twelve rules

The Thirty Rules

In the late 1980s, Makasol provided Schwartz with a copy of a list of thirty rules, typed in both Tok Pisin and English. The document says that Paliau 'introduced' them to 9,000 people 'in the 1946 Movement'. They resemble New Way rules of behaviour, except for the mention of Wing. Conversely, the admonitions to register on the census rolls, pay taxes, and follow doctors' orders make sense in the era of Wing only if construed as referring to Wind Nation records, taxes, and non-Western healing practices. Although he heard many recitations of New Way rules for proper behaviour in 1953–54, Schwartz heard no mention of the list of thirty rules. The rules are as follows, in their original spelling and punctuation:

1. We must unite our people.
2. We must register all our names on the census roll.
3. We must register all men, women, and children on the census roll.
4. We must take good care of the physical health of our men, women, children, and the old men and women.
5. We must obey our leaders.
6. We must follow our leaders orders and directives carefully.
7. We must not allow differences [to] disunite our people.
8. We must work together for our own development.
9. We must move and transport our people together.
10. We must unite all the activities of our people.
11. We must be cooperative and productive at all our gatherings.

12. We must organize sportings and feastivities for all our people to enjoy together.

13. We must eat together.

14. We must sleep together.

15. We must live in peace.

16. We must keep our villages in healthy hyginic conditions.

17. We must construct new roads and maintain them in good order.

18. We must build permanent house for our families.

19. We must build our houses as laid out on the master plan for the village.

20. We must have better food crop gardens.

21. We must develop better avenues of making money.

22. We must generate more revenue.

23. We must pay all taxes together.

24. We must save and spend our money wisely.

25. We must accommodate our families with money and clean clothes.

26. We must take good care of our children with clean clothes and good food.

27. We must use all medicine carefully as prescribed by the doctors.

28. We must leave other people's properties alone.

29. We must obey all orders from our leaders.

30. We must take good care of all things provided by Wing on this earth.

Makasol Study: The Twelve Rules

In the late 1980s, Makasol also provided Schwartz with a copy of the following list of rules, typed in both Tok Pisin and English, under the heading *Makasol Study: The Twelve Rules*. We retain the original spelling and punctuation.

1. You shall look straight respectively towards your parents, kins, teachers and leaders, then there won't be any resentments and conflicts imposed upon you.

2. You shall be willing to love your parents, kins, teachers and leaders, then there won't be any resentments and conflicts imposed upon you.

3. You shall joyfully share mutual pleasures with your parents, kins, teachers and leaders, then there won't be any resentments and conflicts imposed upon you.

4. You shall speak truths your parents, kins, teachers and leaders, then there won't be any resentments and conflicts imposed upon you.

5. Your parents shall show interests and adore you for being very good to them, then there won't be any resentments and conflicts imposed upon you.

6. You shall not be lazy and get bored of your parents, kins, teachers and leaders, then there won't be any resentments and conflicts imposed upon you.

7. You shall not get panic and fear your parents, kins, teachers and leaders, then there won't be any resentments and conflicts imposed upon you.

8. You shall not fell shy and timid towards your parents, kins, teachers and leaders, then there won't be any resentments and conflicts imposed upon you.

9. You shall not tell lies about anyone to parents, kins, teachers and leaders, then there won't be any resentments and conflicts imposed upon you.

10. Your parents shall richly bless you and glorify you for being very good to them, then there won't be any resentments and conflicts imposed upon you.

11. You shall always inform and notify your parents, kins, teachers and leaders, then there won't be any resentments and conflicts imposed upon you.

12. You shall always ask permissions from your parents, kins, teachers and leaders, then there won't be any resentments and conflicts imposed upon you.

All these Rules are Living Rules and True, inspired by Jesus; so if you heed them, Jesus shall always help you. Since you are all the Dwelling Temple of the Holy spirit and Angle [Angel], you are the Prophetic agents from Heaven, therefore you must obey and abide them.

At the bottom of the page appears Paliau's signature over his typed name, OBE, and the title 'The Last Prophet of the World'.

References

Andersen, Barbara, 2017, 'Learning to believe in Papua New Guinea'. In Knut Rio, Michelle MacCarthy, and Ruy Blanes (eds), *Pentecostalism and Witchcraft: Spiritual Warfare in Africa and Melanesia.* New York and London: Palgrave Macmillan, pp. 235–55. doi.org/10.1007/978-3-319-56068-7_10

Andreas, Chris, Sheila Boniface Davies, and Andrew Offenberger (eds), 2008, 'Introduction'. *African Studies* 67(2). doi.org/10.1080/00020180802242517

ANGAU (Australian New Guinea Administrative Unit), 1944, 'History of Admiralty Islands campaign, 29 February – 18 May, 1944'. AWM 54, 80/6/6, DPI: 200. Canberra: Australian War Memorial.

Antrosio, Jason, 2013, 'When culture looks like race: Dobu & reification'. *Living Anthropologically* [blog], posted 16 September 2013, revised 21 July 2019. www.livinganthropologically.com/cultures-islands-dobu/

Aron, Raymond, 2001 [1957], *The Opium of the Intellectuals.* New Brunswick, NJ: Transaction Publishers. doi.org/10.4324/9781315133591

Atran, Scott, 2002, *In Gods We Trust: The Evolutionary Landscape of Religion.* New York: Oxford University Press. doi.org/10.1093/acprof:oso/9780195 178036.001.0001

Bailey, F.G., 1971, 'The management of reputations and the process of change'. In F.G. Bailey (ed.), *Gifts and Poison.* New York: Schocken Books, pp. 281–301.

Bailoenakia, Philip and Francis Koimanrea, 1983, 'The Pomio Kivung Movement'. In Wendy Flannery and Glen W. Bays (eds), *Religious Movements in Melanesia Today* (vol. 1). Goroka, Papua New Guinea: Melanesian Institute for Pastoral and Socio-Economic Service, pp. 171–89.

Bainton, Nicholas A., 2010, *The Lihir Destiny: Cultural Responses to Mining in Melanesia.* Asia-Pacific Environment Monograph No. 5. Canberra: ANU E Press. doi.org/10.22459/LD.10.2010

Banerjee, Konika and Paul Bloom, 2014, 'Why did this happen to me? Religious believers' and non-believers' teleological reasoning about life events'. *Cognition* 133(1): 277–303. doi.org/10.1016/j.cognition.2014.06.017

Barkun, Michael, 1998 [1974], *Disaster and the Millennium*. New Haven, CT: Yale University Press.

Barkun, Michael, 2006 [2003], *A Culture of Conspiracy: Apocalyptic Visions in Contemporary America*. Berkeley and Los Angeles: University of California Press. doi.org/10.1525/california/9780520238053.001.0001

Barrett, Justin L., 2000, 'Exploring the natural foundations of religion'. *Trends in Cognitive Sciences* 4(1): 29–34. doi.org/10.1016/S1364-6613(99)01419-9

Bateson, Gregory, 1958 [1936], *Naven: A Survey of the Problems Suggested by a Composite Picture of the Culture of a New Guinea Tribe Drawn from Three Points of View*. Stanford, CA: Stanford University Press.

Benedict, Ruth, 1934, *Patterns of Culture*. Boston and New York: Houghton Mifflin.

Bercovitch, Eytan, 1994, 'The agent in the gift: Hidden exchange in inner New Guinea'. *Cultural Anthropology* 9: 498–536. doi.org/10.1525/can.1994.9.4.02a00030

Berger, Peter, 1967, *The Sacred Canopy: Elements of a Sociological Theory of Religion*. New York: Anchor Books.

Biersack, Aletta, 1991, 'Prisoners of time: Millenarian praxis in a Melanesian valley'. In Aletta Biersack (ed.), *Clio in Oceania: Toward a Historical Anthropology*. Washington, DC: Smithsonian Institution Press, pp. 231–95.

Biersack, Aletta, 2001, 'Reproducing inequality: The gender politics of male cults in the Papua New Guinea highlands and Amazonia'. In Thomas Gregor and Donald Tuzin (eds), *Gender in Amazonia and Melanesia: An Exploration of the Comparative Method*. Berkeley and Los Angeles: University of California Press, pp. 69–91. doi.org/10.1525/california/9780520228511.003.0004

Biersack, Aletta, 2011a, 'The sun and the shakers, again: Enga, Ipili, and Somaip perspectives on the Cult of Ain. Part one'. *Oceania* 81(2): 113–36. doi.org/10.1002/j.1834-4461.2011.tb00097.x

Biersack, Aletta, 2011b, 'The sun and the shakers, again: Enga, Ipili, and Somaip perspectives on the Cult of Ain. Part two'. *Oceania* 81(3): 225–43. doi.org/10.1002/j.1834-4461.2011.tb00105.x

Biersack, Aletta, 2013, 'Beyond "cargo cult": Interpreting *Mata Kamo*'. In Marc Tabani and Marcellin Abong (eds), *Kago, Kastom, and Kalja: The Study of Indigenous Movements in Melanesia Today*. Marseilles: pacific-credo Publications, pp. 85–121. doi.org/10.4000/books.pacific.164

Biersack, Aletta, 2017, 'Afterword: From witchcraft to the Pentecostal-witchcraft nexus'. In Knut Rio, Michelle MacCarthy, and Ruy Blanes (eds), *Pentecostalism and Witchcraft: Spiritual Warfare in Africa and Melanesia*. New York and London: Palgrave Macmillan, pp. 293–304. doi.org/10.1007/978-3-319-56068-7_13

Biskup, Peter, 1970, 'Foreign coloured labour in German New Guinea: A study in economic development'. *Journal of Pacific History* 5(1): 85–107. doi.org/10.1080/00223347008572166

Blackburn, Simon, 1994, *The Oxford Dictionary of Philosophy*. Oxford and New York: Oxford University Press. doi.org/10.1093/acref/9780198735304.001.0001

Bogen, Emil, n.d., 'The Admiralty Islands and the Admiralty Islanders: Incidental Observations at a Southwest Pacific Naval Base, 1944–1945'. Copy held at the Archive for Melanesian Anthropology, University of California, San Diego.

Bourdieu, Pierre, 1977, *Outline of a Theory of Practice*. Cambridge: Cambridge University Press. doi.org/10.1017/CBO9780511812507

Bowler, Kate, 2013, *Blessed: A History of the American Prosperity Gospel*. New York: Oxford University Press. doi.org/10.1093/acprof:oso/9780199827695.001.0001

Boyer, Pascal, 2001, *Religion Explained: The Evolutionary Origins of Religious Thought*. New York: Basic Books.

Boyer, Paul, 1992, *When Time Shall Be No More: Prophecy Belief in Modern American Culture*. Cambridge, MA: Harvard University Press.

Brison, Karen, 1991, 'Community and prosperity: Social movements among the Kwanga of Papua New Guinea'. *The Contemporary Pacific* 3(2): 325–55.

Burridge, Kenelm O., 1969, *New Heaven, New Earth: A Study of Millenarian Activities*. Oxford: Basil Blackwell.

Burridge, Kenelm O., 1995 [1960], *Mambu: A Melanesian Millennium*. Princeton, NJ: Princeton University Press. doi.org/10.1515/9781400851584

Carrier, James G., 1992, 'Occidentalism: The world turned upside-down'. *American Ethnologist* 19(2): 195–212. doi.org/10.1525/ae.1992.19.2.02a00010

Carrier, James G. and Achsah H. Carrier, 1985, 'A Manus centenary: Production, kinship, and exchange in the Admiralty Islands'. *American Ethnologist* 12(3): 505–22. doi.org/10.1525/ae.1985.12.3.02a00070

Carrier, James G. and Achsah H. Carrier, 1989, *Wage, Trade, and Exchange in Melanesia: A Manus Society in the Modern State*. Berkeley and Los Angeles: University of California Press.

Carter, Joe, 2010, 'Jesus is coming back *when*? A crash course in evangelical views of eschatology'. *First Things*, 22 July. www.firstthings.com/blogs/firstthoughts/2010/07/jesus-is-coming-back-when-a-crash-course-in-evangelical-views-of-eschatology

Chinnery, E.W. and A.C. Haddon, 1917, 'Five new religious cults in New Guinea'. *The Hibbert Journal* 15: 448–63. London: Sherman, French & Co.

Clarke, Arthur C., 1953, *Childhood's End*. New York: Ballantine Books.

Cohn, Norman, 1970, *The Pursuit of the Millennium: Revolutionary millenarians and mystical anarchists of the Middle Ages*. St Albans: Paladin.

Coles, Robert, 1999, *The Secular Mind*. Princeton, NJ: Princeton University Press. doi.org/10.1515/9781400822812

Comaroff, Jean, 2010, 'The politics of conviction: Faith on the neo-liberal frontier'. In Bruce Kapferer, Kari Telle, and Annelin Eriksen (eds), *Contemporary Religiosities: Emergent Socialities and the Post-Nation-State*. New York and Oxford: Berghahn Books, pp. 17–38.

Connell, John, 1997, *Papua New Guinea: The Struggle for Development*. London and New York: Routledge.

Cox, John, 2014, 'The beginnings of a 'Pentecostalite' public realm in Papua New Guinea?' In 'Purging parliament: A new Christian politics in Papua New Guinea?' *State, Society and Governance in Melanesia Discussion Paper* 2014/1. Canberra: The Australian National University, pp. 11–14.

Dalsgaard, Steffen, 2009, 'All the Government's Men: State and Leadership in Manus Province, Papua New Guinea'. PhD thesis. Denmark: University of Aarhus.

Dalton, Douglas, 2004, 'Cargo and cult: The mimetic critique of capitalist culture'. In Holger Jebens (ed.), *Cargo, Cult, and Culture Critique*. Honolulu: University of Hawai'i Press, pp. 187–208. doi.org/10.1515/9780824840440-012

Dalton, Douglas, 2013, 'Between "cargo" and "cult"'. In Marc Tabani and Marcellin Abong (eds), *Kago, Kastom, and Kalja: The Study of Indigenous Movements in Melanesia Today*. Marseilles, France: pacific-credo Publications, pp. 29–58. doi.org/10.4000/books.pacific.160

Dalton, Douglas, 2017 [2005], '"We Are All 'Les' Men": Sorrow and modernism in Melanesia, or humor in paradise'. In Joel Robbins and Holly Wardlow (eds), *The Making of Global and Local Modernities in Melanesia*. New York: Routledge, pp. 103–14.

De Vos, George A., 1976, 'Introduction: Change as a social science problem'. In George A. De Vos (ed.), *Responses to Change: Society, Culture, and Personality*. New York: Van Nostrand, pp. 1–11.

Dean, Jodi, 1998, *Aliens in America: Conspiracy Cultures from Outerspace to Cyberspace*. Ithaca, NY: Cornell University Press.

Deming, W. Edwards, 1982, *Out of the Crisis*. Cambridge, MA: MIT Center for Advanced Engineering Study.

Dennett, Daniel C., 2006, *Breaking the Spell: Religion as a Natural Phenomenon*. New York and London: Viking.

Diamond, Jared, 1997, *Guns, Germs and Steel*. New York: W.W. Norton.

Diamond, Stanley, 1974, *In Search of the Primitive: A Critique of Civilization*. New Brunswick, NJ: Transaction Publishers.

Doctorow, E.L., 2009, *Homer and Langley*. New York: Random House.

Dorney, Sean, 1990, *Papua New Guinea: People, Politics, and History since 1975*. Sydney: Random House.

Douglas, Bronwen, 2001, 'From invisible Christians to gothic theatre: The romance of the millennial in Melanesian anthropology'. *Current Anthropology* 42(5): 615–50. doi.org/10.1086/322556

Douglas, Mary and Baron Isherwood, 1979, *The World of Goods: Toward an Anthropology of Consumption*. New York: W.W. Norton and Company.

Dwyer, Peter and Monica Minnegal, 2000, 'El Niño, Y2K and the "short, fat lady": Drought and agency in a lowland Papua New Guinean community'. *Journal of the Polynesian Society* 109(3): 251–72.

Epstein, Arnold Leonard, 2000–2001, 'The paranoid ethos in Melanesia: The case of the Tolai'. *Journal de la Société des Océanistes* 110: 3–18. doi.org/10.3406/jso.2000.2112

Eriksen, Annelin, 2010, 'Healing the nation: In search of unity through the Holy Spirit in Vanuatu'. In Bruce Kapferer, Kari Telle, and Annelin Eriksen (eds), *Contemporary Religiosities: Emergent Socialities and the Post-Nation-State*. New York and Oxford: Berghahn Books, pp. 66–81.

Ernst, Manfred, 2012, 'Changing Christianity in Oceania: A regional overview'. *Archives de Sciences Sociales des Religions* 157(January–March): 29–45. doi.org/10.4000/assr.23613

Errington, Frederick, 1974, 'Indigenous ideas of order, time, and transition in a New Guinea cargo movement'. *American Ethnologist* 1(2): 255–67. doi.org/10.1525/ae.1974.1.2.02a00030

Errington, Frederick and Deborah Gewertz, 2004, *Yali's Question: Sugar, Culture, and History*. Chicago and London: University of Chicago Press.

Eves, Richard, 2008, 'Cultivating Christian civil society: Fundamentalist Christianity, politics and governance in Papua New Guinea'. *State, Society, and Governance in Melanesia Discussion Paper* 2008/8. Canberra: Research School of Pacific and Asian Studies, The Australian National University.

Eves, Richard and Miranda Forsyth, 2015, 'Developing insecurity: Sorcery, witchcraft and Melanesia economic development'. *State, Society and Governance in Melanesia Discussion Paper* 2015/7. Canberra: The Australian National University. dpa.bellschool.anu.edu.au/sites/default/files/publications/attachments/2015-12/DP-2015-7-Eves%2BForsyth_0.pdf

Eves, Richard, N. Haley, R.J. May, J. Cox, P. Gibbs, F. Merlan, and A. Rumsey, 2014, 'Purging parliament: A new Christian politics in Papua New Guinea?' *State, Society and Governance in Melanesia Discussion Paper* 2014/1. Canberra: The Australian National University. dpa.bellschool.anu.edu.au/sites/default/files/publications/attachments/2015-12/SSGM-DP-2014-1-Eves-et-al-ONLINE3_0.pdf

Fenbury, D.M., 1978, *Practice Without Policy: Genesis of Local Government in Papua New Guinea*. Development Studies Centre Monograph No. 13. Canberra: The Australian National University.

Firth, Stewart, 1973, 'German Recruitment and Employment of Labourers in the Western Pacific before the First World War'. PhD thesis. Oxford: University of Oxford.

Foerstel, Lenora and Angela Gilliam (eds), 1992, *Confronting the Margaret Mead Legacy: Scholarship, Empire, and the South Pacific*. Philadelphia, PA: Temple University Press.

Forsyth, Miranda and Richard Eves (eds), 2015, *Talking it Through: Responses to Sorcery and Witchcraft Beliefs and Practices in Melanesia*. Canberra: ANU Press. doi.org/10.22459/TIT.05.2015

Fortune, Reo, 1932, *Sorcerers of Dobu: The Social Anthropology of the Dobu Islanders of the Western Pacific*. London: Routledge & Keegan Paul.

Fortune, Reo, 1965 [1935], *Manus Religion*. Philadelphia, PA: American Philosophical Society.

Foster, George M., 1976, 'Disease etiologies in non-Western medical systems'. *American Anthropologist* 78(4): 773–82. doi.org/10.1525/aa.1976.78.4.02a 00030

Foster, George M. and Barbara Gallatin Anderson, 1978, *Medical Anthropology*. New York: Wiley.

Foster, Robert J., 2017 [2005], 'Afterword: Frustrating modernity in Melanesia'. In Joel Robbins and Holly Wardlow (eds), *The Making of Global and Local Modernities in Melanesia*. New York: Routledge, pp. 207–16.

Gesch, Patrick, 1990, 'Cultivation of surprise and excess in the Sepik: The encounter of cultures in the Sepik of Papua New Guinea'. In Garry Trompf (ed.), *Cargo Cults and Millenarian Movements: Transoceanic Comparisons of New Religious Movements*. New York: Mouton de Gruyer, pp. 213–38.

Gibbs, Philip J., 1977, 'The cult from Lyeimi and the Ipili'. *Oceania* XLVIII(1): 1–25. doi.org/10.1002/j.1834-4461.1977.tb01315.x

Gibbs, Philip, 2014, 'Papua New Guinea'. In *Worldmark Encyclopedia of Religious Practices* (2nd ed., vol. 3), pp. 637–47. www.philipgibbs.org/pdfs/Papua%20 New%20Guinea_Vol%203_pg%20637%20to%20647.pdf

Gramsci, Antonio, 1971, *Selections from the Prison Notebooks*. New York: International Publishers.

Gregory, C.A., 1982, *Gifts and Commodities*. New York: Academic Press.

Griffin, James, Hank Nelson and Stewart Firth, 1979, *Papua New Guinea: A Political History*. Richmond, Victoria: Heinemann Educational Australia.

Gustafsson, Berit, 1992, *Houses and Ancestors: Continuities and Discontinuities in Leadership among the Manus*. Göteborg, Sweden: Institute for Advanced Studies in Social Anthropology, University of Gothenburg.

Gustafsson, Berit, 1995, 'From God to Win: The rise of a Melanesian religious movement based on Christianity'. In Gören Aijmer (ed.), *Syncretism and the Commerce of Symbols*. Göteborg, Sweden: Institute for Advanced Studies in Social Anthropology, University of Gothenburg, pp. 60–83.

Guthrie, Stewart Elliott, 1993, *Faces in the Clouds: A New Theory of Religion*. New York: Oxford University Press.

Hall, John R., 2009, *Apocalypse: From Antiquity to the Empire of Modernity*. Malden, MA: Polity Press.

Hallowell, A. Irving, 1955, *Culture and Experience*. New York: Schocken Books. doi.org/10.9783/9781512816600

Hallowell, A. Irving, 1960, 'Ojibwa ontology, behavior, and world view'. In Stanley Diamond (ed.), *Culture in History: Essays in Honor of Paul Radin*. New York: Columbia University Press, pp. 19–52.

Hamilton, Malcom B., 2001, 'Sociological dimensions of Christian millenarianism'. In Stephen Hunt (ed.), *Christian Millenarianism: From the Early Church to Waco*. Bloomington, IN: Indiana University Press, pp. 12–25.

Hannerz, Ulf, 1992, *Cultural Complexity*. New York: Columbia University Press.

Harvey, Graham, 2005, *Animism: Respecting the Living World*. Kent Town, South Australia: Wakefield Press.

Hau'ofa, Epeli, 1975, 'Anthropology and Pacific Islanders'. *Oceania*, XLV(4): 283–9. doi.org/10.1002/j.1834-4461.1975.tb01871.x

Heimlich, Russell, 2010, 'Jesus Christ's return to Earth'. Pew Research Center, 14 July. www.pewresearch.org/fact-tank/2010/07/14/jesus-christs-return-to-earth/

Hermann, Elfriede, 2004, 'Dissolving the self-other dichotomy in Western "cargo cult" constructions'. In Holger Jebens (ed.), *Cargo, Cult, and Culture Critique*. Honolulu: University of Hawai'i Press, pp. 36–58. doi.org/10.1515/9780824840440-004

Hickel, Jason, 2014, '"Xenophobia" in South Africa: Order, chaos, and the moral economy of witchcraft'. *Cultural Anthropology* 29(1): 103–27. doi.org/10.14506/ca29.1.07

Hiery, Hermann Joseph, 1995, *The Neglected War: The German South Pacific and the Influence of World War I*. Honolulu: University of Hawai'i Press. doi.org/10.1515/9780824864897

Hofstadter, Richard, 2008 [1965], *The Paranoid Style in American Politics*. Penguin Random House.

Hogbin, H. Ian, 1935, 'Trading expeditions in northern New Guinea'. *Oceania* V(4): 375–407. doi.org/10.1002/j.1834-4461.1935.tb00162.x

Holbraad, Martin and Morten Axel Pedersen, 2017, *The Ontological Turn: An Anthropological Exposition*. Cambridge: Cambridge University Press. doi.org/10.1017/9781316218907

Hood, Bruce M., 2009, *Supersense: Why We Believe in the Unbelievable*. New York: HarperCollins.

Hughes, Colin A., 1965, 'The development of the legislature: Preparing for the House of Assembly'. In David G. Bettison, Colin A. Hughes, and Paul W. van der Veur (eds), *The Papua-New Guinea Elections 1964*. Canberra: The Australian National University, pp. 28–52.

Hunt, Stephen, 2001, 'The Christian millennium: An enduring theme'. In Stephen Hunt (ed.), *Christian Millenarianism: From the Early Church to Waco*. Bloomington, IN: Indiana University Press, pp. 1–11.

Hutchins, Edwin, 1995, *Cognition in the Wild*. Cambridge, MA: MIT Press.

Ingersoll, Julie J., 2015, *Building God's Kingdom: Inside the World of Christian Reconstruction*. Oxford and New York: Oxford University Press. doi.org/10.1093/acprof:oso/9780199913787.001.0001

Jackson, Richard, 1976, 'Lorengau'. In R. Jackson (ed.), *An Introduction to the Urban Geography of Papua New Guinea*. Department of Geography Occasional Paper 13. Port Moresby: University of Papua New Guinea.

Jacoby, Susan, 2008, *The Age of American Unreason*. New York: Pantheon.

Jarvie, I.C., 1984, *Rationality and Relativism: In Search of a Philosophy and History of Anthropology*. London: Routledge & Kegan Paul.

Jebens, Holger, 2000, 'Signs of the Second Coming: On eschatological expectation and disappointment in highland and seaboard Papua New Guinea'. *Ethnohistory* 47(1): 171–204. doi.org/10.1215/00141801-47-1-171

Jebens, Holger, 2004a, 'Introduction: Cargo, cult, and culture critique'. In Holger Jebens (ed.), *Cargo, Cult, and Culture Critique*. Honolulu: University of Hawai'i Press, pp. 1–13. doi.org/10.1515/9780824840440-002

Jebens, Holger, 2004b, 'Talking about cargo cults in Koimumu (West New Britain Province, Papua New Guinea)'. In Holger Jebens (ed.), *Cargo, Cult, and Culture Critique*. Honolulu: University of Hawai'i Press, pp. 157–69. doi.org/10.1515/9780824840440-010

Jebens, Holger, 2005, *Pathways to Heaven: Contesting Mainline and Fundamentalist Christianity in Papua New Guinea*. Oxford: Berghahn Books.

Jolly, Margaret and Nicholas Thomas (eds), 1992, 'The politics of tradition in the South Pacific'. *Oceania* Special Issue 62(4). doi.org/10.1002/j.1834-4461.1992.tb00355.x

Kaima, Sam T., 1991, 'The evolution of cargo cults and the emergence of political parties in Melanesia'. *Journal de la Société des Océanistes* 92–93(1&2): 173–80. doi.org/10.3406/jso.1991.2909

Kais, Kakak, 1998, 'The Paliau Movement'. Papua New Guinea Buai Digital Project. www.pngbuai.com/100philosophy/paliau-movement/

Kanasa, Biama, 1991, 'Paliau Maloat: Tribute to a reformist'. *The Times of Papua New Guinea*, 21 November, pp. 20–1.

Kapferer, Bruce, Annelin Eriksen, and Kari Telle, 2010, 'Introduction: Religiosities toward a future—in pursuit of the new millennium'. In Bruce Kapferer, Kari Telle, and Annelin Eriksen (eds), *Contemporary Religiosities: Emergent Socialities and the Post-Nation-State*. New York and Oxford: Berghahn Books, pp. 1–16. doi.org/10.3167/sa.2009.530101

Keesing, Roger M., 1982, *Kwaio Religion: The Living and the Dead in a Solomon Island Society*. New York: Columbia University Press.

Keesing, Roger M., 1994, 'Theories of culture revisited'. In Robert Borofsky (ed.), *Assessing Cultural Anthropology*. New York: McGraw-Hill, pp. 301–12.

Keesing, Roger and Robert Tonkinson (eds), 1982, 'Reinventing traditional culture: The politics of *kastom* in island Melanesia'. *Mankind* Special Issue 13(4).

Kelsen, Hans, 2012, *Secular Religion: A Polemic against the Misinterpretation of Modern Social Philosophy, Science, and Politics as 'New Religions'*. Berlin and Heidelberg: Springer-Verlag.

Kierkegaard, Søren (Johannes De Silentio), 2012 [1843]. In Dragan Nikolic (ed.), *Fear and Trembling*. Walter Lowie (trans., 1941). Published in the United States by Dragan Nikolic.

King, V.E., 1978, 'The End of an Era: Aspects of the History of the Admiralty Islands, 1898–1908'. Bachelor of Arts (Honours) thesis. Sydney: Macquarie University.

Knauft, Bruce M., 1996, *Genealogies for the Present in Cultural Anthropology.* New York: Routledge.

Knauft, Bruce M., 1999, *From Primitive to Postcolonial in Melanesia and Anthropology.* Ann Arbor, MI: University of Michigan Press. doi.org/10.3998/mpub.10934

Kohl, Karl-Heinz, 2004, 'Mutual hopes: German money and the tree of wealth in East Flores'. In Holger Jebens (ed.), *Cargo, Cult, and Culture Critique.* Honolulu: University of Hawai'i Press, pp. 79–91. doi.org/10.1515/97808 24840440-006

Kuehling, Susanne, 2005, *Dobu: Ethics of Exchange on a Massim Island.* Honolulu: University of Hawai'i Press.

Kuznar, Lawrence A., 1997, *Reclaiming a Scientific Anthropology.* Walnut Creek, CA: AltaMira Press.

La Barre, Weston, 1972 [1970], *The Ghost Dance: The Origins of Religion.* New York: Delta.

Lamy, Philip, 1996, *Millennium Rage: Survivalists, White Supremacists, and the Doomsday Prophecy.* New York: Plenum Press. doi.org/10.1007/978-1-4899-6076-4_1

Landes, Richard, 2011, *Heaven on Earth: The Varieties of the Millennial Experience.* New York: Oxford University Press. doi.org/10.1093/acprof:oso/9780199753598.003.0001

Landman, Marjorie, 1951, 'Special Report on Baluan School, Part 1: Some Notes on Culture Contact in Baluan'. Copy held in the Archive for Melanesian Anthropology, University of California, San Diego.

Lanternari, Vittorio, 1963, *The Religions of the Oppressed: A Study of Modern Messianic Cults.* New York: Knopf.

Latour, Bruno, 1993, *We Have Never Been Modern.* Catherine Porter (trans.). Cambridge, MA: Harvard University Press.

Lattas, Andrew, 1992, 'Hysteria, anthropological disclosure and the concept of the unconscious: Cargo cults and the scientisation of race and colonial power'. *Oceania* 63(1): 1–14. doi.org/10.1002/j.1834-4461.1992.tb00364.x

Lattas, Andrew, 1998, *Cultures of Secrecy: Reinventing Race in Bush Kaliai Cargo Cults*. Madison, WI: University of Wisconsin Press.

Lattas, Andrew, 2001, 'The underground life of capitalism: Space, persons, and money in Bali (West New Britain)'. In Alan Rumsey and James Weiner (eds), *Emplaced Myth: Space, Narrative, and Knowledge in Aboriginal Australia and Papua New Guinea*. Honolulu: University of Hawai'i Press, pp. 161–88. doi.org/10.1515/9780824843946-010

Lawrence, Peter, 1989 [1964], *Road Belong Cargo: A Study of the Cargo Movement in the Southern Madang District, New Guinea*. Long Grove, IL: Waveland Press.

Leavitt, Stephen C., 2004, 'From "cult" to religious conviction: The case for making cargo personal'. In Holger Jebens (ed.), *Cargo, Cult, and Culture Critique*. Honolulu: University of Hawai'i Press, pp. 170–86. doi.org/10.1515/9780824840440-011

Leavitt, Stephen C., 2017 [2005], '"We are not straight": Bumbita Arapesh strategies for self-reflection in the face of images of Western superiority'. In Joel Robbins and Holly Wardlow (eds), *The Making of Global and Local Modernities in Melanesia*. New York: Routledge, pp. 73–84.

Lepowsky, Maria, 2011, 'The boundaries of personhood, the problem of empathy, and "the native's point of view" in the outer islands'. In Douglas W. Hollan and C. Jason Throop (eds), *The Anthropology of Empathy: Experiencing the Lives of Others in Pacific Societies*. New York and Oxford: Berghahn Books, pp. 43–65.

Lewis, Herbert S., 2014, *In Defense of Anthropology: An Investigation of the Critique of Anthropology*. New Brunswick, NJ: Transaction Publishers.

Lewis, James R. (ed.), 2004, *The Oxford Handbook of New Religious Movements*. New York: Oxford University Press.

Lindstrom, Lamont, 1993a, *Cargo Cult: Strange Stories of Desire from Melanesia and Beyond*. Honolulu: University of Hawai'i Press.

Lindstrom, Lamont, 1993b, 'Cargo cult culture: Toward a genealogy of Melanesian kastom'. *Anthropological Forum* 6(4): 495–513. doi.org/10.1080/00664677.1993.9967429

Lindstrom, Lamont, 2004, 'Cargo cult at the third millennium'. In Holger Jebens (ed.), *Cargo, Cult, and Culture Critique*. Honolulu: University of Hawai'i Press, pp. 15–35. doi.org/10.1515/9780824840440-003

Lindstrom, Lamont, 2011, 'Personhood, cargo and Melanesian social unities'. In Edvard Hviding and Knut M. Rio (eds), *Made In Oceania: Social Movements, Cultural Heritage and the State in the Pacific.* Wantage, UK: Sean Kingston Publishing, pp. 253–72.

Lindstrom, Lamont, 2013, 'Even more strange stories of desire: Cargo cult in popular media'. In Marc Tabani and Marcellin Abong (eds), *Kago, Kastom, and Kalja: The Study of Indigenous Movements in Melanesia Today.* Marseilles, France: pacific-credo Publications, pp. 169–85. doi.org/10.4000/books.pacific.170

Lindstrom, Lamont and Geoffrey M. White, 1989, 'War stories'. In Lamont Lindstrom and Geoffrey M. White (eds), *The Pacific Theater: Island Representations of World War II.* Melbourne: Melbourne University Press, pp. 3–40.

Lindstrom, Lamont and Geoffrey M. White (eds), 1994, *Culture, Kastom and Tradition: Cultural Policy in Melanesia.* Suva, Fiji: Institute of Pacific Studies, University of the South Pacific.

Lukas, Paliau, 1983, 'A white man's religion? Challenge by a Melanesian, response from a missionary'. *Catalyst* 13(1). Goroka, Papua New Guinea: Melanesian Institute for Pastoral and Socio-Economic Service, pp. 6–16.

Lutkehaus, Nancy C., 2008, *Margaret Mead: The Making of an American Icon.* Princeton, NJ: Princeton University Press. doi.org/10.1515/9780691190273

Macintyre, Martha, 2010, 'Kago, kastom and kalja: Old theories and new realities in the study of Melanesian movements'. Debates, Remarks and Comments. ASAO Sessions 2009–2010. Unpublished document.

Macintyre, Martha, 2013, 'Instant wealth: Visions of the future on Lihir, New Ireland, Papua New Guinea'. In Marc Tabani and Marcellin Abong (eds), *Kago, Kastom, and Kalja: The Study of Indigenous Movements in Melanesia Today.* Marseilles, France: pacific-credo Publications, pp. 123–46. doi.org/ 10.4000/books.pacific.166

Mair, Lucy, 1948, *Australia in New Guinea.* London: Christophers.

Malinowski, Bronislaw, 1922, *Argonauts of the Western Pacific: An Account of Native Enterprise and Adventure in the Archipelagoes of Melanesian New Guinea.* London: George Routledge & Sons.

Maloat, Paliau, 1970, 'Histori bilong mi taim mi bon na i kamap tede' [The story of my life from the day I was born until the present day]. In Marion W. Ward, Susan C. Tarua, and May Dudley (eds), *The Politics of Melanesia: Papers Delivered at the Fourth Waigani Seminar.* Canberra: Research School of Pacific Studies, The Australian National University, pp. 144–61.

Mauss, Marcel, 1967 [1925], *The Gift: Forms and Functions of Exchange in Archaic Societies*. New York: W.W. Norton and Company.

May, John D'Arcy (ed.), 1985, *Living Theology in Melanesia: A Reader*. Goroka, Papua New Guinea: Melanesian Institute for Pastoral and Socio-Economic Service, pp. 31–43.

May, R.J., 1982, 'Micronationalism in perspective'. In R.J. May (ed.), *Micronationalist Movements in Papua New Guinea*. Political and Social Change Monograph No. 1. Canberra: Research School of Pacific Studies, The Australian National University, pp. 1–28.

McDowell, Nancy, 1988, 'A note on cargo cults and cultural constructions of change'. *Pacific Studies* 11(2): 121–34.

McDowell, Nancy, 2000, 'A brief comment on difference and rationality'. *Oceania* 7(4): 373–80. doi.org/10.1002/j.1834-4461.2000.tb03073.x

McVicar, Michael Joseph, 2015, *Christian Reconstruction: R.J. Rushdoony and American Religious Conservatism*. Chapel Hill, NC: University of North Carolina Press. doi.org/10.5149/northcarolina/9781469622743.001.0001

Mead, Margaret, 1928, *Coming of Age in Samoa*. New York: William Morrow and Company.

Mead, Margaret, 1932, 'An investigation of the thought of primitive children, with special reference to animism'. *Journal of the Royal Anthropological Institute of Great Britain and Ireland* 62(January–June): 173–190. doi.org/10.2307/2843884

Mead, Margaret, 1977, *Letters from the Field: 1925–1975*. New York: Harper and Row.

Mead, Margaret, 2001 [1930], *Growing Up in New Guinea: A Comparative Study of Primitive Education*. New York: Perennial.

Mead, Margaret, 2001 [1956], *New Lives for Old: Cultural Transformation, Manus, 1928–1953*. New York: Perennial.

Mead, Margaret, 2002 [1934], 'Kinship in the Admiralty Islands'. *Anthropological Papers of the American Museum of Natural History* 34(2).

Mead, Margaret and Theodore Schwartz, n.d., 'Admiralty Island political systems'. Copy held in the Archive for Melanesian Anthropology, University of California, San Diego.

Minol, Bernard, Dorcas Pwahau, and Francis Kolpai (eds), 2014, *A Brief History of N'Dranou Local Church*. Port Moresby: University of Papua New Guinea Press.

Moore, Clive, 2003, *New Guinea: Crossing Boundaries and History*. Honolulu: University of Hawai'i Press. doi.org/10.1515/9780824844134

Morris, Adam, 2019, *American Messiahs: False Prophets of a Damned Nation*. New York: Liveright.

Nelson, Hank, 1980, 'As bilong soldia: The raising of the Papuan Infantry Battalion in 1940'. *Yagl-Ambu* 7: 19–24.

Nevermann, Hans, 1934, *Admiralitäts-Inseln. II. Ethnograpphie: A Melanesien. Ergebnisse der Südsee-Expedition, 1908–1910* (vol. 3). G. Thilenius (ed.). Hamburg: Friederichsen, De Gruyter.

Noble, David F., 1997, *The Religion of Technology: The Divinity of Man and the Spirit of Innovation*. New York: Knopf.

Ogan, Eugene, 1972, 'Business and cargo: Socio-economic change among the Nasioi of Bougainville'. *New Guinea Research Bulletin* No. 44. Boroko, Papua New Guinea: New Guinea Research Unit, The Australian National University.

Oldenbourg, Zoé, 1961 [1959], *Massacre at Monségur: A History of the Albigensian Crusade*. Peter Green (trans.). New York: Pantheon Books.

Otto, Ton, 1991, *The Politics of Tradition in Baluan: Social Change and the Construction of the Past in a Manus Society*. Nijmegen, The Netherlands: Centre for Pacific Studies, University of Nijmegen.

Otto, Ton, 1992a, 'From Paliau Movement to Makasol: The politics of representation'. *Canberra Anthropology* 15(2): 46–68. doi.org/10.1080/03149099209508450

Otto, Ton, 1992b, 'Introduction: Imagining cargo cults'. *Canberra Anthropology* 15(2): 1–10. doi.org/10.1080/03149099209508447

Otto, Ton, 1992c, 'The Paliau Movement in Manus and the objectification of tradition'. *History and Anthropology* 5(3–4): 427–54. doi.org/10.1080/0275 7206.1992.9960821

Otto, Ton, 1998, 'Paliau's stories: Autobiography and automythography of a Melanesian prophet'. *Focaal* (32): 71–87.

Otto, Ton, 2004, 'Work, wealth, and knowledge: Enigmas of cargoist identifications'. In Holger Jebens (ed.), *Cargo, Cult, and Culture Critique*. Honolulu: University of Hawai'i Press, pp. 209–26. doi.org/10.1515/9780824840440-013

Otto, Ton, 2010, 'What happened to cargo cults? Material religions in Melanesia and the West'. In Bruce Kapferer, Kari Telle, and Annelin Eriksen (eds), *Contemporary Religiosities: Emergent Socialities and the Post-Nation-State*. New York and Oxford: Berghahn Books, pp. 82–102.

Peires, J.B., 1989, *The Dead Will Arise: Nongqawuse and the Great Xhosa Cattle-Killing Movement of 1856–7*. Johannesburg: Raven Press.

Pokawin, Stephen, 1976, 'The elections in Manus'. In David Stone (ed.), *Prelude to Self-Government: Electoral Politics in Papua New Guinea 1972*. Canberra: Research School of Pacific Studies, The Australian National University, pp. 400–14.

Pokawin, Stephen P., 1983a, 'Community government in Manus: People's participation in government'. *Yagl-Ambu* 10(4): 8–16.

Pokawin, [Stephen] Polonhou, 1983b, 'Wing, Wang, Wong: Developments in the Paliau Movement'. In Wendy Flannery and Glen W. Bays (eds), *Religious Movements in Melanesia Today* (vol. 1). Goroka, Papua New Guinea: Melanesian Institute for Pastoral and Socio-Economic Service, pp. 104–14.

Pokawin, Polonhou S., 1989, 'Manus yearns for quality leadership: A questionable verdict in 1982'. In Peter King (ed.), *Pangu Returns to Power: The 1982 Elections in Papua New Guinea*. Political and Social Change Monograph No. 9. Canberra: Research School of Pacific Studies, The Australian National University, pp. 235–78.

Pouwer, Jan, 2000, 'Review of *Expecting the Day of Wrath: Versions of the Millennium in Papua New Guinea*, Christin Kocher Schmid (ed.)'. *Paideuma: Mitteilungen zur Kulturkunde* 46: 339–44.

Rappaport, Roy A., 1999, *Ritual and Religion in the Making of Humanity*. Cambridge: Cambridge University Press. doi.org/10.1017/CBO97805118 14686

Rasmussen, Anders Emil, 2013, 'Manus canoes: Skill, making, and personhood in Mbuke Islands (Papua New Guinea)'. *Kon-Tiki Museum Occasional Papers* Vol. 13. Oslo, Norway: Kon-Tiki Museum.

Rasmussen, Anders Emil, 2015, *In the Absence of the Gift: New Forms of Value and Personhood in a Papua New Guinea Community*. New York and Oxford: Berghahn Books. doi.org/10.2307/j.ctt9qdb0f

Rio, Knut, Michelle MacCarthy, and Ruy Blanes (eds), 2017, *Pentecostalism and Witchcraft: Spiritual Warfare in Africa and Melanesia*. New York and London: Palgrave Macmillan. doi.org/10.1007/978-3-319-56068-7

Robbins, Joel, 2004a, *Becoming Sinners: Christianity and Moral Torment in a Papua New Guinea Society.* Berkeley and Los Angeles: University of California Press. doi.org/10.1525/9780520937086

Robbins, Joel, 2004b, 'On the critique in cargo and the cargo in critique: Toward a comparative anthropology of critical practice'. In Holger Jebens (ed.), *Cargo, Cult, and Culture Critique.* Honolulu: University of Hawai'i Press, pp. 243–59. doi.org/10.1515/9780824840440-015

Robbins, Joel, 2011, 'On Messianic promise'. In David Lipset and Paul Roscoe (eds), *In Echoes of the Tambaran: Masculinity, History and the Subject in the Work of Donald F. Tuzin.* Canberra: ANU E Press, pp. 183–94. doi.org/10.22459/ET.10.2011.09

Robbins, Joel and Holly Wardlow (eds), 2017 [2005], *The Making of Global and Local Modernities in Melanesia.* New York: Routledge.

Robinson, Neville K., 1981, *Villagers at War: Some Papua New Guinean Experiences in World War II.* Pacific Research Monograph Number Two. Canberra: The Australian National University.

Rodman, Margaret, 1979, 'Introduction'. In Margaret Rodman and Matthew Cooper (eds), *The Pacification of Melanesia.* Association for Social Anthropology in Oceania Monograph No. 7. Ann Arbor, MI: University of Michigan Press, pp. 1–23.

Romanucci Schwartz, Lola, 1966, 'Conflits fonciers á Mokerang, village Matankor des Iles de l'Amirauté'. *L'Homme* 6(2): 32–52. doi.org/10.3406/hom.1966.366784

Romanucci-Ross, Lola, 1985, *Mead's Other Manus: Phenomenology of the Encounter.* South Hadley, MA: Bergin and Garvey.

Rowley, C.D., 1965, *The New Guinea Villager: A Retrospect from 1964.* Melbourne: Cheshire.

Russell, Bertrand, 1997 [1935], *Religion and Science.* New York: Oxford University Press.

Sack, Peter and Dymphna Clark (eds and trans.), 1979, *German New Guinea: The Annual Reports.* Canberra: Australian National University Press.

Sahlins, Marshall, 1992, 'The economics of develop-man in the Pacific'. *Res: Anthropology and aesthetics* 21(Spring): 12–25. doi.org/10.1086/RESv21n1ms20166839

Sahlins, Marshall, 2013, 'Difference'. Association for Social Anthropology in Oceania 2013 Distinguished Lecture. *Oceania* 83(3): 281–94. doi.org/10.1002/ocea.5025

Said, Edward W., 1979 [1978], *Orientalism*. New York: Vintage.

Schmid, Christin Kocher (ed.), 1999, *Expecting the Day of Wrath: Versions of the Millennium in Papua New Guinea*. Boroko, Papua New Guinea: National Research Institute.

Schmid, Christin Kocher and Stefanie Klappa, 1999, 'Profile of a leader, or the world according to Yulu Nuo'. In Christin Kocher Schmid (ed.), *Expecting the Day of Wrath: Versions of the Millennium in Papua New Guinea*. Boroko, Papua New Guinea: National Research Institute, pp. 89–110.

Schwartz, Theodore, 1962, 'The Paliau Movement in the Admiralty Islands, 1946–1954'. *Anthropological Papers of the American Museum of Natural History* 49(2).

Schwartz, Theodore, 1963, 'Systems of areal integration: Some considerations based on the Admiralty Islands of northern Melanesia'. *Anthropological Forum* 1(1): 56–97. doi.org/10.1080/00664677.1963.9967181

Schwartz, Theodore, 1966–67, 'The cooperatives: *Ol i bagarapim mani*'. *New Guinea* 1: 36–47.

Schwartz, Theodore, 1972, 'Distributive models of culture in relation to societal scale'. Paper presented at the De Vos Conference on Psychological Adjustment and Adaptation to Culture Change, Hakone, Japan, 1968, and the 8th International Congress of Anthropological and Ethnological Sciences, Tokyo.

Schwartz, Theodore, 1973, 'Cult and context: The paranoid ethos in Melanesia'. *Ethos* 1(2): 153–74. doi.org/10.1525/eth.1973.1.2.02a00020

Schwartz, Theodore, 1975, 'Cultural totemism: Ethnic identity primitive and modern'. In George De Vos and Lola Ross (eds), *Ethnic Identity in Cultural Continuity and Change*. Palo Alto, CA: Mayfield Press, pp. 106–31.

Schwartz, Theodore, 1976a, 'The cargo cult: A Melanesian type-response to change'. In George De Vos (ed.), *Responses to Change*. New York: Van Nostrand, pp. 157–206.

Schwartz, Theodore, 1976b, 'Relations among generations in time-limited cultures'. In Theodore Schwartz (ed.), *Socialization as Cultural Communication: Development of a Theme in the Work of Margaret Mead*. Berkeley and Los Angeles: University of California Press, pp. 217–30.

Schwartz, Theodore, 1978a, 'Where is the culture? Personality and the distributive locus of culture'. In George D. Spindler (ed.), *The Making of Psychological Anthropology*. Berkeley and Los Angeles: University of California Press.

Schwartz, Theodore, 1978b, 'The size and shape of a culture'. In Fredrik Barth (ed.), *Scale and Social Organization*. Oslo: Universitetsforlaget, pp. 215–52.

Schwartz, Theodore, 1983, 'Anthropology: A quaint science'. *American Anthropologist* 85(4): 919–29. doi.org/10.1525/aa.1983.85.4.02a00190

Schwartz, Theodore, 1991, 'Behavioral evolution beyond the advent of culture'. In L. Bryce Boyer and Ruth M. Boyer (eds), *The Psychoanalytic Study of Society* (vol. 16). New York: Routledge, pp. 183–213. doi.org/10.4324/9781315792057-9

Schwartz, Theodore, 1993, 'Kastom, "custom", and culture: Conspicuous culture and culture-constructs'. *Anthropological Forum* 6(4): 515–40. doi.org/10.1080/00664677.1993.9967430

Schwartz, Theodore and Margaret Mead, 1961, 'Micro- and macro-cultural models for cultural evolution'. *Anthropological Linguistics* 3: 107.

Schwimmer, Eric, 1979, 'The self and the product: Concepts of work in comparative perspective'. In Sandra Wallman (ed.), *Social Anthropology of Work*. New York: Academic Press, pp. 287–315.

Searle, John R., 1995, *The Construction of Social Reality*. New York: The Free Press.

Searle, John R., 2006, 'Reality and social construction: Reply to Friedman'. *Anthropological Theory* 6(1): 81–8. doi.org/10.1177/1463499606061738

Sillitoe, Paul, 1998, *An Introduction to the Anthropology of Melanesia: Culture and Tradition*. Cambridge: Cambridge University Press.

Smith, Michael French, 1982, 'Bloody time and bloody scarcity: Capitalism, authority, and the transformation of temporal experience in a Papua New Guinea village'. *American Ethnologist* 9(3): 503–18. doi.org/10.1525/ae.1982.9.3.02a00040

Smith, Michael French, 1984, '"Wild" villagers and capitalist virtues: Perceptions of Western work habits in a preindustrial community'. *Anthropological Quarterly* 57(4): 125–38. doi.org/10.2307/3317683

Smith, Michael French, 1990, 'Business and the romance of community cooperation on Kairiru Island'. In Nancy Lutkehaus, Christian Kaufman, William E. Mitchell, Douglas Newton, Lita Osmundsen, and Meinhard Schuster (eds), *Sepik Heritage: Tradition and Change in Papua New Guinea*. Durham, NC: Carolina Academic Press, pp. 212–20.

Smith, Michael French, 1994, *Hard Times on Kairiru Island: Poverty, Development, and Morality in a Papua New Guinea Village*. Honolulu: University of Hawai'i Press.

Smith, Michael French, 2002, *Village on the Edge: Changing Times in Papua New Guinea*. Honolulu: University of Hawai'i Press. doi.org/10.1515/9780824865450

Smith, Michael French, 2013, *A Faraway, Familiar Place: An Anthropologist Returns to Papua New Guinea*. Honolulu: University of Hawai'i Press. doi.org/10.21313/hawaii/9780824836863.001.0001

Somare, Michael, 1970, 'Problems of political organisation in diversified tribes in Papua-New Guinea'. In Marion W. Ward, Susan C. Tarua, and May Dudley (eds), *The Politics of Melanesia: Papers Delivered at the Fourth Waigani Seminar*. Canberra: Research School of Pacific Studies, The Australian National University, pp. 489–93.

Souter, Gavin, 1963, *New Guinea: The Last Unknown*. Sydney: Angus and Robertson.

Spiro, Melford E., 1967, *Burmese Supernaturalism: A Study in the Explanation and Reduction of Suffering*. Englewood Cliffs, NJ: Prentice-Hall.

Spiro, Melford E., 1986, 'Cultural relativism and the future of anthropology'. *Cultural Anthropology* 1(3): 259–86. doi.org/10.1525/can.1986.1.3.02a00010

Stanner, W.E.H., 1953, *The South Seas in Transition: A Study of Post-war Rehabilitation and Reconstruction in Three British Pacific Dependencies*. Sydney: Australasian Publishing Company.

Stanner, W.E.H., 1958, 'On the interpretation of cargo cults'. *Oceania* XXIX(1): 1–25. doi.org/10.1002/j.1834-4461.1958.tb02934.x

Stark, Rodney and Roger Finke, 2000, *Acts of Faith: Explaining the Human Side of Religion*. Berkeley and Los Angeles: University of California Press. doi.org/10.1525/9780520924345

Stella, Regis Tove, 2007, *Imagining the Other: The Representation of the Papua New Guinean Subject*. Honolulu: University of Hawai'i Press. doi.org/10.1515/9780824862923

Stewart, Iain, 2012, 'Kelsen, the enlightenment and modern premodernists'. *Australian Journal of Legal Philosophy* 37: 251–78.

Stewart, Kathleen and Susan Harding, 1999, 'Bad endings: American apocalypsis'. *Annual Review of Anthropology* 28: 285–310. doi.org/10.1146/annurev.anthro.28.1.285

Strahan, Lachlan, 2005, *Day of Reckoning*. Canberra: Pandanus Books.

Strathern, Andrew, 1971, *The Rope of Moka: Big-men and Ceremonial Exchange in Mount Hagen New Guinea*. Cambridge: Cambridge University Press. doi.org/10.1017/CBO9780511558160

Strathern, Marilyn, 1975, 'No money on our skins: Hagen migrants in Port Moresby'. *New Guinea Research Bulletin* No. 61. Boroko, Papua New Guinea: New Guinea Research Unit, The Australian National University.

Strathern, Marilyn, 1988, *The Gender of the Gift: Problems with Women and Problems with Society in Melanesia*. Berkeley and Los Angeles: University of California Press. doi.org/10.1525/california/9780520064232.001.0001

Sullivan, Nancy, 2005, 'Cargo and condescension'. *Contemporary PNG Studies: Divine Word University Research Journal* 3(November): 31–46.

Swain, Tony and Garry Trompf, 1995, *The Religions of Oceania*. London and New York: Routledge.

Tabani, Marc, 2013, 'What's the matter with cargo cults today?' In Marc Tabani and Marcellin Abong (eds), *Kago, Kastom, and Kalja: The Study of Indigenous Movements in Melanesia Today*. Marseilles, France: pacific-credo Publications, pp. 7–27. doi.org/10.4000/books.pacific.159

Tanabe, George, Jr, 2005, 'Pono and Kapu: Righteousness and taboo in Hawai'i'. In Wade Clark Roof and Mark Silk (eds), *Religion and Public Life in the Pacific Region: Fluid Identities*. Lanham, MD: AltaMira Press.

Tillich, Paul, 1952, *The Courage To Be*. New Haven, CT: Yale University Press.

Trompf, G.W. (ed.), 1990, *Cargo Cults and Millenarian Movements: Transoceanic Comparisons of New Religious Movements*. Berlin: Mouton de Gruyter. doi.org/10.1515/9783110874419

Trompf, Garry W., 1991, *Melanesian Religion*. Cambridge: Cambridge University Press. doi.org/10.1017/CBO9780511518140

Trompf, Garry W., 1994, *Payback: The Logic of Retribution in Melanesian Religions*. Cambridge: Cambridge University Press. doi.org/10.1017/CBO9780511470141

Turner, Mark, 1990, *Papua New Guinea: The Challenge of Independence*. Ringwood, Victoria: Penguin Books.

Tuzin, Donald F., 1980, *The Voice of the Tambaran: Truth and Illusion in Arapesh Religion*. Berkeley and Los Angeles: University of California Press.

Tuzin, Donald F., 1990, 'Fighting for their lives: The problem of cultural authenticity in today's Sepik region'. In Nancy Lutkehaus, Christian Kaufman, William E. Mitchell, Douglas Newton, Lita Osmundsen, and Meinhard Shuster (eds), *Sepik Heritage: Tradition and Change in Papua New Guinea*. Durham, NC: Carolina Academic Press, pp. 364–9.

Tuzin, Donald F., 1997, *The Cassowary's Revenge: The Life and Death of Masculinity in a New Guinea Society*. Chicago: University of Chicago Press.

Tylor, Edward B., 1871, *Primitive Culture: Researches into the Development of Mythology, Philosophy, Religion, Art, and Custom* (2 vols). London: John Murray.

Uscinski, Joseph E. and Joseph M. Parent, 2014, *American Conspiracy Theories*. London: Oxford University Press. doi.org/10.1093/acprof:oso/9780199351800.001.0001

van der Veur, Paul W., 1965, 'The first two meetings of the House of Assembly'. In David G. Bettison, Colin A. Hughes, and Paul W. van der Veur (eds), *The Papua-New Guinea Elections 1964*. Canberra: The Australian National University, pp. 445–504.

Van Leeuwen, Neil and Michiel van Elk, 2019, 'Seeking the supernatural: The interactive religious experience model'. *Religion, Brain & Behavior* 9(3): 221–51. doi.org/10.1080/2153599X.2018.1453529

van Prooijen, Jan-Willem, Karen M. Douglas, and Clara De Inocencio, 2017, 'Connecting the dots: Illusory pattern perception predicts belief in conspiracies and the supernatural'. *European Journal of Social Psychology* 48(3): 320–35. doi.org/10.1002/ejsp.2331

Wagner, Roy, 1981, *The Invention of Culture*. Chicago: Chicago University Press.

Waiko, John Dademo, 2007, *A Short History of Papua New Guinea* (2nd ed.). Oxford and New York: Oxford University Press.

Walker, Jesse, 2013, *The United States of Paranoia: A Conspiracy Theory*. New York: Harper.

Wallace, Anthony F.C., 1956, 'Revitalization movements'. *American Anthropologist* 58(2): 264–81. doi.org/10.1525/aa.1956.58.2.02a00040

Wanek, Alexander, 1996, *The State and Its Enemies in Papua New Guinea*. Nordic Institute of Asian Studies Monograph Series No. 68. Richmond, Surrey: Curzon Press.

Ward, Marion W., Susan C. Tarua, and May Dudley (eds), 1970, *The Politics of Melanesia: Papers Delivered at the Fourth Waigani Seminar, Port Moresby, Papua New Guinea*. Canberra: Research School of Pacific Studies, The Australian National University.

Wardlow, Holly, 2017 [2005], 'Transformations of desire: Envy and resentment among the Huli of Papua New Guinea'. In Joel Robbins and Holly Wardlow (eds), *The Making of Global and Local Modernities in Melanesia*. New York: Routledge, pp. 57–71.

Watt, Diane, 2001, 'Medieval millenarianism and prophecy'. In Stephen Hunt (ed.), *Christian Millenarianism: From the Early Church to Waco*. Bloomington, IN: Indiana University Press, pp. 88–97.

Waugh, Evelyn, 1938, *Scoop*. London: Chapman and Hall.

West, Paige, 2016, *Dispossession and the Environment: Rhetoric and Inequality in Papua New Guinea*. New York: Columbia University Press. doi.org/10.7312/west17878

White, Geoffrey M. and Lamont Lindstrom (eds), 1993, 'Custom today'. *Anthropological Forum* Special Issue 6(4). doi.org/10.1080/00664677.1993.9967427

White, Osmar, 1965, *Parliament of a Thousand Tribes*. Melbourne: Wren Publishing.

Whitehouse, Harvey, 1995, *Inside the Cult: Religious Innovation and Transmission in Papua New Guinea*. Oxford and New York: Oxford University Press.

Whitehouse, Harvey, 2000, *Arguments and Icons: Divergent Modes of Religiosity*. Oxford: Oxford University Press.

Williams, F.E., 1923, 'The Vailala Madness and the destruction of native ceremonies in the Gulf Division of New Guinea'. *Papuan Anthropological Reports* No. 4. Port Moresby.

Williams, F.E., 1928, *Orokaiva Magic*. London: Humphry Milford.

Williams, F.E., 1934, 'The Vailala Madness in retrospect'. In E.E. Evans-Pritchard (ed.), *Essays Presented to C.G. Seligman*. London: Routledge and Kegan Paul.

Wilson, Bryan, 1961, *Sects and Society*. Heinemann: London.

Worsley, Peter, 1968 [1957], *The Trumpet Shall Sound: A Study of 'Cargo' Cults in Melanesia* (2nd ed., augmented). New York: Schocken Books.

Worsley, Peter, 1999, '"Cargo cults": Forty years on'. In Christin Kocher Schmidt (ed.), *Expecting the Day of Wrath: Versions of the Millennium in Papua New Guinea*. Boroko, Papua New Guinea: National Research Institute, pp. 145–55.

Index

Page numbers that include 'i' are illustrations. A page number containing 'n' indicates a reference appearing in a footnote on that page.

Many Manus personal names are a single name only, so to help identify individuals their village is added to their index entry, for example, 'Bonyalo of Pere'. Some Manus personal names comprise two names, for example 'John Kilepak' [of Pere]. The system used here is to index Manus personal names in natural order, for example, John Kilepak is filed under 'J'. See also footnote 22, page 117. European names are indexed in the conventional way, with surname first, for example, 'Mead, Margaret'.

hereditary rank, 65
House of Assembly, 365–70, 375–76
human behaviour, irrational, 53–58
human cognitive bias, 76–79
Human Development Index, 456–57
Humble, Graeme, 403n13
'humiliation' and modernisation,
    216n15
Hutchins, Edwin, 21, 384

Ilahita Arapesh people, 51
illness
    after feasts, 125, 137
    caused by anger or conflict,
        163n11, 165
    as punishment, 7, 70–71, 72–74,
        97
    and *tingting*, 165–66, 170
    see also paranoid ethos;
        personification
independence, PNG, 23, 364–65
inequality, 457
institutional discipline, 96
irrationality, 53–58

Jakob of Yiru, 259
Japanese forces, World War II, 92–94,
    133–35, 160
Jesus
    communication via ghosts, 270
    kaunsil for the dead, 272
    'Long Story of God', 150–62
    in revelatory dream, 139–42
    visits Lapun of Malei, 282
    see also Christianity; Paliau,
        as Jesus
Johannes Lokes of Pere, 250
Johannes Pominis of Pere, 202, 203,
    472
John (Paliau's son), 122
'John Brown's Body' (song), 158, 202,
    251, 301
John Guise, 366n3

John Kilepak of Pere, 106, 107, 203,
    250, 312–13
Johnston Island
    Cemetery Cult, 323n5, 356
    ghost of Thomas, 269–78, 279,
        329
    ghostly prophecy, 253–54
    influences Patusi village, 308
    new graveyard, 248–50, 278, 303
    Paliau warns of trouble, 347
    uniforms, 286
Joseph Nanei of Lowaya, 284, 285,
    286, 287, 289, 322, 340, 354,
    355, 359, 475
Joseph Pati, 122–23, 124, 127, 129,
    131, 136

Kalopeu: Manus Kastam Kansol Stori,
    390, 400, 477–87
    see also Makasol (Manus Kastam
        Kansol)
Kalowin of Lipan, 123
Kamanra of Johnston Island, 270
Kametan of Bunai, 344
Kampo Monrai of Malei, 265, 475
Kampo of Lahan
    advocates social change, 115–18
    cash economy ambitions, 242
    Cemetery Cult leadership
        ambitions, 292–97, 354
    Cemetery Cult opposition, 268,
        294, 297, 303–5, 313
    Cemetery Cult speeches, 261–62,
        265
    Noise, 178, 205–12
    Paliau Movement, 363
    wife's divine revelation, 258–59,
        280
Kanaw Kampo, 397
Kapo village, 260, 279–80, 286,
    323n5, 325, 337
Karol Manoi of Patusi, 197, 199,
    203, 314

Scholars cited

Landes, Richard, 8n10, 8n11, 12, 13n14, 13n15, 14, 15, 16, 28n2, 45, 50n45, 55, 57, 85, 212, 223, 321, 424, 435, 458, 460–61, 462, 465
Landman, Marjorie, 183n4
Lanternari, Vittorio, 44n33, 458
Latour, Bruno, 462n21
Lattas, Andrew, 14, 45, 49n44, 51, 52n46, 446
Lawrence, Peter, 218n17
Leavitt, Stephen C., 45, 75, 99, 216n15
Lepowsky, Maria, 84, 464
Lewis, Herbert S., 43n28, 47
Lewis, James R., 44, 57n57
Lindstrom, Lamont, 14, 15, 16n21, 38, 39, 40n23, 41, 42, 43, 44, 45, 46, 48, 54, 84n23, 94, 95, 96, 409, 470n2
Lukas, Paliau, 389, 398, 447n14
Lutkehaus, Nancy C., 454n9

Macintyre, Martha, 41, 45
Mair, Lucy, 42
Malinowski, Bronislaw, 98
Maloat, Paliau, 34n14, 416n26
Mauss, Marcel, 49n42, 73, 97, 98
May, John D'Arcy, 477
May, R.J., 17, 223, 460
McDowell, Nancy, 15, 41, 44, 53n49, 54, 218n17
McVicar, Michael Joseph, 28
Mead, Margaret, 1, 2n2, 4, 11n12, 33, 34, 35, 42, 60, 64n3, 65, 68, 70n6, 71, 80, 92, 97, 99, 103, 105, 109, 113, 123n1, 136, 189n6, 202n8, 228n5, 234, 321n4, 366, 371n9, 454
Minnegal, Monica, 218n16
Minol, Bernard, 7n9, 117n23
Moore, Clive, 5n6, 6n7, 27n1, 232n6, 233, 366n4, 380n18
Morris, Adam, 455

Nelson, Hank, 94n12
Nevermann, Hans, 59, 63
Noble, David F., 32n12

Offenberger, Andrew, 57n58
Ogan, Eugene, 215
Oldenbourg, Zoé, 44n29, 268n2
Otto, Ton, 10, 17, 28n2, 35n16, 36n17, 37–38, 39n20, 44, 45, 46n35, 48, 49n44, 65, 81, 122, 123n2, 150, 162n9, 169, 193, 217, 233, 234, 236, 364, 369, 370, 373, 374, 379, 380, 381, 390, 391, 393, 394, 404n15, 405, 406, 409, 412, 420, 421, 422, 423, 439

Parent, Joseph M., 459, 463n23
Pedersen, Morten Axel, 31n9, 215n14
Peires, J.B., 38, 57n58
Pokawin, Stephen, 6n8, 369, 379, 389, 402n12, 406n17, 410, 412, 416n26, 455
Pouwer, Jan, 48

Rappaport, Roy A., 28, 29, 76
Rasmussen, Anders Emil, 81, 364, 439
Rio, Knut, 99n16, 466–67
Robbins, Joel, 14, 45, 216n15, 218n17, 461–62, 467
Robinson, Neville K., 95, 96
Rodman, Margaret, 90
Romanucci Schwartz, Lola, 65
Romanucci-Ross, Lola, 379
Rowley, C.D., 89n4, 100
Russell, Bertrand, 29n5

Sack, Peter, 88n2, 88n3
Sahlins, Marshall, 71, 74n10, 216n15
Said, Edward W., 54n51
Schmid, Christin Kocher, 14n18, 43n26

www.ingramcontent.com/pod-product-compliance
Lightning Source LLC
Chambersburg PA
CBHW051442270326
41932CB00032B/3377

* 9 7 8 1 7 6 0 4 6 4 2 4 0 *